Essentials of
Systems Analysis
and Design

Essentials of Systems Analysis and Design

FIFTH EDITION

Joseph S. Valacich
University of Arizona

Joey F. George
Iowa State University

Jeffrey A. Hoffer
University of Dayton

PEARSON

Boston   Columbus   Indianapolis   New York   San Francisco   Upper Saddle River
Amsterdam   Cape Town   Dubai   London   Madrid   Milan   Munich   Paris   Montreal   Toronto
Delhi   Mexico City   São Paulo   Sydney   Hong Kong   Seoul   Singapore   Taipei   Tokyo

Editorial Director: Sally Yagan
Editor in Chief: Eric Svendsen
Executive Editor: Bob Horan
Editorial Assistant: Ashlee Bradbury
Director of Marketing: Patrice Lumumba Jones
Executive Marketing Manager: Anne Fahlgren
Senior Managing Editor: Judy Leale
Production Project Manager: Kelly Warsak
Senior Operations Supervisor: Arnold Vila
Operations Specialist: Cathleen Petersen
Creative Director: Blair Brown
Senior Art Director/Design Supervisor: Janet Slowik
Text Designer: Michael Fruhbeis
Creative Director/Cover: Jayne Conte
Cover Designer: Suzanne Duda
Cover Art: Fotolia/3d mosaic/©Redshinestudio
Manager, Rights and Permissions: Hessa Albader
Media Project Manager: Lisa Rinaldi
Media Editor: Denise Vaughn
Full-Service Project Management: Tiffany Timmerman/S4Carlisle Publishing Services
Composition: S4Carlisle Publishing Services
Printer/Binder: Courier/Kendallville
Cover Printer: Lehigh-Phoenix Color/Hagerstown
Text Font: ITCCentury Book

Credits and acknowledgments borrowed from other sources and reproduced, with permission, in this textbook appear on appropriate page within text.

Microsoft® and Windows® are registered trademarks of the Microsoft Corporation in the U.S.A. and other countries. Screen shots and icons reprinted with permission from the Microsoft Corporation. This book is not sponsored or endorsed by or affiliated with the Microsoft Corporation.

Many of the designations by manufacturers and seller to distinguish their products are claimed as trademarks. Where those designations appear in this book, and the publisher was aware of a trademark claim, the designations have been printed in initial caps or all caps.

Library of Congress Cataloging-in-Publication Data
Valacich, Joseph S.
   Essentials of systems analysis and design / Joseph S. Valacich,
Joey F. George, Jeffrey A. Hoffer.—5th ed.
       p. cm.
   Includes bibliographical references and index.
   ISBN-13: 978-0-13-706711-4
   ISBN-10: 0-13-706711-9
   1. System design.   2. System analysis.   I. George, Joey F.   II.
Hoffer, Jeffrey A.   III. Title.
   QA76.9.S88V345 2011
   003—dc22
                                        2011008298

10 9 8 7 6 5 4 3 2
ISBN 10:   0-13-706711-9
ISBN 13: 978-0-13-706711-4

To Jackie, Jordan, and James,
for your sacrifices, encouragement,
and support.

—Joe

To Karen, Evan, and Caitlin.

—Joey

To Patty, for her sacrifices,
encouragement, and support.
To my students, for being receptive
and critical, and for challenging me
to be a better teacher.

—Jeff

Brief Contents

Contents

Preface

Our Approach

In today's information- and technology-driven business world, students need to be aware of three key factors. First, it is more crucial than ever to know how to organize and access information strategically. Second, success often depends on the ability to work as part of a team. Third, the Internet will play an important part in their work lives. *Essentials of Systems Analysis and Design, Fifth Edition*, addresses these key factors.

More than 50 years' combined teaching experience in systems analysis and design have gone into creating *Essentials of Systems Analysis and Design, Fifth Edition*, a text that emphasizes hands-on, experimental learning. We provide a clear presentation of the concepts, skills, and techniques students need to become effective systems analysts who work with others to create information systems for businesses. We use the systems development life cycle model as an organizing tool throughout the book to provide a strong conceptual and systematic framework.

Internet coverage is provided in each chapter via an integrated, extended illustrative case (Pine Valley Furniture WebStore) and an end-of-chapter case (Petrie's Electronics).

Many systems analysis and design courses involve lab work and outside reading. Lecture time can be limited. Based on market research and our own teaching experience, we understand the need for a book that combines depth of coverage with brevity. So we have created a ten-chapter book that covers key systems analysis and design content without overwhelming students with unnecessary detail.

New to the Fifth Edition

The following features are new to the Fifth Edition:

- *Emphasis on current changes in systems analysis and design.* The move to structured analysis and design in the late 1970s was considered to be a revolution in systems development. We are undergoing another revolution now, as we move away from complex, plan-driven development to new approaches called "Agile Methodologies." Although the best-known Agile Methodology is eXtreme Programming, many other approaches are also available. The Agile revolution in systems development is acknowledged and briefly explained in Chapter 1 and then explored in much greater depth in Appendix B.

- *Increased focus on make versus buy and systems integration.* More and more systems development involves the use of packages in combination with legacy applications and new modules. Coverage of the make-versus-buy decision and of the multiple sources of software and software components is highlighted in Chapter 2 to show how companies deal with these issues.

- *New end-of-chapter running case.* Petrie's Electronics, a fictional electronics retailer, is a student project case that allows students to study and develop a Web-based customer loyalty program to enhance a customer relationship management system.

- *Updated illustrations of technology.* Screen captures have been updated throughout the text to show examples using the latest versions of programming and Internet development environments, and user interface designs.

- *New entity-relationship notation.* We now use a new notation for entity-relationship diagramming in Chapter 7 and elsewhere. This notation is consistent with that used in *Modern Database Management, Tenth Edition,* by Hoffer, Ramesh, and Topi (2011).

- *Updated content.* Throughout the book, the content in each chapter has been updated where appropriate.

- *End-of-chapter updates.* We have provided extensive updates to existing problems along with several new problems in every chapter.

Themes

Essentials of Systems Analysis and Design, Fifth Edition, is characterized by the following themes:

- *Systems development is firmly rooted in an organizational context.* The successful systems analyst requires a broad understanding of organizations, organizational culture, and operations.

- *Systems development is a practical field.* Coverage of current practices as well as accepted concepts and principles is essential for today's systems analyst.

- *Systems development is a profession.* The text presents standards of practice, and fosters a sense of continuing personal development, ethics, and a respect for and collaboration with the work of others.

- *Systems development has significantly changed with the explosive growth in databases, data-driven architecture for systems, and the Internet.* Systems development and database management can be taught in a highly coordinated fashion. The Internet has rapidly become a common development platform for database-driven electronic commerce systems.

- *Success in systems analysis and design requires not only skills in methodologies and techniques, but also in the management of time, resources, and risks.* Learning systems analysis and design requires a thorough understanding of the process as well as the techniques and deliverables of the profession.

Given these themes, the text emphasizes these approaches:

- A business rather than a technology perspective

- The role, responsibilities, and mind-set of the systems analyst as well as the systems project manager, rather than those of the programmer or business manager

- The methods and principles of systems development rather than the specific tools or tool-related skills of the field

Audience

The book assumes that students have taken an introductory course on computer systems and have experience writing programs in at least one programming language. We review basic system principles for those students who have not been exposed to the material on which systems development methods are based. We also assume that students have a solid background in computing literacy and a general understanding of the core elements of a business, including basic terms associated with the production, marketing, finance, and accounting functions.

Organization

The outline of the book follows the systems development life cycle:

- Part I, "Foundations for Systems Development," gives an overview of systems development and previews the remainder of the book.
- Part II, "Systems Planning and Selection," covers how to assess project feasibility and build the baseline project plan.
- Part III, "Systems Analysis," covers determining system requirements, process modeling, and conceptual data modeling.
- Part IV, "Systems Design," covers how to design the human interface and databases.
- Part V, "Systems Implementation and Operation," covers system implementation, operation, closedown, and system maintenance.
- Appendix A, "Object-Oriented Analysis and Design," and Appendix B, "Agile Methodologies," can be skipped or treated as advanced topics at the end of the course.

Distinctive Features

Here are some of the distinctive features of *Essentials of Systems Analysis and Design, Fifth Edition:*

1. The grounding of systems development in the typical architecture for systems in modern organizations, including database management and Web-based systems.

2. A clear linkage of all dimensions of systems description and modeling— process, decision, and data modeling—into a comprehensive and compatible set of systems analysis and design approaches. Such broad coverage is necessary for students to understand the advanced capabilities of many systems development methodologies and tools that automatically generate a large percentage of code from design specifications.

3. Extensive coverage of oral and written communication skills (including systems documentation), project management, team management, and a variety of systems development and acquisition strategies (e.g., life cycle, prototyping, rapid application development, object orientation, joint application development, participatory design, and business process reengineering).

4. Coverage of rules and principles of systems design, including decoupling, cohesion, modularity, and audits and controls.

5. A discussion of systems development and implementation within the context of management of change, conversion strategies, and organizational factors in systems acceptance.

6. Careful attention to human factors in systems design that emphasize usability in both character-based and graphical user interface situations.

Pedagogical Features

The pedagogical features of *Essentials of Systems Analysis and Design, Fifth Edition*, reinforce and apply the key content of the book.

SDLC Framework

Although several conceptual processes can be used for guiding a systems development effort, the systems development life cycle (SDLC) is arguably the most widely applied method for designing contemporary information systems. We highlight four key SDLC steps (Figure P-1):

- Planning and selection
- Analysis
- Design
- Implementation and operation

FIGURE P-1
The systems development life cycle (SDLC): management is necessary throughout.

We use the SDLC to frame the part and chapter organization of our book. Most chapters open with an SDLC figure with various parts highlighted to show students how these chapters, and each step of the SDLC, systematically builds on the previous one.

Internet Coverage and Features

 Pine Valley Furniture WebStore A furniture company founded in 1980 has decided to explore electronic commerce as an avenue to increase its market share. Should this company sell its products online? How would a team of analysts work together to develop, propose, and implement a plan? Beginning in Chapter 4, we explore the step-by-step process.

 Petrie's Electronics This end-of-chapter fictional case illustrates how a national electronics retailer develops a Web-based customer loyalty program to build and strengthen customer relationships. The case first appears at the end of Chapter 2 and concludes at the end of Chapter 10.

Three Illustrative Fictional Cases

Pine Valley Furniture (PVF) This case is introduced in Chapter 3 and revisited throughout the book. As key systems development life cycle concepts are presented, they are applied and illustrated. For example, in Chapter 3, we explore how PVF implements the purchasing fulfillment system, and in Chapter 4, we explore how PVF implements a customer tracking system. A margin icon identifies the location of the case segments. A case problem related to PVF is included in the end-of-chapter material.

Hoosier Burger (HB) This second illustrative case is introduced in Chapter 6 and revisited throughout the book. Hoosier Burger is a fictional fast-food restaurant in Bloomington, Indiana. We use this case to illustrate how analysts would develop and implement an automated food-ordering system. A margin icon identifies the location of these case segments. A case problem related to HB is included in the end-of-chapter material.

Petrie's Electronics This fictional electronics retailer is used as an extended case at the end of each chapter, beginning with Chapter 2. Designed to bring the chapter concepts to life, this case illustrates how a company initiates, plans, models, designs, and implements a Web-based customer loyalty program. Discussion questions are included to promote critical thinking and class participation. Suggested solutions to the discussion questions are provided in the Instructor's Manual.

End-of-Chapter Material

We have developed an extensive selection of end-of-chapter material designed to accommodate various learning and teaching styles.

Key Points Review This section repeats the learning objectives that appear at the opening of the chapter and summarizes the key points related to the objectives.

Key Terms Checkpoint In this self-test feature, students match each key term in the chapter with its definition.

Review Questions These questions test students' understanding of key concepts.

Problems and Exercises These exercises test students' analytical skills and require them to apply key concepts.

Discussion Questions These questions promote class participation and discussion.

Case Problems These problems require students to apply the concepts of the chapter to fictional cases from various industries. The two illustrative cases from the chapters are revisited—Pine Valley Furniture and Hoosier Burger. Other cases are from various fields such as medicine, agriculture, and technology. Solutions are provided in the Instructor's Manual.

Margin Term Definitions

Each key term and its definition appear in the margin. A glossary of terms appears at the back of the book.

References

Located at the end of the text, references are organized by chapter and list more than 200 books and journals that can provide students and faculty with additional coverage of topics.

The Supplement Package: www.pearsonhighered.com/valacich

A comprehensive and flexible technology support package is available to enhance the teaching and learning experience. Instructor supplements are available at www.pearsonhighered.com/valacich:

- An *Instructor's Resource Manual* provides chapter-by-chapter instructor objectives, teaching suggestions, and answers to all text review questions, problems, and exercises.
- The *Test Item File* and *TestGen* include a comprehensive set of more than 1,500 test questions in multiple-choice, true-false, and short-answer format; questions are ranked according to level of difficulty and referenced with page numbers and topic headings from the text. The Test Item File is available in Microsoft Word and as the computerized Prentice Hall TestGen software. The software is PC/Mac-compatible and preloaded with all of the Test Item File questions. You can manually or randomly view test questions and drag-and-drop to create a test. You can add or modify test-bank questions as needed.
- *PowerPoint Presentation Slides* feature lecture notes that highlight key text terms and concepts. Professors can customize the presentation by adding their own slides or by editing the existing ones.
- The *Image Library* is a collection of the text art organized by chapter. This collection includes all of the figures, tables, and screenshots (as permission allows) from the book. These images can be used to enhance class lectures and PowerPoint slides.

Materials for Your Online Course

Our TestGens are converted for use in BlackBoard and WebCT. These conversions can be found on the Instructor's Resource Center. Conversions to D2L or Angel can be requested through your local Pearson Sales Representative.

CourseSmart

CourseSmart eTextbooks were developed for students looking to save on required or recommended textbooks. Students simply select their eText by title or author and purchase immediate access to the content for the duration of the course using any major credit card. With a CourseSmart eText, students can search for specific keywords or page numbers, take notes online, print out reading assignments that incorporate lecture notes, and bookmark important passages for later review. For more information or to purchase a CourseSmart eTextbook, visit www.coursesmart.com.

Acknowledgments

The authors have been blessed by considerable assistance from many people on all aspects of preparation of this text and its supplements. We are, of course, responsible for what eventually appears between the covers, but the insights, corrections, contributions, and proddings of others have greatly improved our manuscript. The people we recognize here all have a strong commitment to students, to the IS field, and to excellence. Their contributions have stimulated us, and frequently rejuvenated us during periods of waning energy for this project.

We would like to recognize the efforts of the many faculty and practicing systems analysts who have been reviewers of the five editions of this text and its associated text, *Modern Systems Analysis and Design*. We have tried to deal with each reviewer comment, and although we did not always agree with specific points (within the approach we wanted to take with this book), all reviewers made us stop and think carefully about what and how we were writing. The reviewers were:

Richard Allen, *Richland Community College*
Charles Arbutina, *Buffalo State College*
Paula Bell, *Lock Haven University of Pennsylvania*
Sultan Bhimjee, *San Francisco State University*
Bill Boroski, *Trident Technical College*
Nora Braun, *Augsburg College*
Rowland Brengle, *Anne Arundel Community College*
Richard Burkhard, *San Jose State University*
Doloras Carlisle, *Western Oklahoma State College*
Pam Chapman, *Waubonsee Community College*
Edward Chen, *University of Massachusetts Lowell*
Suzanne Clayton, *Drake University*
Garry Dawdy, *Metropolitan State College of Denver*
Thomas Dillon, *James Madison University*
Brad Dyer, *Hazard Community and Technical College*
Veronica Echols-Noble, *DeVry University–Chicago*
Richard Egan, *New Jersey Institute of Technology*
Gerald Evans, *University of Montana*
Lawrence Feidelman, *Florida Atlantic University*
David Firth, *University of Montana*
John Fowler, *Walla Walla Community College*
Larry Fudella, *Erie Community College*
Carol Grimm, *Palm Beach Community College*
Carol Healy, *Drake University*
Lenore Horowitz, *Schenectady County Community College*
Daniel Ivancevich, *University of North Carolina–Wilmington*
Jon Jasperson, *University of Oklahoma*
Len Jessup, *Washington State University*
Rich Kepenach, *St. Petersburg College*
Lin Lin, *Lehigh University*
James Scott Magruder, *University of Southern Mississippi*
Diane Mayne-Stafford, *Grossmont College*

David McNair, *Maryville University*
Loraine Miller, *Cayuga Community College*
Klara Nelson, *University of Tampa*
Max North, *Southern Polytechnic State University*
Doncho Petkov, *Eastern Connecticut State University*
Lou Pierro, *Indiana University*
Selwyn Piramuthu, *University of Florida*
Mitzi Pitts, *University of Memphis*
Richard Platt, *University of West Florida*
James Pomykalski, *Susquehanna University*
Robin Poston, *University of Memphis*
Rao Prabhakar, *Amarillo College*
Mary Prescott, *University of Tampa*
Joseph Rottman, *University of Missouri, St. Louis*
Robert Saldarini, *Bergen Community College*
Howard Schuh, *Rockland Community College*
Elaine Seeman, *Pitt Community College*
Teresa Shaft, *The University of Oklahoma*
Thomas Shaw, *Louisiana State University*
Gary Templeton, *Mississippi State University*
Dominic Thomas, *University of Georgia*
Don Turnbul, *The University of Texas at Austin*
Kathleen Voge, *University of Alaska–Anchorage*
Erica Wagner, *Portland State University*
Sharon Walters, *Southern Illinois University*
Haibo Wang, *Texas A&M International University*
Mark Ward, *Southern Illinois University, Edwardsville*
Merrill Warkentin, *Northeastern University*
June Wei, *University of West Florida*
Mudasser Wyne, *University of Michigan–Flint*
Saeed Yazdain, *Lane College*
Liang Yu, *San Francisco State University*
Steven Zeltmann, *University of Central Arkansas*
Justin Zhang, *Eastern New Mexico University*

We extend a special note of thanks to Jeremy Alexander, who was instrumental in conceptualizing and writing the Pine Valley Furniture WebStore feature that appears in Chapters 3 through 10. The addition of this feature has helped make those chapters more applied and innovative. We also want to thank Ryan Wright, University of San Francisco, for the help he provided with the Visual Basic and .NET related materials, as well as Dave Wilson, Washington State University, and David Gomillion, Florida State University, for assisting with updates to the end-of-chapter problems, exercises, and cases.

In addition, we want to thank Nicholas Romano for his work on the Instructor's Resource Manual for this edition. We also thank John Russo, for his work on the PowerPoint presentations and Test Bank of *Essentials of Systems Analysis and Design*.

We also wish to thank Atish Sinha of the University of Wisconsin–Milwaukee for writing the initial draft of Appendix A on object-oriented analysis and design. Dr. Sinha, who has been teaching this topic for several years to both undergraduates and MBA students, executed a challenging assignment with creativity and cooperation. We are also indebted to our undergraduate and MBA students at the University of Dayton, Florida State University, and Washington State University who have given us many helpful comments as they worked with drafts of this text.

Thanks also go to V. Ramesh (Indiana University) and Heikki Topi (Bentley College) for their assistance in coordinating this text with its companion book—*Modern Database Management*, also by Pearson Prentice Hall.

Finally, we have been fortunate to work with a large number of creative and insightful people at Pearson Prentice Hall, who have added much to the development, format, and production of this text. We have been thoroughly impressed with their commitment to this text and to the IS education market. These people include Bob Horan, Executive Editor; Anne Fahlgren, Executive Marketing Manager; Kelly Loftus, Senior Editorial Project Manager; Judy Leale, Senior Managing Editor; Kelly Warsak, Production Project Manager; Janet Slowik, Senior Art Director; and Denise Vaughn, Media Editor.

The writing of this text has involved thousands of hours of time from the authors and from all of the people listed. Although our names will be visibly associated with this book, we know that much of the credit goes to the individuals and organizations listed here for any success this book might achieve.

About the Authors

Joseph S. Valacich is an Eller Professor of Management Information Systems in the Eller College of Management at the University of Arizona. He has had visiting faculty appointments at Buskerud College (Norway), City University of Hong Kong, Norwegian University of Life Sciences, Riga Technical University (Latvia), and Helsinki School of Economics and Business. He received a Ph.D. degree from the University of Arizona (MIS), and M.B.A. and B.S. (computer science) degrees from the University of Montana. His teaching interests include systems analysis and design, collaborative computing, project management, and management of information systems. Professor Valacich cochaired the national task forces to design *IS 2008: The Model Curriculum and Guidelines for Undergraduate Degree Programs in Information Systems*. He also served on the Executive Committee, funded by the National Science Foundation, to define the *IS Program Accreditation Standards* and on the Board of Directors for CSAB (formally, the Computing Sciences Accreditation Board), representing the Association for Information Systems (AIS). He was the general conference co-chair for the 2003 International Conference on Information Systems (ICIS), and the co-chair for the Americas' Conference on Information Systems (AMCIS) in 2012.

Prior to his academic career, Dr. Valacich worked in the information systems field as a programmer, systems analyst, and technical product manager. He has conducted numerous corporate training and executive development programs for organizations, including AT&T, Boeing, Dow Chemical, EDS, Exxon, FedEx, General Motors, Microsoft, and Xerox.

Dr. Valacich serves on the editorial board of *MIS Quarterly* and was formerly an associate editor for *Information Systems Research*. His research has appeared in publications such as *MIS Quarterly, Information Systems Research, Management Science*, and *Academy of Management Journal*. He is a coauthor of the best-selling *Modern Systems Analysis and Design* (Sixth Edition), as well as *Object-Oriented Systems Analysis and Design, Information Systems Today* (Fifth Edition), and *Information Systems Project Team Management*; all are published by Pearson Prentice Hall.

Joey F. George is professor and Dean's Chair in the Iowa State University College of Business. Dr. George earned his bachelor's degree at Stanford University in 1979 and his Ph.D. in management at the University of California at Irvine in 1986. He was previously the Edward G. Schlieder Chair of Information Systems in the E. J. Ourso College of Business Administration at Louisiana State University. He also served at Florida State University as Chair of the Department of Information and Management Sciences from 1995 to 1998.

Dr. George has published dozens of articles in such journals as *Information Systems Research, Communications of the ACM, MIS Quarterly, Journal of MIS*, and *Communication Research*. His research interests focus on the use of information systems in the workplace, including computer-based monitoring, computer-mediated deceptive communication, and group support systems.

Dr. George is coauthor of the textbooks *Modern Systems Analysis and Design, Sixth Edition*, published in 2010, and *Object-Oriented Systems Analysis and Design, Second Edition*, published in 2007, both from Pearson Prentice Hall. He has served as an associate editor and senior editor for both *MIS Quarterly* and *Information Systems Research*. He served three years as the editor-in-chief of the *Communications of the AIS*. Dr. George was the conference cochair for the 2001 ICIS, held in New Orleans, Louisiana, and the doctoral consortium cochair for the 2003 ICIS, held in Seattle, Washington. He is a Fellow of the Association for Information Systems (AIS) and served as President of AIS in 2010–11.

Jeffrey A. Hoffer is the Sherman–Standard Register Professor of Data Management for the Department of MIS, Operations Management, and Decision Sciences in the School of Business Administration at the University of Dayton. He also taught at Indiana University and Case Western Reserve University. Dr. Hoffer earned his B.A. from Miami University in 1969 and his Ph.D. from Cornell University in 1975.

Dr. Hoffer has coauthored all editions of three college textbooks: *Modern Systems Analysis and Design*, with George and Valacich; *Managing Information Technology: What Managers Need to Know*, with Brown, DeHayes, Martin, and Perkins; and *Modern Database Management*, with Ramesh and Topi, all published by Pearson Prentice Hall. His research articles have appeared in numerous journals, including the *MIS Quarterly–Executive*, *Journal of Database Management*, *Small Group Research*, *Communications of the ACM*, and *Sloan Management Review*. He has received research grants from Teradata (Division of NCR), IBM Corporation, and the U.S. Department of the Navy.

Dr. Hoffer is cofounder of the International Conference on Information Systems and Association for Information Systems and has served as a guest lecturer at the Catholic University of Chile, Santiago, and the Helsinki School of Economics and Business in Mikkeli, Finland.

Joseph S. Valacich, Tucson, Arizona
Joey F. George, Ames, Iowa
Jeffrey A. Hoffer, Dayton, Ohio

Essentials of
Systems Analysis
and Design

one

The Systems Development Environment

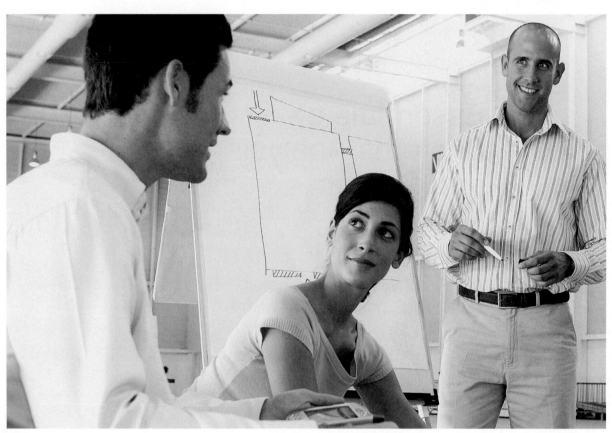

Javier Larrea/AGE Fotostock

Chapter Objectives

After studying this chapter, you should be able to:

- Define information systems analysis and design.

- Discuss the modern approach to systems analysis and design that combines both process and data views of systems.

- Describe the role of the systems analyst in information systems development.

- Describe the information systems development life cycle (SDLC).

- List alternatives to the systems development life cycle, including a description of the role of computer-aided software engineering (CASE) tools in systems development.

Chapter Preview . . .

The key to success in business is the ability to gather, organize, and interpret information. Systems analysis and design is a proven methodology that helps both large and small businesses reap the rewards of utilizing information to its full capacity. As a systems analyst, the person in the organization most involved with systems analysis and design, you will enjoy a rich career path that will enhance both your computer and interpersonal skills.

The systems development life cycle (SDLC) is central to the development of an efficient information system. We will highlight four key SDLC steps: (1) planning and selection, (2) analysis, (3) design, and (4) implementation and operation. Be aware that these steps may vary in each organization, depending on its goals. The SDLC is illustrated in Figure 1-1. Each chapter of this book includes an updated version of the SDLC, highlighting which steps have been covered and which steps remain.

This text requires that you have a general understanding of computer-based information systems as provided in an introductory information systems course. This chapter previews systems analysis and lays the groundwork for the rest of the book.

FIGURE 1-1
The four steps of the systems development life cycle (SDLC): (1) planning and selection, (2) analysis, (3) design, and (4) implementation and operation.

What Is Information Systems Analysis and Design?

Information systems analysis and design is a method used by companies ranging from IBM to PepsiCo to Sony to create and maintain information systems that perform basic business functions such as keeping track of customer names and addresses, processing orders, and paying employees. The main goal of systems analysis and design is to improve organizational systems, typically through applying software that can help employees accomplish key business tasks more easily and efficiently. As a systems analyst, you will be at the center of developing this software. The analysis and design of information systems are based on:

- Your understanding of the organization's objectives, structure, and processes
- Your knowledge of how to exploit information technology for advantage

To be successful in this endeavor, you should follow a structured approach. The SDLC, shown in Figure 1-1, is a four-phased approach to identifying, analyzing, designing, and implementing an information system. Throughout this book, we use the SDLC to organize our discussion of the systems development process. Before we talk about the SDLC, we first describe what is meant by systems analysis and design.

Systems Analysis and Design: Core Concepts

The major goal of systems analysis and design is to improve organizational systems. Often this process involves developing or acquiring **application software** and training employees to use it. Application software, also called a *system*, is designed to support a specific organizational function or process, such as inventory management, payroll, or market analysis. The goal of application software is to turn data into information. For example, software developed for the inventory department at a bookstore may keep track of the number of books in stock of the latest best seller. Software for the payroll department may keep track of the changing pay rates of employees. A variety of off-the-shelf application software can be purchased, including WordPerfect, Excel, and PowerPoint. However, off-the-shelf software may not fit the needs of a particular organization, and so the organization must develop its own product.

In addition to application software, the information system includes:

- The hardware and systems software on which the application software runs. Note that the systems software helps the computer function, whereas the application software helps the user perform tasks such as writing a paper, preparing a spreadsheet, and linking to the Internet.
- Documentation and training materials, which are materials created by the systems analyst to help employees use the software they've helped create.
- The specific job roles associated with the overall system, such as the people who run the computers and keep the software operating.
- Controls, which are parts of the software written to help prevent fraud and theft.
- The people who use the software in order to do their jobs.

The components of a computer-based information system application are summarized in Figure 1-2. We address all the dimensions of the overall system,

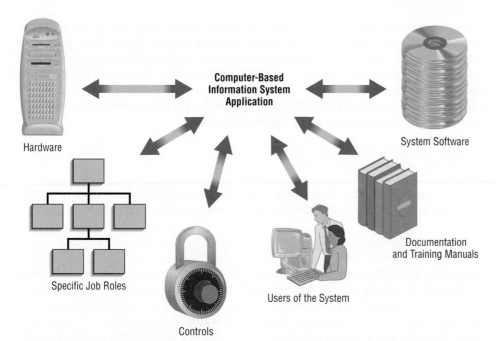

FIGURE 1-2
Components of a computer-based information system application.

Hardware

System Software

Computer-Based
Information System
Application

Specific Job Roles

Controls

Users of the System

Documentation
and Training Manuals

with particular emphasis on application software development—your primary responsibility as a systems analyst.

Our goal is to help you understand and follow the software engineering process that leads to the creation of information systems. As shown in Figure 1-3, proven methodologies, techniques, and tools are central to software engineering processes (and to this book).

Methodologies are a sequence of step-by-step approaches that help develop your final product: the information system. Most methodologies incorporate several development techniques, such as direct observations and interviews with users of the current system.

Techniques are processes that you, as an analyst, will follow to help ensure that your work is well thought-out, complete, and comprehensible to others on your project team. Techniques provide support for a wide range of tasks, including conducting thorough interviews with current and future users of the information system to determine what your system should do, planning and managing the activities in a systems development project, diagramming how the system will function, and designing the reports, such as invoices, your system will generate for its users to perform their jobs.

Tools are computer programs, such as computer-aided software engineering (CASE) tools, that make it easy to use specific techniques. These three elements— methodologies, techniques, and tools—work together to form an organizational approach to systems analysis and design.

Methodologies

Software
Engineering
Process

Techniques

Tools

FIGURE 1-3
The software engineering process uses proven methodologies, techniques, and tools.

In the rest of this chapter, you will learn about approaches to systems development—the data- and process-oriented approaches. You will also identify the various people who develop systems and the different types of systems they develop. The chapter ends with a discussion of some of the methodologies, techniques, and tools created to support the systems development process. Before we talk more about computer-based information systems, let's briefly discuss what we mean by the word *system*.

Systems

The key term used most frequently in this book is *system*. Understanding systems and how they work is critical to understanding systems analysis and design.

Definition of a System and Its Parts

System

A group of interrelated procedures used for a business function, with an identifiable boundary, working together for some purpose.

A **system** is an interrelated set of business procedures (or components) used within one business unit, working together for some purpose. For example, a system in the payroll department keeps track of checks, whereas an inventory system keeps track of supplies. The two systems are separate. A system has nine characteristics, seven of which are shown in Figure 1-4. A detailed explanation of each characteristic follows, but from the figure you can see that a system exists within a larger world, an environment. A boundary separates the system from its environment. The system takes input from outside, processes it, and sends the resulting output back to its environment. The arrows in the figure show this interaction between the system and the world outside of it.

1. Components
2. Interrelated components

FIGURE 1-4
Seven characteristics of a system.

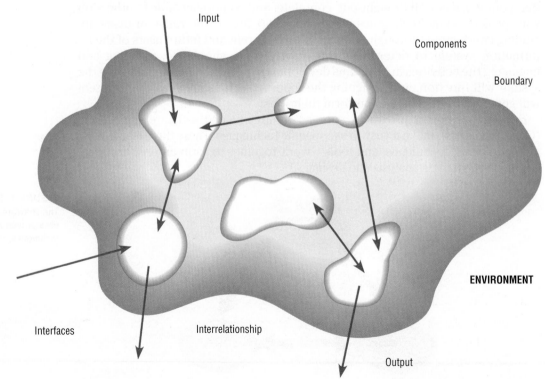

3. Boundary
4. Purpose
5. Environment
6. Interfaces
7. Constraints
8. Input
9. Output

A system is made up of components. A **component** is either an irreducible part or an aggregate of parts, also called a *subsystem*. The simple concept of a component is very powerful. For example, just as with an automobile or a stereo system, with proper design, we can repair or upgrade the system by changing individual components without having to make changes throughout the entire system. The components are **interrelated;** that is, the function of one is somehow tied to the functions of the others. For example, the work of one component, such as producing a daily report of customer orders received, may not progress successfully until the work of another component is finished, such as sorting customer orders by date of receipt. A system has a **boundary,** within which all of its components are contained and which establishes the limits of a system, separating it from other systems. Components within the boundary can be changed, whereas systems outside the boundary cannot be changed. All of the components work together to achieve some overall **purpose** for the larger system: the system's reason for existing.

A system exists within an **environment**—everything outside the system's boundary that influences the system. For example, the environment of a state university includes prospective students, foundations and funding agencies, and the news media. Usually the system interacts with its environment. A university interacts with prospective students by having open houses and recruiting from local high schools. An information system interacts with its environment by receiving data (raw facts) and information (data processed in a useful format). Figure 1-5 shows how a university can be seen as a system. The points at which the system meets its environment are called **interfaces;** an interface also occurs between subsystems.

In its functioning, a system must face **constraints**—the limits (in terms of capacity, speed, or capabilities) to what it can do and how it can achieve its purpose within its environment. Some of these constraints are imposed inside the system (e.g., a limited number of staff available), and others are imposed by the environment (e.g., due dates or regulations). A system takes input from its environment in order to function. People, for example, take in food, oxygen, and water from the environment as input. You are constrained from breathing fresh air if you're in an elevator with someone who is smoking. Finally, a system returns output to its environment as a result of its functioning and thus achieves its purpose. The system is constrained if electrical power is cut.

Component
An irreducible part or aggregation of parts that makes up a system; also called a *subsystem.*

Interrelated
Dependence of one part of the system on one or more other system parts.

Boundary
The line that marks the inside and outside of a system and that sets off the system from its environment.

Purpose
The overall goal or function of a system.

Environment
Everything external to a system that interacts with the system.

Interface
Point of contact where a system meets its environment or where subsystems meet each other.

Constraint
A limit to what a system can accomplish.

Important System Concepts

Systems analysts need to know several other important systems concepts:

- Decomposition
- Modularity
- Coupling
- Cohesion

FIGURE 1-5
A university as a system.

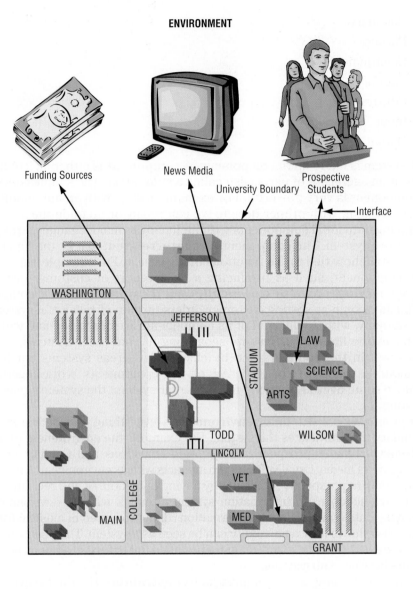

Decomposition
The process of breaking the description of a system down into small components; also known as *functional decomposition*.

Decomposition is the process of breaking down a system into its smaller components. These components may themselves be systems (subsystems) and can be broken down into their components as well. How does decomposition aid understanding of a system? It results in smaller and less complex pieces that are easier to understand than larger, complicated pieces. Decomposing a system also allows us to focus on one particular part of a system, making it easier to think of how to modify that one part independently of the entire system. Decomposition is a technique that allows the systems analyst to:

- Break a system into small, manageable, and understandable subsystems
- Focus attention on one area (subsystem) at a time, without interference from other areas
- Concentrate on the part of the system pertinent to a particular group of users, without confusing users with unnecessary details
- Build different parts of the system at independent times and have the help of different analysts

Figure 1-6 shows the decomposition of a portable MP3 player. Decomposing the system into subsystems reveals the system's inner workings. You can decompose an MP3 player into at least three separate physical subsystems. (Note that decomposing the same MP3 player into *logical* subsystems would result in a different set of subsystems.) One subsystem, the battery, supplies the power for the entire system to operate. A second physical subsystem, the storage system, is made up of a hard drive that stores thousands of MP3 recordings. The third subsystem, the control subsystem, consists of a printed circuit board (PCB), with various chips attached, that controls all of the recording, playback, and access functions. Breaking the subsystems down into their components reveals even more about the inner workings of the system and greatly enhances our understanding of how the overall system works.

Modularity is a direct result of decomposition. It refers to dividing a system into chunks or modules of a relatively uniform size. Modules can represent a system simply, making it easier to understand and easier to redesign and rebuild. For example, each of the separate subsystem modules for the MP3 player in Figure 1-6 shows how decomposition makes it easier to understand the overall system.

Coupling means that subsystems are dependent on each other. Subsystems should be as independent as possible. If one subsystem fails and other subsystems are highly dependent on it, the others will either fail themselves or have problems functioning. Looking at Figure 1-6, we would say the components of a portable MP3 player are tightly coupled. The best example is the control system, made up of the printed circuit board and its chips. Every function the MP3 player can perform is enabled by the board and the chips. A failure in one part of the circuit board would typically lead to replacing the entire board rather than attempting to isolate the problem on the board and fix it. Even though repairing a circuit board in an MP3 player is certainly possible, it is typically not cost-effective; the cost of the labor expended to diagnose and fix the problem may be worth more than the value of the circuit board itself. In a home stereo system, the components are loosely coupled because the subsystems, such as the speakers, the amplifier, the receiver, and the CD player, are all physically separate and function independently. If the amplifier in a home stereo system fails, only the amplifier needs to be repaired.

Modularity
Dividing a system up into chunks or modules of a relatively uniform size.

Coupling
The extent to which subsystems depend on each other.

Battery:
Power system

Hard drive:
Storage system

Printed circuit board:
Control system

FIGURE 1-6
An MP3 player is a system with power supply, storage and control subsystems.

Sources: Shutterstock; ©Harald van Arkel/Chipmunk International.

Cohesion
The extent to which a system or subsystem performs a single function.

Cohesion is the extent to which a subsystem performs a single function. In the MP3 player example, supplying power is a single function.

This brief discussion of systems should better prepare you to think about computer-based information systems and how they are built. Many of the same principles that apply to systems in general apply to information systems as well. In the next section, we review how the information systems development process and the tools that have supported it have changed over the decades.

A Modern Approach to Systems Analysis and Design

Today, systems development focuses on systems integration. Systems integration allows hardware and software from different vendors to work together in an application. It also enables existing systems developed in procedural languages to work with new systems built with visual programming environments. Developers use visual programming environments, such as Visual Basic, to design the user interfaces for systems that run on client/server platforms. In a client/server environment, some of the software runs on the server, a powerful computer designed to allow many people access to software and data stored on it, and some of the software runs on client machines. Client machines are the PCs you use at your desk at work. The database usually resides on the server. These relationships are shown in Figure 1-7. The Internet is also organized in a client/server format. With the browser software on your home PC, you can get files and applications from many different computers throughout the world. Your home PC is the client, and all of the Internet computers are servers.

Alternatively, organizations may purchase an enterprise-wide system from companies such as SAP (Systems, Applications, and Products in Data Processing) or Oracle. Enterprise-wide systems are large, complex systems that consist of a series of independent system modules. Developers assemble systems by choosing and implementing specific modules. Enterprise-wide systems usually contain software to support many different tasks in an organization rather than only one or two functions. For example, an enterprise-wide system may handle all human resources management, payroll, benefits, and retirement functions within a single, integrated system. It is, in fact, increasingly rare for organizations to develop systems in-house anymore. Chapter 2 will introduce you to the

FIGURE 1-7
The client/server model.

Server

Database

Clients

various sources of information systems technology. First, however, you must gain some insight into what your role will be in the systems development process.

Your Role in Systems Development

Although many people in organizations are involved in systems analysis and design, the **systems analyst** has the primary responsibility. A career as a systems analyst will allow you to have a significant impact on how your organization operates. This fast-growing and rewarding position is found in both large and small companies. IDC, a leading consulting group, predicts that growth in information technology (IT) employment will exceed 3 percent per year through at least 2013. The Bureau of Labor Statistics predicts additional increases in the numbers of IT jobs from 2004 to 2014. During this period, the professional IT workforce is projected to add more than 1 million new jobs in the United States. Information technology workers remain in demand.

Systems analyst
The organizational role most responsible for the analysis and design of information systems.

The primary role of a systems analyst is to study the problems and needs of an organization in order to determine how people, methods, and information technology can best be combined to bring about improvements in the organization. A systems analyst helps system users and other business managers define their requirements for new or enhanced information services.

Systems analysts are key to the systems development process. To succeed as a systems analyst, you will need to develop four types of skills: analytical, technical, managerial, and interpersonal. Analytical skills enable you to understand the organization and its functions, to identify opportunities and problems, and to analyze and solve problems. One of the most important analytical skills you can develop is systems thinking, or the ability to see organizations and information systems as systems. Systems thinking provides a framework from which to see the important relationships among information systems, the organizations they exist in, and the environment in which the organizations themselves exist. Technical skills help you understand the potential and the limitations of information technology. As an analyst, you must be able to envision an information system that will help users solve problems and that will guide the system's design and development. You must also be able to work with programming languages such as C++ and Java, various operating systems such as Windows and Linux, and computer hardware platforms such as IBM and Mac. Management skills help you manage projects, resources, risk, and change. Interpersonal skills help you work with end users as well as with other analysts and programmers. As a systems analyst, you will play a major role as a liaison among users, programmers, and other systems professionals. Effective written and oral communication, including competence in leading meetings, interviewing end users, and listening, are key skills that analysts must master. Effective analysts successfully combine these four types of skills, as Figure 1-8 (a typical advertisement for a systems analyst position) illustrates.

Let's consider two examples of the types of organizational problems you could face as a systems analyst. First, you work in the information systems department of a major magazine company. The company is having problems keeping an updated and accurate list of subscribers, and some customers are getting two magazines instead of one. The company will lose money and subscribers if these problems continue. To create a more efficient tracking system, the users of the current computer system as well as financial managers submit their problem to you and your colleagues in the information systems department. Second, you work in the information systems department at a university, where you are called upon to address an organizational problem such as the mailing of student grades to the wrong addresses.

Simon & Taylor, Inc., a candle manufacturer, has an immediate opening for a systems analyst in its Vermont-based office.

The ideal candidate will have:

1. A bachelor's degree in management information systems or computer science.

2. Two years' experience with UNIX/LINUX.

3. Experience with C, Java, and/or other object-oriented programming languages, and with application development environments such as Visual Studio or IBM's Rational Unified Process.

4. LAN-related skills and experience.

5. Familiarity with distribution and manufacturing concepts (allocation, replenishment, shop floor control, and production scheduling).

6. Working knowledge of project management and all phases of the systems development life cycle.

7. Strong communication skills.

We offer a competitive salary, relocation assistance, and the challenges of working in a state-of-the-art IT environment.

E-mail your resume to HR@simontaylor.com.

Simon & Taylor, Inc., is an equal opportunity employer.

When developing information systems to deal with problems such as these, an organization and its systems analysts have several options: They can go to an information technology services firm, such as Accenture or EDS, an HP Company, to have the system developed for them; they can buy the system off the shelf; they can implement an enterprise-wide system from a company such as SAP; they can obtain open-source software; or they can use in-house staff to develop the system. Alternatively, the organization can decide to outsource system development and operation. All of these options are discussed in detail in Chapter 2.

Developing Information Systems and the Systems Development Life Cycle

Systems development methodology
A standard process followed in an organization to conduct all the steps necessary to analyze, design, implement, and maintain information systems.

Systems development life cycle (SDLC)
The series of steps used to mark the phases of development for an information system.

Organizations use a standard set of steps, called a **systems development methodology,** to develop and support their information systems. Like many processes, the development of information systems often follows a life cycle. For example, a commercial product, such as a Nike sneaker or a Honda car, follows a life cycle: It is created, tested, and introduced to the market. Its sales increase, peak, and decline. Finally, the product is removed from the market and is replaced by something else. The **systems development life cycle (SDLC)** is a common methodology for systems development in many organizations. It marks the phases or steps of information systems development: Someone has an idea for an information system and what it should do. The organization that will use the system decides to devote the necessary resources to acquiring it. A careful study is done of how the organization currently handles the work the system will support. Professionals develop a strategy for designing the new system, which is then either built or purchased. Once complete, the system is installed in the organization, and after proper training, the users begin to incorporate the new system into their daily work. Every organization uses a slightly different life-cycle model to model these steps, with anywhere from three to almost twenty identifiable phases. In this book, we highlight four SDLC

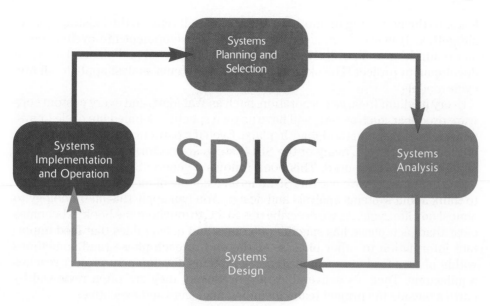

FIGURE 1-9
The systems development life cycle (SDLC).

steps: (1) planning and selection, (2) analysis, (3) design, and (4) implementation and operation (see Figure 1-9).

Although any life cycle appears at first glance to be a sequentially ordered set of phases, it actually is not. The specific steps and their sequence are meant to be adapted as required for a project. For example, in any given SDLC phase, the project can return to an earlier phase, if necessary. Similarly, if a commercial product does not perform well just after its introduction, it may be temporarily removed from the market and improved before being reintroduced. In the systems development life cycle, it is also possible to complete some activities in one phase in parallel with some activities of another phase. Sometimes the life cycle is iterative; that is, phases are repeated as required until an acceptable system is found. Some systems analysts consider the life cycle to be a spiral, in which we constantly cycle through the phases at different levels of detail, as illustrated in Figure 1-10. The circular nature of the life-cycle diagram in Figure 1-10 illustrates how the end of the useful life of one system

FIGURE 1-10
Evolutionary model SDLC.

leads to the beginning of another project that will replace the existing system altogether. However conceived, the systems development life cycle used in an organization is an orderly set of activities conducted and planned for each development project. The skills required of a systems analyst apply to all life-cycle models.

Every medium-to-large corporation, such as Wal-Mart, and every custom software producer, such as SAP, will have its own specific, detailed life cycle or systems development methodology in place. Even if a particular methodology does not look like a cycle, many of the SDLC steps are performed, and SDLC techniques and tools are used. This book follows a generic SDLC model, as illustrated in Figure 1-9. We use this SDLC as an example of methodology and a way to think about systems analysis and design. You can apply this methodology to almost any life cycle. As we describe this SDLC throughout the book, it becomes clear that each phase has specific outcomes and deliverables that feed important information to other phases. At the end of each phase (and sometimes within phases for intermediate steps), a systems development project reaches a milestone. Then, as deliverables are produced, they are often reviewed by parties outside the project team, including managers and executives.

Phase 1: Systems Planning and Selection

Systems planning and selection

The first phase of the SDLC, in which an organization's total information system needs are analyzed and arranged, and in which a potential information systems project is identified and an argument for continuing or not continuing with the project is presented.

The first phase in the SDLC, **systems planning and selection,** has two primary activities. First, someone identifies the need for a new or enhanced system. Information needs of the organization are examined, and projects to meet these needs are identified. The organization's information system needs may result from:

- Requests to deal with problems in current procedures
- The desire to perform additional tasks
- The realization that information technology could be used to capitalize on an existing opportunity

The systems analyst prioritizes and translates the needs into a written plan for the information systems (IS) department, including a schedule for developing new major systems. Requests for new systems spring from users who need new or enhanced systems. During the systems planning and selection phase, an organization determines whether resources should be devoted to the development or enhancement of each information system under consideration. A *feasibility study* is conducted before the second phase of the SDLC to determine the economic and organizational impact of the system.

The second task in the systems planning and selection phase is to investigate the system and determine the proposed system's scope. The team of systems analysts then produces a specific plan for the proposed project for the team to follow. This baseline project plan customizes the standardized SDLC and specifies the time and resources needed for its execution. The formal definition of a project is based on the likelihood that the organization's IS department is able to develop a system that will solve the problem or exploit the opportunity and determine whether the costs of developing the system outweigh the possible benefits. The final presentation to the organization's management of the plan for proceeding with the subsequent project phases is usually made by the project leader and other team members.

Phase 2: Systems Analysis

Systems analysis

Phase of the SDLC in which the current system is studied and alternative replacement systems are proposed.

The second phase of the systems development life cycle is **systems analysis.** During this phase, the analyst thoroughly studies the organization's current procedures and the information systems used to perform tasks such as general ledger, shipping, order entry, machine scheduling, and payroll. Analysis has several subphases. The first subphase involves determining the requirements of the system. In this subphase, you and other analysts work with users to determine what the users want from a proposed system. This subphase involves a careful study of any current systems, manual and computerized, that might be replaced or enhanced as part of this project. Next, you study the requirements and structure them according to their interrelationships, eliminating any redundancies. As part of structuring, you generate alternative initial designs to match the requirements. Then you compare these alternatives to determine which best meets the requirements within the cost, labor, and technical levels the organization is willing to commit to the development process. The output of the analysis phase is a description of the alternative solution recommended by the analysis team. Once the recommendation is accepted by the organization, you can make plans to acquire any hardware and system software necessary to build or operate the system as proposed.

Phase 3: Systems Design

The third phase of the SDLC is called **systems design.** During systems design, analysts convert the description of the recommended alternative solution into logical and then physical system specifications. You must design all aspects of the system from input and output screens to reports, databases, and computer processes.

Logical design is not tied to any specific hardware and systems software platform. Theoretically, the system you design could be implemented on any hardware and systems software. Logical design concentrates on the business aspects of the system; that is, how the system will impact the functional units within the organization. Figure 1-11 shows both the logical design for a product and its physical design, side by side, for comparison. You can see from the comparison that many specific decisions had to be made to move from the logical model to the physical product. The situation is similar in information systems design.

In physical design, you turn the logical design into physical, or technical, specifications. For example, you must convert diagrams that map the origin, flow, and processing of data in a system into a structured systems design that can then be broken down into smaller and smaller units for conversion to instructions written in a programming language. You design the various parts of the system to perform the physical operations necessary to facilitate data capture, processing, and information output. During physical design, the analyst team decides which programming languages the computer instructions will be written in, which database systems and file structures will be used for the data, and which hardware platform, operating system, and network environment the system will run under. These decisions finalize the hardware and software plans initiated at the end of the analysis phase. Now you can acquire any new technology not already present in the organization. The final product of the design phase is the physical system specifications, presented in a form, such as a diagram or written report, ready to be turned over to programmers and other system builders for construction.

Phase 4: Systems Implementation and Operation

The final phase of the SDLC is a two-step process: **systems implementation and operation.** During systems implementation and operation, you turn system specifications into a working system that is tested and then put into use. Implementation includes coding, testing, and installation. During coding, programmers write the programs that make up the system. During testing, programmers and analysts test individual programs and the entire system in

Systems design
Phase of the SDLC in which the system chosen for development in systems analysis is first described independently of any computer platform, (logical design) and is then transformed into technology-specific details (physical design) from which all programming and system construction can be accomplished.

Systems implementation and operation
Final phase of the SDLC, in which the information system is coded, tested, and installed in the organization, and in which the information system is systematically repaired and improved.

FIGURE 1-11
The difference between logical design and physical design: (A) A skateboard ramp blueprint (logical design), (B) A skateboard ramp (physical design).

Source: http://www.tumyeto.com/ tydu/skatebrd/organizations/ plans/14pipe.jpg; www.tumyeto .com/tydu/skatebrd/ organizations/iuscblue.html (accessed September 16, 1999). Reprinted by permission of the International Association of Skateboard Companies.

order to find and correct errors. During installation, the new system becomes a part of the daily activities of the organization. Application software is installed, or loaded, on existing or new hardware; then users are introduced to the new system and trained. Begin planning for both testing and installation as early as the project planning and selection phase, because they both require extensive analysis in order to develop exactly the right approach.

Systems implementation activities also include initial user support such as the finalization of documentation, training programs, and ongoing user assistance. Note that documentation and training programs are finalized during implementation; documentation is produced throughout the life cycle, and training (and education) occurs from the inception of a project. Systems implementation can continue for as long as the system exists because ongoing user support is also part of implementation. Despite the best efforts of analysts, managers, and programmers, however, installation is not always a simple process. Many well-designed systems have failed because the installation process was faulty. Note that even a well-designed system can fail if implementation is not well managed. Because the management of systems implementation is usually done by the project team, we stress implementation issues throughout this book.

The second part of the fourth phase of the SDLC is operation. While a system is operating in an organization, users sometimes find problems with how it works and often think of improvements. During operation, programmers make the changes that users ask for and modify the system to reflect changing business conditions. These changes are necessary to keep the system running and useful. The amount of time and effort devoted to system enhancements during operation depends a great deal on the performance of the previous phases of the life cycle. Inevitably, the time comes when an information system is no longer performing as desired, when the costs of keeping a system running become prohibitive, or when an organization's needs have changed substantially. Such problems indicate that it is time to begin designing the system's replacement, thereby completing the loop and starting the life cycle over again.

The SDLC is a highly linked set of phases whose products feed the activities in subsequent phases. Table 1-1 summarizes the outputs or products of each phase based on the preceding descriptions. The subsequent chapters on the SDLC phases discuss the products of each phase and how they are developed.

Throughout the systems development life cycle, the systems development project itself needs to be carefully planned and managed. The larger the systems project, the greater the need for project management. Several project management techniques have been developed in the last quarter-century, and many have been improved through automation. Chapter 3 contains a more detailed treatment of project planning and management techniques.

TABLE 1-1: Products of the SDLC Phases

Phase	Products, Outputs, or Deliverables
Systems planning and selection	Priorities for systems and projects
	Architecture for data, networks, hardware, and IS management
	Detailed work plan for selected project
	Specification of system scope
	System justification or business case
Systems analysis	Description of current system
	General recommendation on how to fix, enhance, or replace current system
	Explanation of alternative systems and justification for chosen alternative
	Acquisition plan for new technology
Systems design	Detailed specifications of all system elements
Systems implementation and operation	Code
	Documentation
	Training procedures and support capabilities
	New versions or releases of software with associated updates to documentation, training, and support

Alternative Approaches to Development

Prototyping, computer-aided software engineering (CASE) tools, joint application design (JAD), rapid application development (RAD), participatory design (PD), and the use of Agile Methodologies represent different approaches that streamline and improve the systems analysis and design process from different perspectives.

Prototyping

Prototyping
Building a scaled-down version of the desired information system.

Designing and building a scaled-down but working version of a desired system is known as **prototyping.** A prototype can be developed with a CASE tool, a software product that automates steps in the systems development life cycle. CASE tools make prototyping easier and more creative by supporting the design of screens and reports and other parts of a system interface. CASE tools also support many of the diagramming techniques you will learn, such as data-flow diagrams and entity-relationship diagrams.

Figure 1-12 illustrates prototyping. The analyst works with users to determine the initial or basic requirements for the system. The analyst then quickly builds a prototype. When the prototype is completed, the users work with it and tell the analyst what they like and do not like about it. The analyst uses this feedback to improve the prototype and takes the new version back to the users. This iterative process continues until the users are relatively satisfied with what they have seen. The key advantages of the prototyping technique are: (1) it involves the user in analysis and design, and (2) it captures requirements in concrete, rather than verbal or abstract, form. In addition to being used as a stand-alone, prototyping may also be used to augment the SDLC. For example, a prototype of the final system may be developed early in analysis to help the analysts identify what users want. Then the final system is developed based on the specifications of the prototype. We discuss prototyping in greater detail in Chapter 5 and use various prototyping tools in Chapter 9 to illustrate the design of system outputs.

Computer-Aided Software Engineering (CASE) Tools

Computer-aided software engineering (CASE)
Software tools that provide automated support for some portion of the systems development process.

Computer-aided software engineering (CASE) refers to automated software tools used by systems analysts to develop information systems. These tools can be used to automate or support activities throughout the systems development process with the objective of increasing productivity and improving the overall quality of systems. CASE helps provide an engineering-type discipline to software

FIGURE 1-12
The prototyping method.

Source: Adapted from J. D. Naumann and A. M. Jenkins, "Prototyping: The New Paradigm for Systems Development," *MIS Quarterly* 6, no. 3 (1982): 29–44.

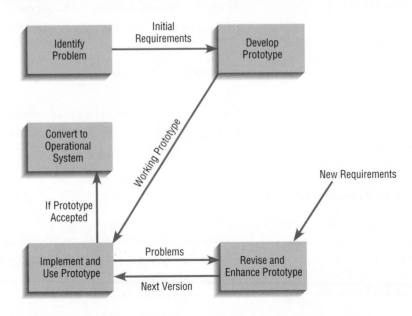

development and to the automation of the entire software life-cycle process, sometimes with a single family of integrated software tools. In general, CASE assists systems builders in managing the complexities of information system projects and helps ensure that high-quality systems are constructed on time and within budget.

Vendors of CASE products have "opened up" their systems through the use of standard databases and data-conversion utilities to share information across products and tools easier. An integrated and standard database called a **repository** is the common method for providing product and tool integration and has been a key factor in enabling CASE to manage larger, more complex projects easier and to seamlessly integrate data across various tools and products. The general types of CASE tools include:

- Diagramming tools that enable system process, data, and control structures to be represented graphically.

- Computer display and report generators that help prototype how systems "look and feel" to users. Display (or form) and report generators also make it easier for the systems analyst to identify data requirements and relationships.

- Analysis tools that automatically check for incomplete, inconsistent, or incorrect specifications in diagrams, forms, and reports.

- A central repository that enables the integrated storage of specifications, diagrams, reports, and project management information.

- Documentation generators that help produce both technical and user documentation in standard formats.

- Code generators that enable the automatic generation of program and database definition code directly from the design documents, diagrams, forms, and reports.

Repository
A centralized database that contains all diagrams, forms and report definitions, data structures, data definitions, process flows and logic, and definitions of other organizational and system components; it provides a set of mechanisms and structures to achieve seamless data-to-tool and data-to-data integration.

Joint Application Design

In the late 1970s, systems development personnel at IBM developed a new process for collecting information system requirements and reviewing system designs. The process is called **joint application design (JAD).** The idea behind JAD is to structure the requirements determination phase of analysis and the reviews that occur as part of the design. Users, managers, and systems developers are brought together for a series of intensive structured meetings run by a JAD session leader. By gathering the people directly affected by an IS in one room at the same time to work together to agree on system requirements and design details, time and organizational resources are better managed. Group members are more likely to develop a shared understanding of what the IS is supposed to do. JAD has become common in certain industries, such as insurance, and in specific companies, such as CIGNA. We discuss JAD in more detail in Chapter 5.

Joint application design (JAD)
A structured process in which users, managers, and analysts work together for several days in a series of intensive meetings to specify or review system requirements.

Rapid Application Development

Prototyping, CASE, and JAD are key tools that support **rapid application development (RAD).** The fundamental principle of any RAD methodology is to delay producing detailed system design documents until after user requirements are clear. The prototype serves as the working description of needs. RAD involves gaining user acceptance of the interface and developing key system capabilities as quickly as possible. RAD is widely used by consulting firms. It is also used as an in-house methodology by firms such as the Boeing Company. RAD sacrifices computer efficiency for gains in human efficiency in rapidly building and rebuilding working systems. On the other hand, RAD methodologies can overlook important systems development principles, which may result in problems with systems developed this way.

Rapid application development (RAD)
Systems development methodology created to radically decrease the time needed to design and implement information systems.

RAD grew out of the convergence of two trends: the increased speed and turbulence of doing business in the late 1980s and early 1990s, and the ready availability of high-powered computer-based tools to support systems development and easy maintenance. As the conditions of doing business in a changing, competitive global environment became more turbulent, management in many organizations began to question whether it made sense to wait two to three years to develop systems that would be obsolete upon completion. On the other hand, CASE tools and prototyping software were diffusing throughout organizations, making it relatively easy for end users to see what their systems would look like before they were completed. Why not use these tools to address the problems of developing systems more productively in a rapidly changing business environment? So RAD was born.

As Figure 1-13 shows, the same phases followed in the traditional SDLC are also followed in RAD, but the phases are combined to produce a more streamlined development technique. Planning and design phases in RAD are shortened by focusing work on system functional and user interface requirements at the expense of detailed business analysis and concern for system performance issues. Also, usually RAD looks at the system being developed in isolation from other systems, thus eliminating the time-consuming activities of coordinating with existing standards and systems during design and development. The emphasis in RAD is generally less on the sequence and structure of processes in the life cycle and more on doing different tasks in parallel with each other and on using prototyping extensively. Notice also, that the iteration in the RAD life cycle is limited to the design and development phases, which is where the bulk of the work in a RAD approach takes place. Although it is possible in RAD to return to planning once design has begun, it is rarely done. Similarly, although it is possible to return to development from the cutover phase (when the system is turned over to the user), RAD is designed to minimize iteration at this point in the life cycle. The high level of user commitment and involvement throughout RAD implies that the system that emerges should be more readily accepted by the user community (and hence more easily implemented during cutover) than would a system developed using traditional techniques.

FIGURE 1-13
RAD systems development life cycle compared to standard SDLC.

Participatory Design

Developed in northern Europe, **participatory design (PD)** represents a viable alternative approach to the SDLC. One of the best-known companies that has used this approach is StatoilHydro, the Norwegian oil company. PD emphasizes the role of the user much more than do traditional North American techniques such as structured analysis and structured design. In some cases, PD may involve the entire user community in the development process. Each user has an equal voice in determining system requirements and in approving system design. In other cases, an elected group of users controls the process. These users represent the larger community, much as a legislature represents the needs and wants of the electorate. Typically, under PD, systems analysts work for the users. The organization's management and outside consultants provide advice rather than control. PD is partly a result of the roles of labor and management in the northern European workplace where labor is more organized, carries more clout, and is more intimately involved with technological changes than is true in North America.

Participatory design (PD)
A systems development approach that originated in northern Europe, in which users and the improvement of their work lives are the central focus.

Agile Methodologies

As you might imagine, many other approaches to systems analysis and design have been developed over the years. These approaches include eXtreme Programming, the Crystal family of methodologies, Adaptive Software Development, Scrum, and Feature Driven Development. In February 2001, many of the proponents of these alternative approaches met in Utah in the United States and reached a consensus on many of the underlying principles their various approaches contained. This consensus turned into a document they called "The Agile Manifesto" (see Appendix B for more detail). These **Agile Methodologies** share three key principles: (1) a focus on adaptive rather than predictive methodologies, (2) a focus on people rather than roles, and (3) a self-adaptive process. Adopting an adaptive rather than predictive methodology refers to the observation that engineering-based methodologies work best when the process and product are predictive. Software tends not to be as predictive as, say, a bridge, especially in today's turbulent business environment. More adaptive methodologies are needed, then, and the Agile Methodologies are based on the ability to adapt quickly. The focus on people rather than roles is also a criticism of engineering-based techniques, where people became interchangeable. An Agile approach views people as talented individuals, not people filling roles, each of whom has unique talents to bring to a development project. Finally, Agile Methodologies promote a self-adaptive software development process. As the methodologies are applied, they should also be adapted by a particular development team working on a particular project in a particular context. No single monolithic methodology effectively fits all developers on all projects at all times. You will learn much more about Agile Methodologies in Appendix B.

Agile Methodologies
A family of development methodologies characterized by short iterative cycles and extensive testing; active involvement of users for establishing, prioritizing, and verifying requirements; and a focus on small teams of talented, experienced programmers.

Key Points Review

1. **Define information systems analysis and design.**
   Systems analysis and design is the complex organizational process whereby computer-based information systems are developed and operated.
2. **Describe the role of the systems analyst in information systems development.**
   Systems analysts play a key organizational role in systems development. They act as liaisons between business users on one hand and technical

personnel on the other. Analysts need to develop four sets of skills in order to succeed: analytical, technical, managerial, and interpersonal.
3. **Describe the information systems development life cycle (SDLC).**
   The SDLC used in this book has four major phases: (1) systems planning and selection, (2) systems analysis, (3) systems design, and (4) systems implementation and operation. In the first phase, which is planning and selection,

analysts make detailed road maps of the system development project. In analysis, analysts work to solve the business problem being studied. In design, the solution to the problem is built. Finally, in the last phase, the system is given to users and kept running.

4. **List alternatives to the SDLC, including a description of the role of computer-aided software engineering (CASE) tools in systems development.**

    The alternative frameworks mentioned in this chapter are prototyping, joint application design (JAD), rapid application development (RAD), participatory design (PD), and Agile Methodologies.

Using prototyping, analysts build a working model of the system. In JAD, analysts and users meet to solve problems and design systems. RAD decreases the time needed to design and implement information systems. In PD, the emphasis is on the user community. Agile Methodologies focus on adaptive rather than predictive methodologies, on people rather than roles. CASE tools represent the use of information technology to assist in the systems development process. They include diagramming tools, screen and report design tools, and other special-purpose tools. CASE tools help programmers and analysts do their jobs efficiently and effectively by automating routine tasks.

Key Terms Checkpoint

Here are the key terms from the chapter. The page where each term is first explained is in parentheses after the term.

1. Agile Methodologies (p. 21)
2. Application software (p. 4)
3. Boundary (p. 7)
4. Cohesion (p. 10)
5. Component (p. 7)
6. Computer-aided software engineering (CASE) (p. 18)
7. Constraint (p. 7)
8. Coupling (p. 9)
9. Decomposition (p. 8)
10. Environment (p. 7)
11. Information systems analysis and design (p. 4)
12. Interface (p. 7)
13. Interrelated (p. 7)
14. Joint application design (JAD) (p. 19)
15. Modularity (p. 9)
16. Participatory design (PD) (p. 21)
17. Prototyping (p. 18)
18. Purpose (p. 7)
19. Rapid application development (RAD) (p. 19)
20. Repository (p. 19)
21. System (p. 6)
22. Systems analysis (p. 14)
23. Systems analyst (p. 11)
24. Systems design (p. 15)
25. Systems development life cycle (SDLC) (p. 12)
26. Systems development methodology (p. 12)
27. Systems implementation and operation (p. 15)
28. Systems planning and selection (p. 14)

Match each of the key terms above with the definition that best fits it.

_____ 1. The first phase of the SDLC in which an organization's total information system needs are analyzed and arranged, and in which a potential information systems project is identified and an argument for continuing or not continuing with the project is presented.

_____ 2. The process of developing and maintaining an information system.

_____ 3. A systems development approach that originated in northern Europe, in which users and the improvement of their work lives are the central focus.

_____ 4. Software designed to process data and support users in an organization. Examples include spreadsheets, word processors, and database management systems.

_____ 5. The organizational role most responsible for the analysis and design of information systems.

_____ 6. A structured process in which users, managers, and analysts work together for several days in a series of intensive meetings to specify or review system requirements.

_____ 7. Building a scaled-down version of the desired information system.

_____ 8. A group of interrelated procedures used for a business function, with an identifiable boundary, working together for some purpose.

_____ 9. An irreducible part or aggregation of parts that make up a system, also called a *subsystem.*

_____ 10. Dependence of one part of the system on one or more other system parts.

_____ 11. The line that marks the inside and outside of a system and that sets off the system from its environment.

_____ 12. The overall goal or function of a system.

_____ 13. Phase of the SDLC, in which the system chosen for development in systems analysis is first described independently of any computer platform and is then transformed into technology-specific details from which all programming and system construction can be accomplished.

_____ 14. Phase of the SDLC, in which the current system is studied and alternative replacement systems are proposed.

_____ 15. Everything external to a system that interacts with the system.

_____ 16. Point of contact where a system meets its environment or where subsystems meet each other.

_____ 17. A limit to what a system can accomplish.

_____ 18. Final phase of the SDLC, in which the information system is coded, tested, and installed in the organization, and in which the information system is systematically repaired and improved.

_____ 19. A standard process followed in an organization to conduct all the steps necessary to analyze, design, implement, and maintain information systems.

_____ 20. The series of steps used to mark the phases of development for an information system.

_____ 21. The process of breaking the description of a system down into small components; also known as *functional decomposition*.

_____ 22. Dividing a system up into chunks or modules of a relatively uniform size.

_____ 23. The extent to which subsystems depend on each other.

_____ 24. The extent to which a system or subsystem performs a single function.

_____ 25. Software tools that provide automated support for some portion of the systems development process.

_____ 26. A centralized database that contains all diagrams, forms and report definitions, data structures, data definitions, process flows and logic, and definitions of other organizational and system components; it provides a set of mechanisms and structures to achieve seamless data-to-tool and data-to-data integration.

_____ 27. Systems development methodology created to radically decrease the time needed to design and implement information systems.

_____ 28. Current approaches to systems development that focus on adaptive methodologies, people instead of roles, and an overall self-adaptive development process.

Review Questions

1. What is information systems analysis and design?
2. What is systems thinking? How is it useful for thinking about computer-based information systems?
3. What is decomposition? Coupling? Cohesion?
4. In what way are organizations systems?
5. List and explain the different phases in the systems development life cycle.
6. What is prototyping?
7. What are CASE tools? What is a CASE repository and how is it used?
8. What is JAD? What is participatory design?
9. What is RAD? How does it compare to the typical SDLC?
10. What are Agile Methodologies?

Problems and Exercises

1. Why is it important to use systems analysis and design methodologies when building a system? Why not just build the system in whatever way seems to be "quick and easy?" What value is provided by using an "engineering" approach?
2. Describe your university or college as a system. What is the input? The output? The boundary? The components? Their interrelationships? The constraints? The purpose? The interfaces? The environment? Draw a diagram of this system.
3. A car is a system with several subsystems, including the braking subsystem, the electrical subsystem, the engine, the fuel subsystem, the climate-control subsystem, and the passenger subsystem. Draw a diagram of a car as a system and label all of its system characteristics.
4. Your personal computer is a system. Draw and label a personal computer as a system as you did for a car in Problem and Exercise 3.
5. Choose a business transaction you undertake regularly, such as using an ATM machine, buying groceries at the supermarket, or buying a ticket for a university's basketball game. For this transaction, define the data, draw the data-flow diagram, and describe processing logic.
6. How is the joint application design (JAD) approach different from the participatory design (PD) approach developed in northern Europe? (You may

have to do some digging at the library to answer this question adequately.) What are the benefits in using these types of approaches in building information systems? What are the barriers?

7. How would you organize a project team of students to work with a small business client? How would you organize a project team if you were working for a professional consulting organization? How might these two methods of organization differ? Why?

8. How might prototyping be used as part of the SDLC?

9. Describe the difference in the role of a systems analyst in the SDLC versus prototyping.

10. Compare Figures 1-9 and 1-10. What similarities and differences do you see?

Discussion Questions

1. If someone at a party asked you what a systems analyst was and why anyone would want to be one, what would you say? Support your answer with evidence from this chapter.

2. Explain how a computer-based information system designed to process payroll is a specific example of a system. Be sure to account for all nine components of any system in your explanation.

3. How does the Internet, and more specifically the World Wide Web, fit into the picture of systems analysis and systems development drawn in this chapter?

4. What do you think systems analysis and design will look like in the next decade? As you saw earlier in the chapter, changes in systems development have been pretty dramatic in the past. A computer programmer suddenly transported from the 1950s to the 2000s would have trouble recognizing the computing environment that had evolved just fifty years later. What dramatic changes might occur in the next ten years?

Case Problems

1. Pine Valley Furniture

Alex Schuster began Pine Valley Furniture (PVF) as a hobby. Initially, Alex would build custom furniture in his garage for friends and family. As word spread about his quality craftsmanship, he began taking orders. The hobby has since evolved into a medium-sized business, employing more than fifty workers.

Over the years, increased demand has forced Alex to relocate several times, increase his sales force, expand his product line, and renovate Pine Valley Furniture's information systems. As the company began to grow, Alex organized the company into functional areas—manufacturing, sales, orders, accounting, and purchasing. Originally, manual information systems were used; however, as the business began to expand rapidly, a minicomputer was installed to automate applications.

In the beginning, a process-oriented approach was utilized. Each separate application had its own data files. The applications automated the manual systems on which they were modeled. In an effort to improve its information systems, PVF recently renovated its information systems, resulting in a company-wide database and applications that work with this database. Pine Valley Furniture's computer-based applications are primarily in the accounting and financial areas. All applications have been built in-house, and when necessary, new information systems staff is hired to support Pine Valley Furniture's expanding information systems.

a. How did PVF go about developing its information systems? Why do you think the company chose this option? What other options were available?

b. One option available to PVF was an enterprise-wide system. What features does an enterprise-wide system, such as SAP, provide? What is the primary advantage of an enterprise-wide system?

c. PVF will be hiring two systems analysts next month. Your task is to develop a job advertisement for these positions. Locate several Web sites or newspapers that have job advertisements for systems analysts. What skills are required?

d. What types of information systems are currently utilized at PVF? Provide an example of each.

2. Hoosier Burger

As college students in the 1970s, Bob and Thelma Mellankamp often dreamed of starting their own business. While on their way to an economics class, Bob and Thelma drove by Myrtle's Family Restaurant and noticed a "for sale" sign in the window.

Bob and Thelma quickly made arrangements to purchase the business, and Hoosier Burger Restaurant was born. The restaurant is moderately sized, consisting of a kitchen, dining room, counter, storage area, and office. Currently, all paperwork is done by hand. Thelma and Bob have discussed the benefits of purchasing a computer system; however, Bob wants to investigate alternatives and hire a consultant to help them.

Perishable food items, such as beef patties, buns, and vegetables are delivered daily to the restaurant. Other items, such as napkins, straws, and cups, are ordered and delivered as needed. Bob Mellankamp receives deliveries at the restaurant's back door and then updates a stock log form. The stock log form helps Bob track inventory items. The stock log form is updated when deliveries are received and also nightly after daily sales have been tallied.

Customers place their orders at the counter and are called when their orders are ready. The orders are written on an order ticket, totaled on the cash register, and then passed to the kitchen where the orders are prepared. The cash register is not capable of capturing point-of-sale information. Once an order is prepared and delivered, the order ticket is placed in the order ticket box. Bob reviews these order tickets nightly and makes adjustments to inventory.

In the past several months, Bob has noticed several problems with Hoosier Burger's current information systems, especially with the inventory control, customer ordering, and management reporting systems. Because the inventory control and customer ordering systems are paper based, errors occur frequently. These errors often affect delivery orders received from suppliers as well as customer orders. Bob has often wanted to have electronic access to forecasting information, inventory usage, and basic sales information. This access is impossible because of the paper-based system.

a. Apply the SDLC approach to Hoosier Burger.
b. Using the Hoosier Burger scenario, identify an example of each system characteristic.
c. Decompose Hoosier Burger into its major subsystems.
d. Briefly summarize the approaches to systems development discussed in this chapter. Which approach do you feel should be used by Hoosier Burger?

3. Natural Best Health Food Stores

Natural Best Health Food Stores is a chain of health food stores serving Oklahoma, Arkansas, and Texas. Garrett Davis opened his first Natural

Best Health Food Store in 1975 and has since opened fifteen stores in three states. Initially, he sold only herbal supplements, gourmet coffees and teas, and household products. In 1990, he expanded his product line to include personal care, pet care, and grocery items.

In the past several months, many of Mr. Davis's customers have requested the ability to purchase prepackaged meals, such as chicken, turkey, fish, and vegetarian, and have these prepackaged meals automatically delivered to their homes weekly, biweekly, or monthly. Mr. Davis feels that this option is viable because Natural Best has an automatic delivery system in place for its existing product lines.

With the current system, a customer can subscribe to the Natural Best Delivery Service (NBDS) and have personal care, pet care, gourmet products, and grocery items delivered on a weekly, biweekly, or monthly basis. The entire subscription process takes approximately five minutes. The salesclerk obtains the customer's name, mailing address, credit card number, desired delivery items and quantity, delivery frequency, and phone number. After the customer's subscription has been processed, delivery usually begins within a week. As customer orders are placed, inventory is automatically updated. The NBDS system is a client/server system. Each store is equipped with a client computer that accesses a centralized database housed on a central server. The server tracks inventory, customer activity, delivery schedules, and individual store sales. Each week the NBDS generates sales summary reports, low-in-stock reports, and delivery schedule reports for each store. The information contained on each of these individual reports is then consolidated into master sales summary, low-in-stock, and forecasting reports. Information contained on these reports facilitates restocking, product delivery, and forecasting decisions. Mr. Davis has an Excel worksheet that he uses to consolidate sales information from each store. He then uses this worksheet to make forecasting decisions for each store.

a. Identify the different types of information systems used at Natural Best Health Food Stores. Provide an example of each. Is an expert system currently used? If not, how could Natural Best benefit from the use of such a system?
b. Figure 1-4 identifies seven characteristics of a system. Using the Natural Best Health Food Stores scenario, provide an example of each system characteristic.
c. What type of computing environment does Natural Best Health Food Stores have?

two

The Sources of Software

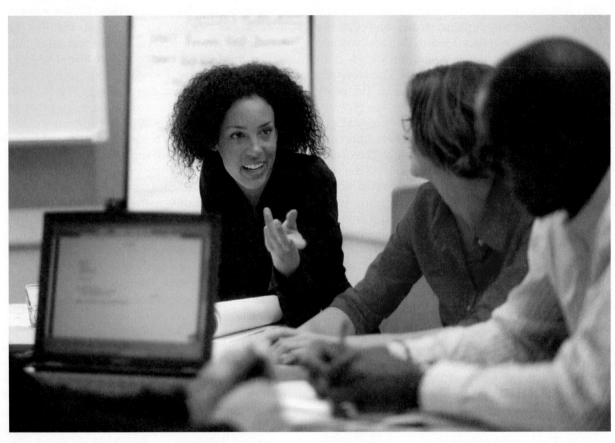

© Ryanstock/Getty Images

After studying this chapter, you should be able to:

- Explain outsourcing.
- Describe six different sources of software.
- Discuss how to evaluate off-the-shelf software.

- Explain reuse and its role in software development.

Chapter Preview . . .

Software is a big part of any business application system. Although most software was once written in-house by a company's own systems analysts and programmers, this practice is certainly not the case today. In today's thriving software industry, you can purchase software for just about any business situation imaginable. However, every business is unique, and no existing software fits a given firm and its needs exactly. Software must be modified to fit a company's specific needs. Many times, a business application is actually a combination of many different bits and pieces of software, purchased or otherwise acquired from many different vendors and integrated by a firm's internal information technology staff. But where does the IT staff find all the software it needs? That is the subject of Chapter 2. Here you will learn about the many sources of software available to today's system analyst.

Introduction

Many different sources of software are available, and many of you reading this book will end up working for firms that produce software rather than working in the information systems department of a corporation. But for those of you who go on to work in a corporate information systems department, the focus is no longer exclusively on in-house development. Instead, the focus will be on where to obtain the many pieces and components that you will combine into the application system you have been asked to create. You and your peers will still write code, mainly to make all the different pieces work together, but more and more of your application software will be written by someone else. Even though you will not write the code, you will still use the basic structure and processes of the systems development life cycle (SDLC) to build the application systems your organization demands. The organizational process of systems development remains the focus for the rest of the book, but first you need to know more about where software originates in today's development environment.

In this chapter, you will learn about the various sources of software for organizations. The first source considered is outsourcing, in which all or part of an organization's information systems, their development, and their maintenance are given over to another organization. You will then read about six different sources of software: (1) information technology services firms, (2) packaged software providers, (3) vendors of enterprise solutions software, (4) cloud computing, (5) open-source software, and (6) the organization itself when it develops software in-house. You will learn of criteria to evaluate software from these different sources. The chapter closes with a discussion of reuse and its impact on software development.

Systems Acquisition

Despite some debate about when and where the first administrative information system was developed, it is generally agreed that the first such system in the United Kingdom was developed at J. Lyons & Sons. In the United States, the first administrative information system was General Electric's (GE) payroll system, which was developed in 1954. At that time, and for many years afterwards, obtaining an information system meant one thing only: in-house development.

The software industry itself did not even come into existence until a decade after GE's payroll system was implemented.

Since GE's payroll system was built, in-house development has become a progressively smaller piece of all the systems development work that takes place in and for organizations. Internal corporate information systems departments now spend a smaller and smaller proportion of their time and effort on developing systems from scratch. Corporate information systems groups reported spending less time and money on traditional software development and maintenance than they used to. Instead, they increased work on packaged applications by a factor of three, and they increased outsourcing by 42 percent. Where in-house development occurred, it was related to Internet technology. Developers probably view Internet-related development as being more challenging and more fun than traditional development.

Organizations today have many choices when seeking an information system. We will start with a discussion of outsourcing development and operation and then present the six categories of software sources mentioned earlier. These various sources represent points along a continuum of options, along with many hybrid combinations as well.

Outsourcing

Outsourcing
The practice of turning over responsibility for some or all of an organization's information systems applications and operations to an outside firm.

If another organization develops or runs a computer application for your organization, that practice is called outsourcing. **Outsourcing** includes a spectrum of working arrangements. At one extreme is having a firm develop and run your application on its computers—you only supply input and take output. A common example is a company that runs payroll applications for clients so that clients don't have to develop an independent in-house payroll system. Instead they simply provide employee payroll information to the company and, for a fee, the company returns completed paychecks, payroll accounting reports, and tax and other statements for employees. For many organizations, the most cost-effective way to manage payroll operations is through outsourcing. In another example of outsourcing arrangements, you hire a company to run your applications at your site on your computers. In some cases, an organization employing such an arrangement will dissolve some or all of its information systems unit and transfer most or all of its information systems employees to the company brought in to run the organization's computing.

Why would an organization outsource its information systems operations? As we saw in the payroll example, outsourcing may be cost effective. If a company specializes in running payroll for other companies, it can leverage the economies of scale it achieves from running one stable computer application for many organizations into low prices. But why would an organization dissolve its entire information processing unit and bring in an outside firm to manage its computer applications? One reason may be to overcome operating problems the organization faces in its information systems unit. For example, the city of Grand Rapids, Michigan, hired an outside firm to run its computing center thirty years ago in order to manage its computing center employees better. Union contracts and civil service constraints, then in force, made it difficult to fire people, so the city brought in a facilities management organization to run its computing operations, and it was able to get rid of problem employees at the same time. Another reason for total outsourcing is that an organization's management may feel its core mission does not involve managing an information systems unit and that it might achieve more effective computing by turning over all of its operations to a more experienced, computer-oriented company. Kodak decided in the late 1980s that it was not in the computer applications business and turned over management of its mainframes to IBM and management of its personal computers to Businessland.

Outsourcing is big business. Some organizations outsource the IT development and many of their IT functions, at a cost of billions of dollars. The traditional outsourcing market is now a $280 billion industry, and the off-shoring market is worth $70 billion. Individual outsourcing vendors sign large contracts for their services. IBM and HP are two of the biggest, best-known global outsourcing firms. Both companies have multiple outsourcing contracts in place with many different firms.

Outsourcing is an alternative that analysts definitely need to be aware of. When generating alternative system development strategies for a system, you as an analyst should consult organizations in your area that provide outsourcing services. It may well be that at least one such organization has already been developed and is running an application similar to what your users are asking for. Perhaps outsourcing the replacement system should be one of your alternatives. Knowing what your system requirements are before you consider outsourcing means that you can carefully assess how well the suppliers of outsourcing services can respond to your needs. However, should you decide not to outsource, you need to consider whether some software components of your replacement system should be purchased and not built.

Sources of Software

We can group organizations that produce software into six major categories: (1) information technology services firms, (2) packaged software providers, (3) vendors of enterprise solutions software, (4) cloud computing, (5) open-source software, and (6) in-house development (Figure 2-1).

Information Technology Services Firms If a company needs an information system but does not have the expertise or the personnel to develop the system in-house and a suitable off-the-shelf system is not available, the company will likely consult an information technology (IT) services firm. IT services firms help companies develop custom information systems for internal use; they develop, host, and run applications for customers, or they provide other services. Note in Table 2-1, a list of the top ten global software firms, that three out of ten specialize in services, which include custom systems development. These firms employ people with expertise in the development of information systems. Their consultants may also have expertise in a given business area. For

IT Services Firms

ASPs/MSPs

Packaged Software Providers

Open Source

ERP Vendors

In-house

FIGURE 2-1
Sources of application software.

example, consultants who work with banks understand financial institutions as well as information systems. Consultants use many of the same methodologies, techniques, and tools that companies use to develop systems in-house.

It may surprise you to see IBM listed as the top global software producer. You may think of IBM as a hardware company primarily. Yet IBM has been moving away from a reliance on hardware development for many years. The purchase of the IT consulting arm of PricewaterhouseCoopers by IBM in 2002 solidified its move into services and consulting. IBM is also well known for its development of Web server and middleware software. Other leading IT services firms include traditional consulting firms such as Accenture. The list also includes HP, another company formerly focused on hardware that has made the transition to an IT services firm.

Packaged Software Producers The growth of the software industry has been phenomenal since its beginnings in the mid-1960s. Now, some of the largest computer companies in the world, as measured by *Software* magazine, are companies that produce software exclusively (see Table 2-1). Software companies develop what are sometimes called *prepackaged* or *off-the-shelf systems*. Microsoft's Project and Intuit's Quicken, QuickPay, and QuickBooks are popular examples of such software. The packaged software development industry serves many market segments. Its software offerings range from general, broad-based packages, such as general ledger, to more narrow, niche packages, such as software to help manage a day-care center. Software companies develop software to run on many different computer platforms, from microcomputers to large mainframes. The companies range in size from just a few people to thousands of employees. Software companies consult with system users after the initial software design has been completed and after an early version of the system has

TABLE 2-1: The 2010 Top 10 Global Software Companies

Rank	Company	2009 Software/ Services Revenue (millions of USD)	Software Business Sector
1	IBM	$74,934	Middleware/Application Server/ Web Server/Services
2	Microsoft	$50,820	Operating Systems
3	HP	$38,265	Systems Integration Services/ IT Consulting
4	Oracle	$23,252	Database
5	Accenture	$21,577	Systems Integration Services/ IT Consulting
6	Computer Sciences Corp.	$16,740	Enterprise Resource Planning
7	SAP AG	$15,235	Enterprise Application/ Data Integration
8	EMC Corp.	$14,026	Information Management
9	Hitachi	$12,254	Other
10	Lockheed Martin Corp.	$12,130	Vertical Industry Applications

Note: All figures in U.S. dollars (USD).
Source: Based on Software Magazine; visit www.softwaremag.com.

been built. The systems are then tested in actual organizations to reveal any problems or determine any improvements that can be made. Until testing is completed, the system is not offered for sale to the public.

Some off-the-shelf software systems cannot be modified to meet the specific, individual needs of a particular organization. Such application systems are sometimes called *turnkey* systems. The producer of a turnkey system will make changes to the software only when a substantial number of users ask for a specific change. Other off-the-shelf application software can be modified or extended, however, by the producer or the user to fit the needs of the organization more closely. Even though many organizations perform similar functions, no two organizations do the same thing in quite the same way. A turnkey system may be good enough for a certain level of performance, but it will never perfectly match the way a given organization does business. A reasonable estimate is that off-the-shelf software can at best meet 70 percent of an organization's needs. Thus, even in the best case, 30 percent of the software systems used don't perfectly match the organization's specifications.

Enterprise Solutions Software   As mentioned earlier, more and more organizations are choosing complete software solutions, called enterprise solutions or **enterprise resource planning (ERP) systems,** to support their operations and business processes. These ERP software solutions consist of a series of integrated modules. Each module supports an individual traditional business function, such as accounting, distribution, manufacturing, and human resources. The difference between the modules and traditional approaches is that the modules are integrated to focus on business processes rather than on business functional areas. For example, a series of modules will support the entire order-entry process, from receiving an order to adjusting inventory to shipping to billing to after-the-sale service. The traditional approach would use different systems in different functional areas of the business, such as a billing system in accounting and an inventory system in the warehouse. Using ERP systems, a firm can integrate all parts of a business process in a unified information system. All aspects of a single transaction occur seamlessly within a single information system, rather than in a series of disjointed, separate systems focused on business functional areas.

Enterprise resource planning (ERP) system
A system that integrates individual traditional business functions into a series of modules so that a single transaction occurs seamlessly within a single information system rather than several separate systems.

The benefits of the enterprise solutions approach include a single repository of data for all aspects of a business process and the flexibility of the modules. A single repository ensures more consistent and accurate data, as well as less maintenance. The modules are flexible because additional modules can be added as needed once the basic system is in place. Added modules are immediately integrated into the existing system.

Enterprise solutions software also involves some disadvantages. The systems are complex, so implementation can take a long time to complete. Organizations typically do not have the necessary expertise in-house to implement the systems, so they must rely on consultants or employees of the software vendor, which can be expensive. In some cases, organizations must change how they do business in order to benefit from a shift toward enterprise solutions.

Several major vendors offer enterprise solutions software. The best-known vendor is probably SAP AG, a German firm, known for its flagship product R/3. SAP stands for Systems, Applications, and Products in Data Processing. SAP AG was founded in 1972, but most of its growth has occurred since 1992. In 2009, SAP America was the seventh largest supplier of software in the world (see Table 2-1). The other major vendor of enterprise solutions is Oracle Corp., a U.S.-based firm, perhaps better known for its database software. Oracle is fourth on the list of the top ten software companies for 2009 (Table 2-1). At the end of 2004, Oracle acquired PeopleSoft, Inc., a U.S. firm founded in 1987. PeopleSoft began with enterprise solutions that focused on human resources management and expanded to cover financials, materials management, distribution, and manufacturing before Oracle acquired it. Just before being purchased by Oracle, PeopleSoft had boosted its corporate strength in 2003 through acquiring another ERP vendor, J.D. Edwards. In 2009, SAP held 31 percent of the global core enterprise applications market. As the higher end of the market has become saturated with ERP systems, most ERP vendors are looking to medium and small businesses for growth.

Cloud Computing   Another method for organizations to obtain applications is to rent them or license them from third-party providers who run the applications at remote sites. Users have access to the applications through the Internet or through virtual private networks (VPNs). The application provider buys, installs, maintains, and upgrades the applications. Users pay on a per-use basis or they license the software, typically month to month. Although this practice has been known by many different names over the years, today it is called **cloud computing**. Cloud computing refers to the provision of applications over the Internet, where customers do not have to invest in the hardware and software resources needed to run and maintain the applications. You may have seen the Internet referred to as a cloud in other contexts, which comes from how the Internet is depicted on computer network diagrams. A well-known example of cloud computing is Google Apps, which provides common personal productivity tools online, while the software runs on Google's servers. Another well-known example is Salesforce.com, which provides customer relationship management (CRM) software online. Cloud computing includes many areas of technology, including software as a service (often referred to as SaaS), which includes Google Apps and Salesforce.com, and hardware as a service, which allows companies to order server capacity and storage on demand.

Merrill Lynch has predicted that by 2013, 12 percent of the world's corporate computing will be done by cloud computing. The total market for cloud computing is expected to be $160 billion, which includes $95 billion in business and $65 billion in online advertising. The companies that are most likely to profit immediately are those that can quickly adjust their product lines to meet the needs of cloud computing. These include such well-known names as IBM, which has built several cloud computing centers worldwide; Microsoft, which in 2008 announced its Azure platform to support the development and operation of business applications and consumer services on its own servers; and Amazon.com, which provides storage and capacity from its own servers to customers.

As these growth forecasts indicate, taking the cloud-computing route has its advantages. The top three reasons for choosing to go with cloud computing, all of which result in benefits for the company, are: (1) freeing internal IT staff, (2) gaining access to applications faster than via internal development, and (3) achieving lower-cost access to corporate-quality applications. Especially appealing is the ability to gain access to large and complex systems without having to go through the expensive and time-consuming process of implementing the systems themselves in-house. Getting your computing through a cloud also makes it easier to walk away from an unsatisfactory systems solution. IT managers do have some concerns, however. The primary concern is reliability, but other concerns include security and compliance with government regulations such as Sarbanes-Oxley.

Open-Source Software   Open-source software is unlike the other types of software you have read about so far. Open-source software is different because it is freely available—not just the final product, but the source code itself. It is also different because it is developed by a community of interested people instead of by employees of a particular company. Open-source software performs the same functions as commercial software, such as operating systems, e-mail, database systems, Web browsers, and so on. Some of the most well-known and popular open-source software names are Linux (the operating system), mySQL (a database system), and Firefox (a Web browser). Open source also applies to software components and objects. Open source is

Cloud computing
The provision of computing resources, including applications, over the Internet, so customers do not have to invest in the computing infrastructure needed to run and maintain the resources.

developed and maintained by communities of people. These communities can sometimes be quite large. Developers often use common Web resources, such as SourceForge.net to organize their activities. In December 2010, SourceForge.net hosted more than 260,000 projects and had over 2.7 million registered users. Without question, the open-source movement would not be having the success it enjoys without the availability of the Internet for providing access and organizing development activities.

If the software is free, you might wonder how anybody makes any money by developing open-source software. Companies and individuals can make money with open source: (1) by providing maintenance and other services, or (2) by providing one version of the software for free and selling a more fully-featured version. Some open-source solutions have more of an impact on the software industry than others. Firefox, for example, has been very successful in the Web browser market, where it is estimated to have 24 percent of the market share. Other open-source software products, such as mySQL, have also been successful, and open source's share of the software industry seems destined to continue growing.

In-House Development We have talked about several different types of external organizations that serve as sources of software, but in-house development remains an option. Of course, in-house development need not entail development of all of the software that will compose the total system. Hybrid solutions involving some purchased and some in-house software components are common. Some in-house software components are reused. Table 2-2 compares the six different software sources.

Choosing Off-the-Shelf Software

Once you have decided to purchase off-the-shelf software rather than write some or all of the software for your new system, how do you decide what to buy? Several criteria need consideration, and special ones may arise with each potential software purchase. For each standard, an explicit comparison should be made between the software package and the process of developing the same application in-house. The most common criteria, highlighted in Figure 2-2, are as follows:

- Cost
- Functionality

TABLE 2-2: Comparison of Six Different Sources of Software Components

Producers	When to Go to This Type of Organization for Software	Internal Staffing Requirements
IT services firms	When task requires custom support and system can't be built internally or system needs to be sourced	Internal staff may be needed, depending on application
Packaged software producers	When supported task is generic	Some IS and user staff to define requirements and evaluate packages
Enterprise solutions vendors	For complete systems that cross functional boundaries	Some internal staff necessary but mostly need consultants
Cloud computing	For instant access to an application; when supported task is generic	Few; frees up staff for other IT work
Open-source software	When supported task is generic but cost is an issue	Some IS and user staff to define requirements and evaluate packages
In-house developers	When resources and staff are available and system can be built from scratch	Internal staff necessary though staff size may vary

FIGURE 2-2
Common criteria for choosing off-the-shelf software.

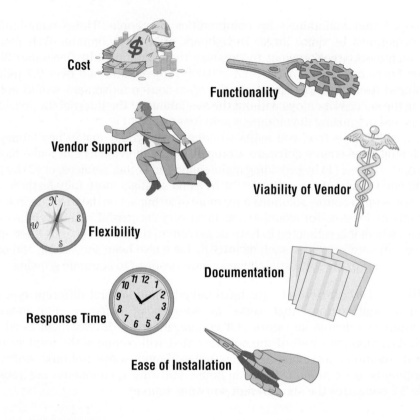

Cost

Functionality

Vendor Support

Viability of Vendor

Flexibility

Documentation

Response Time

Ease of Installation

- Vendor support
- Viability of vendor
- Flexibility
- Documentation
- Response time
- Ease of installation

The relative importance of these standards will vary from project to project and from organization to organization. If you had to choose two criteria that would always be among the most important, those two would probably be vendor support and vendor viability. You don't want to license software from a vendor that has a reputation for poor support. Similarly, you don't want to get involved with a vendor that might not be in business tomorrow. How you rank the importance of the remaining criteria depends primarily on your specific situation.

Cost involves comparing the cost of developing the same system in-house to the cost of purchasing or licensing the software package. Be sure to include a comparison of the cost of purchasing vendor upgrades or annual license fees with the costs you would incur to maintain your own software. Costs for purchasing and developing in-house can be compared based on the economic feasibility measures. Functionality refers to the tasks the software can perform and the mandatory, essential, and desired system features. Can the software package perform all, or just some of the tasks your users need? If some, can it perform the necessary core tasks? Note that meeting user requirements occurs at the end of the analysis phase because you cannot evaluate packaged software until user requirements have been gathered and structured. Purchasing application software is not a substitute for conducting the systems analysis phase.

As we said earlier, vendor support refers to whether the vendor can provide support, and how much. Support includes assistance to install the software, to train user and systems staff on the software, and to provide help as problems arise after installation. Recently, many software companies have significantly reduced the amount of free support they provide customers, so the cost to use telephone, on-site fax, or computer bulletin board support facilities should be considered. Related to support is the vendor's viability. This latter point should not be minimized. The software industry is quite dynamic, and innovative application software is created by entrepreneurs working from home offices—the classic cottage industry. Such organizations, even with outstanding software, often do not have the resources or business management ability to stay in business long. Further, competitive moves by major software firms can render the products of smaller firms outdated or incompatible with operating systems. One software firm we talked to while developing this book was struggling to survive by working to make its software operate on any Windows, Mac OS, or mobile platform. Keeping up with hardware and system software changes may be more than a small firm can handle, and good off-the-shelf application software is lost.

Flexibility refers to how easy it is for you, or the vendor, to customize the software. If the software is not sufficiently flexible, your users may have to adapt the way they work to fit the software. Are they likely to adapt in this manner? Purchased software can be modified in several ways. Sometimes, the vendor will make custom changes for you if you are willing to pay for the redesign and programming. Some vendors design the software for customization. For example, the software may include several different ways of processing data and, at installation time, the customer chooses which to initiate. Also, displays and reports may be easily redesigned if these modules are written in a fourth-generation language. Reports, forms, and displays may be easily customized using a process whereby your company name and chosen titles for reports, displays, forms, and column headings are selected from a table of parameters you provide. You may want to employ some of these same customization techniques for in-house-developed systems so that the software can be easily adapted for different business units, product lines, or departments.

Documentation includes the user's manual as well as technical documentation. How understandable and up to date is the documentation? What is the cost for multiple copies, if required? Response time refers to how long it takes the software package to respond to the user's requests in an interactive session. Another measure of time would be how long it takes the software to complete running a job. Finally, ease of installation is a measure of the difficulty of loading the software and making it operational.

Validating Purchased Software Information   One way to get all of the information you want about a software package is to collect it from the vendor. Some of this information may be contained in the software documentation and technical marketing literature. Other information can be provided upon request. For example, you can send prospective vendors a questionnaire asking specific questions about their packages. This questionnaire may be part of a request for proposal (RFP) or request for quote (RFQ) process your organization requires when major purchases are made.

If you decide that new hardware or system software is a strong possibility, you may want to issue a **request for proposal (RFP)** to vendors. The RFP will ask the vendors to propose hardware and system software that will meet the requirements of your new system. Issuing an RFP gives you the opportunity to have vendors conduct the research you need in order to decide among various options. You can request that each bid submitted by a vendor contain certain information essential for you to decide on what best fits your needs. For example, you can ask for performance information related to speed and number of operations per second. You can ask about machine reliability and service availability and whether an installation is located nearby that you can visit for more information. You can ask to take part in a demonstration of the hardware. The bid will also include information on cost.

Request for proposal (RFP)
A document provided to vendors to ask them to propose hardware and system software that will meet the requirements of a new system.

Of course, actually using the software yourself and running it through a series of tests based on the criteria for selecting software may provide the best route for evaluation. Remember to test not only the software, but also the documentation, the training materials, and even the technical support facilities. One requirement you can place on prospective software vendors as part of the bidding process is that they install (free or at an agreed-upon cost) their software for a limited amount of time on your computers. This way you can determine how their software works in your environment, not in some optimized environment they have.

One of the most reliable and insightful sources of feedback is other users of the software. Vendors will usually provide a list of customers (remember, they will naturally tell you about satisfied customers, so you may have to probe for a cross section of customers) and people who are willing to be contacted by prospective customers. Here is where your personal network of contacts, developed through professional groups, college friends, trade associations, or local business clubs, can be a resource; do not hesitate to find some contacts on your own. Such current or former customers can provide a depth of insight on the use of a package at their organizations.

To gain a range of opinions about possible packages, you can use independent software testing services that periodically evaluate software and collect user opinions. Such surveys are available for a fee either as subscription services or on demand. Occasionally, unbiased surveys appear in trade publications. Often, however, articles in trade publications, even software reviews, are actually seeded by the software manufacturer and are not unbiased.

If you are comparing several software packages, you can assign scores for each package on each criterion and compare the scores using the quantitative method (see Chapter 7) for comparing alternative system design strategies.

Reuse

Reuse
The use of previously written software resources, especially objects and components, in new applications.

Reuse is the use of previously written software resources in new applications. Because so many bits and pieces of applications are relatively generic across applications, it seems intuitive that great savings can be achieved in many areas if those generic bits and pieces do not have to be written anew each time they are needed. Reuse should increase programmer productivity, because being able to use existing software for some functions means they can perform more work in the same amount of time. Reuse should also decrease development time, minimizing schedule overruns. Because existing pieces of software have already been tested, reusing them tends to result in higher-quality software with lower defect rates, decreasing maintenance costs.

Although reuse can conceivably apply to many different aspects of software, typically it is most commonly applied to two different development technologies: object-oriented and component-based development. For example, consider an object class created to model an employee. The object class Employee would contain both the data about employees and the instructions necessary for calculating payroll for a variety of job types. The object class could be used in any application that dealt with employees, but if changes had to be made in calculating payroll for different types of employees, the changes would only have to be made to the object class and not to the various applications that used it. By definition, using the Employee object class in more than one application constitutes reuse.

Component-based development is similar to object-oriented development in that the focus is on creating general-purpose pieces of software that can be used interchangeably in many different programs. Components can be as small as objects or as large as pieces of software that handle single business functions, such as currency conversion. The idea behind component-based development is the assembly of an application from many different components at many different levels of complexity and size. Many vendors are working on developing libraries of components that can be retrieved and assembled as needed into desired applications.

Some evidence suggests that reuse can be effective, especially for object classes. For example, one laboratory study found that reuse of object class libraries resulted in increased productivity, reduced defect density, and reduced rework. For HP, a reuse program resulted in cutting time to market for certain products by a factor of three or more, from eighteen months to less than five months. However, for reuse to work in an organizational setting, many different issues must be addressed. Technical issues include the current lack of a methodology for creating and clearly defining and labeling reusable components for placement in a library and the small number of reusable and reliable software resources currently available. Key organizational issues include the lack of commitment to reuse, as well as the lack of proper training and rewards needed to promote it, the lack of organizational support for institutionalizing reuse, and the difficulty in measuring the economic gains from reuse. Because of the considerable costs of developing a reusable component, most organizations cannot compete economically with established commercial organizations that focus on selling components as their main line of business. Success depends on being able to leverage the cost of components across a large user and project base (Figure 2-3). Key legal and contractual issues concerning the reuse of object classes and components originally used in other applications must also be addressed.

When an organization's management decides to pursue reuse as a strategy, it is important for the organization to match its approach to reuse with its strategic business goals. The benefits of reuse grow as more corporate experience is gained from it, but so do the costs and the amount of resources necessary for reuse to work well. Software reuse has three basic steps: abstraction, storage, and recontextualization. Abstraction involves the design of a reusable piece of software, starting from existing software assets or from scratch. Storage involves making software assets available for others to use. Although it sounds like a simple problem, storage can actually be very challenging. The problem is not simply putting software assets on a shelf; the problem is correctly labeling and cataloging assets so that others can find the ones they want to use. Once an asset has been found, recontextualization, or making the reusable asset understandable to developers who want to use it in their systems, becomes important. Software is complex, and a software asset developed for a particular system under system-specific circumstances may not at all be the asset it appears to be. What seems to be a generic asset called "Customer" may actually be something quite different, depending on the context in which it was developed. It may often appear to be easier to simply build your own assets rather than invest the time and energy it takes to establish a good understanding of software someone else has developed. A key part of a reuse strategy, as mentioned previously, is establishing rewards, incentives, and organizational support for reuse to help make it more worthwhile than developing your own assets.

FIGURE 2-3
Investments necessary to achieve reusable components.

Source: Royce, W. 1998. *Software Project Management: A Unified Framework.* Boston, MA: Addison-Wesley. Used by permission.

TABLE 2-3: Approaches to Reuse

Approach	Reuse Level	Cost	Policies & Procedures
Ad hoc	None to low	Low	None
Facilitated	Low	Low	Developers are encouraged to reuse but are not required to do so.
Managed	Moderate	Moderate	Development, sharing, and adoption of reusable assets are mandated; organizational policies are established for documentation, packaging, and certification.
Designed	High	High	Reuse is mandated; policies are put in place so that reuse effectiveness can be measured; code must be designed for reuse during initial development, regardless of the application it is originally designed for; there may be a corporate office for reuse.

Source: Based on Griss, 2003.

An organization can take one of four approaches to reuse (see Table 2-3). The *ad hoc reuse* approach is not really an approach at all, at least from an official organizational perspective. With this approach, individuals are free to find or develop reusable assets on their own, but few, if any, organizational rewards are offered for reusing assets. Storage is not an issue, because individuals keep track of and distribute their own software assets. For such an ad hoc, individually driven approach, it is difficult to measure any potential benefits to the company.

Another approach to reuse is *facilitated reuse*. With this approach, developers are not required to practice reuse, but they are encouraged to do so. The organization makes available some tools and techniques that enable the development and sharing of reusable assets, and one or more employees may be assigned the role of evangelist to publicize and promote the program. Little is done to track the quality and use of reusable assets; however, the overall corporate investment is small.

Managed reuse is a more structured, and more expensive, mode of managing software reuse. With managed reuse, the development, sharing, and adoption of reusable assets is mandated. The organization establishes processes and policies for ensuring that reuse is practiced and that the results are measured. The organization also establishes policies and procedures for ensuring the quality of its reusable assets. The focus is on identifying existing assets that can be potentially reused from various sources, including from utility asset libraries that come with operating systems, from companies that sell assets, from the open-source community, from internal repositories, from scouring existing legacy code, and so on.

The most expensive and extensive approach to reuse is *designed reuse*. In addition to mandating reuse and measuring its effectiveness, the designed reuse approach takes the extra step of mandating that assets be designed for reuse as they are being designed for specific applications. The focus is more on developing reusable assets than on finding existing assets that might be candidates for reuse. A corporate reuse office may be established to monitor and manage the overall methodology. Under such an approach, as much as 90 percent of software assets may be reused across different applications.

Each approach to reuse has its advantages and disadvantages. No single approach is a silver bullet that will solve the reuse puzzle for all organizations and for all situations. Successful reuse requires an understanding of how reuse fits within larger organizational goals and strategies as well as an understanding of the social and technical world into which the reusable assets must fit.

Even though reuse is valuable to many organizations, it turns out it is not as valuable to all developers in any given organization. Novice developers are more likely to reuse code and components than are more experienced developers. Novice developers are more risk averse and do not want to make mistakes, so they tend to reuse an existing code that has already been tested and verified. More experienced developers tend to trust their own coding skills more than they trust the skills of others, so they prefer to write and test their own code. Differences in reuse across different types of development teams are also common. Transient project teams, which will only exist a short time, are more likely to reuse than are established, more permanent project teams.

Key Points Review

1. **Explain outsourcing.**

   Outsourcing is the practice of turning over to another organization all or part of the responsibility for your information systems' development, operation, and maintenance. Outsourcing can be done through many different organizational arrangements, all of which are governed through contractual agreements. Outsourcing is big business, with large computer firms such as IBM and HP each handling several contracts worth billions of dollars per year. As an analyst, you need to consider outsourcing seriously as an alternative way to get things done.

2. **Describe six different sources of software.**

   As a systems analyst, you must be aware of where you can obtain software that meets some or all of an organization's needs. You can obtain application (and system) software from information technology services firms, packaged software providers, vendors of enterprise solutions software, cloud computing, and open-source software providers, as well as from internal systems

development resources, including the reuse of existing software components.

3. **Discuss how to evaluate off-the-shelf software.**

   You must also know the criteria to use when choosing among off-the-shelf software products. These criteria include cost, functionality, vendor support, vendor viability, flexibility, documentation, response time, and ease of installation. Requests for proposals are one way you can collect more information about system software, its performance, and its costs.

4. **Explain reuse and its role in software development.**

   Reuse is the use of previously written software resources in new applications. Reuse should increase programmer productivity, decrease development time, and result in higher-quality software with lower defect rates, decreasing maintenance costs. Some evidence suggests that reuse can be effective, especially for object classes. However, when an organization pursues reuse as a strategy, its reuse strategy should match its strategic business goals.

Key Terms Checkpoint

Here are the key terms from the chapter. The page where each term is first explained is in parentheses after the term.

1. Cloud computing (p. 32)
2. Enterprise resource planning (ERP) system (p. 31)
3. Outsourcing (p. 28)
4. Request for proposal (RFP) (p. 35)
5. Reuse (p. 36)

Match each of the key terms above with the definition that best fits it.

_____ 1. The practice of turning over responsibility of some or all of an organization's information systems applications and operations to an outside firm.

_____ 2. A system that integrates individual traditional business functions into a series of modules so that a single transaction occurs seamlessly within a single information system rather than several separate systems.

_____ 3. A document provided to vendors to ask them to propose hardware and system

software that will meet the requirements of your new system.

_____ 4. The use of previously written software resources, especially objects and components, in new applications.

_____ 5. The provision of computing resources over the Internet, so customers do not have to invest in the computing infrastructure needed to run and maintain the resources.

Review Questions

1. Describe and compare the six sources of software.
2. How can you decide among various off-the-shelf software options? What criteria should you use?
3. What is an RFP, and how do analysts use one to gather information about hardware and system software?
4. What methods can a systems analyst employ to verify vendor claims about a software package?
5. What are ERP systems? What are the benefits and disadvantages of such systems as a design strategy?
6. Explain reuse and its advantages and disadvantages.
7. Compare and contrast the four approaches to reuse.
8. Why would a company rely on cloud computing for its software needs?

Problems and Exercises

1. Research how to prepare an RFP.
2. Review the criteria for selecting off-the-shelf software presented in this chapter. Use your experience and imagination and describe other criteria that are or might be used to select off-the-shelf software in the "real world." For each new criterion, explain how use of this criterion might be functional (i.e., it is useful to use this criterion), dysfunctional, or both.
3. In the section on choosing off-the-shelf software, eight criteria are proposed for evaluating alternative packages. Suppose the choice is between alternative custom software developers rather than prewritten packages. What criteria would be appropriate to select and compare among competing bidders for custom development of an application? Define each of these criteria.
4. How might the project team recommending an ERP design strategy justify its recommendation as compared with other types of design strategies?

Field Exercises

1. Interview businesspeople who participate in the purchase of off-the-shelf software in their organizations. Review with them the criteria for selecting off-the-shelf software presented in this chapter. Have them prioritize the list of criteria as they are used in their organization and provide an explanation of the rationale for each criterion's ranking. Ask them to list and describe any other criteria that are used in their organization.
2. Obtain copies of actual RFPs used for information systems developments or purchases. If possible, obtain RFPs from public and private organizations. Find out how they are used. What are the major components of these proposals? Do these proposals seem to be useful? Why or why not? How and why do RFPs from public and private organizations differ?
3. Contact an organization that has or is implementing an integrated ERP application. Why did it choose this design strategy? How has it managed this development project differently from prior large projects? What organizational changes have occurred due to this design strategy? How long did the implementation last and why?

CASE: PETRIE'S ELECTRONICS

The Sources of Software

Jim Watanabe looked around his new office. He couldn't believe that he was the assistant director of information technology at Petrie's Electronics, his favorite consumer electronics retail store. He always bought his new DVDs and video games for his Xbox 360 at Petrie's. In fact, he had bought his Blu-ray player and his Xbox 360 at Petrie's, along with his surround sound system and his 40" flat-screen HD LED TV. And now he worked there too. The employee discount was a nice perk[1] of his new job, but he was also glad that his technical and people skills were finally recognized by the people at Petrie's. He had worked for five years at Broadway Entertainment Company

[1] perquisite

as a senior systems analyst, and it was clear that he was not going to be promoted there. He was really glad he had put his résumé up on Monster.com and that now he had a bigger salary and a great job with more responsibility at Petrie's.

Petrie's Electronics had started as a single electronics store in 1984 in San Diego, California. The store was started by Jacob Rosenstein in a strip mall. It was named after Rob Petrie, the TV writer played by Dick Van Dyke in the TV show named after himself. Rosenstein always liked that show. When he had grown the store to a chain of thirteen stores in the Southern California area, it was too much for Rosenstein to handle. He sold out in 1992, for a handsome profit, to the Matsutoya Corporation, a huge Japanese conglomerate that saw the chain of stores as a place to sell its many consumer electronics goods in the U.S.

Matsutoya aggressively expanded the chain to 218 stores nationwide by the time they sold the chain in 2002, for a handsome profit, to Sam and Harry's, a maker and seller of ice cream. Sam and Harry's was looking for a way to diversify and invest the considerable cash they had made creating and selling ice cream, with flavors named after actors and actresses, like their best selling Lime Neeson and Jim Carrey-mel. Sam and Harry's brought in professional management to run the chain, and since they bought it, they added fifteen more stores, including one in Mexico and three in Canada. Even though they originally wanted to move the headquarters to their home state of Delaware, Sam and Harry decided to keep Petrie's headquartered in San Diego.

The company had made some smart moves and had done well, Jim knew, but he also knew that competition was fierce. Petrie's competitors included big electronics retail chains like Best Buy. In California, Fry's was a ferocious competitor. Other major players in the arena included the electronics departments of huge chains like Wal-Mart and Target and online vendors like Amazon.com. Jim knew that part of his job in IT was to help the company grow and prosper and beat the competition—or at least survive.

Just then, as Jim was trying to decide if he needed a bigger TV, Ella Whinston, the chief operations officer at Petrie's, walked into his office. "How's it going, Jim? Joe keeping you busy?" Joe was Joe Swanson, Jim's boss, the director of IT. Joe was away for the week, at a meeting in Pullman, Washington. Jim quickly pulled his feet off his desk.

"Hi, Ella. Oh, yeah, Joe keeps me busy. I've got to get through the entire corporate strategic IT plan before he gets back—he's going to quiz me—and then there's the new help-desk training we are going to start next week."

"I didn't know we had a strategic IT plan," Ella teased. "Anyway, what I came in here for is to give you some good news. I have decided to make you the project manager for a project that is crucial to our corporate survival."

"Me?" Jim said. "But I just got here."

"Who better than you? You have a different perspective, new ideas. You aren't chained down by the past and by the Petrie's way of doing things, like the rest of us. Not that it matters, since you don't have a choice. Joe and I both agree that you are the best person for the job."

"So," Jim asked, "what's the project about?"

"Well," Ella began, "the executive team has decided that the number one priority we have right now is to not only survive but to thrive and to prosper, and the way to do that is to develop closer relationships with our customers. The other person on the executive team, who is even more excited about this than me, is John [John Smith, the head of marketing]. We want to attract new customers, like all of our competitors. But also like our competitors, we want to keep our customers for life, kind of like a frequent flier program, but better. Better for us and for our loyal customers. And we want to reward most, the customers who spend the most. We are calling the project 'No Customer Escapes.'"

"I hope that's only an internal name," Jim joked. "Seriously, I can see how something like this would be good for Petrie's, and I can see how IT would play an important, no, crucial role in making something like this happen. OK, then, let's get started."

Case Questions

1. How do information systems projects get started in organizations?
2. How are organizational information systems related to company strategy? How does strategy affect the information systems a company develops and uses?
3. Research customer loyalty programs in retail firms. How common are they? What are their primary features?
4. What do you think Jim's next step would be? Why?
5. Why would a systems analyst new to a company be a good choice to lead an important systems development effort?

three

Managing the Information Systems Project

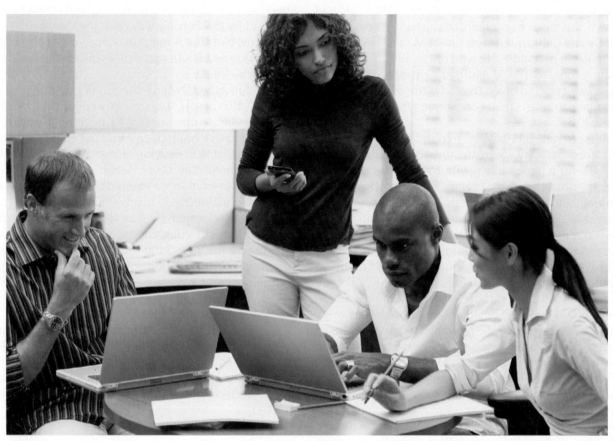

© LWA/Getty Images

After studying this chapter, you should be able to:

- Describe the skills required to be an effective project manager.

- List and describe the skills and activities of a project manager during project initiation, project planning, project execution, and project closedown.

- Explain what is meant by critical path scheduling and describe the process of creating Gantt charts and Network diagrams.

- Explain how commercial project management software packages can be used to assist in representing and managing project schedules.

Chapter Preview . . .

In Chapter 1, we introduced the four phases of the systems development life cycle (SDLC) and explained how an information system project moves through those four phases. In this chapter, we focus on the systems analyst's role as project manager of information systems projects. Throughout the SDLC, the project manager is responsible for initiating, planning, executing, and closing down the systems development project. Figure 3-1 illustrates these four functions.

We use two fictional companies in this book—Pine Valley Furniture and Hoosier Burger—to help illustrate key SDLC concepts. Icons appear in the margins to make references to these companies easy to spot while you read. The next section gives you background on Pine Valley Furniture, a manufacturing company. Next, we describe the project manager's role and the project management process. The subsequent section examines techniques for reporting project plans using Gantt charts and Network diagrams. At the end of the chapter, we discuss commercially available project management software that a systems analyst can use in a wide variety of project management activities.

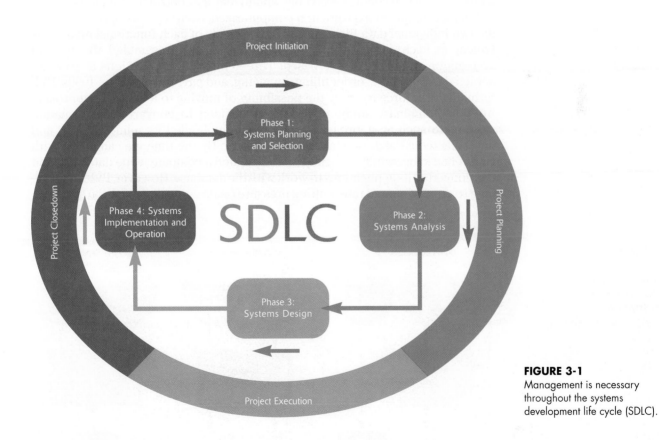

FIGURE 3-1
Management is necessary throughout the systems development life cycle (SDLC).

Pine Valley Furniture Company Background

Pine Valley Furniture (PVF) Company manufactures high-quality wood furniture and distributes it to retail stores within the United States. Its product lines include dinette sets, stereo cabinets, wall units, living room furniture, and bedroom furniture. In the early 1980s, PVF's founder, Alex Schuster, started to make and sell custom furniture in his garage. Alex managed invoices and kept track of customers by using file folders and a filing cabinet. By 1984, business expanded and Alex had to rent a warehouse and hire a part-time bookkeeper. PVF's product line had multiplied, sales volume had doubled, and staff had increased to fifty employees. By 1990, PVF moved into its third and present location. Because of the added complexity of the company's operations, Alex reorganized the company into the following functional areas:

- Manufacturing, which was further subdivided into three separate functions—fabrication, assembling, and finishing
- Sales
- Orders
- Accounting
- Purchasing

Alex and the heads of the functional areas established manual information systems, such as accounting ledgers and file folders, which worked well for a time. Eventually, however, PVF selected and installed a minicomputer to automate invoicing, accounts receivable, and inventory control applications.

When the applications were first computerized, each separate application had its own individual data files tailored to the needs of each functional area. As is typical in such situations, the applications closely resembled the manual systems on which they were based. Three computer applications at PVF are depicted in Figure 3-2: order filling, invoicing, and payroll. In the late 1990s, PVF formed a task force to study the possibility of moving to a database approach. After a preliminary study, management decided to convert its information systems to such an approach. The company upgraded its minicomputer and implemented a database management system. By the time we caught up with PVF, it had successfully designed and populated a company-wide database, and had converted its applications to work with the database. However, PVF is continuing to grow at a rapid rate, putting pressure on its current application systems.

FIGURE 3-2
Three computer applications at Pine Valley Furniture: order filling, invoicing, and payroll.

Source: Hoffer, Ramesh, and Topi, 2011.

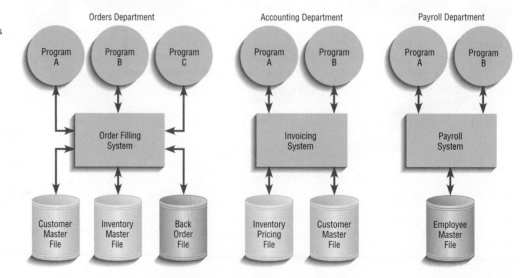

The computer-based applications at PVF support its business processes. When customers order furniture, their orders must be processed appropriately: Furniture must be built and shipped to the right customer and the right invoice mailed to the right address. Employees have to be paid for their work. Given these tasks, most of PVF's computer-based applications are located in the accounting and financial areas. The applications include order filling, invoicing, accounts receivable, inventory control, accounts payable, payroll, and general ledger. At one time, each application had its own data files. For example, PVF had a customer master file, an inventory master file, a back-order file, an inventory pricing file, and an employee master file. The order filling system uses data from three files: customer master, inventory master, and back order. With PVF's new centralized database, data are organized around entities, or subjects, such as customers, invoices, and orders.

Pine Valley Furniture Company, like many firms, decided to develop its application software in-house; that is, it hired staff and bought computer hardware and software necessary to build application software suited to its own needs. (Other methods used to obtain application software were explained in Chapter 2.) Although PVF continues to grow at a rapid rate, market conditions are becoming extremely competitive, especially with the advent of the Internet and the World Wide Web. Let's see how a project manager plays a key role in developing a new information system for PVF.

Managing the Information Systems Project

Project management is an important aspect of the development of information systems and a critical skill for a systems analyst. The focus of project management is to ensure that system development projects meet customer expectations and are delivered within budget and time constraints.

The **project manager** is a systems analyst with a diverse set of skills—management, leadership, technical, conflict management, and customer relationship—who is responsible for initiating, planning, executing, and closing down a project. As a project manager, your environment is one of continual change and problem solving. In some organizations, the project manager is a senior systems analyst who "has been around the block" a time or two. In others, both junior and senior analysts are expected to take on this role, managing parts of a project or actively supporting a more senior colleague who is assuming this role. Understanding the project management process is a critical skill for your future success.

Creating and implementing successful projects requires managing resources, activities, and tasks needed to complete the information systems project. A **project** is a planned undertaking of a series of related activities, having a beginning and an end, to reach an objective. The first questions you might ask yourself are, Where do projects come from? and, after considering all the different things that you could be asked to work on within an organization, How do I know which projects to work on? The ways in which each organization answers these questions vary.

In the rest of this section, we describe the process followed by Juanita Lopez and Chris Martin during the development of Pine Valley Furniture's Purchasing Fulfillment System. Juanita works in the purchasing department, and Chris is a systems analyst.

Juanita observed problems with the way orders were processed and reported: sales growth had increased the workload for the manufacturing department, and the current systems no longer adequately supported the tracking of orders.

It was becoming more difficult to track orders and get the right furniture and invoice to the right customers. Juanita contacted Chris, and together they developed a system that corrected these purchasing department problems.

Project manager

A systems analyst with a diverse set of skills—management, leadership, technical, conflict management, and customer relationship—who is responsible for initiating, planning, executing, and closing down a project.

Project

A planned undertaking of related activities, having a beginning and an end, to reach an objective.

 PINE VALLEY FURNITURE

The first **deliverable,** or end product, produced by Chris and Juanita was a system service request (SSR), a standard form PVF uses for requesting systems development work. Figure 3-3 shows an SSR for purchasing a fulfillment system. The form includes the name and contact information of the person requesting the system, a statement of the problem, and the name and contact information of the liaison and sponsor.

This request was then evaluated by the Systems Priority Board of PVF. Because all organizations have limited time and resources, not all requests can be approved. The board evaluates development requests in relation to the business problems or opportunities the system will solve or create. It also considers how the proposed project fits within the organization's information systems architecture and long-range development plans. The review board selects those projects that best meet overall organizational goals. In the case of the Purchasing Fulfillment System request, the board found merit in the request and approved

FIGURE 3-3
System service request for purchasing fulfillment with name and contact information of the person requesting the system, a statement of the problem, and the name and contact information of the liaison and sponsor.

Pine Valley Furniture
System Service Request

REQUESTED BY ____Juanita Lopez____ DATE ____November 2, 2012____

DEPARTMENT ____Purchasing, Manufacturing Support____

LOCATION ____Headquarters, 1-322____

CONTACT ____Tel: 4-3267   FAX: 4-3270   e-mail: jlopez@pvf.com____

TYPE OF REQUEST	URGENCY
[X] New System	[ ] Immediate—Operations are impaired or opportunity lost
[ ] System Enhancement	[ ] Problems exist, but can be worked around
[ ] System Error Correction	[X] Business losses can be tolerated until new system installed

PROBLEM STATEMENT

Sales growth at PVF has caused greater volume of work for the manufacturing support unit within Purchasing. Further, more concentration on customer service has reduced manufacturing lead times, which puts more pressure on purchasing activities. In addition, cost-cutting measures force Purchasing to be more agressive in negotiating terms with vendors, improving delivery times, and lowering our investments in inventory. The current modest systems support for manufacturing purchasing is not responsive to these new business conditions. Data are not available, information cannot be summarized, supplier orders cannot be adequately tracked, and commodity buying is not well supported. PVF is spending too much on raw materials and not being responsive to manufacturing needs.

SERVICE REQUEST

I request a thorough analysis of our current operations with the intent to design and build a completely new information system. This system should handle all purchasing transactions, support display and reporting of critical purchasing data, and assist purchasing agents in commodity buying.

IS LIAISON ____Chris Martin (Tel: 4-6204   FAX: 4-6200   e-mail: cmartin@pvf.com)____

SPONSOR ____Sal Divario, Director, Purchasing____

-   TO BE COMPLETED BY SYSTEMS PRIORITY BOARD   -

[   ] Request approved   Assigned to _____

[   ] Recommend revision   Start date _____

[   ] Suggest user development

[   ] Reject for reason   _____

_____

_____

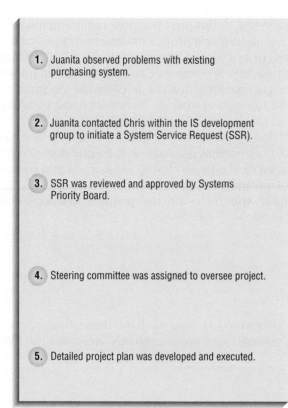

1. Juanita observed problems with existing purchasing system.

2. Juanita contacted Chris within the IS development group to initiate a System Service Request (SSR).

3. SSR was reviewed and approved by Systems Priority Board.

4. Steering committee was assigned to oversee project.

5. Detailed project plan was developed and executed.

FIGURE 3-4
A graphical view of the five steps followed during the project initiation of the purchasing fulfillment system.

a more detailed **feasibility study.** A feasibility study, conducted by the project manager, involves determining whether the information system makes sense for the organization from an economic and operational standpoint. The study takes place before the system is constructed. Figure 3-4 is a graphical view of the steps followed during the project initiation of the Purchasing Fulfillment System.

Feasibility study
Determines whether the information system makes sense for the organization from an economic and operational standpoint.

In summary, systems development projects are undertaken for two primary reasons: to take advantage of business opportunities and to solve business problems. Taking advantage of an opportunity might mean providing an innovative service to customers through the creation of a new system. For example, PVF may want to create a Web page so that customers can easily access its catalog and place orders at any time. Solving a business problem could involve modifying how an existing system processes data so that more accurate or timely information is provided to users. For example, a company such as PVF may create a password-protected intranet site that contains important announcements and budget information.

Projects are not always initiated for the rational reasons (taking advantage of business opportunities or solving business problems) previously stated. For example, in some instances organizations and government undertake projects to spend resources, attain or pad budgets, keep people busy, or help train people and develop their skills. Our focus in this chapter is not on how and why organizations identify projects but on the management of projects once they have been identified.

Once a potential project has been identified, an organization must determine the resources required for its completion by analyzing the scope of the project and determining the probability of successful completion. After getting this information, the organization can then determine whether taking advantage of an opportunity or solving a particular problem is feasible within time and resource constraints. If deemed feasible, a more detailed project analysis is then conducted.

As you will see, determining the size, scope, and resource requirements for a project are just a few of the many skills that a project manager must possess. A project manager is often referred to as a juggler keeping aloft many balls, which reflect the various aspects of a project's development, as depicted in Figure 3-5.

To successfully orchestrate the construction of a complex information system, a project manager must have interpersonal, leadership, and technical skills. Table 3-1 lists the project manager's common activities and skills. Note that many of the skills are related to personnel or general management, not simply technical skills. Table 3-1 shows that not only does an effective project manager have varied skills, but he or she is also the most instrumental person to the successful completion of any project.

The remainder of this chapter will focus on the **project management** process, which involves four phases:

1. Initiating the project
2. Planning the project
3. Executing the project
4. Closing down the project

Several activities must be performed during each of these four phases. Following this formal project management process greatly increases the likelihood of project success.

Project management
A controlled process of initiating, planning, executing, and closing down a project.

FIGURE 3-5
A project manager juggles numerous activities.

TABLE 3-1: Common Activities and Skills of a Project Manager

Activity	Description	Skill
Leadership	Influencing the activities of others toward the attainment of a common goal through the use of intelligence, personality, and abilities	Communication; liaison between management, users, and developers; assigning activities; monitoring progress
Management	Getting projects completed through the effective utilization of resources	Defining and sequencing activities; communicating expectations; assigning resources to activities; monitoring outcomes
Customer relations	Working closely with customers to ensure project deliverables meet expectations	Interpreting system requests and specifications; site preparation and user training; contact point for customers
Technical problem solving	Designing and sequencing activities to attain project goals	Interpreting system requests and specifications; defining activities and their sequence; making trade-offs between alternative solutions; designing solutions to problems
Conflict management	Managing conflict within a project team to ensure that conflict is not too high or too low	Problem solving; smoothing out personality differences; compromising; goal setting
Team management	Managing the project team for effective team performance	Communication within and between teams; peer evaluations; conflict resolution; team building; self-management
Risk and change management	Identifying, assessing, and managing the risks and day-to-day changes that occur during a project	Environmental scanning; risk and opportunity identification and assessment; forecasting; resource redeployment

Initiating the Project

During **project initiation** the project manager performs several activities that assess the size, scope, and complexity of the project, and establishes procedures to support subsequent activities. Depending on the project, some initiation activities may be unnecessary and some may be more involved. The types of activities you will perform when initiating a project are summarized in Figure 3-6 and are described next.

1. *Establishing the project initiation team.* This activity involves organizing an initial core of project team members to assist in accomplishing the

Project initiation
The first phase of the project management process in which activities are performed to assess the size, scope, and complexity of the project and to establish procedures to support later project activities.

Project Initiation

1. Establishing the Project Initiation Team

2. Establishing a Relationship with the Customer

3. Establishing the Project Initiation Plan

4. Establishing Management Procedures

5. Establishing the Project Management Environment and Project Workbook

6. Developing the Project Charter

FIGURE 3-6
Six project initiation activities.

project initiation activities. For example, during the Purchasing Fulfillment System project at PVF, Chris Martin was assigned to support the purchasing department. It is a PVF policy that all initiation teams consist of at least one user representative, in this case Juanita Lopez, and one member of the IS development group. Therefore, the project initiation team consisted of Chris and Juanita; Chris was the project manager.

2. *Establishing a relationship with the customer.* A thorough understanding of your customer builds stronger partnerships and higher levels of trust. At PVF, management has tried to foster strong working relationships between business units (such as purchasing) and the IS development group by assigning a specific individual to work as a liaison between both groups. Because Chris had been assigned to the purchasing unit for some time, he was already aware of some of the problems with the existing purchasing systems. PVF's policy of assigning specific individuals to each business unit helped to ensure that both Chris and Juanita were comfortable working together prior to the initiation of the project. Many organizations use a similar mechanism for establishing relationships with customers.

3. *Establishing the project initiation plan.* This step defines the activities required to organize the initiation team while it is working to define the scope of the project. Chris's role was to help Juanita translate her business requirements into a written request for an improved information system. This task required the collection, analysis, organization, and transformation of a lot of information. Because Chris and Juanita were already familiar with each other and their roles within a development project, they next needed to define when and how they would communicate, define deliverables and project steps, and set deadlines. Their initiation plan included agendas for several meetings. These steps eventually led to the creation of their system service request (SSR) form.

4. *Establishing management procedures.* Successful projects require the development of effective management procedures. Within PVF, many of these management procedures had been established as standard operating procedures by the Systems Priority Board and the IS development group. For example, all project development work is charged to the functional unit requesting the work. In other organizations, each project may have unique procedures tailored to its needs. Yet, in general, when establishing procedures, you are concerned with developing team communication and reporting procedures, job assignments and roles, project change procedures, and determining how project funding and billing will be handled. It was fortunate for Chris and Juanita that most of these procedures were already established at PVF, allowing them to move quickly on to other project activities.

5. *Establishing the project management environment and project workbook.* The focus of this activity is to collect and organize the tools that you will use while managing the project and to construct the **project workbook.** For example, most diagrams, charts, and system descriptions provide much of the project workbook contents. Thus, the project workbook serves as a repository for all project correspondence, inputs, outputs, deliverables, procedures, and standards established by the project team. The project workbook can be stored as an online electronic document, a Web site, or in a large three-ring binder. The project workbook is used by all team members and is useful for project audits, orientation of new team members, communication with management and customers, identification of future projects, and performance of postproject reviews. The establishment and diligent recording of all

Project workbook
An online or hard-copy repository, for all project correspondence, inputs, outputs, deliverables, procedures, and standards, that is used for performing project audits, orienting new team members, communicating with management and customers, identifying future projects, and performing postproject reviews.

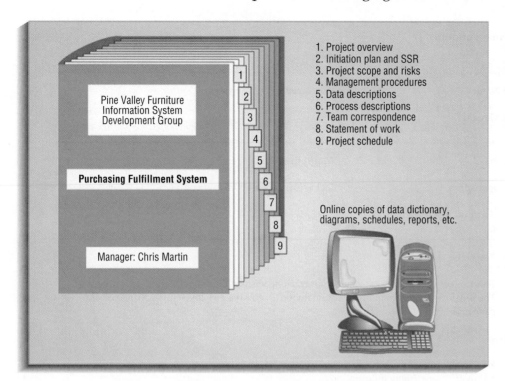

FIGURE 3-7
The project workbook for the Purchase Fulfillment System project contains nine key documents in both hard-copy and electronic form.

Pine Valley Furniture Information System Development Group

Purchasing Fulfillment System

Manager: Chris Martin

1. Project overview
2. Initiation plan and SSR
3. Project scope and risks
4. Management procedures
5. Data descriptions
6. Process descriptions
7. Team correspondence
8. Statement of work
9. Project schedule

Online copies of data dictionary, diagrams, schedules, reports, etc.

project information in the workbook are two of the most important activities you will perform as project manager.

Figure 3-7 shows the project workbook for the Purchasing Fulfillment System. It consists of both a large hard-copy binder and online storage where the system data dictionary, a catalog of data stored in the database, and diagrams are stored. For this system, all project documents can fit into a single binder. It is not unusual, however, for project documentation to be spread over several binders. As more information is captured and recorded electronically, however, fewer hard-copy binders may be needed. Many project teams keep their project workbooks on the Web. A Web site can be created so that all project members can easily access all project documents. This Web site can be a simple repository of documents or an elaborate site with password protection and security levels. The best feature of using the Web as your repository is that it allows all project members and customers to review a project's status and all related information continually.

6. *Developing the project charter.* The **project charter** is a short (typically one page), high-level document prepared for the customer that describes what the project will deliver and outlines many of the key elements of the project. A project charter can vary in the amount of detail it contains, but often includes the following elements:

- Project title and date of authorization
- Project manager name and contact information
- Customer name and contact information
- Projected start and completion dates
- Project description and objectives
- Key assumptions or approach
- Key stakeholders, roles, responsibilities and signatures

The project charter ensures that both you and your customer gain a common understanding of the project. It is also a useful communication tool; it helps to announce to the organization that a particular project has been chosen for development. A sample project charter is shown in Figure 3-8.

Project charter
A short, high-level document prepared for both internal and external stakeholders to formally announce the establishment of the project and to briefly describe its objective, key assumptions, and stakeholders.

Pine Valley Furniture

Project Charter   **Prepared:**   November 2, 2012

Project Name: Customer Tracking System

Project Manager: Jim Woo (jwoo@pvf.com)

Customer: **Marketing**

Project Sponsor: Jackie Judson (jjudson@pvf.com)

Project Start/End (projected):   10/2/12–2/1/13

Project Overview:

This project will implement a customer tracking system for the marketing department. The purpose of this system is to automate the . . . to save employee time, reduce errors, have more timely information . . .

Objectives:

- Minimize data entry errors
- Provide more timely information
- . . .

Key Assumptions:

- System will be built in-house
- Interface will be a Web-browser
- System will access customer database
- . . .

Stakeholders and Responsibilities

Stakeholder	Role	Responsibility	Signatures
Jackie Judson	VP Marketing	Project Vision, Resources	*Jackie Judson*
Alex Datta	CIO	Monitoring, Resources	*Alex Datta*
Jim Woo	Project Manager	Plan, Monitor, Execute Project	*Jim Woo*
James Jordan	Director of Sales	System Functionality	*James Jordan*
Mary Shide	VP Human Resoures	Staff Assignments	*Mary Shide*

FIGURE 3-8
A project charter for a proposed information systems project.

Project initiation is complete once these six activities have been performed. Before moving on to the next phase of the project, the work performed during project initiation is reviewed at a meeting attended by management, customers, and project team members. An outcome of this meeting is a decision to continue the project, modify it, or abandon it. In the case of the Purchasing Fulfillment System project at Pine Valley Furniture, the board accepted the SSR and selected a project steering committee to monitor project progress and to provide guidance to the team members during subsequent activities. If the scope of the project is modified, it may be necessary to return to project initiation activities and collect additional information. Once a decision is made to continue the project, a much more detailed project plan is developed during the project planning phase.

Planning the Project

The next step in the project management process is **project planning.** Project planning involves defining clear, discrete activities and the work needed to complete each activity within a single project. It often requires you to make numerous assumptions about the availability of resources such as hardware, software, and personnel. It is much easier to plan nearer-term activities than those occurring in the longer term. In actual fact, you often have to construct longer-term plans that are more general in scope and nearer-term plans that are more detailed. The repetitive nature of the project management process requires that plans be constantly monitored throughout the project and periodically updated (usually after each phase) based upon the most recent information.

Figure 3-9 illustrates the principle that nearer-term plans are typically more specific and firmer than longer-term plans. For example, it is virtually impossible to rigorously plan activities late in the project without first completing earlier activities. Also, the outcome of activities performed earlier in the project are likely to affect later activities. In other words, it is difficult, and likely inefficient, to try to plan detailed solutions for activities that will occur far in the future.

As with the project initiation process, varied and numerous activities must be performed during project planning. For example, during the Purchasing Fulfillment System project, Chris and Juanita developed a ten-page plan. However, project plans for large systems may be several hundred pages in length. The types of activities that you can perform during project planning are summarized in Figure 3-10 and are described in the following list:

1. *Describing project scope, alternatives, and feasibility.* The purpose of this activity is to understand the content and complexity of the project. Within PVF's system development methodology, one of the first meetings must focus on defining a project's scope. Although project scope information was not included in the SSR developed by Chris and Juanita, it is important that both share the same vision for the project before moving too far along. During this activity, you should reach agreement on the following questions:

   - What problem or opportunity does the project address?
   - What are the quantifiable results to be achieved?

Project planning
The second phase of the project management process, which focuses on defining clear, discrete activities and the work needed to complete each activity within a single project.

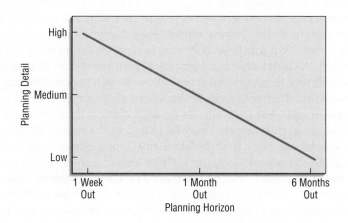

FIGURE 3-9
Level of project planning detail should be high in the short term, with less detail as time goes on.

FIGURE 3-10
Ten project planning activities.

Project Planning

1. Describing Project Scope, Alternatives, and Feasibility

2. Dividing the Project into Manageable Tasks

3. Estimating Resources and Creating a Resource Plan

4. Developing a Preliminary Schedule

5. Developing a Communication Plan

6. Determining Project Standards and Procedures

7. Identifying and Assessing Risk

8. Creating a Preliminary Budget

9. Developing a Project Scope Statement

10. Setting a Baseline Project Plan

- What needs to be done?
- How will success be measured?
- How will we know when we are finished?

After defining the scope of the project, your next objective is to identify and document general alternative solutions for the current business problem or opportunity. You must then assess the feasibility of each alternative solution and choose which to consider during subsequent SDLC phases. In some instances, off-the-shelf software can be found. It is also important that any unique problems, constraints, and assumptions about the project be clearly stated.

2. *Dividing the project into manageable tasks.* This activity is critical during the project planning process. Here, you must divide the entire project into manageable tasks and then logically order them to ensure a smooth evolution between tasks. The definition of tasks and their sequence is referred to as the **work breakdown structure (WBS).** Some tasks may be performed in parallel, whereas others must follow one another sequentially. Task sequence depends on which tasks produce deliverables needed in other tasks, when critical resources are available, the constraints placed on the project by the client, and the process outlined in the SDLC.

For example, suppose that you are working on a new development project and need to collect system requirements by interviewing users of the new system and reviewing reports they currently use to do their job. A work breakdown for these activities is represented in a Gantt chart in Figure 3-11. A **Gantt chart** is a graphical representation of a project that shows each task as a horizontal bar whose length is proportional to its time for completion. Different colors, shades, or shapes can be used to highlight each kind of task. For example, those activities on the critical path (defined later in this chapter) may be in red, and a summary task could have a special bar. Note that the black horizontal bars—rows 1, 2, and 6 in Figure 3-11—represent summary tasks. Planned versus actual times or progress for an activity can be compared by parallel bars of different colors, shades, or shapes. Gantt charts do not show how tasks must be ordered (precedence) but simply show when an activity should begin

Work breakdown structure (WBS)
The process of dividing the project into manageable tasks and logically ordering them to ensure a smooth evolution between tasks.

Gantt chart
A graphical representation of a project that shows each task as a horizontal bar whose length is proportional to its time for completion.

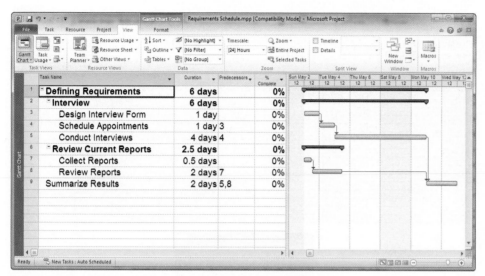

FIGURE 3-11
Gantt chart showing project tasks,
duration times for those tasks,
and predecessors.

and end. In Figure 3-11, the task duration is shown in the second column, in days, and necessary prior tasks are noted in the third column as predecessors. Most project management software tools support a broad range of task durations, including minutes, hours, days, weeks, and months. As you will learn in later chapters, the SDLC consists of several phases, which you need to break down into activities. Creating a work breakdown structure requires that you decompose phases into activities—summary tasks—and activities into specific tasks. For example, Figure 3-11 shows that the activity Interviewing consists of three tasks: design interview form, schedule appointments, and conduct interviews.

Defining tasks in too much detail will make the management of the project unnecessarily complex.

What are the characteristics of a task? A task:

- Can be done by one person or a well-defined group
- Has a single and identifiable deliverable (the task, however, is the process of creating the deliverable)
- Has a known method or technique
- Has well-accepted predecessor and successor steps
- Is measurable so that percent completed can be determined

Through experience, you will develop the skill of discovering the optimal level of detail for representing tasks. For example, it may be difficult to list tasks that require less than one hour of time to complete in a final work breakdown structure. Alternatively, choosing tasks that are too large in scope (e.g., several weeks long) will not provide you with a clear sense of the status of the project or of the interdependencies between tasks.

3. *Estimating resources and creating a resource plan.* The goal of this activity is to estimate resource requirements for each project activity and use this information to create a project resource plan. The resource plan helps assemble and deploy resources in the most effective manner. For example, you would not want to bring additional programmers onto the project at a rate faster than you could prepare work for them. Project managers use a variety of tools to assist in making estimates of project size and costs. The most widely used method is called **COCOMO** (**CO**nstructive **CO**st **MO**del), which uses parameters that were derived from prior projects of differing

COCOMO
A method for estimating a
software project's size and cost.

FIGURE 3-12
COCOMO is used by many project managers to estimate project resources.

complexity. COCOMO uses these different parameters to predict human resource requirements for basic, intermediate, and complex systems (see Figure 3-12).

People are the most important and expensive part of project resource planning. Project time estimates for task completion and overall system quality are significantly influenced by the assignment of people to tasks. It is important to give people tasks that allow them to learn new skills. It is equally important to make sure that project members are not in "over their heads" or working on a task that is not well suited to their skills. Resource estimates may need to be revised based upon the skills of the actual person (or people) assigned to a particular activity. Figure 3-13 indicates the relative programming speed versus the relative programming quality of three programmers. The figure suggests that Carl should not be assigned tasks in which completion time is critical and that Brenda should be assigned to tasks in which high quality is most vital.

FIGURE 3-13
Trade-offs between the quality of the program code versus the speed of programming.

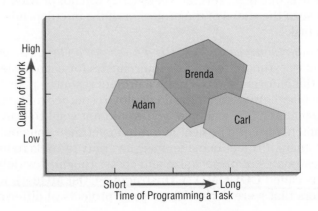

One approach to assigning tasks is to assign a single task type (or only a few task types) to each worker for the duration of the project. For example, you could assign one worker to create all computer displays and another to create all system reports. Such specialization ensures that both workers become efficient at their own particular tasks. A worker may become bored if the task is too specialized or is long in duration, so you could assign workers to a wider variety of tasks. However, this approach may lead to lowered task efficiency. A middle ground would be to make assignments with a balance of both specialization and task variety. Assignments depend upon the size of the development project and the skills of the project team. Regardless of the manner in which you assign tasks, make sure that each team member works only on one task at a time. Exceptions to this rule can occur when a task occupies only a small portion of a team member's time (e.g., testing the programs developed by another team member) or during an emergency.

4. *Developing a preliminary schedule.* During this activity, you use the information on tasks and resource availability to assign time estimates to each activity in the work breakdown structure. These time estimates will allow you to create target starting and ending dates for the project. Target dates can be revisited and modified until a schedule produced is acceptable to the customer. Determining an acceptable schedule may require that you find additional or different resources or that the scope of the project be changed. The schedule may be represented as a Gantt chart, as illustrated in Figure 3-11, or as a Network diagram, as illustrated in Figure 3-14. A **Network diagram** is a graphical depiction of project tasks and their interrelationships. As with a Gantt chart, each type of task can be highlighted by different features on the Network diagram. The distinguishing feature of a Network diagram is that the ordering of tasks is shown by connecting tasks—depicted as rectangles or ovals—with its predecessor and successor tasks. However, the relative size of a node (representing a task) or a gap between nodes does not imply the task's duration. We describe both of these charts later in this chapter.

Network diagram
A diagram that depicts project tasks and their interrelationships.

5. *Developing a communication plan.* The goal of this activity is to outline the communication procedures among management, project team members, and the customer. The communication plan includes when and how written and oral reports will be provided by the team, how team members will coordinate work, what messages will be sent to announce

FIGURE 3-14
A Network diagram illustrates tasks with rectangles (or ovals) and the relationships and sequences of those activities with arrows.

the project to interested parties, and what kinds of information will be shared with vendors and external contractors involved with the project. It is important that free and open communication occurs among all parties, with respect for proprietary information and confidentiality with the customer. When developing a communication plan, numerous questions must be answered in order to ensure that the plan is comprehensive and complete, including:

- Who are the stakeholders for this project?
- What information does each stakeholder need?
- When, and at what interval, does this information need to be produced?
- What sources will be used to gather and generate this information?
- Who will collect, store, and verify the accuracy of this information?
- Who will organize and package this information into a document?
- Who will be the contact person for each stakeholder, should any questions arise?
- What format will be used to package this information?
- What communication medium will be most effective for delivering this information to the stakeholder?

Once these questions are answered for each stakeholder, a comprehensive communication plan can be developed. In this plan, a summary of communication documents, work assignments, schedules, and distribution methods will be outlined. Additionally, a project communication matrix that provides a summary of the overall communication plan can be developed (see Figure 3-15). This matrix

FIGURE 3-15
The project communication matrix provides a high-level summary of the communication plan.

Stakeholder	Document	Format	Team Contact	Date Due
Team Members	Project Status Report	Project Intranet	Juan Kim	First Monday of Month
Management Supervisor	Project Status Report	Hard Copy	Juan Kim	First Monday of Month
User	Project Status Report	Hard Copy	James Kim	First Monday of Month
Internal IT Staff	Project Status Report	E-mail	Jackie James	First Monday of Month
IT Manager	Project Status Report	Hard Copy	Juan Jeremy	First Monday of Month
Contract Programmers	Software Specifications	E-mail/Project Intranet	Jordan Kim	October 4, 2012
Training Subcontractor	Implementation and Training Plan	Hard Copy	Jordan James	January 10, 2013

can be easily shared among team members, and verified by stakeholders outside the project team, so that the right people are getting the right information at the right time, and in the right format.

6. *Determining project standards and procedures.* During this activity, you specify how various deliverables are produced and tested by you and your project team. For example, the team must decide on which tools to use, how the standard SDLC might be modified, which SDLC methods will be used, documentation styles (e.g., type fonts and margins for user manuals), how team members will report the status of their assigned activities, and terminology. Setting project standards and procedures for work acceptance is a way to ensure the development of a high-quality system. Also, it is much easier to train new team members when clear standards are in place. Organizational standards for project management and conduct make the determination of individual project standards easier and the interchange or sharing of personnel among different projects feasible.

7. *Identifying and assessing risk.* The goal of this activity is to identify sources of project risk and to estimate the consequences of those risks. Risks might arise from the use of new technology, prospective users' resistance to change, availability of critical resources, competitive reactions or changes in regulatory actions due to the construction of a system, or team member inexperience with technology or the business area. You should continually try to identify and assess project risk.

   The identification of project risks is required to develop PVF's new Purchasing Fulfillment System. Chris and Juanita met to identify and describe possible negative outcomes of the project and their probabilities of occurrence. Although we list the identification of risks and the outline of project scope as two discrete activities, they are highly related and often concurrently discussed.

8. *Creating a preliminary budget.* During this phase, you need to create a preliminary budget that outlines the planned expenses and revenues associated with your project. The project justification will demonstrate that the benefits are worth these costs. Figure 3-16 shows a cost-benefit analysis for a new development project. This analysis shows net present value calculations of the project's benefits and costs, as well as a return on investment and cash flow analysis. We discuss project budgets fully in Chapter 4.

9. *Developing a project scope statement.* An important activity that occurs near the end of the project planning phase is the development of the *project scope statement*. Developed primarily for the customer, this document outlines work that will be done and clearly describes what the project will deliver. The project scope statement is useful to make sure that you, the customer, and other project team members have a clear understanding of the intended project size, duration, and outcomes.

10. *Setting a baseline project plan.* Once all of the prior project planning activities have been completed, you will be able to develop a *baseline project plan*. This baseline plan provides an estimate of the project's tasks and resource requirements and is used to guide the next project phase—execution. As new information is acquired during project execution, the baseline plan will continue to be updated.

    At the end of the project planning phase, a review of the baseline project plan is conducted to double-check all the information in the plan. As with the project initiation phase, it may be necessary to modify the plan, which means returning to prior project planning activities before proceeding. As with the Purchasing Fulfillment System project, you may

FIGURE 3-16
A financial cost-benefit analysis for a systems development project.

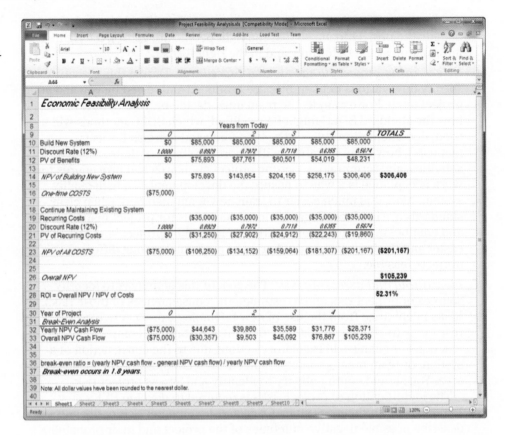

submit the plan and make a brief presentation to the project steering committee at this time. The committee can endorse the plan, ask for modifications, or determine that it is not wise to continue the project as currently outlined.

Executing the Project

Project execution The third phase of the project management process, in which the plans created in the prior phases (project initiation and planning) are put into action.

Project execution puts the baseline project plan into action. Within the context of the SDLC, project execution occurs primarily during the analysis, design, and implementation phases. During the development of the Purchasing Fulfillment System, Chris Martin was responsible for five key activities during project execution. These activities are summarized in Figure 3-17 and are described in the remainder of this section:

1. *Executing the baseline project plan.* As project manager, you oversee the execution of the baseline plan: You initiate the execution of project activities, acquire and assign resources, orient and train new team members, keep the project on schedule, and ensure the quality of project deliverables. This formidable task is made much easier through the use of sound project management techniques. For example, as tasks are completed during a project, they can be "marked" as completed on the project schedule. In Figure 3-18, tasks 3 and 7 are marked as completed by showing 100 percent in the "% Complete" column. Members of the project team will come and go. You are responsible for initiating new team members by providing them with the resources they need and helping them assimilate into the team. You may want to plan social events, regular team project status meetings, team-level reviews of project deliverables, and other group events to mold the group into an effective team.

Project Execution

1. Executing the Baseline Project Plan

2. Monitoring Project Progress Against the Baseline Project Plan

3. Managing Changes to the Baseline Project Plan

4. Maintaining the Project Workbook

5. Communicating the Project Status

FIGURE 3-17
Five project execution activities.

2. *Monitoring project progress against the baseline project plan.* While you execute the baseline project plan, you should monitor your progress. If the project gets ahead of (or behind) schedule, you may have to adjust resources, activities, and budgets. Monitoring project activities can result in modifications to the current plan. Measuring the time and effort expended on each activity helps you improve the accuracy of estimations for future projects. It is possible with project schedule charts, like Gantt, to show progress against a plan; and it is easy with Network diagrams to understand the ramifications of delays in an activity. Monitoring progress also means that the team leader must evaluate and appraise each team member, occasionally change work assignments or request changes in personnel, and provide feedback to the employee's supervisor.

3. *Managing changes to the baseline project plan.* You will encounter pressure to make changes to the baseline plan. At PVF, policies dictate that only approved changes to the project specification can be made, and all changes must be reflected in the baseline plan and project workbook, including all charts. For example, if Juanita suggests a significant change to the existing design of the Purchasing Fulfillment System, a formal change request must be approved by the steering committee. The request should explain why changes are desired and describe all possible impacts on prior and subsequent activities, project resources, and the overall project schedule. Chris would have to help Juanita develop such a request.

FIGURE 3-18
Gantt chart with tasks 3 and 7 completed.

This information allows the project steering committee to more easily evaluate the costs and benefits of a significant midcourse change.

In addition to changes occurring through formal request, changes may also occur because of events outside of your control. In fact, numerous events may initiate a change to the baseline project plan, including the following possibilities:

- A slipped completion date for an activity
- A bungled activity that must be redone
- The identification of a new activity that becomes evident later in the project
- An unforeseen change in personnel due to sickness, resignation, or termination

When an event occurs that delays the completion of an activity, you typically have two choices: devise a way to get back on schedule or revise the plan. Devising a way to get back on schedule is the preferred approach because no changes to the plan will have to be made. The ability to head off and smoothly work around problems is a critical skill that you need to master.

As you will see later in the chapter, project schedule charts are helpful in assessing the impact of change. Using such charts, you can quickly see whether the completion time of other activities will be affected by changes in the duration of a given activity or if the whole project completion date will change. Often you will have to find a way to rearrange the activities because the ultimate project completion date may be rather fixed. The organization may even incur a penalty (even legal action) if the expected completion date is not met.

4. *Maintaining the project workbook.* As in all project phases, maintaining complete records of all project events is necessary. The workbook provides the documentation new team members require to assimilate project tasks quickly. It explains why design decisions were made and is a primary source of information for producing all project reports.

5. *Communicating the project status.* The project manager is responsible for keeping all team members—system developers, managers, and customers—abreast of the project status. Clear communication is required to create a shared understanding of the activities and goals of the project; such an understanding ensures better coordination of activities. This means that the entire project plan should be shared with the entire project team, and any revisions to the plan should be communicated to all interested parties so that everyone understands how the plan is evolving. Procedures for communicating project activities vary from formal meetings to informal hallway discussions. Some procedures are useful for informing others of project status, others for resolving issues, and others for keeping permanent records of information and events. Two types of information are routinely exchanged throughout the project: (1) *work results*, or the outcomes of the various tasks and activities that are performed to complete the project, and (2) the *project plan*, which is the formal comprehensive document used to execute the project. The project plan contains numerous items including the project charter, project schedule, budgets, risk plan, and so on. Table 3-2 lists numerous communication procedures, their level of formality, and most likely use. Whichever procedure you use, frequent communication helps to ensure project success.

This section outlined your role as the project manager during the execution of the baseline project plan. The ease with which the project can be managed is significantly influenced by the quality of prior project phases. If you develop a

TABLE 3-2:   Project Team Communication Methods

Procedure	Formality	Use
Project workbook	High	Inform; permanent record
Meetings	Medium to high	Resolve issues
Seminars and workshops	Low to medium	Inform
Project newsletters	Medium to high	Inform
Status reports	High	Inform
Specification documents	High	Inform; permanent record
Minutes of meetings	High	Inform; permanent record
Bulletin boards	Low	Inform
Memos	Medium to high	Inform
Brown bag lunches	Low	Inform
Hallway discussions	Low	Inform; resolve issues

high-quality project plan, it is much more likely that the project will be successfully executed. The next section describes your role during project closedown, the final phase of the project management process.

Closing Down the Project

The focus of **project closedown** is to bring the project to an end. Projects can conclude with a natural or unnatural termination. A natural termination occurs when the requirements of the project have been met—the project has been completed and is a success. An unnatural termination occurs when the project is stopped before completion. Several events can cause an unnatural termination of a project. For example, it may be learned that the assumption used to guide the project proved to be false, or that the performance of the system or development group was somehow inadequate, or that the requirements are no longer relevant or valid in the customer's business environment. The most likely reasons for the unnatural termination of a project relate to running out of time or money, or both. Regardless of the project termination outcome, several activities must be performed: closing down the project, conducting postproject reviews, and closing the customer contract. Within the context of the SDLC, project closedown occurs after the implementation phase. The system maintenance phase typically represents an ongoing series of projects, each needing to be individually managed. Figure 3-19 summarizes the project closedown activities that are described more fully in the remainder of this section:

1. *Closing down the project.* During closedown, you perform several diverse activities. For example, if you have several team members working with

Project closedown
The final phase of the project management process, which focuses on bringing a project to an end.

Project Closedown

1. Closing Down the Project
2. Conducting Postproject Reviews
3. Closing the Customer Contract

FIGURE 3-19
Three project closedown activities.

you, project completion may signify job and assignment changes for some members. You will likely be required to assess each team member and provide an appraisal for personnel files and salary determination. You may also want to provide career advice to team members, write letters to superiors praising special accomplishments of team members, and send thank-you letters to those who helped but were not team members.

As project manager, you must be prepared to handle possible negative personnel issues, such as job termination, especially if the project was not successful. When closing down the project, it is also important to notify all interested parties that the project has been completed and to finalize all project documentation and financial records so that a final review of the project can be conducted. You should also celebrate the accomplishments of the team. Some teams will hold a party, and each team member may receive memorabilia (e.g., a T-shirt with "I survived the X project"). The goal is to celebrate the team's effort in bringing a difficult task to a successful conclusion.

2. *Conducting postproject reviews.* Once you have closed down the project, final reviews of the project should be conducted with management and customers. The objective of these reviews is to determine the strengths and weaknesses of project deliverables, the processes used to create them, and the project management process. It is important that everyone understands what went right and what went wrong, in order to improve the process for the next project. Remember, the systems development methodology adopted by an organization is a living guideline that must undergo continual improvement.

3. *Closing the customer contract.* The focus of this final activity is to ensure that all contractual terms of the project have been met. A project governed by a contractual agreement is typically not completed until agreed to by both parties, often in writing. Thus, it is paramount that you gain agreement from your customer that all contractual obligations have been met and that further work is either their responsibility or covered under another system service request or contract.

Closedown is an important activity. A project is not complete until it is closed, and it is at closedown that projects are deemed a success or failure. Completion also signifies the chance to begin a new project and apply what you have learned. Now that you have an understanding of the project management process, the next section describes specific techniques used in systems development for representing and scheduling activities and resources.

Representing and Scheduling Project Plans

A project manager has a wide variety of techniques available for depicting and documenting project plans. These planning documents can take the form of graphical or textual reports, although graphical reports have become most popular for depicting project plans. The most commonly used methods are Gantt charts and Network diagrams. Because Gantt charts do not show how tasks must be ordered (precedence) but simply show when a task should begin and when it should end, they are often more useful for depicting relatively simple projects or subparts of a larger project, the activities of a single worker, or for monitoring the progress of activities compared to scheduled completion dates (see Figure 3-20A). Recall that a Network diagram shows the ordering of activities by connecting a task to its predecessor and successor tasks (see Figure 3-20B). Sometimes a Network diagram is preferable; other times a

FIGURE 3-20
Graphical diagrams that depict project plans: (A) A Gantt chart, (B) A Network diagram.

Gantt chart more easily shows certain aspects of a project. Here are the key differences between these two representations:

- A Gantt chart shows the duration of tasks, whereas a Network diagram shows the sequence dependencies between tasks.

- A Gantt chart shows the time overlap of tasks, whereas a Network diagram does not show time overlap but does show which tasks could be done in parallel.

- Some forms of Gantt charts can show slack time available within an earliest start and latest finish date. A Network diagram shows these data within activity rectangles.

FIGURE 3-21
A screen from Microsoft Project for Windows summarizes all project activities, their durations in weeks, and their scheduled starting and ending dates.

Source: Reprinted with permission of Microsoft.

Project managers also use textual reports that depict resource utilization by tasks, complexity of the project, and cost distributions to control activities. For example, Figure 3-21 shows a screen from Microsoft Project for Windows that summarizes all project activities, their durations in weeks, and their scheduled starting and ending dates. Most project managers use computer-based systems to help develop their graphical and textual reports. Later in this chapter, we discuss these automated systems in more detail.

A project manager will periodically review the status of all ongoing project task activities to assess whether the activities will be completed early, on time, or late. If early or late, the duration of the activity, depicted in column 2 of Figure 3-21, can be updated. Once changed, the scheduled start and finish times of all subsequent tasks will also change. Making such a change will also alter a Gantt chart or Network diagram used to represent the project tasks. The ability to easily make changes to a project is a powerful feature of most project management environments. It allows the project manager to determine easily how changes in task duration affect the project completion date. It is also useful for examining the impact of "what if" scenarios for adding or reducing resources, such as personnel, for an activity.

Resources

Any person, group of people, piece of equipment, or material used in accomplishing an activity.

Critical path scheduling

A scheduling technique in which the order and duration of a sequence of task activities directly affect the completion date of a project.

Representing Project Plans

Project scheduling and management requires that time, costs, and resources be controlled. **Resources** are any person, group of people, piece of equipment, or material used in accomplishing an activity. Network diagramming is a **critical path scheduling** technique used for controlling resources. A critical path refers to a sequence of task activities whose order and durations directly affect the completion date of a project. A Network diagram is one of the most widely used and best-known scheduling methods.

A major strength of Network diagramming is its ability to represent how completion times vary for activities. Because of this, it is more often used than Gantt charts to manage projects such as information systems development where

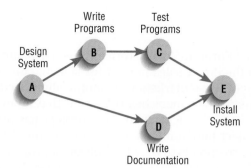

FIGURE 3-22
A Network diagram showing activities (represented by circles) and sequence of those activities (represented by arrows).

variability in the duration of activities is the norm. Network diagrams are composed of circles or rectangles representing activities and connecting arrows showing required work flows, as illustrated in Figure 3-22.

Calculating Expected Time Durations Using PERT

One of the most difficult and most error-prone activities when constructing a project schedule is the determination of the time duration for each task within a work breakdown structure. It is particularly problematic to make these estimates when a high degree of complexity and uncertainty characterize a task. **PERT (program evaluation review technique)** is a technique that uses optimistic, pessimistic, and realistic time estimates to calculate the *expected time* for a particular task. This technique helps you obtain a better time estimate when you are uncertain as to how much time a task will require to be completed.

The optimistic (o) and pessimistic (p) times reflect the minimum and maximum possible periods of time for an activity to be completed. The realistic time (r), or most likely time, reflects the project manager's "best guess" of the amount of time the activity will require for completion. Once each of these estimates is made for an activity, an expected completion time (ET) can be calculated for that activity. Because the expected completion time should be closer to the realistic time (r), the realistic time is typically weighted 4 times more than the optimistic (o) and pessimistic (p) times. Once you add these values together, it must be divided by 6 to determine the ET. This equation is shown in the following formula:

$$ET = \frac{o + 4r + p}{6}$$

where
    ET = expected time for the completion for an activity
    o = optimistic completion time for an activity
    r = realistic completion time for an activity
    p = pessimistic completion time for an activity

For example, suppose that your instructor asked you to calculate an expected time for the completion of an upcoming programming assignment. For this assignment, you estimate an optimistic time of 2 hours, a pessimistic time of 8 hours, and a most likely time of 6 hours. Using PERT, the expected time for completing this assignment is 5.67 hours. Commercial project management software such as Microsoft Project assists you in using PERT to make expected time calculations. Additionally, many commercial tools allow you to customize the weighing of optimistic, pessimistic, and realistic completion times.

PERT (Program Evaluation Review Technique)
A technique that uses optimistic, pessimistic, and realistic time estimates to calculate the expected time for a particular task.

Constructing a Gantt Chart and Network Diagram at Pine Valley Furniture

Although Pine Valley Furniture has historically been a manufacturing company, it recently entered the direct sales market for selected target markets. One of the fastest growing of these markets is economically priced furniture suitable for college students. Management has requested that a new Sales Promotion Tracking System (SPTS) be developed. This project has already successfully moved through project initiation and is currently in the detailed project planning stage, which corresponds to the SDLC phase of project initiation and planning. The SPTS will be used to track the sales purchases by college students for the next fall semester. Students typically purchase low-priced beds, bookcases, desks, tables, chairs, and dressers. Because PVF does not normally stock a large quantity of lower-priced items, management feels that a tracking system will help provide information about the college student market that can be used for follow-up sales promotions (e.g., a midterm futon sale).

The project is to design, develop, and implement this information system before the start of the fall term in order to collect sales data at the next major buying period. This deadline gives the project team twenty-four weeks to develop and implement the system. The Systems Priority Board at PVF wants to make a decision this week based on the feasibility of completing the project within the twenty-four-week deadline. Using PVF's project planning methodology, the project manager, Jim Woo, knows that the next step is to construct a Gantt chart and a Network diagram of the project to represent the baseline project plan so that he can use these charts to estimate the likelihood of completing the project within twenty-four weeks. A major activity of project planning focuses on dividing the project into manageable activities, estimating times for each, and sequencing their order. Here are the steps Jim followed:

1. *Identify each activity to be completed in the project.* After discussing the new Sales Promotion Tracking System with PVF's management, sales, and development staff, Jim identified the following major activities for the project:
   - Requirements collection
   - Screen design
   - Report design
   - Database design
   - User documentation creation
   - Software programming
   - System testing
   - System installation

2. *Determine time estimates and calculate the expected completion time for each activity.* After identifying the major project activities, Jim established optimistic, realistic, and pessimistic time estimates for each activity. These numbers were then used to calculate the expected completion times for all project activities. Figure 3-23 shows the estimated time calculations for each activity of the Sales Promotion Tracking System project.

3. *Determine the sequence of the activities and precedence relationships among all activities by constructing a Gantt chart and Network diagram.* This step helps you understand how various activities are related. Jim starts by determining the order in which activities should take place. The results of this analysis for the SPTS project are shown in Figure 3-24. The first row of this figure shows that no activities precede requirements collection. Row 2 shows that screen design must be preceded by requirements collection. Row 4 shows that both screen

ACTIVITY	TIME ESTIMATE (in weeks)			EXPECTED TIME (ET) $\dfrac{o + 4r + p}{6}$
	o	r	p	
1. Requirements Collection	1	5	9	5
2. Screen Design	5	6	7	6
3. Report Design	3	6	9	6
4. Database Design	1	2	3	2
5. User Documentation	2	6	7	5.57
6. Programming	4	5	6	5
7. Testing	1	3	5	3
8. Installation	1	1	1	1

FIGURE 3-23
Expected time calculations for the SPTS project.

ACTIVITY	PRECEDING ACTIVITY
1. Requirements Collection	—
2. Screen Design	1
3. Report Design	1
4. Database Design	2,3
5. User Documentation	4
6. Programming	4
7. Testing	6
8. Installation	5,7

FIGURE 3-24
Sequence of activities within the SPTS project.

and report design must precede database design. Thus, activities may be preceded by zero, one, or more activities.

Using the estimated times and activity sequencing information from Figures 3-23 and 3-24, Jim can now construct a Gantt chart and Network diagram of the project's activities. To construct the Gantt chart, a horizontal bar is drawn for each activity that reflects its sequence and duration, as shown in Figure 3-25. The Gantt chart may not, however, show direct interrelationships between activities. For example, just because the database design activity begins right after the screen design and report design bars finish does not imply that

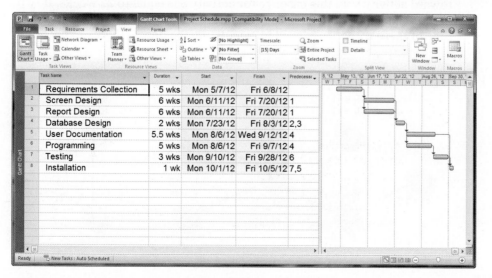

FIGURE 3-25
Gantt chart that illustrates the sequence and duration of each activity of the SPTS project.

FIGURE 3-26
A Network diagram that illustrates the activities (circles) and the sequence (arrows) of those activities.

these two activities must finish before database design can begin. To show such precedence relationships, a Network diagram must be used. The Gantt chart in Figure 3-25 does, however, show precedence relationships.

Network diagrams have two major components: arrows and nodes. Arrows reflect the sequence of activities, whereas nodes reflect activities that consume time and resources. A Network diagram for the SPTS project is shown in Figure 3-26. This diagram has eight nodes labeled 1 through 8.

4. *Determine the critical path.* The critical path of a Network diagram is represented by the sequence of connected activities that produces the shortest overall time period. All nodes and activities within this sequence are referred to as being "on" the **critical path.** The critical path represents the shortest time in which a project can be completed. In other words, any activity on the critical path that is delayed in completion delays the entire project. Nodes not on the critical path, however, can be delayed (for some amount of time) without delaying the final completion of the project. Nodes not on the critical path contain **slack time** and allow the project manager some flexibility in scheduling.

Figure 3-27 shows the Network diagram that Jim constructed to determine the critical path and expected completion time for the SPTS project. To determine the critical path, Jim calculated the earliest and latest expected completion time for each activity. He found each activity's earliest expected completion time (T_E) by summing the expected completion times (ET) of the activity and each preceding activity from left to right (i.e., in precedence order), starting at activity 1 and working toward activity 8. In this case, T_E for activity 8 is equal to 22 weeks. If two or more activities precede an activity, the largest expected completion time of these activities is used in calculating the new activity's expected

Critical path
The shortest time in which a project can be completed.

Slack time
The amount of time that an activity can be delayed without delaying the project.

FIGURE 3-27
A Network diagram for the SPTS project showing estimated times for each activity and the earliest and latest expected completion time for each activity.

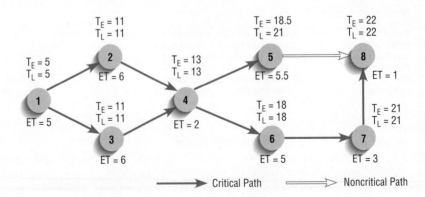

ACTIVITY	T_E	T_L	SLACK $T_L - T_E$	ON CRITICAL PATH
1	5	5	0	✓
2	11	11	0	✓
3	11	11	0	✓
4	13	13	0	✓
5	18.5	21	2.5	
6	18	18	0	✓
7	21	21	0	✓
8	22	22	0	✓

FIGURE 3-28
Activity slack time calculations for the SPTS project all activities except number 5 are on the critical path.

completion time. For example, because activity 8 is preceded by both activities 5 and 7, the largest expected completion time between 5 and 7 is 21, so T_E for activity 8 is $21 + 1$, or 22. The earliest expected completion time for the last activity of the project represents the amount of time the project should take to complete. Because the time of each activity can vary, however, the projected completion time represents only an estimate. The project may, in fact, require more or less time for completion.

The latest expected completion time (T_L) refers to the time in which an activity can be completed without delaying the project. To find the values for each activity's T_L, Jim started at activity 8 and set T_L equal to the final T_E (22 weeks). Next, he worked right to left toward activity 1 and subtracted the expected time for each activity. The slack time for each activity is equal to the difference between its latest and earliest expected completion times ($T_L - T_E$). Figure 3-28 shows the slack time calculations for all activities of the SPTS project. All activities with a slack time equal to zero are on the critical path. Thus, all activities except 5 are on the critical path. Part of the diagram in Figure 3-27 shows two critical paths, between activities 1-2-4 and 1-3-4, because both of these parallel activities have zero slack.

In addition to the possibility of having multiple critical paths, two types of slack are actually possible. *Free slack* refers to the amount of time a task can be delayed without delaying the early start of any task immediately following. *Total slack* refers to the amount of time a task can be delayed without delaying the completion of the project. Understanding free and total slack allows the project manager to better identify where trade-offs can be made if changes to the project schedule are needed. For more information about understanding slack and how it can be used to manage tasks, see *Information Systems Project Management* (© 2008) by Mark A. Fuller, Joseph S. Valacich, and Joey F. George (Upper Saddle River, NJ: Prentice Hall).

Using Project Management Software

A wide variety of automated project management tools are available to help you manage a development project. New versions of these tools are continuously being developed and released by software vendors. Most of the available tools have a common set of features that include the ability to define and order tasks, assign resources to tasks, and easily modify tasks and resources. Project management tools are available to run on Windows-compatible personal computers, the Macintosh, and larger mainframe and workstation-based systems. These systems vary in the number of task activities supported, the complexity of relationships, system processing and storage requirements, and, of course, cost. Prices for these systems can range from a few hundred dollars for personal computer–based systems to more than $100,000 for large-scale multiproject

FIGURE 3-29
Establishing a project starting date in Microsoft Project for Windows.

Source: Reprinted with permission of Microsoft.

systems. Yet, a lot can be done with systems like Microsoft Project as well as public domain and shareware systems. For example, numerous shareware project management programs (e.g., OpenProj or EasyProjectPlan) can be downloaded from the World Wide Web (e.g., at www.download.com). Because these systems are continuously changing, you should comparison shop before choosing a particular package.

We now illustrate the types of activities you would perform when using project management software. Microsoft Project for Windows is a project management system that has earned consistently high marks in computer publication reviews (see www.microsoft.com and search for "project"—also, if you search the Web, you can find many useful tutorials for improving your Microsoft Project skills). When using this system to manage a project, you need to perform at least the following activities:

- Establish a project starting or ending date.
- Enter tasks and assign task relationships.
- Select a scheduling method to review project reports.

Establishing a Project Starting Date

Defining the general project information includes obtaining the name of the project and project manager and the starting or ending date of the project. Starting and ending dates are used to schedule future activities or backdate others (see following) based upon their duration and relationships to other activities. An example from Microsoft Project for Windows of the data-entry screen for establishing a project starting or ending date is shown in Figure 3-29. This screen shows PVF's Purchasing Fulfillment System project. Here, the starting date for the project is Monday, November 5, 2012.

Entering Tasks and Assigning Task Relationships

The next step in defining a project is to define project tasks and their relationships. For the Purchasing Fulfillment System project, Chris defined 11 tasks to be completed when he performed the initial system analysis activities of the project (Task 1—Start Analysis Phase—is a summary task that is used to group related tasks). The task entry screen, shown in Figure 3-30, is similar to a financial spreadsheet program. The user moves the cursor to a cell with arrow keys or the mouse and then simply enters a textual Task Name and a numeric Duration for each activity. Scheduled Start and Scheduled Finish are automatically entered based upon the project start date and duration. To set an activity

FIGURE 3-30
Entering tasks and assigning task relationships in Microsoft Project for Windows.

Source: Reprinted with permission of Microsoft.

relationship, the ID number (or numbers) of the activity that must be completed before the start of the current activity is entered in the Predecessors column. Additional codes under this column make the precedence relationships more precise. For example, consider the Predecessor column for ID 6. The entry in this cell says that activity 6 cannot start until one day before the finish of activity 5. (Microsoft Project provides many different options for precedence and delays such as in this example, but discussion of these is beyond the scope of our coverage.) The project management software uses this information to construct Gantt charts, Network diagrams, and other project-related reports.

Selecting a Scheduling Method to Review Project Reports

Once information about all the activities for a project has been entered, it is easy to review the information in a variety of graphical and textual formats using displays or printed reports. For example, Figure 3-30 shows the project information in a Gantt chart screen, whereas Figure 3-31 shows the project information as a Network diagram. You can easily change how you view the information by making a selection from the View menu shown in Figure 3-31.

As mentioned in the chapter, interim project reports to management will often compare actual progress to plans. Figure 3-32 illustrates how Microsoft Project

FIGURE 3-31
Viewing project information as a Network diagram in Microsoft Project for Windows.

Source: Reprinted with permission of Microsoft.

FIGURE 3-32
Gantt chart showing progress of
activities (right frame) versus
planned activities (left frame).

shows progress with a solid line within the activity bar. In this figure, task 2 is completed and task 3 is almost completed, but there remains a small percentage of work, as shown by the incomplete solid lines within the bar for this task. Assuming that this screen represents the status of the project on Friday, November 16, 2012, the third activity is approximately on schedule. Tabular reports can summarize the same information.

This brief introduction to project management software has only scratched the surface to show you the power and the features of these systems. Other features widely available and especially useful for multi-person projects relate to resource usage and utilization. Resource-related features allow you to define characteristics such as standard costing rates and daily availability via a calendar that records holidays, working hours, and vacations. These features are particularly useful for billing and estimating project costs. Often, resources are shared across multiple projects, which could significantly affect a project's schedule. Depending upon how projects are billed within an organization, assigning and billing resources to tasks is a time-consuming activity for most project managers. The features provided in these powerful tools can greatly ease both the planning and managing of projects so that both project and management resources are effectively utilized.

Key Points Review

1. **Describe the skills required to be an effective project manager.**

   A project manager has both technical and managerial skills and is ultimately responsible for determining the size, scope, and resource requirements for a project. Once a project is deemed feasible by an organization, the project manager ensures that the project meets the customer's needs and is delivered within budget and time constraints.

2. **List and describe the skills and activities of a project manager during project initiation, project planning, project execution, and project closedown.**

   To manage the project, the project manager must execute four primary activities: project

initiation, project planning, project execution, and project closedown. The focus of project initiation is on assessing the size, scope, and complexity of a project and establishing procedures to support later project activities. The focus of project planning is on defining clear, discrete activities and the work needed to complete each activity. The focus of project execution is on putting the plans developed in project initiation and planning into action. Project closedown focuses on bringing the project to an end.

3. **Explain what is meant by critical path scheduling and describe the process of creating Gantt charts and Network diagrams.**

   Critical path scheduling refers to planning methods whereby the order and duration of the project's activities directly affect the completion date of the project. Gantt charts and Network diagrams are powerful graphical techniques used in planning and controlling projects. Both Gantt and Network diagramming scheduling techniques require that a project have activities that can be defined as having a clear beginning and end, can be worked on independently of other activities, are ordered, and are such that their completion signifies the end of the project. Gantt charts use horizontal bars to represent the beginning, duration, and ending of an activity. Network diagramming is a critical path scheduling method that shows the interrelationships between activities. These charts show when activities can begin and end, which activities cannot be delayed without delaying the whole project, how much slack time each activity has, and progress against planned activities. Network diagramming's ability to use estimated completion times, based on optimistic, pessimistic, and most likely completion times, when determining critical paths.

4. **Explain how commercial project management software packages can be used to assist in representing and managing project schedules.**

A wide variety of automated tools for assisting the project manager are available. Most tools have common features, including the ability to define and order tasks, assign resources to tasks, and modify tasks and resources. Systems vary regarding the number of activities supported, the complexity of relationships, processing and storage requirements, and cost.

Key Terms Checkpoint

Here are the key terms from the chapter. The page where each term is first explained is in parentheses after the term.

1. COCOMO (p. 55)
2. Critical path (p. 70)
3. Critical path scheduling (p. 66)
4. Deliverable (p. 46)
5. Feasibility study (p. 47)
6. Gantt chart (p. 54)
7. Network diagram (p. 57)
8. PERT (Program Evaluation Review Technique) (p. 67)
9. Project (p. 45)
10. Project charter (p. 51)
11. Project closedown (p. 63)
12. Project execution (p. 60)
13. Project initiation (p. 49)
14. Project management (p. 48)
15. Project manager (p. 45)
16. Project planning (p. 53)
17. Project workbook (p. 50)
18. Resources (p. 66)
19. Slack time (p. 70)
20. Work breakdown structure (WBS) (p. 54)

Match each of the key terms above with the definition that best fits it.

_____ 1. An online or hard-copy repository for all project correspondence, inputs, outputs, deliverables, procedures, and standards that is used for performing project audits, orienting new team members, communicating with management and customers, identifying future projects, and performing postproject reviews.

_____ 2. An end product in a phase of the SDLC.

_____ 3. Determines whether the information system makes sense for the organization from an economic and operational standpoint.

_____ 4. A controlled process of initiating, planning, executing, and closing down a project.

_____ 5. The third phase of the project management process in which the plans created in the prior phases (project initiation and planning) are put into action.

_____ 6. The first phase of the project management process in which activities are performed to assess the size, scope, and complexity of the project and to establish procedures to support later project activities.

_____ 7. A diagram that depicts project tasks and their interrelationships.

_____ 8. A planned undertaking of related activities to reach an objective that has a beginning and an end.

_____ 9. The amount of time that an activity can be delayed without delaying the project.

_____ 10. The process of dividing the project into manageable tasks and logically ordering them to ensure a smooth evolution between tasks.

_____ 11. The final phase of the project management process, which focuses on bringing a project to an end.

____ 12. A graphical representation of a project that shows each task activity as a horizontal bar whose length is proportional to its time for completion.

____ 13. Any person, group of people, piece of equipment, or material used in accomplishing an activity.

____ 14. A scheduling technique in which the order and duration of a sequence of activities directly affect the completion date of a project.

____ 15. A systems analyst with a diverse set of skills—management, leadership, technical, conflict management, and customer relationship—who is responsible for initiating, planning, executing, and closing down a project.

____ 16. The second phase of the project management process, which focuses on defining clear, discrete activities and the work needed to complete each activity within a single project.

____ 17. The shortest time in which a project can be completed.

____ 18. A technique that uses optimistic, pessimistic, and realistic time estimates to calculate the expected time for a particular task.

____ 19. A short document prepared for the customer during project initiation that describes what the project will deliver and outlines generally at a high level all work required to complete the project.

____ 20. A method for estimating a software project's size and cost.

Review Questions

1. Discuss the reasons why organizations undertake information system projects.
2. List and describe the common skills and activities of a project manager. Which skill do you think is most important? Why?
3. Describe the activities performed by the project manager during project initiation.
4. Describe the activities performed by the project manager during project planning.
5. Describe the activities performed by the project manager during project execution.
6. List various project team communication methods, and describe an example of the type of information that might be shared among team members using each method.
7. Describe the activities performed by the project manager during project closedown.
8. What characteristics must a project have in order for critical path scheduling to be applicable?
9. Describe the steps involved in making a Gantt chart.
10. Describe the steps involved in making a Network diagram.
11. In which phase of the systems development life cycle does project planning typically occur? In which phase is project management necessary?
12. What are some reasons why one activity may have to precede another activity before the second activity can begin? In other words, what causes precedence relationships between project activities?

Problems and Exercises

1. Which of the four phases of the project management process do you feel is most challenging? Why?
2. What are some sources of risk in a systems analysis and design project, and how does a project manager cope with risk during the stages of project management?
3. Search the Web for recent reviews of project management software. Which packages seem to be most popular? What are the relative strengths and weaknesses of each package? What advice would you give to someone intending to buy project management software for his or her PC? Why?
4. Suppose that you have been contracted by a jewelry store to manage a project to create a new inventory tracking system. Describe your initial approach to the project. What should your first activity be? What information would you need? To whom might you need to speak?
5. Can a project have two critical paths? Why or why not? Give a brief example to illustrate your point.
6. Calculate the expected time for the following tasks.

Task	Optimistic Time	Most Likely Time	Pessimistic Time	Expected Time
A	3	7	11	
B	5	9	13	
C	1	2	9	
D	2	3	16	
E	2	4	18	
F	3	4	11	
G	1	4	7	
H	3	4	5	
I	2	4	12	
J	4	7	9	

7. A project has been defined to contain the following list of activities along with their required times for completion.

Activity No.	Activity	Time (weeks)	Immediate Predecessors
1	Collect requirements	3	
2	Analyze processes	2	1
3	Analyze data	2	2
4	Design processes	6	2
5	Design data	3	3
6	Design screens	2	3,4
7	Design reports	4	4,5
8	Program	5	6,7
9	Test and Document	7	7
10	Install	2	8,9

a. Draw a Network diagram for the activities.
b. Calculate the earliest expected completion time.
c. Show the critical path.
d. What would happen if activity 6 were revised to take 6 weeks instead of 2 weeks?

8. Construct a Gantt chart for the project defined in Problem and Exercise 7.
9. Look again at the activities outlined in Problem and Exercise 7. Assume that your team is in its first week of the project and has discovered that each of the activity duration estimates is wrong. Activities 4 and 7 will each take three times longer than anticipated. All other activities will take twice as long to complete as previously estimated. In addition, a new activity, number 11, has been added. It will take one week to complete, and its immediate predecessors are activities 10 and 9. Adjust the Network diagram and recalculate the earliest expected completion times.
10. Construct a Gantt chart and Network diagram for a project you are or will be involved in.

Choose a project of sufficient depth at either work, home, or school. Identify the activities to be completed, determine the sequence of the activities, and construct a diagram reflecting the starting, ending, duration, and precedence (Network diagram only) relationships among all activities. For your Network diagram, use the procedure in this chapter to determine time estimates for each activity and calculate the expected time for each activity. Now determine the critical path and the early and late starting and finishing times for each activity. Which activities have slack time?

11. For the project you described in Problem and Exercise 10, assume that the worst has happened. A key team member has dropped out of the project and has been assigned to another project in another part of the country. The remaining team members are having personality clashes. Key deliverables for the project are now due much earlier than expected. In addition, you have just determined that a key phase in the early life of the project will now take much longer than you had originally expected. To make matters worse, your boss absolutely will not accept that this project cannot be completed by the old deadline. What will you do to account for these project changes and problems? Begin by reconstructing your Gantt chart and Network diagram and determining a strategy for dealing with the specific changes and problems described here. If new resources are needed to meet the old deadline, outline the rationale that you will use to convince your boss that these additional resources are critical to the success of the project.

12. Assume you have a project with seven activities labeled A–G (following). Derive the earliest completion time (or early finish—EF), latest completion time (or late finish—LF), and slack for each of the following tasks (begin at time = 0). Which tasks are on the critical path? Draw a Gantt chart for these tasks.

Task	Preceding Event	Expected Duration	EF	LF	Slack	Critical Path?
A	—	2				
B	A	3				
C	A	4				
D	C	6				
E	B,C	4				
F	D	1				
G	D,E,F	5				

13. Draw a Network diagram for the tasks shown in Problem and Exercise 12. Highlight the critical path.

14. Assume you have a project with ten activities labeled A–J. Derive the earliest completion time (or early finish—EF), latest completion time (or late finish—LF), and slack for each of the following tasks (begin at time = 0). Which tasks are on the critical path? Highlight the critical path on your Network diagram.

Activity	Preceding Event	Expected Duration	EF	LF	Slack	Critical Path?
A	—	4				
B	A	5				
C	A	6				
D	A	7				
E	A,D	6				
F	C,E	5				
G	D,E	4				
H	E	3				
I	F,G	4				
J	H,I	5				

15. Draw a Gantt chart for the tasks shown in Problem and Exercise 14.

16. Assume you have a project with ten activities labeled A–J. Derive the earliest completion time (or early finish—EF), latest completion time (or late finish—LF), and slack for each of the following tasks (begin at time = 0). Which tasks are on the critical path? Draw both a Gantt chart and a Network diagram for these tasks, and make sure you highlight the critical path on your Network diagram.

Activity	Preceding Event	Expected Duration	EF	LF	Slack	Critical Path?
A	—	3				
B	A	1				
C	A	2				
D	B,C	5				
E	C	3				
F	D	2				
G	E,F	3				
H	F,G	5				
I	G,H	5				
J	I	2				

17. Make a list of the tasks that you performed when designing your schedule of classes for this term. Develop a table showing each task, its duration, preceding event(s), and expected duration. Develop a Network diagram for these tasks. Highlight the critical path on your Network diagram.

18. Fully decompose a project you've done in another course (e.g., a semester project or term paper). Discuss the level of detail where you stopped decomposing and explain why.

19. Create a work breakdown structure based on the decomposition you carried out for the previous question.

20. Working in a small group, pick a project (it could be anything, such as planning a party, writing a group term paper, developing a database application, etc.) and then write the various tasks that need to be done to accomplish the project on Post-Its (one task per Post-It). Then, use the Post-Its to create a work breakdown structure for the project. Was it complete? Add missing tasks if necessary. Were some tasks at a lower level in the WBS than others? What was the most difficult part of doing this exercise?

Discussion Questions

1. You interview for a job and the employer asks you if the project management process for systems development should be a structured, formal process. What will your answer be?

2. Do you agree that breaking projects down into small, manageable tasks is an important part of managing a project? What are the pros and cons of this type of breakdown?

3. Microsoft Project is powerful but expensive. Assume you are in charge of researching and purchasing a project management application. Would you select Microsoft Project? Why or why not? If you were to select Microsoft Project, how would you justify its cost to your manager?

4. When completing a project, some tasks are independent of others, whereas some are interdependent. What does task interdependence mean in regards to slack? How are slack and the critical path related?

Case Problems

1. Pine Valley Furniture

   In an effort to better serve the various departments at Pine Valley Furniture, the PVF information systems department assigns one of its systems analysts to serve as a liaison to a particular business unit. Chris Martin is currently the liaison to the purchasing department.

   After graduating from Valley State University, Chris began working at Pine Valley Furniture. He began his career at Pine Valley Furniture as a programmer/analyst I. This job assignment required him to code and maintain financial application systems in COBOL. In the six years he has been at PVF, he has been promoted several times; his most recent promotion was to a junior systems analyst position. During his tenure at PVF, Chris has worked on several important projects, including serving as a team member on a project that developed a five-year plan that would renovate the manufacturing information systems.

   Chris enjoys his work at Pine Valley Furniture and wishes to continue moving up the information systems ladder. Over the past three years, Chris has often thought about becoming certified by the Project Management Institute. He has taken several courses toward his MBA, has attended three technology-related seminars, and has helped the local Feed the Hungry chapter develop, implement, and maintain its computerized information system.

   a. While eating lunch one day, Juanita asked Chris about the benefits of becoming a project management professional. Briefly make a case for becoming a project management professional.
   b. What are the project management professional eligibility criteria for Chris? What documentation must he provide?
   c. Assume Chris has obtained his certification. What are PDUs, and how many must Chris acquire over a three-year period?
   d. Several activity categories are listed as qualifying for PDUs on the Project Management Institute's Web site. Identify these categories. In which categories would you place Chris's experience?

2. Hoosier Burger

   Bob and Thelma Mellankamp have come to realize that the current problems with their inventory control, customer ordering, and management reporting systems are seriously affecting Hoosier Burger's day-to-day operations. At the close of business one evening, Bob and Thelma decide to hire the Build a Better System (BBS) consulting firm. Harold Parker and Lucy Chen, two of BBS's owners, are frequent Hoosier Burger customers. Bob and Thelma are aware of the excellent consulting service BBS is providing to the Bloomington area.

   Build a Better System is a medium-size consulting firm based in Bloomington, Indiana. Six months ago, BBS hired you as a junior systems analyst for the firm. Harold and Lucy were impressed with your résumé, course work, and systems analysis and design internship. During your six months with BBS, you have had the opportunity to work alongside several senior systems analysts and observe the project management process.

   On a Friday afternoon, you learn that you have been assigned to the Hoosier Burger project and that the lead analyst on the project is Juan Rodriquez. A short while later, Juan stops by your desk and mentions that you will be participating in the project management process. Mr. Rodriquez has scheduled a meeting with you for 10:00 A.M. on Monday to review the project management process with you. You know from your brief discussion with Mr. Rodriquez that you will be asked to prepare various planning documents, particularly a Gantt chart and a Network diagram.

   a. In an effort to learn more about project management, you decide to research this topic over the weekend. Locate articles that discuss project management. Summarize your findings.
   b. At your meeting on Monday, Mr. Rodriquez asks you to prepare a Gantt chart for the Hoosier Burger project. Using the following information, prepare a Gantt chart.

Activity No.	Activity	Time (weeks)	Immediate Predecessors
1	Requirements collection	1	—
2	Requirements structuring	2	1
3	Alternative generation	1	2
4	Logical design	2	3
5	Physical design	3	4
6	Implementation	2	5

   c. Using the information provided in part b, prepare a Network diagram.
   d. After reviewing the Gantt chart and a Network diagram, Mr. Rodriquez feels that alternative generation should take only one-half week and that implementation may take three weeks. Modify your charts to reflect these changes.

3. Lilly Langley's Baking Goods Company

In 1919 Lionel Langley opened his first bakery store, which he named after his wife, Lilly. Initially he sold only breads, cakes, and flour to his customers. Through the years, the business expanded rapidly by opening additional bakeries, acquiring flour mills, and acquiring food-processing companies. After 81 years in business, the company is now a well-known, highly reputable, international corporation. Lilly Langley's Baking Goods Company (LLBGC) has more than 15,000 employees, operates in 50 countries, and offers a wide variety of products.

Frederica Frampton, LLBGC's chief information officer, has just returned from a meeting with Chung Lau, LLBGC's director of operations. They discussed the many problems the company is having with getting supplies and distributing products. In essence, the end users of the current operations/manufacturing systems are demanding information that the current system just cannot provide. The current information systems are inflexible.

- Combining data housed in separate plant databases is difficult, if not impossible.
- End users have difficulty generating ad hoc reports.
- Scheduling the production lines is becoming quite tedious.

Costs to enhance the systems are becoming unwieldy, so now it is time to consider renovating these systems. Because of a top management directive, the systems must be operational within nine months.

Frederica Frampton recognizes the importance of the LLBGC operations/manufacturing systems renovation. She decides to assemble a team of her best systems analysts to develop new operations/manufacturing systems for LLBGC. You are assigned as a member of this team.

a. Lorraine Banderez, the project manager, has asked you to investigate how other companies have used project management software, particularly Microsoft Project. Investigate two companies and provide a brief summary of how each has used project management software.

b. Part of your responsibility is to assist in the preparation of the planning documents. Using the following information, prepare a Gantt chart.

Activity No.	Activity	Time (weeks)	Immediate Predecessors
1	Requirements collection	3	—
2	Requirements structuring	4	1
3	Process analysis	3	2
4	Data analysis	3	2
5	Logical design	5	3,4
6	Physical design	5	5
7	Implementation	6	6

c. Using the information from part b, prepare a Network diagram. Identify the critical path.

d. After reviewing your planning documents, Lorraine decides to modify several of the activity times. Revise both your Gantt chart and Network diagram to reflect these modifications.

Activity	Time (weeks)
Requirements collection	4
Requirements structuring	3
Process analysis	4
Data analysis	4.5
Logical design	5
Physical design	5.5
Implementation	7

CASE: PETRIE'S ELECTRONICS

Managing the Information Systems Project

Jim Watanabe, the assistant director of information technology at Petrie's Electronics, a Southern California–based electronics retail store, walked into his building's conference room. It was early in the morning for Jim, but the meeting was important for him. Jim was going to put together his team for the customer relationship project he had just been named

to manage. It was Jim's first big project to manage at Petrie's, and he was excited about getting started.

"Hi Jim," said Ella Whinston, the chief operations officer. With Ella was a guy Jim did not know. "Jim, this is Bob Petroski. I've asked that he be on your project team, to represent me."

Jim and Bob shook hands. "Nice to meet you, Jim. I'm looking forward to working with you on this project."

"And Bob knows how important this project is to me," Ella said, "so I expect him to keep me informed about your progress." Ella smiled.

Great, Jim thought, more pressure. That's all I need.

Just then, John Smith, the head of marketing walked into the conference room. With him was a young woman Jim recognized, but he wasn't sure from where.

"Jim," John said, "Let me introduce you to Sally Fukuyama. She is the assistant director of marketing. She will be representing marketing, and me, on your 'No Customer Escapes' project."

"Hi Jim," Sally said, "I have a lot of ideas about what we can do. Even though I still have my regular job to worry about, I'm excited about working on this project."

"Who else will be on your team?" Ella asked.

"I am bringing Sanjay Agarwal from IT," Jim said. "He is in charge of systems integration in the IT department and reports to me. In addition to myself and Sanjay and Sally and Bob, we will also have a store manager on the team. I'm trying to get Carmen Sanchez, the manager of the store in Irvine (California). Like the rest of us, she is really busy, but I think we have to have a store manager on the team."

"Irvine?" Ella asked. "That's one of our top stores. Carmen should have a lot of insight into the issues related to keeping customers, if she is managing the Irvine store. And you are right, she is going to be very busy."

"So," John asked, "When is your first meeting?"

Case Questions

1. What qualities might Jim possess that would make him a successful project manager?
2. How do you think Jim should respond to Ella's implied pressure about the importance of the project to her?
3. What strategies might Jim employ to deal with a very busy team member such as Carmen Sanchez?
4. What should Jim do next to complete the project initiation?
5. List five team communication methods that Jim might use throughout this project. What are some pros and cons of each?

four
Systems Planning and Selection

Comstock/Thinkstock

After studying this chapter, you should be able to:

Chapter Objectives

- Describe the steps involved when identifying and selecting projects and initiating and planning projects.

- Explain the need for and the contents of a project scope statement and baseline project plan.

- List and describe various methods for assessing project feasibility.

- Describe the differences between tangible and intangible benefits and costs, and the differences between one-time and recurring costs.

- Perform cost-benefit analysis and describe what is meant by the time value of money, present value, discount rate, net present value, return on investment, and break-even analysis.

- Describe the activities and participant roles within a structured walkthrough.

Chapter Preview . . .

The acquisition, development, and maintenance of information systems consume substantial resources for most organizations. Organizations can benefit from following a formal process for identifying, selecting, initiating, and planning projects. The first phase of the systems development life cycle—systems planning and selection—deals with this issue. As you can see in Figure 4-1, this phase consists of two primary activities. In the next section, you learn about the first activity, a general method for identifying and selecting projects and the deliverables and outcomes from this process. Next, we review the second activity, project initiation and planning, and present several techniques for assessing project feasibility. The information uncovered during feasibility analysis is organized into a document called a baseline project plan. The process of building this plan is discussed next. Before the project can evolve to the next phase of the systems development life cycle—systems analysis—the project plan must be reviewed and accepted. In the final major section of the chapter, we provide an overview of the project review process.

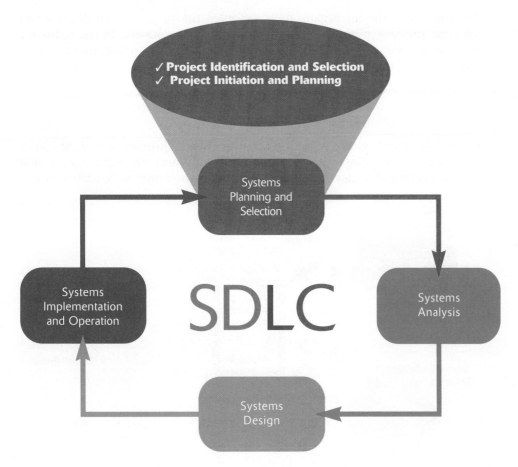

FIGURE 4-1
Systems development life cycle phase 1, systems planning and selection. Phase 1 activities are project identification and selection and project initiation and planning.

Identifying and Selecting Projects

The first activity of the systems planning and selection phase of the SDLC is project identification and selection. During this activity, a senior manager, a business group, an IS manager, or a steering committee identifies and assesses all possible systems development projects that a business unit could undertake. Next, those projects deemed most likely to yield significant organizational benefits, given available resources, are selected. Organizations vary in their approach to identifying and selecting projects. In some organizations, project identification and selection is a formal process in which projects are outcomes of a larger overall planning process. For example, a large organization may follow a formal project identification process that involves rigorously comparing all competing projects. Alternatively, a small organization may use informal project selection processes that allow the highest-ranking IS manager to select projects independently or allow individual business units to decide on projects after agreeing on funding.

Requests for information systems development can come from three key sources, as depicted in Figure 4-2:

1. Managers and business units who want to replace or extend an existing system in order to gain needed information or to provide a new service to customers

2. Information systems managers who want to make a system more efficient, less costly to operate, or want to move a system to a new operating environment

3. Formal planning groups that want to improve an existing system in order to help the organization meet its corporate objectives, such as providing better customer service

Regardless of how an organization executes the project identification and selection process, a common sequence of activities occurs. In the following sections, we describe a general process for identifying and selecting projects, and producing the deliverables and outcomes of this process.

The Process of Identifying and Selecting Information Systems Development Projects

Project identification and selection consists of three primary activities: identifying potential development projects, classifying and ranking projects, and selecting projects for development. Each of these activities is described next.

FIGURE 4-2
Three key sources for information systems projects.

Managers and Business Units

Project 1
Project 2
Project 3
...
Project *N*

Formal Planning Groups

Information Systems Managers

1. *Identifying potential development projects.* Organizations vary as to how they identify projects. This process can be performed by:

   - A key member of top management, either the CEO of a small or medium-size organization or a senior executive in a larger organization
   - A steering committee, composed of a cross section of managers with an interest in systems
   - User departments, in which either the head of the requesting unit or a committee from the requesting department decides which projects to submit (as a systems analyst, you will help users prepare such requests)
   - The development group or a senior IS manager

   Each identification method has strengths and weaknesses. For example, projects identified by top management have a strategic organizational focus. Alternatively, projects identified by steering committees reflect the diversity of the committee and therefore have a cross-functional focus. Projects identified by individual departments or business units have a narrow, tactical focus. The development group identifies projects based on the ease with which existing hardware and systems will integrate with the proposed project. Other factors, such as project cost, duration, complexity, and risk, also influence the people who identify a project. Table 4-1 summarizes the characteristics of each selection method.

   Of all the possible project sources, those identified by top management and steering committees most often reflect the broader needs of the organization. These groups have a better understanding of overall business objectives and constraints. Projects identified by top management or by a diverse steering committee are therefore referred to as coming from a top-down source.

   Projects identified by a functional manager, a business unit, or the information systems development group are often designed for a particular business need within a given business unit and may not reflect the overall objectives of the organization. It's not that projects identified by individual managers, business units, or the IS development group are deficient, but rather that they may not consider broader organizational issues. Project initiatives stemming from managers, business units, or the development group are referred to as coming from a bottom-up source. As a systems analyst, you provide ongoing support for users of these types of projects and are involved early in the life cycle. You help managers describe their information needs and the reasons for doing the project. These descriptions are evaluated in selecting which projects will be approved to move into the project initiation and planning activities.

   In sum, projects are identified by both top-down and bottom-up initiatives. The formality of identifying and selecting projects can vary substantially across organizations. Because limited resources preclude the

TABLE 4-1: Common Characteristics of Alternative Methods for Making Information Systems Identification and Selection Decisions

Project Source	Cost	Duration	Complexity	System Size	Focus
Top management	Highest	Longest	Highest	Largest	Strategic
Steering committee	High	Long	High	Large	Cross-functional
User department	Low	Short	Low	Small	Departmental
Development group	Low–high	Short–long	Low–high	Small–large	Integration with existing systems

development of all proposed systems, most organizations have some process of classifying and ranking each project's merit. Those projects deemed to be inconsistent with overall organizational objectives, redundant in functionality to some existing system, or unnecessary will not be considered.

2. *Classifying and ranking IS development projects.* Assessing the merit of potential projects is the second major activity in the project identification and selection phase. As with project identification, classifying and ranking projects can be performed by top managers, a steering committee, business units, or the IS development group. The criteria used to assign the merit of a given project can vary based on the size of the organization. Table 4-2 summarizes the criteria commonly used to evaluate projects. In any given organization, one or several criteria might be used during the classifying and ranking process.

   As with project identification, the criteria used to evaluate projects will vary by organization. If, for example, an organization uses a steering committee, it may choose to meet monthly or quarterly to review projects and use a wide variety of evaluation criteria. At these meetings, new project requests are reviewed relative to projects already identified, and ongoing projects are monitored. The relative ratings of projects are used to guide the final activity of this identification process—project selection.

3. *Selecting IS development projects.* The selection of projects is the final activity in the project identification and selection phase. The short- and long-term projects most likely to achieve business objectives are considered. As business conditions change over time, the relative importance of any single project may substantially change. Thus, the identification and selection of projects is an important and ongoing activity.

   Numerous factors must be considered when selecting a project, as illustrated in Figure 4-3. These factors include:

   ■ Perceived needs of the organization
   ■ Existing systems and ongoing projects
   ■ Resource availability
   ■ Evaluation criteria
   ■ Current business conditions
   ■ Perspectives of the decision makers

TABLE 4-2: Possible Evaluation Criteria When Classifying and Ranking Projects

Evaluation Criteria	Description
Value chain analysis	Extent to which activities add value and costs when developing products and/or services; information systems projects providing the greatest overall benefits will be given priority over those with fewer benefits
Strategic alignment	Extent to which the project is viewed as helping the organization achieve its strategic objectives and long-term goals
Potential benefits	Extent to which the project is viewed as improving profits, customer service, etc., and the duration of these benefits
Resource availability	Amount and type of resources the project requires and their availability
Project size/duration	Number of individuals and the length of time needed to complete the project
Technical difficulty/risks	Level of technical difficulty to complete the project successfully within given time and resource constraints

FIGURE 4-3
Numerous factors must be considered when selecting a project. Decisions can result in one of seven outcomes.

This decision-making process can lead to numerous outcomes. Of course, projects can be accepted or rejected. Acceptance of a project usually means that funding to conduct the next SDLC activity has been approved. Rejection means that the project will no longer be considered for development. However, projects may also be conditionally accepted; projects may be accepted pending the approval or availability of needed resources or the demonstration that a particularly difficult aspect of the system can be developed. Projects may also be returned to the original requesters who are told to develop or purchase the requested system themselves. Finally, the requesters of a project may be asked to modify and resubmit their request after making suggested changes or clarifications.

Deliverables and Outcomes

The primary deliverable, or end product, from the project identification and selection phase is a schedule of specific IS development projects. These projects come from both top-down and bottom-up sources, and once selected they move into the second activity within this SDLC phase—project initiation and planning. This sequence of events is illustrated in Figure 4-4. An outcome of this activity is the assurance that people in the organization gave careful

FIGURE 4-4
Information systems development projects come from both top-down and bottom-up initiatives.

consideration to project selection and clearly understood how each project could help the organization reach its objectives. Because of the principle of incremental commitment, a selected project does not necessarily result in a working system. **Incremental commitment** means that after each subsequent SDLC activity, you, other members of the project team, and organization officials will reassess your project. This reassessment will determine whether the business conditions have changed or whether a more detailed understanding of a system's costs, benefits, and risks would suggest that the project is not as worthy as previously thought. In the next section, we discuss several techniques for gaining a thorough understanding of your development project.

Incremental commitment
A strategy in systems analysis and design in which the project is reviewed after each phase, and continuation of the project is rejustified in each of these reviews.

Initiating and Planning Systems Development Projects

Many activities performed during initiation and planning could also be completed during the next phase of the SDLC—systems analysis. Proper and insightful project initiation and planning, including determining project scope and identifying project activities, can reduce the time needed to complete later project phases, including systems analysis. For example, a careful feasibility analysis conducted during initiation and planning could lead to rejecting a project and saving a considerable expenditure of resources. The actual amount of time expended will be affected by the size and complexity of the project as well as by the experience of your organization in building similar systems. A rule of thumb is that between 10 and 20 percent of the entire development effort should be expended on initiation and planning. In other words, you should not be reluctant to spend considerable time and energy early in the project's life in order to fully understand the motivation for the requested system.

Most organizations assign an experienced systems analyst, or team of analysts for large projects, to perform project initiation and planning. The analyst will work with the proposed customers—managers and users in a business unit—of the system and other technical development staff in preparing the final plan. Experienced analysts working with customers who well understand their information services needs should be able to perform a detailed analysis with relatively little effort. Less experienced analysts with customers who only vaguely understand their needs will likely expend more effort in order to be certain that the project scope and work plan are feasible.

The objective of project initiation and planning is to transform a vague system request document into a tangible project description, as illustrated in Figure 4-5. Effective communication among the systems analysts, users, and management is crucial to the creation of a meaningful project plan. Getting all parties to agree on the direction of a project may be difficult for cross-department projects when different parties have different business objectives. Projects at large, complex organizations require systems analysts to take more time to analyze both the current and proposed systems.

In the remainder of this chapter, we describe how a systems analyst develops a clear project description.

The Process of Initiating and Planning Systems Development Projects

As its name implies, two major activities occur during project initiation and project planning. Project initiation focuses on activities that will help organize a team to conduct project planning. During initiation, one or more analysts are assigned to work with a customer to establish work standards and communication procedures. Table 4-3 summarizes six activities performed during project initiation.

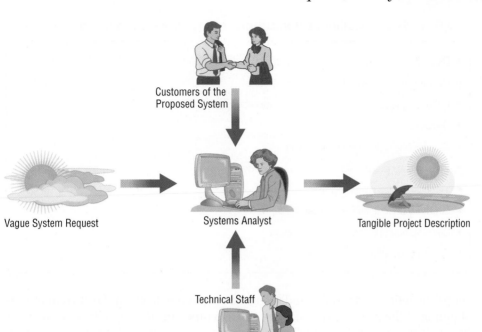

FIGURE 4-5
The systems analyst transforms
a vague systems request into a
tangible project description during
project initiation and planning.

Customers of the
Proposed System

Vague System Request   Systems Analyst   Tangible Project Description

Technical Staff

The second activity, project planning, focuses on defining clear, discrete tasks and the work needed to complete each task. The objective of the project planning process is to produce two documents: a *baseline project plan* (BPP) and the *project scope statement* (PSS). The BPP becomes the foundation for the remainder of the development project. It is an internal document used by the development team but not shared with customers. The PSS, produced by the project team, clearly outlines the objectives of the project for the customer. As with the project initiation process, the size, scope, and complexity of a project dictate the comprehensiveness of the project planning process and the resulting documents. Further, numerous assumptions about resource availability and potential problems will have to be made. Analysis of these assumptions and system costs and benefits forms a **business case.** Table 4-4 lists the activities performed during project planning.

Deliverables and Outcomes

The major outcomes and deliverables from project initiation and planning are the baseline project plan and the project scope statement. The **baseline project plan (BPP)** contains all information collected and analyzed during the project initiation and planning activity. The plan contains the best estimate of the project's

Business case
A written report that outlines the justification for an information system. The report highlights economic benefits and costs and the technical and organizational feasibility of the proposed system.

Baseline project plan (BPP)
One of the major outcomes and deliverables from the project initiation and planning phase. It contains the best estimate of the project's scope, benefits, costs, risks, and resource requirements.

TABLE 4-3:   Types of Activities Performed during Project Initiation

- Establishing the project initiation team
- Establishing a relationship with the customer
- Establishing the project initiation plan
- Establishing management procedures
- Establishing the project management environment and project workbook
- Developing the project charter

TABLE 4-4: Activities Performed during Project Planning

- Describing the project scope, alternatives, and feasibility
- Dividing the project into manageable tasks
- Estimating resources and creating a resource plan
- Developing a preliminary schedule
- Developing a communication plan
- Determining project standards and procedures
- Identifying and assessing risk
- Creating a preliminary budget
- Developing a project scope statement
- Setting a baseline project plan

scope, benefits, costs, risks, and resource requirements given the current understanding of the project. The BPP specifies detailed project activities for the next life cycle phase—systems analysis—and provides less detail for subsequent project phases (because these depend on the results of the analysis phase). Similarly, benefits, costs, risks, and resource requirements will become more specific and quantifiable as the project progresses. The project selection committee uses the BPP to help decide whether to continue, redirect, or cancel a project. If selected, the BPP becomes the foundation document for all subsequent SDLC activities; however, it is updated as new information is learned during subsequent SDLC activities. We explain how to construct the BPP later in the chapter.

Assessing Project Feasibility

Most information systems projects have budgets and deadlines. Assessing project feasibility is a required task that can be a large undertaking because it requires you, as a systems analyst, to evaluate a wide range of factors. Although the specifics of a given project will dictate which factors are most important, most feasibility factors fall into the following six categories:

- Economic
- Operational
- Technical
- Schedule
- Legal and contractual
- Political

The analysis of these six factors forms the business case that justifies the expenditure of resources on the project. In the remainder of this section, we examine various feasibility studies, beginning with economic feasibility.

PINE VALLEY FURNITURE

To help you better understand the feasibility assessment process, we examine a project at Pine Valley Furniture. Jackie Judson, Pine Valley Furniture's (PVF) vice president of marketing, prepares a system service request (SSR), illustrated in Figure 4-6, to develop a customer tracking system. Jackie feels that this system would allow PVF's marketing group to better track customer purchase activity and sales trends. She also feels that, if implemented, the Customer Tracking System (CTS) would help improve revenue, a tangible benefit, and improve employee morale, an intangible benefit. PVF's Systems Priority Board selected this project for an initiation and planning study. The board assigned senior systems

Pine Valley Furniture
System Service Request

REQUESTED BY ___Jackie Judson___ DATE: September 1, 2012

DEPARTMENT ___Marketing___

LOCATION ___Headquarters, 570c___

CONTACT ___Tel: 4-3290   FAX: 4-3270   e-mail: jjudson@pvf.com___

TYPE OF REQUEST   URGENCY
[X] New System   [   ] Immediate—Operations are impaired or opportunity lost
[   ] System Enhancement   [   ] Problems exist, but can be worked around
[   ] System Error Correction   [X] Business losses can be tolerated until new system installed

PROBLEM STATEMENT

Sales growth at PVF has caused a greater volume of work for the marketing department. This volume of work has greatly increased the volume and complexity of the data we need to deal with and understand. We are currently using manual methods and a complex PC-based electronic spreadsheet to track and forecast customer buying patterns. This method of analysis has many problems: (1) We are slow to catch buying trends as there is often a week or more delay before data can be taken from the point-of-sale system and manually entered into our spreadsheet; (2) the process of manual data entry is prone to errors (which makes the results of our subsequent analysis suspect); and (3) the volume of data and the complexity of analyses conducted in the system seem to be overwhelming our current system—sometimes the program starts recalculating and never returns anything, or it returns information that we know cannot be correct.

SERVICE REQUEST

I request a thorough analysis of our current method of tracking and analysis of customer purchasing activity with the intent to design and build a completely new information system. This system should handle all customer purchasing activity, support display and reporting of critical sales information, and assist marketing personnel in understanding the increasingly complex and competitive business environment. I feel that such a system will improve the competitiveness of PVF, particularly in our ability to better serve our customers.

IS LIAISON   Jim Woo (Tel: 4-6207 FAX: 4-6200 e-mail: jwoo@pvf.com)

SPONSOR   Jackie Judson, Vice President of Marketing

------------------------ TO BE COMPLETED BY SYSTEMS PRIORITY BOARD ------------------------

[   ] Request approved   Assigned to _____
                             Start date _____
[   ] Recommend revision
[   ] Suggest user development
[   ] Reject for reason _____
       _____

FIGURE 4-6
System service request (SSR) for the Customer Tracking System at Pine Valley Furniture. The SSR includes contact information, a problem statement, service request statement, and liaison contact information.

analyst Jim Woo to work with Jackie to initiate and plan the project. At this point in the project, all project initiation activities have been completed: Jackie prepared an SSR, the selection board reviewed the SSR, and Jim Woo was assigned to work on the project. Jackie and Jim can now focus on project planning activities, which will lead to the baseline project plan.

Assessing Economic Feasibility

A study of economic feasibility is required for the baseline project plan. The purpose for assessing **economic feasibility** is to identify the financial benefits and costs associated with the development project. Economic feasibility is often referred to as *cost-benefit analysis*. During project initiation and planning, it will be impossible for you to define precisely all benefits and costs related to a particular project. Yet, it is important that you identify and quantify benefits and costs, or it will be impossible for you to conduct a sound economic analysis and determine whether one project is more feasible than another. Next, we review worksheets you can use to record costs and benefits, and techniques for making cost-benefit calculations. These worksheets and techniques are used after each SDLC phase to decide whether to continue, redirect, or kill a project.

Determining Project Benefits An information system can provide many benefits to an organization. For example, a new or renovated IS can automate monotonous jobs, reduce errors, provide innovative services to customers and suppliers, and improve organizational efficiency, speed, flexibility, and morale. These benefits are both tangible and intangible. A **tangible benefit** is an item that can be measured in dollars and with certainty. Examples of tangible benefits include reduced personnel expenses, lower transaction costs, or higher profit margins. It is important to note that not all tangible benefits can be easily quantified. For example, a tangible benefit that allows a company to perform a task 50 percent of the time may be difficult to quantify in terms of hard dollar savings. Most tangible benefits fit in one or more of the following categories:

- Cost reduction and avoidance
- Error reduction
- Increased flexibility
- Increased speed of activity
- Improvement of management planning and control
- Opening new markets and increasing sales opportunities

Jim and Jackie identified several tangible benefits of the Customer Tracking System at PVF and summarized them in a worksheet, shown in Figure 4-7. Jackie and Jim collected information from users of the current customer tracking system in order to create the worksheet. They first interviewed the person responsible for collecting, entering, and analyzing the correctness of the current customer tracking data. This person estimated that he spent 10 percent of his

Economic feasibility
A process of identifying the financial benefits and costs associated with a development project.

Tangible benefit
A benefit, derived from the creation of an information system, that can be measured in dollars and with certainty.

FIGURE 4-7
Tangible benefits worksheet for the Customer Tracking System at Pine Valley Furniture.

TANGIBLE BENEFITS WORKSHEET	
Customer Tracking System Project	
	Year 1 through 5
A. Cost reduction or avoidance	$ 4,500
B. Error reduction	2,500
C. Increased flexibility	7,500
D. Increased speed of activity	10,500
E. Improvement in management planning or control	25,000
F. Other _____	0
TOTAL Tangible Benefits	**$50,000**

time correcting data-entry errors. This person's salary is $25,000, so Jackie and Jim estimated an error reduction benefit of $2,500 (10 percent of $25,000). Jackie and Jim also interviewed managers who used the current customer tracking reports to estimate other tangible benefits. They learned that cost reduction or avoidance benefits could be gained with better inventory management. Also, increased flexibility would likely occur from a reduction in the time normally taken to reorganize data manually for different purposes. Further, improvements in management planning or control should result from a broader range of analyses in the new system. This analysis forecasts that benefits from the system would be approximately $50,000 per year.

Jim and Jackie also identified several intangible benefits of the system. Although they could not quantify these benefits, they will still be described in the final BPP. **Intangible benefits** refer to items that cannot be easily measured in dollars or with certainty. Intangible benefits may have direct organizational benefits, such as the improvement of employee morale, or they may have broader societal implications, such as the reduction of waste creation or resource consumption. Potential tangible benefits may have to be considered intangible during project initiation and planning because you may not be able to quantify them in dollars or with certainty at this stage in the life cycle. During later stages, such intangibles can become tangible benefits as you better understand the ramifications of the system you are designing. Intangible benefits include:

- Competitive necessity
- Increased organizational flexibility
- Increased employee morale
- Promotion of organizational learning and understanding
- More timely information

After determining project benefits, project costs must be identified.

Determining Project Costs   An information system can have both tangible and intangible costs. A **tangible cost** refers to an item that you can easily measure in dollars and with certainty. From a systems development perspective, tangible costs include items such as hardware costs, labor costs, and operational costs from employee training and building renovations. Alternatively, an **intangible cost** refers to an item that you cannot easily measure in terms of dollars or with certainty. Intangible costs can include loss of customer goodwill, employee morale, or operational inefficiency.

Besides tangible and intangible costs, you can distinguish system-related development costs as either one-time or recurring. A **one-time cost** refers to a cost associated with project initiation and development and the start-up of the system. These costs typically encompass the following activities:

- System development
- New hardware and software purchases
- User training
- Site preparation
- Data or system conversion

When conducting an economic cost-benefit analysis, you should create a worksheet for capturing these expenses. This worksheet can be a two-column document or a multicolumn spreadsheet. For large projects, one-time costs may be staged over one or more years. In these cases, a separate one-time cost worksheet should be created for each year. This separation would make it easier to perform present-value calculations (see the following section "Time Value of

Intangible benefit
A benefit derived from the creation of an information system, that cannot be easily measured in dollars or with certainty.

Tangible cost
A cost associated with an information system that can be easily measured in dollars and with certainty.

Intangible cost
A cost associated with an information system, that cannot be easily measured in terms of dollars or with certainty.

One-time cost
A cost associated with project initiation and development, or system start-up.

Recurring cost
A cost resulting from the ongoing evolution and use of the system.

Money"). A **recurring cost** refers to a cost resulting from the ongoing evolution and use of the system. Examples of these costs typically include:

- Application software maintenance
- Incremental data storage expense
- Incremental communications
- New software and hardware leases
- Consumable supplies and other expenses (e.g., paper, forms, data-center personnel)

Both one-time and recurring costs can consist of items that are fixed or variable in nature. Fixed costs refer to costs that are billed or incurred at a regular interval and usually at a fixed rate. A facility lease payment is an example of a fixed cost. Variable costs refer to items that vary in relation to usage. Long-distance phone charges are variable costs.

Jim and Jackie identified both one-time and recurring costs for the Customer Tracking System project. Figure 4-8 shows that this project will incur a one-time cost of $42,500. Figure 4-9 shows a recurring cost of $28,500 per year. One-time costs were established by discussing the system with Jim's boss, who felt that the system would require approximately four months to develop (at $5,000 per month). To run the new system effectively, the marketing department would need to upgrade at least five of its current workstations (at $3,000 each). Additionally, software licenses for each workstation (at $1,000 each) and modest user training fees (10 users at $250 each) would be necessary.

As you can see from Figure 4-9, Jim and Jackie estimate that the proposed system will require, on average, five months of annual maintenance, primarily for enhancements that users will request from the IS department. Other ongoing expenses such as increased data storage, communications equipment, and supplies should also be expected.

You should now have an understanding of the types of benefit and cost categories associated with an information systems project. In the next section, we address the relationship between time and money.

The Time Value of Money Most techniques used to determine economic feasibility encompass the concept of the **time value of money (TVM)**. TVM refers to comparing present cash outlays to future expected returns. As we've seen, the development of an information system has both one-time and recurring costs. Furthermore, benefits from systems development will likely occur sometime in the future. Because many projects may be competing for the

Time value of money (TVM)
The process of comparing present cash outlays to future expected returns.

FIGURE 4-8
One-time costs worksheet for the Customer Tracking System at Pine Valley Furniture.

ONE-TIME COSTS WORKSHEET *Customer Tracking System Project*	
	Year 0
A. Development costs	$20,000
B. New hardware	15,000
C. New (purchased) software, if any	
1. Packaged applications software	5,000
2. Other _____	0
D. User training	2,500
E. Site preparation	0
F. Other _____	0
TOTAL One-Time Costs	**$42,500**

RECURRING COSTS WORKSHEET
Customer Tracking System Project

	Year 1 through 5
A. Application software maintenance	$25,000
B. Incremental data storage required: 20 GB × $50 (estimated cost/GB = $50)	1,000
C. Incremental communications (lines, messages, ...)	2,000
D. New software or hardware leases	0
E. Supplies	500
F. Other_____	0
TOTAL Recurring Costs	**$28,500**

FIGURE 4-9
Recurring costs worksheet for the Customer Tracking System at Pine Valley Furniture.

same investment dollars and may have different useful life expectancies, all costs and benefits must be viewed in relation to their present, rather than future value when comparing investment options.

A simple example will help you understand the concept of TVM. Suppose you want to buy a used car from an acquaintance, and she asks that you make three payments of $1,500 for three years, beginning next year, for a total of $4,500. If she would agree to a single lump-sum payment at the time of sale (and if you had the money!), what amount do you think she would agree to? Should the single payment be $4,500? Should it be more or less? To answer this question, we must consider the time value of money. Most of us would gladly accept $4,500 today rather than three payments of $1,500, because a dollar today (or $4,500 for that matter) is worth more than a dollar tomorrow or next year, because money can be invested. The interest rate at which money can be borrowed or invested, the cost of capital, is called the **discount rate** for TVM calculations. Let's suppose that the seller could put the money received for the sale of the car in the bank and receive a 10 percent return on her investment. A simple formula can be used when figuring out the **present value** of the three $1,500 payments:

Discount rate
The interest rate used to compute the present value of future cash flows.

$$PV_n = Y \times \frac{1}{(1 + i)^n}$$

Present value
The current value of a future cash flow.

where PV_n is the present value of Y dollars n years from now, when i is the discount rate.

From our example, the present value of the three payments of $1,500 can be calculated as:

$$PV_1 = 1,500 \times \frac{1}{(1 + .10)^1} = 1,500 \times .9091 = 1,363.65$$

$$PV_2 = 1,500 \times \frac{1}{(1 + .10)^2} = 1,500 \times .8264 = 1,239.60$$

$$PV_3 = 1,500 \times \frac{1}{(1 + .10)^3} = 1,500 \times .7513 = 1,126.95$$

where $PV_1, PV_2,$ and PV_3 reflect the present value of each $1,500 payment in year 1, 2, and 3, respectively.

To calculate the net present value (NPV) of the three $1,500 payments, simply add the present values calculated (NPV $= PV_1 + PV_2 + PV_3 = 1,363.65 + 1,239.60 + 1,126.95 = \$3,730.20$). In other words, the seller could accept a lump sum payment of $3,730.20 as equivalent to the three payments of $1,500, given a discount rate of 10 percent.

Now that we know the relationship between time and money, the next step in performing the economic analysis is to create a summary worksheet that reflects the present values of all benefits and costs. PVF's Systems Priority Board feels that the useful life of many information systems may not exceed five years. Therefore, all cost-benefit analysis calculations will be made using a five-year time horizon as the upper boundary on all time-related analyses. In addition, the management of PVF has set its cost of capital to be 12 percent (i.e., PVF's discount rate). The worksheet constructed by Jim is shown in Figure 4-10.

Cell H11 of the worksheet displayed in Figure 4-10 summarizes the NPV of the total tangible benefits from the project over five years ($180,239). Cell H19 summarizes the NPV of the total costs from the project. The NPV for the project, indicated in cell H22 ($35,003), shows that benefits from the project exceed costs.

The overall return on investment (ROI) for the project is also shown on the worksheet in cell H25 (0.24). Because alternative projects will likely have different benefit and cost values and, possibly, different life expectancies, the overall ROI value is useful for making project comparisons on an economic basis. Of course, this example shows ROI for the overall project over five years. An ROI analysis could be calculated for each year of the project.

The last analysis shown in Figure 4-10, on line 34, is a **break-even analysis.** The objective of the break-even analysis is to discover at what point (if ever) cumulative benefits equal costs (i.e., when break-even occurs). To conduct this analysis, the NPV of the yearly cash flows is determined. Here, the yearly cash flows are calculated by subtracting both the one-time cost and the present values of the recurring costs from the present value of the yearly benefits. The overall NPV of the cash flows reflect the total cash flows for all preceding

Break-even analysis
A type of cost-benefit analysis to identify at what point (if ever) benefits equal costs.

FIGURE 4-10
Worksheet reflecting the present value calculations of all benefits and costs for the Customer Tracking System at Pine Valley Furniture. This worksheet indicates that benefits from the project over five years exceed its costs by $35,003.

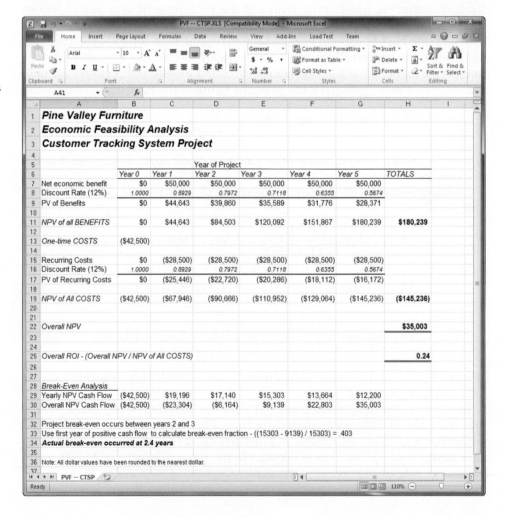

years. If you examine line 30 of the worksheet, you'll see that break-even occurs between years two and three. Because year three is the first year in which the overall NPV cash flows figure is non-negative, identifying the point when break-even occurs can be derived as follows:

$$\text{Break-Even Ratio} = \frac{\text{Yearly NPV Cash Flow} - \text{Overall NPV Cash Flow}}{\text{Yearly NPV Cash Flow}}$$

Using data from Figure 4-10,

$$\text{Break-Even Ratio} = \frac{15{,}303 - 9{,}139}{15{,}303} = .403$$

Project break-even occurs at approximately 2.4 years. A graphical representation of this analysis is shown in Figure 4-11. Using the information from the economic analysis, PVF's Systems Priority Board will be in a much better position to understand the potential economic impact of the Customer Tracking System. Without this information, it would be virtually impossible to know the cost-benefits of a proposed system and would be impossible to make an informed decision on approving or rejecting the service request.

You can use many techniques to compute a project's economic feasibility. Because most information systems have a useful life of more than one year and will provide benefits and incur expenses for more than one year, most techniques for analyzing economic feasibility employ the concept of the time value of money, TVM. Table 4-5 describes three commonly used techniques for conducting economic feasibility analysis. (For a more detailed discussion of TVM or cost-benefit analysis techniques in general, the interested reader is encouraged to review an introductory finance or managerial accounting textbook.)

To be approved for continuation, a systems project may not have to achieve break-even or have an ROI greater than estimated during project initiation and planning. Because you may not be able to quantify many benefits or costs at this point in a project, such financial hurdles for a project may be unattainable. In this case, simply doing as thorough an economic analysis as possible, including producing a long list of intangibles, may be sufficient for the project to progress. One other option is to run the type of economic analysis shown in Figure 4-10 using pessimistic, optimistic, and expected benefit and cost estimates during project initiation and planning. This range of possible outcomes, along with the list of intangible benefits and the support of the requesting business unit, will often be enough to allow the project to continue to the analysis-phase. You must, however, be as precise as you can with the economic analysis, especially when investment capital is scarce. In this case, it may be necessary to conduct some typical analysis-phase activities during project initiation and planning in order to clearly identify inefficiencies and shortcomings with the existing system and to explain how a new system will overcome these problems.

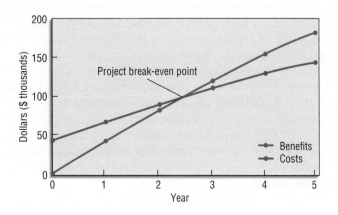

FIGURE 4-11
Break-even analysis for the Customer Tracking System at Pine Valley Furniture.

TABLE 4-5: Commonly Used Economic Cost-Benefit Analysis Techniques: Net Present Value, Return on Investment, and Break-Even Analysis

Analysis Technique	Description
Net present value (NPV)	NPV uses a discount rate determined from the company's cost of capital to establish the present value of a project. The discount rate is used to determine the present value of both cash receipts and outlays.
Return on investment (ROI)	ROI is the ratio of the net cash receipts of the project divided by the cash outlays of the project. Trade-off analysis can be made among projects competing for investment by comparing their representative ROI ratios.
Break-even analysis (BEA)	BEA finds the amount of time required for the cumulative cash flow from a project to equal its initial and ongoing investment.

Operational feasibility
The process of assessing the degree to which a proposed system solves business problems or takes advantage of business opportunities.

Technical feasibility
The process of assessing the development organization's ability to construct a proposed system.

Schedule feasibility
The process of assessing the degree to which the potential time frame and completion dates for all major activities within a project meet organizational deadlines and constraints for effecting change.

Legal and contractual feasibility
The process of assessing potential legal and contractual ramifications due to the construction of a system.

Political feasibility
The process of evaluating how key stakeholders within the organization view the proposed system.

Assessing Other Feasibility Concerns

You may need to consider other feasibility studies when formulating the business case for a system during project planning. **Operational feasibility** is the process of examining the likelihood that the project will attain its desired objectives. The goal of this study is to understand the degree to which the proposed system will likely solve the business problems or take advantage of the opportunities outlined in the system service request or project identification study. In other words, assessing operational feasibility requires that you gain a clear understanding of how an IS will fit into the current day-to-day operations of the organization.

The goal of **technical feasibility** is to understand the development organization's ability to construct the proposed system. This analysis should include an assessment of the development group's understanding of the possible target hardware, software, and operating environments to be used, as well as, system size, complexity, and the group's experience with similar systems. **Schedule feasibility** considers the likelihood that all potential time frames and completion-date schedules can be met and that meeting these dates will be sufficient for dealing with the needs of the organization. For example, a system may have to be operational by a government-imposed deadline by a particular point in the business cycle (such as the beginning of the season when new products are introduced), or at least by the time a competitor is expected to introduce a similar system.

Assessing **legal and contractual feasibility** requires that you gain an understanding of any potential legal and contractual ramifications due to the construction of the system. Considerations might include copyright or nondisclosure infringements, labor laws, antitrust legislation (which might limit the creation of systems to share data with other organizations), foreign trade regulations (e.g., some countries limit access to employee data by foreign corporations), and financial reporting standards as well as current or pending contractual obligations. Typically, legal and contractual feasibility is a greater consideration if your organization has historically used an outside organization for specific systems or services that you now are considering handling yourself. Assessing **political feasibility** involves understanding how key stakeholders within the organization view the proposed system. Because an information system may affect the distribution of information within the organization, and thus the distribution of power, the construction of an IS can have political ramifications. Those stakeholders not supporting the project may take steps to block, disrupt, or change the project's intended focus.

In summary, numerous feasibility issues must be considered when planning a project. This analysis should consider economic, operational, technical, schedule, legal, contractual, and political issues related to the project. In addition to these considerations, project selection by an organization may be influenced by issues beyond those discussed here. For example, projects may be selected for construction given high project costs and high technical risk if the system is viewed as a strategic necessity, that is, the project is viewed by the organization as being critical to its survival. Alternatively, projects may be selected because they are deemed to require few resources and have little risk. Projects may also be selected because of the power or persuasiveness of the manager proposing the system. This means that project selection may be influenced by factors beyond those discussed here and beyond items that can be analyzed. Your role as a systems analyst is to provide a thorough examination of the items that can be assessed so that a project review committee can make informed decisions. In the next section, we discuss how project plans are typically constructed.

Building the Baseline Project Plan

All the information collected during project initiation and planning is collected and organized into a document called the *baseline project plan*. Once the BPP is completed, a formal review of the project can be conducted with customers. This presentation, a walkthrough, is discussed later in the chapter. The focus of the walkthrough is to verify all information and assumptions in the baseline plan before moving ahead with the project. An outline of a baseline project plan, shown in Figure 4-12, contains four major sections:

1. Introduction
2. System description
3. Feasibility assessment
4. Management issues

The purpose of the *introduction* is to provide a brief overview of the entire document and outline a recommended course of action for the project. The introduction is often limited to only a few pages. Although it is sequenced as the first section of the BPP, it is often the final section to be written. It is only after performing most of the project planning activities that a clear overview and recommendation can be created. One initial activity that should be performed is the definition of the project scope, its range, which is an important part of the BPP's introduction section.

When defining the scope for the Customer Tracking System within PVF, Jim Woo first needed to gain a clear understanding of the project's objectives. Jim interviewed Jackie Judson and several of her colleagues to gain a good idea of their needs. He also reviewed the existing system's functionality, processes, and data-use requirements for performing customer tracking activities. These activities provided him with the information needed to define the project scope and to identify possible alternative solutions. Alternative system solutions can relate to different system scopes, platforms for deployment, or approaches to acquiring the system. We elaborate on the idea of alternative solutions, called *design strategies*, in Chapter 7. During project initiation and planning, the most crucial element of the design strategy is the system's scope. Scope depends on the answers to these questions:

- Which organizational units (business functions and divisions) might be affected by or use the proposed system or system change?
- With which current systems might the proposed system need to interact or be consistent, or which current systems might be changed because of a replacement system?

BASELINE PROJECT PLAN REPORT

1.0 *Introduction*
   A. Project Overview—Provides an executive summary that specifies the project's scope, feasibility, justification, resource requirements, and schedules. Additionally, a brief statement of the problem, the environment in which the system is to be implemented, and constraints that affect the project are provided.
   B. Recommendation—Provides a summary of important findings from the planning process and recommendations for subsequent activities.

2.0 *System Description*
   A. Alternatives—Provides a brief presentation of alternative system configurations.
   B. System Description—Provides a description of the selected configuration and a narrative of input information, tasks performed, and resultant information.

3.0 *Feasibility Assessment*
   A. Economic Analysis—Provides an economic justification for the system using cost-benefit analysis.
   B. Technical Analysis—Provides a discussion of relevant technical risk factors and an overall risk rating of the project.
   C. Operational Analysis—Provides an analysis of how the proposed system solves business problems or takes advantage of business opportunities in addition to an assessment of how current day-to-day activities will be changed by the system.
   D. Legal and Contractual Analysis—Provides a description of any legal or contractual risks related to the project (e.g., copyright or nondisclosure issues, data capture or transferring, and so on).
   E. Political Analysis—Provides a description of how key stakeholders within the organization view the proposed system.
   F. Schedules, Timeline, and Resource Analysis—Provides a description of potential time frame and completion-date scenarios using various resource allocation schemes.

4.0 *Management Issues*
   A. Team Configuration and Management—Provides a description of the team member roles and reporting relationships.
   B. Communication Plan—Provides a description of the communication procedures to be followed by management, team members, and the customer.
   C. Project Standards and Procedures—Provides a description of how deliverables will be evaluated and accepted by the customer.
   D. Other Project-Specific Topics—Provides a description of any other relevant issues related to the project uncovered during planning.

FIGURE 4-12
An outline of a baseline project plan contains four major sections: introduction, system description, feasibility assessment, and management issues.

- Who inside and outside the requesting organization (or the organization as a whole) might care about the proposed system?
- What range of potential system capabilities is to be considered?

The statement of project scope for the Customer Tracking System project at PVF is shown in Figure 4-13. A **project scope statement** is a short document prepared primarily for the customer to clearly describe what the project will deliver and outline generally at a high level all the work required for completing the project. It is therefore a useful communication tool. The project scope statement ensures that both you and your customer gain a common understanding of the project size, duration, and outcomes. The project scope statement is an

Project scope statement
A document prepared for the customer that describes what the project will deliver and outlines generally at a high level all work required to complete the project.

Pine Valley Furniture *Project Scope Statement*	Prepared by: Jim Woo Date: September 20, 2012

General Project Information
    Project Name: Customer Tracking System
    Sponsor: Jackie Judson, VP Marketing
    Project Manager: Jim Woo

Problem/Opportunity Statement:
    Sales growth has outpaced the marketing department's ability to track and forecast customer buying trends accurately. An improved method for performing this process must be found in order to reach company objectives.

Project Objectives:
    To enable the marketing department to track and forecast customer buying patterns accurately in order to better serve customers with the best mix of products. This will also enable PVF to identify the proper application of production and material resources.

Project Description:
    A new information system will be constructed that will collect all customer purchasing activity, support display and reporting of sales information, aggregate data, and show trends in order to assist marketing personnel in understanding dynamic market conditions. The project will follow PVF's systems development life cycle.

Business Benefits:
    Improved understanding of customer buying patterns
    Improved utilization of marketing and sales personnel
    Improved utilization of production and materials

Project Deliverables:
    Customer tracking system analysis and design
    Customer tracking system programs
    Customer tracking documentation
    Training procedures

Estimated Project Duration:
    5 months

FIGURE 4-13
Project scope statement for the Customer Tracking System at Pine Valley Furniture.

easy document to create because it typically consists of a high-level summary of the baseline project plan (BPP) information (described next).

Depending upon your relationship with your customer, the role of the project scope statement may vary. At one extreme, the project scope statement can be used as the basis of a formal contractual agreement outlining firm deadlines, costs, and specifications. At the other extreme, the project scope statement can simply be used as a communication vehicle to outline the current best estimates of what the project will deliver, when it will be completed, and the resources it may consume. A contract programming or consulting firm, for example, may establish a formal relationship with a customer and use a project charter that is more extensive and formal. Alternatively, an internal development group may develop a project scope statement that is shorter and less formal, as it will be intended to inform customers rather than to set contractual obligations and deadlines.

For the Customer Tracking System (CTS), project scope was defined using only textual information. It is not uncommon, however, to define project scope using tools such as data-flow diagrams and entity-relationship models. For example, Figure 4-14 shows a context-level data-flow diagram used to define system scope for PVF's Purchasing Fulfillment System. As shown in Figure 4-14, the Purchasing Fulfillment System interacts with the production schedulers, suppliers, and engineering. You will learn much more about data-flow diagrams in Chapter 6. The other items in the introduction section of the BPP are simply executive summaries of the other sections of the document.

The second section of the BPP is the *system description*, in which you outline possible alternative solutions to the one deemed most appropriate for the given situation. Note that this description is at a high level, mostly narrative in form. Alternatives may be stated as simply as this:

1. Web-based online system
2. Mainframe with central database
3. Local area network with decentralized databases
4. Batch data input with online retrieval
5. Purchasing of a prewritten package

If the project is approved for construction or purchase, you will need to collect and structure information in a more detailed and rigorous manner during the systems analysis phase and evaluate in greater depth these and other alternatives for the system.

When Jim and Jackie were considering system alternatives for the CTS, they focused on two primary issues. First, they discussed how the system would be acquired and considered three options: (1) purchase the system if one could be found that met PVF's needs, (2) outsource the development of the system to an outside organization, or (3) build the system within PVF. Next, Jim and Jackie defined the comprehensiveness of the system's functionality. To complete this task, Jackie wrote a series of statements listing the types of tasks that she thought marketing personnel would be able to accomplish when using the CTS. This list became the basis of the system description and was instrumental in helping them make the acquisition decision. After considering the unique needs of the marketing group, they decided that the best decision was to build the system within PVF.

FIGURE 4-14
Context-level data-flow diagram showing project scope for the purchasing fulfillment system at Pine Valley Furniture.

In the third section of the BPP, *feasibility assessment*, the systems analyst outlines project costs and benefits and technical difficulties. This section is where high-level project schedules are specified using Network diagrams and Gantt charts. Recall from Chapter 3 that this process is referred to as a *work breakdown structure*. During project initiation and planning, task and activity estimates are generally not detailed. An accurate work breakdown can be done only for the next one or two life-cycle activities—systems analysis and systems design. After defining the primary tasks for the project, an estimate of the resource requirements can be made. As with defining tasks and activities, this activity involves obtaining estimates of the human resource requirements, because people are typically the most expensive resource element of a project. Once you define the major tasks and resource requirements, a preliminary schedule can be developed. Defining an acceptable schedule may require that you find additional or different resources or that the scope of the project be changed. The greatest amount of project planning effort is typically expended on feasibility assessment activities.

The final section of the BPP, *management issues*, outlines the concerns that management has about the project. It will be a short section if the proposed project is going to be conducted exactly as prescribed by the organization's standard systems development methodology. Most projects, however, have some unique characteristics that require minor to major deviation from the standard methodology. In the team configuration and management portion, you identify the types of people to work on the project, who will be responsible for which tasks, and how work will be supervised and reviewed (see Figure 4-15). In the communication

Project: WebStore		Prepared by: Juan Gonzales				Legend: P = Primary S = Support	
Manager: Juan Gonzales		Page: 1 of 1					
		Responsibility Matrix					
Task ID	Task	Jordan	James	Jackie	Jeremy	Kim	Juan
A	Collect requirements	P	S				S
B	Develop data model			P		S	S
C	Program interface		P		S		S
D	Build database			S		P	S
F	Design test scenarios	S	S	S	P	S	S
G	Run test scenarios	S	S	S	S	S	P
H	User documentation	P	S				S
I	Install system	S	P			S	S
J	Customer support	S	P			S	S

FIGURE 4-15
Task-responsibility matrix.

Stakeholder	Document	Format	Team Contact	Date Due
Team Members	Project Status Report	Project Intranet	Juan Kim	First Monday of Month
Management Supervisor	Project Status Report	Hard Copy	Juan Kim	First Monday of Month
User	Project Status Report	Hard Copy	James Kim	First Monday of Month
Internal IT Staff	Project Status Report	E-mail	Jackie James	First Monday of Month
IT Manager	Project Status Report	Hard Copy	Juan Jeremy	First Monday of Month
Contract Programmers	Software Specifications	E-mail/Project Intranet	Jordan Kim	October 4, 2012
Training Subcontractor	Implementation and Training Plan	Hard Copy	Jordan James	January 10, 2012

FIGURE 4-16
The Project Communication Matrix provides a high-level summary of the communication plan.

plan portion, you explain how the user will be kept informed about project progress, such as periodic review meetings or even a newsletter, and which mechanisms will be used to foster sharing of ideas among team members, such as a computer-based conference facility (see Figure 4-16). An example of the type of information contained in the project standards and procedures portion would be procedures for submitting and approving project change requests and any other issues deemed important for the project's success.

You should now have a feel for how a BPP is constructed and the types of information it contains. Its creation is not meant to be a project in and of itself but rather a step in the overall systems development process. Developing the BPP has two primary objectives. First, it helps to assure that the customer and development group share a common understanding of the project. Second, it helps to provide the sponsoring organization with a clear idea of the scope, benefits, and duration of the project. Meeting these objectives creates the foundation for a successful project.

Reviewing the Baseline Project Plan

Before phase 2 of the SDLC analysis can begin, the users, management, and development group must review and approve the baseline project plan. This review takes place before the BPP is submitted or presented to some project approval body, such as an IS steering committee or the person who must fund the project. The objective of this review is to ensure that the proposed system conforms to organizational standards and to make sure that all relevant parties understand and agree with the information contained in the baseline project plan. A common method for performing this review (as well as reviews during subsequent life-cycle phases) is called a **walkthrough.** Walkthroughs, also called *structured walkthroughs*, are peer group reviews of any product created during the systems development process. They are widely used by professional development organizations, such as IBM, Xerox, and the U.S. government, and have proven effective in ensuring the quality of an information system. As a systems analyst, you will frequently be involved in walkthroughs.

Walkthrough
A peer group review of any product created during the systems development process; also called a *structured walkthrough*.

Although walkthroughs are not rigidly formal or exceedingly long in duration, they have a specific agenda that highlights what is to be covered and the expected completion time. Individuals attending the meeting have specific roles. These roles can include the following:

- *Coordinator:* This person plans the meeting and facilitates discussions. This person may be the project leader or a lead analyst responsible for the current life-cycle step.
- *Presenter:* This person describes the work product to the group. The presenter is usually an analyst who has done all or some of the work being presented.
- *User:* This person (or group) makes sure that the work product meets the needs of the project's customers. This user would usually be someone not on the project team.
- *Secretary:* This person takes notes and records decisions or recommendations made by the group. This may be a clerk assigned to the project team or one of the analysts on the team.
- *Standards bearer:* This person ensures that the work product adheres to organizational technical standards. Many larger organizations have staff groups within the unit responsible for establishing standard procedures, methods, and documentation formats. For example, within Microsoft, user interface standards are developed and rigorously enforced on all development projects. As a result, all systems have the same look and feel to users. These standards bearer validate the work so that it can be used by others in the development organization.
- *Maintenance oracle:* This person reviews the work product in terms of future maintenance activities. The goal is to make the system and its documentation easy to maintain.

After Jim and Jackie completed their BPP for the Customer Tracking System, Jim approached his boss and requested that a walkthrough meeting be scheduled and a walkthrough coordinator be assigned to the project. PVF provides the coordinator with a Walkthrough Review Form, shown in Figure 4-17. Using this form, the coordinator can easily make sure that a qualified individual is assigned to each walkthrough role; that each member has been given a copy of the review materials; and that each member knows the agenda, date, time, and location of the meeting. At the meeting, Jim presented the BPP, and Jackie

---

Pine Valley Furniture
Walkthrough Review Form

Session Coordinator:

Project/Segment:

Coordinator's Checklist:

1. Confirmation with producer(s) that material is ready and stable:_____
2. Issue invitations, assign responsibilities, distribute materials: [ ] Y   [ ] N
3. Set date, time, and location for meeting:

Date: ___ / ___ / ___   Time: _____ A.M. / P.M. (circle one)

Location: _____

Responsibilities	Participants	Can Attend	Received Materials
Coordinator	_____	[ ] Y [ ] N	[ ] Y [ ] N
Presenter	_____	[ ] Y [ ] N	[ ] Y [ ] N
User	_____	[ ] Y [ ] N	[ ] Y [ ] N
Secretary	_____	[ ] Y [ ] N	[ ] Y [ ] N
Standards	_____	[ ] Y [ ] N	[ ] Y [ ] N
Maintenance	_____	[ ] Y [ ] N	[ ] Y [ ] N

Agenda:
____ 1. All participants agree to follow PVF's Rules of a Walkthrough
____ 2. New material: Walkthrough of all material
____ 3. Old material: Item-by-item checkoff of previous action list
____ 4. Creation of new action list (contribution by each participant)
____ 5. Group decision (see below)
____ 6. Deliver copy of this form to the project control manager

Group Decision:
_____ Accept product as-is
_____ Revise (no further walkthrough)
_____ Review and schedule another walkthrough

Signatures		

FIGURE 4-17
Walkthrough Review Form for the Customer Tracking System at Pine Valley Furniture.

added comments from a user perspective. Once the walkthrough presentation was completed, the coordinator polled each representative for his or her recommendation concerning the work product. The results of this voting may result in validation of the work product, validation pending changes suggested during the meeting, or a suggestion that the work product requires major revision before being presented for approval. In the last case, substantial changes to the work product are usually requested, after which another walkthrough must be scheduled before the project can be proposed to the Systems Priority Board (steering committee). In the case of the Customer Tracking System, the BPP was supported by the walkthrough panel pending some minor changes to the duration estimates of the schedule. These suggested changes were recorded by the secretary on a Walkthrough Action List, shown in Figure 4-18, and given

Pine Valley Furniture *Walkthrough Action List*	
Session Coordinator:	
Project/Segment:	
Date and Time of Walkthrough: Date: ___ / ___ / ___ Time: _____ A.M. / P.M. (circle one)	
Fixed (✓)	**Issues raised in review:**

FIGURE 4-18
Walkthrough Action List for Pine Valley Furniture.

to Jim to incorporate into the next version of the baseline plan presented to the steering committee.

Walkthrough meetings are a common occurrence in most systems development groups. In addition to reviewing the BPP, these meetings can be used for the following activities:

- System specifications
- Logical and physical designs
- Code or program segments
- Test procedures and results
- Manuals and documentation

One of the key advantages to using a structured review process is to ensure that formal review points occur during the project. At each subsequent phase of the project, a formal review should be conducted (and shown on the project schedule) to make sure that all aspects of the project are satisfactorily accomplished before assigning additional resources to the project. This conservative approach of reviewing each major project activity with continuation contingent on successful completion of the prior phase is called *incremental commitment*. It is much easier to stop or redirect a project at any point when using this approach.

Walkthroughs are used throughout the duration of the project for briefing team members and external stakeholders. These presentations can provide many benefits to the team but, unfortunately, are often not well done. With the proliferation of computer technology and the availability of powerful software to assist in designing and delivering presentations, making an effective presentation has never been easier. Microsoft's PowerPoint has emerged as the de facto standard for creating computer-based presentations. Although this program is relatively easy to use, it can also be misused such that the "bells and whistles" added to a computer-based presentation actually detract from the presentation. Like any project, to make an effective presentation it must be planned, designed, and delivered. Planning and designing your presentation is equally important as delivering it. If your slides are poorly laid out, hard to read, or inconsistent, it won't matter how good your delivery is; your audience will think more about the poor quality of the slides, than about what you are saying. Fortunately, with a little work it is easy to design a high-quality presentation if you follow a few simple steps that are outlined in Table 4-6.

Pine Valley Furniture WebStore: Systems Planning and Selection

PINE
VALLEY
FURNITURE

Most businesses have discovered the power of Internet-based electronic commerce as a means to communicate efficiently with customers and to extend their marketing reach. As a systems analyst, you and a project team may be asked by your employer to help determine whether an Internet-based electronic commerce application fits the goals of the company and, if so, how that application should be implemented.

The systems planning and selection process for an Internet-based electronic commerce application is no different than the process followed for other applications. Nonetheless, you should take into account special issues when developing an Internet-based application. In this section, we highlight those issues.

Internet Basics

Internet
A network of interconnected individual networks that use a common protocol to communicate with each other; a global computing network to support business-to-consumer electronic commerce.

The term *Internet* is derived from the term *internetworking*. The **Internet** is a global network comprised of thousands of interconnected individual

TABLE 4-6:   Guidelines for Making an Effective Presentation

Presentation Planning

Who is the audience?	To design the most effective presentation, you need to consider the audience (e.g., What do they know about your topic? What is their education level?).
What is the message?	Your presentation should be designed with a particular objective in mind.
What is the presentation environment?	Knowledge of the room size, shape, and lighting is valuable information for designing an optimal presentation.

Presentation Design

Organize the sequence	Organize your presentation so that related elements or topics are found in one place instead of scattered throughout the material in random fashion.
Keep it simple	Make sure that you don't pack too much information onto a slide so that it is difficult to read. Also, work to have as few slides as possible; in other words, only include information that you absolutely need.
Be consistent	Make sure that you are consistent in the types of fonts, font sizes, colors, design approach, and backgrounds.
Use variety	Use both textual and graphical slides to convey information in the most meaningful format.
Don't rely on the spell checker alone	Make sure you carefully review your presentation for typographical and grammatical errors.
Use bells and whistles sparingly	Make sure that you use familiar graphical icons to guide and enhance slides; don't lose sight of your message as you add bells and whistles. Also, take great care when making transitions between slides and elements so that "special effects" don't take away from your message.
Supplemental materials	Take care when using supplemental materials so that they don't distract the audience. For example, don't provide handouts until you want the audience to actually read this material.
Have a clear beginning and end	At the beginning, introduce yourself and your teammates (if any), thank your audience for being there, and provide a clear outline of what will be covered during the presentation. At the conclusion, have a concluding slide so that the audience clearly sees that the presentation is over.

Presentation Delivery

Practice	Make sure that you thoroughly test your completed work on yourself and others to be sure it covers your points and presents them in an effective manner within the time frame required.
Arrive early and cue up your presentation	It is good practice when feasible to have your presentation ready to go prior to the arrival of the audience.
Learn to use the special software keys	Using special keys to navigate the presentation will allow you to focus on your message and not on the software.
Have a backup plan	Have a backup plan in case technology fails or your presentation is lost when traveling.
Delivery	To make an effective presentation, you must become an effective public speaker through practice.
Personal appearance	Your appearance and demeanor can go a long way toward enhancing how the audience receives your presentation.

networks that communicate with each other through *TCP/IP* (transmission control protocol/Internet protocol). Using the Internet and other technologies to support day-to-day business activities, such as communicating with customers and selling goods and services online, is referred to as **electronic commerce (EC),** also called e-commerce. Note that EC can also refer to the use of non-Internet technologies such as telephone voice-messaging systems

Electronic commerce (EC)
Internet-based communication and other technologies that support day-to-day business activities.

FIGURE 4-19
Three possible modes of electronic commerce.

that route and process customer requests and inquiries. Nonetheless, for our purposes, we will use *EC* to mean Internet-enabled business. The three classes of Internet EC applications are Internet, intranet, and extranet, as illustrated in Figure 4-19. Internet-based EC is transactions between individuals and businesses. **Intranet** refers to the use of the Internet within the same business. **Extranet** refers to Internet-based communication to support business-to-business activities.

Intranets and extranets are examples of two ways organizations communicate via technology. Having an intranet is a lot like having a "global" local area network. A company may create an intranet to house commonly used forms, up-to-date information on sales, and human resource information so that employees can access them easily and at any time. Organizations that have intranets dictate: (1) what applications will run over the intranet—such as electronic mail or an inventory control system, and (2) the speed and quality of the hardware connected to the intranet. Intranets are a new way of using information systems to support business activities within a single organization. Extranets are another new way of using an established computing model, **electronic data interchange (EDI).** EDI refers to the use of telecommunication technologies to transfer business documents directly between organizations. Using EDI, trading partners—suppliers, manufacturers, and customers—establish computer-to-computer links that allow them to exchange data electronically. For example, a car manufacturer using EDI may send an electronic purchase order to a steel or tire supplier instead of a paper request. The paper order may take several days to arrive at the supplier, whereas an EDI purchase order will take only a few seconds. EDI is fast becoming the standard by which organizations will communicate with each other in the world of electronic commerce.

When developing either an intranet or an extranet, developers know who the users are, what applications will be used, the speed of the network connection, and the type of communication devices (e.g., Web browsers such as Firefox, Chrome, or Internet Explorer, smart phones such as an iPhone). On the other hand, when developing an Internet EC application, developers have to discern countless unknowns in order to build a useful system. Table 4-7 lists several unknowns you and your project team may deal with when designing and building an EC. These unknowns may result in making trade-offs based on a careful analysis of who the users are likely to be, where they are likely to be located, and how they are likely to be connected to the Internet. Even with all these difficulties to contend with, you will find no shortage of Internet ECs springing up all across the world. One company that has decided to get onto the Web with its own EC site is Pine Valley Furniture.

Pine Valley Furniture WebStore

The PVF board of directors has requested that a project team be created to explore the opportunity to develop an EC system. Specifically, market research

Intranet
Internet-based communication to support business activities within a single organization.

Extranet
Internet-based communication to support business-to-business activities.

Electronic data interchange (EDI)
The use of telecommunication technologies to transfer business documents directly between organizations.

TABLE 4-7: Unknowns That Must Be Dealt with When Designing and Building Internet Applications

User	Concern: Who is the user?
	Examples: Where is the user located? What is their expertise, education, or expectations?
Connection Speed	Concern: What is the speed of the connection and what information can be effectively displayed?
	Examples: modem, cable modem, satellite, broadband, cellular
Access Method	Concern: What is the method of accessing the Internet?
	Examples: Web browser, personal digital assistant (PDA), Web-enabled cellular phone, Web-enabled television

has found a good opportunity for online furniture purchases, especially in the areas of:

- Corporate furniture buying
- Home-office furniture purchasing
- Student furniture purchasing

The board wants to incorporate all three target markets into its long-term EC plan but wants to focus initially on the corporate furniture buying system. The board feels that this segment has the greatest potential to provide an adequate return on investment and would be a good building block for moving into the customer-based markets. Because the corporate furniture buying system will be specifically targeted to the business furniture market, it will be easier to define the system's operational requirements. Additionally, this EC system should integrate nicely with two currently existing systems, Purchasing Fulfillment and Customer Tracking. Together, these attributes make it an ideal candidate for initiating PVF's Web strategy.

Initiating and Planning PVF's E-Commerce System Given the high priority of this project, Jackie Judson, vice president of marketing, and senior systems analyst Jim Woo were assigned to work on this project. As for the Customer Tracking System described earlier in the chapter, their first activity was to begin the project's initiation and planning activity. Over the next few days, Jim and Jackie met several times to initiate and plan the proposed system. At the first meeting, they agreed that "WebStore" would be the proposed system project name. Next, they worked on identifying potential benefits, costs, and feasibility concerns. Jim developed a list of potential costs the company would incur to develop Web-based systems that he shared with Jackie and the other project team members (see Table 4-8).

WebStore Project Walkthrough After meeting with the project team, Jim and Jackie established an initial list of benefits and costs (see Table 4-9) as well as several feasibility concerns (see Table 4-10). Next, Jim worked with several of PVF's technical specialists to develop an initial project schedule. Figure 4-20 shows the Gantt chart for this 84-day schedule. Finally, Jim and Jackie presented their initial project plans in a walkthrough to PVF's board of directors and senior management. All were excited about the project plan and approval was given to move the WebStore project on to the analysis phase.

TABLE 4-8: Web-Based System Costs

Cost Category	Examples
Platform costs	Web-hosting service
	Web server
	Server software
	Software plug-ins
	Firewall server
	Router
	Internet connection
Content and service	Creative design and development
	Ongoing design fees
	Web project manager
	Technical site manager
	Content staff
	Graphics staff
	Support staff
	Site enhancement funds
	Fees to license outside content
	Programming, consulting, and research
	Training and travel
Marketing	Direct mail
	Launch and ongoing public relations
	Print advertisement
	Paid links to other Web sites
	Promotions
	Marketing staff
	Advertising sales staff

TABLE 4-9: PVF WebStore Project Benefits and Costs

Tangible Benefits	Intangible Benefits
Lower per-transaction overhead cost	First to market
Repeat business	Foundation for complete Web-based IS
Tangible Costs (one-time)	Simplicity for customers
Internet service setup fee	**Intangible Costs**
Hardware	No face-to-face interaction
Development cost	Not all customers use Internet
Data entry	
Tangible Costs (recurring)	
Internet service hosting fee	
Software	
Support	
Maintenance	
Decreased sales via traditional channels	

TABLE 4-10:   PVF WebStore Feasibility Concerns

Feasibility Concern	Description
Operational	Online store open 24/7/365; returns/customer support
Technical	New skill set for development, maintenance, and operation
Schedule	Must be open for business by Q3
Legal	Credit card fraud
Political	Traditional distribution channel loses business

FIGURE 4-20
Gantt chart showing the schedule for the WebStore project.

Key Points Review

1. **Describe the steps involved when identifying and selecting projects and initiating and planning projects.**

   Project identification and selection consists of three primary activities: identifying potential development projects, classifying and ranking projects, and selecting projects for development. A variety of organizational members or units can be assigned to perform this process, including top management, a diverse steering committee, business units and functional managers, the development group, or the most senior IS executive. Potential projects can be evaluated and selected using a broad range of criteria such as value chain analysis, alignment with business strategy, potential benefits, resource availability and requirements, and risks. Project initiation and planning is a critical activity in the life of a project. At this point, projects are accepted for development, rejected as infeasible, or redirected. The objective of this process is to transform a vague system request into a tangible system description, clearly outlining the objectives, feasibility issues, benefits, costs, and time schedules for the project. Project initiation includes forming the project initiation team, establishing customer relationships, developing a plan to get the project started, setting project management procedures, and creating an overall project management environment. After project initiation, project planning focuses on assessing numerous feasibility issues associated with the project in order to create a clear baseline project plan.

2. **Explain the need for and the contents of a project scope statement and a baseline project plan.**

   A project scope statement and a baseline project plan are created during project initiation and planning. The project scope statement is a short document prepared for the customer that describes what the project will deliver and outlines all work required to complete the project; it ensures that both you and your customer gain a common understanding of the project. The baseline project plan contains an introduction, a high-level description of the proposed system or system change, an outline of the various feasibilities, and an overview of management issues specific to the project. Before the development of an information system can begin, the users, management, and development group must review and agree on this specification.

3. **List and describe various methods for assessing project feasibility.**

    Assessing project feasibility can include an examination of economic, operational, technical, schedule, legal and contractual, and political aspects of the project. This assessment is influenced by the project size, the type of system proposed, and the collective experience of the development group and potential customers of the system. High project costs and risks are not necessarily bad; rather it is more important that the organization understands the costs and risks associated with a project and with the portfolio of active projects before proceeding.

4. **Describe the differences between tangible and intangible benefits and costs, and the differences between one-time and recurring costs.**

    Tangible benefits can be easily measured in dollars and with certainty. Intangible benefits cannot be easily measured in dollars or with certainty. Tangible costs can be easily measured in dollars and with certainty. Intangible costs cannot be easily measured in terms of dollars or with certainty. One-time costs are associated with project start-up and development. Recurring costs result from the ongoing evolution and use of a system.

5. **Perform cost-benefit analysis and describe what is meant by the time value of money, present value, discount rate, net present value, return on investment, and break-even analysis.**

    The time value of money refers to comparing present cash outlays to future expected returns. Thus, the present value represents the current value of a future cash flow. The discount rate refers to the rate of return used to compute the present value of future cash flows. The net present value uses a discount rate to gain the present value of a project's overall benefits and costs. The return on investment is the ratio of the cash benefits of a project divided by the cash costs; trade-off analysis can be made among projects by comparing their representative ROI ratios. Break-even analysis finds the amount of time required for the cumulative incoming cash flow (the benefits) from a project to equal its initial and ongoing investment (the costs).

6. **Describe the activities and participant roles within a structured walkthrough.**

    A walkthrough assesses the merits of the project and ensures that the project, if accepted for development, conforms to organizational standards and goals. An objective of this process is also to make sure that all relevant parties understand and agree with the information contained in the baseline project plan before subsequent development activities begin. Several individuals participate in a walkthrough, including the coordinator, presenter, user, secretary, standards bearer, and maintenance oracle. Each plays a specific role to make sure that the walkthrough is a success. Walkthroughs are used to assess all types of project deliverables, including system specifications, logical and physical designs, code and program segments, test procedures and results, and manuals and documentation.

Key Terms Checkpoint

Here are the key terms from the chapter. The page where each term is first explained is in parentheses after the term.

1. Baseline project plan (BPP) (p. 89)
2. Break-even analysis (p. 96)
3. Business case (p. 89)
4. Discount rate (p. 95)
5. Economic feasibility (p. 92)
6. Electronic commerce (EC) (p. 109)
7. Electronic data interchange (EDI) (p. 110)
8. Extranet (p. 110)
9. Incremental commitment (p. 88)
10. Intangible benefit (p. 93)
11. Intangible cost (p. 93)
12. Internet (p. 108)

13. Intranet (p. 110)
14. Legal and contractual feasibility (p. 98)
15. One-time cost (p. 93)
16. Operational feasibility (p. 98)
17. Political feasibility (p. 98)
18. Present value (p. 95)
19. Project scope statement (p. 100)
20. Recurring cost (p. 94)
21. Schedule feasibility (p. 98)
22. Tangible benefit (p. 92)
23. Tangible cost (p. 93)
24. Technical feasibility (p. 98)
25. Time value of money (TVM) (p. 94)
26. Walkthrough (p. 105)

Match each of the key terms above with the definition that best fits it.

_____ 1. The process of evaluating how key stakeholders within the organization view the proposed system.

_____ 2. A document prepared for the customer that describes what the project will deliver and outlines generally at a high level all work required to complete the project.

_____ 3. A written report that outlines the justification for an information system. This report highlights economic benefits and costs and the technical and organizational feasibility of the proposed system.

_____ 4. A process of identifying the financial benefits and costs associated with a development project.

_____ 5. A strategy in systems analysis and design in which the project is reviewed after each phase, and continuation of the project is rejustified in each of these reviews.

_____ 6. A cost resulting from the ongoing evolution and use of the system.

_____ 7. The interest rate used to compute the present value of future cash flows.

_____ 8. A benefit derived from the creation of an information system, that cannot be easily measured in dollars or with certainty.

_____ 9. A network of interconnected individual networks that use a common protocol to communicate with each other; a global computing network to support business-to-consumer electronic commerce.

_____ 10. The process of assessing the degree to which the potential time frame and completion dates for all major activities within a project meet organizational deadlines and constraints for affecting change.

_____ 11. A cost associated with an information system, that can be easily measured in dollars and with certainty.

_____ 12. Internet-based communication and other technologies that support day-to-day business activities.

_____ 13. A peer group review of any product created during the systems development process.

_____ 14. A process of assessing the development organization's ability to construct a proposed system.

_____ 15. A cost associated with project initiation and development, or system start-up.

_____ 16. The current value of a future cash flow.

_____ 17. Internet-based communication to support business activities within a single organization.

_____ 18. A benefit derived from the creation of an information system, that can be measured in dollars and with certainty.

_____ 19. The process of assessing potential legal and contractual ramifications due to the construction of a system.

_____ 20. A cost associated with an information system, that cannot be easily measured in terms of dollars or with certainty.

_____ 21. One of the major outcomes and deliverables from the project initiation and planning phase. It contains the best estimate of the project's scope, benefits, costs, risks, and resource requirements.

_____ 22. The process of assessing the degree to which a proposed system solves business problems or takes advantage of business opportunities.

_____ 23. The process of comparing present cash outlays to future expected returns.

_____ 24. A type of cost-benefit analysis to identify at what point (if ever) benefits equal costs.

_____ 25. Internet-based communication to support business-to-business activities.

_____ 26. The use of telecommunications technologies to transfer business documents directly between organizations.

Review Questions

1. Describe the project identification and selection process.
2. Describe several project evaluation criteria.
3. List and describe the steps in the project initiation and planning process.
4. What is contained in a baseline project plan? Are the content and format of all baseline plans the same? Why or why not?
5. Describe three commonly used methods for performing economic cost-benefit analysis.
6. List and discuss the different types of project feasibility factors. Is any factor most important? Why or why not?
7. What are the potential consequences of not assessing the technical risks associated with an information systems development project?
8. What are the types or categories of benefits from an IS project?
9. What intangible benefits might an organization obtain from the development of an IS?
10. Describe the concept of the time value of money. How does the discount rate affect the value of $1 today versus one year from today?
11. Describe the structured walkthrough process. What roles need to be performed during a walkthrough?

Problems and Exercises

1. The economic analysis carried out during project identification and selection is rather superficial. Why is this? Consequently, what factors do you think tend to be most important for a potential project to survive this first phase of the life cycle?
2. Consider your use of a PC at either home or work and list tangible benefits from an information system. Based on this list, does your use of a PC seem to be beneficial? Why or why not?
3. Assume you are put in charge of launching a new Web site for a local nonprofit organization. What costs would you need to account for? Make a list of expected costs and benefits for the project. You don't need to list values, just sources of expense. Consider both one-time and recurring costs.
4. Consider the situation you addressed in Problem and Exercise 3. Create numeric cost estimates for each of the costs you listed. Calculate the net present value and return on investment. Include a break-even analysis. Assume a 10 percent discount rate and a five-year time horizon.
5. Consider the situation you addressed in Problem and Exercise 3. Create a sample project scope statement, following the structure shown in Figure 4-13.
6. Assuming monetary benefits of an information system at $85,000 per year, one-time costs of $75,000, recurring costs of $35,000 per year, a discount rate of 12 percent, and a five-year time horizon, calculate the net present value of these costs and benefits of an information system. Also calculate the overall return on investment of the project and then present a break-even analysis. At what point does break-even occur?
7. Use the outline for the baseline project plan provided in Figure 4-12 to present the system specifications for the information system you chose for Problem and Exercise 3.
8. Change the discount rate for Problem and Exercise 6 to 10 percent and redo the analysis.
9. Change the recurring costs in Problem and Exercise 6 to $40,000 and redo the analysis.
10. Change the time horizon in Problem and Exercise 6 to three years and redo the analysis.
11. Assume monetary benefits of an information system of $40,000 the first year and increasing benefits of $10,000 a year for the next five years (year 1 = $50,000, year 2 = $60,000, year 3 = $70,000, year 4 = $80,000, year 5 = $90,000). One-time development costs were $80,000 and recurring costs were $45,000 over the duration of the system's life. The discount rate for the company was 11 percent. Using a six-year time horizon, calculate the net present value of these costs and benefits. Also, calculate the overall return on investment and then present a break-even analysis. At what point does break-even occur?
12. Change the discount rate for Problem and Exercise 11 to 12 percent and redo the analysis.
13. Change the recurring costs in Problem and Exercise 11 to $40,000 and redo the analysis.
14. For the system you chose for Problem and Exercise 3, complete section 1.0.A, the project overview, of the baseline project plan report. How important is it that this initial section of the baseline project plan report be done well? What could go wrong if this section is incomplete or incorrect?

15. For the system you chose for Problem and Exercise 3, complete section 2.0.A, the alternatives, of the baseline project plan report. Without conducting a full-blown feasibility analysis, what is your gut feeling as to the feasibility of this system?

16. For the system you chose for Problem and Exercise 3, complete section 3.0.A–F, the feasibility analysis, of the baseline project plan report. How does this feasibility analysis compare with your gut feeling from the previous question? What might go wrong if you rely on your gut feeling in determining system feasibility?

17. For the system you chose for Problem and Exercise 3, complete section 4.0.A–C, management issues, of the baseline project plan report. Why might people sometimes feel that these additional steps in the project plan are a waste of time? What could you say to convince them that these steps are important?

Discussion Questions

1. Imagine that you are the chief information officer (CIO) of a company and are responsible for making all technology investment decisions. Would you ever agree to build an information system that had a negative net present value? If so, why? If not, why not? How would you justify your decision?

2. Imagine that you are interviewing for a job when the interviewer asks you which cost-benefit analysis technique is best for assessing a project's economic feasibility. What would your response be?

3. Imagine you are a member of the project approval committee. An ambitious young manager in the marketing department is well connected with the top management team in your company. He catches you in the hall and mentions that he is frustrated with how long it takes to get a simple system enhancement through the "bureaucratic" approval process. He wonders whether you could sign off on a small enhancement request for his team's reporting application. With a wink, he promises to "owe you one." What would you say to him and why?

4. Of the six methods for assessing project feasibility, which is the most important? In which situation is each method more or less important?

Case Problems

1. Pine Valley Furniture

   Pine Valley Furniture recently implemented a new internship program and has begun recruiting interns from nearby university campuses. As part of this program, interns have the opportunity to work alongside a systems analyst. This shadowing opportunity provides invaluable insights into the systems analysis and design process. Recently you were selected for a six-month internship at Pine Valley Furniture, and Jim Woo has been assigned as your supervisor.

   At an initial meeting with Jim Woo, he explains that Pine Valley Furniture is currently involved with two important systems development projects, the Customer Tracking System and WebStore. The purpose of the Customer Tracking System is to enable the PVF marketing group to track customer purchase activity and sales trends better. The WebStore project will help move the company into the twenty-first century by facilitating online furniture purchases, with an initial focus on corporate furniture buying. During your meeting with Mr. Woo, he reviews the documentation assembled for both systems. Mr. Woo hands you a copy of the Customer Tracking System's economic feasibility analysis. He mentions that he would like to modify the spreadsheet to reflect the information provided in the following table. Because you are familiar with a spreadsheet product, you volunteer to make the modifications for him.

	Year 0	Year 1	Year 2	Year 3	Year 4	Year 5
Net economic benefit	$ 0	$50,000	$50,000	$50,000	$50,000	$50,000
One-time costs	$47,500					
Recurring costs	$ 0	$32,000	$32,000	$32,000	$32,000	$32,000

   a. How were Pine Valley Furniture's projects initiated? What is the focus for each of the new systems?

b. Modify the Customer Tracking System's economic feasibility analysis to reflect the modifications mentioned in this case problem. Use a discount rate of 10 percent. After the changes are made, what are the new overall NPV, ROI, and break-even point?

c. Modify the worksheet created in part b using discount rates of 12 and 14 percent. What impact do these values have on the overall NPV, ROI, and break-even point?

d. Jim Woo would like to investigate how other online stores are targeting the business furniture market. Identify and evaluate two online stores that sell business furniture. Briefly summarize your findings.

2. Hoosier Burger

The Hoosier Burger project development team has met several times with Bob and Thelma Mellankamp. During these meetings, Bob has stressed the importance of improving Hoosier Burger's inventory control, customer ordering, and management reporting systems. Demand for Hoosier Burger food is at an all-time high, and this increased demand is creating problems for Hoosier Burger's staff, creating stock-out problems and impacting sales.

During rush periods, customers sometimes wait fifteen minutes to place an order and may wait an additional twenty-five minutes to receive their order. Low-in-stock inventory items are often not reordered in a timely fashion, thus creating problems with the food preparation. For instance, vanilla ice cream is used to prepare vanilla malts, an item that accompanies the Hoosier Burger Special. Last week, Bob did not order enough vanilla ice cream, resulting in a last-minute dash to the grocery store.

Bob and Thelma have expressed their feelings that a new information system will be beneficial in the areas of inventory management, marketing, customer service, and food preparation. Additionally, the project team discussed with Bob and Thelma the possibility of implementing a point-of-sale system as an alternative design strategy.

a. How was the Hoosier Burger project identified and selected? What focus will the new system have?

b. Identify the Hoosier Burger project's scope.

c. Using the six feasibility factors presented in the chapter, assess the Hoosier Burger project's feasibility.

d. Using Figure 4-13 as a guide, develop a project scope statement for the Hoosier Burger project.

3. American Labs

American Labs provides lab testing services for a variety of clients, mostly doctors' offices and other small medical businesses throughout the Midwest. Clients send test vials containing blood samples or other test requests to American Labs' testing center, where the requested tests are performed, after which the results are sent back to the client via fax.

Jim Larsen, the head technician in the testing facility at American Labs has approached you for help with the company's outdated inventory tracking system. Business has picked up recently, and the turnaround for clients' requested tests has been lengthening. To make matters worse, the lab technicians are seldom able to give customers an answer regarding where their requests fall in the testing queue or how long they can expect the turnaround to be. Much of this stems from an old, mostly paper-based inventory tracking system, which includes hand-written labels put on each of the incoming test vials and a logbook with entries made for each vial at each stage of the testing process.

Jim would like to streamline the inventory tracking process with an updated information system that uses barcodes and a modern database to keep track of customer test requests and the accompanying vials. He would like to enable technicians to provide accurate status updates and turnaround estimates, and generally shorten the turnaround time for test requests.

After an initial analysis, you make the following estimations. You will use these data as part of your initial feasibility assessment.

	Year 0	Year 1	Year 2	Year 3	Year 4	Year 5
Net economic benefit	$0	$50,000	$50,000	$50,000	$50,000	$50,000
One-time costs	$80,000					
Recurring costs	$0	$25,000	$25,000	$25,000	$25,000	$25,000

a. Identify several benefits and costs associated with implementing this new system.

b. Using Figure 4-10 as a guide, prepare an economic feasibility analysis worksheet for American Labs. Using a discount rate of 10 percent, what are the overall NPV and ROI? When will break-even occur?

c. Modify the spreadsheet developed for part b to reflect discount rates of 11 and 14 percent. What impact will these new rates have on the economic analysis?

CASE: PETRIE'S ELECTRONICS

Systems Planning and Selection

Now that the "No Customer Escapes" project team has been formed and a plan has been developed for distributing project information, Jim began working on the project scope statement, workbook, and baseline project plan. He first drafted the project scope statement and posted it on the project's intranet (see PE Figure 4-1). Once posted on the intranet, he sent a short e-mail message to all team members requesting feedback. Minutes after sending the e-mail, Jim's office phone rang.

"Jim, it's Sally. I just looked over the scope statement and have a few comments."

"Great," replied Jim, "it's just a draft. What do you think?"

"Well, I think that we need to explain more about how the system will work and why we think this new system will more than pay for itself."

"Those are good suggestions; I am sure many others will also want to know that information. However, the scope statement is a pretty high-level document and doesn't get into too much detail. Basically, its purpose is to just formally announce the project, providing a very high-level description as well as briefly listing the objectives, key assumptions, and stakeholders. The other documents that I am working on, the workbook and the baseline project plan, are intended to provide more details on specific deliverables, costs, benefits, and so on. So, anyway, that type of more detailed information will be coming next."

"Oh, OK, that makes sense. I have never been on a project like this, so this is all new to me," said Sally.

"Don't worry," replied Jim, "getting that kind of feedback from you and the rest of the team will be key for us doing a thorough feasibility analysis. I am going to need a lot of your help in identifying possible costs and benefits of the system. When we develop the baseline project plan, we do a very thorough feasibility analysis—we examine financial, technical, operational, schedule, legal and contractual feasibility, as well as potential political issues arising through the development of the system."

"Wow, we have to do all that? Why can't we just build the system? I think we all know what we want," replied Sally.

"That is another great question," replied Jim. "I used to think exactly the same way, but what I learned in my last job was that there are great benefits to following a fairly formal project management process with a new system. By moving forward with care, we are much more likely to have the right system, on time and on budget."

"So," asked Sally, "what is the next step?"

"Well, we need to do the feasibility analyses I just mentioned, which become part of the project's baseline project plan. Once this is completed, we will have a walkthrough presentation to management to make sure they agree with and understand the scope, risks, and costs associated with making 'No Customer Escapes' a reality," said Jim.

"This is going to be a lot of work, but I am sure I am going to learn a lot," replied Sally.

"So, let me get to work on the feasibility analyses," said Jim. "I will be sending requests out to all the team members to get their ideas. I should have this e-mail ready within an hour or so."

"Great, I'll look for it and respond as soon as I can," answered Sally.

"Thanks, the faster we get this background work done, the sooner we will be able to move on to what the system will do," replied Jim.

"Sounds good, talk to you later. Bye," Sally said.

"Bye Sally, and thanks for your quick feedback," answered Jim.

Case Questions

1. Look over the scope statement (PE Figure 4-1). If you were an employee at Petrie's Electronics, would you want to work on this project? Why or why not?

2. If you were part of the management team at Petrie's Electronics, would you approve the project outlined in the scope statement in PE Figure 4-1? What changes, if any, need to be made to the document?

3. Identify a preliminary set of tangible and intangible costs you think would occur for this project and the system it describes. What intangible benefits do you anticipate for the system?

4. What do you consider to be the risks of the project as you currently understand it? Is this a low-, medium-, or high-risk project? Justify your answer. Assuming you were part of Jim's team, would you have any particular risks?

5. If you were assigned to help Jim with this project, how would you utilize the concept of incremental commitment in the design of the baseline project plan?

Petrie's Electronics

Scope Statement | **Prepared:** February 6, 2012

Project Name:	No Customer Escapes
Project Manager:	Jim Watanabe (jwatanabe@petries.com)

Customer:	**Operations**
Project Sponsor:	Ella Whinston (ewhinston@petries.com)
Project Start/End (projected):	2/5/12 – 7/30/12

Project Overview:

This project will design and implement a customer relationship management system in order to provide superior customer service by rewarding our most loyal customers. Specifically, the system will track customer purchases, assign points for cumulative purchases, and allow points to be redeemed for "rewards" at local stores. The goal of this system is to provide an incentive to customers to choose Petrie's Electronics as their first and only choice for making electronic purchases. The system will provide Petrie's management with improved information on the purchase behavior of our most loyal customers.

Objectives:

- Track customer purchases
- Accumulate redeemable points
- Reward customer loyalty and provide incentives to customers to remain loyal
- Provide improved management information

Key Assumptions:

- System development will be outsourced
- Interface will be a Web browser
- System will access existing customer sales databases

Stakeholders and Responsibilities

Stakeholder	Role	Responsibility	Signatures
Ella Whinston	Chief Operating Officer	Project Vision, Executive Sponsor	*Ella Whinston*
Bob Petroski	Senior Operations Manager	Monitoring, Resources	*Bob Petroski*
Jim Watanabe	Project Manager	Plan, Monitor, Execute Project	*Jim Watanabe*
Sally Fukuyama	Assistant Director, Marketing	System Functionality	*Sally Fukuyama*
Sanjay Agarwal	Lead Analyst	Technical Architect	*Sanjay Agarwal*

PE FIGURE 4-1
A scope statement for Petrie's customer relationship management system.

6. If you were assigned to Jim's team for this project, when in the project schedule (in what phase or after which activities are completed) do you think you could develop an economic analysis of the proposed system? What economic feasibility factors do you think would be relevant?

7. If you were assigned to Jim's team for this project, what activities would you conduct in order to prepare the details for the baseline project plan? Explain the purpose of each activity and show a timeline or schedule for these activities.

8. In Question 4, you analyzed the risks associated with this project. Once deployed, what are the potential operational risks of the proposed system? How do you factor operational risks into a systems development plan?

five

Determining System Requirements

© Jim Craigmyle/Corbis

After studying this chapter, you should be able to:

■ Describe options for designing and conducting interviews and develop a plan for conducting an interview to determine system requirements.

■ Explain the advantages and pitfalls of observing workers and analyzing business documents to determine system requirements.

■ Participate in and help plan a joint application design (JAD) session.

■ Use prototyping during requirements determination.

■ Select the appropriate methods to elicit system requirements.

■ Explain business process reengineering (BPR) and how it affects requirements determination.

■ Understand how requirements determination techniques apply to development of Internet applications.

Chapter Preview . . .

Systems analysis is the part of the systems development life cycle in which you determine how a current information system in an organization functions. Then you assess what users would like to see in a new system. As you learned in Chapter 1, the two parts to analysis are determining requirements and structuring requirements. Figure 5-1 illustrates these parts and highlights our focus in this chapter—determining system requirements.

Techniques used in requirements determination have become more structured over time. As we see in this chapter, current methods increasingly rely on computers for support. We first study the more traditional requirements determination methods, which include interviewing, observing users in their work environment, and collecting procedures and other written documents. We then discuss modern methods for collecting system requirements. The first of these methods is joint application design (JAD), which you first read about in Chapter 1. Next, you read about how analysts rely more and more on information systems to help them perform analysis. You learn how prototyping can be used as a key tool for some requirements determination efforts. We end the chapter with a discussion of how requirements determination continues to be a major part of systems analysis and design, even when organizational change is radical, as with business process reengineering, and new, as with developing Internet applications.

FIGURE 5-1
The four steps of the systems development life cycle (SDLC): (1) planning and selection, (2) analysis, (3) design, and (4) implementation and operation.

123

Performing Requirements Determination

As stated earlier and shown in Figure 5-1, the two parts to systems analysis are determining requirements and structuring requirements. We address these as two separate steps, but you should consider these steps as somewhat parallel and repetitive. For example, as you determine some aspects of the current and desired system(s), you begin to structure these requirements or to build prototypes to show users how a system might behave. Inconsistencies and deficiencies discovered through structuring and prototyping lead you to explore further the operation of the current system(s) and the future needs of the organization. Eventually your ideas and discoveries meet on a thorough and accurate depiction of current operations and the requirements for the new system. In the next section, we discuss how to begin the requirements determination process.

The Process of Determining Requirements

At the end of the systems planning and selection phase of the SDLC, management can grant permission to pursue development of a new system. A project is initiated and planned (as described in Chapter 4), and you begin determining what the new system should do. During requirements determination, you and other analysts gather information on what the system should do from as many sources as possible. Such sources include users of the current system, reports, forms, and procedures. All of the system requirements are carefully documented and made ready for structuring. Structuring means taking the system requirements you find during requirements determination and ordering them into tables, diagrams, and other formats that make them easier to translate into technical system specifications. We discuss structuring in detail in Chapters 6 and 7.

In many ways, gathering system requirements is like conducting any investigation. Have you read any of the Sherlock Holmes or similar mystery stories? Do you enjoy solving puzzles? The characteristics you need to enjoy solving mysteries and puzzles are the same ones you need to be a good systems analyst during requirements determination. These characteristics include:

- *Impertinence:* You should question everything. Ask such questions as "Are all transactions processed the same way?" "Could anyone be charged something other than the standard price?" "Might we someday want to allow and encourage employees to work for more than one department?"

- *Impartiality:* Your role is to find the best solution to a business problem or opportunity. It is not, for example, to find a way to justify the purchase of new hardware or to insist on incorporating what users think they want into the new system requirements. You must consider issues raised by all parties and try to find the best organizational solution.

- *Relaxing of constraints:* Assume anything is possible and eliminate the infeasible. For example, do not accept this statement: "We've always done it that way, so we have to continue the practice." Traditions are different from rules and policies. Traditions probably started for a good reason, but as the organization and its environment change, they may turn into habits rather than sensible procedures.

- *Attention to details:* Every fact must fit with every other fact. One element out of place means that the ultimate system will fail at some time. For example, an imprecise definition of who a customer is may mean that you purge customer data when a customer has no active orders; yet these past customers may be vital contacts for future sales.

- *Reframing:* Analysis is, in part, a creative process. You must challenge yourself to look at the organization in new ways. Consider how each user views his or her requirements. Be careful not to jump to this conclusion: "I worked on a system like that once—this new system must work the same way as the one I built before."

Deliverables and Outcomes

The primary deliverables from requirements determination are the types of information gathered during the determination process. The information can take many forms: transcripts of interviews; notes from observation and analysis of documents; sets of forms, reports, job descriptions, and other documents; and computer-generated output such as system prototypes. In short, anything that the analysis team collects as part of determining system requirements is included in these deliverables. Table 5-1 lists examples of some specific information that might be gathered at this time.

The deliverables summarized in Table 5-1 contain the information you need for systems analysis. In addition, you need to understand the following components of an organization:

- The business objectives that drive what and how work is done
- The information people need to do their jobs
- The data handled within the organization to support the jobs
- When, how, and by whom or what the data are moved, transformed, and stored
- The sequence and other dependencies among different data-handling activities
- The rules governing how data are handled and processed
- Policies and guidelines that describe the nature of the business, the market, and the environment in which it operates
- Key events affecting data values and when these events occur

TABLE 5-1: Deliverables for Requirements Determination

Types of Deliverables	Specific Deliverables
Information collected from conversations with users	Interview transcripts
	Notes from observations
	Meeting notes
Existing documents and files	Business mission and strategy statement
	Sample business forms and reports, and computer displays
	Procedure manuals
	Job descriptions
	Training manuals
	Flowcharts and documentation of existing systems
	Consultant reports
Computer-based information	Results from joint application design (JAD) sessions
	CASE repository contents and reports of existing systems
	Displays and reports from system prototypes

Such a large amount of information must be organized in order to be useful, which is the purpose of the next part of systems analysis—requirements structuring.

Requirements Structuring

The amount of information gathered during requirements determination could be huge, especially if the scope of the system under development is broad. The time required to collect and structure a great deal of information can be extensive and, because it involves so much human effort, quite expensive. Too much analysis is not productive, and the term *analysis paralysis* has been coined to describe a project that has become bogged down in an abundance of analysis work. Because of the dangers of excessive analysis, today's systems analysts focus more on the system to be developed than on the current system. Later in the chapter, you learn about joint application design (JAD) and prototyping, techniques developed to keep the analysis effort at a minimum yet still be effective. Other processes have been developed to limit the analysis effort even more, providing an alternative to the SDLC. Many of these are included under the name of *Agile Methodologies* (see Appendix B). Before you can fully appreciate alternative approaches, you need to learn traditional fact-gathering techniques.

Traditional Methods for Determining Requirements

Collection of information is at the core of systems analysis. At the outset, you must collect information about the information systems that are currently in use. You need to find out how users would like to improve the current systems and organizational operations with new or replacement information systems. One of the best ways to get this information is to talk to those directly or indirectly involved in the different parts of the organization affected by the possible system changes. Another way is to gather copies of documentation relevant to current systems and business processes. In this chapter, you learn about traditional ways to get information directly from those who have the information you need: interviews and direct observation. You learn about collecting documentation on the current system and organizational operation in the form of written procedures, forms, reports, and other hard copy. These traditional methods of collecting system requirements are listed in Table 5-2.

Interviewing and Listening

Interviewing is one of the primary ways analysts gather information about an information systems project. Early in a project, an analyst may spend a large amount of time interviewing people about their work, the information they use to

TABLE 5-2: Traditional Methods of Collecting System Requirements

Traditional Method	Activities Involved
Interviews with individuals	Interview individuals informed about the operation and issues of the current system and needs for systems in future organizational activities.
Observations of workers	Observe workers at selected times to see how data are handled and what information people need to do their jobs.
Business documents	Study business documents to discover reported issues, policies, rules, and directions, as well as, concrete examples of the use of data and information in the organization.

TABLE 5-3: Guidelines for Effective Interviewing

Guidelines	What Is Involved
Plan the interview	Prepare interviewee by making an appointment and explaining the purpose of the interview. Prepare a checklist, an agenda, and questions.
Be neutral	Avoid asking leading questions.
Listen and take notes	Give your undivided attention to the interviewee and take notes or tape-record the interview (if permission is granted).
Review notes	Review your notes within forty-eight hours of the meeting. If you discover follow-up questions or need additional information, contact the interviewee.
Seek diverse views	Interview a wide range of people, including potential users and managers.

do it, and the types of information processing that might supplement their work. Others are interviewed to understand organizational direction, policies, and expectations that managers have of the units they supervise. During interviewing, you gather facts, opinions, and speculation and observe body language, emotions, and other signs of what people want and how they assess current systems.

Interviewing someone effectively can be done in many ways, and no one method is necessarily better than another. Some guidelines to keep in mind when you interview are summarized in Table 5-3 and are discussed next.

First, prepare thoroughly before the interview. Set up an appointment at a time and for a duration that is convenient for the interviewee. The general nature of the interview should be explained to the interviewee in advance. You may ask the interviewee to think about specific questions or issues, or to review certain documentation to prepare for the interview. Spend some time thinking about what you need to find out, and write down your questions. Do not assume that you can anticipate all possible questions. You want the interview to be natural and, to some degree, you want to direct the interview spontaneously as you discover what expertise the interviewee brings to the session.

Prepare an interview guide or checklist so that you know in which sequence to ask your questions and how much time to spend in each area of the interview. The checklist might include some probing questions to ask as follow-up if you receive certain anticipated responses. You can, to some extent, integrate your interview guide with the notes you take during the interview, as depicted in a sample guide in Figure 5-2. This same guide can serve as an outline for a summary of what you discover during an interview.

The first page of the sample interview guide contains a general outline of the interview. Besides basic information on who is being interviewed and when, list major objectives for the interview. These objectives typically cover the most important data you need to collect, a list of issues on which you need to seek agreement (e.g., content for certain system reports), and which areas you need to explore. Also, include reminder notes to yourself on key information about the interviewee (e.g., job history, known positions taken on issues, and role with current system). This information helps you to be personal, shows that you consider the interviewee important, and may assist in interpreting some answers. Also included is an agenda with approximate time limits for different sections of the interview. You may not follow the time limits precisely, but the schedule helps you cover all areas during the time the interviewee is available. Space is also allotted for general observations that do not fit under specific questions

Interview Outline	
Interviewee: *Name of person being interviewed*	Interviewer: *Name of person leading interview*
Location/Medium: *Office, conference room, or phone number*	Appointment Date: Start Time: End Time:
Objectives: *What data to collect* *On what to gain agreement* *What areas to explore*	Reminders: *Background/experience of interviewee* *Known opinions of interviewee*

Agenda:
 Introduction
 Background on Project
 Overview of Interview
    Topics to Be Covered
    Permission to Tape Record
 Topic 1 Questions
 Topic 2 Questions
 …
 Summary of Major Points
 Questions from Interviewee
 Closing
	Approximate Time:
	 1 minute
	 2 minutes
	
	 1 minute
	
	 5 minutes
	 7 minutes
	 …
	 2 minutes
	 5 minutes
	 1 minute

General Observations: Interviewee seemed busy—probably need to call in a few days for follow-up questions because he gave only short answers. PC was turned off—probably not a regular PC user.	
Unresolved Issues, Topics Not Covered: He needs to look up sales figures from 2010. He raised the issue of how to handle returned goods, but we did not have time to discuss.	

(continues on next page)

FIGURE 5-2
A typical interview guide.

and for notes taken during the interview about topics skipped or issues raised that could not be resolved.

On subsequent pages, list specific questions. The sample form in Figure 5-2 includes space for taking notes on these questions. Because the interviewee may provide information you were not expecting, you may not follow the guide in sequence. You can, however, check off questions you have asked and write reminders to yourself to return to or skip other questions as the interview takes place.

Choosing Interview Questions You need to decide on the mix and sequence of open-ended and closed-ended questions to use. **Open-ended questions** are usually used to probe for information when you cannot anticipate all possible responses or when you do not know the precise question to ask. The person being interviewed is encouraged to talk about whatever interests him or her within the general bounds of the question. An example is, "What would you say is the best thing about the information system you currently use to do your job?" or "List the three most frequently used menu

Open-ended questions

Questions in interviews and on questionnaires that have no prespecified answers.

Interviewee:	Date:
Questions:	Notes:

When to ask question, if conditional
Question: 1
 	
    Have you used the current sales tracking system? If so, how often?
 	
If yes, go to Question 2
	Answer
	   Yes, I ask for a report on my product line weekly.
	
	Observations
	
	   Seemed anxious—may be overestimating usage frequency

Question: 2
 	
    What do you like least about this system?
	Answer
	   Sales are shown in units, not dollars.
	
	Observations
	
	   System can show sales in dollars, but user does not know this.

FIGURE 5-2
(continued)

options." You must react quickly to answers and determine whether any follow-up questions are needed for clarification or elaboration. Sometimes body language will suggest that a user has given an incomplete answer or is reluctant to provide certain information. If so, a follow-up question might result in more information. One advantage of open-ended questions is that previously unknown information can surface. You can then continue exploring along unexpected lines of inquiry to reveal even more new information. Open-ended questions also often put the interviewees at ease because they are able to respond in their own words using their own structure. Open-ended questions give interviewees more of a sense of involvement and control in the interview. A major disadvantage of open-ended questions is the length of time it can take for the questions to be answered. They also can be difficult to summarize.

Closed-ended questions provide a range of answers from which the interviewee may choose. Here is an example:

Which of the following would you say is the one best thing about the information system you currently use to do your job (pick only one)?

a. Having easy access to all of the data you need

b. The system's response time

c. The ability to run the system concurrently with other applications

Closed-ended questions
Questions in interviews and on questionnaires that ask those responding to choose from among a set of specified responses.

Closed-ended questions work well when the major answers to questions are well known. Another plus is that interviews based on closed-ended questions do not necessarily require a large time commitment—more topics can be covered. Closed-ended questions can also be an easy way to begin an interview and to determine which line of open-ended questions to pursue. You can include an "other" option to encourage the interviewee to add unexpected responses. A major disadvantage of closed-ended questions is that useful information that does not quite fit the defined answers may be overlooked as the respondent tries to make a choice instead of providing his or her best answer.

Like objective questions on an examination, closed-ended questions can follow several forms, including these choices:

- True or false
- Multiple choice (with only one response or selecting all relevant choices)
- Rating a response or idea on some scale, say, from bad to good or strongly agree to strongly disagree (each point on the scale should have a clear and consistent meaning to each person, and there is usually a neutral point in the middle of the scale)
- Ranking items in order of importance

Interview Guidelines   First, with either open- or closed-ended questions, do not phrase a question in a way that implies a right or wrong answer. Respondents must feel free to state their true opinions and perspectives and trust that their ideas will be considered. Avoid questions such as "Should the system continue to provide the ability to override the default value, even though most users now do not like the feature?" because such wording predefines a socially acceptable answer.

Second, listen carefully to what is being said. Take careful notes or, if possible, record the interview on a tape recorder (be sure to ask permission first!). The answers may contain extremely important information for the project. Also, this may be your only chance to get information from this particular person. If you run out of time and still need more information from the person you are talking to, ask to schedule a follow-up interview.

Third, once the interview is over, go back to your office and key in your notes within forty-eight hours with a word processing program such as Microsoft Word. For numerical data, you can use a spreadsheet program such as Microsoft Excel. If you recorded the interview, use the recording to verify your notes. After forty-eight hours, your memory of the interview will fade quickly. As you type and organize your notes, write down any additional questions that might arise from lapses in your notes or ambiguous information. Separate facts from your opinions and interpretations. Make a list of unclear points that need clarification. Call the person you interviewed and get answers to these new questions. Use the phone call as an opportunity to verify the accuracy of your notes. You may also want to send a written copy of your notes to the person you interviewed to check your notes for accuracy. Finally, make sure to thank the person for his or her time. You may need to talk to your respondent again. If the interviewee will be a user of your system or is involved in some other way in the system's success, you want to leave a good impression.

Fourth, be careful during the interview not to set expectations about the new or replacement system unless you are sure these features will be part of the delivered system. Let the interviewee know that there are many steps to the project. Many people will have to be interviewed. Choices will have to be made from among many technically possible alternatives. Let respondents know that their ideas will be carefully considered. Because of the repetitive nature of the systems development process, however, it is premature to say now exactly what the ultimate system will or will not do.

Fifth, seek a variety of perspectives from the interviews. Talk to several different people: potential users of the system, users of other systems that might be affected by this new system, managers and superiors, information systems staff, and others. Encourage people to think about current problems and opportunities and what new information services might better serve the organization. You want to understand all possible perspectives so that later you will have information on which to base a recommendation or design decision that everyone can accept.

Directly Observing Users

Interviewing involves getting people to recall and convey information they have about organizational processes and the information systems that support them. People, however, are not always reliable, even when they try to be and say what they think is the truth. As odd as it may sound, people often do not have a completely accurate appreciation of what they do or how they do it, especially when infrequent events, issues from the past, or issues for which people have considerable passion are involved. Because people cannot always be trusted to interpret and report their own actions reliably, you can supplement what people tell you by watching what they do in work situations.

For example, one possible view of how a hypothetical manager does her job is that a manager carefully plans her activities, works long and consistently on solving problems, and controls the pace of her work. A manager might tell you that is how she spends her day. Several studies have shown, however, that a manager's day is actually punctuated by many, many interruptions. Managers work in a fragmented manner, focusing on a problem or a communication for only a short time before they are interrupted by phone calls or visits from subordinates and other managers. An information system designed to fit the work environment described by our hypothetical manager would not effectively support the actual work environment in which that manager finds herself.

As another example, consider the difference between what another employee might tell you about how much he uses electronic mail and how much electronic mail use you might discover through more objective means. An employee might tell you he is swamped with e-mail messages and spends a significant proportion of time responding to e-mail messages. However, if you were able to check electronic mail records, you might find that this employee receives only three e-mail messages per day on average and that the most messages he has ever received during one eight-hour period is ten. In this case, you were able to obtain an accurate behavioral measure of how much e-mail this employee copes with, without having to watch him read his e-mail.

The intent behind obtaining system records and direct observation is the same, however, and that is to obtain more firsthand and objective measures of employee interaction with information systems. In some cases, behavioral measures will more accurately reflect reality than what employees themselves believe. In other cases, the behavioral information will substantiate what employees have told you directly. Although observation and obtaining objective measures are desirable ways to collect pertinent information, such methods are not always possible in real organizational settings. Thus, these methods are not totally unbiased, just as no one data-gathering method is unbiased.

For example, observation can cause people to change their normal operating behavior. Employees who know they are being observed may be nervous and make more mistakes than normal. On the other hand, employees under observation may follow exact procedures more carefully than they typically do. They may work faster or slower than normal. Because observation typically cannot be continuous, you receive only a snapshot image of the person or task you observe. Such a view may not include important events or activities. Due to time constraints, you observe for only a limited time, a limited number of people, and a limited number of sites. Observation yields only a small segment of data from a possibly vast variety of data sources. Exactly which people or sites to observe is a difficult selection problem. You want to pick both typical and atypical people and sites and observe during normal and abnormal conditions and times to receive the richest possible data from observation.

Analyzing Procedures and Other Documents

As previously noted, interviewing people who use a system every day or who have an interest in a system is an effective way to gather information about current and future systems. Observing current system users is a more direct way of seeing how an existing system operates. Both interviewing and observing have limitations. Methods for determining system requirements can be enhanced by examining system and organizational documentation to discover more details about current systems and the organization they support.

We discuss several important types of documents that are useful in understanding system requirements, but our discussion is not necessarily exhaustive. In addition to the few specific documents we mention, other important documents need to be located and considered, including organizational mission statements, business plans, organization charts, business policy manuals, job descriptions, internal and external correspondence, and reports from prior organizational studies.

What can the analysis of documents tell you about the requirements for a new system? In documents you can find information about:

- Problems with existing systems (e.g., missing information or redundant steps)
- Opportunities to meet new needs if only certain information or information processing were available (e.g., analysis of sales based on customer type)
- Organizational direction that can influence information system requirements (e.g., trying to link customers and suppliers more closely to the organization)
- Titles and names of key individuals who have an interest in relevant existing systems (e.g., the name of a sales manager who has led a study of buying behavior of key customers)
- Values of the organization or individuals who can help determine priorities for different capabilities desired by different users (e.g., maintaining market share even if it means lower short-term profits)
- Special information-processing circumstances that occur irregularly that may not be identified by any other requirements determination technique (e.g., special handling needed for a few large-volume customers who require use of customized customer ordering procedures)
- The reason why current systems are designed as they are, which can suggest features left out of current software that may now be feasible and desirable (e.g., data about a customer's purchase of competitors' products not available when the current system was designed; these data now available from several sources)
- Data, rules for processing data, and principles by which the organization operates that must be enforced by the information system (e.g., each customer assigned exactly one sales department staff member as primary contact if customer has any questions)

One type of useful document is a written work procedure for an individual or a work group. The procedure describes how a particular job or task is performed, including data and information used and created in the process of performing the job. For example, the procedure shown in Figure 5-3 includes data (list of features and advantages, drawings, inventor name, and witness names) required to prepare an invention disclosure. It also indicates that besides the inventor, the vice president for research, the department head, and the dean must review the material and that a witness is required for any filing of an invention disclosure. These insights clearly affect what data must be kept, to whom information must be sent, and the rules that govern valid forms.

GUIDE FOR PREPARATION OF INVENTION DISCLOSURE
(See FACULTY and STAFF MANUALS for detailed Patent Policy and routing procedures.)

(1) DISCLOSE ONLY ONE INVENTION PER FORM.

(2) PREPARE COMPLETE DISCLOSURE.

The disclosure of your invention is adequate for patent purposes ONLY if it enables a person skilled in the art to understand the invention.

(3) CONSIDER THE FOLLOWING IN PREPARING A COMPLETE DISCLOSURE:

(a) All essential elements of the invention, their relationship to one another, and their mode of operation

(b) Equivalents that can be substituted for any elements

(c) List of features believed to be new

(d) Advantages this invention has over the prior art

(e) Whether the invention has been built and/or tested

(4) PROVIDE APPROPRIATE ADDITIONAL MATERIAL.

Drawings and descriptive material should be provided as needed to clarify the disclosure. Each page of this material must be signed and dated by each inventor and properly witnessed. A copy of any current and/or planned publication relating to the invention should be included.

(5) INDICATE PRIOR KNOWLEDGE AND INFORMATION.

Pertinent publications, patents or previous devices, and related research or engineering activities should be identified.

(6) HAVE DISCLOSURE WITNESSED.

Persons other than co-inventors should serve as witnesses and should sign each sheet of the disclosure only after reading and understanding the disclosure.

(7) FORWARD ORIGINAL PLUS ONE COPY (two copies if supported by grant/contract) TO VICE PRESIDENT FOR RESEARCH VIA DEPARTMENT HEAD AND DEAN.

FIGURE 5-3
Example of a written work procedure for an invention disclosure.

Procedures are not trouble-free sources of information, however. Sometimes your analysis of several written procedures reveals a duplication of effort in two or more jobs. You should call such duplication to the attention of management as an issue to be resolved before system design can proceed. That is, it may be necessary to redesign the organization before the redesign of an information system can achieve its full benefits. Another problem you may encounter is a missing procedure. Again, it is not your job to create a document for a missing procedure—that is up to management. A third and common problem happens when the procedure is out of date, which you may realize in your interview of the person responsible for performing the task described in the procedure. Once again, the decision to rewrite the procedure so that it matches reality is made by management, but you may make suggestions based upon your understanding of the organization. A fourth problem often encountered is that the formal procedures may contradict information you collected from interviews, questionnaires, and observation about how the organization operates and what information is required. As in the other cases, resolution rests with management.

All of these problems illustrate the difference between formal systems and informal systems. A **formal system** is one an organization has documented; an **informal system** is the way in which the organization actually works. Informal systems develop because of inadequacies of formal procedures and individual work habits, preferences, and resistance to control. It is important to understand both formal and informal systems because each provides insight into information requirements and what is necessary to convert from present to future systems.

A second type of document useful to systems analysts is a business form, illustrated in Figure 5-4. Forms are used for all types of business functions, from recording an order to acknowledging the payment of a bill to indicating what goods have been shipped. Forms are important for understanding a system because they explicitly indicate what data flow in or out of a system. In the sample invoice form in Figure 5-4, we see space for data such as invoice number, the "bill to" address, the quantity of items ordered, their descriptions, rates, and amounts.

A printed form may correspond to a computer display that the system will generate for someone to enter and maintain data or to display data to online users. The most useful forms contain actual organizational data that allow you to determine the data characteristics actually used by the application. The ways in which people use forms change over time, and data that were needed when a form was designed may no longer be required.

A third type of useful document is a report generated by current systems. As the primary output for some types of systems, a report enables you to work backward from the information on the report to the data that must have been necessary to generate it. Figure 5-5 presents an example of a common financial accounting report, the statement of cash flows. You analyze such reports to determine which data need to be captured over what time period and what manipulation of these raw data is necessary to produce each field on the report.

If the current system is computer based, a fourth set of useful documents is one that describes the current information systems—how they were designed and how they work. Several different types of documents fit this description, everything from flowcharts to data dictionaries to user manuals. An analyst who has access to such documents is fortunate because many in-house-developed information systems lack complete documentation. Analysis of organizational documents and observation, along with interviewing and distributing questionnaires, are the methods used most for gathering system requirements. Table 5-4 (page 137) summarizes the comparative features of observation and analysis of organizational documents.

Formal system
The official way a system works, as described in organizational documentation.

Informal system
The way a system actually works.

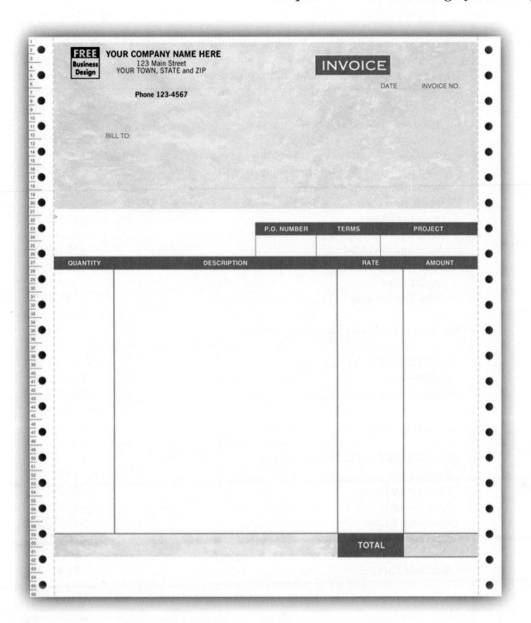

FIGURE 5-4
An example of a business form—an invoice form for QuickBooks.

Source: http://jnk.btobsource.com/NASApp/enduser/products/product_detail.jsp?pc=13050M#.
Reprinted with permission.

Modern Methods for Determining System Requirements

Even though we called interviews, questionnaires, observation, and document analysis traditional methods for determining a system's requirements, all of these methods are still used by analysts to collect important information. Today, however, additional techniques are available to collect information about the current system, the organizational area requesting the new system, and what the new system should be like. In this section, you learn about two modern information-gathering techniques for analysis: joint application design (JAD) and prototyping. These techniques can support effective information collection and structuring while reducing the amount of time required for analysis.

Mellankamp Industries
Statement of Cash Flows
October 1 through December 31, 2012

	Oct. 1–Dec. 31, 2012
OPERATING ACTIVITIES	
Net Income	$38,239.15
Adjustments to reconcile Net Income	
to Net cash provided by Operating Activities:	
Accounts Receivable	–$46,571.69
Employee Loans	–$62.00
Inventory Asset	–$18,827.16
Retainage	–$2,461.80
Accounts Payable	$29,189.66
Business Credit Card	$70.00
BigOil Card	–$18.86
Sales Tax Payable	$687.65
Net cash provided by Operating Activities	$244.95
INVESTING ACTIVITIES	
Equipment	–$44,500.00
Prepaid Insurance	$2,322.66
Net cash provided by Investing Activities	–$42,177.34
FINANCING ACTIVITIES	
Bank Loan	–$868.42
Emergency Loan	$3,911.32
Note Payable	–$17,059.17
Equipment Loan	$43,013.06
Opening Balance Equity	–$11,697.50
Owner's Equity: Owner's Draw	–$6,000.00
Retained Earning	$8,863.39
Net cash provided by Financing Activities	$20,162.68
Net cash increase for period	–$21,769.71
Cash at beginning of period	–$21,818.48
Cash at end of period	**–$43,588.19**

Joint Application Design

You were introduced to joint application design or JAD, in Chapter 1. There you
learned JAD started in the late 1970s at IBM as a means to bring together the key
users, managers, and systems analysts involved in the analysis of a current system. Since the 1970s, JAD has spread throughout many companies and industries. For example, it is quite popular in the insurance industry. The primary
purpose of using JAD in the analysis phase is to collect systems requirements
simultaneously from the key people involved with the system. The result is an
intense and structured, but highly effective, process. Having all the key people

TABLE 5-4: Comparison of Observation and Document Analysis

Characteristic	Observation	Document Analysis
Information richness	High (many channels)	Low (passive) and old
Time required	Can be extensive	Low to moderate
Expense	Can be high	Low to moderate
Chance for follow-up and probing	Good: Opportunity for probing and clarification questions during or after observation	Limited: Probing possible only if original author is available
Confidentiality	Observee is known to observer; observee may change behavior when observed	Depends on nature of document; does not change simply by being read
Involvement of subject	Observees' involvement dependent on whether they know they are being observed	None, no clear commitment
Potential audience	Limited numbers and limited time (snapshot) of each	Potentially biased by which documents were kept or because document not created for this purpose

together in one place at one time allows analysts to see the areas of agreement and the areas of conflict. Meeting with all these important people for over a week of intense sessions allows you the opportunity to resolve conflicts or at least to understand why a conflict may not be simple to resolve.

JAD sessions are usually conducted in a location away from where the people involved normally work, in order to limit distractions and help participants better concentrate on systems analysis. A JAD may last anywhere from four hours to an entire week and may consist of several sessions. A JAD employs thousands of dollars of corporate resources, the most expensive of which is the time of the people involved. Other expenses include the costs associated with flying people to a remote site and putting them up in hotels and feeding them for several days.

The following is a list of typical JAD participants:

- **JAD session leader:** The JAD leader organizes and runs the JAD. This person has been trained in group management and facilitation as well as in systems analysis. The JAD leader sets the agenda and sees that it is met. He or she remains neutral on issues and does not contribute ideas or opinions, but rather concentrates on keeping the group on the agenda, resolving conflicts and disagreements, and soliciting all ideas.

- *Users:* The key users of the system under consideration are vital participants in a JAD. They are the only ones who clearly understand what it means to use the system on a daily basis.

- *Managers:* Managers of the work groups who use the system in question provide insight into new organizational directions, motivations for and organizational impacts of systems, and support for requirements determined during the JAD.

- *Sponsor:* As a major undertaking, because of its expense, a JAD must be sponsored by someone at a relatively high level in the company such as a vice president or chief executive officer. If the sponsor attends any sessions, it is usually only at the beginning or the end.

- *Systems analysts:* Members of the systems analysis team attend the JAD, although their actual participation may be limited. Analysts are

JAD session leader
The trained individual who plans and leads joint application design sessions.

Scribe

The person who makes detailed notes of the happenings at a joint application design session.

there to learn from users and managers, not to run or dominate the process.

- **Scribe:** The scribe takes notes during the JAD sessions, usually on a personal computer or laptop.
- *IS staff:* Besides systems analysts, other IS staff, such as programmers, database analysts, IS planners, and data-center personnel, may attend the session. Their purpose is to learn from the discussion and possibly to contribute their ideas on the technical feasibility of proposed ideas or on the technical limitations of current systems.

JAD sessions are usually held in special-purpose rooms where participants sit around horseshoe-shaped tables, as in Figure 5-6. These rooms are typically equipped with whiteboards (possibly electronic, with a printer to make copies of what is written on the board). Other audiovisual tools may be used, such as magnetic symbols that can be easily rearranged on a whiteboard, flip charts, and computer-generated displays. Flip-chart paper is typically used for keeping track of issues that cannot be resolved during the JAD, or for those issues requiring additional information that can be gathered during breaks in the proceedings. Computers may be used to create and display form or report designs or to diagram existing or replacement systems. In general, however, most JADs do not benefit much from computer support. The end result of a completed JAD is a set of documents that detail the workings of the current system and the features of a replacement system. Depending on the exact purpose of the JAD, analysts may gain detailed information on what is desired of the replacement system.

FIGURE 5-6
A typical room layout for a JAD session.
Source: Based on Wood and Silver, 1989.

Taking Part in a JAD   Imagine that you are a systems analyst taking part in your first JAD. What might participating in a JAD be like? Typically, JADs are held off-site, in comfortable conference facilities. On the first morning of the JAD, you and your fellow analysts walk into a room that looks much like the one depicted in Figure 5-6. The JAD facilitator is already there. She is finishing writing the day's agenda on a flip chart. The scribe is seated in a corner with a laptop, preparing to take notes on the day's activities. Users and managers begin to enter in groups and seat themselves around the U-shaped table. You and the other analysts review your notes describing what you have learned so far about the information system you are all there to discuss. The session leader opens the meeting with a welcome and a brief rundown of the agenda. The first day will be devoted to a general overview of the current system and major problems associated with it. The next two days will be devoted to an analysis of current system screens. The last two days will be devoted to analysis of reports.

The session leader introduces the corporate sponsor, who talks about the organizational unit and current system related to the systems analysis study and the importance of upgrading the current system to meet changing business conditions. He leaves and the JAD session leader takes over. She yields the floor to the senior analyst, who begins a presentation on key problems with the system, which have already been identified. After the presentation, the session leader opens the discussion to the users and managers in the room.

After a few minutes of talk, a heated discussion begins between two users from different corporate locations. One user, who represents the office that served as the model for the original systems design, argues that the system's perceived lack of flexibility is really an asset, not a problem. The other user, who represents an office that was part of another company before a merger, argues that the current system is so inflexible as to be virtually unusable. The session leader intervenes and tries to help the users isolate particular aspects of the system that may contribute to the system's perceived lack of flexibility.

Questions arise about the intent of the original developers. The session leader asks the analysis team about their impressions of the original system design. If these questions cannot be answered during this meeting because none of the original designers are present nor are the original design documents readily available, the session leader assigns the question about intent to the "to-do" list. This question becomes the first item on a flip-chart sheet of to-do items, and the session leader gives you the assignment of finding out about the intent of the original designers. She writes your name next to the to-do item on the list and continues with the session. Before the end of the JAD, you must get an answer to this question.

The JAD will continue in this manner for its duration. Analysts will make presentations, help lead discussions of form and report design, answer questions from users and managers, and take notes on what is being said. After each meeting, the analysis team will meet, usually informally, to discuss what has occurred that day and to consolidate what they have learned. Users will continue to contribute during the meetings, and the session leader will facilitate, intervening in conflicts, seeing that the group follows the agenda. When the JAD is over, the session leader and her assistants must prepare a report that documents the findings in the JAD and then circulate it among users and analysts.

Using Prototyping during Requirements Determination

You were introduced to prototyping in Chapter 1 (see Figure 1-12 for an overview of prototyping). There you learned that prototyping is a repetitive process in which analysts and users build a rudimentary version of an information system based on user feedback. You also learned that prototyping could replace the systems development life cycle or augment it. In this section, we see how prototyping can augment the requirements determination process.

To establish requirements for prototyping, you still have to interview users and collect documentation. Prototyping, however, allows you to quickly convert basic requirements into a working, though limited, version of the desired information system. The user then views and tests the prototype. Typically, seeing verbal descriptions of requirements converted into a physical system prompts the user to modify existing requirements and generate new ones. For example, in the initial interviews, a user might have said he wanted all relevant utility billing information on a single computer display form, such as the client's name and address, the service record, and payment history. Once the same user sees how crowded and confusing such a design would be in the prototype, he might change his mind and instead ask for the information to be organized on several screens but with easy transitions from one screen to another. He might also be reminded of some important requirements (data, calculations, etc.) that had not surfaced during the initial interviews.

You would then redesign the prototype to incorporate the suggested changes. Once modified, users would again view and test the prototype. Once again, you would incorporate their suggestions for change. Through such a repetitive process, the chances are good that you will be able to better capture a system's requirements. The goal with using prototyping to support requirements determination is to develop concrete specifications for the ultimate system, not to build the ultimate system.

Prototyping is most useful for requirements determination when:

- User requirements are not clear or well understood, which is often the case for totally new systems or systems that support decision making.
- One or a few users and other stakeholders are involved with the system.
- Possible designs are complex and require concrete form to evaluate fully.
- Communication problems have existed in the past between users and analysts, and both parties want to be sure that system requirements are as specific as possible.
- Tools (such as form and report generators) and data are readily available to rapidly build working systems.

Prototyping also has some drawbacks as a tool for requirements determination. They include the following:

- A tendency to avoid creating formal documentation of system requirements, which can then make the system more difficult to develop into a fully working system.
- Prototypes can become idiosyncratic to the initial user and difficult to diffuse or adapt to other potential users.
- Prototypes are often built as stand-alone systems, thus ignoring issues of sharing data and interactions with other existing systems.
- Checks in the SDLC are bypassed so that some more subtle, but still important, system requirements might be forgotten (e.g., security, some data-entry controls, or standardization of data across systems).

Radical Methods for Determining System Requirements

Whether traditional or modern, the methods for determining system requirements that you have read about in this chapter apply to any requirements determination effort, regardless of its motivation. Yet, most of what you have learned has traditionally been applied to systems development projects that involve automating existing processes. Analysts use system requirements determination to understand current problems and opportunities, as well as what is needed and desired in future systems. Typically, the current way of doing things has a large impact on the new system. In some organizations, though, management is looking for new ways to perform current tasks. These ways may be radically different from how things are done now, but the payoffs may be enormous: Fewer people may be needed to do the same work; relationships with customers may improve dramatically; and processes may become much more efficient and effective, all of which can result in increased profits. The overall process by which current methods are replaced with radically new methods is referred to as **business process reengineering (BPR).**

To better understand BPR, consider the following analogy. Suppose you are a successful European golfer who has tuned your game to fit the style of golf courses and weather in Europe. You have learned how to control the flight of the ball in heavy winds, roll the ball on wide-open greens, putt on large and undulating greens, and aim at a target without the aid of the landscaping common on North American courses. When you come to the United States to make your fortune on the U.S. tour, you discover that improving your putting, driving accuracy, and sand shots will help, but the new competitive environment is simply not suited to your playing style. You need to reengineer your whole approach, learning how to aim at targets, spin and stop a ball on the green, and manage the distractions of crowds and press. If you are good enough, you may survive, but without reengineering, you will never become a winner.

Just as the competitiveness of golf forces good players to adapt their games to changing conditions, the competitiveness of our global economy has driven most companies into a mode of continuously improving the quality of their products and services. Organizations realize that creatively using information technologies can significantly improve most business processes. The idea behind BPR is not just to improve each business process but, in a systems-modeling sense, to reorganize the complete flow of data in major sections of an organization to eliminate unnecessary steps, combine previously separate steps, and become more responsive to future changes. Companies such as IBM, Procter & Gamble, Wal-Mart, and Ford have had great success in actively pursuing BPR efforts. Yet, many other companies have found difficulty in applying BPR principles. Nonetheless, BPR concepts are actively applied in both corporate strategic planning and information systems planning as a way to improve business processes radically (as described in Chapter 6).

BPR advocates suggest that radical increases in the quality of business processes can be achieved through creatively applying information technologies. BPR advocates also suggest that radical improvement cannot be achieved by making minor changes in existing processes but rather by using a clean sheet of paper and asking, "If we were a new organization, how would we accomplish this activity?" Changing the way work is performed also changes the way information is shared and stored, which means that the results of many BPR efforts are the development of information system maintenance requests, or requests for system replacement. You likely have encountered or will encounter BPR initiatives in your own organization. A recent survey of IS executives found that they view BPR to be a top IS priority for the coming years.

Identifying Processes to Reengineer

A first step in any BPR effort is to understand what processes need to change, what are the **key business processes** for the organization. Key business processes are the structured set of measurable activities designed to produce a

Business process reengineering (BPR)
The search for, and implementation of, radical change in business processes to achieve breakthrough improvements in products and services.

Key business processes
The structured, measured set of activities designed to produce a specific output for a particular customer or market.

specific output for a particular customer or market. The important aspect of this definition is that key processes are focused on some type of organizational outcome such as the creation of a product or the delivery of a service. Key business processes are also customer focused. In other words, key business processes would include all activities used to design, build, deliver, support, and service a particular product for a particular customer. BPR, therefore, requires you first to understand those activities that are part of the organization's key business processes and then to alter the sequence and structure of activities to achieve radical improvements in speed, quality, and customer satisfaction. The same techniques you learned to use for system requirements determination can be applied to discovering and understanding key business processes: interviewing key individuals, observing activities, reading and studying organizational documents, and conducting JAD sessions.

After identifying key business processes, the next step is to identify specific activities that can be radically improved through reengineering. Michael Hammer and James Champy, two academics who coined the term *BPR*, suggest systems analysts ask three questions to identify activities for radical change:

1. How important is the activity to delivering an outcome?
2. How feasible is changing the activity?
3. How dysfunctional is the activity?

The answers to these questions provide guidance for selecting which activities to change. Those activities deemed important, changeable, yet dysfunctional, are primary candidates for alteration. To identify dysfunctional activities, Hammer and Champy suggest you look for activities that involve excessive information exchanges between individuals, information that is redundantly recorded or needs to be rekeyed, excessive inventory buffers or inspections, and a lot of rework or complexity. An example of a dysfunctional process and how BPR is used to change it is presented at the end of Chapter 6.

Disruptive Technologies

Once key business processes and activities have been identified, information technologies must be applied to improve business processes radically. Hammer and Champy suggest that organizations think "inductively" about information technology. Induction is the process of reasoning from the specific to the general, which means that managers must learn about the power of new technologies and think of innovative ways to alter the way work is done. This approach is contrary to deductive thinking, in which problems are first identified and solutions then formulated.

Disruptive technologies
Technologies that enable the breaking of long-held business rules that inhibit organizations from making radical business changes.

Hammer and Champy suggest that managers especially consider disruptive technologies when applying deductive thinking. **Disruptive technologies** are those that enable the breaking of long-held business rules that inhibit organizations from making radical business changes. For example, Toyota is using production schedule databases and electronic data interchange (EDI)—an information system that allows companies to link their computers directly to suppliers—to work with its suppliers as if they and Saturn were one company. Suppliers do not wait until Saturn sends them a purchase order for more parts but simply monitor inventory levels and automatically send shipments as needed. Table 5-5 shows several long-held business rules and beliefs that constrain organizations from making radical process improvements. For example, the first rule suggests that information can appear in only one place at a time. However, the advent of distributed databases, which allow business units to share a common database, has "disrupted" this long-held business belief.

TABLE 5-5: Long-Held Organizational Rules That Are Being Eliminated through Disruptive Technologies

Rule	Disruptive Technology
Information can appear in only one place at a time.	Distributed databases allow the sharing of information.
Only experts can perform complex work.	Expert systems can aid nonexperts.
Businesses must choose between centralization and decentralization.	Advanced telecommunications networks can support dynamic organizational structures.
Managers must make all decisions.	Decision-support tools can aid nonmanagers.
Field personnel need offices where they can receive, store, retrieve, and transmit information.	Wireless data communication and portable computers provide a "virtual" office for workers.
The best contact with a potential buyer is personal contact.	Interactive communication technologies allow complex messaging capabilities.
You have to find out where things are.	Automatic identification and tracking technology knows where things are.
Plans get revised periodically.	High-performance computing can provide real-time updating.

Pine Valley Furniture WebStore: Determining System Requirements

In the last chapter, you read how Pine Valley Furniture's management began the WebStore project—to sell furniture products over the Internet. Here we examine the process followed by PVF to determine system requirements and highlight some of the issues and capabilities that you may want to consider when developing your own Internet-based application.

To collect system requirements as quickly as possible, Jim Woo and Jackie Judson decided to hold a three-day JAD session. In order to get the most out of these sessions, they invited a broad range of people, including representatives from sales and marketing, operations, and information systems. Additionally, they asked an experienced JAD facilitator, Cheri Morris, to conduct the session. Together with Cheri, Jim and Jackie developed an ambitious and detailed agenda for the session. Their goal was to collect requirements on the following items:

- System layout and navigation characteristics
- WebStore and site management system capabilities
- Customer and inventory information
- System prototype evolution

In the remainder of this section, we briefly highlight the outcomes of the JAD session.

System Layout and Navigation Characteristics

As part of the process of preparing for the JAD session, all participants were asked to visit several established retail Web sites, including www.amazon.com, www.landsend.com, www.sony.com, and www.pier1.com. At the JAD session, participants were asked to identify characteristics of these sites that they found

TABLE 5-6: Desired Layout and Navigation Feature of WebStore

Layout and Design

Navigation menu and logo placement should remain consistent throughout the entire site (this allows users to maintain familiarity while using the site and minimizes the number who get "lost" in the site).

Graphics should be lightweight to allow for quick page display.

Text should be used over graphics whenever possible.

Navigation

Any section of the store should be accessible from any other section via the navigation menu.

Users should always be aware of what section they are currently in.

appealing and those they found cumbersome; this allowed participants to identify and discuss those features that they wanted the WebStore to possess. The outcomes of this activity are summarized in Table 5-6.

WebStore and Site Management System Capabilities

After agreeing to the general layout and navigational characteristics of the WebStore, the session then turned its focus to the basic system capabilities. To assist in this process, systems analysts from the information systems department developed a draft skeleton of the WebStore based on the types of screens and capabilities of popular retail Web sites. For example, many retail Web sites have a "shopping cart" feature that allows customers to accumulate multiple items before checking out rather than buying a single item at a time. After some discussion, the participants agreed that the system structure shown in Table 5-7 would form the foundation for the WebStore system.

TABLE 5-7: System Structure of the WebStore and Site Management Systems

WebStore System	Site Management System
Main Page	User profile manager
Product line (catalog)	Order maintenance manager
• Desks	Content (catalog) manager
• Chairs	Reports
• Tables	Total hits
• File cabinets	Most-frequent page views
Shopping cart	User/time of day
Checkout	Users/day of week
Account profile	Shoppers not purchasing (used shopping cart—did not check out)
Order status/history	Feedback analysis
Customer comments	
Company information	
Feedback	
Contact information	

In addition to the WebStore capabilities, members of the sales and marketing department described several reports that would be necessary to manage customer accounts and sales transactions effectively. In addition, the department wants to be able to conduct detailed analyses of site visitors, sales tracking, and so on. Members of the operations department expressed a need to update the product catalog easily. These collective requests and activities were organized into a system design structure called the *Site Management* system, summarized in Table 5-7. The structures of both the WebStore and Site Management systems will be given to the information systems department as the baseline for further analysis and design activities.

Customer and Inventory Information

The WebStore will be designed to support the furniture purchases of three distinct types of customers:

- Corporate customers
- Home-office customers
- Student customers

To track the sales to these different types of customers effectively, the system must capture and store distinct information. Table 5-8 summarizes this information for each customer type identified during the JAD session. Orders reflect the range of product information that must be specified to execute a sales transaction. Thus, in addition to capturing the customer information, product and sales data must also be captured and stored; Table 5-8 lists the results of this analysis.

System Prototype Evolution

As a final activity, the JAD participants discussed, along with extensive input from the information systems staff, how the system implementation should evolve. After completing analysis and design activities, they agreed that the system implementation should progress in three main stages so that requirement changes could be more easily identified and implemented. Table 5-9 summarizes these stages and the functionality incorporated at each one.

At the conclusion of the JAD session, all the participants felt good about the progress that had been made and about the clear requirements that had been identified. With these requirements in hand, Jim and the information systems staff could begin to turn these lists of requirements into formal analysis and

TABLE 5-8: Customer and Inventory Information for WebStore

Corporate Customer	Home-Office Customer	Student Customer	Inventory Information
Company name	Name	Name	SKU
Company address	Doing business as (company name)	School	Name
Company phone	Address	Address	Description
Company fax	Phone	Phone	Finished product size
Preferred shipping method	Fax	E-mail	Finished product weight
Buyer name	E-mail		Available materials
Buyer phone			Available colors
Buyer e-mail			Price
			Lead time

TABLE 5-9 Stages of System Implementation of WebStore

Stage 1 (Basic Functionality)

Simple catalog navigation; two products per section—limited attribute set

25 sample users

Simulated credit card transaction

Full shopping cart functionality

Stage 2 (Look and Feel)

Full product attribute set and media (images, video)—commonly referred to as "product data catalog"

Full site layout

Simulated integration with Purchasing Fulfillment and Customer Tracking Systems

Stage 3 (Staging/Preproduction)

Full integration with Purchasing Fulfillment and Customer Tracking Systems

Full credit card processing integration

Full product data catalog

---

design specifications. To show how information flows through the WebStore, Jim and his staff will produce data-flow diagrams (Chapter 6). To show a conceptual model of the data used within the WebStore, they will generate an entity-relationship diagram (Chapter 7). Both of these analysis documents will become the foundation for detailed system design and implementation.

As we saw in Chapter 1, the systems analysis phase of the systems development life cycle includes determining requirements and structuring requirements. Chapter 5 focuses on requirements determination, the gathering of information about current systems, and the need for replacement systems. Chapters 6 and 7 address techniques for structuring the information discovered during requirements determination.

Key Points Review

1. **Describe options for designing and conducting interviews and develop a plan for conducting an interview to determine system requirements.**

   Interviews can involve open-ended and closed-ended questions. In either case, you must be precise in formulating a question in order to avoid ambiguity and to ensure a proper response. Making a list of questions is just one activity necessary to prepare for an interview. You must also create a general interview guide (see Figure 5-2) and schedule the interview.

2. **Explain the advantages and pitfalls of observing workers and analyzing business documents to determine system requirements.**

   During observation, you must try not to intrude or interfere with normal business activities so

that the people being observed do not modify their activities from normal processes. Observation can be expensive because it is so labor intensive. Analyzing documents may be much less expensive, but any insights gained will be limited to what is available, based on the reader's interpretation. Often the creator of the document is not there to answer questions.

3. **Participate in and help plan a joint application design session.**

   Joint application design (JAD) brings together key users and adds structure and a JAD session leader to it. Typical JAD participants include the session leader, a scribe, key users, managers, a sponsor, systems analysts, and IS staff members. JAD sessions are usually held off-site and may last as long as one week.

4. **Use prototyping during requirements determination.**

   You read how information systems can support requirements determination with prototyping. As part of the prototyping process, users and analysts work closely together to determine requirements that the analyst then builds into a model. The analyst and user then work together on revising the model until it is close to what the user desires.

5. **Select the appropriate methods to elicit system requirements.**

   For requirements determination, the traditional sources of information about a system include interviews, questionnaires, observation, and procedures, forms, and other useful documents. Often many or even all of these sources are used to gather perspectives on the adequacy of current systems and the requirements for replacement systems. Each form of information collection has its advantages and disadvantages, which were summarized in Table 5-4. Selecting the methods to use depends on the need for rich or thorough information, the time and budget available, the need to probe deeper once initial information is collected, the need for confidentiality for those providing assessments of system requirements, the desire to get people involved and committed to a project, and the potential audience from which requirements should be collected.

6. **Explain business process reengineering and how it affects requirements determination.**

   Business process reengineering (BPR) is an approach to changing business processes radically.

7. **Understand how requirements determination techniques apply to development for Internet applications.**

   Most of the same techniques used for requirements determination for traditional systems can also be fruitfully applied to the development of Internet applications. Accurately capturing requirements in a timely manner for Internet applications is just as important as for more traditional systems.

Key Terms Checkpoint

Here are the key terms from the chapter. The page where each term is first explained is in parentheses after the term.

1. Business process reengineering (BPR) (p. 141)
2. Closed-ended questions (p. 129)
3. Disruptive technologies (p. 142)
4. Formal system (p. 134)
5. Informal system (p. 134)
6. JAD session leader (p. 137)
7. Key business processes (p. 141)
8. Open-ended questions (p. 128)
9. Scribe (p. 138)

Match each of the key terms above with the definition that best fits it.

_____ 1. The search for, and implementation of, radical change in business processes to achieve breakthrough improvements in products and services.

_____ 2. The person who makes detailed notes of the happenings at a joint application design session.

_____ 3. Technologies that enable the breaking of long-held business rules that inhibit organizations from making radical business changes.

_____ 4. The way a system actually works.

_____ 5. The official way a system works as described in organizational documentation.

_____ 6. The structured, measured set of activities designed to produce a specific output for a particular customer or market.

_____ 7. Questions in interviews and on questionnaires that ask those responding to choose from among a set of specified responses.

_____ 8. Questions in interviews and on questionnaires that have no prespecified answers.

_____ 9. The trained individual who plans and leads joint application design sessions.

Review Questions

1. Describe systems analysis and the major activities that occur during this phase of the systems development life cycle.
2. What are some useful character traits for an analyst involved in requirements determination?
3. Describe three traditional techniques for collecting information during analysis. When might one be better than another?
4. What are the general guidelines for conducting interviews?
5. What are the general guidelines for collecting data through observing workers?
6. What are the general guidelines for collecting data through analyzing documents?
7. Compare collecting information through observation and through document analysis. Describe a hypothetical situation in which each of these methods would be an effective way to collect information system requirements.
8. What is JAD? How is it better than traditional information-gathering techniques? What are its weaknesses?
9. How has computing been used to support requirements determination?
10. Describe how prototyping can be used during requirements determination. How is it better or worse than traditional methods?
11. When conducting a business process reengineering study, what should you look for when trying to identify business processes to change? Why?
12. What are disruptive technologies, and how do they enable organizations to change their business processes radically?

Problems and Exercises

1. One of the potential problems mentioned in this chapter with gathering information requirements by observing potential system users is that people may change their behavior when observed. What could you do to overcome this potentially confounding factor in accurately determining information requirements?
2. Summarize the problems with the reliability and usefulness of analyzing business documents as a method for gathering information requirements. How could you cope with these problems to use business documents effectively as a source of insights on system requirements?
3. Suppose you were asked to lead a JAD session. List ten guidelines you would follow in playing the proper role of a JAD session leader.
4. Prepare a plan, similar to Figure 5-2, for an interview with your academic adviser to determine which courses you should take to develop the skills you need to be hired as a programmer/analyst.
5. Figure 5-2 shows part of a guide for an interview. How might an interview guide differ when a group interview is to be conducted?
6. JADs are powerful ways to collect system requirements, but special problems arise during group requirements collection sessions. Summarize these special interviewing and group problems, and suggest ways that you, as a group facilitator, might deal with them.
7. Suppose you are a systems analyst charged with gathering information requirements. You decide that you want to use prototyping to gather these requirements. It provides benefits beyond interviews and observations but also presents unique challenges. Discuss the challenges you expect to face and what processes you will put in place to prevent them from harming your information system.
8. Questionnaires can be administered both on paper and via the Internet. Online questionnaires allow for the use of complex analysis tools and real-time results. However, online questionnaires have idiosyncratic challenges. Three such challenges can be computer access concerns, getting users to participate, and employee concerns for privacy of results. Discuss when each concern is likely to impact the online questionnaire and how you would address each challenge.

Discussion Questions

1. The methods of data collection discussed in this chapter take a lot of time. What are some ways analysts can still collect the information they need for systems analysis but also save time? What methods can you think of that would improve upon both traditional and newer techniques?
2. Some of the key problems with information systems that show up later in the systems

development life cycle can be traced back to in-adequate work during requirements determination. How might this issue be avoided?

3. Survey the literature on JAD in the academic and popular press and determine the "state of the art." How is JAD being used to help determine system requirements? Is using JAD for this process beneficial? Why or why not? Present your analysis to the IS manager at your work or at your university. Does your analysis of JAD fit with his or her perception? Why or why not? Is he or she currently using JAD, or a JAD-like method, for determining system requirements? Why or why not?

4. Is business process reengineering a business fad or is there more to it? Explain and justify your answer.

Case Problems

1. Pine Valley Furniture

Jackie Judson, vice president of marketing, and Jim Woo, a senior systems analyst, have been involved with Pine Valley Furniture's Customer Tracking System since the beginning of the project. After receiving project approval from the Systems Priority Board, Jim and his project development team turned their attention toward analyzing the Customer Tracking System.

During a Wednesday afternoon meeting, Jim and his project team members decide to utilize several requirements determination methods. Because the Customer Tracking System will facilitate the tracking of customer purchasing activity and help identify sales trends, various levels of end users will benefit from the new system. Therefore, the project team feels it is necessary to collect requirements from these potential end users. The project team will use interviews, observations, questionnaires, and JAD sessions as data-gathering tools.

Jim assigns you the task of interviewing Stacie Walker, a middle manager in the marketing department; Pauline McBride, a sales representative; and Tom Percy, assistant vice president of marketing. Tom is responsible for preparing the sales forecasts. In addition, Jim assigns Pete Polovich, a project team member, the task of organizing the upcoming JAD sessions.

a. Because Pete Polovich is organizing a JAD session for the first time, he would like to locate additional information about organizing and conducting a JAD session. Find information on JAD on the Web, and provide Pete with several recommendations for conducting and organizing a JAD session.

b. When conducting your interviews, what guidelines should you follow?

c. As part of the requirements determination process, what business documents should be reviewed?

d. Is prototyping an appropriate requirements determination method for this project?

2. Hoosier Burger

Juan Rodriquez has assigned you the task of requirements determination for the Hoosier Burger project. You are looking forward to this opportunity because it will allow you to meet and interact with Hoosier Burger employees. Besides interviewing Bob and Thelma Mellankamp, you decide to collect information from Hoosier Burger's waiters, cooks, and customers.

Mr. Rodriquez suggests that you formally interview Bob and Thelma Mellankamp and perhaps observe them performing their daily management tasks. You decide that the best way to collect requirements from the waiters and cooks is to interview and observe them. You realize that discussing the order-taking process with Hoosier Burger employees and then observing them in action will provide you with a better idea of where potential system improvements can be made. You also decide to prepare a questionnaire to distribute to Hoosier Burger customers. Because Hoosier Burger has a large customer base, it would be impossible to interview every customer; therefore, you feel that a customer satisfaction survey will suffice.

a. Assume you are preparing the customer satisfaction questionnaire. What types of questions would you include? Prepare five questions that you would ask.

b. What types of questions would you ask the waiters? What types of questions would you ask the cooks? Prepare five questions that you would ask each group.

c. What types of documents are you likely to obtain for further study? What types of documents will most likely not be available? Why?

d. What modern requirements determination methods are appropriate for this project?

3. Clothing Shack

The Clothing Shack is an online retailer of men's, women's, and children's clothing. The company has been in business for four years and makes a modest profit from its online sales.

However, in an effort to compete successfully against online retailing heavyweights, the Clothing Shack's marketing director, Makaya O'Neil, has determined that the Clothing Shack's marketing information systems need improvement.

Ms. O'Neil feels that the Clothing Shack should begin sending out catalogs to its customers, keep better track of its customer's buying habits, perform target marketing, and provide a more personalized shopping experience for its customers. Several months ago, Ms. O'Neil submitted a systems service request (SSR) to the Clothing Shack's steering committee. The committee unanimously approved this project. You were assigned to the project at that time and have since helped your project team successfully complete the project initiation and planning phase. Your team is now ready to move into the analysis phase and begin identifying requirements for the new system.

a. Whom would you interview? Why?
b. What requirements determination methods are appropriate for this project?
c. Based on the answers provided for Question b, which requirements determination methods are appropriate for the individuals identified in Question a?
d. Identify the requirements determination deliverables that will likely result from this project.

CASE: PETRIE'S ELECTRONICS

Determining Systems Requirements

Although the customer loyalty project at Petrie's Electronics had gone slowly at first, the past few weeks had been fast paced and busy, Jim Watanabe, the project manager, thought to himself. He had spent much of his time planning and conducting interviews with key stakeholders inside the company. He had also worked with the marketing group to put together some focus groups made up of loyal customers, to get some ideas about what they would value in a customer loyalty program. Jim had also spent some time studying customer loyalty programs at other big retail chains and those in other industries as well, such as the airlines, known for their extensive customer loyalty programs. As project manager, he had also supervised the efforts of his team members. Together, they had collected a great deal of data. Jim had just finished creating a high-level summary of the information into a table he could send to his team members (PE Table 5-1).

From the list of requirements, it was clear that he and his team did not favor building a system from scratch in-house. Jim was glad that the team felt that

PE TABLE 5-1:   Requirements and Constraints for Petrie's Customer Loyalty Project

Requirements

- Effective customer incentives—System should be able to effectively store customer activity and convert to rewards and other incentives

- Easy for customers to use—Interface should be intuitive for customer use

- Proven performance—System as proposed should have been used successfully by other clients

- Easy to implement—Implementation should not require outside consultants or extraordinary skills on the part of our staff or require specialized hardware

- Scalable—System should be easily expandable as the number of participating customers grows

- Vendor support—Vendor should have proven track record of reliable support and infrastructure in place to provide it

Constraints

- Cost to buy—Licenses for one year should be under $500,000

- Cost to operate—Total operating costs should be no more than $1 million per year

- Time to implement—Duration of implementation should not exceed three months

- Staff to implement—Implementation should be successful with the staff we have and with the skills they already possess

PE TABLE 5-2: Alternatives for Petrie's Customer Loyalty Project

Alternative A

Data warehousing-centered system designed and licensed by Standard Basic Systems, Inc. (SBSI). The data warehousing tools at the heart of the system were designed and developed by SBSI, and work with standard relational DBMSs and relational/OO hybrid DBMSs. The SBSI tools and approach have been used for many years and are well known in the industry, but SBSI-certified staff are essential for implementation, operation, and maintenance. The license is relatively expensive. The customer loyalty application using the SBSI data warehousing tools is an established application, used by many retail businesses in other industries.

Alternative B

Customer relationship management (CRM)-centered system designed and licensed by XRA Corporation. XRA is a pioneer in CRM systems, so its CRM is widely recognized as an industry leader. The system includes tools that support customer loyalty programs. The CRM system itself is large and complex, but pricing in this proposal is based only on modules used for the customer loyalty application.

Alternative C

Proprietary system designed and licensed by Nova Innovation Group, Inc. The system is relatively new and leading edge, so it has only been implemented in a few sites. The vendor is truly innovative but small and inexperienced. The customer interface, designed for a standard Web browser, is stunning in its design and is extremely easy for customers to use to check on their loyalty program status. The software runs remotely, in the "cloud," and data related to the customer loyalty program would be stored in the cloud too.

way. Not only was building a system like this in-house an antiquated practice, it was expensive and time consuming. As nice as it might have been to develop a unique system just for Petrie's, there was little point in reinventing the wheel. The IT staff would customize the system interface, and there would be lots of work for Sanjay's staff in integrating the new system and its related components with Petrie's existing systems, but the core of the system would have already been developed by someone else.

Just as he was finishing the e-mail he would send to his team about the new system's requirements and constraints, he received a new message from Sanjay. He had asked Sanjay to take the lead in scouting out existing customer loyalty systems that Petrie's could license. Sanjay had conducted a preliminary investigation that was now complete. His e-mail contained the descriptions of three of the systems he had found and studied (PE Table 5-2). Obviously, Jim and his team would need to have a lot more information about these alternatives, but Jim was intrigued by the possibilities. He sent a reply to Sanjay, asking him to pass the alternatives on to the team, and also

asking him to prepare a briefing for the team that would include more detailed information about each alternative.

Case Questions

1. What do you think are the sources of the information Jim and his team collected? How do you think they collected all of that information?
2. Examine PE Table 5-1. Are there any requirements or constraints that you can think of that were overlooked? List them.
3. If you were looking for alternative approaches for Petrie's customer loyalty program, where would you look for information? Where would you start? How would you know when you were done?
4. Using the Web, find three customizable customer loyalty program systems being sold by vendors. Create a table like PE Table 5-2 that compares them.
5. Why shouldn't Petrie's staff build their own unique system in-house?

SIX
Structuring System Requirements: Process Modeling

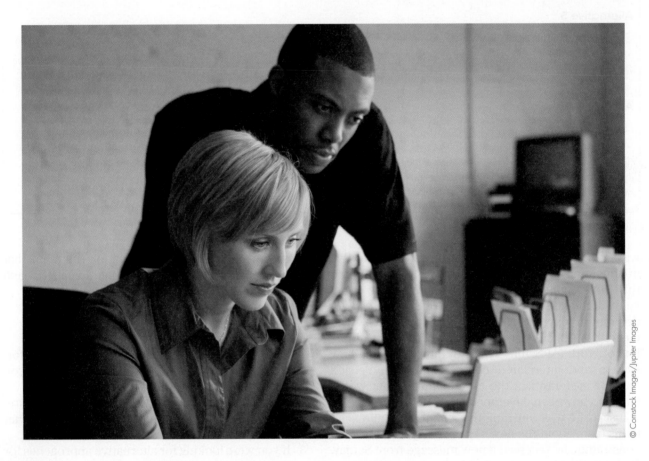

© Comstock Images/Jupiter Images

After studying this chapter, you should be able to:

- Understand the logical modeling of processes through studying examples of data-flow diagrams.

- Draw data-flow diagrams following specific rules and guidelines that lead to accurate and well-structured process models.

- Decompose data-flow diagrams into lower-level diagrams.

- Balance higher-level and lower-level data-flow diagrams.

- Use data-flow diagrams as a tool to support the analysis of information systems.

- Use decision tables to represent process logic.

Chapter Preview . . .

In the previous chapter, you learned about various methods that systems analysts use to collect the information they need to determine systems requirements. In this chapter, we continue our focus on the systems analysis part of the SDLC, which is highlighted in Figure 6-1. Note the two parts to the analysis phase, determining requirements and structuring requirements. We focus on a tool analysts use to structure information—data-flow diagrams (DFDs). Data-flow diagrams allow you to model how data flow through an information system, the relationships among the data flows, and how data come to be stored at specific locations. Data-flow diagrams also show the processes that change or transform data. Because data-flow diagrams concentrate on the movement of data between processes, these diagrams are called *process models*.

As the name indicates, a data-flow diagram is a graphical tool that allows analysts (and users) to show the flow of data in an information system. The system can be physical or logical, manual or computer based. In this chapter, you learn the mechanics of drawing and revising data-flow diagrams, as well as the basic symbols and set of rules for drawing them. We also alert you to pitfalls. You learn two important concepts related to data-flow diagrams: balancing and decomposition. At the end of the chapter, you learn how to use data-flow diagrams as part of the analysis of an information system and as a tool for supporting business process reengineering. You also are briefly introduced to a method for modeling the logic inside processes, decision tables.

FIGURE 6-1
Systems analysis, within the analysis phase of the systems development life cycle, we focus on structuring requirements in this chapter.

Process Modeling

Process modeling involves graphically representing the processes, or actions, that capture, manipulate, store, and distribute data between a system and its environment and among components within a system. A common form of a process model is a **data-flow diagram (DFD).** A data-flow diagram is a graphic that illustrates the movement of data between external entities and the processes and data stores within a system. Although several different tools have been developed for process modeling, we focus solely on data-flow diagrams because they are useful tools for process modeling.

Data-flow diagramming is one of several structured analysis techniques used to increase software development productivity. Although not all organizations use each structured analysis technique, collectively, these techniques, like data-flow diagrams, have had a significant impact on the quality of the systems development process.

Modeling a System's Process

The analysis team begins the process of structuring requirements with an abundance of information gathered during requirements determination. As part of structuring, you and the other team members must organize the information into a meaningful representation of the information system that exists and of the requirements desired in a replacement system. In addition to modeling the processing elements of an information system and transformation of data in the system, you must also model the structure of data within the system (which we review in Chapter 7). Analysts use both process and data models to establish the specification of an information system. With a supporting tool, such as a CASE tool, process and data models can also provide the basis for the automatic generation of an information system.

Deliverables and Outcomes

In structured analysis, the primary deliverables from process modeling are a set of coherent, interrelated data-flow diagrams. Table 6-1 lists the progression of deliverables that result from studying and documenting a system's process. First, a context data-flow diagram shows the scope of the system, indicating which elements are inside and outside the system. Second, data-flow diagrams of the current system specify which people and technologies are used in which processes to move and transform data, accepting inputs and producing outputs. The detail of these diagrams allows analysts to understand the current system and eventually to determine how to convert the current system into its replacement. Third, technology-independent, or logical, data-flow diagrams show the data-flow, structure, and functional requirements of the new system. Finally, entries for all of the objects in all diagrams are included in the project dictionary or CASE repository.

TABLE 6-1: Deliverables for Process Modeling

1. Context DFD
2. DFDs of current physical system
3. DFDs of new logical system
4. Thorough descriptions of each DFD component

This logical progression of deliverables helps you to understand the existing system. You can then reduce this system into its essential elements to show the way in which the new system should meet its information processing requirements, as they were identified during requirements determination. In later steps in the systems development life cycle, you and other project team members make decisions on exactly how the new system will deliver these new requirements in specific manual and automated functions. Because requirements determination and structuring are often parallel steps, data-flow diagrams evolve from the more general to the more detailed as current and replacement systems are better understood.

Even though data-flow diagrams remain popular tools for process modeling and can significantly increase software development productivity, they are not used in all systems development methodologies. Some organizations, such as EDS, have developed their own type of diagrams to model processes. Some methodologies, such as rapid application development (RAD), do not model processes separately at all. Instead, RAD builds processes—the work or actions that transform data so that they can be stored or distributed—into the prototypes created as the core of its development life cycle. However, even if you never formally use data-flow diagrams in your professional career, they remain a part of systems development's history. DFDs illustrate important concepts about the movement of data between manual and automated steps and are a way to depict work flow in an organization. DFDs continue to benefit information systems professionals as tools for both analysis and communication. For that reason, we devote this entire chapter to DFDs.

Data-Flow Diagramming Mechanics

Data-flow diagrams are versatile diagramming tools. With only four symbols, data-flow diagrams can represent both physical and logical information systems. The four symbols used in DFDs represent data flows, data stores, processes, and sources/sinks (or external entities). The set of four symbols we use in this book was developed by Gane and Sarson (1979) and is illustrated in Figure 6-2.

A data flow is data that are in motion and moving as a unit from one place in a system to another. A data flow could represent data on a customer order form or a payroll check. It could also represent the results of a query to a database, the contents of a printed report, or data on a data-entry computer display form. A data flow can be composed of many individual pieces of data that are generated at the same time and that flow together to common destinations.

FIGURE 6-2
Gane and Sarson identified four symbols to use in data-flow diagrams to represent the flow of data: data-flow symbol, data-store symbol, process symbol, and source/sink symbol. We use the Gane and Sarson symbols in this book.

Data store
Data at rest, which may take the form of many different physical representations.

Process
The work or actions performed on data so that they are transformed, stored, or distributed.

Source/sink
The origin and/or destination of data; sometimes referred to as external entities.

A **data store** is data at rest. A data store may represent one of many different physical locations for data, including a file folder, one or more computer-based file(s), or a notebook. To understand data movement and handling in a system, the physical configuration is not really important. A data store might contain data about customers, students, customer orders, or supplier invoices.

A **process** is the work or actions performed on data so that they are transformed, stored, or distributed. When modeling the data processing of a system, it doesn't matter whether a process is performed manually or by a computer.

Finally, a **source/sink** is the origin and/or destination of the data. Source/sinks are sometimes referred to as *external entities* because they are outside the system. Once processed, data or information leave the system and go to some other place. Because sources and sinks are outside the system we are studying, many of their characteristics are of no interest to us. In particular, we do not consider the following:

- Interactions that occur between sources and sinks

- What a source or sink does with information or how it operates (i.e., a source or sink is a "black box")

- How to control or redesign a source or sink because, from the perspective of the system we are studying, the data a sink receives and often what data a source provides are fixed

- How to provide sources and sinks direct access to stored data because, as external agents, they cannot directly access or manipulate data stored within the system; that is, processes within the system must receive or distribute data between the system and its environment

Definitions and Symbols

Among the DFD symbols presented in Figure 6-2, a data flow is depicted as an arrow. The arrow is labeled with a meaningful name for the data in motion; for example, *customer order*, *sales receipt*, or *paycheck*. The name represents the aggregation of all the individual elements of data moving as part of one packet, that is, all the data moving together at the same time. A rectangle or square is used for sources/sinks, and its name states what the external agent is, such as customer, teller, Environmental Protection Agency (EPA) office, or inventory control system. The symbol for a process is a rectangle with rounded corners. Inside the rectangle are written both the number of the process and a name, which indicates what the process does. For example, the process may generate paychecks, calculate overtime pay, or compute grade-point average. The symbol for a data store is a rectangle with the right vertical line missing. Its label includes the number of the data store (e.g., D1 or D2) and a meaningful label, such as *student file*, *transcripts*, or *roster of classes*.

As stated earlier, sources/sinks are always outside the information system and define the system's boundaries. Data must originate outside a system from one or more sources, and the system must produce information to one or more sinks. (These principles of open systems describe almost every information system.) If any data processing takes place inside the source/sink, we are not interested in it, because this processing takes place outside of the system we are diagramming. A source/sink might consist of the following:

- Another organization or organizational unit that sends data to or receives information from the system you are analyzing (e.g., a supplier or an academic department—in either case, this organization is external to the system you are studying)

- A person inside or outside the business unit supported by the system you are analyzing and who interacts with the system (e.g., a customer or a loan officer)
- Another information system with which the system you are analyzing exchanges information

Many times, students learning how to use DFDs become confused about whether a person or activity is a source/sink or a process within a system. This dilemma occurs most often when a system's data flow across office or departmental boundaries. In such a case, some processing occurs in one office, and the processed data are moved to another office, where additional processing occurs. Students are tempted to identify the second office as a source/sink to emphasize that the data have been moved from one physical location to another. Figure 6-3A illustrates an incorrectly drawn DFD showing a process, 3.0 Update Customer Master, as a source/sink, Accounting Department. The reference numbers "1.0" and "2.0" uniquely identify each process. D1 identifies the first data store in the diagram. However, we are not concerned with where the data are physically located. We are more interested in how they are moving through the system and how they are being processed. If the processing of data in the other office is part of your system, then you should represent the second office as one or more processes on your DFD. Similarly, if the work done in the second office might be redesigned to become part of the system you are analyzing,

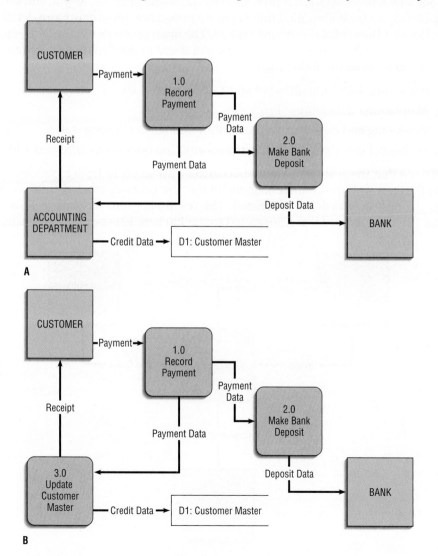

FIGURE 6-3
(A) An incorrectly drawn DFD showing a process as a source/sink,
(B) A DFD showing proper use of a process.

then that work should be represented as one or more processes on your DFD. However, if the processing that occurs in the other office takes place outside the system you are working on, then it should be a source/sink on your DFD. Figure 6-3B is a DFD showing proper use of a process.

Developing DFDs: An Example

Let's work through an example to see how DFDs are used to model the logic of data flows in information systems. Consider Hoosier Burger, a fictional fast-food restaurant in Bloomington, Indiana. Hoosier Burger is owned by Bob and Thelma Mellankamp and is a favorite of students at nearby Indiana University. Hoosier Burger uses an automated food-ordering system. The boundary or scope of this system, and the system's relationship to its environment, is represented by a data-flow diagram called a **context diagram.** A context diagram is shown in Figure 6-4. Notice that this context diagram contains only one process, no data stores, four data flows, and three sources/sinks. The single process, labeled "0," represents the entire system; all context diagrams have only one process labeled "0." The sources/sinks represent its environmental boundaries. Because the data stores of the system are conceptually inside the one process, no data stores appear on a context diagram.

After drawing the context diagram, the next step for the analyst is to think about which processes are represented by the single process. As you can see in Figure 6-5, we have identified four separate processes, providing more detail of the Hoosier Burger food-ordering system. The main processes in the DFD represent the major functions of the system, and these major functions correspond to such actions as the following:

1. Capturing data from different sources (Process 1.0)
2. Maintaining data stores (Processes 2.0 and 3.0)
3. Producing and distributing data to different sinks (Process 4.0)
4. High-level descriptions of data transformation operations (Process 1.0)

We see that the system in Figure 6-5 begins with an order from a customer, as was the case with the context diagram. In the first process, labeled "1.0," we see that the customer order is processed. The results are four streams or flows of data: (1) The food order is transmitted to the kitchen, (2) the customer order is

Context diagram
A data-flow diagram of the scope of an organizational system that shows the system boundaries, external entities that interact with the system, and the major information flows between the entities and the system.

FIGURE 6-4
A context diagram of Hoosier Burger's food-ordering system. The system includes one process (food-ordering system), four data flows (customer order, receipt, food order, management reports), and three sources/sinks (customer, kitchen, and restaurant manager).

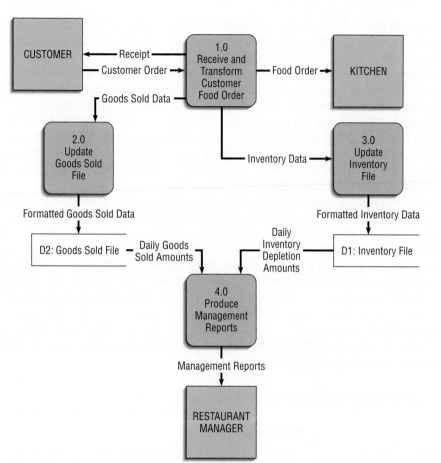

FIGURE 6-5
Four separate processes of the
Hoosier Burger food-ordering
system.

transformed into a list of goods sold, (3) the customer order is transformed into inventory data, and (4) the process generates a receipt for the customer.

Notice that the sources/sinks are the same in the context diagram (Figure 6-4) and in this diagram: the customer, the kitchen, and the restaurant's manager. A context diagram is a DFD that provides a general overview of a system. Other DFDs can be used to focus on the details of a context diagram. A **level-0 diagram,** illustrated in Figure 6-4, is an example of such a DFD. Compare the level of detail in Figure 6-5 with that of Figure 6-4. A level-0 diagram represents the primary individual processes in the system at the highest possible level of detail. Each process has a number that ends in .0 (corresponding to the level number of the DFD).

Two of the data flows generated by the first process, Receive and Transform Customer Food Order, go to external entities (Customer and Kitchen), so we no longer have to worry about them. We are not concerned about what happens outside of our system. Let's trace the flow of the data represented in the other two data flows. First, the data labeled Goods Sold go to Process 2.0, Update Goods Sold File. The output for this process is labeled Formatted Goods Sold Data. This output updates a data store labeled Goods Sold File. If the customer order were for two cheeseburgers, one order of fries, and a large soft drink, each of these categories of goods sold in the data store would be incremented appropriately. The Daily Goods Sold Amounts are then used as input to Process 4.0, Produce Management Reports. Similarly, the remaining data flow generated by Process 1.0, called Inventory Data, serves as input for Process 3.0, Update Inventory File. This process updates the Inventory File data store, based on the inventory that would have been used to create the customer order. For example, an order of two cheeseburgers would mean that Hoosier Burger now has two fewer hamburger patties, two fewer burger buns, and four fewer slices of

Level-0 diagram
A data-flow diagram that represents a system's major processes, data flows, and data stores at a high level of detail.

American cheese. The Daily Inventory Depletion Amounts are then used as input to Process 4.0. The data flow leaving Process 4.0, Management Reports, goes to the sink Restaurant Manager.

Figure 6-5 illustrates several important concepts about information movement. Consider the data flow Inventory Data moving from Process 1.0 to Process 3.0. We know from this diagram that Process 1.0 produces this data flow and that Process 3.0 receives it. However, we do not know the timing of when this data flow is produced, how frequently it is produced, or what volume of data is sent. Thus, this DFD hides many physical characteristics of the system it describes. We do know, however, that this data flow is needed by Process 3.0 and that Process 1.0 provides this needed data.

Also, implied by the Inventory Data data flow is that whenever Process 1.0 produces this flow, Process 3.0 must be ready to accept it. Thus, Processes 1.0 and 3.0 are coupled to each other. In contrast, consider the link between Process 2.0 and Process 4.0. The output from Process 2.0, Formatted Goods Sold Data, is placed in a data store and, later, when Process 4.0 needs such data, it reads Daily Goods Sold Amounts from this data store. In this case, Processes 2.0 and 4.0 are decoupled by placing a buffer, a data store (Goods Sold File), between them. Now, each of these processes can work at its own pace, and Process 4.0 does not have to be vigilant by being able to accept input at any time. Further, the Goods Sold File becomes a data resource that other processes could potentially draw upon for data.

TABLE 6-2: Rules Governing Data-Flow Diagramming

Process

A. No process can have only outputs. It is making data from nothing (a miracle). If an object has only outputs, then it must be a source.

B. No process can have only inputs (a black hole). If an object has only inputs, then it must be a sink.

C. A process has a verb-phrase label.

Data Store

D. Data cannot move directly from one data store to another data store. Data must be moved by a process.

E. Data cannot move directly from an outside source to a data store. Data must be moved by a process that receives data from the source and places the data into the data store.

F. Data cannot move directly to an outside sink from a data store. Data must be moved by a process.

G. A data store has a noun-phrase label.

Source/Sink

H. Data cannot move directly from a source to a sink. They must be moved by a process if the data are of any concern to our system. Otherwise, the data flow is not shown on the DFD.

I. A source/sink has a noun-phrase label.

Data Flow

J. A data flow has only one direction of flow between symbols. It may flow in both directions between a process and a data store to show a read before an update. The latter is usually indicated, however, by two separate arrows because the read and update usually happen at different times.

K. A fork in a data flow means that exactly the same data go from a common location to two or more different processes, data stores, or sources/sinks (it usually indicates different copies of the same data going to different locations).

L. A join in a data flow means that exactly the same data come from any of two or more different processes, data stores, or sources/sinks to a common location.

M. A data flow cannot go directly back to the same process it leaves. At least one other process must handle the data flow, produce some other data flow, and return the original data flow to the beginning process.

N. A data flow to a data store means update (delete or change).

O. A data flow from a data store means retrieve or use.

P. A data flow has a noun-phrase label. More than one data-flow noun phrase can appear on a single arrow as long as all of the flows on the same arrow move together as one package.

Source: Based on J. Celko, "I. Data Flow Diagrams," *Computer Language* 4 (January 1987), 41–43.

Data-Flow Diagramming Rules

You must follow a set of rules when drawing data-flow diagrams. These rules, listed in Table 6-2, allow you to evaluate DFDs for correctness. Figure 6-6 illustrates incorrect ways to draw DFDs and the corresponding correct application of the rules. The rules that prescribe naming conventions (rules C,

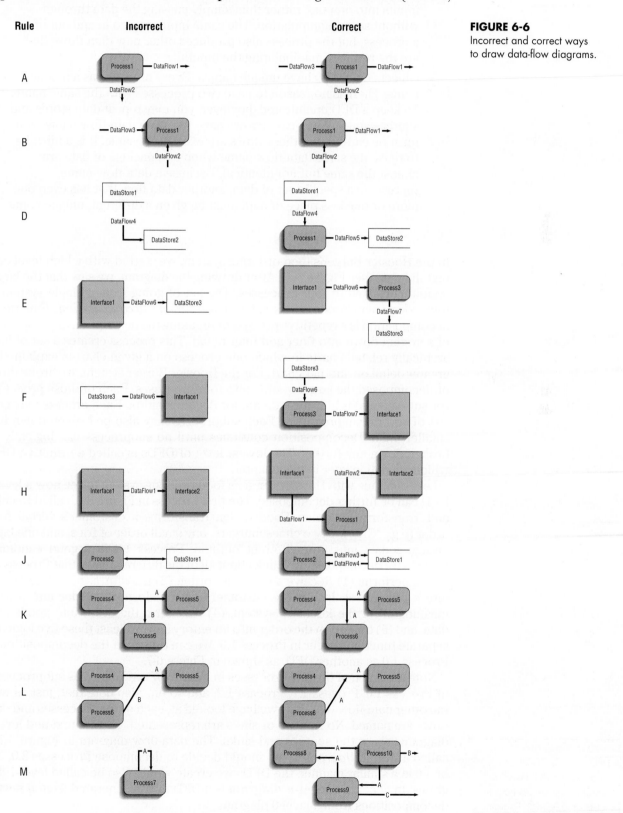

FIGURE 6-6
Incorrect and correct ways to draw data-flow diagrams.

G, I, and P in Table 6-2) and those that explain how to interpret data flows in and out of data stores (rules N and O in Table 6-2) are not illustrated in Figure 6-6. Besides the rules in Table 6-2, two DFD guidelines apply most of the time:

- The inputs to a process are different from the outputs of that process: The reason is that processes, to have a purpose, typically transform inputs into outputs, rather than simply passing the data through without some manipulation. The same input may go in and out of a process, but the process also produces other new data flows that are the result of manipulating the inputs.

- Objects on a DFD have unique names: Every process has a unique name. There is no reason to have two processes with the same name. To keep a DFD uncluttered, however, you may repeat data stores and sources/sinks. When two arrows have the same data-flow name, you must be careful that these flows are exactly the same. It is a mistake to reuse the same data-flow name when two packets of data are almost the same but not identical. Because a data-flow name represents a specific set of data, another data flow that has even one more or one less piece of data must be given a different, unique name.

Decomposition of DFDs

In the Hoosier Burger's food-ordering system, we started with a high-level context diagram (see Figure 6-4). After drawing the diagram, we saw that the larger system consisted of four processes. The act of going from a single system to four component processes is called *(functional) decomposition*. Functional decomposition is a repetitive process of breaking the description or perspective of a system down into finer and finer detail. This process creates a set of hierarchically related charts in which one process on a given chart is explained in greater detail on another chart. For the Hoosier Burger system, we broke down or decomposed the larger system into four processes. Each of those processes (or subsystems) is also a candidate for decomposition. Each process may consist of several subprocesses. Each subprocess may also be broken down into smaller units. Decomposition continues until no subprocess can logically be broken down any further. The lowest level of DFDs is called a primitive DFD, which we define later in this chapter.

Let's continue with Hoosier Burger's food-ordering system to see how a level-0 DFD can be further decomposed. The first process in Figure 6-5, called Receive and Transform Customer Food Order, transforms a customer's verbal food order (e.g., "Give me two cheeseburgers, one small order of fries, and one large orange soda") into four different outputs. Process 1.0 is a good candidate process for decomposition. Think about all of the different tasks that Process 1.0 has to perform: (1) Receive a customer order, (2) transform the entered order into a printed receipt for the customer, (3) transform the order into a form meaningful for the kitchen's system, (4) transform the order into goods sold data, and (5) transform the order into inventory data. At least these five logically separate functions occur in Process 1.0. We can represent the decomposition of Process 1.0 as another DFD, as shown in Figure 6-7.

Note that each of the five processes in Figure 6-7 are labeled as subprocesses of Process 1.0: Process 1.1, Process 1.2, and so on. Also note that, just as with the other data-flow diagrams we have looked at, each of the processes and data flows are named. No sources or sinks are represented. The context and level-0 diagrams show the sources and sinks. The data-flow diagram in Figure 6-7 is called a *level-1 diagram*. If we should decide to decompose Processes 2.0, 3.0, or 4.0 in a similar manner, the DFDs we create would also be called level-1 diagrams. In general, a **level-*n* diagram** is a DFD that is generated from *n* nested decompositions from a level-0 diagram.

Level-*n* diagram
A DFD that is the result of *n* nested decompositions of a series of subprocesses from a process on a level-0 diagram.

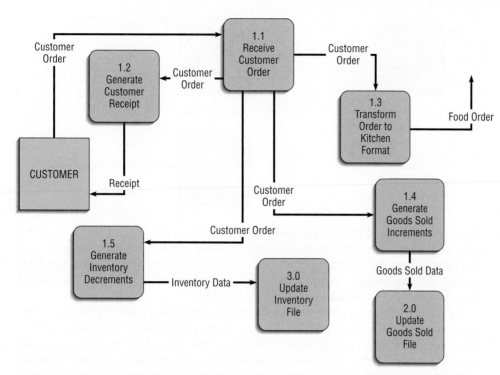

FIGURE 6-7
Level-1 DFD showing the decomposition of process 1.0 from the level-0 diagram for Hoosier Burger's food-ordering system.

Processes 2.0 and 3.0 perform similar functions in that they both use data input to update data stores. Because updating a data store is a singular logical function, neither of these processes needs to be decomposed further. We can, on the other hand, decompose Process 4.0, Produce Management Reports, into at least three subprocesses: Access Goods Sold and Inventory Data, Aggregate Goods Sold and Inventory Data, and Prepare Management Reports. The decomposition of Process 4.0 is shown in the level-1 diagram of Figure 6-8.

Each level-1, -2, or -*n* DFD represents one process on a level-(*n*-1) DFD; each DFD should be on a separate page. As a rule of thumb, no DFD should have more than about seven processes in it, because the diagram would be too crowded and difficult to understand.

To continue with the decomposition of Hoosier Burger's food-ordering system, we examine each of the subprocesses identified in the two level-1

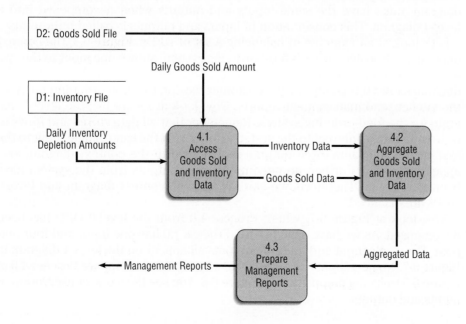

FIGURE 6-8
Level-1 diagram showing the decomposition of process 4.0 from the level-0 diagram for Hoosier Burger's food-ordering system.

FIGURE 6-9
Level-2 diagram showing the decomposition of process 4.3 from the level-1 diagram for process 4.0 for Hoosier Burger's food-ordering system.

diagrams, one for Process 1.0 and one for Process 4.0. To further decompose any of these subprocesses, we would create a level-2 diagram showing that decomposition. For example, if we decided to further decompose Process 4.3 in Figure 6-8, we would create a diagram that looks something like Figure 6-9. Again, notice how the subprocesses are labeled.

Just as the labels for processes must follow numbering rules for clear communication, process names should also be clear, yet concise. Typically, process names begin with an action verb, such as *receive, calculate, transform, generate,* or *produce.* Often process names are the same as the verbs used in many computer programming languages. Examples include *merge, sort, read, write,* and *print.* Process names should capture the essential action of the process in just a few words, yet be descriptive enough of the action of the process so that anyone reading the name gets a good idea of what the process does. Many times, students just learning DFDs will use the names of people who perform the process or the department in which the process is performed as the process name. This practice is not especially useful, because we are more interested in the action the process represents than the person performing it or the place where it occurs.

Balancing DFDs

When you decompose a DFD from one level to the next, a conservation principle is at work. You must conserve inputs and outputs to a process at the next level of decomposition. In other words, Process 1.0, which appears in a level-0 diagram, must have the same inputs and outputs when decomposed into a level-1 diagram. This conservation of inputs and outputs is called **balancing.**

Let's look at an example of balancing a set of DFDs. Figure 6-4, the context diagram for Hoosier Burger's food-ordering system, shows one input to the system, the customer order, which originates with the customer. Notice also the diagram shows three outputs: the customer receipt, the food order intended for the kitchen, and management reports. Now look at Figure 6-5, the level-0 diagram for the food-ordering system. Remember that all data stores and flows to or from them are internal to the system. Notice that the same single input to the system and the same three outputs represented in the context diagram also appear at level-0. Further, no new inputs to or outputs from the system have been introduced. Therefore, we can say that the context diagram and level-0 DFDs are balanced.

Now look at Figure 6-7, where Process 1.0 from the level-0 DFD has been decomposed. As we have seen before, Process 1.0 has one input and four outputs. The single input and multiple outputs all appear on the level-1 diagram in Figure 6-7. No new inputs or outputs have been added. Compare Process 4.0 in Figure 6-5 to its decomposition in Figure 6-8. You see the same conservation of inputs and outputs.

Balancing
The conservation of inputs and outputs to a data-flow diagram process when that process is decomposed to a lower level.

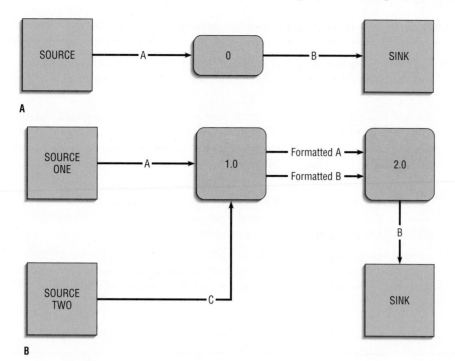

FIGURE 6-10
An unbalanced set of data-flow diagrams: (A) A context diagram, (B) A level-0 diagram.

Figure 6-10A shows you one example of what an unbalanced DFD could look like. Here, the context diagram contains one input to the system, A, and one output, B. Yet, in the level-0 diagram, Figure 6-10B, we see an additional input, C, and flows A and C come from different sources. These two DFDs are not balanced. If an input appears on a level-0 diagram, it must also appear on the context diagram. What happened in this example? Perhaps when drawing the level-0 DFD, the analyst realized that the system also needed C in order to compute B. A and C were both drawn in the level-0 DFD, but the analyst forgot to update the context diagram. In making corrections, the analyst should also include SOURCE ONE and SOURCE TWO on the context diagram. It is very important to keep DFDs balanced, from the context diagram all the way through each level of the diagram you must create.

A data flow consisting of several subflows on a level-n diagram can be split apart on a level-$n + 1$ diagram for a process that accepts this composite data flow as input. For example, consider the partial DFDs from Hoosier Burger illustrated in Figure 6-11. In Figure 6-11A, we see that the payment and coupon always flow together and are input to the process at the same time. In Figure 6-11B, the process is decomposed (sometimes called *exploded* or *nested*) into two subprocesses, and each subprocess receives one of the components of the

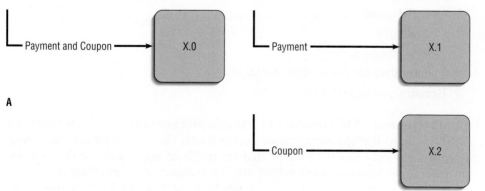

FIGURE 6-11
Example of a data-flow splitting: (A) Composite data flow, (B) Disaggregated data flows.

TABLE 6-3:   Advanced Rules Governing Data-Flow Diagramming

Q. A composite data flow on one level can be split into component data flows at the next level, but no new data can be added, and all data in the composite must be accounted for in one or more subflows.

R. The input to a process must be sufficient to produce the outputs (including data placed in data stores) from the process. Thus, all outputs can be produced, and all data in inputs move somewhere, either to another process or to a data store outside the process or on a more detailed DFD showing a decomposition of that process.

S. At the lowest level of DFDs, new data flows may be added to represent data that are transmitted under exceptional conditions; these data flows typically represent error messages (e.g., "Customer not known; do you want to create a new customer?") or confirmation notices (e.g., "Do you want to delete this record?").

T. To avoid having data-flow lines cross each other, you may repeat data store or sources/sinks on a DFD. Use an additional symbol, like a double line on the middle vertical line of a data-store symbol, or a diagonal line in a corner of a source/sink square, to indicate a repeated symbol.

Source: Based on J. Celko, "I. Data Flow Diagrams," *Computer Language* 4 (January 1987), 41–43.

composite data flow from the higher-level DFD. These diagrams are still balanced because exactly the same data are included in each diagram.

The principle of balancing and the goal of keeping a DFD as simple as possible lead to four additional, advanced, rules for drawing DFDs, summarized in Table 6-3. Rule Q covers the situation illustrated in Figure 6-11. Rule R covers a conservation principle about process inputs and outputs. Rule S addresses one exception to balancing. Rule T tells you how you can minimize clutter on a DFD.

Using Data-Flow Diagramming in the Analysis Process

Learning the mechanics of drawing data-flow diagrams is important to you because data-flow diagrams are essential tools for the structured analysis process. In addition to drawing DFDs that are mechanically correct, you must be concerned about whether the DFDs are complete and consistent across levels. You also need to consider how you can use them as a tool for analysis.

Guidelines for Drawing DFDs

In this section, we consider additional guidelines for drawing DFDs that extend beyond the simple mechanics of drawing diagrams and making sure that the rules listed in Tables 6-2 and 6-3 are followed. These additional guidelines include:

1. Completeness
2. Consistency
3. Timing considerations
4. The iterative nature of drawing DFDs
5. Drawing primitive DFDs

DFD completeness

The extent to which all necessary components of a data-flow diagram have been included and fully described.

Completeness   The concept of **DFD completeness** refers to whether your DFDs include all of the components necessary for the system you are modeling. If your DFD contains data flows that do not lead anywhere, or data stores, processes, or external entities that are not connected to anything else, your DFD is not complete. Most CASE tools have built-in facilities to help find incompleteness in your DFDs. When you draw many DFDs for a system, it is not uncommon to make errors; either CASE-tool analysis functions or walkthroughs with other analysts can help you identify such problems.

Not only must all necessary elements of a DFD be present, each of the components must be fully described in the project dictionary. For most CASE tools, when you define a process, data flow, source/sink, or data store on a DFD, an entry is automatically created in the tool's repository for that element. You must then enter the repository and complete the element's description. Different descriptive information can be kept about each of the four types of elements on a DFD, and each CASE tool has different entry information. A data-flow repository entry includes:

- The label or name for the data flow as entered on DFDs
- A short description defining the data flow
- A list of other repository objects grouped into categories by type of object
- The composition or list of data elements contained in the data flow
- Notes supplementing the limited space for the description that go beyond defining the data flow to explaining the context and nature of this repository object
- A list of locations (the names of the DFDs) on which this data flow appears and the names of the sources and destinations for the data flow on each of these DFDs

Consistency   The concept of **DFD consistency** refers to whether the depiction of the system shown at one level of a DFD is compatible with the depictions of the system shown at other levels. A gross violation of consistency would be a level-1 diagram with no level-0 diagram. Another example of inconsistency would be a data flow that appears on a higher-level DFD but not on lower levels (a violation of balancing). Yet, another example is a data flow attached to one object on a lower-level diagram but attached to another object at a higher level. For example, a data flow named Payment, which serves as input to Process 1 on a level-0 DFD, appears as input to Process 2.1 on a level-1 diagram for Process 2.

You can use the analysis facilities of CASE tools to detect such inconsistencies across nested (or decomposed) data-flow diagrams. For example, to avoid making DFD consistency errors when you draw a DFD using a CASE tool, most tools will automatically place the inflows and outflows of a process on the DFD you create when you inform the tool to decompose that process. In manipulating the lower-level diagram, you could accidentally delete or change a data flow, which would cause the diagrams to be out of balance; thus, a consistency check facility with a CASE tool is quite helpful.

Timing   You may have noticed in some of the DFD examples we have presented that DFDs do not do a good job of representing time. A given DFD provides no indication of whether a data flow occurs constantly in real time, once per week, or once per year. No indication of when a system would run is given either. For example, many large transaction-based systems may run several large, computing-intensive jobs in batch mode at night, when demands on the computer system are lighter. A DFD has no way of indicating such overnight batch processing. When you draw DFDs, then, draw them as if the system you are modeling has never started and will never stop.

Iterative Development   The first DFD you draw will rarely perfectly capture the system you are modeling. You should count on drawing the same diagram over and over again, in an iterative fashion. With each attempt, you will come closer to a good approximation of the system or aspect of the system you are

DFD consistency
The extent to which information contained on one level of a set of nested data-flow diagrams is also included on other levels.

modeling. Iterative DFD development recognizes that requirements determination and requirements structuring are interacting, not sequential, subphases of the analysis phase of the SDLC. One rule of thumb is that it should take you about three revisions for each DFD you draw. Fortunately, CASE tools make revising drawings a lot easier than if you had to draw each revision with pencil and template.

Primitive DFDs   One of the more difficult decisions you need to make when drawing DFDs is when to stop decomposing processes. One rule is to stop drawing when you have reached the lowest logical level; however, it is not always easy to know what the lowest logical level is. Other more concrete rules for when to stop decomposing are:

- When you have reduced each process to a single decision or calculation or to a single database operation, such as retrieve, update, create, delete, or read
- When each data store represents data about a single entity, such as a customer, employee, product, or order
- When the system user does not care to see any more detail, or when you and other analysts have documented sufficient detail to do subsequent systems development tasks
- When every data flow does not need to be split further to show that different data are handled in various ways
- When you believe that you have shown each business form or transaction, computer online display, and report as a single data flow (e.g., often means that each system display and report title corresponds to the name of an individual data flow)
- When you believe a separate process is shown for each choice on all lowest-level menu options

By the time you stop decomposing DFDs, a DFD can become quite detailed. Seemingly simple actions, such as generating an invoice, may pull information from several entities and may also return different results depending on the specific situation. For example, the final form of an invoice may be based on the type of customer (which would determine such things as discount rate), where the customer lives (which would determine such things as sales tax), and how the goods are shipped (which would determine such things as the shipping and handling charges). At the lowest-level DFD, called a **primitive DFD,** all of these conditions would have to be met. Given the amount of detail required in a primitive DFD, perhaps you can see why many experts believe analysts should not spend their time diagramming the current physical information system completely: much of the detail will be discarded when the current logical DFD is created.

Using these guidelines will help you create DFDs that are more than just mechanically correct. Your data-flow diagrams will also be robust and accurate representations of the information system you are modeling. Such primitive DFDs also facilitate consistency checks with the documentation produced from other requirements structuring techniques, as well as make it easy for you to transition to system design steps. Having mastered the skills of drawing good DFDs, you can now use them to support the analysis process, the subject of the next section.

Primitive DFD
The lowest level of decomposition for a data-flow diagram.

Using DFDs as Analysis Tools

We have seen that data-flow diagrams are versatile tools for process modeling and that they can be used to model both physical and logical systems. Data-flow diagrams can also be used for a process called **gap analysis.** In gap analysis, the analyst's role is to discover discrepancies between two or more sets of data-flow diagrams or discrepancies within a single DFD.

Once the DFDs are complete, examine the details of individual DFDs for such problems as redundant data flows, data that are captured but not used by the system, and data that are updated identically in more than one location. These problems may not have been evident to members of the analysis team or to other participants in the analysis process when the DFDs were created. For example, redundant data flows may have been labeled with different names when the DFDs were created. Now that the analysis team knows more about the system it is modeling, analysts can detect such redundancies. Many CASE tools can generate a report listing all the processes that accept a given data element as input (remember, a list of data elements is likely part of the description of each data flow). From the label of these processes, you can determine whether the data are captured redundantly or if more than one process is maintaining the same data stores. In such cases, the DFDs may accurately mirror the activities occurring in the organization. As the business processes being modeled took many years to develop, with participants in one part of the organization sometimes adapting procedures in isolation from other participants, redundancies and overlapping responsibilities may well have resulted. The careful study of the DFDs created as part of the analysis can reveal these procedural redundancies and allow them to be corrected as part of the system design.

A wide variety of inefficiencies can also be identified by studying DFDs. Some inefficiencies relate to violations of DFD drawing rules. Consider rule R from Table 6-3: The inputs to a process must be sufficient to produce the outputs from the process. A violation of rule R could occur because obsolete data are captured but never used within a system. Other inefficiencies are due to excessive processing steps. For example, consider the correct DFD in rule M of Figure 6-6: A data flow cannot go directly back to the same process it leaves. Although this flow is mechanically correct, such a loop may indicate potential delays in processing data or unnecessary approval operations.

Similarly, comparing a set of DFDs that models the current logical system to DFDs that model the new logical system can better determine which processes systems developers need to add or revise while building the new system. Processes for which inputs, outputs, and internal steps have not changed can possibly be reused in the construction of the new system. You can compare alternative logical DFDs to identify those few elements that must be discussed in evaluating competing opinions on system requirements. The logical DFDs for the new system can also serve as the basis for developing alternative design strategies for the new physical system. As we saw with the Hoosier Burger example, a process on a new logical DFD can be implemented in several different physical ways.

Using DFDs in Business Process Reengineering

Data-flow diagrams also make a useful tool for modeling processes in business process reengineering (BPR), which you read about in Chapter 5. To illustrate their usefulness, let's look at an example from M. Hammer and J. Champy, two experts of business redesign processes and authors of reengineering books. Hammer and Champy (1993) use IBM Credit Corporation as an example of a firm that successfully reengineered its primary business process. IBM Credit Corporation provides financing for customers making large purchases of IBM computer equipment. Its job is to analyze deals proposed by salespeople and write the final contracts governing those deals.

According to Hammer and Champy, IBM Credit Corporation typically took six business days to process each financing deal. The process worked like this: First,

Gap analysis
The process of discovering discrepancies between two or more sets of data-flow diagrams or discrepancies within a single DFD.

the salesperson called in with a proposed deal. The call was taken by one of six people sitting around a conference table. Whoever received the call logged it and wrote the details on a piece of paper. A clerk then carried the paper to a second person, who initiated the next step in the process by entering the data into a computer system and checking the client's creditworthiness. This person then wrote the details on a piece of paper and carried the paper, along with the original documentation, to a loan officer. In step 3, the loan officer modified the standard IBM loan agreement for the customer. This involved a separate computer system from the one used in step 2. Details of the modified loan agreement, along with the other documentation, were then sent on to the next station in the process, where a different clerk determined the appropriate interest rate for the loan. Step 4 also involved its own information system. In step 5, the interest rate from step 4 and all of the paper generated up to this point were then used to create the quote letter. Once complete, the quote letter was sent via overnight mail back to the salesperson.

Only reading about this process makes it seem complicated. We can use data-flow diagrams, as illustrated in Figure 6-12, to illustrate how the overall process worked. DFDs help us see that the process is not as complicated as it is tedious and wasteful, especially when you consider that so many different people and computer systems were used to support the work at each step.

According to Hammer and Champy, two IBM managers decided one day to see if they could improve the overall process at IBM Credit Corporation. They took a call from a salesperson and walked him through the system. These managers found that the actual work being done on a contract took only ninety minutes. For much of the rest of the six days it took to process the deal, the various bits of documentation were sitting in someone's in-basket, waiting to be processed.

IBM Credit Corporation management decided to reengineer its entire process. The five sets of task specialists were replaced with generalists. Now each call from the field comes to a single clerk, who does all the work necessary to process the contract. Instead of having different people check for creditworthiness, modify the basic loan agreement, and determine the

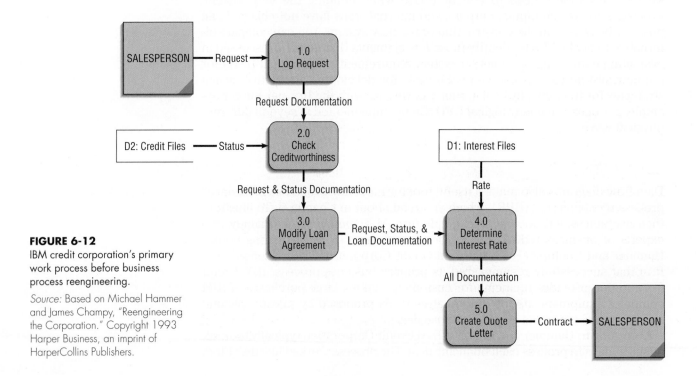

FIGURE 6-12
IBM credit corporation's primary work process before business process reengineering.

Source: Based on Michael Hammer and James Champy, "Reengineering the Corporation." Copyright 1993 Harper Business, an imprint of HarperCollins Publishers.

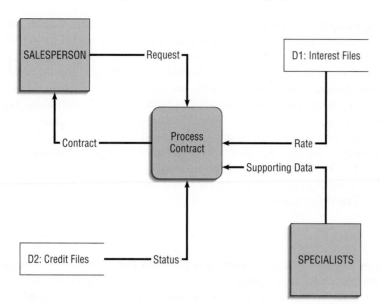

FIGURE 6-13
IBM credit corporation's primary work process after business process reengineering.

Source: Based on Michael Hammer and James Champy, "Reengineering the Corporation." Copyright 1993 Harper Business, an imprint of HarperCollins Publishers.

appropriate interest rate, now one person does it all. IBM Credit Corporation still has specialists for the few cases that are significantly different from what the firm routinely encounters. The process also uses a single supporting computer system. The new process is modeled by the DFD in Figure 6-13. The most striking difference between the DFDs in Figures 6-12 and 6-13, other than the number of process boxes in each one, is the lack of documentation flow in Figure 6-13. The resulting process is much simpler and cuts down dramatically on any chance of documentation getting lost between steps. Redesigning the process from beginning to end allowed IBM Credit Corporation to increase the number of contracts it could handle by a hundred fold—not 100 percent, which would only be doubling the amount of work. BPR allowed IBM Credit Corporation to handle a hundred times more work in the same amount of time and with fewer people!

Logic Modeling

Before we move on to logical methods for representing data, we first introduce the topic of logic modeling. Although data-flow diagrams are good for identifying processes, they do not show the logic inside the processes. Even the processes on the primitive-level data-flow diagrams do not show the most fundamental processing steps. Just what occurs within a process? How are the input data converted to the output information? Because data-flow diagrams are not really designed to show the detailed logic of processes, you must model process logic using other techniques.

Logic modeling involves representing the internal structure and functionality of the processes represented on data-flow diagrams. These processes appear on DFDs as little more than black boxes, in that we cannot tell from only their names precisely what they do and how they do it. Yet, the structure and functionality of a system's processes are a key element of any information system. Processes must be clearly described before they can be translated into a programming language.

We introduce you to a common method for modeling system logic. Decision tables allow you to represent in a tabular format a set of conditions and the actions that follow from them. When several conditions and several possible actions can occur, decision tables help you keep track of the possibilities in a clear and concise manner.

Creating diagrams of process logic is not an end in itself. Rather, these diagrams are created ultimately to serve as part of a clear and thorough explanation of the system's specifications. These specifications are used to explain the system requirements to developers, whether people or automated code generators. Users, analysts, and programmers use logic diagrams throughout analysis to incrementally specify a shared understanding of requirements. Logic diagrams do not take into account specific programming languages or development environments. Such diagrams may be discussed during JAD sessions or project review meetings. Alternatively, system prototypes generated from such diagrams may be reviewed, and requested changes to a prototype will be implemented by changing logic diagrams and generating a new prototype from a CASE tool or other code generator.

Modeling Logic with Decision Tables

Decision table

A matrix representation of the logic of a decision, which specifies the possible conditions for the decision and the resulting actions.

Condition stubs

That part of a decision table that lists the conditions relevant to the decision.

Action stubs

That part of a decision table that lists the actions that result for a given set of conditions.

Rules

That part of a decision table that specifies which actions are to be followed for a given set of conditions.

Sometimes the logic of a process can become quite complex. Research has shown, for example, that people become confused in trying to interpret more than three nested IF statements. A **decision table** is a diagram of process logic where the logic is reasonably complicated. All of the possible choices and the conditions the choices depend on are represented in tabular form, as illustrated in the decision table in Figure 6-14.

The decision table in Figure 6-14 models the logic of a generic payroll system. The three parts to the table include the **condition stubs,** the **action stubs,** and the **rules.** The condition stubs contain the various conditions that apply in the situation the table is modeling. In Figure 6-14, two condition stubs correspond to employee type and hours worked. Employee type has two values: "S," which stands for salaried, and "H," which stands for hourly. Hours worked has three values: less than 40, exactly 40, and more than 40. The action stubs contain all the possible courses of action that result from combining values of the condition stubs. Four possible courses of action are indicated in this table: pay base salary, calculate hourly wage, calculate overtime, and produce Absence Report. You can see that not all actions are triggered by all combinations of conditions. Instead, specific combinations trigger specific actions. The part of the table that links conditions to actions is the section that contains the rules.

To read the rules, start by reading the values of the conditions as specified in the first column: Employee type is "S," or salaried, and hours worked are less than 40. When both of these conditions occur, the payroll system is to pay the base salary. In the next column, the values are "H" and "<40," meaning an hourly worker who worked fewer than 40 hours. In such a situation, the payroll system calculates the hourly wage and makes an entry in the Absence Report. Rule 3 addresses the situation when a salaried employee works exactly 40 hours. The system pays the base salary, as was the case for rule 1. For an hourly worker who has worked exactly 40 hours, rule 4 calculates the hourly wage. Rule 5 pays the

FIGURE 6-14
Complete decision table for payroll system example.

Conditions/ Courses of Action		Rules					
		1	2	3	4	5	6
Condition Stubs	Employee type	S	H	S	H	S	H
	Hours worked	< 40	< 40	40	40	> 40	> 40
Action Stubs	Pay base salary	X		X		X	
	Calculate hourly wage		X		X		X
	Calculate overtime						X
	Produce Absence Report		X				

base salary for salaried employees who work more than 40 hours. Rule 5 has the same action as rules 1 and 3 and governs behavior with regard to salaried employees. The number of hours worked does not affect the outcome for rules 1, 3, or 5. For these rules, hours worked is an **indifferent condition,** in that its value does not affect the action taken. Rule 6 calculates hourly pay and overtime for an hourly worker who has worked more than 40 hours.

Because of the indifferent condition for rules 1, 3, and 5, we can reduce the number of rules by condensing rules 1, 3, and 5 into one rule, as shown in Figure 6-15. The indifferent condition is represented with a dash. Whereas we started with a decision table with six rules, we now have a simpler table that conveys the same information with only four rules.

In constructing these decision tables, we have actually followed a set of basic procedures, as follows:

1. *Name the conditions and the values each condition can assume.* Determine all of the conditions that are relevant to your problem, and then determine all of the values each condition can take. For some conditions, the values will be simply "yes" or "no" (called a *limited entry*). For others, such as the conditions in Figures 6-14 and 6-15, the conditions may have more values (called an *extended entry*).

2. *Name all possible actions that can occur.* The purpose of creating decision tables is to determine the proper course of action given a particular set of conditions.

3. *List all possible rules.* When you first create a decision table, you have to create an exhaustive set of rules. Every possible combination of conditions must be represented. It may turn out that some of the resulting rules are redundant or make no sense, but these determinations should be made only after you have listed every rule so that no possibility is overlooked. To determine the number of rules, multiply the number of values for each condition by the number of values for every other condition. In Figure 6-14, we have two conditions, one with two values and one with three, so we need 2×3, or 6, rules. If we added a third condition with three values, we would need $2 \times 3 \times 3$, or 18, rules.

When creating the table, alternate the values for the first condition, as we did in Figure 6-14 for type of employee. For the second condition, alternate the values but repeat the first value for all values of the first condition, then repeat the second value for all values of the first condition, and so on. You essentially follow this procedure for all subsequent conditions. Notice how we alternated the values of hours worked in Figure 6-14. We repeated "<40" for both values of type of employee, "S" and "H." Then we repeated "40," and then ">40."

Indifferent condition
In a decision table, a condition whose value does not affect which actions are taken for two or more rules.

Conditions/	Rules			
Courses of Action	1	2	3	4
Employee type	S	H	H	H
Hours worked	–	< 40	40	> 40
Pay base salary	X			
Calculate hourly wage		X	X	X
Calculate overtime				X
Produce Absence Report		X		

FIGURE 6-15
Reduced decision table for payroll system example.

4. *Define the actions for each rule.* Now that all possible rules have been identified, provide an action for each rule. In our example, we were able to figure out what each action should be and whether all of the actions made sense. If an action doesn't make sense, you may want to create an "impossible" row in the action stubs in the table to keep track of impossible actions. If you can't tell what the system ought to do in that situation, place question marks in the action stub spaces for that particular rule.

5. *Simplify the decision table.* Make the decision table as simple as possible by removing any rules with impossible actions. Consult users on the rules where system actions aren't clear, and either decide on an action or remove the rule. Look for patterns in the rules, especially for indifferent conditions. We were able to reduce the number of rules in the payroll example from six to four, but often greater reductions are possible.

Let's look at an example from Hoosier Burger. The Mellankamps are trying to determine how they reorder food and other items they use in the restaurant. If they are going to automate the inventory control functions at Hoosier Burger, they need to articulate their reordering process. In thinking through the problem, the Mellankamps realize that how they reorder depends on whether the item is perishable. If an item is perishable, such as meat, vegetables, or bread, the Mellankamps have a standing order with a local supplier stating that a prespecified amount of food is delivered each weekday for that day's use and each Saturday for weekend use. If the item is not perishable, such as straws, cups, and napkins, an order is placed when the stock on hand reaches a certain predetermined minimum reorder quantity. The Mellankamps also realize the importance of the seasonality of their work. Hoosier Burger's business is not as good during the summer months when the students are off-campus as it is during the academic year. They also note that business falls off during Christmas and spring breaks. Their standing orders with all their suppliers are reduced by specific amounts during the summer and holiday breaks. Given this set of conditions and actions, the Mellankamps put together an initial decision table (see Figure 6-16).

Three things are distinctive about Figure 6-16. First, the values for the third condition repeat, providing a distinctive pattern for relating the values for all three conditions to one another. Every possible rule is clearly provided in this table. Second, there are 12 rules. Two values for the first condition (type of item)

FIGURE 6-16
Complete decision table for Hoosier Burger's inventory reordering system.

Conditions/ Courses of Action	Rules											
	1	2	3	4	5	6	7	8	9	10	11	12
Type of item	P	N	P	N	P	N	P	N	P	N	P	N
Time of week	D	D	W	W	D	D	W	W	D	D	W	W
Season of year	A	A	A	A	S	S	S	S	H	H	H	H
Standing daily order	X				X				X			
Standing weekend order			X				X				X	
Minimum order quantity		X		X		X		X		X		X
Holiday reduction									X		X	
Summer reduction					X		X					

Type of item:
P = perishable
N = nonperishable

Time of week:
D = weekday
W = weekend

Season of year:
A = academic year
S = summer
H = holiday

Conditions/ Courses of Action	Rules						
	1	2	3	4	5	6	7
Type of item	P	P	P	P	P	P	N
Time of week	D	W	D	W	D	W	–
Season of year	A	A	S	S	H	H	–
Standing daily order	X		X		X		
Standing weekend order		X		X		X	
Minimum order quantity							X
Holiday reduction					X	X	
Summer reduction			X	X			

FIGURE 6-17
Reduced decision table for Hoosier Burger's inventory reordering system.

times two values for the second condition (time of week) times three values for the third condition (season of year) equals 12 possible rules. Third, the action for nonperishable items is the same, regardless of the day of the week or the time of year. For nonperishable goods, both time-related conditions are indifferent. Collapsing the decision table accordingly gives us the decision table in Figure 6-17. Now it contains only 7 rules instead of 12.

You have now learned how to draw and simplify decision tables. You can also use decision tables to specify additional decision-related information. For example, if the actions that should be taken for a specific rule are more complicated than one or two lines of text can convey, or if some conditions need to be checked only when other conditions are met (nested conditions), you may want to use separate, linked decision tables. In your original decision table, you can specify an action in the action stub that says "Perform Table B." Table B could contain an action stub that returns to the original table, and the return would be the action for one or more rules in Table B. Another way to convey more information in a decision table is to use numbers that indicate sequence rather than Xs where rules and action stubs intersect. For example, for rules 3 and 4 in Figure 6-17, it would be important for the Mellankamps to account for the summer reduction to modify the existing standing order for supplies. "Summer reduction" would be marked with a "1" for rules 3 and 4, whereas "standing daily order" would be marked with a "2" for rule 3, and "standing weekend order" would be marked with a "2" for rule 4.

You have seen how decision tables can model the relatively complicated logic of a process. Decision tables are useful for representing complicated logic in that they convey information in a tabular rather than a linear, sequential format. As such, decision tables are compact; you can pack a lot of information into a small table. Decision tables also allow you to check for the extent to which your logic is complete, consistent, and not redundant.

Pine Valley Furniture WebStore: Process Modeling

In the last chapter, you read how Pine Valley Furniture determined the system requirements for its WebStore project—a project to sell furniture products over the Internet. In this section, we analyze the WebStore's high-level system structure and develop a level-0 DFD for those requirements.

PINE
VALLEY
FURNITURE

Process Modeling for Pine Valley Furniture's WebStore

After completing the JAD session, senior systems analyst Jim Woo went to work on translating the WebStore system structure into a data-flow diagram. His first step was to identify the level-0—major system—processes. To begin, he

TABLE 6-4:   System Structure of the WebStore and Corresponding Level-0 Processes

WebStore System	Processes
Main page	Information display (minor/no processes)
Product line (Catalog)	1.0 Browse Catalog
• Desks	2.0 Select Item for Purchase
• Chairs	
• Tables	
• File cabinets	
Shopping cart	3.0 Display Shopping Cart
Checkout	4.0 Check Out/Process Order
Account profile	5.0 Add/Modify Account Profile
Order status/history	6.0 Order Status Request
Customer comments	Information display (minor/no processes)
Company information	
Feedback	
Contact information	

carefully examined the outcomes of the JAD session that focused on defining the system structure of the WebStore. From this analysis, he identified six high-level processes that would become the foundation of the level-0 DFD. These processes, listed in Table 6-4, were the "work" or "action" parts of the Web site; note that these processes correspond to the major processing items listed in the system structure.

Next, Jim determined that it would be most efficient if the WebStore system exchanged information with existing PVF systems rather than capturing and storing redundant information. This analysis concluded that the Web-Store should exchange information with the Purchasing Fulfillment System—a system for tracking orders (discussed in Chapter 3)—and the Customer Tracking System (discussed in Chapter 4). These two existing systems will be "sources" (providers) and "sinks" (receivers) of information for the WebStore system. When a customer opens an account, his or her information will be passed from the WebStore system to the Customer Tracking System. When an order is placed (or when a customer requests status information on a prior order), information will be stored in and retrieved from the Purchasing Fulfillment System.

Finally, Jim found that the system would need to access two additional data sources. First, in order to produce an online product catalog, the system would need to access the inventory database. Second, to store the items a customer wants to purchase in the WebStore's shopping cart, a temporary database would need to be created. Once the transaction was completed, the shopping cart data could be deleted. With this information, Jim was then able to develop the level-0 DFD for the WebStore system, shown in Figure 6-18. He understood how information would flow through the WebStore, how a customer would interact with the system, and how the WebStore would share information with existing PVF systems.

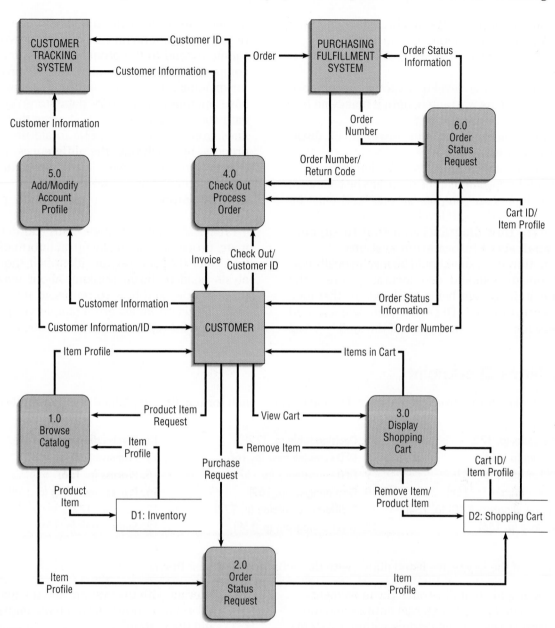

FIGURE 6-18
Level-0 DFD for the WebStore system.

Key Points Review

Data-flow diagrams, or DFDs, are useful for representing the overall data flows into, through, and out of an information system. Data-flow diagrams rely on only four symbols to represent the four conceptual components of a process model: data flows, data stores, processes, and sources/sinks.

1. **Understand the logical modeling of processes through studying examples of data-flow diagrams.**

   Data-flow diagrams are hierarchical in nature, and each level of a DFD can be decomposed into smaller, simpler units on a lower-level diagram. You begin with a context diagram, which shows the entire system as a single process. The next step

is to generate a level-0 diagram, which shows the most important high-level processes in the system.

2. **Draw data-flow diagrams following specific rules and guidelines that lead to accurate and well-structured process models.**

   Several rules govern the mechanics of drawing DFDs. These are listed in Tables 6-2 and 6-3 and many are illustrated in Figure 6-6. Most of these rules are about the ways in which data can flow from one place to another within a DFD.

3. **Decompose data-flow diagrams into lower-level diagrams.**

   Starting with a level-0 diagram, decompose each process, as warranted, until it makes no logical sense to go any further.

4. **Balance higher-level and lower-level data-flow diagrams.**

   When decomposing DFDs from one level to the next, it is important that the diagrams be balanced; that is, inputs and outputs on one level must be conserved on the next level.

5. **Use data-flow diagrams as a tool to support the analysis of information systems.**

   Data-flow diagrams should be mechanically correct, but they should also accurately reflect the information system being modeled. To that end, you need to check DFDs for completeness and consistency and draw them as if the system being

modeled were timeless. You should be willing to revise DFDs several times. Complete sets of DFDs should extend to the primitive level where every component reflects certain irreducible properties; for example, a process represents a single database operation, and every data store represents data about a single entity. Following these guidelines, you can produce DFDs to aid the analysis process by analyzing the differences between existing procedures and desired procedures and between current and new systems.

6. **Use decision tables to represent process logic.**

   Process modeling helps isolate and define the many processes that make up an information system. Once the processes are identified, though, analysts need to begin thinking about what each process does and how to represent that internal logic. Decision tables are a simple yet powerful technique for representing process logic.

Key Terms Checkpoint

Here are the key terms from the chapter. The page where each term is first explained is in parentheses after the term.

1. Action stubs (p. 172)	7. Decision table (p. 172)	13. Level-*n* diagram (p. 162)
2. Balancing (p. 164)	8. DFD completeness (p. 166)	14. Primitive DFD (p. 168)
3. Condition stubs (p. 172)	9. DFD consistency (p. 167)	15. Process (p. 156)
4. Context diagram (p. 158)	10. Gap analysis (p. 169)	16. Process modeling (p. 154)
5. Data-flow diagram (DFD) (p. 154)	11. Indifferent condition (p. 173)	17. Rules (p. 172)
6. Data store (p. 156)	12. Level-0 diagram (p. 159)	18. Source/sink (p. 156)

Match each of the key terms listed above with the definition that best fits it.

_____ 1. A graphic that illustrates the movement of data between external entities and the processes and data stores within a system.

_____ 2. The conservation of inputs and outputs to a data-flow diagram process when that process is decomposed to a lower level.

_____ 3. That part of a decision table that lists the conditions relevant to the decision.

_____ 4. A data-flow diagram that represents a system's major processes, data flows, and data stores at a high level of detail.

_____ 5. The origin and/or destination of data; sometimes referred to as external entities.

_____ 6. In a decision table, a condition whose value does not affect which actions are taken for two or more rules.

_____ 7. A data-flow diagram of the scope of an organizational system that shows the system boundaries, external entities that

interact with the system, and the major information flows between the entities and the system.

_____ 8. The lowest level of decomposition for a data-flow diagram.

_____ 9. The extent to which all necessary components of a data-flow diagram have been included and fully described.

_____ 10. A matrix representation of the logic of a decision, which specifies the possible conditions for the decision and the resulting actions.

_____ 11. The extent to which information contained on one level of a set of nested data-flow diagrams is also included on other levels.

_____ 12. A DFD that is the result of *n* nested decompositions of a series of subprocesses from a process on a level-0 diagram.

____ 13. The work or actions performed on data so that they are transformed, stored, or distributed.

____ 14. That part of a decision table that specifies which actions are to be followed for a given set of conditions.

____ 15. Data at rest, which may take the form of many different physical representations.

____ 16. Graphically representing the processes that capture, manipulate, store, and

distribute data between a system and its environment and among components within a system.

____ 17. The process of discovering discrepancies between two or more sets of data-flow diagrams or discrepancies within a single DFD.

____ 18. That part of a decision table that lists the actions that result for a given set of conditions.

Review Questions

1. What is a data-flow diagram? Why do systems analysts use data-flow diagrams?
2. Explain the rules for drawing good data-flow diagrams.
3. What is decomposition? What is balancing? How can you determine if DFDs are not balanced?
4. Explain the convention for naming different levels of data-flow diagrams.
5. How can data-flow diagrams be used as analysis tools?
6. Explain the guidelines for deciding when to stop decomposing DFDs.
7. How do you decide whether a system component should be represented as a source/sink or as a process?
8. What unique rules apply to drawing context diagrams?
9. Explain what the term *DFD consistency* means and provide an example.
10. Explain what the term *DFD completeness* means and provide an example.
11. How well do DFDs illustrate timing considerations for systems? Explain your answer.
12. How can data-flow diagrams be used in business process reengineering?
13. What are the steps in creating a decision table? How do you reduce the size and complexity of a decision table?
14. What formula is used to calculate the number of rules a decision table must cover?

Problems and Exercises

1. Using the example of an online cell phone apps store, list relevant data flows, data stores, processes, and sources/sinks. Draw a context diagram and a level-0 diagram that represent the apps store. Explain why you chose certain elements as processes versus sources/sinks.
2. Using the example of checking out a book from your university or college library, draw a context diagram and a level-0 diagram.
3. Evaluate your level-0 DFD from Problem and Exercise 2 using the rules for drawing DFDs in this chapter. Edit your DFD so that it does not break any of these rules.
4. Choose an example like that in Problem and Exercise 2, and draw a context diagram. Decompose this diagram until it doesn't make sense to continue. Be sure that your diagrams are balanced, as discussed in this chapter.
5. Refer to Figure 6-19, which contains drafts of a context and level-0 DFD for a university class

registration system. Identify and explain potential violations of rules and guidelines on these diagrams.
6. What is the benefit of creating multiple levels of DFDs? Consider the concept of DFD consistency, as described on page 167. Why is consistency important to take advantage of the multiple levels of DFDs that may be created?
7. Why do you think analysts have different types of diagrams and other documentation to depict different views (e.g., process, logic, and data) of an information system?
8. Consider the DFD in Figure 6-20. List three errors (rule violations) on this DFD.
9. Consider the three DFDs in Figure 6-21. List three errors (rule violations) on these DFDs.
10. Starting with a context diagram, draw as many nested DFDs as you consider necessary to represent all of the details of the patient flow management system described in the following narrative.

FIGURE 6-19
Context and level-0 DFDs for a
university class registration system.

A

B

FIGURE 6-20

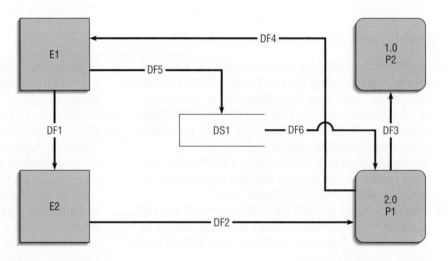

You must draw at least a context diagram and a
level-0 diagram. In drawing these diagrams, if you
discover that the narrative is incomplete, make
up reasonable explanations to complete the story.
Provide these extra explanations along with the
diagrams.

Dr. Frank's walk-in clinic has decided to go pa-
perless and will use an information system to
help move patients through the clinic as efficiently as possible. Patients are entered into the
system by the front desk personnel. If this is the
first time the patient has been seen, insurance

Level 0

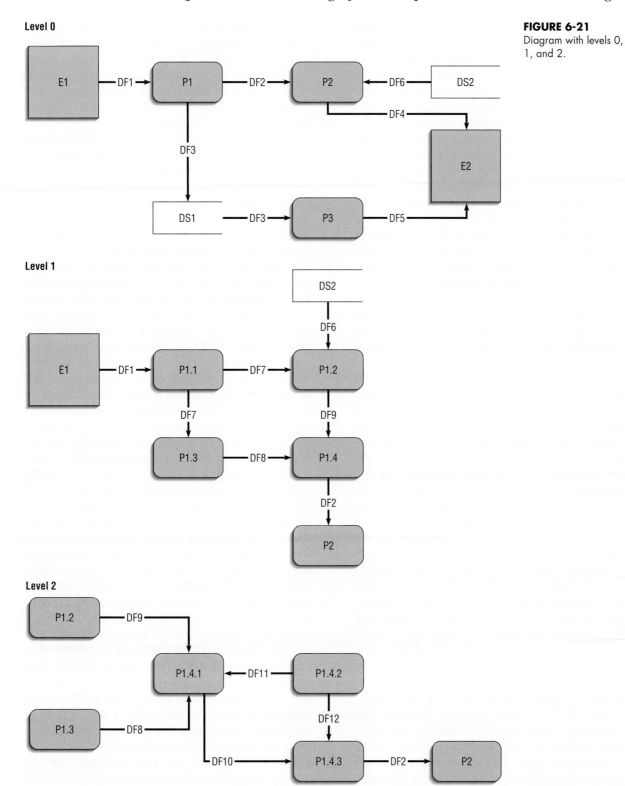

FIGURE 6-21
Diagram with levels 0, 1, and 2.

and basic demographic information is collected from the patient. If the patient has been seen previously, the patient is asked to verify the information. The front desk person then ensures that the patient has a chart in the electronic medical records system; if not, a new medical record is started. The patient is then entered into a queue to wait for a medical technician who will collect health history, weight, height, temperature, blood pressure, and other medical information, placing it into the patient's medical record. Next, the patient is placed into the queue to see a doctor. The first available doctor sees the patient, prescribes medication or treatment when appropriate, and sends the patient to checkout. The person at checkout collects the payment for the services, prints out any prescriptions for medications or treatments, and provides a printed record of the health services received.

11. a. Starting with a context diagram, draw as many nested DFDs as you consider necessary to represent all of the details of the engineering document management system described in the following narrative. You must draw at least a context diagram and a level-0 diagram. In drawing these diagrams, if you discover that the narrative is incomplete, make up reasonable explanations to complete the story. Provide these extra explanations along with the diagrams.

Projects, Inc. is an engineering firm with approximately 500 engineers that provide mechanical engineering assistance to organizations, which requires managing many documents. Projects, Inc. is known for its strong emphasis on change management and quality assurance procedures. The customer provides detailed information when requesting a document through a web portal. The company liaison (a position within Projects, Inc.) assigns an engineer to write the first draft of the requested document. Upon completion, two peer engineers review the document to ensure that it is correct and meets the requirements. These reviewers may require changes or may approve the document as is. The original engineer updates the document until the reviewers are satisfied with the quality of the document. The document is then sent to the company liaison, who performs a final quality check and ensures that the document meets the requirements specified by the customer. Finally, the customer liaison sends the document to the customer for approval. The customer can require changes or accept the document. When the customer requires changes, the company liaison assigns an engineer to make the changes to the document. When those changes are made, two other engineers must review them. When those reviewers are satisfied with the changes, the document is sent back to the company liaison, who sends the document back to the customer. This may happen through several iterations until the customer is satisfied with the document.

b. Analyze the DFDs you created in part a. What recommendations for improvements can you make based on this analysis? Draw new logical DFDs that represent the requirements you would suggest for an improved document management system. Remember, these are to be logical DFDs, so consider improvements independent of technology that can be used to support the management of these documents.

12. A company has various rules for how payments to suppliers are to be authorized. Some payments are in response to an approved purchase order. For approved purchase orders under $5,000, the accounting clerk can immediately issue a check against that purchase order and sign the check. For approved purchase orders between $5,000 and $10,000, the accounting clerk can immediately issue a check but must additionally obtain a second signature. Payments for approved purchase orders over $10,000 always require the approval of the accounting manager to issue the check as well as the signature of two accounting clerks. Payments that are not covered by a purchase order that are under $5,000 must be approved by the accounting manager and a departmental manager that will absorb the cost of the payment into that department's budget. Such checks can be signed by a single accounting clerk. Payments that are not covered by a purchase order that are between $5,000 and $10,000 must be approved by the accounting manager and a departmental manager, and the check must have two signatures. Finally, payments exceeding $10,000 that are not covered by a purchase order must be approved by a department manager, the accounting manager, and the chief financial officer. Such checks require two signatures. Use a decision table to represent the logic in this process. Write down any assumptions you have to make.

13. A relatively small company that sells eyeglasses to the public wants to incentivize its sales staff to sell customers higher quality frames, lenses, and options. To do this, the company has decided to pay the sales representatives based on a percentage of the profit earned on the glasses. All sales representatives will earn 15% of the profit on the eyeglasses. However, the owners are concerned that the sales staff will fear earning less than they do now. Therefore, those who were already working at the company are grandfathered into an arrangement where the workers are guaranteed to earn at least their base salary. Newly hired employees, however, are guaranteed only minimum wage based on the hours worked. To ensure only productive employees are retained, employees who are underperforming for three months in a row are automatically terminated. For those employees who are grandfathered in, any month where the representative earns only the salary is

considered underperforming. For newer employees, the bottom quarter of the employees based on profit earned per hour worked are considered underperforming. Use a decision table to represent the logic in this process. Write down any assumptions you have to make.

14. A large technology company receives thousands of applications per day from software engineers who hope to work for that company. To help manage the constant flow of applications, a process has been created to streamline identifying applicants for specific openings as they occur. Those applications that are not in an approved file format are discarded and not processed in any way. All applications are first fact-checked automatically by detecting any inconsistencies with the application and the résumé, as well as other résumé sites available online. For any applications with more than one inconsistency, the application is automatically rejected as untruthful. Next, the application is checked against the database of other applications already in the system. If such an application exists, the older application is purged and the new application continues processing. Any applications that do not contain at least fifteen of the top 200 keywords that the company is looking for are rejected. Next, the phone numbers of references are checked to ensure they are a valid, working phone number. These applicants are then retained in a searchable database. When managers send a hiring request, the fifty best applications that most closely match the desired attributes are sent to the manager. That manager selects the top ten applications, which are then screened for bad credit, with credit scores below 500 eliminated from the hiring process. If there are at least five remaining candidates, they are all invited to participate in phone interviews. If there are fewer than five remaining candidates, the next ten best matches are added to the pool and screened for poor credit, and any remaining candidates are invited to participate in phone interviews. Present this logic in a decision table. Write down any assumptions you have to make.

15. A huge retail store must carefully manage its inventory levels. Stock-outs (where there is none of an item on a shelf) can cause missed sales, while too much inventory costs the company money in storage, ties up capital, and carries the risk of the products losing value. To balance these requirements, the store has chosen to use just-in-time ordering. To accomplish this, reorders are automatically generated by an information system (called the reorder system). Each item has a floor value, which is the fewest units of an item that should be in the store at all times, as well as a ceiling value, which is the maximum number of units that can be stored on the allocated shelf space. Vendors are required to commit to delivering product in either two days or one week. For vendors of the two-day plan, the reorder system calculates the amount of product purchased by customers in the past week, doubles the quantity, and then adds to the inventory floor. The quantity on hand is then subtracted. This is the desired order quantity. If this quantity added to the current inventory is greater than the ceiling, then the order quantity is reduced to the ceiling value less on-hand quantity. If the desired order quantity is greater than the sales for the previous month, a special report is generated and provided to management and the order must be approved before being sent to the vendor. All other orders are automatically placed with the vendor. However, if a product experiences a stock-out, an emergency order is automatically generated for the ceiling amount or the quantity sold in the last month, whichever is less. For vendors on the one-week plan, the reorder system calculates the amount of inventory sold in the last two weeks, doubles the quantity, and then adds to the floor to create the desired stock level. If this level is greater than the ceiling, the desired stock level is lowered to the ceiling and a report is generated for management to determine if more space should be allocated. The on-hand stock is subtracted from the desired stock level, yielding the desired order level. If the desired order level is greater than the number of units sold in the last two months, a special report is generated and provided to management and the order must be approved before being sent to the vendor. All other orders are automatically placed with the vendor. However, if a product experiences a stock-out, an emergency order is automatically generated for the ceiling amount or the quantity sold in the last month, whichever is less. Present this logic in a decision table. Write down any assumptions you have to make.

Discussion Questions

1. Discuss the importance of diagramming tools for process modeling. Without such tools, what would an analyst do to model diagrams?

2. Think and write about how data-flow diagrams might be modified to allow for time considerations to be adequately incorporated.

3. How would you answer someone who told you that data-flow diagrams were too simple and took too long to draw to be of much use? What if they also said that keeping data-flow diagrams up to date took too much effort, compared to the potential benefits?

4. Find another example of where data-flow diagrams were successfully used to support business process reengineering. Write a report, complete with DFDs, about what you found.

Case Problems

1. Pine Valley Furniture

As a Pine Valley Furniture intern, you have gained valuable insights into the systems development process. Jim Woo has made it a point to discuss with you both the WebStore and the Customer Tracking System projects. The data requirements for both projects have been collected and are ready to be organized into data-flow diagrams. Jim has prepared the data-flow diagrams for the WebStore; however, he has requested your help in preparing the data-flow diagrams for the Customer Tracking System.

You recall that Pine Valley Furniture distributes its products to retail stores, sells directly to customers, and is in the process of developing its WebStore, which will support online sales in the areas of corporate furniture buying, home-office furniture purchasing, and student furniture purchasing. You also know that the Customer Tracking System's primary objective is to track and forecast customer buying patterns.

Information collected during the requirements determination activity suggests that the Customer Tracking System should collect customer purchasing activity data. Customers will be tracked based on a variety of factors, including customer type, geographic location, type of sale, and promotional item purchases. The Customer Tracking System should support trend analysis, facilitate sales information reporting, enable managers to generate ad hoc queries, and interface with the WebStore.

a. Construct a context data-flow diagram, illustrating the Customer Tracking System's scope.
b. Construct a level-0 diagram for the Customer Tracking System.
c. Using the level-0 diagram that you previously constructed, select one of the level-0 processes and prepare a level-1 diagram.
d. Exchange your diagrams with another class member. Ask your classmate to review your diagrams for completeness and consistency. What errors did he or she find? Correct these errors.

2. Hoosier Burger

As one of Build a Better System's lead analysts on the Hoosier Burger project, you have spent significant time discussing the current and future needs of the restaurant with Bob and Thelma Mellankamp. In one of these conversations, Bob and Thelma mentioned that they were in the process of purchasing the empty lot next to Hoosier Burger. In the future, they would like to expand Hoosier Burger to include a drive-through, build a larger seating area in the restaurant, include more items on the Hoosier Burger menu, and provide delivery service to Hoosier Burger customers. After several discussions and much thought, the decision was made to implement the drive-through and delivery service and wait on the activities requiring physical expansion. Implementing the drive-through service will require only minor physical alterations to the west side of the Hoosier Burger building. Many of Hoosier Burger's customers work in the downtown area, so Bob and Thelma think a noon delivery service will offer an additional convenience to their customers.

One day while having lunch at Hoosier Burger with Bob and Thelma, you discuss how the new delivery and drive-through services will work. Customer order-taking via the drive-through window will mirror in-house dining operations. Therefore, drive-through window operations will not require information system modifications. Until a new system is implemented, the delivery service will be operated manually; each night Bob will enter necessary inventory data into the current system.

Bob envisions the delivery system operating as follows. When a customer calls and places a delivery order, a Hoosier Burger employee records the order on a multiform order ticket. The employee captures such details as customer name, business or home address, phone number, order placement time, items ordered, and amount of sale. The multiform document is sent to the kitchen where it is separated when the order is ready for delivery. Two copies accompany the order; a third copy is placed in a reconciliation box. When the order is prepared, the delivery person delivers the order to the customer, removes one order ticket from the food bag, collects payment for the order, and returns to Hoosier Burger. Upon arriving at Hoosier Burger, the delivery person gives the order ticket and the payment to Bob. Each evening Bob reconciles the order tickets stored in the reconciliation box with the delivery payments and matching order tickets returned by the delivery person. At the close of business each evening, Bob uses the data from the order tickets to update the goods sold and inventory files.

a. Modify the Hoosier Burger context-level dataflow diagram (Figure 6-4) to reflect the changes mentioned in the case.
b. Modify Hoosier Burger's level-0 diagram (Figure 6-5) to reflect the changes mentioned in the case.
c. Prepare level-1 diagrams to reflect the changes mentioned in the case.
d. Exchange your diagrams with those of another class member. Ask your classmate to review your diagrams for completeness and consistency. What errors did he or she find? Correct these errors.

3. Evergreen Nurseries

Evergreen Nurseries offers a wide range of lawn and garden products to its customers. Evergreen Nurseries conducts both wholesale and retail operations. Although the company serves as a wholesaler to nurseries all over the United States, the company's founder and president has restricted its retail operations to California, the company's home state. The company is situated on 150 acres and wholesales its bulbs, perennials, roses, trees, shrubs, and Evergreen Accessory products. Evergreen Accessory products include a variety of fertilizers, plant foods, pesticides, and gardening supplies.

In the past five years, the company has seen a phenomenal sales growth. Unfortunately, its information systems have been left behind. Although many of Evergreen Nurseries' processing activities are computerized, these activities require reengineering. You are part of the project team hired by Seymour Davis, the company's president, to renovate its wholesale division. Your project team was hired to renovate the billing, order taking, and inventory control systems.

From requirements determination, you discovered the following. An Evergreen Nurseries customer places a call to the nursery. A sales representative takes the order, verifies the customer's credit standing, determines whether the items are in stock, notifies the customer of the product's status, informs the customer if any special discounts are in effect, and communicates the total payment due. Once an order is entered into the system, the customer's account is updated, product inventory is adjusted, and ordered items are pulled from stock. Ordered items are then packed and shipped to the customer. Once each month, a billing statement is generated and sent to the customer. The customer has thirty days to remit payment in full; otherwise, a 15 percent penalty is applied to the customer's account.

a. Construct a context data-flow diagram, illustrating Evergreen Nurseries' wholesale system.
b. Construct a level-0 diagram for Evergreen Nurseries' wholesale system.
c. Using the level-0 diagram that you constructed in part b, select one of the level-0 processes and prepare a level-1 diagram.
d. Exchange your diagrams with those of another class member. Ask your classmate to review your diagrams for completeness and consistency. What errors did he or she find? Correct these errors.

CASE: PETRIE'S ELECTRONICS

Structuring Systems Requirements: Process Modeling

Jim and Sanjay chatted in Jim's office while they waited for Sally to arrive.

"Good work on researching those alternatives," Jim said.

"Thanks," replied Sanjay. "There are a lot of alternatives out there. I think we found the best three, considering what we are able to pay."

Just then Sally walked in. "Sorry I'm late. Things are getting really busy in marketing right now. I've been putting out fires all morning."

Sally sat down at the table across from Jim.

PE TABLE 6-1: Four Core Functions of Petrie's Customer Loyalty System

Function	Description
Record customer activities	When a customer makes a purchase, the transaction must be recorded in the customer loyalty system, as the rewards the system generates are driven by purchases. Similarly, when a customer uses a coupon generated by the system, it must also be recorded, so that the customer activity records can be updated to show that the coupon has been used and is now invalid.
Send promotions	Data about customer activities provide information about what types of products customers tend to buy and in what quantities. This information helps determine what sales promotion materials are best targeted at what customers. Customers who buy lots of video games should receive promotions about games, game platforms and HD TVs, for example.
Generate point-redemption coupons	Data about customer activities is used to generate coupons for future purchases. Those coupons must be made available to customers, either as paper coupons sent in the mail or online, in the customer's private account area. Once created, the customer activity database needs to be updated to show the creation of the coupon. The loyalty points needed to create the coupon must be deducted from the customer's total points.
Generate customer reports	From time to time, either in the mail or electronically, customers need to be sent account reports that show their recent purchases, the coupons they have been issued that have not yet been redeemed, and the total points they have amassed from their purchases.

"I understand," Jim said. "But to stay on schedule, we need to start focusing on the specifics of what we want our system to do. Remember when you wanted more details on what the system would do? Well, now we start to spend some serious energy on getting that done."

"Awesome," replied Sally, as she pulled a Red Bull out of her oversized bag and popped it open.

"I've got a list here of four core functions the system must perform," said Sanjay, pulling copies of a list from a folder on the table (PE Table 6-1). "Let's look at these."

After reviewing the list Sanjay had given them, Jim said, "Nice job, Sanjay. But we need to put this in graphical format, so that everyone can see what the inputs and outputs are for each function and how they are related to each other. We also need to see how the new system fits in with our existing data sources. We need . . ."

"Some data-flow diagrams," Sanjay interrupted.

"Exactly," said Jim.

"They are already done," replied Sanjay, handing diagrams to both Jim and Sally. "I've already created a first draft of the context diagram [PE Figure 6-1] and a level-1 diagram [PE Figure 6-2]. You can see how I've defined the boundaries of our system, and I've included our existing product and marketing databases."

PE FIGURE 6-1
Context diagram.

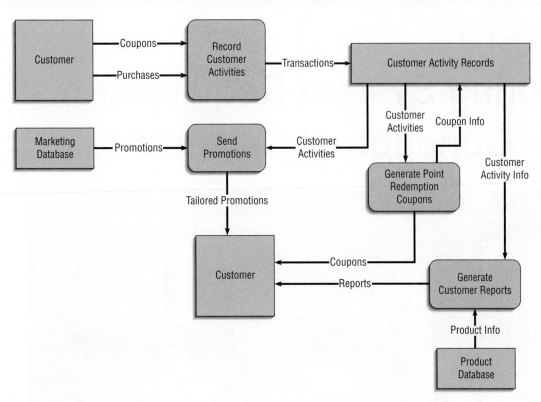

"What can I say?" Jim said. "Again, a nice job on your part. These diagrams are both good places for us to start. Let's get copies of all of this to the team."

"I'll be right back," Sally said, standing up. "I need to get some coffee."

Case Questions

1. Are the DFDs in PE Figures 6-1 and 6-2 balanced? Show that they are, or are not. If they are not balanced, how can they be fixed?

2. Decompose each of the core processes in PE Figure 6-2 and draw a new DFD for each core process.

3. Has the team overlooked any core processes in the system that should be in PE Table 6-1 and PE Figure 6-2? What would they be? Add them to PE Table 6-1 and PE Figure 6-2.

4. Redesign PE Figures 6-1 and 6-2 so that they are clearer, more efficient, and more comprehensive.

5. Why is it important for the team to create DFDs if they are not going to write the actual system code themselves?

seven
Structuring System Requirements: Conceptual Data Modeling

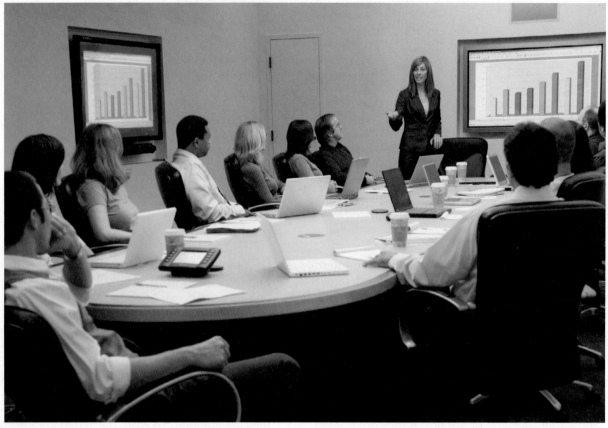

© Corbis

Chapter Objectives

After studying this chapter, you should be able to:

- Concisely define each of the following key data-modeling terms: *conceptual data model, entity-relationship diagram, entity type, entity instance, attribute, candidate key, multivalued attribute, relationship, degree, cardinality*, and *associative entity*.

- Ask the right kinds of questions to determine data requirements for an information system.

- Draw an entity-relationship (E-R) diagram to represent common business situations.

- Explain the role of conceptual data modeling in the overall analysis and design of an information system.

- Distinguish between unary, binary, and ternary relationships, and give an example of each.

- Distinguish between a relationship and an associative entity, and use associative entities in a data model when appropriate.

- Relate data modeling to process and logic modeling as different ways of describing an information system.

- Generate at least three alternative design strategies for an information system.

- Select the best design strategy using both qualitative and quantitative methods.

Chapter Preview . . .

In Chapter 6 you learned how to model and analyze the flow of data (data in motion) between manual or automated steps and how to show data stores (data at rest) in a data-flow diagram. Data-flow diagrams show how, where, and when data are used or changed in an information system, but they do not show the definition, structure, and relationships within the data. Data modeling, the subject of this chapter, develops this missing, and crucial, piece of the description of an information system.

Systems analysts perform data modeling during the systems analysis phase, as highlighted in Figure 7-1. Data modeling is typically done at the same time as other requirements structuring steps. Many systems developers believe that a data model is the most important part of the information system requirements statement for four reasons. First, the characteristics of data captured during data modeling are crucial in the design of databases, programs, computer screens, and printed reports. For example, facts such as these—a data element is numeric, a product can be in only one product line at a time, a line item on a customer order can never be moved to another customer order—are all essential in ensuring an information system's data integrity.

Second, data rather than processes are the most complex aspects of many modern information systems. For example, transaction processing systems can have considerable complexity in validating data, reconciling errors, and coordinating the movement of data to various databases. Management information systems (such as sales tracking), decision support systems (such as short-term cash investment), and executive support systems (such as product planning)

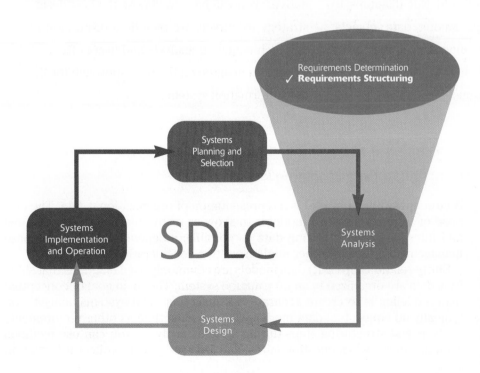

FIGURE 7-1
Systems analysts perform data modeling during the systems analysis phase. Data modeling typically occurs in parallel with other requirements structuring steps.

189

are data intensive and require extracting data from various data sources.

Third, the characteristics about data (such as format and relationships with other data) are rather permanent. In contrast, who receives which data, the format of reports, and what reports are used change constantly over time. A data model explains the inherent nature of the organization, not its transient form. So, an information system design based on data, rather than processes or logic, should have a longer useful life.

Finally, structural information about data is essential to generate programs automatically. For example, the fact that a customer order has many line items as opposed to just one affects the automatic design of a computer form in Microsoft Access for entry of customer orders.

In this chapter, we discuss the key concepts of data modeling, including the most common format used for data modeling—entity-relationship (E-R) diagramming. During the systems analysis phase of the SDLC, you use data-flow diagrams to show data in motion and E-R diagrams to show the relationships among data objects. We also illustrate E-R diagrams drawn using Microsoft's Visio tool, highlighting this tool's capabilities and limitations.

You have now reached the point in the analysis phase where you are ready to transform all of the information you have gathered and structured into some concrete ideas about the design for the new or replacement information system. This aspect is called the design strategy. From requirements determination, you know what the current system does. You also know what the users would like the replacement system to do. From requirements structuring, you know what forms the replacement system's process flow and data should take, at a logical level independent of any physical implementation. To bring analysis to a conclusion, your job is to take these structured requirements and transform them into several alternative design strategies. One of these strategies will be pursued in the design phase of the life cycle. In this chapter, you learn why you need to come up with alternative design strategies and about guidelines for generating alternatives. You then learn the different issues that must be addressed for each alternative. Once you have generated your alternatives, you will have to choose the best design strategy to pursue. We include a discussion of one technique that analysts and users often use to help them agree on the best approach for the new information system.

Conceptual Data Modeling

Conceptual data model
A detailed model that shows the overall structure of organizational data while being independent of any database management system or other implementation considerations.

A **conceptual data model** is a representation of organizational data. The purpose of a conceptual data model is to show as many rules about the meaning and interrelationships among data as possible, independent of any database management system or other implementation considerations.

Entity-relationship (E-R) data models are commonly used diagrams that show how data are organized in an information system. The main goal of conceptual data modeling is to create accurate E-R diagrams. As a systems analyst, you typically do conceptual data modeling at the same time as other requirements analysis and structuring steps during systems analysis. You can use methods such as interviewing, questionnaires, and JAD sessions to collect information for conceptual data modeling. On larger systems development teams, a subset of the project team concentrates on data modeling while other team members focus attention on process or logic modeling. You develop (or use from prior systems development) a conceptual data model for the current system and build a conceptual data model that supports the scope and requirements for the proposed or enhanced system.

The work of all team members is coordinated and shared through the project dictionary or repository. As discussed in Chapter 3, this repository and associated diagrams may be maintained by a CASE tool or a specialized tool such as Microsoft's Visio. Whether automated or manual, the process flow, decision logic, and data-model descriptions of a system must be consistent and complete, because each describes different but complementary views of the same information system. For example, the names of data stores on primitive-level DFDs often correspond to the names of data entities in entity-relationship diagrams, and the data elements in data flows on DFDs must be attributes of entities and relationships in entity-relationship diagrams.

The Process of Conceptual Data Modeling

You typically begin conceptual data modeling by developing a data model for the system being replaced, if a system exists. This phase is essential for planning the conversion of the current files or database into the database of the new system. Further, it is a good, but not a perfect, starting point for your understanding of the new system's data requirements. Then, you build a new conceptual data model that includes all of the data requirements for the new system. You discovered these requirements from the fact-finding methods used during requirements determination. Today, given the popularity of prototyping and other rapid development methodologies, these requirements often evolve through various iterations of a prototype, so the data model is constantly changing.

Conceptual data modeling is only one kind of data modeling and database design activity done throughout the systems development process. Figure 7-2 shows the different kinds of data modeling and database design that occur during the systems development life cycle. The conceptual data-modeling methods we discuss in this chapter are suitable for various tasks in the planning and analysis phases. These phases of the SDLC address issues of system scope, general requirements, and content. An E-R data model evolves from project identification and selection through analysis as it becomes more specific and is validated by more detailed analysis of system needs.

In the design phase, the final E-R model developed in analysis is matched with designs for systems inputs and outputs and is translated into a format that enables physical data storage decisions. During physical design, specific data storage architectures are selected, and then, in implementation, files and databases are defined as the system is coded. Through the use of the project repository, a field in a physical data record can, for example, be traced back to the conceptual data attribute that represents it on an E-R diagram. Thus, the data modeling and design steps in each of the SDLC phases are linked through the project repository.

Deliverables and Outcomes

Most organizations today do conceptual data modeling using entity-relationship modeling, which uses a special notation of rectangles, diamonds, and lines to represent as much meaning about data as possible. Thus, the primary deliverable from the conceptual data-modeling step within the analysis phase is an

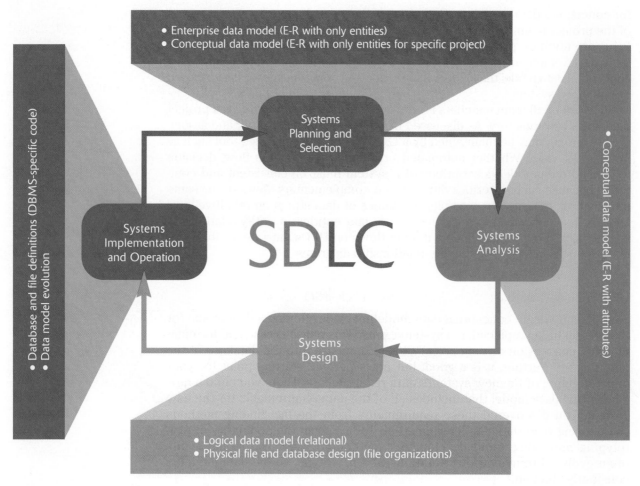

FIGURE 7-2
Relationship between data modeling and the systems development life cycle.

entity-relationship (E-R) diagram. A sample E-R diagram appears in Figure 7-3A. This figure shows the major categories of data (rectangles in the diagram) and the business relationships between them (lines connecting rectangles). For example, Figure 7-3A describes that, for the business represented, a SUPPLIER sometimes supplies ITEMs to the company, and an ITEM is always supplied by one to four SUPPLIERS. The fact that a supplier only sometimes supplies items implies that the business wants to keep track of some suppliers without designating what they can supply. This diagram includes two names on each line, giving you explicit language to read a relationship in each direction. For simplicity, we will not typically include two names on lines in E-R diagrams in this book; however, many organizations use this standard.

It is common that E-R diagrams are developed using CASE tools or other smart drawing packages. These tools provide functions to facilitate consistency of data models across different systems development phases, reverse engineering an existing database definition into an E-R diagram, and provide documentation of objects on a diagram. One popular tool is Microsoft Visio. Figure 7-3B shows the equivalent of Figure 7-3A using Visio. This diagram is developed using the Database Model Diagram tool. The Database|Options|Document settings are specified as relational symbol set, conceptual names on the diagram, optionality is shown, and relationships are shown using the crow's-foot notation with forward and inverse relationship names. These settings cause Visio to draw an E-R diagram that most closely resembles the standards used in this text.

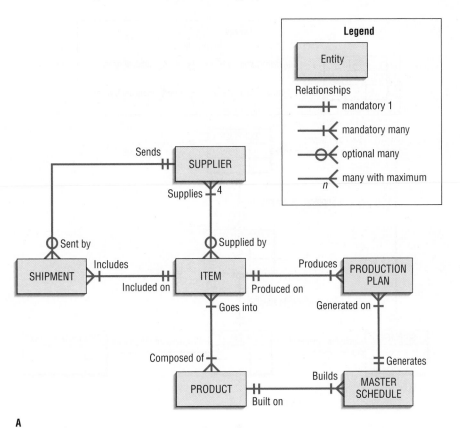

FIGURE 7-3
Sample conceptual data model diagrams: (A) Standard E-R notation.

A

Some key differences distinguish the standard E-R notation illustrated in Figure 7-3A from the notation used in Visio, including:

- Relationships such as Supplies/Supplied by between SUPPLIER and ITEM in Figure 7-3A require an intermediate category of data (called SUPPLIED ITEM in Figure 7-3B because Visio does not support representing these so-called many-to-many relationships.

- Relationships may be named in both directions, but these names appear near the relationship line, separated by a forward slash.

- Limitations, such as an ITEM is always supplied by at most four SUPPLIERS, are not shown on the diagram but rather are documented in the Miscellaneous set of Database Properties of the relationship, which are part of Visio's version of a CASE repository.

- The symbol for each category of data (e.g., SHIPMENT) includes space for listing other properties of each data category (such as all the attributes or columns of data we know about that data category); we will illustrate these components later in this chapter.

We concentrate on the traditional E-R diagramming notation in this chapter; however, we will include the equivalent Visio version on several occasions so you can see how to show data-modeling concepts in this popular database design tool.

As many as four E-R diagrams may be produced and analyzed during conceptual data modeling:

1. An E-R diagram that covers just the data needed in the project's application. (This first diagram allows you to concentrate on the data requirements without being constrained or confused by unnecessary details.)

FIGURE 7-3
Sample conceptual data model
diagrams: (B) Visio E-R notation.

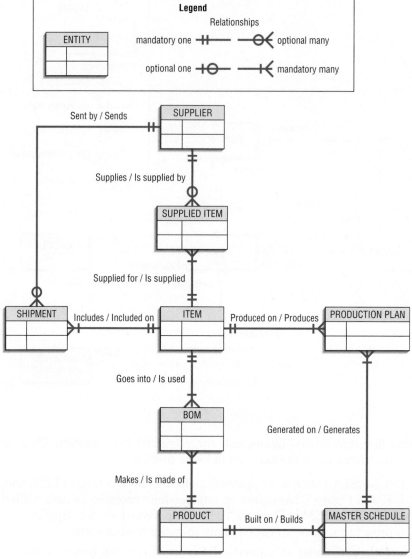

B

2. An E-R diagram for the application system being replaced. (Differences between this diagram and the first show what changes you have to make to convert databases to the new application.) This version is, of course, not produced if the proposed system supports a completely new business function.

3. An E-R diagram for the whole database from which the new application's data are extracted. (Because many applications share the same database or even several databases, this and the first diagram show how the new application shares the contents of more widely-used databases.)

4. An E-R diagram for the whole database from which data for the application system being replaced is drawn. (Again, differences between this diagram and the third show what global database changes you have to make to implement the new application.) Even if no system is being replaced, an understanding of the existing data systems is necessary to see where the new data will fit in or if existing data structures must change to accommodate new data.

The other deliverable from conceptual data modeling is a set of entries about data objects to be stored in the project dictionary or repository. The repository is the mechanism to link data, process, and logic models of an information system. For example, explicit links can be shown between a data model and a data-flow diagram. Some important links are briefly explained here.

- Data elements included in data flows also appear in the data model, and vice versa. You must include in the data model any raw data captured and retained in a data store. The data model can include only data that have been captured or are computed from captured data. Because a data model is a general business picture of data, both manual and automated data stores will be included.

- Each data store in a process model must relate to business objects (what we call *data entities*) represented in the data model. For example, in Figure 6-5, the Inventory File data store must correspond to one or several data objects in a data model.

Gathering Information for Conceptual Data Modeling

Requirements determination methods must include questions and investigations that take a data focus rather than only a process and logic focus. For example, during interviews with potential system users, you must ask specific questions to gain the perspective on data needed to develop a data model. In later sections of this chapter, we introduce some specific terminology and constructs used in data modeling. Even without this specific data-modeling language, you can begin to understand the kinds of questions that must be answered during requirements determination. These questions relate to understanding the rules and policies by which the area supported by the new information system operates. That is, a data model explains what the organization does and what rules govern how work is performed in the organization. You do not, however, need to know how or when data are processed or used to do data modeling.

You typically do data modeling from a combination of perspectives. The first perspective is called the *top-down approach*. It derives the data model from an intimate understanding of the nature of the business, rather than from any specific information requirements in computer displays, reports, or business forms. Table 7-1 summarizes key questions to ask system users and business managers so that you can develop an accurate and complete data model. The questions are purposely posed in business terms. Of course, technical terms do not mean much to a business manager, so you must learn how to frame your questions in business terms.

Alternatively, you can gather the information for data modeling by reviewing specific business documents—computer displays, reports, and business forms—handled within the system. This second perspective of gaining an understanding of data is often called a *bottom-up approach*. These business documents will appear as data flows on DFDs and will show the data processed by the system, which probably are the data that must be maintained in the system's database. Consider, for example, Figure 7-4, which shows a customer order form used at Pine Valley Furniture.

From the form in Figure 7-4, we determine that the following data must be kept in the database:

ORDER NO	CUSTOMER NO
ORDER DATE	NAME
PROMISED DATE	ADDRESS
PRODUCT NO	CITY-STATE-ZIP
DESCRIPTION	
QUANTITY ORDERED	
UNIT PRICE	

PINE VALLEY FURNITURE

TABLE 7-1: Questions to Ask to Develop Accurate and Complete Data Models

Category of Questions	Questions to Ask System Users and Business Managers
1. Data entities and their descriptions	What are the subjects/objects of the business? What types of people, places, things, and materials are used or interact in this business about which data must be maintained? How many instances of each object might exist?
2. Candidate key	What unique characteristics distinguish each object from other objects of the same type? Could any such distinguishing feature change over time or is it permanent? Could this characteristic of an object be missing even though we know the object exists?
3. Attributes and secondary keys	What characteristic describes each object? On what basis are objects referenced, selected, qualified, sorted, and categorized? What must we know about each object in order to run the business?
4. Security controls and understanding who really knows the meaning of data	How do you use these data? That is, are you the source of the data for the organization, do you refer to the data, do you modify them, and do you destroy them? Who is not permitted to use these data? Who is responsible for establishing legitimate values for these data?
5. Cardinality and time dimensions of data	Over what period of time are you interested in these data? Do you need historical trends, current "snapshot" values, and/or estimates or projections? If a characteristic of an object changes over time, must you know the obsolete values?
6. Relationships and their cardinality and degrees	What events occur that imply associations between various objects? What natural activities or transactions of the business involve handling data about several objects of the same or different type?
7. Integrity rules, minimum and maximum cardinality, time dimensions of data	Is each activity or event always handled the same way, or are there special circumstances? Can an event occur with only some of the associated objects, or must all objects be involved? Can the associations between objects change over time (e.g., employees change departments)? Are values for data characteristics limited in any way?

FIGURE 7-4
Customer order form used at Pine Valley Furniture.

PVF CUSTOMER ORDER

ORDER NO: 61384   CUSTOMER NO: 1273

NAME: Contemporary Designs
ADDRESS: 123 Oak St.
CITY-STATE-ZIP: Austin, TX 28384

ORDER DATE: 11/04/2012   PROMISED DATE: 11/21/2012

PRODUCT NO	DESCRIPTION	QUANTITY ORDERED	UNIT PRICE
M128	Bookcase	4	200.00
B381	Cabinet	2	150.00
R210	Table	1	500.00

We also see that each order is from one customer, and an order can have multiple line items, each for one product. We use this kind of understanding of an organization's operation to develop data models.

Introduction to Entity-Relationship Modeling

The basic entity-relationship modeling notation uses three main constructs: data entities, relationships, and their associated attributes. Several different E-R notations exist, and many CASE tools support multiple notations. For simplicity, we have adopted one common notation for this book, the so-called crow's-foot notation. If you use another notation in courses or work, you should be able to easily translate between notations.

An **entity-relationship diagram** (or **E-R diagram**) is a detailed, logical, and graphical representation of the data for an organization or business area. The E-R diagram is a model of entities in the business environment, the relationships or associations among those entities, and the attributes or properties of both the entities and their relationships. A rectangle is used to represent an entity, and lines are used to represent the relationship between two or more entities. The notation for E-R diagrams appears in Figure 7-5.

Entities

An **entity** is a person, place, object, event, or concept in the user environment about which the organization wishes to maintain data. As noted in Table 7-1, the first requirements determination question an analyst should ask concerns data

Entity-relationship diagram (E-R diagram)
A graphical representation of the entities, associations, and data for an organization or business area; it is a model of entities, the associations among those entities, and the attributes of both the entities and their associations.

Entity
A person, place, object, event, or concept in the user environment about which the organization wishes to maintain data.

FIGURE 7-5
Entity-relationship diagram notations: basic symbols, relationship degree, and relationship cardinality.

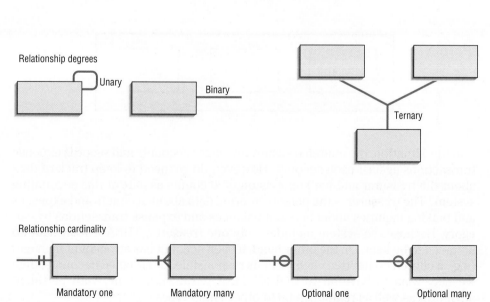

entities. An entity has its own identity, which distinguishes it from every other entity. Some examples of entities follow:

- Person: EMPLOYEE, STUDENT, PATIENT
- Place: STATE, REGION, COUNTRY, BRANCH
- Object: MACHINE, BUILDING, AUTOMOBILE, PRODUCT
- Event: SALE, REGISTRATION, RENEWAL
- Concept: ACCOUNT, COURSE, WORK CENTER

Entity type
A collection of entities that share common properties or characteristics.

You need to recognize an important distinction between entity *types* and entity *instances*. An **entity type** is a collection of entities that share common properties or characteristics. Each entity type in an E-R model is given a name. Because the name represents a set of entities, it is singular. Also, because an entity is an object, we use a simple noun to name an entity type. We use capital letters in naming an entity type, and in an E-R diagram, the name is placed inside a rectangle representing the entity, for example:

Entity instance (instance)
A single occurrence of an entity type.

An **entity instance** (or **instance**) is a single occurrence of an entity type. An entity type is described just once in a data model, whereas many instances of that entity type may be represented by data stored in the database. For example, most organizations have one EMPLOYEE entity type, but hundreds (or even thousands) of instances of this entity type may be stored in the database.

A common mistake made in learning to draw E-R diagrams, especially if you already know how to do data-flow diagramming, is to confuse data entities with sources/sinks, system outputs, or system users, and to confuse relationships with data flows. A simple rule to avoid such confusion is that a true data entity will have many possible instances, each with a distinguishing characteristic, as well as one or more other descriptive pieces of data. Consider the following entity types that might be associated with a church expense system:

In this situation, the church treasurer manages accounts and records expense transactions against each account. However, do we need to keep track of data about the treasurer and her supervision of accounts as part of this accounting system? The treasurer is the person entering data about accounts and expenses and making inquiries about account balances and expense transactions by category. Because the system includes only one treasurer, TREASURER data do not need to be kept. On the other hand, if each account has an account manager (e.g., a church committee chair) who is responsible for assigned accounts, then we may wish to have an ACCOUNT MANAGER entity type, with pertinent attributes as well as relationships to other entity types.

In this same situation, is an expense report an entity type? Because an expense report is computed from expense transactions and account balances, it is a data flow, not an entity type. Even though multiple instances of expense reports will occur over time, the report contents are already represented by the ACCOUNT and EXPENSE entity types.

Often when we refer to entity types in subsequent sections, we simply say *entity*. This shorthand reference is common among data modelers. We will clarify that we mean an entity by using the term *entity instance*.

Attributes

Each entity type has a set of attributes associated with it. An **attribute** is a property or characteristic of an entity that is of interest to the organization (relationships may also have attributes, as we see in the section on relationships). Asking about attributes is the third question noted in Table 7-1 (see page 196). Following are some typical entity types and associated attributes:

> STUDENT: Student_ID, Student_Name, Address, Phone_Number, Major
> AUTOMOBILE: Vehicle_ID, Color, Weight, Horsepower
> EMPLOYEE: Employee_ID, Employee_Name, Address, Skill

We use nouns with an initial capital letter followed by lowercase letters in naming an attribute. In E-R diagrams, we represent an attribute by placing its name inside the rectangle that represents the associated entity. In many E-R drawing tools, such as Microsoft Visio, attributes are listed within the entity rectangle under the entity name.

Candidate Keys and Identifiers

Every entity type must have an attribute or set of attributes that distinguishes one instance from other instances of the same type. A **candidate key** is an attribute (or combination of attributes) that uniquely identifies each instance of an entity type. A candidate key for a STUDENT entity type might be Student_ID.

Sometimes more than one attribute is required to identify a unique entity. For example, consider the entity type GAME for a basketball league. The attribute Team_Name is clearly not a candidate key, because each team plays several games. If each team plays exactly one home game against every other team, then the combination of the attributes Home_Team and Visiting_Team is a candidate key for GAME.

Some entities may have more than one candidate key. One candidate key for EMPLOYEE is Employee_ID; a second is the combination of Employee_Name and Address (assuming that no two employees with the same name live at the same address). If more than one candidate key is involved, the designer must choose one of the candidate keys as the identifier. An **identifier** is a candidate key that has been selected to be used as the unique characteristic for an entity type.

Identifiers should be selected carefully because they are critical for the integrity of data. You should apply the following identifier selection rules:

1. Choose a candidate key that will not change its value over the life of each instance of the entity type. For example, the combination of Employee_Name and Address would probably be a poor choice as a primary key for EMPLOYEE because the values of Employee_Name and Address could easily change during an employee's term of employment.

2. Choose a candidate key such that for each instance of the entity, the attribute is guaranteed to have valid values and not be null. To ensure valid values, you may have to include special controls in data entry and maintenance routines to eliminate the possibility of errors. If the

---

Attribute
A named property or characteristic of an entity that is of interest to the organization.

Candidate key
An attribute (or combination of attributes) that uniquely identifies each instance of an entity type.

Identifier
A candidate key that has been selected as the unique, identifying characteristic for an entity type.

candidate key is a combination of two or more attributes, make sure that all parts of the key have valid values.

3. Avoid the use of so-called intelligent keys, whose structure indicates classifications, locations, and other entity properties. For example, the first two digits of a key for a PART entity may indicate the warehouse location. Such codes are often modified as conditions change, which renders the primary key values invalid.

4. Consider substituting single-attribute surrogate keys for large composite keys. For example, an attribute called Game_ID could be used for the entity GAME instead of the combination of Home_Team and Visiting_Team.

For each entity, the name of the identifier is underlined on an E-R diagram. The following diagram shows the representation for a STUDENT entity type using E-R notation:

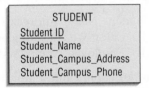

The equivalent representation using Microsoft Visio is the following:

In the Visio notation, the primary key is listed immediately below the entity name with the notation PK, and the primary key is underlined. All required attributes (that is, an instance of STUDENT must have values for Student_ID and Name) are in bold.

Multivalued Attributes

Multivalued attribute
An attribute that may take on more than one value for each entity instance.

A **multivalued attribute** may take on more than one value for each entity instance. Suppose that, Skill is one of the attributes of EMPLOYEE. If each employee can have more than one Skill, then it is a multivalued attribute. During conceptual design, two common special symbols or notations are used to highlight multivalued attributes. The first is to use curly brackets around the name of the multivalued attribute, so that the EMPLOYEE entity with its attributes is diagrammed as follows:

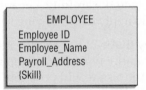

Many E-R drawing tools, such as Microsoft Visio, do not support multivalued attributes within an entity. Thus, a second approach is to separate the repeating data into another entity, called a *weak* (or *attributive*) entity, and then using a relationship (relationships are discussed in the next section), link the weak entity to its associated regular entity. The approach also easily handles several attributes that repeat together, called a **repeating group.** Consider an EMPLOYEE and his or her dependents. Dependent name, age, and relation to employee (spouse, child, parent, etc.) are multivalued attributes about an employee, and these attributes repeat together. We can show this repetition using an attributive entity, DEPENDENT, and a relationship, shown here simply by a line between DEPENDENT and EMPLOYEE. The crow's-foot next to DEPENDENT means that many DEPENDENTs may be associated with the same EMPLOYEE. Likewise, a DEPENDENT may be associated with more than one EMPLOYEE (i.e., two different EMPLOYEES are parents to a specific DEPENDENT).

Repeating group
A set of two or more multivalued attributes that are logically related.

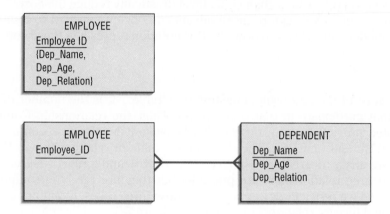

Relationships

Relationships are the glue that hold together the various components of an E-R model. In Table 7-1 (see page 196), questions 5, 6, and 7 deal with relationships. A **relationship** is an association between the instances of one or more entity types that are of interest to the organization. An association usually means that an event has occurred or that some natural linkage exists between entity instances. For this reason, relationships are labeled with verb phrases. For example, a training department in a company is interested in tracking which training courses each of its employees has completed. This information leads to a relationship (called Completes) between the EMPLOYEE and COURSE entity types that we diagram as follows:

Relationship
An association between the instances of one or more entity types that is of interest to the organization.

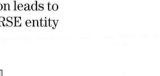

As indicated by the lines, this relationship is considered a many-to-many relationship: Each employee may complete more than one course, and each course may be completed by more than one employee. More significantly, we can use the Completes relationship to determine the specific courses that a given employee has completed. Conversely, we can determine the identity of each employee who has completed a particular course.

Conceptual Data Modeling and the E-R Model

The last section introduced the fundamentals of the E-R data modeling notation—entities, attributes, and relationships. The goal of conceptual data modeling is to capture as much of the meaning of data as possible. The more details (or what some systems analysts call *business rules*) about data that we can model, the better the system we can design and build. Further, if we can include all these details in an automated repository, such as a CASE tool, and if a CASE tool can generate code for data definitions and programs, then the more we know about data, the more code can be generated automatically, making the system building more accurate and faster. More importantly, if we can keep a thorough repository of data descriptions, we can regenerate the system as needed as the business rules change. Because maintenance is the largest expense with any information system, the efficiencies gained by maintaining systems at the rule, rather than code, level drastically reduce the cost.

In this section, we explore more advanced concepts needed to more thoroughly model data and learn how the E-R notation represents these concepts.

Degree of a Relationship

Degree
The number of entity types that participate in a relationship.

The **degree** of a relationship, question 6 in Table 7-1, is the number of entity types that participate in that relationship. Thus, the relationship Completes, illustrated previously, is of degree two because it involves two entity types: EMPLOYEE and COURSE. The three most common relationships in E-R diagrams are unary (degree one), binary (degree two), and ternary (degree three). Higher-degree relationships are possible, but they are rarely encountered in practice, so we restrict our discussion to these three cases. Examples of unary, binary, and ternary relationships appear in Figure 7-6.

Unary relationship (recursive relationship)
A relationship between the instances of one entity type.

Unary Relationship Also called a **recursive relationship,** a **unary relationship** is a relationship between the instances of one entity type. Two examples are shown in Figure 7-6. In the first example, Is_married_to is shown as a one-to-one relationship between instances of the PERSON entity type. That is, each person may be currently married to one other person. In the second example, Manages is shown as a one-to-many relationship between instances of the EMPLOYEE entity type. Using this relationship, we could identify (for example) the employees who report to a particular manager or, reading the Manages relationship in the opposite direction, who the manager is for a given employee.

FIGURE 7-6
Examples of the three most common relationships in E-R diagrams: unary, binary, and ternary.

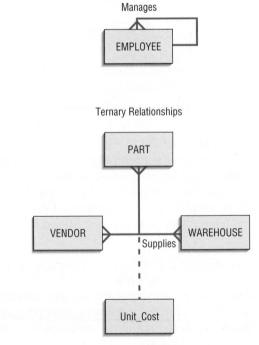

Binary Relationship A **binary relationship** is a relationship between instances of two entity types and is the most common type of relationship encountered in data modeling. Figure 7-6 shows three examples. The first (one-to-one) indicates that an employee is assigned one parking place, and each parking place is assigned to one employee. The second (one-to-many) indicates that a product line may contain several products, and each product belongs to only one product line. The third (many-to-many) shows that a student may register for more than one course and that each course may have many student registrants.

Binary relationship
A relationship between instances of two entity types.

Ternary Relationship A **ternary relationship** is a simultaneous relationship among instances of three entity types. In the example shown in Figure 7-6, the relationship Supplies tracks the quantity of a given part that is shipped by a particular vendor to a selected warehouse. Each entity may be a one or a many participant in a ternary relationship (in Figure 7-6, all three entities are many participants).

Ternary relationship
A simultaneous relationship among instances of three entity types.

Note that a ternary relationship is not the same as three binary relationships. For example, Unit_Cost is an attribute of the Supplies relationship in Figure 7-6. Unit_Cost cannot be properly associated with any of the three possible binary relationships among the three entity types (such as that between PART and VENDOR) because Unit_Cost is the cost of a particular PART shipped from a particular VENDOR to a particular WAREHOUSE.

Cardinalities in Relationships

Suppose that two entity types, A and B, are connected by a relationship. The **cardinality** of a relationship (see the fifth, sixth, and seventh questions in Table 7-1) is the number of instances of entity B that can (or must) be associated with each instance of entity A. For example, consider the following relationship for DVDs and movies:

Cardinality
The number of instances of entity B that can (or must) be associated with each instance of entity A.

Clearly, a video store may stock more than one DVD of a given movie. In the terminology we have used so far, this example is intuitively a "many" relationship. Yet, it is also true that the store may not have a single DVD of a particular movie in stock. We need a more precise notation to indicate the range of cardinalities for a relationship. This notation of relationship cardinality was introduced in Figure 7-5, which you may want to review at this point.

Minimum and Maximum Cardinalities The minimum cardinality of a relationship is the minimum number of instances of entity B that may be associated with each instance of entity A. In the preceding example, the minimum number of DVDs available for a movie is zero, in which case we say that DVD is an optional participant in the Is_stocked_as relationship. When the minimum cardinality of a relationship is one, then we say entity B is a mandatory participant in the relationship. The maximum cardinality is the maximum number of instances. For our example, this maximum is "many" (an unspecified number greater than one). Using the notation from Figure 7-5, we diagram this relationship as follows:

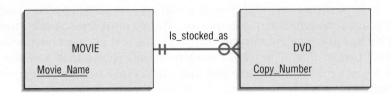

The zero through the line near the DVD entity means a minimum cardinality of zero, whereas the crow's-foot notation means a "many" maximum cardinality. It is possible for the maximum cardinality to be a fixed number, not an arbitrary "many" value. For example, see the Supplies relationship in Figure 7-3A, which indicates that each item involves at most four suppliers.

Associative Entities   As seen in the examples of the Supplies ternary relationship in Figure 7-6, attributes may be associated with a many-to-many relationship as well as with an entity. For example, suppose that the organization wishes to record the date (month and year) when an employee completes each course. Some sample data follow:

Employee_ID	Course_Name	Date_Completed
549–23–1948	Basic Algebra	March 2012
629–16–8407	Software Quality	June 2012
816–30–0458	Software Quality	Feb 2012
549–23–1948	C Programming	May 2012

From this limited data, you can conclude that the attribute Date_Completed is not a property of the entity EMPLOYEE (because a given employee, such as 549–23–1948, has completed courses on different dates). Nor is Date_Completed a property of COURSE, because a particular course (such as Software Quality) may be completed on different dates. Instead, Date_Completed is a property of the relationship between EMPLOYEE and COURSE. The attribute is associated with the relationship and diagrammed as follows:

Because many-to-many and one-to-one relationships may have associated attributes, the E-R diagram poses an interesting dilemma: Is a many-to-many relationship actually an entity in disguise? Often the distinction between entity and relationship is simply a matter of how you view the data. An **associative entity** is a relationship that the data modeler chooses to model as an entity type. Figure 7-7 shows the E-R notation for representing the Completes relationship as an associative entity. The lines from CERTIFICATE to the two entities are not two separate binary relationships, so they do not have labels. Note that EMPLOYEE and COURSE have mandatory-one cardinality, because an instance

Associative entity

An entity type that associates the instances of one or more entity types and contains attributes that are peculiar to the relationship between those entity instances.

FIGURE 7-7
Example of an associative entity.

of Completes must have an associated EMPLOYEE and COURSE. The implicit identifier of Completes is the combination of the identifiers of EMPLOYEE and COURSE, Employee_ID, and Course_ID, respectively. The explicit identifier is Certificate_Number, as shown in Figure 7-7.

E-R drawing tools that do not support many-to-many relationships require that any such relationship be converted into an associative entity, whether it has attributes or not. You have already seen an example of this in Figure 7-3 for Microsoft Visio, in which the Supplies/Supplied by relationship from Figure 7-3A was converted in Figure 7-3B into the SUPPLIED ITEM entity (actually, associative entity) and two mandatory one-to-many relationships.

One situation in which a relationship must be turned into an associative entity is when the associative entity has other relationships with entities besides the relationship that caused its creation. For example, consider the E-R model, which represents price quotes from different vendors for purchased parts stocked by Pine Valley Furniture, shown in Figure 7-8A.

Now, suppose that we also need to know which price quote is in effect for each part shipment received. This additional data requirement necessitates that the relationship between VENDOR and PART be transformed into an associative entity. This new relationship is represented in Figure 7-8B.

A Many-to-many relationship with attributes

FIGURE 7-8
An E-R model that represents each price quote for each part shipment received by Pine Valley Furniture.

B Associative entity with separate relationship

In this case, PRICE QUOTE is not a ternary relationship. Rather, PRICE QUOTE is a binary many-to-many relationship (associative entity) between VENDOR and PART. In addition, each PART RECEIPT, based on Amount, has an applicable, negotiated Price. Each PART RECEIPT is for a given PART from a specific VENDOR, and the Amount of the receipt dictates the purchase price in effect by matching with the Quantity attribute. Because the PRICE QUOTE pertains to a given PART and given VENDOR, PART RECEIPT does not need direct relationships with these entities.

An Example of Conceptual Data Modeling at Hoosier Burger

Chapter 6 structured the process and data-flow requirements for a food-ordering system for Hoosier Burger. Figure 7-9 describes requirements for a new system using Microsoft Visio. The purpose of this system is to monitor and report changes in raw material inventory levels and to issue material orders and payments to suppliers. Thus, the central data entity for this system will be an INVENTORY ITEM, shown in Figure 7-10, corresponding to data store D1 in Figure 7-9.

Changes in inventory levels are due to two types of transactions: receipt of new items from suppliers and consumption of items from sales of products. Inventory is added upon receipt of new raw materials, for which Hoosier Burger receives a supplier INVOICE (see Process 1.0 in Figure 7-9). Figure 7-10 shows that each INVOICE indicates that the supplier has sent a specific quantity of one or more INVOICE ITEMs, which correspond to Hoosier's INVENTORY ITEMs. Inventory is used when customers order and pay for PRODUCTs. That is, Hoosier makes a SALE for one or more ITEM SALEs,

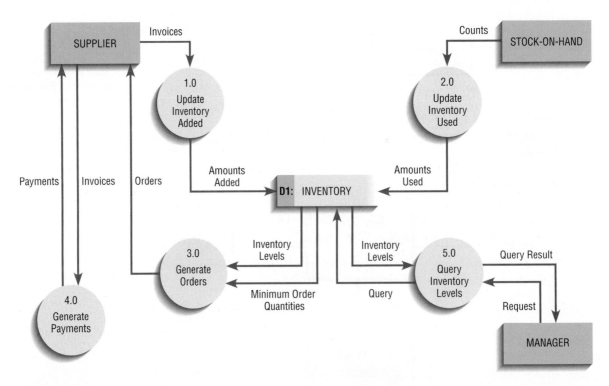

FIGURE 7-9
Level-0 data-flow diagram for Hoosier Burger's new logical inventory control system.

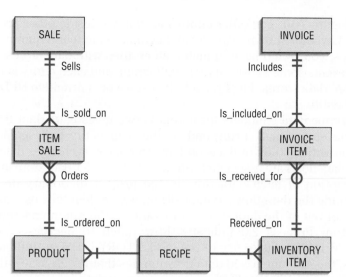

FIGURE 7-10
Preliminary E-R diagram for
Hoosier Burger's inventory
control system.

each of which corresponds to a food PRODUCT. Because the real-time customer-order processing system is separate from the inventory control system, a source, STOCK-ON-HAND in Figure 7-9, represents how data flow from the order processing to the inventory control system. Finally, because food PRODUCTs are made up of various INVENTORY ITEMs (and vice versa), Hoosier Burger maintains a RECIPE to indicate how much of each INVENTORY ITEM goes into making one PRODUCT. From this discussion, we have identified the data entities required in a data model for the new Hoosier Burger inventory control system: INVENTORY ITEM, INVOICE, INVOICE ITEM, PRODUCT, SALE, ITEM SALE, and RECIPE. To complete the E-R diagram, we must determine necessary relationships among these entities as well as attributes for each entity.

The wording in the previous description tells us much of what we need to know to determine relationships:

- An INVOICE includes one or more INVOICE ITEMs, each of which corresponds to an INVENTORY ITEM. Obviously, an INVOICE ITEM cannot exist without an associated INVOICE, and over time the result will be zero-to-many receipts, or INVOICE ITEMs, for an INVENTORY ITEM.

- Each PRODUCT is associated with INVENTORY ITEMs.

- A SALE indicates that Hoosier Burger sells one or more ITEM SALEs, each of which corresponds to a PRODUCT. An ITEM SALE cannot exist without an associated SALE, and over time the result will be zero-to-many ITEM SALEs for a PRODUCT.

Figure 7-10 shows an E-R diagram with the entities and relationships previously described. We include on this diagram two labels for each relationship, one to be read in either relationship direction (e.g., an INVOICE Includes one-to-many INVOICE ITEMs, and an INVOICE ITEM Is_included_on exactly one INVOICE). Now that we understand the entities and relationships, we must decide which data elements are associated with the entities and associative entities in this diagram.

You may wonder at this point why only the INVENTORY data store is shown in Figure 7-9 when seven entities and associative entities are on the E-R diagram. The INVENTORY data store corresponds to the INVENTORY ITEM entity in Figure 7-10. The other entities are hidden inside other processes for which we have not shown lower-level diagrams. In actual requirements structuring steps, you would have to match all entities with data stores: Each data store represents some subset of an E-R diagram, and each entity is included in one or more data stores. Ideally, each data store on a primitive DFD will be an individual entity.

To determine data elements for an entity, we investigate data flows in and out of data stores that correspond to the data entity and supplement this information with a study of decision logic that uses or changes data about the entity. Six data flows are associated with the INVENTORY data store in Figure 7-9. The description of each data flow in the project dictionary or repository would include the data flow's composition, which then tells us what data are flowing in or out of the data store. For example, the Amounts Used data flow coming from Process 2.0 indicates how much to decrease an attribute STOCK_ON_HAND due to use of the INVENTORY ITEM to fulfill a customer sale. Thus, the Amounts Used data flow implies that Process 2.0 will first read the relevant INVENTORY ITEM record, then update its STOCK_ON_HAND attribute, and finally store the updated value in the record. Each data flow would be analyzed similarly (space does not permit us to show the analysis for each data flow).

After having considered all data flows in and out of data stores related to data entities, plus all decision logic related to inventory control, we derive the full E-R diagram, with attributes, shown in Figure 7-11. In Visio, the ITEM SALE, RECIPE, and INVOICE ITEM entities participate in what are called *identifying relationships*. Thus, Visio treats them as associative entities, not just the RECIPE entity. Visio automatically includes the primary keys of the identifying entities as primary keys in the identified (associative) entities. Also note that in Visio, because it cannot represent many-to-many relationships, there are two mandatory relationships on either side of RECIPE.

FIGURE 7-11

Final E-R diagram for Hoosier Burger's inventory control system.

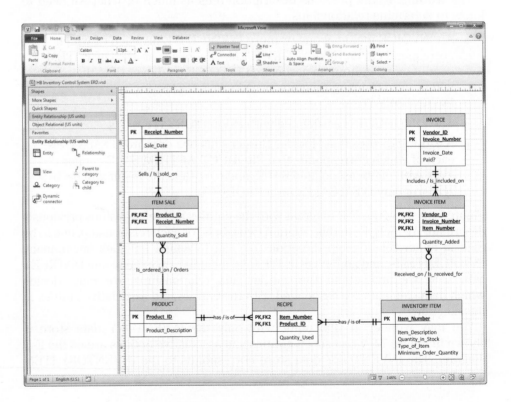

PVF WebStore: Conceptual Data Modeling

Conceptual data modeling for an Internet-based electronic commerce application is no different from the process followed when analyzing the data needs for other types of applications. In the last chapter, you read how Jim Woo analyzed the flow of information within the WebStore and developed a data-flow diagram. In this section, we examine the process he followed when developing the WebStore's conceptual data model.

Conceptual Data Modeling for Pine Valley Furniture's WebStore

To better understand what data would be needed within the WebStore, Jim Woo carefully reviewed the information from the JAD session and his previously developed data-flow diagram. Table 7-2 summarizes the customer and inventory information identified during the JAD session. Jim wasn't sure whether this information was complete but knew that it was a good starting place for identifying what information the WebStore needed to capture, store, and process. To identify additional information, he carefully studied the level-0 DFD shown in Figure 7-12. In this diagram, two data stores—Inventory and Shopping Cart—are clearly identified; both were strong candidates to become entities within the conceptual data model. Finally, Jim examined the data flows from the DFD as additional possible sources for entities. Hence, he identified five general categories of information to consider:

- Customer
- Inventory
- Order
- Shopping Cart
- Temporary User/System Messages

After identifying these multiple categories of data, his next step was to define each item carefully. He again examined all data flows within the DFD and recorded each one's source and destination. By carefully listing these flows, he could move more easily through the DFD and understand more thoroughly what information was needed to move from point to point. This activity resulted in the creation of two tables that documented Jim's growing understanding of the WebStore's requirements. The first, Table 7-3, lists each of the data flows within

TABLE 7-2:   Customer and Inventory Information for WebStore

Corporate Customer	Home-Office Customer	Student Customer	Inventory Information
Company name	Name	Name	SKU
Company address	Doing business as (company's name)	School	Name
Company phone		Address	Description
Company fax	Address	Phone	Finished product size
Company preferred shipping method	Phone	E-mail	Finished product weight
	Fax		Available materials
Buyer name	E-mail		Available colors
Buyer phone			Price
Buyer e-mail			Lead time

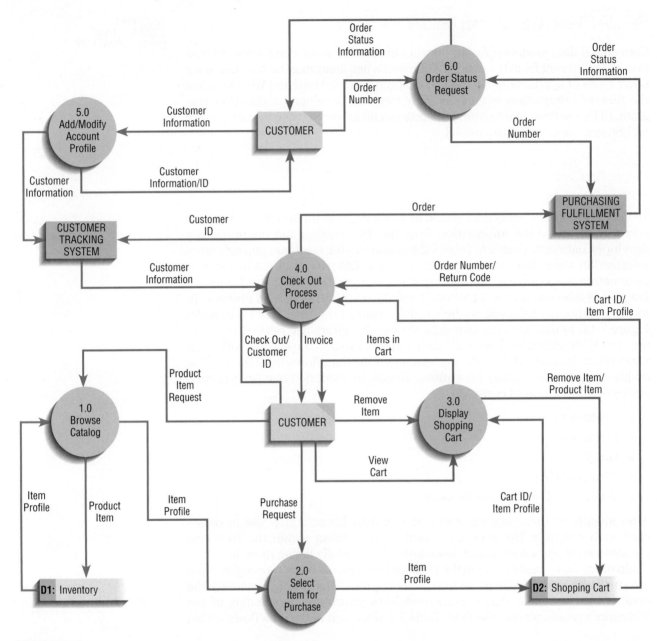

FIGURE 7-12
Level-0 data-flow diagram for the WebStore.

each data category and its corresponding description. The second, Table 7-4, lists each of the unique data flows within each data category. Jim then felt ready to construct an entity-relationship diagram for the WebStore.

He concluded that Customer, Inventory, and Order were all unique entities and would be part of his E-R diagram. Recall that an entity is a person, place, or object; all three of these items meet this criteria. Because the Temporary User/System Messages data were not permanently stored items—nor were they a person, place, or object—he concluded that this should not be an entity in the conceptual data model. Alternatively, although the shopping cart was also a temporarily stored item, its contents needed to be stored for at least the duration of a customer's visit to the WebStore and should be considered an object. As shown in Figure 7-12, Process 4, Check Out/Process Order, moves the Shopping Cart contents to the Purchasing Fulfillment System, where the order details are stored. Thus, he concluded that Shopping Cart—along with Customer, Inventory, and Order—would be entities in his E-R diagram.

TABLE 7-3: Data Category, Data Flow, and Data-Flow Descriptions for the WebStore DFD

Data Category	
Data Flow	**Description**
Customer Related	
Customer ID	Unique identifier for each customer (generated by Customer Tracking System)
Customer Information	Detailed customer information (stored in Customer Tracking System)
Inventory Related	
Product Item	Unique identifier for each product item (stored in Inventory Database)
Item Profile	Detailed product information (stored in Inventory Database)
Order Related	
Order Number	Unique identifier for an order (generated by Purchasing Fulfillment System)
Order	Detailed order information (stored in Purchasing Fulfillment System)
Return Code	Unique code for processing customer returns (generated by/stored in Purchasing Fulfillment System)
Invoice	Detailed order summary statement (generated from order information stored in Purchasing Fulfillment System)
Order Status Information	Detailed summary information on order status (stored/generated by Purchasing Fulfillment System)
Shopping Cart	
Cart ID	Unique identifier for shopping cart
Temporary User/System Messages	
Product Item Request	Request to view information on a catalog item
Purchase Request	Request to move an item into the shopping cart
View Cart	Request to view the contents of the shopping cart
Items in Cart	Summary report of all shopping cart items
Remove Item	Request to remove item from shopping cart
Check Out	Request to check out and process order

The final step was to identify the interrelationships between these four entities. After carefully studying all the related information, he concluded the following:

1. Each Customer <u>owns</u> *zero-to-many* Shopping Cart Instances; each Shopping Cart Instance <u>is-owned-by</u> *one-and-only-one* Customer.

2. Each Shopping Cart Instance <u>contains</u> *one-and-only-one* Inventory item; each Inventory item <u>is-contained-in</u> *zero-to-many* Shopping Cart Instances.

3. Each Customer <u>places</u> *zero-to-many* Orders; each Order <u>is-placed-by</u> *one-and-only-one* Customer.

4. Each Order <u>contains</u> *one-to-many* Shopping Cart Instances; each Shopping Cart Instance <u>is-contained-in</u> *one-and-only-one* Order.

With these relationships defined, Jim drew the E-R diagram shown in Figure 7-13. Through it, he demonstrated his understanding of the requirements, the flow of information within the WebStore, the flow of information between the WebStore and existing PVF systems, and now the conceptual data model.

TABLE 7-4:   Data Category, Data Flow, and the Source/Destination of Data Flows within the WebStore DFD

Data Category

Data Flow	From/To
Customer Reated	
Customer ID	From Customer to Process 4.0
	From Process 4.0 to Customer Tracking System
	From Process 5.0 to Customer
Customer Information	From Customer to Process 5.0
	From Process 5.0 to Customer
	From Process 5.0 to Customer Tracking System
	From Customer Tracking System to Process 4.0
Inventory Related	
Product Item	From Process 1.0 to Data Store D1
	From Process 3.0 to Data Store D2
Item Profile	From Data Store D1 to Process 1.0
	From Process 1.0 to Process 2.0
	From Process 2.0 to Data Store D2
	From Data Store D2 to Process 3.0
	From Data Store D2 to Process 4.0
Order Related	
Order Number	From Purchasing Fulfillment System to Process 4.0
	From Customer to Process 6.0
	From Process 6.0 to Purchasing Fulfillment System
Order	From Process 4.0 to Purchasing Fulfillment System
Return Code	From Purchasing Fulfillment System to Process 4.0
Invoice	From Process 4.0 to Customer
Order Status Information	From Process 6.0 to Customer
	From Purchasing Fulfillment System to Process 6.0
Shopping Cart	
Cart ID	From Data Store D2 to Process 3.0
	From Data Store D2 to Process 4.0
Temporary User/System Messages	
Product Item Request	From Customer to Process 1.0
Purchase Request	From Customer to Process 2.0
View Cart	From Customer to Process 3.0
Items in Cart	From Process 3.0 to Customer
Remove Item	From Customer to Process 3.0
	From Process 3.0 to Data Store D2
Check Out	From Customer to Process 4.0

Over the next few hours, Jim planned to refine his understanding further by listing the specific attributes for each entity and then comparing these lists with the existing inventory, customer, and order database tables. He had to make sure that all attributes were accounted for before determining a final design strategy.

FIGURE 7-13
Entity-relationship diagram
for the WebStore system.

Selecting the Best Alternative Design Strategy

Selecting the best alternative system involves at least two basic steps: (1) generating a comprehensive set of alternative design strategies, and (2) selecting the one that is most likely to result in the desired information system, given all of the organizational, economic, and technical constraints that limit what can be done. A system **design strategy** represents a particular approach to developing the system. Selecting a strategy requires you to answer questions about the system's functionality, hardware and system software platform, and method for acquisition. We use the term *design strategy* in this chapter rather than *alternative system* because, at the end of analysis, we are still quite a long way from specifying an actual system. This delay is purposeful because we do not want to invest in design efforts until some agreement is reached on which direction to take the project and the new system. The best we can do at this point is to outline, rather broadly, the approach we can take in moving from logical system specifications to a working physical system. The overall process of selecting the best system strategy and the deliverables from this step in the analysis process are discussed next.

Design strategy
A particular approach to developing an information system. It includes statements on the system's functionality, hardware and system software platform, and method for acquisition.

The Process of Selecting the Best Alternative Design Strategy

Systems analysis involves determining requirements and structuring requirements. After the system requirements have been structured in terms of process flow and data, analysts again work with users to package the requirements into different system configurations. Shaping alternative system design strategies involves the following processes:

- Dividing requirements into different sets of capabilities, ranging from the bare minimum that users would accept (the required features) to the most elaborate and advanced system the company could afford to develop (which includes all the features desired by all users). Alternatively, different sets of capabilities may represent the position of different organizational units with conflicting notions about what the system should do.

- Enumerating different potential implementation environments (hardware, system software, and network platforms) that could be used to deliver the different sets of capabilities. (Choices on the implementation environment may place technical limitations on the subsequent design phase activities.)

- Proposing different ways to source or acquire the various sets of capabilities for the different implementation environments.

In theory, if the system includes three sets of requirements, two implementation environments, and four sources of application software, twenty-four design strategies would be possible. In practice, some combinations are usually infeasible, and only a small number—typically three—can be easily considered.

Selecting the best alternative is usually done with the help of a quantitative procedure, an example of which comes later in the chapter. Analysts will recommend what they believe to be the best alternative, but management (a combination of the steering committee and those who will fund the rest of the project) will make the ultimate decision about which system design strategy to follow. At this point in the life cycle, it is also certainly possible for management to end a project before the more expensive phases of system design or system implementation and operation are begun. Reasons for ending a project might include the costs or risks outweighing the benefits, the needs of the organization having changed since the project began, or other competing projects having become more important while development resources remain limited.

Generating Alternative Design Strategies

The solution to an organizational problem may seem obvious to an analyst. Typically, the analyst is familiar with the problem, having conducted an extensive analysis of it and how it has been solved in the past. On the other hand, the analyst may be more familiar with a particular solution that he or she attempts to apply to all organizational problems encountered. For example, if an analyst is an expert at using advanced database technology to solve problems, then he or she tends to recommend advanced database technology as a solution to every possible problem. Or if the analyst designed a similar system for another customer or business unit, the "natural" design strategy would be the one used before. Given the role of the analysts' experience in the solutions they suggest, analysis teams typically generate at least two alternative solutions for every problem they work on.

A good number of alternatives for analysts to generate is three. Why three? Because three alternatives can neatly represent low, middle, and high ranges of potential solutions. One alternative represents the low end of the range. Low-end alternatives are the most conservative in terms of the effort, cost, and technology involved in developing a new system. Some low-end solutions may not involve computer technology at all, focusing instead on making paper flows more efficient or reducing redundancies in current processes. A low-end strategy provides all the required functionality users demand with a system that is minimally different from the current system.

Another alternative represents the high end of the range. High-end alternatives go beyond simply solving the problem in question and focus instead on systems that contain many extra features users may desire. Functionality, not cost, is the primary focus of high-end alternatives. A high-end alternative will provide all desired features using advanced technologies that often allow the system to expand to meet future requirements. Finally, the third alternative lies between the extremes of the low-end and high-end systems. Such alternatives combine the frugality of low-end alternatives with the focus on functionality of high-end alternatives. Midrange alternatives represent compromise solutions. Other possible solutions exist outside of these three alternatives, of course. Defining the low, middle, and high possibilities allows the analyst to draw bounds around what can be reasonably done.

How do you know where to draw bounds around the potential solution space? The analysis team has already gathered the information it needs to identify the solution, but first that information must be systematically organized. The first of two major considerations in this process is to determine the minimum requirements for the new system. These features are mandatory, and if any of them are missing, the design strategy is useless. Mandatory features are the ones that everyone agrees are necessary to solve the problem or meet the opportunity. Which features are mandatory can be determined from a survey of users and others who have been involved in requirements determination. You would conduct this survey near the end of the analysis phase after all requirements have been structured and analyzed. In this survey, users rate features discovered during requirements determination or categorize features on some scale, and an arbitrary breakpoint is used to divide mandatory from desired features. Some organizations will break the features into three categories: mandatory, essential, and desired. Whereas mandatory features screen out possible solutions, essential features are the important capabilities of a system that serve as the primary basis for comparison of different design strategies. Desired features are those that users could live without but that are used to select between design strategies that are of almost equal value in terms of essential features. Features can take many different forms, as illustrated in Figure 7-14, and might include:

- *Data kept in system files:* For example, multiple customer addresses so that bills can be sent to addresses different from where we ship goods.
- *System outputs:* Printed reports, online displays, transaction documents (for example, a paycheck or sales summary graph).
- *Analyses to generate the information in system outputs:* For example, a sales forecasting module or an installment billing routine.
- *Expectations on accessibility, response time, or turnaround time for system functions:* For example, online, real-time updating of inventory files.

The second consideration in drawing bounds around alternative design strategies is determining the constraints on system development. Constraints, some of which also appear in Figure 7-14, may include:

- *A date when the replacement system is needed.*
- *Available financial and human resources.*
- *Elements of the current system that cannot change.*
- *Legal and contractual restrictions:* For example, a software package bought off the shelf cannot be legally modified, or a license to use a particular software package may limit the number of concurrent users to twenty-five.
- *The importance or dynamics of the problem that may limit how the system can be acquired:* For example, a strategically important system that uses highly proprietary data probably cannot be outsourced or purchased.

Features

Database

Data   Output   Analyses

Constraints

Time   Financial   Legal

FIGURE 7-14
Essential features to consider during systems development include data (such as customer addresses), output (such as a printed report like a sales summary graph), and analyses (such as a sales forecast). Constraints on systems development may include time, finances, and legal issues.

Remember, be impertinent and question whether stated constraints are firm. You may want to consider some design alternatives that violate constraints you consider to be flexible.

Developing Design Strategies for Hoosier Burger's New Inventory Control System

As an example of alternative generation and selection, let's look at an inventory control system that Hoosier Burger wants developed. Figure 7-15 lists ranked requirements and constraints for the enhanced information system being considered by Hoosier Burger. The requirements represent a sample of those developed from the requirements determination and structuring carried out in prior analysis steps. The system in question is an upgrade to the company's existing inventory system. Before deciding to get a new inventory system, Bob Mellankamp, one of the owners of Hoosier Burger, had to follow several steps in his largely manual inventory control system, as identified in Figure 7-16.

Using the current manual system, Bob first receives invoices from suppliers, and he records their receipt on an invoice log sheet. He puts the actual invoices in his accordion file. Using the invoices, Bob records the amount of stock delivered on the stock logs, paper forms posted near the point of storage for each inventory item. The stock logs include minimum order quantities, as well as spaces for posting the starting amount, amount delivered, and the amount used for each item. Amounts delivered are entered on the sheet when Bob logs stock deliveries; amounts used are entered after Bob has compared

FIGURE 7-15
Ranked system requirements and constraints for Hoosier Burger's inventory system.

SYSTEM REQUIREMENTS (in descending priority)	SYSTEM CONSTRAINTS (in descending order)
1. Must be able to easily enter shipments into system as soon as they are received.	1. System development can cost no more than $50,000.
2. System must automatically determine whether and when a new order should be placed.	2. New hardware can cost no more than $50,000.
3. Management should be able to determine at any time approximately what inventory levels are for any given item in stock.	3. The new system must be operational in no more than six months from the start of the contract.
	4. Training needs must be minimal (i.e., the new system must be easy to use).

FIGURE 7-16
The steps in Hoosier Burger's inventory control system.

1. Meet delivery trucks before opening restaurant.
2. Unload and store deliveries.
3. Log invoices and file in accordion file.
4. Manually add amounts received to stock logs.
5. After closing, print inventory report.
6. Count physical inventory amounts.
7. Compare inventory reports totals to physical count totals.
8. Compare physical count totals to minimum order quantities; if the amount is less, make order; if not, do nothing.
9. Pay bills that are due and record them as paid.

the amounts of stock used, according to a physical count and according to the numbers on the inventory report generated by the food-ordering system. Some Hoosier Burger items, especially perishable goods, have standing orders for daily delivery.

The Mellankamps want to improve their inventory system so that new orders are immediately accounted for, so that the system can determine when new orders should be placed, and so that management can obtain accurate inventory levels at any time of the day. All three of these system requirements have been ranked in order of descending priority in Figure 7-15. A logical data-flow diagram showing the key processes in the desired inventory system is shown in Figure 7-17. The goal of having new orders automatically accounted for is reflected in Process 1.0. The goal of having the system determine when new orders should be placed is realized in Process 3.0. The third goal for the new system, of allowing managers to obtain accurate inventory levels at any time, is captured by Process 5.0. The two other processes in Figure 7-17, generating payments (4.0) and updating inventory levels due to usage (2.0), are part of the existing manual system.

The constraints on developing an enhanced inventory system at Hoosier Burger are also listed in Figure 7-15, again in order of descending priority. The first two constraints cover costs for systems development and for new computer hardware. Development can cost no more than $50,000. New hardware can cost no more than $50,000. The third constraint involves time for development—Hoosier Burger wants the system to be installed and in operation in no more than six months from the beginning of the development project. Finally, Hoosier Burger would prefer that training for the system be simple; the new system must be designed so that it is easy to use. However, because it is the fourth most important constraint, the demands it makes are more flexible than those contained in the other three.

Any set of alternative solutions to Hoosier Burger's inventory system problems must be developed with the company's prioritized requirements and

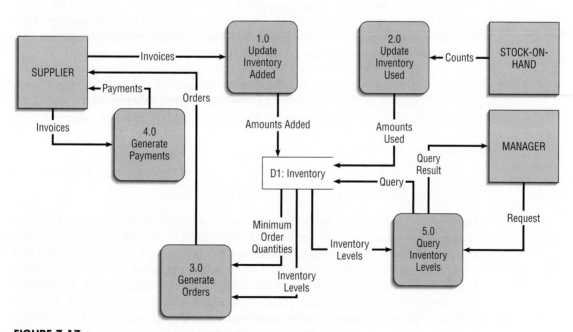

FIGURE 7-17
A logical data-flow diagram showing the key processes in Hoosier Burger's desired inventory system.

CRITERIA	ALTERNATIVE A	ALTERNATIVE B	ALTERNATIVE C
Requirements			
1. Easy real-time entry of new shipment data	Yes	Yes	Yes
2. Automatic reorder decisions	For some items	For all items	For all items
3. Real-time data on inventory levels	Not available	Available for some items only	Fully available
Constraints			
1. Cost to develop	$25,000	$50,000	$65,000
2. Cost of hardware	$25,000	$50,000	$50,000
3. Time to operation	Three months	Six months	Nine months
4. Ease of training	One week of training	Two weeks of training	One week of training

FIGURE 7-18
Description of three alternative systems that could be developed for Hoosier Burger's inventory system.

constraints in mind. Figure 7-18 illustrates how each of three possible alternatives meets (or exceeds) the criteria implied in Hoosier Burger's requirements and constraints. Alternative A is a low-end solution. It meets only the first requirement completely and partially satisfies the second requirement, but it does not meet the final one. However, Alternative A is relatively inexpensive to develop and requires hardware that is much less expensive than the largest amount Hoosier Burger is willing to pay. Alternative A also meets the requirements for the other two constraints: It will take only 3 months to become operational, and users will require only 1 week of training. Alternative C is the high-end solution. Alternative C meets all of the requirements criteria. On the other hand, Alternative C violates two of the four constraints: Development costs are high at $65,000, and time to operation is 9 months. If Hoosier Burger really wants to satisfy all three of its requirements for its new inventory system, the company will have to pay more than it wants and will have to wait longer for development. Once operational, however, Alternative C will take just as much time to train people to use as Alternative A. Alternative B is in the middle. This alternative solution meets the first two requirements, partially satisfies the third, and does not violate any of the constraints.

Now that three plausible alternative solutions have been generated for Hoosier Burger, the analyst hired to study the problem has to decide which one to recommend to management for development. Management will then decide whether to continue with the development project (incremental commitment) and whether the system recommended by the analyst should be developed.

Selecting the Most Likely Alternative

One method we can use to decide among the alternative solutions to Hoosier Burger's inventory system problem is illustrated in Figure 7-19. On the left, you see that we have listed all three system requirements and all four constraints from Figure 7-15. These are our decision criteria. We have weighted requirements as a group and constraints as a group equally; that is, we believe that requirements are just as important as constraints. We do not have to weight requirements and constraints equally; it is certainly possible to make requirements more or less important than constraints. Weights are arrived at

Criteria	Weight	Alternative A		Alternative B		Alternative C	
		Rating	Score	Rating	Score	Rating	Score
Requirements							
Real-time data entry	18	5	90	5	90	5	90
Auto reorder	18	3	54	5	90	5	90
Real-time data query	14	1	14	3	42	5	70
	50		158		222		250
Constraints							
Development costs	20	5	100	4	80	3	60
Hardware costs	15	5	75	4	60	4	60
Time to operation	10	5	50	4	40	3	30
Ease of training	5	5	25	3	15	5	25
	50		250		195		175
Total	100		408		417		425

FIGURE 7-19
Weighted approach for comparing the three alternative systems for Hoosier Burger's inventory system.

in discussions among the analysis team, users, and sometimes managers. Weights tend to be fairly subjective, and for that reason, should be determined through a process of open discussion to reveal underlying assumptions, followed by an attempt to reach consensus among stakeholders. We have also assigned weights to each individual requirement and constraint. Notice that the total of the weights for both requirements and constraints is 50. Our weights correspond with our prioritization of the requirements and constraints.

Our next step is to rate each requirement and constraint for each alternative, on a scale of 1 to 5. A rating of 1 indicates that the alternative does not meet the requirement well or that the alternative violates the constraint. A rating of 5 indicates that the alternative meets or exceeds the requirement or clearly abides by the constraint. Ratings are even more subjective than weights and should also be determined through open discussion among users, analysts, and managers. The next step is to multiply the rating for each requirement and each constraint by its weight and follow this procedure for each alternative. The final step is to add up the weighted scores for each alternative. Notice that we have included three sets of totals: for requirements, for constraints, and for overall totals. If you look at the totals for requirements, Alternative C is the best choice (score of 250), because it meets or exceeds all requirements. However, if you look only at constraints, Alternative A is the best choice (score of 250), as it does not violate any constraints. When we combine the totals for requirements and constraints, we see that the best choice is Alternative C (score of 425), even though it had the lowest score for constraints, as it has the highest overall score.

Alternative C, then, appears to be the best choice for Hoosier Burger. Whether Alternative C is actually chosen for development is another issue. The Mellankamps may be concerned that Alternative C violates two constraints, including the most important one, development costs. On the other hand, the owners (and chief users) at Hoosier Burger may want the full functionality Alternative C offers that they are willing to ignore the constraints violations. Or Hoosier Burger's management may be so interested in cutting costs that it prefers Alternative A, even though its functionality is severely limited. What may appear to be the best choice for a systems development project may not always be the one that ends up being developed.

Key Points Review

1. **Concisely define each of the following key data-modeling terms:** *conceptual data model, entity-relationship diagram, entity type, entity instance, attribute, candidate key, multivalued attribute, relationship, degree, cardinality,* **and** *associative entity.*

   A conceptual data model represents the overall structure of organizational data, independent of any database technology. An E-R diagram is a detailed representation of the entities, associations, and attributes for an organization or business area. An entity type is a collection of entities that share common properties or characteristics. An attribute is a named property or characteristic of an entity. One or a combination of attributes that uniquely identifies each instance of an entity type is called a candidate key. A multivalued attribute may take on more than one value for an entity instance. A relationship is an association between the instances of one or more entity types, and the number of entity types participating in a relationship is the degree of the relationship. Cardinality is the number of instances of entity B that can (or must) be associated with each instance of entity A. Data that are simultaneously associated with several entity instances are stored in an associative entity.

2. **Ask the right kinds of questions to determine data requirements for an information system.**

   Information is gathered for conceptual data modeling as part of each phase of the systems development life cycle. You must ask questions in business, rather than data modeling, terms so that business managers can explain the nature of the business; the systems analyst represents the objects and events of the business through a data model. Questions include: What are the objects of the business? What uniquely characterizes each object? What characteristics describe each object? How are data used? What history of data must be retained? What events occur that relate different kinds of data, and are there special data-handling procedures? (See Table 7-1 for details.)

3. **Draw an entity-relationship (E-R) diagram to represent common business situations.**

   An E-R diagram uses symbols for entity, relationship, identifier, attribute, multivalued attribute, and associative entity and shows the degree and cardinality of relationships (see Figure 7-5 for all the symbols discussed in this chapter, and see Figures 7-3 and 7-11 for example diagrams). Exercises at the end of this chapter give you practice at drawing E-R diagrams.

4. **Explain the role of conceptual data modeling in the overall analysis and design of an information system.**

   Conceptual data modeling occurs in parallel with other requirements analysis and structuring steps during systems development. Information for conceptual data modeling is collected during interviews, from questionnaires, and in JAD sessions. Conceptual data models may be developed for a new information system and for the system it is replacing, as well as for the whole database for current and new systems. A conceptual data model is useful input to subsequent data-oriented steps in the analysis, design, and implementation phases of systems development where logical data models, physical file designs, and database file coding are done.

5. **Distinguish between unary, binary, and ternary relationships and give an example of each.**

   A unary relationship is between instances of the same entity type (e.g., Is_married_to relates different instances of a PERSON entity type). A binary relationship is between instances of two entity types (e.g., Registers_for relates instances of STUDENT and COURSE entity types). A ternary relationship is a simultaneous association among instances of three entity types (e.g., Supplies relates instances of PART, VENDOR, and WAREHOUSE entity types).

6. **Distinguish between a relationship and an associative entity, and use associative entities in a data model when appropriate.**

   Sometimes many-to-many and one-to-one relationships have associated attributes. When this occurs, it is best to change the relationship into an associative entity. For example, if we needed to know the date an employee completed a course, Date_Completed is neither an attribute of EMPLOYEE nor COURSE but of the relationship between these entities. In this case, we would create a CERTIFICATE associative entity (see Figure 7-7), associate Date_Completed with CERTIFICATE, and draw mandatory one relationships from CERTIFICATE to each of EMPLOYEE and COURSE. An associative entity, like any entity, then may be related to other entities, as shown in Figure 7-8.

7. **Relate data modeling to process and logic modeling as different ways of describing an information system.**

   Process and logic modeling represent the movement and use of data, whereas data modeling represents the meaning and structure of data.

A data model is usually a more permanent representation of the data requirements of an organization than are models of data flow and use. Still, consistency between these models of different views of an information system is required. For example, all the data in an E-R diagram for an information system must be in data stores on associated data-flow diagrams.

8. **Generate at least three alternative design strategies for an information system.**

    Generating different alternatives is something you would do in actual systems analysis or as part of a class project. Three is not a magic number.

It represents instead the endpoints and midpoint of a series of alternatives, such as the most expensive, the least expensive, and an alternative somewhere in the middle.

9. **Select the best design strategy using both qualitative and quantitative methods.**

    Once developed, alternatives can be compared to each other through quantitative methods, but the actual decision may depend on other criteria, such as organizational politics. In this chapter, you were introduced to one way to compare alternative design strategies quantitatively.

Key Terms Checkpoint

Here are the key terms from the chapter. The page where each term is first explained is in parentheses after the term.

1. Associative entity (p. 204)
2. Attribute (p. 199)
3. Binary relationship (p. 203)
4. Candidate key (p. 199)
5. Cardinality (p. 203)
6. Conceptual data model (p. 190)
7. Degree (p. 202)
8. Design strategy (p. 213)
9. Entity (p. 197)
10. Entity instance (instance) (p. 198)
11. Entity-relationship diagram (E-R diagram) (p. 197)
12. Entity type (p. 198)
13. Identifier (p. 199)
14. Multivalued attribute (p. 200)
15. Relationship (p. 201)
16. Repeating group (p. 201)
17. Ternary relationship (p. 203)
18. Unary relationship (recursive relationship) (p. 202)

Match each of the key terms above with the definition that best fits it.

_____ 1. A graphical representation of the entities, associations, and data for an organization or business area; it is a model of entities, the associations among those entities, and the attributes of both the entities and their associations.

_____ 2. A single occurrence of an entity type.

_____ 3. An attribute that may take on more than one value for each entity instance.

_____ 4. A simultaneous relationship among instances of three entity types.

_____ 5. A collection of entities that share common properties or characteristics.

_____ 6. A relationship between instances of two entity types.

_____ 7. An entity type that associates the instances of one or more entity types and contains attributes that are peculiar to the relationship between those entity instances.

_____ 8. A named property or characteristic of an entity that is of interest to the organization.

_____ 9. The number of instances of entity B that can (or must) be associated with each instance of entity A.

_____ 10. A candidate key that has been selected as the unique, identifying characteristic for an entity type.

_____ 11. An association between the instances of one or more entity types that is of interest to the organization.

_____ 12. An attribute (or combination of attributes) that uniquely identifies each instance of an entity type.

_____ 13. The number of entity types that participate in a relationship.

_____ 14. A relationship between the instances of one entity type.

_____ 15. A detailed model that shows the overall structure of organizational data but is independent of any database management system or other implementation considerations.

_____ 16. A set of two or more multivalued attributes that are logically related.

_____ 17. A person, place, object, event, or concept in the user environment about which the organization wishes to maintain data.

_____ 18. A particular approach to developing an information system. It includes statements on the system's functionality, hardware and system software platform, and method for acquisition.

Review Questions

1. What characteristics of data are represented in an E-R diagram?
2. What elements of a data-flow diagram should be analyzed as part of data modeling?
3. Explain why a ternary relationship is not the same as three binary relationships.
4. When must a many-to-many relationship be modeled as an associative entity?
5. Which of the following types of relationships can have attributes associated with them: one-to-one, one-to-many, many-to-many?
6. What is the degree of a relationship? Give an example of each of the relationship degrees illustrated in this chapter.
7. Give an example of a ternary relationship (different from any example in this chapter).
8. List the deliverables from conceptual data modeling.
9. Explain the relationship between minimum cardinality and optional and mandatory participation.
10. List the ideal characteristics of an entity identifier attribute.
11. List the four types of E-R diagrams produced and analyzed during conceptual data modeling.
12. What notation is used on an E-R diagram to show the minimum and maximum cardinalities on a one-to-many relationship?
13. Explain the difference between a candidate key and the identifier of an entity type.
14. What distinguishes a repeating group from a simple multivalued attribute?
15. How do analysts generate alternative solutions to information systems problems?
16. How do managers decide which alternative design strategy to develop?

Problems and Exercises

1. Assume that at Pine Valley Furniture each product (described by Product No., Description, and Cost) consists of at least three components (described by Component No., Description, and Unit of Measure), and components are used to make one or many products (i.e., must be used in at least one product). In addition, assume that components are used to make other components and that raw materials are also considered to be components. In both cases of components being used to make products and components being used to make other components, we need to keep track of how many components go into making something else. Draw an E-R diagram for this situation and place minimum and maximum cardinalities on the diagram.
2. A performance venue hosts many concert series a year. Performers have a name and perform several times in a concert series (each constituting a performance with a different date). Concert series have one or more performers and have a name and a specified seating arrangement. A concert series is held in one (and only one) of several concert halls, each of which has a room number. Represent this situation of concerts and performers with an E-R diagram.
3. A restaurant chain has several store locations in a city (with a name and zip code stored for each), and each is managed by one manager. Managers manage only one store. Each restaurant location has its own unique set of menus. Most have more than one menu (e.g., lunch and dinner menus). Each menu has many menu items, and items can appear on multiple menus, and with different prices on different menus. Represent this situation of restaurants with an E-R diagram.
4. Consider the E-R diagram in Figure 7-7.
   a. What is the identifier for the CERTIFICATE associative entity?
   b. Now, assume that the same employee may take the same course multiple times, on different dates. Does this change your answer to part a? Why or why not?
   c. Now, assume we do know the instructor who issues each certificate to each employee for each course. Include this new entity in Figure 7-7 and relate it to the other entities. How did you choose to relate INSTRUCTOR to CERTIFICATE and why?
5. Consider the E-R diagram in Figure 7-20. Based on this E-R diagram, answer the following questions:
   a. How many EMPLOYEES can work on a project?
   b. What is the degree of the Used_on relationship?
   c. Do any associative entities appear in this diagram? If so, name them.
   d. How else could the attribute Skill be modeled?
   e. What attributes might be attached to the Works_on relationship?
   f. Could TOOL be modeled as an associative entity? Why or why not?

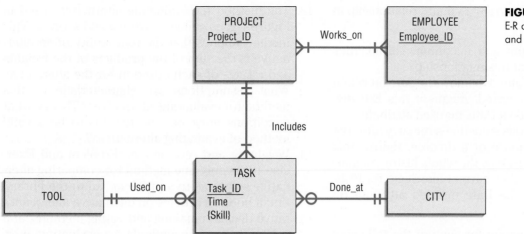

FIGURE 7-20
E-R diagram for Problem and Exercise 5.

6. A car rental is an association between a customer, sales agent, and a car. Select a few pertinent attributes for each of these entity types and represent a rental in an E-R diagram.

7. Consider the E-R diagram in Figure 7-21. Are all three relationships—Holds, Goes_on, and Transports—necessary (i.e., can one of these be deduced from the other two)? What, if any, reasonable assumptions make all three relationships necessary?

8. Draw an E-R diagram to represent the sample customer order in Figure 7-4.

9. A company database contains an entity called EMPLOYEE. Among other information, the company records information about any degrees each employee has earned, along with the graduation date for the degree.

a. Represent the EMPLOYEE entity and its degree attributes using the notation for multi-valued attributes.

b. Represent the EMPLOYEE entity and its degree attributes using two entity types.

c. Finally, assume the company decides to also keep data about the institution from which the employees' degrees were earned, including name of the institution, city, and state where the institution is located. Augment your answer to part b to accommodate this new entity type.

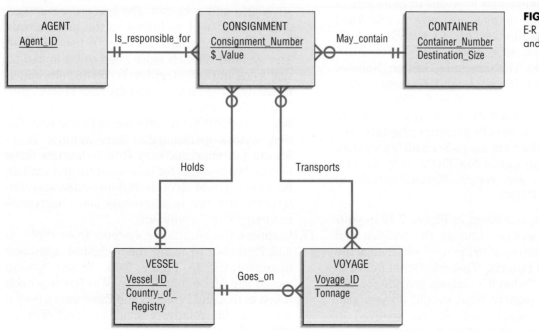

FIGURE 7-21
E-R diagram for Problem and Exercise 7.

10. Consider the Is_married_to unary relationship in Figure 7-6.

    a. Draw minimum and maximum cardinalities for each end of this relationship.
    b. Assume we wanted to know the date on which a marriage occurred. Augment this E-R diagram to include a Date_married attribute.
    c. Because persons sometimes remarry after the death of a spouse or a divorce, redraw this E-R diagram to show the whole history of marriages (not just the current marriage) for PERSONs. Show the Date_married attribute on this diagram.

11. Draw an E-R diagram for each of the following situations:

    a. A laboratory has several chemists who work on one or more projects. Chemists also may use certain kinds of equipment on each project. Attributes of CHEMIST include Employee_ID (identifier), Name, and Phone_No. Attributes of PROJECT include Project_ID (identifier) and Start_Date. Attributes of EQUIPMENT include Serial_No and Cost. The organization wishes to record Assign_Date—that is, the date when a given equipment item was assigned to a particular chemist working on a specified project. A chemist must be assigned to at least one project and one equipment item. A given equipment item need not be assigned, and a given project need not be assigned either a chemist or an equipment item. Provide good definitions for all of the relationships in this situation.
    b. A college course may have one or more scheduled sections or may not have a scheduled section. Attributes of COURSE include Course_ID, Course_Name, and Units. Attributes of SECTION include Section_Number and Semester_ID. Semester_ID is composed of two parts: Semester and Year. Section_Number is an integer (such as "1" or "2") that distinguishes one section from another for the same course but does not uniquely identify a section. How did you model SECTION? Why did you choose this way versus alternative ways to model SECTION?

12. Recreate the spreadsheet in Figure 7-19 in your spreadsheet package. Change the weights and compare the outcome to Figure 7-19. Change the rankings. Add criteria. What additional information does this "what if" analysis provide for you as a decision maker? What insight do you gain into the decision-making process involved in choosing the best alternative system design?

13. The method for evaluating alternatives used in Figure 7-19 is called weighting and scoring. This method implies that the total utility of an alternative is the sum of the products of the weights and ratings of each criterion for the alternative. What assumptions are characteristic of this method for evaluating alternatives? That is, what conditions must be true for this to be a valid method of evaluating alternatives?

14. Weighting and scoring (see Problem and Exercise 13) is only one method for comparing alternative solutions to a problem. Go to the library, find a book or articles on qualitative and quantitative decision making and voting methods, and outline two other methods for evaluating alternative solutions to a problem. What are the pros and cons of these methods compared to the weighting and scoring method? Under weighting and scoring and the other alternatives you find, how would you incorporate the opinions of multiple decision makers?

15. Prepare an agenda for a meeting at which you would present the findings of the analysis phase of the SDLC to Bob Mellankamp concerning his request for a new inventory control system. Use information provided in Chapters 5 through 7 as background in preparing this agenda. Concentrate on which topics to cover, not the content of each topic.

16. The owner of two pizza parlors located in adjacent towns wants to computerize and integrate sales transactions and inventory management within and between both stores. The point-of-sale component must be easy to use and flexible enough to accommodate a variety of pricing strategies and coupons. The inventory management, which will be linked to the point-of-sale component, must also be easy to use and fast. The systems at each store need to be linked so that sales and inventory levels can be determined instantly for each store and for both stores combined. The owner can allocate $40,000 for hardware and $20,000 for software and must have the new system operational in three months. Training must be short and easy. Briefly describe three alternative systems for this situation and explain how each would meet the requirements and constraints. Are the requirements and constraints realistic? Why or why not?

17. Compare the alternative systems from Problem and Exercise 16 using the weighted approach demonstrated in Figure 7-19. Which system would you recommend? Why? Was the approach taken in this and Problem and Exercise 16 useful even for this relatively small system? Why or why not?

18. Suppose that an analysis team did not generate alternative design strategies for consideration by a project steering committee or client. What might the consequences be of having only one design strategy? What might happen during the oral presentation of project progress if only one design strategy is offered?

19. Assume you are designing a database for a local used car dealership. Attributes for a car include the vehicle identification number, stock number, make, model, year, and trim. What would you use for the primary key in this entity? What attributes are likely to be foreign keys associated with other entities?

Discussion Questions

1. Discuss why some systems developers believe that a data model is one of the most important parts of the statement of information system requirements.

2. Using Table 7-1 as a guide, develop a script of at least ten questions you would ask during an interview of the customer-order processing department manager at Pine Valley Furniture. Assume the focus is on analyzing the requirements for a new order-entry system. The purpose of the interview is to develop a preliminary E-R diagram for this system.

3. If possible, contact a systems analyst in a local organization. Discuss with this systems analyst the role of conceptual data modeling in the overall systems analysis and design of information systems at his or her company. How, and by whom, is conceptual data modeling performed? What training in this technique is given? At what point(s) is this done in the development process? Why?

4. Talk to MIS professionals at a variety of organizations and determine the extent to which CASE tools are used in the creation and editing of entity-relationship diagrams. Try to determine whether they use CASE tools for this purpose; which CASE tools are used; and why, when, and how they are used. In companies that do not use CASE tools for this purpose, determine why not

and what would have to change in order to use them.

5. Ask a systems analyst to give you a copy of the standard notation he or she uses to draw E-R diagrams. In what ways is this notation different from notation in this text? Which notation do you prefer and why? What is the meaning of any additional notation?

6. Consider the purchase of a new PC to be used by you at your work (or by you at a job that you would like to have). Describe in detail three alternatives for this new PC that represent the low, middle, and high points of a continuum of potential solutions. Be sure that the low-end PC meets at least your minimum requirements and the high-end PC is at least within a reasonable budget. At this point, without quantitative analysis, which alternative would you choose?

7. For the new PC described in Question 6, develop ranked lists of your requirements and constraints as displayed in Figure 7-19. Display the requirements and constraints, along with the three alternatives, as done in Figure 7-19, and note how each alternative is rated on each requirement and constraint. Calculate scores for each alternative on each criterion and compute total scores. Which alternative has the highest score? Why? Does this choice fit with your selection in the previous question? Why or why not?

Case Problems

1. Pine Valley Furniture

   In order to determine the requirements for the new Customer Tracking System, several JAD sessions, interviews, and observations were conducted. Resulting information from these requirements determination methods was useful in the preparation of the Customer Tracking System's data-flow diagrams.

   One afternoon while you are working on the Customer Tracking System's data-flow diagrams, Jim Woo stops by your desk and assigns you the task of preparing a conceptual entity-relationship diagram for the Customer Tracking System. Later that afternoon, you review the

requirements-determination phase deliverables, including the data-flow diagrams you have just finished preparing.

   Your review of these deliverables suggests that the Customer Tracking System's primary objective is to track and forecast customer buying patterns. Additionally, in order to track a customer's buying habits, an order history must be established, satisfaction levels assessed, and a variety of demographic data collected. The demographic data will categorize the customer according to type, geographic location, and type of purchase. Customer Tracking System information will enable Pine Valley Furniture to better forecast its product demand, control its inventory, and solicit customers. Also, the Customer Tracking System's ability to interface with the WebStore is important to the project.

a. What entities are identified in the previous scenario? Can you think of additional entities? What interrelationships exist between the entities?
b. For each entity, identify its set of associated attributes. Specify identifiers for each entity.
c. Based on the case scenario and your answers to parts a and b, prepare an entity-relationship diagram. Be sure to specify the cardinalities for each relationship.
d. How does this conceptual model differ from the WebStore's conceptual model?

2. Hoosier Burger

Although Hoosier Burger is well recognized for its fast foods, especially the Hoosier Burger Special, plate lunches are also offered. These include such main menu items as barbecue ribs, grilled steak, meat loaf, and grilled chicken breast. The customer can choose from a variety of side items, including roasted garlic mashed potatoes, twice-baked potatoes, coleslaw, corn, baked beans, and Caesar salad.

Many downtown businesses often call and place orders for Hoosier Mighty Meals. These are combination meals consisting of a selection of main menu items and three side orders. The customer can request Hoosier Mighty Meals to feed 5, 10, 15, or 20 individuals. As a convenience to its business customers, Bob and Thelma allow business customers to charge their order. Once each month, a bill is generated and sent to those business customers who have charged their orders. Bob and Thelma have found that many of their business customers are repeat customers and often place orders for the same Hoosier Mighty Meals. Bob asks you if it is possible to track a customer's order history, and you indicate that it is indeed possible.

a. Based on the information provided in the case scenario, what entities will Hoosier Burger need to store information about?
b. For the entities identified in part a, identify a set of attributes for each entity.
c. Specify an identifier for each entity. What rules did you apply when selecting the identifier?
d. Modify Figure 7-10 to reflect the addition of these new entities. Be sure to specify the cardinalities for each relationship.

3. Corporate Technology Center

Five years ago, Megan Thomas was a busy executive seeking to keep herself and her employees current with new technology. She

realized that many small companies were facing the same dilemma. Using her life savings and money from investors, Megan founded Corporate Technology Center. Corporate Technology Center's primary objective is to offer technology update seminars to local business executives and their employees. A wide variety of seminars are offered, including ones covering operating systems, spreadsheets, word processing, database management, Internet, Web page design, and telecommunications.

Although Corporate Technology Center offers seminars at its own campus, it also provides on-site training for local companies. One-day, two-day, or four-day seminars are offered. Courses are open to a minimum of twenty students and a maximum of forty students. Although several staff members are capable of teaching any given course, generally only one staff member teaches a given course on a given date.

a. What entities are identified in the previous scenario? Can you identify additional entities?
b. For each entity identified in part a, specify a set of associated attributes.
c. Select an identifier for each entity. What rules did you apply when selecting the identifier?
d. Based on the case scenario and your answers to a, b, and c, prepare an entity-relationship diagram. Be sure to specify the cardinalities for each relationship.

4. Pine Valley Furniture

During your time as a Pine Valley Furniture intern, you have learned much about the systems analysis and design process. You have been able to observe Jim Woo as he serves as the lead analyst on the WebStore project, and you have also received hands-on experience with the Customer Tracking System project. The requirements determination and requirements structuring activities for the Customer Tracking System are now complete, and it is time to begin generating alternative design strategies.

On Monday afternoon, Jim Woo stops by your desk and requests that you attend a meeting scheduled for tomorrow morning. He mentions that during tomorrow's meeting, the Customer Tracking System's requirements and constraints, weighting criteria, and alternative design strategy ratings will be discussed. He also mentions that during the previously conducted systems planning and selection phase, Jackie Judson and he prepared a baseline project plan. At the time the initial baseline project plan was prepared, the in-house development option was the preferred design strategy. The marketing group's unique information needs seemed to indicate that in-house development was the best option. However, other alternative design strategies have since been investigated.

During Tuesday's meeting, several end users, managers, and systems development team members meet, discuss, and rank the requirements and constraints for the new Customer Tracking System. Also, weights and rankings are assigned to the three alternative design strategies. At the end of the meeting, Jim Woo assigns you the task of arranging this information into a table and calculating the overall scores for each alternative. He would like to review this information later in the afternoon. Tables 7-5 and 7-6 summarize the information obtained from Tuesday's meeting.

a. Generally speaking, what alternative design strategies were available to Pine Valley Furniture?
b. Of the alternative design strategies available to Pine Valley Furniture, which were the most viable? Why?
c. Using the information provided in Table 7-6, calculate the scores for each alternative.
d. Based on the information provided in Tables 7-5 and 7-6, which alternative do you recommend?

5. Hoosier Burger

As the lead analyst on the Hoosier Burger project, you have been busy collecting, structuring, and evaluating the new system's requirements. During a Monday morning meeting with Bob and Thelma, the three of you review the system requirements, system constraints, and alternative design strategies. The proposed alternative design strategies address low-end, midrange, and high-end solutions. Additionally, weights are assigned to the evaluation criteria, and the alternatives are ranked according to the criteria.

Bob has stated repeatedly that his main priority is to implement an inventory control system. However, you are aware that, if at all possible, Bob would like to also implement a delivery system. You inform Bob that two of the alternative design strategies support a delivery system but will increase the system's development cost by at least $20,000 and will add $10,000 in recurring costs to the new system. Bob feels that the addition of the new delivery system will result in $25,000 in yearly benefits over the life of the new system.

The inclusion of a delivery system necessitates the addition of several new requirements and the modification of system constraints. Table 7-7

TABLE 7-5: Pine Valley Furniture Requirements and Constraints

Criteria	Alternative A	Alternative B	Alternative C
New Requirements			
Ease of use	Acceptable	Fair	Good
Easy real-time updating of customer profiles	Yes	Yes	Yes
Tracks customer purchasing activity	No	Yes	Yes
Supports sales forecasting	Some forecasting models are supported	Some forecasting models are supported	Provides support for all necessary forecasting models
Ad hoc report generation	No	Yes	Yes
Constraints			
Must interface with existing systems	Requires significant modifications	Minor modifications	Minor modifications
Costs to develop	$150,000	$200,000	$350,000
Cost of hardware	$80,000	$80,000	$100,000
Time to operation	6 months	7 months	9 months
Must interface with existing systems	Requires significant modifications	Minor modifications	Minor modifications
Ease of training	3 weeks of training	3 weeks of training	2 weeks of training
Legal restrictions	Cannot be modified	Allows for customization	None

TABLE 7-6:   Pine Valley Furniture Multi-Criteria Analysis

Criteria	Weight	Alternative A		Alternative B		Alternative C	
		Rating	Score	Rating	Score	Rating	Score
Requirements							
Ease of use	15	2		3		5	
Real-time customer profile updating	12	3		3		4	
Tracks customer purchasing activity	12	1		3		3	
Sales forecasting	8	2		2		3	
Ad hoc report generation	3	1		2		3	
Total	50						
Constraints							
Interfaces with existing systems	15	3		4		2	
Development costs	10	5		4		2	
Hardware costs	10	5		4		2	
Time to operation	5	4		1		2	
Ease of training	5	2		2		4	
Legal restrictions	5	1		2		5	
Total	50						

outlines these changes. The weights, ratings, and scores also require adjustments. Table 7-8 contains information about these adjustments.

a. Generally speaking, what alternative design strategies are available to Hoosier Burger?
b. Is an enterprise resource planning system a viable option for Hoosier Burger? Why or why not?

c. Modify Figure 7-19 to incorporate the criteria mandated by the new delivery system. Which alternative should be chosen?
d. Assuming that Alternative C is still chosen, update Hoosier Burger's economic feasibility analysis to reflect the changes mentioned in this scenario.

TABLE 7-7:   Hoosier Burger Requirements and Constraints

Criteria	Alternative A	Alternative B	Alternative C
New Requirements			
Easy real-time entry of new shipment data	Yes	Yes	Yes
Automatic reorder decisions	For some items	For all items	For all items
Real-time data on inventory levels	Not available	Available for some items only	Fully available
Facilitates forecasting	Not available	Available	Available
Track delivery sales	Available	Available	Available
Customer billing	Not available	Not available	Available
Constraints			
Costs to develop	$45,000	$70,000	$85,000
Cost of hardware	$25,000	$50,000	$50,000
Time to operation	4 months	7 months	10 months
Ease of training	1 week of training	3 weeks of training	3 weeks of training

TABLE 7-8: Hoosier Burger Multi-Criteria Analysis

Criteria	Weight	Alternative A		Alternative B		Alternative C	
		Rating	Score	Rating	Score	Rating	Score
Requirements							
Real-time data entry	12	5		5		5	
Auto reorder	12	3		5		5	
Real-time data query	10	1		3		5	
Facilitates forecasting	8	1		2		3	
Track delivery sales	5	3		3		3	
Customer billing	3	1		1		3	
Total	50						
Constraints							
Development costs	20	5		4		2	
Hardware costs	15	5		4		3	
Time to operation	10	5		4		3	
Ease of training	5	2		1		5	
Total	50						

CASE: PETRIE'S ELECTRONICS

Structuring Systems Requirements: Conceptual Data Modeling

Jim Watanabe, manager of the "No Customer Escapes" project, and assistant director of IT for Petrie's Electronics, was sitting in the company cafeteria. He had just finished his house salad and was about to go back to his office when Stephanie Welch sat down at his table. Jim had met Stephanie once, back when he started work at Petrie's. He remembered she worked for the database administrator.

"Hi, Jim, remember me?" she asked.

"Sure, Stephanie, how are you? How are things in database land?"

"Can't complain. Sanjay asked me to talk to you about the database needs for your new customer loyalty system." Stephanie's phone binged. She pulled it out of her oversize bag and looked at it. She started to text as she continued to talk to Jim. "How far along are you on your database requirements?"

That's kinda rude, Jim thought. Oh well. "We are still in the early stages. I can send you a very preliminary E-R diagram we have [PE Figure 7-1], along with a description of the major entities."

"OK, that will help. I suspect that you won't have too many new entities to add to what's already in the system," Stephanie responded, still looking at her phone and still texting. She briefly looked up at Jim and smiled slightly before going back to texting. "Just send the E-R to me, and I'll let you know if I have any questions." She stood up, still looking at her phone. "Gotta go," she said, and she walked away.

OK, Jim thought, I need to remember to send Stephanie the preliminary E-R we have. I should probably send her the entity descriptions too (PE Table 7-1), just in case. Jim stood up, carried his tray over to the recycling area of the cafeteria, and went back to his office.

When Jim got back to his office, Sanjay was waiting for him.

"I've got more information on those alternatives we talked about earlier," Sanjay said. "I had one of my employees gather some data on how the alternatives might satisfy our needs." (See the descriptions of the alternatives in PE Table 5-2.) Sanjay handed Jim a short report. "The matrix shows the requirements and constraints for each alternative and makes it relatively easy to compare them." (See PE Figure 7-2.)

PE FIGURE 7-1
Initial E-R for Petrie's customer loyalty program.

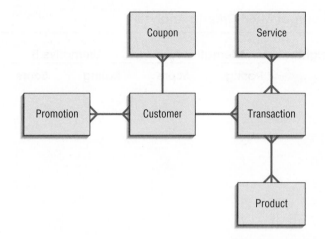

PE TABLE 7-1: Entity Descriptions for the Preliminary E-R Diagram for Petrie's Customer Loyalty System

Entity	Description
Coupon	A coupon is a special promotion created specifically for an individual customer. A coupon is for a set dollar amount, for example, $10. The customer may use it like cash or like a dollars-off promotion when purchasing products or services. Coupons can only be created for an individual customer based on the points in his or her customer loyalty account. For each dollar value of a coupon, a certain number of points must be redeemed. Coupons must be accounted for when created and when redeemed.
Customer	A customer is someone who buys products and/or services from Petrie's Electronics. Customers include both online customers and those who shop in Petrie's Brick-and-Mortar stores.
Product	An item made available for sale to a Petrie's customer. For example, a product is a 40" Sony LCD HD television. Products can be purchased online or in Brick-and-Mortar stores.
Promotion	A promotion is a special incentive provided to a customer to entice the customer into buying a specific product or service. For example, a promotion intended to sell Blu-ray disks may involve 2-for-1 coupons. Promotions are targeted to all customers, or to subsets of customers, not just to individual customers.
Service	A job performed by one of Petrie's associates for a customer. For example, upgrading the memory in a computer by installing new memory cards is a service that Petrie's provides for a fee. Services may only be ordered and performed in Brick-and-Mortar stores, not online.
Transaction	A record that a particular product or service was sold to a specified customer on a particular date. A transaction may involve more than one product or service, and it may involve more than one of a particular kind of product or service. For example, one transaction may involve blank DVDs and prerecorded DVDs, and the prerecorded DVDs may all be of the same movie. For members of the loyalty program, each transaction is worth a number of points, depending on the dollar value of the transaction.

"The matrix favors the XRA CRM system," Jim said, after looking over the report. "It looks like their proposal meets our requirements the best, but the Nova group's proposal does the best job with the constraints."

"Yes, but just barely," Sanjay said. "There is only a five-point difference between XRA and Nova, so they are pretty comparable when it comes to constraints. But I think the XRA system has a pretty clear advantage in meeting our requirements."

"XRA seems to be pretty highly rated in your matrix in terms of all of the requirements. You have them ranked better than the other two proposals for implementation, scalability, and vendor support," Jim said. "The '5' you gave them for proven performance is one of the few '5s' you have in your whole matrix."

"That's because they are one of the best companies in the industry to work with," Sanjay responded, "Their reputation is stellar."

"This looks really promising," Jim said. "Let's see if reality matches what we have here. It's time to put together the formal request for proposal. I'll get that work started today. I hope that all three of these companies decide to bid."

Criteria	Weight	Alternative A	SBSI	Alternative B	XRA	Alternative C	Nova
		Rating	Score	Rating	Score	Rating	Score
Requirements							
Effective customer incentives	15	5	75	4	60	4	60
Easy for customers to use	10	3	30	4	40	5	50
Proven performance	10	4	40	5	50	3	30
Easy to implement	5	3	15	4	20	3	15
Scalable	10	3	30	4	40	3	30
Vendor support	10	3	30	4	40	3	30
	60		220		250		215
Constraints							
Cost to buy	15	3	45	4	60	5	75
Cost to operate	10	3	30	4	40	4	40
Time to implement	5	3	15	3	15	3	15
Staff to implement	10	3	30	4	40	3	30
	40		120		155		160
Total	100		340		405		375

PE FIGURE 7-2
Evaluation matrix for customer loyalty proposals.

Case Questions

1. Review the data-flow diagrams you developed for questions in the Petrie's Electronics case at the end of Chapter 6 (or diagrams given to you by your instructor). Study the data flows and data stored on these diagrams and decide whether you agree with the team's conclusion that the only six entity types needed are listed in the case and in PE Figure 7-1. If you disagree, define additional entity types, explain why they are necessary, and modify PE Figure 7-1 accordingly.

2. Again, review the DFDs you developed for the Petrie's Electronics case (or those given to you by your instructor). Use these DFDs to identify the attributes of each of the six entities listed in this case plus any additional entities identified in your answer to Question 1. Write an unambiguous definition for each attribute. Then, redraw PE Figure 7-1 by placing the six (and additional) entities in this case on the diagram along with their associated attributes.

3. Using your answer to Question 2, designate which attribute or attributes form the identifier for each entity type. Explain why you chose each identifier.

4. Using your answer to Question 3, draw the relationships between entity types needed by the system. Remember, a relationship is needed only if the system wants data about associated entity instances. Give a meaningful name to each relationship. Specify cardinalities for each relationship and explain how you decided on each minimum and maximum cardinality at each end of each relationship. State any assumptions you made if the Petrie's Electronics cases you have read so far and the answers to questions in these cases do not provide the evidence to justify the cardinalities you choose. Redraw your final E-R diagram in Microsoft Visio.

5. Now that you have developed in your answer to Question 4 a complete E-R diagram for the Petrie's Electronics database, what are the consequences of not having an employee entity type in this diagram? Assuming only the attributes you show on the E-R diagram, would any attribute be moved from the entity it is currently associated with to an employee entity type if it were in the diagram? Why or why not?

6. Write project dictionary entries (using standards given to you by your instructor) for all the entities, attributes, and relationships shown in the E-R diagram in your answer to Question 4. How detailed are these entries at this point? What other details still must be filled in? Are any of the entities on the E-R diagram in your answer to Question 4 weak entities? Why? In particular, is the SERVICE entity type a weak entity? If so, why? If not, why not?

7. What date-related attributes did you identify in each of the entity types in your answer to Question 4? Why are each of these needed? Can you make some observations about why date attributes must be kept in a database, based on your analysis of this database?

eight

Designing the Human Interface

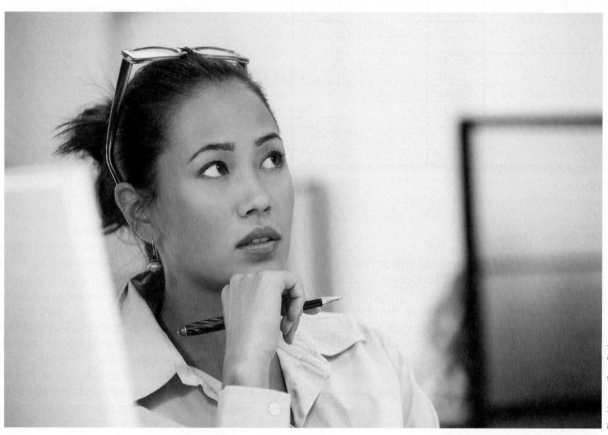

Blend Images/SuperStock

Chapter Preview . . .

Analysts must complete two important activities in the systems design phase, as illustrated in Figure 8-1: designing the human interface and designing databases. In this chapter, you learn guidelines to follow when designing the human-computer interface. In the first section, we describe the process of designing forms and reports and provide guidance on the deliverables produced during this process. Properly formatted segments of information are the building blocks for designing all forms and reports. We present guidelines for formatting information and for designing interfaces and dialogues. Next, we show you a method for representing human-computer dialogues called *dialogue diagramming*. Finally, we close the chapter by examining various human-computer interface design issues for Internet-based applications, specifically as they apply to Pine Valley Furniture's WebStore.

FIGURE 8-1
The systems design phase consists of two important activities: designing the human interface and designing databases.

Designing Forms and Reports

System inputs and outputs—forms and reports—are produced at the end of the systems analysis phase of the SDLC. During systems analysis, however, you may not have been concerned with the precise appearance of forms and reports. Instead, you focused on which forms and reports needed to exist and the content they needed to contain. You may have distributed to users the prototypes of forms and reports that emerged during analysis as a way to confirm requirements. Forms and reports are integrally related to the DFD and E-R diagrams developed during requirements structuring. For example, every input form is associated with a data flow entering a process on a DFD, and every output form or report is a data flow produced by a process on a DFD. Therefore, the contents of a form or report correspond to the data elements contained in the associated data flow. Further, the data on all forms and reports must consist of data elements in data stores and on the E-R data model for the application or else be computed from these data elements. (In rare instances, data simply go from system input to system output without being stored within the system.) It is common to discover flaws in DFDs and E-R diagrams as you design forms and reports; these diagrams should be updated as designs evolve.

If you are unfamiliar with computer-based information systems, it will be helpful to clarify exactly what we mean by a form or report. A **form** is a business document containing some predefined data and often includes some areas where additional data are to be filled in. Most forms have a stylized format and are usually not in simple rows and columns. Examples of business forms are product order forms, employment applications, and class registration sheets. Traditionally, forms have been displayed on a paper medium, but today, video display technology allows us to duplicate the layout of almost any printed form, including an organizational logo or any graphic, on a video display terminal. Forms on a video display may be used for data display or data entry. Additional examples of forms are an electronic spreadsheet, computer sign-on or menu, and an automated teller machine (ATM) transaction layout. On the Internet, form interaction is the standard method of gathering and displaying information when consumers order products, request product information, or query account status.

A **report** is a business document containing only predefined data; it is a passive document used solely for reading or viewing. Examples of reports are invoices, weekly sales summaries by region and salesperson, and a pie chart of population by age categories. We usually think of a report as printed on paper, but it may be printed to a computer file, a visual display screen, or some other medium such as microfilm. Often a report has rows and columns of data, but a report may consist of any format—for example, mailing labels. Frequently, the differences between a form and a report are subtle. A report is only for reading and often contains data about multiple unrelated records in a computer file. On the other hand, a form typically contains data from only one record or is, at least, based on one record, such as data about one customer, one order, or one student. The guidelines for the design of forms and reports are similar.

The Process of Designing Forms and Reports

Designing forms and reports is a user-focused activity that typically follows a prototyping approach (see Figure 1-12 to review the prototyping method). First, you must gain an understanding of the intended user and task objectives during the requirements determination process. During this process, the intended user must answer several questions that attempt to answer the who, what, when, where, and how related to the creation of all forms or reports, as listed in Table 8-1. Gaining an understanding of these questions is a required first step in the creation of any form or report.

Form

A business document that contains some predefined data and may include some areas where additional data are to be filled in; typically based on one database record.

Report

A business document that contains only predefined data; it is a passive document used only for reading or viewing; typically contains data from many unrelated records or transactions.

TABLE 8-1: Fundamental Questions When Designing Forms and Reports

1. Who will use the form or report?
2. What is the purpose of the form or report?
3. When is the form or report needed and used?
4. Where does the form or report need to be delivered and used?
5. How many people need to use or view the form or report?

Understanding the skills and abilities of the users helps you create an effective design. Are your users experienced computer users or novices? What is their educational level, business background, and task-relevant knowledge? Answers to these questions provide guidance for both the format and the content of your designs. Also, what is the purpose of the form or report? What task will users be performing, and what information is needed to complete this task? Other questions are also important to consider. Where will the users be when performing this task? Will users have access to online systems or will they be in the field? How many people will need to use this form or report? If, for example, a report is being produced for a single user, the design requirements and usability assessment will be relatively simple. A design for a larger audience, however, may need to go through a more extensive requirements collection and usability assessment process.

After collecting the initial requirements, you structure and refine this information into an initial prototype. Structuring and refining the requirements are completed without assistance from the users, although you may occasionally need to contact users to clarify some issue overlooked during analysis. Finally, you ask users to review and evaluate the prototype; then they may accept the design or request that changes be made. If changes are needed, repeat the construction-evaluate-refinement cycle until the design is accepted. Usually, several repetitions of this cycle occur during the design of a single form or report. As with any prototyping process, you should make sure that these iterations occur rapidly in order to gain the greatest benefit from this design approach.

The initial prototype may be constructed in numerous environments, including Visual Basic, Java, or HTML. The obvious choice is to employ standard development tools used within your organization. Often, initial prototypes are simply mock screens that are not working modules or systems. Mock screens can also be produced from a word processor, computer graphics design package, or presentation, software. It is important to remember that the focus of this phase within the SDLC is on the *design*—content and layout. How specific forms or reports are implemented (e.g., the programming language or screen painter code) is left for a later stage. Nonetheless, tools for designing forms and reports are rapidly evolving. In the past, inputs and outputs of all types were typically designed by hand on a coding or layout sheet. For example, Figure 8-2 shows the layout of a data input form using a coding sheet.

Although coding sheets are still used, their importance has diminished because of significant changes in system operating environments and the evolution of automated design tools. Prior to the creation of graphical operating environments, for example, analysts designed many inputs and outputs that were 80 columns (characters) by 25 rows, the standard dimensions for most video displays. These limits in screen dimensions are radically different in graphical operating environments such as Mac OS or Windows where font sizes and screen dimensions can often be changed from user to user. Consequently, the creation of new tools and development environments was needed to help analysts and programmers develop these graphical and flexible designs.

FIGURE 8-2
The layout of a data input form using a coding sheet.

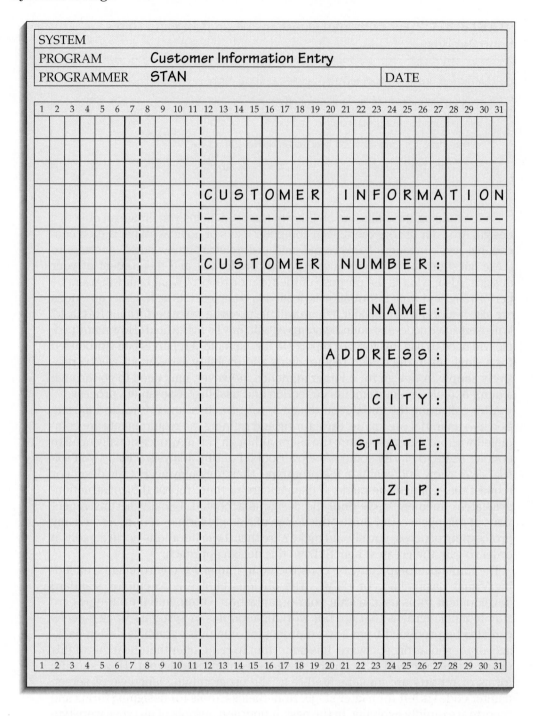

Figure 8-3 shows an example of the same data input form as designed in Microsoft's Visual Basic.Net. Note the variety of fonts, sizes, and highlighting that was used. Online graphical tools for designing forms and reports are rapidly becoming the standard in most professional development organizations.

Deliverables and Outcomes

Each SDLC activity helps you to construct a system. In order to move from phase to phase, each activity produces some type of deliverable that is used in a later activity. For example, within the systems planning and selection phase of the SDLC, the baseline project plan serves as input to many subsequent SDLC activities. In the case of designing forms and reports, design specifications are

FIGURE 8-3
A data input screen designed in Microsoft's Visual Basic.Net.

the major deliverables and are inputs to the system implementation and operation phase. Design specifications have three sections:

1. Narrative overview
2. Sample design
3. Testing and usability assessment

The narrative overview provides a general overview of the characteristics of the target users, tasks, system, and environmental factors in which the form or report will be used. Its purpose is to explain to those who will actually develop the final form, why this form exists, and how it will be used so that they can make the appropriate implementation decisions. In this section, you list general information and the assumptions that helped shape the design. For example, Figure 8-4 shows an excerpt of a design specification for a Customer Account Status form for Pine Valley Furniture. The first section of the specification, Figure 8-4A, provides a narrative overview containing the information relevant to developing and using the form within PVF. The overview explains the tasks supported by the form, where and when the form is used, characteristics of the people using the form, the technology delivering the form, and other pertinent information. For example, if the form is delivered on a visual display terminal, this section would describe the capabilities of this device, such as navigation and whether it has a touch screen and whether color and a mouse are available.

In the second section of the specification, Figure 8-4B, a sample design of the form is shown. This design may be hand-drawn using a coding sheet, although, in most instances, it is developed using standard development tools. Using actual development tools allows the design to be more thoroughly tested and assessed. The final section of the specification, Figure 8-4C, provides all testing and usability assessment information. Some specification information may be irrelevant when designing certain forms and reports. For example, the design of a simple yes/no

PINE
VALLEY
FURNITURE

FIGURE 8-4
A design specification for a Customer Account Status form for Pine Valley Furniture: (A) The narrative overview containing the information relevant to developing and using the form within PVF, (B) A sample design of the PVF form, (C) Testing and usability assessment information.

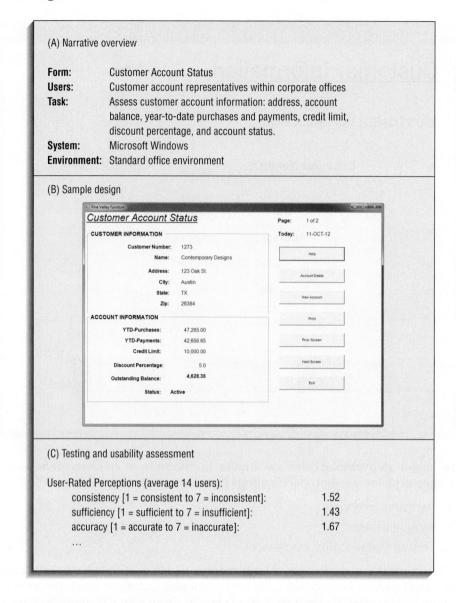

(A) Narrative overview

Form: Customer Account Status
Users: Customer account representatives within corporate offices
Task: Assess customer account information: address, account balance, year-to-date purchases and payments, credit limit, discount percentage, and account status.
System: Microsoft Windows
Environment: Standard office environment

(B) Sample design

Pine Valley Furniture

Customer Account Status

CUSTOMER INFORMATION

Customer Number: 1273
Name: Contemporary Designs
Address: 123 Oak St.
City: Austin
State: TX
Zip: 28384

ACCOUNT INFORMATION

YTD-Purchases: 47,285.00
YTD-Payments: 42,656.65
Credit Limit: 10,000.00
Discount Percentage: 5.0
Outstanding Balance: 4,628.35
Status: Active

Page: 1 of 2
Today: 11-OCT-12

Help
Account Details
New Account
Print
Prior Screen
Next Screen
Exit

(C) Testing and usability assessment

User-Rated Perceptions (average 14 users):
     consistency [1 = consistent to 7 = inconsistent]:   1.52
     sufficiency [1 = sufficient to 7 = insufficient]:   1.43
     accuracy [1 = accurate to 7 = inaccurate]:   1.67
     …

selection form may be so straightforward that no usability assessment is needed. Also, much of the narrative overview may be unnecessary unless intended to highlight some exception that must be considered during implementation.

Formatting Forms and Reports

A wide variety of information can be provided to users of information systems, ranging from text to video to audio. As technology continues to evolve, a greater variety of data types will be used. A definitive set of rules for delivering every type of information to users has yet to be defined because these rules are continuously evolving along with the rapid changes in technology. Research conducted by computer scientists on human-computer interaction has provided numerous general guidelines for formatting information. Many of these guidelines undoubtedly will apply to the formatting of all evolving information types on yet-to-be-determined devices. Keep in mind that designing usable forms and reports requires your active interaction with users. If this single and fundamental activity occurs, you will likely create effective designs.

For example, the human-computer interface is one of the greatest challenges for designing mobile applications that run on devices such as the iPhone. In particular, the small video display of these devices presents significant challenges for application designers. Nevertheless, as these and other computing devices evolve and gain popularity, standard guidelines will emerge to make the process of designing interfaces much less challenging.

General Formatting Guidelines Over the past several years, industry and academic researchers have investigated how information formatting influences individual task performance and perceptions of usability. Through this work, several guidelines for formatting information have emerged, as highlighted in Table 8-2. These guidelines reflect some of the general truths of formatting most types of information. The differences between a well-designed form or report and a poorly designed one often will be obvious. For example, Figure 8-5A shows a poorly designed form for viewing a current account balance for a PVF customer. Figure 8-5B is a better design, incorporating several general guidelines from Table 8-2.

The first major difference between the two forms has to do with the title. The title in Figure 8-5A (Customer Information) is ambiguous, whereas the title in Figure 8-5B (Detail Customer Account Information) clearly and specifically describes the contents of the form. The form in Figure 8-5B also includes the date (October 11, 2012) the form was generated so that, if printed, it will be clear to the reader when this occurred. Figure 8-5A displays the account status and customer address, information that is extraneous to viewing the current account balance, which is the intent of the form and provides information that is not in the most useful format for the user. For example, Figure 8-5A provides all customer data, as well as account transactions and a summary of year-to-date purchases and payments. The form does not, however, provide the current outstanding balance of the account, leaving the reader to perform a manual calculation. The layout of information between the two forms also varies in balance and information density. Gaining an understanding of the skills of the

TABLE 8-2: Guidelines for Designing Forms and Reports

Guideline	Description
Use meaningful titles	Clear and specific titles describing content and use of form or report
	Revision date or code to distinguish a form or report from prior versions
	Current date that identifies when the form or report was generated
	Valid date that identifies on what date (or time) the data in the form or report were accurate
Include meaningful information	Only needed information displayed
	Information provided in a usable manner without modification
Balance the layout	Information balanced on the screen or page
	Adequate spacing and margins used
	All data and entry fields clearly labeled
Design an easy navigation system	Clearly show how to move forward and backward
	Clearly show where you are (e.g., page 1 of 3)
	Notify user of the last page of a multipage sequence

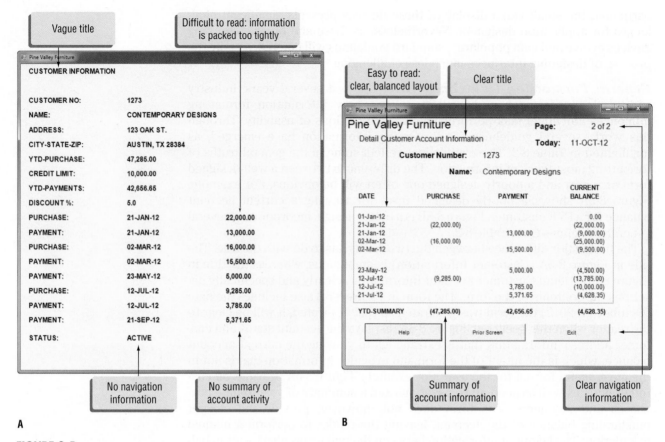

FIGURE 8-5
Contrast of a poorly designed and a well-designed form: (A) A poorly designed form for viewing a current account balance
for a PVF customer, (B) A better design that incorporates several general guidelines from Table 8-2.

intended system users and the tasks they will be performing is invaluable when constructing a form or report. By following these general guidelines, your chances of creating effective forms and reports will be enhanced. In the next sections, we discuss specific guidelines for highlighting information, displaying text, and presenting numeric tables and lists.

Highlighting Information   As display technologies continue to improve, a greater variety of methods will be available to highlight information. Table 8-3 lists the most commonly used methods for highlighting information. Given this vast array of options, it is important to consider how highlighting can be used to enhance an output without being a distraction. In general, highlighting should be used sparingly to draw the user to or away from certain information and to group together related information. In several situations, highlighting can be a valuable technique for conveying special information:

- Notifying users of errors in data entry or processing
- Providing warnings to users regarding possible problems, such as unusual data values or an unavailable device
- Drawing attention to keywords, commands, high-priority messages, and data that have changed or gone outside normal operating ranges

Highlighting techniques can be used singularly or in tandem, depending upon the level of emphasis desired by the designer. Figure 8-6 shows a form where several types of highlighting are used. In this example, columns clarify different categories of data; capital letters and different fonts distinguish labels from actual data; and bolding is used to draw attention to important data.

TABLE 8-3: Methods of Highlighting

Blinking and audible tones

Color differences

Intensity differences

Size differences

Font differences

Reverse video

Boxing

Underlining

All capital letters

Offsetting the position of nonstandard information

Highlighting should be used conservatively. For example, blinking and audible tones should be used only to highlight critical information requiring the user's immediate response. Once a response is made, these highlights should be turned off. Additionally, highlighting methods should be consistently selected and used based upon the level of importance of the emphasized information. It is also important to examine how a particular highlighting method appears on

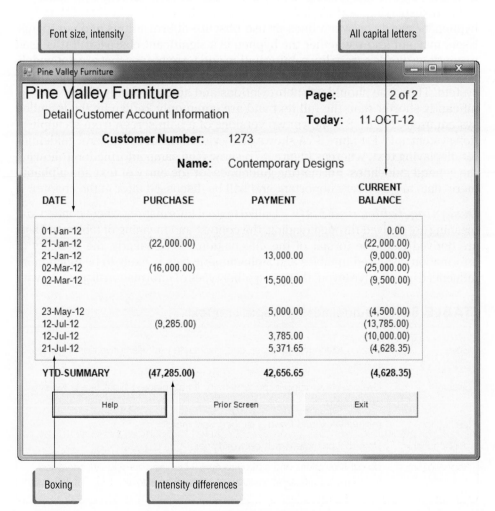

Font size, intensity

All capital letters

FIGURE 8-6
A form in which several types of highlighting are used.

Boxing

Intensity differences

all possible output devices that could be used with the system. For example, some color combinations may convey appropriate information on one display configuration but wash out and reduce legibility on another.

Recent advances in the development of graphical operating environments such as Windows, Mac OS, or Linux provide designers with some standard highlighting guidelines. However, because these guidelines are continuously evolving, they are often quite vague and leave a great deal of control in the hands of the systems developer. To realize the benefits of using standard graphical operating environments—such as reduced user training time and interoperability among systems—you must be disciplined in how you use highlighting.

Displaying Text   In business-related systems, textual output is becoming increasingly important as text-based applications, such as electronic mail, blogs, and information services (e.g., Dow Jones Industrial Average stock index), are more widely used. The display and formatting of system help screens, which often contain lengthy textual descriptions and examples, is one example of textual data that can benefit from following the simple guidelines that have emerged from systems design research. These guidelines appear in Table 8-4. The first one is simple: You should display text using common writing conventions such as mixed upper- and lowercase and appropriate punctuation. For large blocks of text, and if space permits, text should be double spaced. However, if the text is short, or rarely used, it may make sense to use single spacing and place a blank line between each paragraph. You should also left-justify text with a ragged right margin—research shows that a ragged right margin makes it easier to find the next line of text when reading than when text is both left- and right-justified.

When displaying textual information, you should also be careful not to hyphenate words between lines or use obscure abbreviations and acronyms. Users may not know whether the hyphen is a significant character if it is used to continue words across lines. Information and terminology that are not widely understood by the intended users may significantly influence the usability of the system. Thus, you should use abbreviations and acronyms only if they are significantly shorter than the full text and are commonly known by the intended system users. Figure 8-7 shows two versions of a help screen from an application system at PVF. Figure 8-7A shows many violations of the general guidelines for displaying text, whereas Figure 8-7B shows the same information following the general guidelines. Formatting guidelines for the entry of text and alphanumeric data are also very important and will be discussed later in the chapter.

Designing Tables and Lists   Unlike textual information, where context and meaning are derived through reading, the context and meaning of tables and lists are derived from the format of the information. Consequently, the usability of information displayed in tables and alphanumeric lists is likely to be much more influenced by effective layout than most other types of information display. As with

TABLE 8-4:   Guidelines for Displaying Text

Case	Display text in mixed upper- and lowercase and use conventional punctuation.
Spacing	Use double spacing if space permits. If not, place a blank line between paragraphs.
Justification	Left-justify text and leave a ragged right margin.
Hyphenation	Do not hyphenate words between lines.
Abbreviations	Use abbreviations and acronyms only when they are widely understood by users and are significantly shorter than the full text.

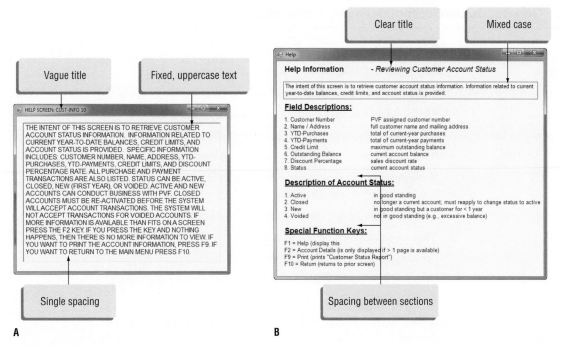

FIGURE 8-7
Contrasting two help screens from an application system at PVF: (A) A poorly designed help screen with many violations of the general guidelines for displaying text, (B) An improved design for a help screen.

the display of textual information, tables and lists can also be greatly enhanced by following a few simple guidelines. These are summarized in Table 8-5.

Figure 8-8 displays two versions of a form design from a Pine Valley Furniture application system that displays customer year-to-date transaction information in a table format. Figure 8-8A displays the information without consideration of the guidelines presented in Table 8-5, and Figure 8-8B (only page 2 of 2 is shown) displays this information after consideration of these guidelines.

One key distinction between these two display forms relates to labeling. The information reported in Figure 8-8B has meaningful labels that stand out more clearly compared to the display in Figure 8-8A. Transactions are sorted by date and transaction type, and numeric data are right-justified and aligned by decimal point in Figure 8-8B, which helps to facilitate scanning. Adequate space is left between columns, and blank lines are inserted after every five rows in Figure 8-8B to help ease the finding and reading of information. Such spacing also provides room for users to annotate data that catch their attention. Using the guidelines presented in Table 8-5 helped create an easy-to-read layout of the information for the user.

Most of the guidelines in Table 8-5 are rather obvious, but this and other tables serve as a quick reference to validate that your form and report designs will be usable. It is beyond our scope here to discuss each of these guidelines, but you should read each carefully and think about why it is appropriate. For example, why should labels be repeated on subsequent screens and pages (the first guideline in Table 8-5)? One explanation is that pages may be separated or copied, and the original labels will no longer be readily accessible to the reader of the data. Why should long alphanumeric data (see the last guideline) be broken into small groups? (If you have a credit card or bank check, look at how your account number is displayed.) Two reasons are that the characters will be easier to remember as you read and type them, and this approach provides a natural and consistent place to pause when you speak them over the phone (e.g., when you are placing a phone order for products in a catalog).

TABLE 8-5: General Guidelines for Displaying Tables and Lists

Guideline	Description
Use meaningful labels	All columns and rows should have meaningful labels.
	Labels should be separated from other information by using highlighting.
	Redisplay labels when the data extend beyond a single screen or page.
Format columns, rows, and text	Sort in a meaningful order (e.g., ascending, descending, or alphabetical).
	Place a blank line between every five rows in long columns.
	Similar information displayed in multiple columns should be sorted vertically (i.e., read from top to bottom, not left to right).
	Columns should have at least two spaces between them.
	Allow white space on printed reports for user to write notes.
	Use a single typeface, except for emphasis.
	Use same family of typefaces within and across displays and reports.
	Avoid overly fancy fonts.
Format numeric, textual, and alphanumeric data	Right-justify *numeric data* and align columns by decimal points or other delimiter.
	Left-justify *textual data*. Use short line length, usually 30 to 40 characters per line (this guideline is what newspapers use, and it is easy to speed-read).
	Break long sequences of *alphanumeric data* into small groups of three to four characters each.

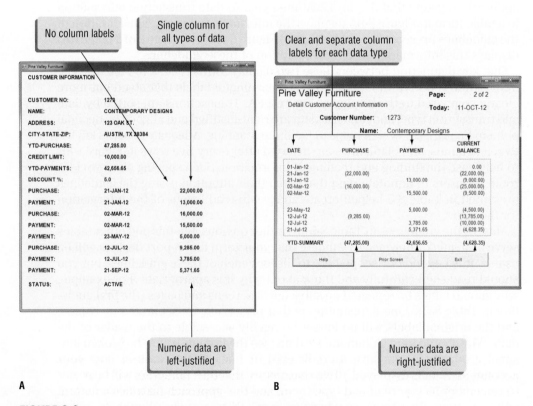

FIGURE 8-8
Contrasting two Pine Valley Furniture forms: (A) A poorly designed form, (B) An improved design form.

Place meaningful labels on all columns and rows

Alphabetic text is left-justified

Use a meaningful title

Box the table data to improve the appearance of the table

Pine Valley Furniture
Salesperson Annual Summary Report, 2012

January 10, 2013   Page 1 of 2

Region	Salesperson	SSN	Quarterly Actual Sales			
			First	Second	Third	Fourth
Northwest & Mountain						
	Baker	999-99-9999	195,000	146,000	133,000	120,000
	Hawthorne	999-99-9999	220,000	175,000	213,000	198,000
	Hodges	999-99-9999	110,000	95,000	170,000	120,000
Midwest & Mid-Atlantic						
	Franklin	999-99-9999	110,000	120,000	170,000	90,000
	Stephenson[1]	999-99-9999	75,000	66,000	80,000	80,000
	Swenson	999-99-9999	110,000	98,000	100,000	90,000
New England						
	Brightman	999-99-9999	250,000	280,000	260,000	330,000
	Kennedy	999-99-9999	310,000	190,000	270,000	280,000

[1]Sales reflect May 1, 2012–December 31, 2012.

Superscript characters can be used to alert reader of more detailed information

Sort columns in some meaningful order (names are sorted alphabetically within region)

Long sequence of alphanumeric data is grouped into smaller segments

Right-justify all numeric data

Try to fit table onto a single page to help in making comparisons

FIGURE 8-9
Tabular report illustrating good report design guidelines.

When you design the display of numeric information, you must determine whether a table or a graph should be used. In general, tables are best when the user's task involves finding an individual data value from a larger data set, whereas line and bar graphs are more appropriate for analyzing data changes over time. For example, if the marketing manager for Pine Valley Furniture needed to review the actual sales of a particular salesperson for a particular quarter, a tabular report such as the one shown in Figure 8-9 would be most useful. This report has been annotated to emphasize good report design practices. The report has both a printed date as well as a clear indication, as part of the report title, of the period over which the data apply. Sufficient white space also provides some room for users to add personal comments and observations. Often, to provide such white space, a report must be printed in landscape, rather than portrait, orientation. Alternatively, if the marketing manager wished to compare the overall sales performance of each sales region, a line or bar graph would be more appropriate, as illustrated in Figure 8-10.

Paper versus Electronic Reports   When a report is produced on paper rather than on a computer display, you need to consider some additional things. For example, laser printers (especially color laser printers) and ink-jet printers allow you to produce a report that looks exactly as it does on the display screen. Thus, when using these types of printers, you can follow our general design guidelines to create a report with high usability. However, other types of

FIGURE 8-10
Graphs showing quarterly sales at Pine Valley Furniture: (A) Line graph, (B) Bar graph.

printers cannot closely reproduce the display screen image onto paper. For example, many business reports are produced using high-speed impact printers that produce characters and a limited range of graphics by printing a fine pattern of dots. The advantages of impact printers are that they are fast, reliable, and relatively inexpensive. Their drawbacks are that they have a limited ability to produce graphics and have a somewhat lower print quality. In other words, they are good at rapidly producing reports that contain primarily alphanumeric information but cannot exactly replicate a screen report onto paper. For this reason, impact printers are mostly used for producing large batches of reports, such as a batch of phone bills for your telephone company, on a wide range of paper widths and types. When designing reports for impact printers, you use a coding sheet similar to the one displayed in Figure 8-2, although coding sheets for designing printer reports typically can have up to 132 columns. Like the process for designing all forms and reports, you follow a prototyping process and carefully control the spacing of characters in order to produce a high-quality report. However, unlike other form and report designs, you may be limited in the range of formatting, text types, and highlighting options. Nonetheless, you can easily produce a highly usable report of any type if you carefully and creatively use the available formatting options.

Designing Interfaces and Dialogues

Interface and dialogue design focuses on how information is provided to and captured from users. Dialogues are analogous to a conversation between two people. The grammatical rules followed by each person during a conversation are analogous to the human-computer interface. The design of interfaces and dialogues involves defining the manner in which humans and computers exchange information. A good human-computer interface provides a uniform structure for finding, viewing, and invoking the different components of a system. In this section we describe how to design interfaces and dialogues.

The Process of Designing Interfaces and Dialogues

Similar to designing forms and reports, the process of designing interfaces and dialogues is a user-focused activity. You follow a prototyping methodology of iteratively collecting information, constructing a prototype, assessing usability, and making refinements. To design usable interfaces and dialogues, you must answer the same who, what, when, where, and how questions used to guide the

Design Specification

1. Narrative Overview
   a. Interface/Dialogue Name
   b. User Characteristics
   c. Task Characteristics
   d. System Characteristics
   e. Environmental Characteristics

2. Interface/Dialogue Designs
   a. Form/Report Designs
   b. Dialogue Sequence Diagram(s) and Narrative Description

3. Testing and Usability Assessment
   a. Testing Objectives
   b. Testing Procedures
   c. Testing Results
       i)   Time to Learn
       ii) Speed of Performance
       iii) Rate of Errors
       iv) Retention over Time
       v)   User Satisfaction and Other Perceptions

FIGURE 8-11
An outline for a design specification for interfaces and dialogues.

design of forms and reports (see Table 8-1). Thus, this process parallels that of designing forms and reports.

Deliverables and Outcomes

The deliverable and outcome from system interface and dialogue design is the creation of a design specification. This specification is similar to the specification produced for form and report designs—with one exception. Recall that the design specification for forms and reports had three sections (see Figure 8-4):

1. Narrative overview
2. Sample design
3. Testing and usability assessment

For interface and dialogue designs, one additional subsection is included: a section outlining the dialogue sequence—the ways a user can move from one display to another. Later in the chapter you will learn how to design a dialogue sequence by using dialogue diagramming. An outline for a design specification for interfaces and dialogues is shown in Figure 8-11.

Designing Interfaces

In this section we discuss the design of interface layouts. This discussion provides guidelines for structuring and controlling data-entry fields, providing feedback, and designing online help. Effective interface design requires you to gain a thorough understanding of each of these concepts.

Designing Layouts   To ease user training and data recording, use standard formats for computer-based forms and reports similar to paper-based forms and reports for recording or reporting information. A typical paper-based form for

PINE
VALLEY
FURNITURE

FIGURE 8-12
Paper-based form for reporting customer sales activity at Pine Valley Furniture.

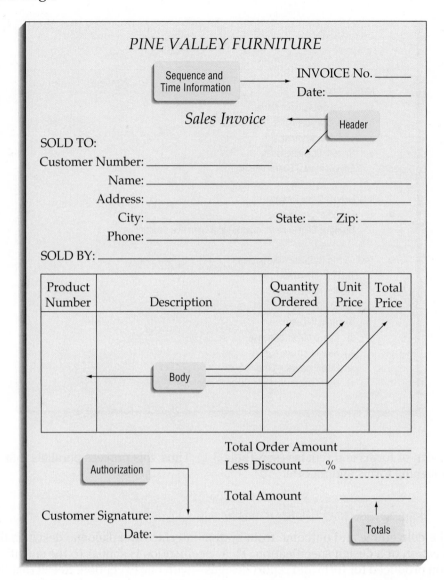

reporting customer sales activity is shown in Figure 8-12. This form has several general areas common to most forms:

- Header information
- Sequence and time-related information
- Instruction or formatting information
- Body or data details
- Totals or data summary
- Authorization or signatures
- Comments

In many organizations, data are often first recorded on paper-based forms and then later recorded within application systems. When designing layouts to record or display information on paper-based forms, try to make both as similar as possible. Additionally, data-entry displays should be consistently formatted across applications to speed data entry and reduce errors. Figure 8-13 shows an equivalent computer-based form to the paper-based form shown in Figure 8-12.

The design of between-field navigation is another item to consider when designing the layout of computer-based forms. Because you can control the

FIGURE 8-13
Computer-based form for reporting customer sales activity at Pine Valley Furniture.

sequence for users to move between fields, standard screen navigation should flow from left-to-right and top-to-bottom just as when you work on paper-based forms. For example, Figure 8-14 contrasts the flow between fields on a form used to record business contacts. Figure 8-14A uses a consistent left-to-right, top-to-bottom flow. Figure 8-14B uses a flow that is nonintuitive. When appropriate, you should also group data fields into logical categories with labels describing the contents of the category. Areas of the screen not used for data entry or commands should be inaccessible to the user.

When designing the navigation procedures within your system, flexibility and consistency are primary concerns. Users should be able to move freely forward and backward or to any desired data-entry fields. Users should be able to navigate each form in the same way or in as similar a manner as possible. Additionally, data should not usually be permanently saved by the system until the user makes an explicit request to do so. This option allows the user to abandon a data-entry screen, back up, or move forward without adversely impacting the contents of the permanent data.

Consistency extends to the selection of keys and commands. Assign each key or command only one function. This assignment should be consistent throughout the entire system and across systems, if possible. Depending upon the application, various types of functional capabilities will be required to provide smooth navigation and data entry. Table 8-6 provides a checklist for testing

A   B

FIGURE 8-14
Contrasting the navigation flow within a data-entry form: (A) Proper flow between data-entry fields with a consistent left-to-right, top-to-bottom flow, (B) Poor flow between data-entry fields with inconsistent flow.

the functional capabilities for providing smooth and easy navigation within a form. For example, a good interface design provides a consistent way for moving the cursor to different places on the form, editing characters and fields, moving among form displays, and obtaining help. These functions may be provided by keystrokes, mouse, menu, or function keys. It is possible that, for a single application, not all capabilities listed in Table 8-6 may be needed in order

TABLE 8-6: Checklist for Validating the Usability of User Interface

Cursor-Control Capabilities

Move the cursor forward to the next data field.

Move the cursor backward to the previous data field.

Move the cursor to the first, last, or some other designated data field.

Move the cursor forward one character in a field.

Move the cursor backward one character in a field.

Editing Capabilities

Delete the character to the left of the cursor.

Delete the character under the cursor.

Delete the whole field.

Delete data from the whole form (empty the form).

Exit Capabilities

Transmit the screen to the application program.

Move to another screen/form.

Confirm the saving of edits or go to another screen/form.

Help Capabilities

Get help on a data field.

Get help on a full screen/form.

Source: Based on J. S. Dumas (1988). *Designing User Interfaces for Software*. Upper Saddle River, NJ: Prentice Hall.

to create a good user interface. Yet, the capabilities that are used should be consistently applied to provide an optimal user environment. Table 8-6 provides you with a checklist for validating the usability of user interface designs.

Structuring Data Entry   You should consider several guidelines when structuring data-entry fields on a form. These guidelines are listed in Table 8-7. The first is simple, yet, is often violated by designers. To minimize data-entry errors and user frustration, never require the user to enter information that is already available within the system or information that can be easily computed by the system. For example, never require the user to enter the current date and time, because each of these values can be easily retrieved from the computer system's internal calendar and clock. By allowing the system to do these tasks, the user simply confirms that the calendar and clock are working properly.

Other guidelines are equally important. For example, suppose that a bank customer is repaying a loan on a fixed schedule with equal monthly payments. Each month when a payment is sent to the bank, a clerk needs to record that the payment has been received into a loan-processing system. Within such a system, default values for fields should be provided whenever appropriate, which allows the clerk to enter specific data into the system only when the customer pays more or less than the scheduled amount. In all other cases, the clerk simply verifies that the check is for the default amount provided by the system and presses a single key to confirm the receipt of payment.

When entering data, do not require the user to specify the dimensional units of a particular value, for example, whether an amount is in dollars or a weight is in tons. Use field formatting and the data-entry prompt to make clear the type of data being requested. In other words, place a caption describing the data to be entered adjacent to each data field so that the user knows what type of data is being requested. As with the display of information, all data entered onto a form should automatically justify in a standard format (e.g., date, time, money).

TABLE 8-7: Guidelines for Structuring Data-Entry Fields

Entry	Never request data that are already online or that can be computed, for example, do not request customer data on an order form if that data can be retrieved from the database, and do not request extended prices that can be computed from quantity sold and unit prices.
Defaults	Always provide default values when appropriate, for example, assume today's date for a new sales invoice, or use the standard product price unless overridden.
Units	Make clear the type of data units requested for entry, for example, indicate quantity in tons, dozens, pounds, etc.
Replacement	Use character replacement when appropriate, for example, allow the user to look up the value in a table or automatically fill in the value once the user enters enough significant characters.
Captioning	Always place a caption adjacent to fields; see Table 8-8 for caption options.
Format	Provide formatting examples when appropriate, for example, automatically show standard embedded symbols, decimal points, credit symbols, or dollar signs.
Justify	Automatically justify data entries; numbers should be right-justified and aligned on decimal points, and text should be left-justified.
Help	Provide context-sensitive help when appropriate, for example, provide a hot key, such as the F1 key, that opens the help system on an entry that is most closely related to where the cursor is on the display.

TABLE 8-8:   Display Design Options for Entering Text

Options	Example
Line caption	Phone Number ( ) - _____
Drop caption	( ) - _____
	Phone Number
Boxed caption	Phone Number
Delimited characters	|(| | | |)| | | |-| | | |
	Phone Number
Check-off boxes	Method of payment (check one)
	❏ Check
	❏ Cash
	❏ Credit card: Type

Table 8-8 illustrates display design options for printed forms. For data entry on video display terminals, highlight the area in which text is entered so that the exact number of characters per line and number of lines are clearly shown. You can also use check-off boxes or radio buttons to allow users to choose standard textual responses. Use data-entry controls to ensure that the proper type of data (alphabetic or numeric, as required) is entered. Data-entry controls are discussed next.

Controlling Data Input   One objective of interface design is to reduce data-entry errors. As data are entered into an information system, steps must be taken to ensure that the input is valid. As a systems analyst, you must anticipate the types of errors users may make and design features into the system's interfaces to avoid, detect, and correct data-entry mistakes. Several types of data errors are summarized in Table 8-9. Data errors can occur from appending extra data onto a field, truncating characters off a field, transcripting the wrong characters into a field, or transposing one or more characters within a field. Systems designers have developed numerous tests and techniques for detecting invalid data before saving or transmission, thus improving the likelihood that data will be valid. Table 8-10 summarizes these techniques. These tests and techniques are often incorporated into both data-entry screens and when data are transferred from one computer to another.

Correcting erroneous data is much easier to accomplish before it is permanently stored in a system. Online systems can notify a user of input problems as data are being entered. When data are processed online as events occur, it is much less likely that data-validity errors will occur and not be caught. In an online system, most problems can be easily identified and resolved before permanently saving data to a storage device using many of the techniques

TABLE 8-9:   Types of Data Errors

Data Error	Description
Appending	Adding additional characters to a field
Truncating	Losing characters from a field
Transcripting	Entering invalid data into a field
Transposing	Reversing the sequence of one or more characters in a field

TABLE 8-10: Techniques Used by Systems Designers to Detect Data Errors before Saving or Transmission

Validation Test	Description
Class or composition	Test to ensure that data are of proper type (e.g., all numeric, all alphabetic, alphanumeric)
Combinations	Test to see that value combinations of two or more data fields are appropriate or make sense (e.g., does the quantity sold make sense given the type of product?)
Expected values	Test to see whether data are what is expected (e.g., match with existing customer names, payment amount, etc.)
Missing data	Test for existence of data items in all fields of a record (e.g., is there a quantity field on each line item of a customer order?)
Pictures/templates	Test to ensure that data conform to a standard format (e.g., are hyphens in the right places for a student ID number?)
Range	Test to ensure data are within a proper range of values (e.g., is a student's grade-point average between 0 and 4.0?)
Reasonableness	Test to ensure data are reasonable for situation (e.g., pay rate for a specific type of employee)
Self-checking digits	Technique by which extra digits, derived using a standard formula (see Figure 8-15), are added to a numeric field before transmission and checked after transmission
Size	Test for too few or too many characters (e.g., is social security number exactly nine digits?)
Values	Test to make sure values come from a set of standard values (e.g., two-letter state codes)

described in Table 8-10. However, in systems where data inputs are stored and entered (or transferred) in batches, the identification and notification of errors are more difficult. Batch processing systems can, however, reject invalid inputs and store them in a log file for later resolution.

Most of the straightforward tests and techniques shown in Table 8-10 are widely used. Some can be handled by data-management technologies, such as a database management system (DBMS), to ensure that they are applied for all data-maintenance operations. If a DBMS cannot perform these tests, then you must design the tests into program modules. Self-checking digits, shown in Figure 8-15, is an example of a sophisticated program. The figure provides a description and an outline of how to apply the technique. A short example then shows how a check digit is added to a field before data entry or transfer. Once entered or transferred, the check digit algorithm is again applied to the field to "check" whether the check digit received obeys the calculation. If it does, it is likely (but not guaranteed, because two different values could yield the same check digit) that no data transmission or entry error occurred. If not equal, then some type of error occurred.

In addition to validating the data values entered into a system, controls must be established to verify that all input records are correctly entered and processed only once. A common method used to enhance the validity of entering batches of data records is to create an **audit trail** of the entire sequence of data entry, processing, and storage. In such an audit trail, the actual sequence, count, time, source location, and human operator are recorded in a separate transaction log in the event of a data input or processing error. If an error occurs, corrections can be made by reviewing the contents of the log. Detailed

Audit trail
A record of the sequence of data entries and the date of those entries.

FIGURE 8-15
How check digits are calculated.

Description	Techniques where extra digits are added to a field to assist in verifying its accuracy
Method	1. Multiply each digit of a numeric field by weighting factor (e.g., 1,2,1,2, . . .). 2. Sum the results of weighted digits. 3. Divide sum by modulus number (e.g., 10). 4. Subtract remainder of division from modulus number to determine check digit. 5. Append check digits to field.

Example	Assume a numeric part number of: 12473
	 1–2. Multiply each digit of part number by weighting factor from right to left and sum the results of weighted digits:
	
	 $$\begin{array}{ccccc} 1 & 2 & 4 & 7 & 3 \\ \times 1 & \times 2 & \times 1 & \times 2 & \times 1 \\ \hline 1 \; + & 4 \; + & 4 \; + & 14 \; + & 3 \end{array} = 26$$
	
	 3. Divide sum by modulus number.
	   26/10 = 2 remainder 6
	 4. Subtract remainder from modulus number to determine check digit.
	   check digit = 10 − 6 = 4
	 5. Append check digits to field.
	   Field value with appended check digit = 124734

logs of data inputs not only are useful for resolving batch data-entry errors and system audits, but also serve as a powerful method for performing backup and recovery operations in the case of a catastrophic system failure.

Providing Feedback   When you talk with friends, you expect them to give you feedback by nodding and replying to your questions and comments. Without feedback, you would be concerned that they were not listening. Similarly, when designing system interfaces, providing appropriate feedback is an easy way to make a user's interaction more enjoyable; not providing feedback is a sure way to frustrate and confuse. System feedback can consist of three types:

1. Status information

2. Prompting cues

3. Error and warning messages

1. *Status Information.* Providing status information is a simple technique for keeping users informed of what is going on within a system. For example, relevant status information, such as displaying the current customer name or time, placing appropriate titles on a menu or screen, and identifying the number of screens following the current one (e.g., Screen 1 of 3), all provide needed feedback to the user. Providing status information during processing operations is especially important if the operation takes longer than a second or two. For example, when opening a file, you might display, "Please wait while I open the file," or when performing a large calculation, flash the message "Working . . ." to the user. Further, it is important to tell the user that besides working, the system has accepted the user's input and the input was in the correct form. Sometimes it is important to give the user a chance to obtain more feedback. For example, a function key could toggle between showing

a "Working . . ." message and giving more specific information as each intermediate step is accomplished. Providing status information reassures users that nothing is wrong and makes them feel in command of the system, not vice versa.

2. *Prompting Cues.* A second feedback method is to display prompting cues. When prompting the user for information or action, it is useful to be specific in your request. For example, suppose a system prompted users with the following request:

READY FOR INPUT: _____

   With such a prompt, the designer assumes that the user knows exactly what to enter. A better design would be specific in its request, possibly providing an example, default values, or formatting information. An improved prompting request might be as follows:

   Enter the customer account number (123-456-7):____-___-_

3. *Error and Warning Messages.* A final method available to you for providing system feedback is using error and warning messages. Following a few simple guidelines can greatly improve the usefulness of these messages. First, make messages specific and free of error codes and jargon. Additionally, messages should never scold the user but attempt to guide the user toward a resolution. For example, a message might say, "No customer record found for that customer ID. Please verify that digits were not transposed." Messages should be in user, not computer, terms. Terms such as *end of file, disk I/O error,* or *write protected* may be too technical and not helpful for many users. Multiple messages can be useful so that a user can get more detailed explanations if wanted or needed. Also, make sure error messages appear in roughly the same format and placement each time so that they are recognized as error messages and not as some other information. Examples of bad and good messages are provided in Table 8-11. Use these guidelines to provide useful feedback in your designs. A special type of feedback is answering help requests from users. This important topic is described next.

Providing Help   Designing a help system is one of the most important interface design issues you will face. When designing help, you need to put yourself in the user's place. When accessing help, the user likely does not know what to do next, does not understand what is being requested, or does not know how the requested information needs to be formatted. A user requesting help is much like a ship in distress, sending an SOS. In Table 8-12, we provide our SOS guidelines for the design of system help: Simplify, Organize, and Show. Our first

TABLE 8-11:   Examples of Poor and Improved Error Messages

Poor Error Messages	Improved Error Messages
ERROR 56 OPENING FILE	The file name you typed was not found. Press F2 to list valid file names.
WRONG CHOICE	Please enter an option from the menu.
DATA ENTRY ERROR	The prior entry contains a value outside the range of acceptable values. Press F9 for list of acceptable values.
FILE CREATION ERROR	The file name you entered already exists. Press F10 if you want to overwrite it. Press F2 if you want to save it with a new name.

TABLE 8-12:   Guidelines for Designing System Help

Guideline	Explanation
Simplify	Use short, simple wording, common spelling, and complete sentences. Give users only what they need to know, with ability to find additional information.
Organize	Use lists to break information into manageable pieces.
Show	Provide examples of proper use and the outcomes of such use.

guideline, *simplify*, suggests that help messages should be short, to the point, and use words that users can understand. The second guideline, *organize*, means that the information in help messages should be easy for users to absorb. Long paragraphs of text are often difficult for people to understand. A better design organizes lengthy information in a manner easier for users to digest through the use of bulleted and ordered lists. Finally, it is often useful to explicitly *show* users how to perform an operation and the outcomes of procedural steps. Figure 8-16 contrasts the designs of two help screens, one that employs our guidelines and one that does not.

Many commercially available systems provide extensive system help. For example, Table 8-13 lists the range of help available in a popular electronic spreadsheet. Many systems are also designed so that users can vary the level of detail provided. Help may be provided at the system level, screen or form level, and individual field level. The ability to provide field-level help is often referred to as *context-sensitive* help. For some applications, providing context-sensitive help for all system options is a tremendous undertaking that is virtually a project in itself. If you do decide to design an extensive help system with many levels of detail, you must be sure that you know exactly what the user needs help with, or your efforts may confuse users more than help them. After leaving a help screen, users should always return back to where they were prior to

A

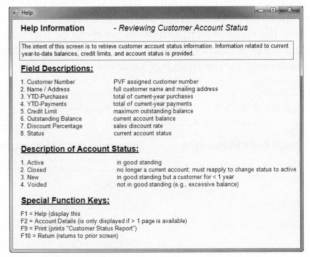

B

FIGURE 8-16

Contrasting help screens: (A) A poorly designed help screen, (B) An improved design for a help screen.

TABLE 8-13: Types of Help

Type of Help	Example of Question
Help on help	How do I get help?
Help on concepts	What is a customer record?
Help on procedures	How do I update a record?
Help on messages	What does "Invalid File Name" mean?
Help on menus	What does "Graphics" mean?
Help on function keys	What does each function key do?
Help on commands	How do I use the "Cut" and "Paste" commands?
Help on words	What do "merge" and "sort" mean?

requesting help. If you follow these simple guidelines, you will likely design a highly usable help system.

As with the construction of menus, many programming environments provide powerful tools for designing system help. For example, Microsoft's HTML Help SDK allows you to construct hypertext-based help systems quickly. In this environment, you use a text editor to construct help pages that can be easily linked to other pages containing related or more specific information. Linkages are created by embedding special characters into the text document that make words hypertext buttons—that is, direct linkages—to additional information. The HTML Help SDK transforms the text document into a hypertext document. For example, Figure 8-17 shows a hypertext-based help screen from Microsoft.

FIGURE 8-17
Hypertext-based help system from Microsoft.

Source: Copyright © 2011 Microsoft Corporation. All rights reserved. Protected by the copyright laws of the United States and international treaties.

Hypertext-based help systems have become the standard environment for most commercial operating environments for two primary reasons. First, standardizing system help across applications eases user training. Second, hypertext allows users to selectively access the level of help they need, making it easier to provide effective help for both novice and experienced users within the same system.

Designing Dialogues

Dialogue
The sequence of interaction between a user and a system.

The process of designing the overall sequences that users follow to interact with an information system is called *dialogue design*. A **dialogue** is the sequence in which information is displayed to and obtained from a user. As with other design processes, designing dialogues is a three-step process:

1. Designing the dialogue sequence
2. Building a prototype
3. Assessing usability

The primary design guideline for designing dialogues is consistency; dialogues need to be consistent in sequence of actions, keystrokes, and terminology. In other words, use the same labels for the same operations on all screens and the same location of the same information on all displays.

One example of these guidelines concerns removing data from a database or file (see the Reversal entry in Table 8-14). It is good practice to display the information that will be deleted before making a permanent change to the file. For

TABLE 8-14: Guidelines for the Design of Human-Computer Dialogues

Guideline	Explanation
Consistency	Dialogues should be consistent in sequence of actions, keystrokes, and terminology (e.g., use the same labels for the same operations on all screens and the same location of the same information on all displays).
Shortcuts and sequence	Allow advanced users to take shortcuts using special keys (e.g., CTRL-C to copy highlighted text). A natural sequence of steps should be followed (e.g., enter first name before last name, if appropriate).
Feedback	Feedback should be provided for every user action (e.g., confirm that a record has been added, rather than simply putting another blank form on the screen).
Closure	Dialogues should be logically grouped and have a beginning, middle, and end (e.g., the last in the sequence of screens should indicate that there are no more screens).
Error handling	All errors should be detected and reported; suggestions on how to proceed should be made (e.g., suggest why such errors occur and what the user can do to correct the error). Synonyms for certain responses should be accepted (e.g., accept either "t," "T," or "TRUE").
Reversal	Dialogues should, when possible, allow the user to reverse actions (e.g., undo a deletion); data should not be deleted without confirmation (e.g., display all the data for a record the user has indicated is to be deleted).
Control	Dialogues should make the user (especially an experienced user) feel in control of the system (e.g., provide a consistent response time at a pace acceptable to the user).
Ease	Dialogues should provide simple means for users to enter information and navigate between screens (e.g., provide means to move forward, backward, and to specific screens, such as first and last).

Source: Based on B. Shneiderman, C. Plaisant, M. Cohen, and S. Jacobs (2009). *Designing the User Interface: Strategies for Effective Human-Computer Interaction, 5th Edition.* Reading, MA: Addison-Wesley.

example, if the customer service representative wanted to remove a customer from the database, the system should ask only for the customer ID in order to retrieve the correct customer account. Once found, and before allowing the confirmation of the deletion, the system should display the account information. For actions making permanent changes to system data files and when the action is not commonly performed, many system designers use the double-confirmation technique by which the users must confirm their intention twice before being allowed to proceed.

Designing the Dialogue Sequence   Your first step in dialogue design is to define the sequence. In other words, you must have a clear understanding of the user, task, technological, and environmental characteristics when designing dialogues. Suppose that the marketing manager at Pine Valley Furniture (PVF) wants sales and marketing personnel to be able to review the year-to-date transaction activity for any PVF customer. After talking with the manager, you both agree that a typical dialogue between a user and the Customer Information System for obtaining this information might proceed as follows:

PINE VALLEY FURNITURE

1. Request to view individual customer information
2. Specify the customer of interest
3. Select the year-to-date transaction summary display
4. Review customer information
5. Leave system

As a designer, once you understand how a user wishes to use a system, you can then transform these activities into a formal dialogue specification.

A method for designing and representing dialogues is **dialogue diagramming.** Dialogue diagrams, illustrated in Figure 8-18, have only one symbol, a box with three sections; each box represents one display (which might be a full screen or a specific form or window) within a dialogue. The three sections of the box are used as follows:

Dialogue diagramming
A formal method for designing and representing human-computer dialogues using box-and-line diagrams.

1. Top: Contains a unique display reference number used by other displays for referencing it
2. Middle: Contains the name or description of the display
3. Bottom: Contains display reference numbers that can be accessed from the current display

All lines connecting the boxes within dialogue diagrams are assumed to be bidirectional and, thus, do not need arrowheads to indicate direction. With this capability, users are allowed to always move forward and backward between adjacent displays. If you desire only unidirectional flows within a dialogue, arrowheads should be placed at one end of the line. Within a dialogue diagram, you can easily represent the sequencing of displays, the selection of one display over another, or the repeated use of a single display (e.g., a data-entry display). These three concepts—sequence, selection, and iteration—are illustrated in Figure 8-19.

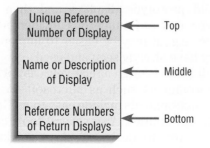

FIGURE 8-18
A dialogue-diagramming box has three sections.

FIGURE 8-19
Dialogue diagram illustrating
sequence, selection, and iteration.

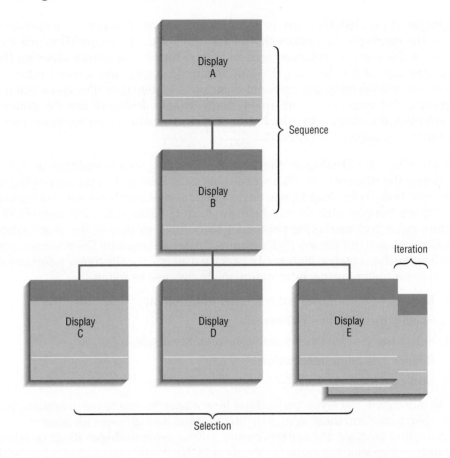

Continuing with our PVF example, Figure 8-20 shows a partial dialogue diagram for processing the marketing manager's request. In this diagram, the analyst placed the request to view year-to-date customer information within the context of the overall Customer Information System. The user must first gain access to the system through a log-on procedure (item 0). If log-on is successful, a main menu is displayed that has four items (item 1). Once the user selects the Individual Customer Information display (item 2), control is transferred to the Select Customer display (item 2.1). After a customer is selected, the user is presented with an option to view customer information four different ways (item 2.1.1). Once the user views the customer's year-to-date transaction activity (item 2.1.1.2), the system will allow the user to back up to select a different customer or back up to the main menu (see bottom of item 2.1.1.2).

Building Prototypes and Assessing Usability Building dialogue prototypes and assessing usability are often optional activities. Some systems may be simple and straightforward. Others may be more complex but are extensions to existing systems where dialogue and display standards have already been established. In either case, you may not be required to build prototypes and do a formal assessment. However, for many other systems, it is critical that you build prototype displays and then assess the dialogue; developing a prototype can pay numerous dividends later in the systems development life cycle (e.g., it may be easier to implement a system or train users on a system they have already seen and used).

Building prototype displays is often a relatively easy activity if you use graphical development environments such as Microsoft's Visual Basic.Net. Some systems development environments include easy-to-use input and output (form, report, or window) design utilities. Also several tools called "Prototypers" or "Demo Builders" allow you to design displays quickly and show how an

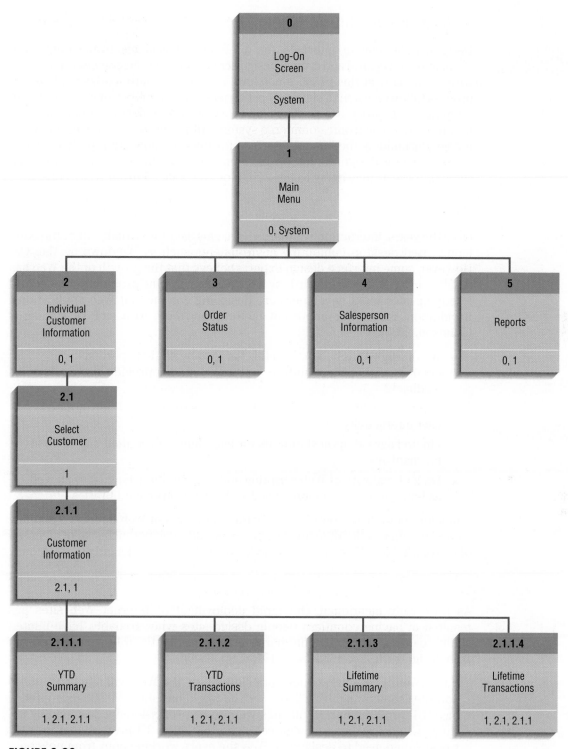

FIGURE 8-20
Dialogue diagram for the Customer Information System at Pine Valley Furniture.

interface will work within a full system. These demo systems allow users to enter data and move through displays as if they were using the actual system. Such activities are useful not only for showing how an interface will look and feel but also for assessing usability and performing user training long before actual systems are completed.

Pine Valley Furniture WebStore: Designing the Human Interface

Designing the human interface for an Internet-based electronic commerce application is a central and critical design activity. Because customers will interact with a company at this point, much care must be put into its design. Like the process followed when designing the interface for other types of systems, a prototyping design process is most appropriate when designing the human interface for an Internet electronic commerce system. Although the techniques and technology for building the human interface for Internet sites are rapidly evolving, several general design guidelines have emerged. In this section, we examine some of these as they apply to the design of Pine Valley Furniture's WebStore.

General Guidelines for Designing Web Interfaces

Over the years, interaction standards have emerged for virtually all of the commonly used desktop computing environments such as Windows or Mac OS. However, some interface design experts believe that the growth of the Web has resulted in a big step backward for interface design. One problem is that countless nonprofessional developers are designing commercial Web applications. In addition, four other important factors contribute to a lack of standards (Johnson, 2007):

- Web's single "click-to-act" method of loading static hypertext documents (i.e., most buttons on the Web do not provide click feedback)
- Limited capabilities of most Web browsers to support finely grained user interactivity
- Limited agreed-upon standards for encoding Web content and control mechanisms
- Lack of maturity of Web scripting and programming languages as well as limitations in commonly used Web GUI component libraries

In addition to these contributing factors, designers of Web interfaces and dialogues are often guilty of many design errors. Although not inclusive of all possible errors, Table 8-15 summarizes those errors that are particularly troublesome.

General Guidelines for Web Layouts

As previously mentioned, the rapid deployment of Internet Web sites has resulted in having countless people design sites who, arguably, have limited ability to do so. To put this into perspective, consider the following quote from Web design guru, Jakob Nielsen (1999a, pp. 65–66):

> If the [Web's] growth rate does not slow down, the Web will reach 200 million sites sometime during 2003. . . . The world has about 20,000 user interface [UI] professionals. If all sites were to be professionally designed by a single UI professional, we can conclude that every UI professional in the world would need to design one Web site every working hour from now on to meet demand. This is obviously not going to happen. . . .

Continued growth in the number of unique Web sites, estimated to exceed 250 million in early 2011, makes this problem increasingly dire. Three possible solutions to the problem include the following:

- Make it possible to design reasonably usable sites without having UI expertise
- Train more people in good Web design
- Live with poorly designed sites that are hard to use

TABLE 8-15:   Common Errors When Designing the Interface and Dialogues of Web Sites

Error	Description
Opening new browser window	Avoid opening a new browser window when a user clicks on a link unless it is clearly marked that a new window will be opened; users may not see that a new window has been opened, which will complicate navigation, especially when moving backward.
Breaking or slowing down the back button	Make sure users can use the back button to return to prior pages. Avoid opening new browser window; using immediate redirect where and when a user clicks the back button, they are pushed forward to an undesired location; or prevent caching such that each click of the back button requires a new trip to the server.
Complex URLs	Avoid overly long and complex URLs that make it more difficult for users to understand where they are and can cause problems if users want to e-mail page locations to others.
Orphan pages	Avoid having pages with no "parent" that can be reached by using a back button; requires users to "hack" the end of the URL to get back to a prior page.
Scrolling navigation pages	Avoid placing navigational links below where a page opens, because many users may miss these important options that are not immediately visible.
Lack of navigation support	Make sure your pages conform to user expectations by providing commonly used icon links, such as a site logo at the top of major elements. Also place these elements on pages in a consistent manner.
Hidden links	Make sure you leave a border around images that are links, don't change link colors from normal defaults, and avoid embedding links within long blocks of text.
Links that don't provide enough information	Avoid not turning off link-marking borders so that links clearly show which links users have clicked and which they have not. Make sure users know which links are internal anchor points versus external links, and indicate if a link brings up a separate browser window from those that do not. Finally, make sure link images and text provide enough information to the user so that they understand the meaning of the link.
Buttons that provide no click feedback	Avoid using image buttons that don't clearly change when being clicked; use Web GUI toolkit button, HTML from-submit buttons, or simple textual links.

Designing forms and reports may lead to errors that are specific to Web site design. It is unfortunately beyond the scope of this book to critically examine all possible design problems with contemporary Web sites. Here, we will simply summarize those errors that commonly occur and are particularly detrimental to the user's experience (see Table 8-16). Fortunately, numerous excellent sources are available for learning more about designing useful Web sites (Ash, 2008; Loveday and Niehaus, 2007; Nielsen and Loranger, 2006; Veeny, 2008; www.useit.com; www.webpagesthatsuck.com).

Designing the Human Interface at Pine Valley Furniture

The first design activity that Jim Woo and the PVF development team focused on was the human-computer interface. To begin, they reviewed many popular electronic commerce Web sites and established the following design guidelines:

- Menu-driven navigation with cookie crumbs
- Lightweight graphics
- Forms and data integrity rules
- Template-based HTML

In order to ensure that all team members understood what was meant by each guideline, Jim organized a design briefing to explain how each would be incorporated into the WebStore interface design.

TABLE 8-16: Common Errors When Designing the Layout of Web Pages

Error	Recommendation
Nonstandard use of GUI widgets	Make sure that when using standard design items, that they behave in accordance to major interface design standards. For example, the rules for radio buttons state that they are used to select one item among a set of items that is, not confirmed until "OK'ed" by a user. In many Web sites, selecting radio buttons are used as both *selection* and *action*.
Anything that looks like advertising	Because research on Web traffic has shown that many users have learned to stop paying attention to Web advertisement, make sure that you avoid designing any legitimate information in a manner that resembles advertising (e.g., banners, animations, pop-ups).
Bleeding-edge technology	Make sure that users don't need the latest browsers or plug-ins to view your site.
Scrolling text and looping animators	Avoid scrolling text and animations because they are both hard to read and often equated by users with advertising.
Nonstandard link colors	Avoid using nonstandard colors to show links and for showing links that users have already used; nonstandard colors will confuse the user and reduce ease of use.
Outdated information	Make sure that your site is continuously updated so that users "feel" that the site is regularly maintained and updated. Outdated content is a sure way to lose credibility.
Slow download times	Avoid using large images, lots of images, unnecessary animations, or other time-consuming content that will slow the downloading time of a page.
Fixed-formatted text	Avoid fixed-formatted text that requires users to scroll horizontally to view contents or links.
Displaying long lists as long pages	Avoid requiring users to scroll down a page to view information, especially navigational controls. Manage information by showing only *N* items at a time, using multiple pages, or by using a scrolling container within the window.

Menu-Driven Navigation with Cookie Crumbs

After reviewing several sites, the team concluded that menus should stay in the exact same place throughout the entire site. They concluded that placing a menu in the same location on every page will help customers to become familiar with the site more quickly and therefore to navigate through the site more rapidly. Experienced Web developers know that the quicker customers can reach a specific destination at a site, the quicker they can purchase the product they are looking for or get the information they set out to find. Jim emphasized this point by stating, "These details may seem silly, but the second users find themselves 'lost' in our site, they're gone. One mouse click and they're no longer shopping at Pine Valley Furniture but at one of our competitor's sites."

A second design feature, and one that is being used on many electronic commerce sites, is cookie crumbs. **Cookie crumbs** are a technique for showing users where they are in the site by placing "tabs" on a Web page that remind users where they are and where they have been. These tabs are hypertext links that can allow users to move backward quickly in the site. For example, suppose that a site is four levels deep, with the top level called "Entrance," the second "Products," the third "Options," and the fourth "Order." As the user moves deeper into the site, a tab is displayed across the top of the page showing the user where she is and giving her the ability to jump backward quickly one or more levels. In other words, when first entering the store, a tab is displayed at the top (or some other standard place) of the screen with the word "Entrance." After moving down a level, two tabs are displayed, "Entrance" and "Products." After selecting a product on the second level, a third level is displayed where a user can choose product options. When this level is displayed, a third tab is

Cookie crumbs
A technique for showing users where they are in a Web site by placing a series of "tabs" on a Web page that shows users where they are and where they have been.

produced with the label "Options." Finally, if the customer decides to place an order and selects this option, a fourth-level screen is displayed and a fourth tab displayed with the label "Order." In summary:

Level 1: Entrance
Level 2: Entrance → Products
Level 3: Entrance → Products → Options
Level 4: Entrance → Products → Options → Order

By using cookie crumbs, users know exactly how far they have wandered from "home." If each tab is a link, users can quickly jump back to a broader part of the store should they not find exactly what they are looking for. Cookie crumbs serve two important purposes. First, they allow users to navigate to a point previously visited and will ensure that they are not lost. Second, it clearly shows users where they have been and how far they have gone from home.

Lightweight Graphics

In addition to easy menu and page navigation, the PVF development team wants a system where Web pages load quickly. A technique to assist in making pages load quickly is **lightweight graphics.** Lightweight graphics are the use of small simple images that allow a page to load as quickly as possible. "Using lightweight graphics allows pages to load quickly and helps users to reach their final location in the site—hopefully the point-of-purchase area—as quickly as possible. Large color images will only be used for displaying detailed product pictures that customers explicitly request to view," Jim explained. Experienced Web designers have found that customers are not willing to wait at each hop of navigation for a page to load, just so they have to click and wait again. The quick feedback that a Web site with lightweight graphics can provide will help to keep customers at the WebStore longer.

Lightweight graphics
The use of small simple images to allow a Web page to be displayed more quickly.

Forms and Data Integrity

Because the goal of the WebStore is to have users place orders for products, all forms that request information should be clearly labeled and provide adequate room for input. If a specific field requires a specific input format such as a date of birth or phone number, it must provide a clear example for the user so that data errors can be reduced. Additionally, the site must clearly designate which fields are optional, which are required, and which have a range of values.

Jim emphasized, "All of this to me seems a bit like overkill, but it makes processing the data much simpler. Our site checks all data before submitting it to the server for processing. This allows us to provide quicker feedback to the user on any data-entry error and eliminate the possibility of writing erroneous data into the permanent database. Additionally, we want to provide a disclaimer to reassure our customers that the data will be used only for processing orders, will never be sold to marketers, and will be kept strictly confidential."

Template-Based HTML

When Jim talked with the consultants about the WebStore during the analysis phase, they emphasized the advantages of using **template-based HTML.** He was told that when displaying individual products, it would be advantageous to try to have a few "templates" that could be used to display the entire product line. In other words, not every product needs its own page; the development time for that would be far too great. Jim explained, "We need to look for ways to write a module once and reuse it. This way, a change requires modifying one page, not seven hundred. Using HTML templates will help us create an interface that is easy to maintain. For example, a desk and a filing cabinet are two

Template-based HTML
Templates to display and process common attributes of higher-level, more abstract items.

completely different products. Yet, both have an array of finishes to choose from. Logically, each item requires the same function—namely: 'display all finishes.' If designed correctly, this function can be applied to all products in the store. On the other hand, if we write a separate module for each product, it would require us to change each and every module every time we make a product change, like adding a new finish. But a function such as 'display all finishes,' written once and associated with all appropriate products, will require the modification of one generic or 'abstract' function, not hundreds."

Key Points Review

1. **Explain the process of designing forms and reports, and the deliverables for their creation.**

    Forms and reports are created through a prototyping process. Once created, designs may be stand-alone or integrated into actual working systems. The purpose of the prototyping process, however, is to show users what a form or report will look like when the system is implemented. The outcome of this activity is the creation of a specification document where characteristics of the users, tasks, system, and environment are outlined along with each form and report design. Performance testing and usability assessments may also be included in the design specification.

2. **Apply the general guidelines for formatting forms and reports.**

    Guidelines should be followed when designing forms and reports. These guidelines, proven over years of experience with human-computer interaction, help to create professional, usable systems. Guidelines are available for the use of titles, layout of fields, navigation between pages or screens, highlighting information, format of text, and the appropriate use and layout of tables and lists.

3. **Format text, tables, and lists effectively.**

    Textual output is becoming increasingly important as text-based applications such as electronic mail, bulletin boards, and information services become more popular. Text should be displayed using common writing conventions such as mixed uppercase and lowercase, appropriate punctuation, left-justified, and a minimal amount of obscure abbreviations. Words should not be hyphenated between lines, and blocks of text should be double-spaced or, minimally, a blank line should be placed between each paragraph. Tables and lists should have meaningful labels that clearly stand out. Information should be sorted and arranged in a meaningful way. Numeric data should be right-justified.

4. **Explain the process of designing interfaces and dialogues, and the deliverables for their creation.**

    Designing interfaces and dialogues is a user-focused activity that follows a prototyping methodology of iteratively collecting information, constructing a prototype, assessing usability, and making refinements. The deliverable and outcome from interface and dialogue design is the creation of a specification that can be used to implement the design.

5. **Describe and apply the general guidelines for interface design, including guidelines for layout design, structuring data-entry-fields, providing feedback, and system help.**

    To have a usable interface, users must be able to move the cursor position, edit data, exit with different consequences, and obtain help. Numerous techniques for structuring and controlling data entry, as well as providing feedback, prompting, error messages, and a well-organized help function can be used to enhance usability.

6. **Design human-computer dialogues, including the use of dialogue diagramming.**

    Human-computer dialogues should be consistent in design, allowing for shortcuts, providing feedback and closure on tasks, handling errors, allowing for action reversal, and giving the user a sense of control and ease of navigation. Dialogue diagramming is a technique for representing human-computer dialogues. The technique uses boxes to represent screens, forms, or reports and lines to show the flow between each.

7. **Discuss interface design guidelines unique to the design of Internet-based electronic commerce systems.**

    The human-computer interface is a central and critical aspect of any Internet-based electronic commerce system. Using menu-driven navigation with cookie crumbs ensures that users can easily understand and navigate a system. Using lightweight graphics ensures that Web pages load quickly. Ensuring data integrity means that customer information is processed quickly, accurately, and securely. Using common templates ensures a consistent interface that is easy to maintain.

Key Terms Checkpoint

Here are the key terms from the chapter. The page where each term is first explained is in parentheses after the term.

1. Audit trail (p. 253)
2. Cookie crumbs (p. 264)
3. Dialogue (p. 258)
4. Dialogue diagramming (p. 259)
5. Form (p. 234)
6. Lightweight graphics (p. 265)
7. Report (p. 234)
8. Template-based HTML (p. 265)

Match each of the key terms above with the definition that best fits it.

_____ 1. Templates to display and process common attributes of higher-level, more abstract items.

_____ 2. A formal method for designing and representing human-computer dialogues using box and line diagrams.

_____ 3. A business document that contains only predefined data; it is a passive document used only for reading or viewing; typically contains data from many unrelated records or transactions.

_____ 4. A technique for showing users where they are in a Web site by placing a series of "tabs" on a Web page that shows users where they are and where they have been.

_____ 5. The sequence of interaction between a user and a system.

_____ 6. A business document that contains some predefined data and may include some areas where additional data are to be filled in; typically based on one database record.

_____ 7. A record of the sequence of data entries and the date of those entries.

_____ 8. The use of small simple images to allow a Web page to be displayed more quickly.

Review Questions

1. Describe the prototyping process of designing forms and reports. What deliverables are produced from this process? Are these deliverables the same for all types of system projects? Why or why not?

2. To which initial questions must the analyst gain answers in order to build an initial prototype of a system output?

3. How should textual information be formatted on a help screen?

4. What type of labeling can you use in a table or list to improve its usability?

5. What column, row, and text formatting issues are important when designing tables and lists?

6. Describe how numeric, textual, and alphanumeric data should be formatted in a table or list.

7. Provide some examples where variations in user, task, system, and environmental characteristics might impact the design of system forms and reports.

8. Describe the process of designing interfaces and dialogues. What deliverables are produced from this process? Are these deliverables the same for all types of system projects? Why or why not?

9. List and describe the functional capabilities needed in an interface for effective entry and navigation. Which capabilities are most important? Why? Will this be the same for all systems? Why or why not?

10. Describe the general guidelines for structuring data-entry fields. Can you think of any instances when it would be appropriate to violate these guidelines?

11. Describe four types of data errors.

12. Describe the types of system feedback. Is any form of feedback more important than the others? Why or why not?

13. Describe the general guidelines for designing usable help. Can you think of any instances when it would be appropriate to violate these guidelines?

14. What steps do you need to follow when designing a dialogue? Of the guidelines for designing a dialogue, which is most important? Why?

15. Describe what is meant by a cookie crumb. How do these help prevent users from getting lost?

16. Describe why you might want to use lightweight graphics on some Web pages and large detailed graphics on others.

17. Why is it especially important to eliminate data-entry errors on an electronic commerce Web site?

18. How can template-based HTML help to make a large electronic commerce site more maintainable?

Problems and Exercises

1. Imagine that you are to design a budget report for a colleague at work using a spreadsheet package. Following the prototyping discussed in the chapter (see also Figure 1-12), describe the steps you would take to design a prototype of this report.

2. Consider a system that produces inventory reports at a local retailer. Alternatively, consider a system that produces student academic records for the records office at a university. For whichever system you choose, answer the following design questions: Who will use the output? What is the purpose of the output? When is the output needed, and when is the information that will be used within the output available? Where does the output need to be delivered? How many people need to view the output?

3. Imagine the worst possible reports from a system. What is wrong with them? List as many problems as you can. What are the consequences of such reports? What could go wrong as a result? How does the prototyping process help guard against each problem?

4. Given the guidelines presented in this chapter, identify flaws in the design of the Report of Employees shown below. What assumptions about users and tasks did you make in order to assess this design? Redesign this report to correct these flaws.

5. Consider the design of a registration system for a hotel. Following design specification items in Figure 8-11, briefly describe the relevant users, tasks, and displays involved in such a system.

6. Obtain a report of some information, either from your employer (e.g., a budget or project report) or from your school (e.g., your student academic record). Evaluate the design of the report using the general guidelines in Table 8-2.

7. Design one sample data-entry screen for a hotel registration system using the data-entry guidelines provided in this chapter (see Table 8-7). Support your design with arguments for each of the design choices you made.

8. Describe some typical dialogue scenarios between users and a hotel registration system. For hints, reread the section in this chapter that provides sample dialogue between users and the Customer Information System at Pine Valley Furniture.

9. Represent the dialogues from the previous question through the use of dialogue diagrams.

10. Think of an online retailer you've recently used or considered using for a purchase. Why is good design of that retailer's interface important for the retailer? Visit the online retailer and evaluate the interface, highlighting several good things and several bad things.

Report of Employees-1-2-08

Em_ID	Name, Title
0124543	John Smith, VP Marketing
2345645	Jared Wright, Project Manager
2342456	Jennifer Chang, Systems Analyst
4564234	Mark Walters, Software Engineer
7875468	Nick Shelley, BI Analyst
4446789	Kim Eagar, HR Manager
4678899	Emily Graham, Receptionist
4452378	Matt Hoffman, Network Operations Specialist

Discussion Questions

1. Discuss the differences between a form and a report. What characteristics make a form or report good (bad) and effective (ineffective)?

2. Discuss the various ways that information can be highlighted on a computer display. Which methods are most effective? Are some methods better than others? If so, why and when?

3. What problems can occur if a system fails to provide clear feedback and error messages to users?

4. Use a search engine to find recommendations for good design of Web interfaces. How are these recommendations similar to those discussed in this chapter? How do they differ?

Case Problems

1. **Pine Valley Furniture**

   Pine Valley Furniture's Customer Tracking System project is now ready to move into the systems design phase. You are excited because this phase involves designing the new system's forms, reports, and databases. During this morning's meeting with Jim Woo, he asked you to design several forms and reports for the new Customer Tracking System.

   During the requirements determination phase, Jackie Judson requested that a customer profile be created for each customer. The customer profile is established when new customers place their first order. Customers will have the option of not completing a profile; however, to encourage customer participation, a 10 percent discount on the customer's total order will be given to each customer who completes a profile. In the beginning, existing customers will also be given the opportunity to participate in the customer profiling process. Customer profile information will be collected via a Customer Profile Form.

   Gracie Breshers, a marketing executive, has requested that the Customer Tracking System generate a Products by Demographics Summary Report. This summary report should identify Pine Valley Furniture's major furniture categories, such as business furniture, living room, dining room, home office, and kitchen. Within each furniture category, she would like the total sales by region and customer age reported. She has also requested that several detailed reports be prepared; these reports will associate customer demographics with specific furniture category items.

   Thi Hwang, a Pine Valley Furniture sales executive, would like to know, in a Customer Purchasing Frequency Report, how many of Pine Valley Furniture's customers are repeat customers, in terms of percentages, and how often they make purchases. Additionally, he would like to have this information categorized by customer type. For each customer type, he would like to know the frequency of the purchases. For instance, does this type of customer place an order at least once a month, at least every six months, at least once a year, or longer than one year? To be considered a repeat customer, the customer must have made two separate purchases within a two-year period.

   a. What data will the Customer Profile Form need to collect? Using the guidelines presented in the chapter, design the Customer Profile Form.
   b. Using the guidelines presented in the chapter, design the Products by Demographics Summary Report.
   c. Using the guidelines presented in the chapter, design the Customer Purchasing Frequency Report.
   d. Modify the dialogue diagram presented in Figure 8-20 to reflect the addition of the Customer Profile Form, Products by Demographics Summary Report, and the Customer Purchasing Frequency Report.

2. **Hoosier Burger**

   As the lead analyst for the Hoosier Burger project, you have worked closely with Bob and Thelma Mellankamp. Having completed the systems analysis phase, you are now ready to begin designing the new Hoosier Burger information system. As the lead analyst on this project, you are responsible for overseeing the development of the forms, reports, and databases required by the new system. Because the inventory system is being automated and a new delivery system is being implemented, the Hoosier Burger system requires the development of several forms and reports.

   Using your data-flow diagrams and entity-relationship diagrams, you begin the task of identifying all the necessary forms and reports. You readily identify the need for a Delivery Customer Order Form, a Customer Account Balance Form, a Low-in-Stock Report, and a Daily Delivery Summary Report. The Delivery Customer Order Form will capture order details for those customers placing delivery orders. Bob will use the Customer Account Balance Form to look up a customer's current account balance. The Low-in-Stock Report will be generated daily to identify all food items or supplies that are low in stock. The Daily Delivery Summary Report will summarize each day's delivery sales by menu item sold.

   a. What data will the Delivery Customer Order Form need to collect? Using the design guidelines presented in the chapter, design the Delivery Customer Order Form.
   b. What data will the Customer Account Balance Form need to show? Using the design guidelines presented in the chapter, design the Customer Account Balance Form.
   c. Using the design guidelines presented in the chapter, design the Daily Delivery Summary Report.
   d. Using the design guidelines presented in the chapter, design the Low-in-Stock Report.

3. **Pet Nanny**

   Pet owners often have difficulty locating pet-sitters for their pets, boarding their pets, or just getting the pets to the veterinarian. Recognizing these needs, Gladys Murphy decided to open Pet Nanny, a business providing specialized pet-care services to busy pet owners. The company provides a multitude of services, including pet grooming, massage, day care, home care, aromatherapy, boarding, and pickup and delivery. The company has been experiencing a steady increase in demand for its services.

Initially, when the company was founded, all pet-care records were kept manually. However, Gladys recognized the need to update Pet Nanny's existing systems and hired your consulting firm to design the system changes. Your analyst team has just completed the requirements structuring phase and has selected an alternative design strategy. You are now ready to begin the systems design phase.

During the analysis phase, you determined that several forms and reports were necessary, including a Pet Enrollment Form, Pet Service Form, Pickup and Delivery Schedule Report, and Daily Boarding Report. When a customer wishes to use Pet Nanny's services for a new pet, the customer must provide basic information about the pet. For instance, the customer is asked to

provide his or her name, address, phone number, the pet's name, birth date (if known), and special care instructions. When a customer requests a special service for the pet, such as grooming or a massage, a service record is created. Because the pickup and delivery service is one of the most popular services offered by Pet Nanny, Gladys wants to make sure that no pets are forgotten. Each morning a report listing the pet pickups and deliveries is created. She also needs a report listing the pets being boarded, their special needs, and their length of stay.

a. What data should the Pet Enrollment Form collect? Using the guidelines provided in the chapter, design the Pet Enrollment Form.
b. What data should the Pet Service Form collect? Using the guidelines provided in the chapter, design the Pet Service Form.
c. Using the guidelines provided in the chapter, design the Pickup and Delivery Schedule Report.
d. Using the guidelines provided in the chapter, design the Daily Boarding Report.

CASE: PETRIE'S ELECTRONICS

Designing the Human Interface

Jim Watanabe, project director for the "No Customer Escapes" customer loyalty system for Petrie's Electronics, walked into the conference room. Sally Fukuyama, from marketing, and Sanjay Agarwal, from IT, were already there. Also at the meeting was Sam Waterston, one of Petrie's key interface designers.

"Good morning," Jim said. "I'm glad everyone could be here today. I know you are all busy, but we need to make some real progress on the customer account area for 'No Customer Escapes.' We have just awarded the development of the system to XRA, and once all the documents are signed, they will be coming over to brief us on the implementation process and our role in it."

"I'm sorry," Sally said, "I don't understand. If we are licensing their system, what's left for us to do? Don't we just install the system and we're done?" Sally took a big gulp of coffee from her cup.

"I wish it was that easy," Jim said. "While it is true that we are licensing their system, there are many parts of it that we need to customize for our own particular needs. One obvious area where we need to customize is all of the human interfaces. We don't want the system to look generic to our loyal customers—we need to make it unique to Petrie's."

"And we have to integrate the XRA system with our own operations," added Sanjay. "For example, we have to integrate our existing marketing and product databases with the XRA CRM (see PE Figure 6-2). That's just one piece of all the technical work we have to do."

"We've already done some preliminary work on system functionality and the conceptual database," Jim said. "I want to start working on interface issues now. That's why Sam is here. What we want to do today is start work on how the customer account area should look and operate. And Sally, the customer loyalty site is a great opportunity for marketing. We can advertise specials and other promotions to our best customers on this site. Maybe we could use it to show offers that are only good for members of our loyalty program."

"Oh yeah," Sally replied, "that's a great idea. How would that look?"

"I have ideas," said Sam. Using a drawing program on a tablet PC, he started to draw different zones that would be part of the interface. "Here at the top we would have a simple banner that says 'Petrie's' and the name of the program."

"It's not really going to be called 'No Customer Escapes,' is it?" asked Sally.

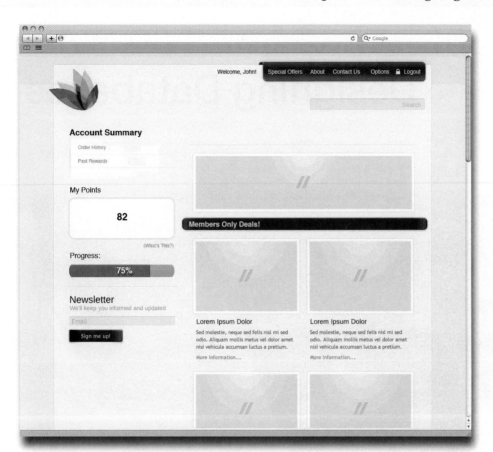

PE FIGURE 8-1
Preliminary design for the customer account area.

"No, that's an internal name," replied Jim, "but I don't know what the real name will be yet."

"OK, so the real name of the program will go in the banner, after 'Petrie's.' Then on the left side, we'll have a sidebar that has overview information about the customer account, things like name and points balance," said Sam, drawing in a sidebar on the left of the screen. "There will also be links to more detailed information about the account, so the customer can see more details on past transactions and on his or her profile."

"So the rest of the screen is open. That would be a perfect place for marketing information," suggested Sally. "Would we want just one big window for marketing? Maybe we could divide it up into additional windows, so we could use one to focus on general promotions and one to advertise 'member only' promotions?"

"Yeah, we can do that," said Sam.

Just then Jim's phone beeped. Jim looked at it. Uh-oh, it was an urgent message from his boss, the director of IT. "Sorry, I need to take care of this immediately," he told the group. "Can you guys work on this some more and then send me some of the screen designs you come up with?"

Later that afternoon, after the crisis was over, Jim sat back down at his desk for the first time in what seemed like a very long time. He glanced over his e-mail and noticed there was a message from Sam. Attached was a preliminary design for the customer account area. Jim opened it and looked it over (PE Figure 8-1). Hmmm, not bad, he thought. This is a good place for us to start.

Case Questions

1. Using the guidelines from this chapter and other sources, evaluate the usability of the page design depicted in PE Figure 8-1.
2. Chapter 8 encourages the design of a help system early in the design of the human interface. How would you incorporate help into the interface as shown in PE Figure 8-1?
3. Describe how cookie crumbs could be used in this system. Are cookie crumbs a desirable navigation aid for this system? Why or why not?
4. The page design depicted in PE Figure 8-1 links to an Order History page. Sketch a similar layout for the Order History page, following guidelines from Chapter 8.
5. Describe how the use of template-based HTML might be leveraged in the design of the "No Customer Escapes" system.

nine

Designing Databases

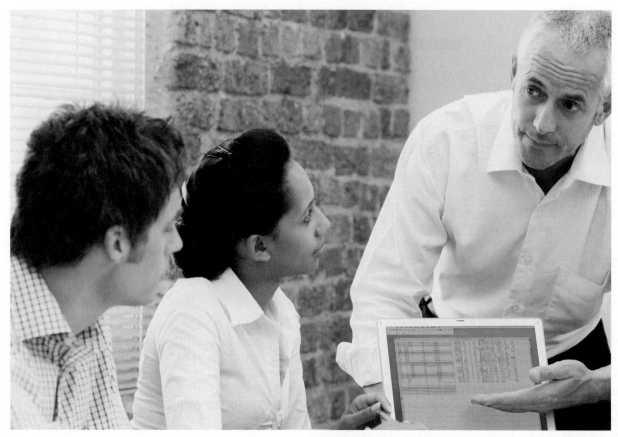

Monkey Business Images/Shutterstock

After studying this chapter, you should be able to:

- Concisely define each of the following key database design terms: *relation, primary key, functional dependency, foreign key, referential integrity, field, data type, null value, denormalization, file organization, index,* and *secondary key.*

- Explain the role of designing databases in the analysis and design of an information system.

- Transform an entity-relationship (E-R) diagram into an equivalent set of well-structured (normalized) relations.

- Merge normalized relations from separate user views into a consolidated set of well-structured relations.

- Choose storage formats for fields in database tables.

- Translate well-structured relations into efficient database tables.

- Explain when to use different types of file organizations to store computer files.

- Describe the purpose of indexes and the important considerations in selecting attributes to be indexed.

Chapter Preview . . .

In Chapter 7 you learned how to represent an organization's data graphically using an entity-relationship (E-R) diagram and Microsoft Visio. In this chapter, you learn guidelines for clear and efficient data files and about logical and physical database design. It is likely that the human interface and database design steps will happen in parallel, as illustrated in the SDLC in Figure 9-1.

Logical and physical database design has five purposes:

1. Structure the data in stable structures that are not likely to change over time and that have minimal redundancy.

2. Develop a logical database design that reflects the actual data requirements that exist in the forms (hard copy and computer displays) and reports of an information system. For this reason, database design is often done in parallel with the design of the human interface of an information system.

3. Develop a logical database design from which we can do physical database design. Because most information systems today use relational database management systems, logical database design usually uses a relational database model, which represents data in simple tables with common columns to link related tables.

4. Translate a relational database model into a technical file and database design.

5. Choose data-storage technologies (such as hard disk, CD-ROM, or flash disk) that will efficiently, accurately, and securely process database activities.

The implementation of a database (i.e., creating and loading data into files and databases) is done during the next phase of the systems development life cycle. Because implementation is technology specific, we address implementation issues only at a general level in Chapter 10.

FIGURE 9-1
Systems development life cycle. Systems analysts design databases during the systems design phase. Database design typically occurs in parallel with other design steps.

Database Design

File and database design occurs in two steps. You begin by developing a logical database model, which describes data using a notation that corresponds to a data organization used by a database management system. This system software is responsible for storing, retrieving, and protecting data (such as Microsoft Access, Oracle, or SQL Server). The most common style for a logical database model is the relational database model. Once you develop a clear and precise logical database model, you are ready to prescribe the technical specifications for computer files and databases in which to store the data ultimately. A physical database design provides these specifications.

You typically do logical and physical database design in parallel with other systems design steps. Thus, you collect the detailed specifications of data necessary for logical database design as you design system inputs and outputs. Logical database design is driven not only from the previously developed E-R data model for the application but also from form and report layouts. You study data elements on these system inputs and outputs and identify interrelationships among the data. As with conceptual data modeling, the work of all systems development team members is coordinated and shared through the project dictionary or repository. The designs for logical databases and system inputs and outputs are then used in physical design activities to specify to computer programmers, database administrators, network managers, and others how to implement the new information system. We assume for this text that the design of computer programs and distributed information processing and data networks are topics of other courses, so we concentrate on the aspect of physical design most often undertaken by a systems analyst—physical file and database design.

The Process of Database Design

Figure 9-2 shows that database modeling and design activities occur in all phases of the systems development process. In this chapter we discuss methods that help you finalize logical and physical database designs during the design phase. In logical database design you use a process called *normalization*, which is a way to build a data model that has the properties of simplicity, nonredundancy, and minimal maintenance.

In most situations, many physical database design decisions are implicit or eliminated when you choose the data-management technologies to use with the application. We concentrate on those decisions you will make most frequently and use Microsoft Access to illustrate the range of physical database design parameters you must manage. The interested reader is referred to Hoffer, Ramesh, and Topi (2011) for a more thorough treatment of techniques for logical and physical database design.

Four steps are key to logical database modeling and design:

1. Develop a logical data model for each known user interface (form and report) for the application, using normalization principles.
2. Combine normalized data requirements from all user interfaces into one consolidated logical database model; this step is called *view integration*.
3. Translate the conceptual E-R data model for the application, developed without explicit consideration of specific user interfaces, into normalized data requirements.
4. Compare the consolidated logical database design with the translated E-R model and produce, through view integration, one final logical database model for the application.

During physical database design, you use the results of these four key logical database design steps. You also consider definitions of each attribute; descriptions

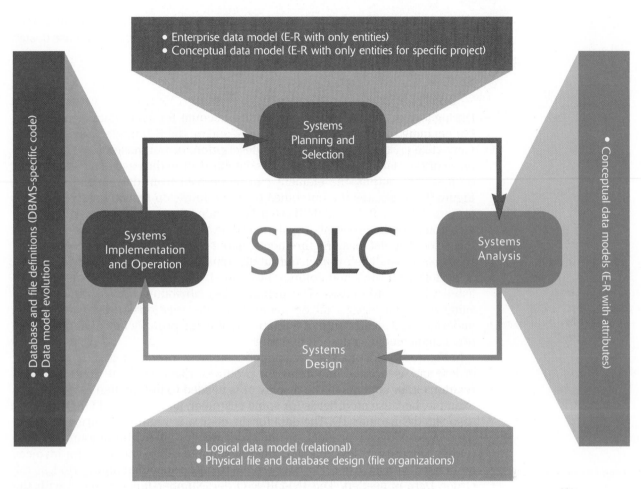

FIGURE 9-2
Relationship between data modeling and the systems development life cycle.

of where and when data are entered, retrieved, deleted, and updated; expectations for response time and data integrity; and descriptions of the file and database technologies to be used. These inputs allow you to make key physical database design decisions, including the following:

1. Choosing the storage format (called *data type*) for each attribute from the logical database model; the format is chosen to minimize storage space and to maximize data quality. Data type involves choosing length, coding scheme, number of decimal places, minimum and maximum values, and potentially many other parameters for each attribute.

2. Grouping attributes from the logical database model into physical records (in general, this is called *selecting a stored record*, or *data structure*).

3. Arranging related records in secondary memory (hard disks and magnetic tapes) so that individual and groups of records can be stored, retrieved, and updated rapidly (called *file organizations*). You should also consider protecting data and recovering data after errors are found.

4. Selecting media and structures for storing data to make access more efficient. The choice of media affects the utility of different file organizations. The primary structure used today to make access to data more rapid is key indexes, on unique and nonunique keys.

In this chapter we show how to do each of the logical database design steps and discuss factors to consider in making each physical file and database design decision.

PINE
VALLEY
FURNITURE

Deliverables and Outcomes

During logical database design, you must account for every data element on a system input or output—form or report—and on the E-R model. Each data element (like customer name, product description, or purchase price) must be a piece of raw data kept in the system's database, or in the case of a data element on a system output, the element can be derived from data in the database. Figure 9-3 illustrates the outcomes from the four-step logical database design process. Figures 9-3A and 9-3B (step 1) contain two sample system outputs for a customer order processing system at Pine Valley Furniture. A description of the associated database requirements, in the form of what we call *normalized relations*, is listed below each output diagram. Each relation (think of a relation as a table with rows and columns) is named, and its attributes (columns) are listed within parentheses. The **primary key** attribute—that attribute whose value is unique across all occurrences of the relation—is indicated by an underline, and an attribute of a relation that is the primary key of another relation is indicated by a dashed underline.

Primary key

An attribute whose value is unique across all occurrences of a relation.

In Figure 9-3A data are shown about customers, products, and the customer orders and associated line items for products. Each of the attributes of each relation either appears in the display or is needed to link related relations. For example, because an order is for some customer, an attribute of ORDER is the associated Customer_ID. The data for the display in Figure 9-3B are more complex. A backlogged product on an order occurs when the amount ordered (Order_Quantity) is less than the amount shipped (Ship_Quantity) for invoices associated with an order. The query refers to only a specified time period, so the Order_Date is needed. The INVOICE Order_Number links invoices with the associated order.

Figure 9-3C (step 2) shows the result of integrating these two separate sets of normalized relations. Figure 9-3D (step 3) shows an E-R diagram for a customer order processing application that might be developed during conceptual data modeling along with equivalent normalized relations. Figure 9-3E (step 4) shows a set of normalized relations that would result from reconciling the logical database designs of Figures 9-3C and 9-3D. Normalized relations like those in Figure 9-3E are the primary deliverable from logical database design.

Finally, Figure 9-3F shows the E-R diagram drawn in Microsoft Visio. Visio actually shows the tables and relationships between the tables from the normalized relations. Thus, the associative entities, LINE ITEM and SHIPMENT, are shown as entities on the Visio diagram; we do not place relationship names on either side of these entities on the Visio diagram because these represent associative entities. Visio also shows for these entities the primary keys of the associated ORDER, INVOICE, and PRODUCT entities. Also, note that the lines for the Places and Bills relationships are dashed. This Visio notation indicates that ORDER and INVOICE have their own primary keys that do not include the primary keys of CUSTOMER and ORDER, respectively (what Visio calls non-identifying relationships). Because LINE ITEM and SHIPMENT both include in their primary keys the primary keys of other entities (which is common for associative entities), the relationships around LINE ITEM and SHIPMENT are identifying, and hence the relationship lines are solid.

It is important to remember that relations do not correspond to computer files. In physical database design, you translate the relations from logical database design into specifications for computer files. For most information

A

HIGHEST VOLUME CUSTOMER

ENTER PRODUCT ID.:	M128
START DATE:	11/01/2012
END DATE:	12/31/2012

- - - - - - - - - - - - - - - - - - - -

CUSTOMER ID.:	1256
NAME:	Commonwealth Builder
VOLUME:	30

FIGURE 9-3
Simple example of logical data modeling: (A) Highest-volume customer query screen, (B) Backlog summary report, (C) Integrated set of relations, (D) Conceptual data model and transformed relations, (E) Final set of normalized relations, (F) Microsoft Visio E-R diagram.

This inquiry screen shows the customer with the largest volume total sales of a specified product during an indicated time period.

Relations:
    CUSTOMER(Customer_ID,Name)
    ORDER(Order_Number,Customer_ID,Order_Date)
    PRODUCT(Product_ID)
    LINE ITEM(Order_Number,Product_ID,Order_Quantity)

B

```
                                                    PAGE 1
                    BACKLOG SUMMARY REPORT
                         11/30/2012

                                    BACKLOG
                    PRODUCT ID      QUANTITY
                        B381            0
                        B975            0
                        B985            6
                        E125           30
                         ⋮
                        M128            2
                         ⋮
```

This report shows the unit volume of each product that has been ordered less than amount shipped through the specified date.

Relations:
    PRODUCT(Product_ID)
    LINE ITEM(Product_ID,Order_Number,Order_Quantity)
    ORDER(Order_Number,Order_Date)
    SHIPMENT(Product_ID,Invoice_Number,Ship_Quantity)
    INVOICE(Invoice_Number,Invoice_Date,Order_Number)

C
    CUSTOMER(Customer_ID,Name)
    PRODUCT(Product_ID)
    INVOICE(Invoice_Number,Invoice_Date,Order_Number)
    ORDER(Order_Number,Customer_ID,Order_Date)
    LINE ITEM(Order_Number,Product_ID,Order_Quantity)
    SHIPMENT(Product_ID,Invoice_Number,Ship_Quantity)

FIGURE 9-3
(*continued*)

D

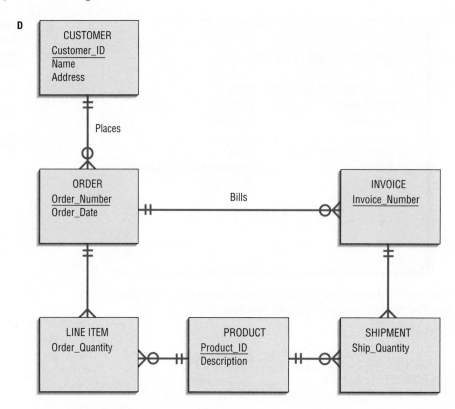

E
CUSTOMER(Customer_ID,Name,Address)
PRODUCT(Product_ID,Description)
ORDER(Order_Number,Customer_ID,Order_Date)
LINE ITEM(Order_Number,Product_ID,Order_Quantity)
INVOICE(Invoice_Number,Order_Number,Invoice_Date)
SHIPMENT(Invoice_Number,Product_ID,Ship_Quantity)

F

A   B

FIGURE 9-4

Definition of SHIPMENT table in Microsoft Access: (A) Table with invoice_number properties, (B) Invoice_number lookup properties.

systems, these files will be tables in a relational database. These specifications are sufficient for programmers and database analysts to code the definitions of the database. The coding, done during systems implementation, is written in special database definition and processing languages, such as Structured Query Language (SQL), or by filling in table definition forms, such as with Microsoft Access. Figure 9-4 shows a possible definition for the SHIPMENT relation from Figure 9-3E using Microsoft Access. This display of the SHIPMENT table definition illustrates choices made for several physical database design decisions.

- All three attributes from the SHIPMENT relation, and no attributes from other relations, have been grouped together to form the fields of the SHIPMENT table.

- The Invoice_Number field has been given a data type of Text, with a maximum length of 10 characters.

- The Invoice_Number field is required because it is part of the primary key for the SHIPMENT table (the value that makes every row of the SHIPMENT table unique is a combination of Invoice_Number and Product_ID).

- An index is defined for the Invoice_Number field, but because there may be several rows in the SHIPMENT table for the same invoice (different products on the same invoice), duplicate index values are allowed (so Invoice_Number is what we will call a *secondary key*).

- The Invoice_Number, because it references the Invoice_Number from the INVOICE table, is defined as a Lookup to the first column (Invoice_Number) of the INVOICE table; in this way, all values that are placed in the Invoice_Number field of the SHIPMENT table must correspond to a previously entered invoice.

Many other physical database design decisions were made for the SHIPMENT table, but they are not apparent on the display in Figure 9-4. Further, this table is only one table in the PVF Order Entry database, and other tables and structures for this database are not illustrated in this figure.

Relational Database Model

Many different database models are in use and are the basis for database technologies. Although hierarchical and network models have been popular in the past, they are not often used today for new information systems. Object-oriented database models are emerging but are still not common. The vast majority of information systems today use the relational database model.

FIGURE 9-5
EMPLOYEE1 relation with sample data.

EMPLOYEE1

Emp_ID	Name	Dept	Salary
100	Margaret Simpson	Marketing	42,000
140	Allen Beeton	Accounting	39,000
110	Chris Lucero	Info Systems	41,500
190	Lorenzo Davis	Finance	38,000
150	Susan Martin	Marketing	38,500

Relational database model

Data represented as a set of related tables or relations.

Relation

A named, two-dimensional table of data. Each relation consists of a set of named columns and an arbitrary number of unnamed rows.

The **relational database model** represents data in the form of related tables or relations. A **relation** is a named, two-dimensional table of data. Each relation (or table) consists of a set of named columns and an arbitrary number of unnamed rows. Each column in a relation corresponds to an attribute of that relation. Each row of a relation corresponds to a record that contains data values for an entity.

Figure 9-5 shows an example of a relation named EMPLOYEE1. This relation contains the following attributes describing employees: Emp_ID, Name, Dept, and Salary. The table contains five sample rows, corresponding to five employees.

You can express the structure of a relation by a shorthand notation in which the name of the relation is followed (in parentheses) by the names of the attributes in the relation. The identifier attribute (called the *primary key* of the relation) is underlined. For example, you would express EMPLOYEE1 as follows:

Employee (Emp_ID, Name, Dept, Salary)

Not all tables are relations. Relations have several properties that distinguish them from nonrelational tables:

1. Entries in cells are simple. An entry at the intersection of each row and column has a single value.

2. Entries in columns are from the same set of values.

3. Each row is unique. Uniqueness is guaranteed because the relation has a nonempty primary key value.

4. The sequence of columns can be interchanged without changing the meaning or use of the relation.

5. The rows may be interchanged or stored in any sequence.

Well-Structured Relations

Well-structured relation (or table)

A relation that contains a minimum amount of redundancy and allows users to insert, modify, and delete the rows without errors or inconsistencies.

What constitutes a **well-structured relation** (or **table**)? Intuitively, a well-structured relation contains a minimum amount of redundancy and allows users to insert, modify, and delete the rows in a table without errors or inconsistencies. EMPLOYEE1 (Figure 9-5) is such a relation. Each row of the table contains data describing one employee, and any modification to an employee's data (such as a change in salary) is confined to one row of the table.

In contrast, EMPLOYEE2 (Figure 9-6) contains data about employees and the courses they have completed. Each row in this table is unique for the combination of Emp_ID and Course, which becomes the primary key for the table. It is not a well-structured relation, however. If you examine the sample data in the table, you notice a considerable amount of redundancy. For example, the Emp_ID, Name, Dept, and Salary values appear in two separate rows for employees 100, 110, and 150. Consequently, if the salary for employee 100 changes, we must record this fact in two rows (or more, for some employees).

The problem with this relation is that it contains data about two entities: EMPLOYEE and COURSE. You will learn to use principles of normalization to divide EMPLOYEE2 into two relations. One of the resulting relations is

EMPLOYEE2

Emp_ID	Name	Dept	Salary	Course	Date_Completed
100	Margaret Simpson	Marketing	42,000	SPSS	6/19/2012
100	Margaret Simpson	Marketing	42,000	Surveys	10/7/2012
140	Alan Beeton	Accounting	39,000	Tax Acc	12/8/2012
110	Chris Lucero	Info Systems	41,500	SPSS	1/12/2012
110	Chris Lucero	Info Systems	41,500	C++	4/22/2012
190	Lorenzo Davis	Finance	38,000	Investments	5/7/2012
150	Susan Martin	Marketing	38,500	SPSS	6/19/2012
150	Susan Martin	Marketing	38,500	TQM	8/12/2012

FIGURE 9-6
Relation with redundancy.

EMPLOYEE1 (Figure 9-5). The other we will call EMP COURSE, which appears with sample data in Figure 9-7. The primary key of this relation is the combination of Emp_ID and Course (we emphasize this by underlining the column names for these attributes).

Normalization

We have presented an intuitive discussion of well-structured relations, however, we need rules and a process for designing them. **Normalization** is a process for converting complex data structures into simple, stable data structures. For example, we used the principles of normalization to convert the EMPLOYEE2 table with its redundancy to EMPLOYEE1 (Figure 9-5) and EMP COURSE (Figure 9-7).

Normalization
The process of converting complex data structures into simple, stable data structures.

Rules of Normalization

Normalization is based on well-accepted principles and rules. The many normalization rules, are too numerous to cover in this text (see Hoffer, Ramesh, and Topi [2011] for more complete coverage). Besides the five properties of relations outlined previously, two other rules are frequently used.

1. *Second normal form (2NF).* Each nonprimary key attribute is identified by the whole key (what we call *full functional dependency*).
2. *Third normal form (3NF).* Nonprimary key attributes do not depend on each other (what we call *no transitive dependencies*).

The result of normalization is that every nonprimary key attribute depends upon the whole primary key and nothing but the primary key. We discuss second and third normal form in more detail next.

EMP COURSE

Emp_ID	Course	Date_Completed
100	SPSS	6/19/2012
100	Surveys	10/7/2012
140	Tax Acc	12/8/2012
110	SPSS	1/22/2012
110	C++	4/22/2012
190	Investments	5/7/2012
150	SPSS	6/19/2012
150	TQM	8/12/2012

FIGURE 9-7
EMP COURSE relation.

Functional Dependence and Primary Keys

Normalization is based on the analysis of functional dependence. A **functional dependency** is a particular relationship between two attributes. In a given relation, attribute B is functionally dependent on attribute A if, for every valid value of A, that value of A uniquely determines the value of B. The functional dependence of B on A is represented by an arrow, as follows: A→B (e.g., Emp_ID→Name in the relation of Figure 9-5). Functional dependence does not imply mathematical dependence—that the value of one attribute may be computed from the value of another attribute; rather, functional dependence of B on A means that there can be only one value of B for each value of A. Thus, for a given Emp_ID value, only one Name value can be associated with it; the value of Name, however, cannot be derived from the value of Emp_ID. Other examples of functional dependencies from Figure 9-3B are in ORDER, Order_Number→Order_Date, and in INVOICE, Invoice_Number→Invoice_Date and Order_Number.

An attribute may be functionally dependent on two (or more) attributes, rather than on a single attribute. For example, consider the relation EMP COURSE (Emp_ID, Course, Date_Completed) shown in Figure 9-7. We represent the functional dependency in this relation as follows: Emp_ID, Course Date_Completed. In this case, Date_Completed cannot be determined by either Emp_ID or Course alone, because Date_Completed is a characteristic of an employee taking a course.

You should be aware that the instances (or sample data) in a relation do not prove that a functional dependency exists. Only knowledge of the problem domain, obtained from a thorough requirements analysis, is a reliable method for identifying a functional dependency. However, you can use sample data to demonstrate that a functional dependency does not exist between two or more attributes. For example, consider the sample data in the relation EXAMPLE (A, B, C, D) shown in Figure 9-8. The sample data in this relation prove that attribute B is not functionally dependent on attribute A, because A does not uniquely determine B (two rows with the same value of A have different values of B).

Second Normal Form

A relation is in **second normal form (2NF)** if every nonprimary key attribute is functionally dependent on the whole primary key. Thus, no nonprimary key attribute is functionally dependent on a part, but not all, of the primary key. Second normal form is satisfied if any one of the following conditions apply:

1. The primary key consists of only one attribute (such as the attribute Emp_ID in relation EMPLOYEE1).

2. No nonprimary key attributes exist in the relation.

3. Every nonprimary key attribute is functionally dependent on the full set of primary key attributes.

FIGURE 9-8
EXAMPLE relation.

EXAMPLE

A	B	C	D
X	U	X	Y
Y	X	Z	X
Z	Y	Y	Y
Y	Z	W	Z

EMPLOYEE2 (Figure 9-6) is an example of a relation that is not in second normal form. The shorthand notation for this relation is:

EMPLOYEE2(Emp_ID, Name, Dept, Salary, Course, Date_Completed)

The functional dependencies in this relation are the following:

Emp_ID→Name, Dept, Salary
Emp_ID, Course→Date_Completed

The primary key for this relation is the composite key Emp_ID, Course. Therefore, the nonprimary key attributes Name, Dept, and Salary are functionally dependent on only Emp_ID but not on Course. EMPLOYEE2 has redundancy, which results in problems when the table is updated.

To convert a relation to second normal form, you decompose the relation into new relations using the attributes, called *determinants*, that determine other attributes; the determinants are the primary keys of these relations. EMPLOYEE2 is decomposed into the following two relations:

1. EMPLOYEE1(Emp_ID, Name, Dept, Salary): This relation satisfies the first second normal form condition (sample data shown in Figure 9-5).
2. EMP COURSE(Emp_ID, Course, Date_Completed): This relation satisfies second normal form condition three (sample data appear in Figure 9-7).

Third Normal Form

A relation is in **third normal form (3NF)** if it is in second normal form with no functional dependencies between two (or more) nonprimary key attributes (a functional dependency between nonprimary key attributes is also called a *transitive dependency*). For example, consider the relation SALES(Customer_ID, Customer_Name, Salesperson, Region) (sample data shown in Figure 9-9A).

The following functional dependencies exist in the SALES relation:

> **Third normal form (3NF)**
> A relation that is in second normal form and has no functional (transitive) dependencies between two (or more) nonprimary key attributes.

1. Customer_ID→Customer_Name, Salesperson, Region (Customer_ID is the primary key.)
2. Salesperson→Region (Each salesperson is assigned to a unique region.)

Notice that SALES is in second normal form because the primary key consists of a single attribute (Customer_ID). However, Region is functionally dependent on Salesperson, and Salesperson is functionally dependent on Customer_ID. As a result, data maintenance problems arise in SALES.

1. A new salesperson (Robinson) assigned to the North region cannot be entered until a customer has been assigned to that salesperson (because a value for Customer_ID must be provided to insert a row in the table).
2. If customer number 6837 is deleted from the table, we lose the information that salesperson Hernandez is assigned to the East region.
3. If salesperson Smith is reassigned to the East region, several rows must be changed to reflect that fact (two rows are shown in Figure 9-9A).

These problems can be avoided by decomposing SALES into the two relations, based on the two determinants, shown in Figure 9-9(B). These relations are the following:

SALES1(Customer_ID, Customer_Name, Salesperson)
SPERSON(Salesperson, Region)

> **Foreign key**
> An attribute that appears as a nonprimary key attribute in one relation and as a primary key attribute (or part of a primary key) in another relation.

Note that Salesperson is the primary key in SPERSON. Salesperson is also a foreign key in SALES1. A **foreign key** is an attribute that appears as a nonprimary key attribute in one relation (such as SALES1) and as a primary key

FIGURE 9-9
Removing transitive dependencies: (A) Relation with transitive dependency, (B) Relations in 3NF.

SALES

Customer_ID	Customer_Name	Salesperson	Region
8023	Anderson	Smith	South
9167	Bancroft	Hicks	West
7924	Hobbs	Smith	South
6837	Tucker	Hernandez	East
8596	Eckersley	Hicks	West
7018	Arnold	Faulb	North

A

SALES1

Customer_ID	Customer_Name	Salesperson
8023	Anderson	Smith
9167	Bancroft	Hicks
7924	Hobbs	Smith
6837	Tucker	Hernandez
8596	Eckersley	Hicks
7018	Arnold	Faulb

SPERSON

Salesperson	Region
Smith	South
Hicks	West
Hernandez	East
Faulb	North

B

Referential integrity

An integrity constraint specifying that the value (or existence) of an attribute in one relation depends on the value (or existence) of the same attribute in another relation.

attribute (or part of a primary key) in another relation. You designate a foreign key by using a dashed underline.

A foreign key must satisfy **referential integrity,** which specifies that the value of an attribute in one relation depends on the value of the same attribute in another relation. Thus, in Figure 9-9B, the value of Salesperson in each row of table SALES1 is limited to only the current values of Salesperson in the SPERSON table. Referential integrity is one of the most important principles of the relational model.

Transforming E-R Diagrams into Relations

Normalization produces a set of well-structured relations that contains all of the data mentioned in system inputs and outputs developed in human interface design. Because these specific information requirements may not represent all future information needs, the E-R diagram you developed in conceptual data modeling is another source of insight into possible data requirements for a new application system. To compare the conceptual data model and the normalized relations developed so far, your E-R diagram must be transformed into relational notation, normalized, and then merged with the existing normalized relations.

Transforming an E-R diagram into normalized relations and then merging all the relations into one final, consolidated set of relations can be accomplished in four steps. These steps are summarized briefly here, and then steps 1, 2, and 4 are discussed in detail in subsequent sections of this chapter.

1. *Represent entities.* Each entity type in the E-R diagram becomes a relation. The identifier of the entity type becomes the primary key of the relation, and other attributes of the entity type become nonprimary key attributes of the relation.

2. *Represent relationships.* Each relationship in an E-R diagram must be represented in the relational database design. How we represent a relationship depends on its nature. For example, in some cases we represent a relationship by making the primary key of one relation a foreign key of another relation. In other cases, we create a separate relation to represent a relationship.

3. *Normalize the relations.* The relations created in steps 1 and 2 may have unnecessary redundancy. So, we need to normalize these relations to make them well structured.

4. *Merge the relations.* So far in database design we have created various relations from both a bottom-up normalization of user views and from transforming one or more E-R diagrams into sets of relations. Across these different sets of relations, redundant relations (two or more relations that describe the same entity type) may need to be merged and renormalized to remove the redundancy.

Represent Entities

Each regular entity type in an E-R diagram is transformed into a relation. The identifier of the entity type becomes the primary key of the corresponding relation. Each nonkey attribute of the entity type becomes a nonkey attribute of the relation. You should check to make sure that the primary key satisfies the following two properties:

1. The value of the key must uniquely identify every row in the relation.
2. The key should be nonredundant; that is, no attribute in the key can be deleted without destroying its unique identification.

Some entities may have keys that include the primary keys of other entities. For example, an EMPLOYEE DEPENDENT may have a Name for each dependent, but, to form the primary key for this entity, you must include the Employee_ID attribute from the associated EMPLOYEE entity. Such an entity whose primary key depends upon the primary key of another entity is called a *weak entity*.

Representation of an entity as a relation is straightforward. Figure 9-10A shows the CUSTOMER entity type for Pine Valley Furniture. The corresponding CUSTOMER relation is represented as follows:

CUSTOMER(Customer_ID, Name, Address, City_State_ZIP, Discount)

In this notation, the entity type label is translated into a relation name. The identifier of the entity type is listed first and underlined. All nonkey attributes are listed after the primary key. This relation is shown as a table with sample data in Figure 9-10B.

FIGURE 9-10
Transforming an entity type to a relation:
(A) E-R diagram,
(B) Relation.

A
CUSTOMER
Customer_ID
Name
Address
City_State_Zip
Discount

CUSTOMER

Customer_ID	Name	Address	City_State_Zip	Discount
1273	Contemporary Designs	123 Oak St.	Austin, TX 28384	5%
6390	Casual Corner	18 Hoosier Dr.	Bloomington, IN 45821	3%

B

Represent Relationships

The procedure for representing relationships depends on both the degree of the relationship—unary, binary, ternary—and the cardinalities of the relationship.

Binary 1:N and 1:1 Relationships A binary one-to-many (1:*N*) relationship in an E-R diagram is represented by adding the primary key attribute (or attributes) of the entity on the one side of the relationship as a foreign key in the relation that is on the many side of the relationship.

Figure 9-11A, an example of this rule, shows the Places relationship (1:*N*) linking CUSTOMER and ORDER at Pine Valley Furniture. Two relations, CUSTOMER and ORDER, were formed from the respective entity types (see Figure 9-11B). Customer_ID, which is the primary key of CUSTOMER (on the one side of the relationship) is added as a foreign key to ORDER (on the many side of the relationship).

One special case under this rule was mentioned in the previous section. If the entity on the many side needs the key of the entity on the one side as part of its primary key (this is a so-called weak entity), then this attribute is added not as a nonkey but as part of the primary key.

For a binary or unary one-to-one (1:1) relationship between the two entities A and B (for a unary relationship, A and B would be the same entity type), the relationship can be represented by any of the following choices:

1. Adding the primary key of A as a foreign key of B
2. Adding the primary key of B as a foreign key of A
3. Both of the above

Binary and Higher-Degree **M:N** ***Relationships*** Suppose that a binary many-to-many (*M:N*) relationship (or associative entity) exists between two entity types A and B. For such a relationship, we create a separate relation C. The primary key of this relation is a composite key consisting of the primary key for each of the two entities in the relationship.

FIGURE 9-11
Representing a 1:*N* relationship:
(A) E-R diagram, (B) Relations.

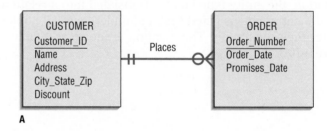

A

CUSTOMER

Customer_ID	Name	Address	City_State_ZIP	Discount
1273	Contemporary Designs	123 Oak St.	Austin, TX 28384	5%
6390	Casual Corner	18 Hoosier Dr.	Bloomington, IN 45821	3%

ORDER

Order_Number	Order_Date	Promised_Date	Customer_ID
57194	3/15/12	3/28/12	6390
63725	3/17/12	4/01/12	1273
80149	3/14/12	3/24/12	6390

B

PRODUCT
Product_ID
Description
Room
City_State_Zip
(Other Attributes)

Requests

Ordered_Quantity

ORDER
Order_Number
Order_Date
Promises_Date

A

ORDER

Order_Number	Order_Date	Promised_Date
61384	2/17/2012	3/01/2012
62009	2/13/2012	2/27/2012
62807	2/15/2012	3/01/2012

ORDER LINE

Order_Number	Product_ID	Quantity_Ordered
61384	M128	2
61384	A261	1

PRODUCT

Product_ID	Description	(Other Attributes)
M128	Bookcase	—
A261	Wall unit	—
R149	Cabinet	—

B

FIGURE 9-12

Representing an *M:N* relationship: (A) E-R diagram, (B) Relations.

Any nonkey attributes that are associated with the *M:N* relationship are included with the relation C.

Figure 9-12A, an example of this rule, shows the Requests relationship (*M:N*) between the entity types ORDER and PRODUCT for Pine Valley Furniture. Figure 9-12B shows the three relations (ORDER, ORDER LINE, and PRODUCT) that are formed from the entity types and the Requests relationship. A relation (called ORDER LINE in Figure 9-12B) is created for the Requests relationship. The primary key of ORDER LINE is the combination (Order_Number, Product_ID), which consists of the respective primary keys of ORDER and PRODUCT. The nonkey attribute Quantity_Ordered also appears in ORDER LINE.

Occasionally, the relation created from an *M:N* relationship requires a primary key that includes more than just the primary keys from the two related relations. Consider, for example, the following situation:

CUSTOMER
Customer_ID
Name

SHIPMENT
Date
Amount

VENDOR
Vendor_ID
Address

In this case, Date must be part of the key for the SHIPMENT relation to uniquely distinguish each row of the SHIPMENT table, as follows:

SHIPMENT(Customer_ID, Vendor_ID, Date, Amount)

If each shipment has a separate nonintelligent key (a system-assigned unique value that has no business meaning; e.g., order number, customer number), say a shipment number, then Date becomes a nonkey and Customer_ID and Vendor_ID become foreign keys, as follows:

SHIPMENT(Shipment_Number, Customer_ID, Vendor_ID, Date, Amount)

In some cases, a relationship may be found among three or more entities. In such cases, we create a separate relation that has as a primary key the composite of the primary keys of each of the participating entities (plus any necessary additional key elements). This rule is a simple generalization of the rule for a binary *M:N* relationship.

Unary Relationships To review, a unary relationship is a relationship between the instances of a single entity type, which are also called *recursive relationships*. Figure 9-13 shows two common examples. Figure 9-13A shows a one-to-many relationship named Manages that associates employees with another employee who is their manager. Figure 9-13B shows a many-to-many relationship that associates certain items with their component items. This relationship is called a *bill-of-materials structure*.

For a unary 1:*N* relationship, the entity type (such as EMPLOYEE) is modeled as a relation. The primary key of that relation is the same as for the entity type. Then a foreign key is added to the relation that references the primary key values. A **recursive foreign key** is a foreign key in a relation that references the primary key values of that same relation. We can represent the relationship in Figure 9-13A as follows:

> EMPLOYEE(Emp_ID, Name, Birthdate, Manager_ID)

In this relation, Manager_ID is a recursive foreign key that takes its values from the same set of worker identification numbers as Emp_ID.

For a unary *M:N* relationship, we model the entity type as one relation. Then we create a separate relation to represent the *M:N* relationship. The primary key of this new relation is a composite key that consists of two attributes (which need not have the same name) that both take their values from the same primary key. Any attribute associated with the relationship (such as Quantity in Figure 9-13B) is included as a nonkey attribute in this new relation. We can express the result for Figure 9-13B as follows:

> ITEM(Item_Number, Name, Cost)
> ITEM-BILL(Item_Number, Component_Number, Quantity)

Summary of Transforming E-R Diagrams to Relations

We have now described how to transform E-R diagrams to relations. Table 9-1 lists the rules discussed in this section for transforming entity-relationship diagrams into equivalent relations. After this transformation, you should check the resulting relations to determine whether they are in third normal form and, if necessary, perform normalization as described earlier in the chapter.

Recursive foreign key
A foreign key in a relation that references the primary key values of that same relation.

FIGURE 9-13
Two unary relations: (A) EMPLOYEE with manages relationship (1:*N*), (B) Bill-of-materials structure (*M:N*).

TABLE 9-1: E-R to Relational Transformation

E-R Structure	Relational Representation
Regular entity	Create a relation with primary key and nonkey attributes.
Weak entity	Create a relation with a composite primary key (which includes the primary key of the entity on which this weak entity depends) and nonkey attributes.
Binary or unary 1:1 relationship	Place the primary key of either entity in the relation for the other entity or do it for both entities.
Binary 1:*N* relationship	Place the primary key of the entity on the one side of the relationship as a foreign key in the relation for the entity on the many side.
Binary or unary *M:N* relationship or associative entity	Create a relation with a composite primary key using the primary keys of the related entities, plus any nonkey attributes of the relationship or associative entity.
Binary or unary *M:N* relationship or associative entity with additional key(s)	Create a relation with a composite primary key using the primary keys of the related entities and additional primary key attributes associated with the relationship or associative entity, plus any nonkey attributes of the relationship or associative entity.
Binary or unary *M:N* relationship or associative entity with its own key	Create a relation with the primary key associated with the relationship or associative entity, plus any nonkey attributes of the relationship or associative entity and the primary keys of the related entities (as nonkey attributes).

Merging Relations

As part of the logical database design, normalized relations likely have been created from a number of separate E-R diagrams and various user interfaces. Some of the relations may be redundant—they may refer to the same entities. If so, you should merge those relations to remove the redundancy. This section describes merging relations, or *view integration*, which is the last step in logical database design and prior to physical file and database design.

An Example of Merging Relations

Suppose that modeling a user interface or transforming an E-R diagram results in the following 3NF relation:

EMPLOYEE1(<u>Emp_ID</u>, Name, Address, Phone)

Modeling a second user interface might result in the following relation:

EMPLOYEE2(<u>Emp_ID</u>, Name, Address, Jobcode, Number_of_Years)

Because these two relations have the same primary key (Emp_ID) and describe the same entity, they should be merged into one relation. The result of merging the relations is the following relation:

EMPLOYEE(<u>Emp_ID</u>, Name, Address, Phone, Jobcode, Number_of_Years)

Notice that an attribute that appears in both relations (such as Name in this example) appears only once in the merged relation.

View Integration Problems

When integrating relations, you must understand the meaning of the data and must be prepared to resolve any problems that may arise in that process. In this section, we describe and illustrate three problems that arise in view integration: synonyms, homonyms, and dependencies between nonkeys.

Synonyms   In some situations, two or more attributes may have different names but the same meaning, as when they describe the same characteristic of an entity. Such attributes are called **synonyms.** For example, Emp_ID and Employee_Number may be synonyms.

When merging the relations that contain synonyms, you should obtain, if possible, agreement from users on a single standardized name for the attribute and eliminate the other synonym. Another alternative is to choose a third name to replace the synonyms. For example, consider the following relations:

> STUDENT1(<u>Student_ID</u>, Name)
> STUDENT2(<u>Matriculation_Number</u>, Name, Address)

In this case, the analyst recognizes that both the Student_ID and the Matriculation_Number are synonyms for a person's social security number and are identical attributes. One possible resolution would be to standardize on one of the two attribute names, such as Student_ID. Another option is to use a new attribute name, such as SSN, to replace both synonyms. Assuming the latter approach, merging the two relations would produce the following result:

> STUDENT(SSN, Name, Address)

Homonyms   In other situations, a single attribute name, called a **homonym,** may have more than one meaning or describe more than one characteristic. For example, the term *account* might refer to a bank's checking account, savings account, loan account, or other type of account; therefore, *account* refers to different data, depending on how it is used.

You should be on the lookout for homonyms when merging relations. Consider the following example:

> STUDENT1(<u>Student_ID</u>, Name, Address)
> STUDENT2(<u>Student_ID</u>, Name, Phone_Number, Address)

In discussions with users, the systems analyst may discover that the attribute Address in STUDENT1 refers to a student's campus address, whereas in STUDENT2 the same attribute refers to a student's home address. To resolve this conflict, we would probably need to create new attribute names and the merged relation would become:

> STUDENT(<u>Student_ID</u>, Name, Phone_Number, Campus_Address,
>   Permanent_Address)

Dependencies between Nonkeys   When two 3NF relations are merged to form a single relation, dependencies between nonkeys may result. For example, consider the following two relations:

> STUDENT1(<u>Student_ID</u>, <u>Major</u>)
> STUDENT2(<u>Student_ID</u>, Adviser)

Because STUDENT1 and STUDENT2 have the same primary key, the two relations may be merged:

> STUDENT(<u>Student_ID</u>, Major, Adviser)

Synonyms
Two different names that are used for the same attribute.

Homonym
A single attribute name that is used for two or more different attributes.

However, suppose that each major has exactly one adviser. In this case, Adviser is functionally dependent on Major:

Major→Adviser

If the previous dependency exists, then STUDENT is in 2NF but not 3NF, because it contains a functional dependency between nonkeys. The analyst can create 3NF relations by creating two relations with Major as a foreign key in STUDENT:

STUDENT(Student_ID, Major)
MAJOR ADVISER(Major, Adviser)

Logical Database Design for Hoosier Burger

In Chapter 7 we developed an E-R diagram for a new inventory control system at Hoosier Burger (Figure 9-14 repeats the diagram from Chapter 7). In this section we show how this E-R model is translated into normalized relations and how to normalize and then merge the relations for a new report with the relations from the E-R model.

In this E-R model, four entities exist independently of other entities: SALE, PRODUCT, INVOICE, and INVENTORY ITEM. Given the attributes shown in Figure 9-14, we can represent these entities in the following four relations:

SALE(Receipt_Number, Sale_Date)
PRODUCT(Product_ID, Product_Description)
INVOICE(Vendor_ID, Invoice_Number, Invoice_Date, Paid?)
INVENTORY ITEM(Item_Number, Item_Description, Quantity_in_Stock,
    Minimum_Order_Quantity, Type_of_Item)

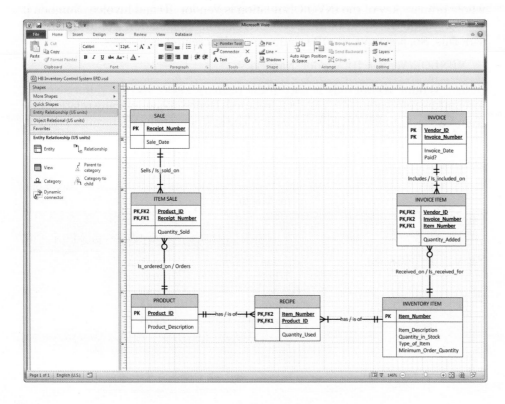

FIGURE 9-14
Final E-R diagram for Hoosier Burger's inventory control system.

The entities ITEM SALE and INVOICE ITEM as well as the associative entity RECIPE each have composite primary keys taken from the entities to which they relate, so we can represent these three entities in the following three relations:

> ITEM SALE(<u>Receipt_Number, Product_ID</u>, Quantity_Sold)
> INVOICE ITEM(<u>Vendor_ID, Invoice_Number, Item_Number</u>, Quantity_ Added)
> RECIPE(<u>Product_ID, Item_Number</u>, Quantity_Used)

Because no many-to-many, one-to-one, or unary relationships are involved, we have now represented all the entities and relationships from the E-R model. Also, each of the previous relations is in 3NF because all attributes are simple, all nonkeys are fully dependent on the whole key, and there are no dependencies between nonkeys in the INVOICE and INVENTORY ITEM relations.

Now suppose that Bob Mellankamp wanted an additional report that was not previously known by the analyst who designed the inventory control system for Hoosier Burger. A rough sketch of this new report, listing volume of purchases from each vendor by type of item in a given month, appears in Figure 9-15. In this report, the same type of item may appear many times if multiple vendors supply the same type of item.

This report contains data about several relations already known to the analyst, including:

> INVOICE(<u>Vendor_ID, Invoice_Number</u>, Invoice_Date): primary keys and the date are needed to select invoices in the specified month of the report
> INVENTORY ITEM(<u>Item_Number</u>, Type_of_Item): primary key and a nonkey in the report
> INVOICE ITEM(<u>Vendor_ID, Invoice_Number, Item_Number</u>, Quantity_Added): primary keys and the raw quantity of items invoiced that are subtotaled by vendor and type of item in the report

In addition, the report includes a new attribute: Vendor_Name. After some investigation, an analyst determines that Vendor_ID→Vendor_Name. Because the whole primary key of the INVOICE relation is Vendor_ID and Invoice_Number, if Vendor_Name were part of the INVOICE relation, this relation would violate the 3NF rule. So, a new VENDOR relation must be created as follows:

> VENDOR(<u>Vendor_ID</u>, Vendor_Name)

Now, Vendor_ID not only is part of the primary key of INVOICE but also is a foreign key referencing the VENDOR relation. Hence, a one-to-many relationship from VENDOR to INVOICE is necessary. The systems analyst determines that an

FIGURE 9-15
Hoosier Burger monthly vendor load report.

| | Monthly Vendor Load Report | for Month: xxxxx | Page *x* of *n* |

Vendor			
ID	Name	Type of Item	Total Quantity Added
V1	V1name	aaa	nnn1
		bbb	nnn2
		ccc	nnn3
V2	V2name	bbb	nnn4
		mmm	nnn5

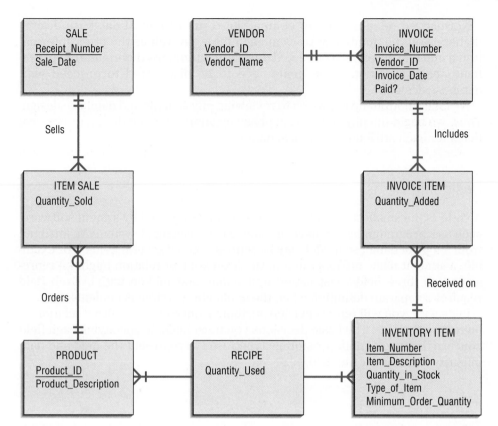

FIGURE 9-16
E-R diagram corresponding to normalized relations of Hoosier Burger's inventory control system.

invoice must come from a vendor, and keeping data about a vendor is not necessary unless the vendor invoices Hoosier Burger. An updated E-R diagram, reflecting these enhancements for new data needed in the monthly vendor load report, appears in Figure 9-16. The normalized relations for this database are:

    SALE(Receipt_Number, Sale_Date)
    PRODUCT(Product_ID, Product_Description)
    INVOICE(Vendor_ID, Invoice_Number, Invoice_Date, Paid?)
    INVENTORY ITEM(Item_Number, Item_Description, Quantity_in_Stock,
        Type_of_Item, Minimum_Order_Quantity)
    ITEM SALE(Receipt_Number, Product_ID, Quantity_Sold)
    INVOICE ITEM(Vendor_ID, Invoice_Number, Item_Number, Quantity_Added)
    RECIPE(Product_ID, Item_Number, Quantity_Used)
    VENDOR(Vendor_ID, Vendor_Name)

Physical File and Database Design

Designing physical files and databases requires certain information that should have been collected and produced during prior SDLC phases. This information includes:

- Normalized relations, including volume estimates
- Definitions of each attribute
- Descriptions of where and when data are used: entered, retrieved, deleted, and updated (including frequencies)
- Expectations or requirements for response time and data integrity
- Descriptions of the technologies used for implementing the files and database so that the range of required decisions and choices for each is known

Normalized relations are, of course, the result of logical database design. Statistics on the number of rows in each table, as well as the other information listed may have been collected during requirements determination in systems analysis. If not, these items need to be discovered to proceed with database design.

We take a bottom-up approach to reviewing physical file and database design. Thus, we begin the physical design phase by addressing the design of physical fields for each attribute in a logical data model.

Designing Fields

Field

The smallest unit of named application data recognized by system software.

A **field** is the smallest unit of application data recognized by system software, such as a programming language or database management system. An attribute from a logical database model may be represented by several fields. For example, a student name attribute in a normalized student relation might be represented as three fields: last name, first name, and middle initial. Each field requires a separate definition when the application system is implemented.

In general, you will represent each attribute from each normalized relation as one or more fields. The basic decisions you must make in specifying each field concern the type of data (or storage type) used to represent the field and data integrity controls for the field.

Choosing Data Types

Data type

A coding scheme recognized by system software for representing organizational data.

A **data type** is a coding scheme recognized by system software for representing organizational data. The bit pattern of the coding scheme is usually immaterial to you, but the space to store data and the speed required to access data are of consequence in the physical file and database design. The specific file or database management software you use with your system will dictate which choices are available to you. For example, Table 9-2 lists the data types available in Microsoft Access.

Selecting a data type balances four objectives that will vary in degree of importance for different applications:

1. Minimize storage space
2. Represent all possible values of the field
3. Improve data integrity for the field
4. Support all data manipulations desired on the field

You want to choose a data type for a field that minimizes space, represents every possible legitimate value for the associated attribute, and allows the data to be manipulated as needed. For example, suppose a "quantity sold" field can be represented by a Number data type. You would select a length for this field that would handle the maximum value, plus some room for growth of the business. Further, the Number data type will restrict users from entering inappropriate values (text), but it does allow negative numbers (if this is a problem, application code or form design may be required to restrict the values to positive).

Be careful—the data type must be suitable for the life of the application; otherwise, maintenance will be required. Choose data types for future needs by anticipating growth. Also, be careful that date arithmetic can be done so that dates can be subtracted or time periods can be added to or subtracted from a date.

Several other capabilities of data types may be available with some database technologies. We discuss a few of the most common of these features next: calculated fields and coding and compression techniques.

TABLE 9-2: Microsoft Access Data Types

Data Type	Description
Text	Text or combinations of text and numbers, as well as numbers that don't require calculations, such as phone numbers. A specific length is indicated, with a maximum number of characters of 255. One byte of storage is required for each character used.
Memo	Lengthy (up to 65,535 characters) text or combinations of text and numbers. One byte of storage is required for each character used.
Number	Numeric data used in mathematical calculations. Either 1, 2, 4, or 8 bytes of storage space is required, depending on the specified length of the number.
Date/Time	Date and time values for the years 100 through 9999. Eight bytes of storage space is required.
Currency	Currency values and numeric data used in mathematical calculations involving data with one to four decimal places. Accurate to 15 digits on the left side of the decimal separator and to 4 digits on the right side. Eight bytes of storage space is required.
Autonumber	A unique sequential (incremented by 1) number or random number assigned by Microsoft Access whenever a new record is added to a table. Typically, 4 bytes of storage is required.
Yes/No	Yes and No values and fields that contain only one of two values (Yes/No, True/False, or On/Off). One bit of storage is required.
OLE Object	An object (such as a Microsoft Excel spreadsheet, a Microsoft Word document, graphics, sounds, or other binary data) linked to or embedded in a Microsoft Access table. Up to 1 gigabyte of storage possible.
Hyperlink	Text or combinations of text and numbers stored as text and used as a hyperlink address (typical URL form).
Lookup Wizard	Creates a field that allows you to choose a value from another table (the table's primary key) or from a list of values by using a list box or combo box. Clicking this option starts the Lookup Wizard, which creates a Lookup field. After you complete the wizard, Microsoft Access sets the data type based on the values selected in the wizard. Used for foreign keys to enforce referential integrity. Space requirement depends on length of foreign key or lookup value.

Calculated Fields It is common that an attribute is mathematically related to other data. For example, an invoice may include a "total due" field, which represents the sum of the amount due on each item on the invoice. A field that can be derived from other database fields is called a **calculated** (or **computed** or **derived**) **field** (recall that a functional dependency between attributes does not imply a calculated field). Some database technologies allow you to explicitly define calculated fields along with other raw data fields. If you specify a field as calculated, you would then usually be prompted to enter the formula for the calculation; the formula can involve other fields from the same record and possibly fields from records in related files. The database technology will either store the calculated value or compute it when requested.

Calculated (or computed or derived) field
A field that can be derived from other database fields.

Coding and Compression Techniques Some attributes have few values from a large range of possible values. For example, although a six-digit field (five numbers plus a value sign) can represent numbers -99999 to 99999, maybe only 100 positive values within this range will ever exist. Thus, a Number data type does not adequately restrict the permissible values for data integrity, and storage space for five digits plus a value sign is wasteful. To use space more efficiently (and less space may mean faster access because the data you need are closer together), you can define a field for an attribute so that the possible attribute values are not represented literally but rather are abbreviated. For example, suppose in Pine Valley Furniture each product has a finish attribute, with possible values Birch, Walnut, Oak, and so forth. To store this attribute as Text might require 12, 15, or even 20 bytes to represent the longest finish value.

Suppose that even a liberal estimate is that Pine Valley Furniture will never have more than twenty-five finishes. Thus, a single alphabetic or alphanumeric character would be more than sufficient. We not only reduce storage space but also increase integrity (by restricting input to only a few values), which helps to achieve two of the physical file and database design goals. Codes also have disadvantages. If used in system inputs and outputs, they can be more difficult for users to remember, and programs must be written to decode fields if codes will not be displayed.

Controlling Data Integrity

We have already explained that data typing helps control data integrity by limiting the possible range of values for a field. You can use additional physical file and database design options to ensure higher-quality data. Although these controls can be imposed within application programs, it is better to include these as part of the file and database definitions so that the controls are guaranteed to be applied all the time, as well as uniformly for all programs. The five popular data integrity control methods are default value, input mask, range control, referential integrity, and null value control.

Default value

The value a field will assume unless an explicit value is entered for that field.

Input mask

A pattern of codes that restricts the width and possible values for each position of a field.

- *Default value:* A **default value** is the value a field will assume unless an explicit value is entered for the field. For example, the city and state of most customers for a particular retail store will likely be the same as the store's city and state. Assigning a default value to a field can reduce data-entry time (the field can simply be skipped during data entry) and data-entry errors, such as typing *IM* instead of *IN* for *Indiana*.

- *Input mask:* Some data must follow a specified pattern. An **input mask** (or field template) is a pattern of codes that restricts the width and possible values for each position within a field. For example, a product number at Pine Valley Furniture is four alphanumeric characters—the first is alphabetic and the next three are numeric—defined by an input mask of L999, where L means that only alphabetic characters are accepted, and 9 means that only numeric digits are accepted. M128 is an acceptable value, but 3128 or M12H would be unacceptable. Other types of input masks can be used to convert all characters to uppercase, indicate how to show negative numbers, suppress showing leading zeros, or indicate whether entry of a letter or digit is optional.

- *Range control:* Both numeric and alphabetic data may have a limited set of permissible values. For example, a field for the number of product units sold may have a lower bound of 0, and a field that represents the month of a product sale may be limited to the values JAN, FEB, and so forth.

- *Referential integrity:* As noted earlier in this chapter, the most common example of referential integrity is cross-referencing between relations. For example, consider the pair of relations in Figure 9-17A. In this case, the values for the foreign key Customer_ID field within a customer order must be limited to the set of Customer_ID values from the customer relation; we would not want to accept an order for a nonexisting or unknown customer. Referential integrity may be useful in other instances. Consider the employee relation example in Figure 9-17B. In this example, the employee relation has a field of Supervisor_ID. This field refers to the Employee_ID of the employee's supervisor and should have referential integrity on the Employee_ID field within the same relation. Note in this case that because some employees do not

CUSTOMER(**Customer_ID**,Cust_Name,Cust_Address,...)

CUST_ORDER(Order_ID,<u>**Customer_ID**</u>,Order_Date,...)

A   and Customer_ID may not be null because every order must be for some existing customer

EMPLOYEE(**Employee_ID**,<u>**Supervisor_ID**</u>,Empl_Name,...)

B   and Supervisor_ID may be null because not all employees have supervisors

FIGURE 9-17
Examples of referential integrity field controls: (A) Referential integrity between relations, (B) Referential integrity within a relation.

have supervisors, this referential integrity constraint is weak because the value of a Supervisor_ID field may be empty.

- *Null value control:* A **null value** is a special field value, distinct from 0, blank, or any other value, that indicates that the value for the field is missing or otherwise unknown. It is not uncommon that when it is time to enter data—for example, a new customer—you might not know the customer's phone number. The question is whether a customer, to be valid, must have a value for this field. The answer for this field is probably initially no, because most data processing can continue without knowing the customer's phone number. Later, a null value may not be allowed when you are ready to ship product to the customer. On the other hand, you must always know a value for the Customer_ID field. Because of referential integrity, you cannot enter any customer orders for this new customer without knowing an existing Customer_ID value, and the customer's name is essential for visual verification of correct data entry. Besides using a special null value when a field is missing its value, you can also estimate the value, produce a report indicating rows of tables with critical missing values, or determine whether the missing value matters in computing needed information.

Null value
A special field value, distinct from 0, blank, or any other value, that indicates that the value for the field is missing or otherwise unknown.

Designing Physical Tables

A relational database is a set of related tables (tables are related by foreign keys referencing primary keys). In logical database design, you grouped into a relation those attributes that concern some unifying, normalized business concept, such as a customer, product, or employee. In contrast, a **physical table** is a named set of rows and columns that specifies the fields in each row of the table. A physical table may or may not correspond to one relation. Whereas normalized relations possess properties of well-structured relations, the design of a physical table has two goals different from those of normalization: efficient use of secondary storage and data-processing speed.

Physical table
A named set of rows and columns that specifies the fields in each row of the table.

The efficient use of secondary storage (disk space) relates to how data are loaded on disks. Disks are physically divided into units (called *pages*) that can be read or written in one machine operation. Space is used efficiently when the physical length of a table row divides close to evenly into the length of the storage unit. For many information systems, this even division is difficult to achieve because it depends on factors, such as operating system parameters, outside the control of each database. Consequently, we do not discuss this factor of physical table design in this text.

A second and often more important consideration when selecting a physical table design is efficient data processing. Data are most efficiently processed

Denormalization

The process of splitting or combining normalized relations into physical tables based on affinity of use of rows and fields.

when they are stored close to one another in secondary memory, thus minimizing the number of input/output (I/O) operations that must be performed. Typically, the data in one physical table (all the rows and fields in those rows) are stored close together on disk. **Denormalization** is the process of splitting or combining normalized relations into physical tables based on affinity of use of rows and fields. Consider Figure 9-18. In Figure 9-18A, a normalized product relation is split into separate physical tables with each containing only engineering, accounting, or marketing product data; the primary key must be included in each table. Note, the Description and Color attributes are repeated in both the engineering and marketing tables because these attributes relate to both kinds of data. In Figure 9-18B, a customer relation is denormalized by putting rows from different geographic regions into separate tables. In both cases, the goal is to create tables that contain only the data used together in programs. By placing data used together close to one another on disk, the number of disk I/O operations needed to retrieve all the data needed in a program is minimized.

Denormalization can increase the chance of errors and inconsistencies that normalization avoided. Further, denormalization optimizes certain data processing at the expense of others, so if the frequencies of different processing activities change, the benefits of denormalization may no longer exist.

FIGURE 9-18
Examples of denormalization:
(A) Denormalization by columns,
(B) Denormalization by rows.

Normalized Product Relation

PRODUCT(Product_ID,Description,Drawing_Number,Weight,Color,Unit_Cost,Burden_Rate,Price,Product_Manager)

Denormalized Functional Area Product Relations for Tables

Engineering: E_PRODUCT(Product_ID,Description,Drawing_Number,Weight,Color)
Accounting: A_PRODUCT(Product_ID,Unit_Cost,Burden_Rate)
Marketing: M_PRODUCT(Product_ID,Description,Color,Price,Product_Manager)

A

Normalized Customer Table

CUSTOMER

Customer_ID	Name	Region	Annual_Sales
1256	Rogers	Atlantic	10,000
1323	Temple	Pacific	20,000
1455	Gates	South	15,000
1626	Hope	Pacific	22,000
2433	Bates	South	14,000
2566	Bailey	Atlantic	12,000

Denormalized Regional Customer Tables

A_CUSTOMER

Customer_ID	Name	Region	Annual_Sales
1256	Rogers	Atlantic	10,000
2566	Bailey	Atlantic	12,000

P_CUSTOMER

Customer_ID	Name	Region	Annual_Sales
1323	Temple	Pacific	20,000
1626	Hope	Pacific	22,000

S_CUSTOMER

Customer_ID	Name	Region	Annual_Sales
1455	Gates	South	15,000
2433	Bates	South	14,000

B

Various forms of denormalization can be done, but no hard-and-fast rules will help you decide when to denormalize data. Here are three common situations in which denormalization often makes sense (see Figure 9-19 for illustrations):

1. *Two entities with a one-to-one relationship.* Figure 9-19A shows student data with optional data from a standard scholarship application a student may complete. In this case, one record could be formed with four fields from the STUDENT and SCHOLARSHIP APPLICATION FORM normalized relations. (*Note:* In this case, fields from the optional entity must have null values allowed.)

2. *A many-to-many relationship (associative entity) with nonkey attributes.* Figure 9-19B shows price quotes for different items from different vendors. In this case, fields from ITEM and PRICE QUOTE relations might be combined into one physical table to avoid having to combine all three tables together. (*Note:* It may create considerable duplication of data—in the example, the ITEM fields, such as Description, would repeat for each price quote—and excessive updating if duplicated data changes.)

3. *Reference data.* Figure 9-19C shows that several ITEMs have the same STORAGE INSTRUCTIONS, and STORAGE INSTRUCTIONS relate only to ITEMs. In this case, the storage instruction data could be stored in the ITEM table, thus reducing the number of tables to access but also creating redundancy and the potential for extra data maintenance.

Arranging Table Rows

The result of denormalization is the definition of one or more physical files. A computer operating system stores data in a **physical file,** which is a named set of table rows stored in a contiguous section of secondary memory. A file contains rows and columns from one or more tables, as produced from denormalization. To the operating system—like Windows, Linux, or Mac OS—each table may be one file or the whole database may be in one file, depending on how the database technology and database designer organize data. The way the operating system arranges table rows in a file is called a **file organization.** With some database technologies, the systems designer can choose among several organizations for a file.

If the database designer has a choice, he or she chooses a file organization for a specific file to provide:

1. Fast data retrieval
2. High throughput for processing transactions
3. Efficient use of storage space
4. Protection from failures or data loss
5. Minimal need for reorganization
6. Accommodation of growth
7. Security from unauthorized use

Often these objectives conflict, and you must select an organization for each file that provides a reasonable balance among the criteria within the resources available.

To achieve these objectives, many file organizations utilize the concept of a pointer. A **pointer** is a field of data that can be used to locate a related field or row of data. In most cases, a pointer contains the address of the associated data, which has no business meaning. Pointers are used in file organizations when it is not possible to store related data next to each other. Because such situations are often the case, pointers are common. In most cases, fortunately, pointers are hidden from a programmer. Yet, because a database designer may need to decide whether and how to use pointers, we introduce the concept here.

Physical file
A named set of table rows stored in a contiguous section of secondary memory.

File organization
A technique for physically arranging the records of a file.

Pointer
A field of data that can be used to locate a related field or row of data.

FIGURE 9-19
Possible denormalization situations: (A) Two entities with a one-to-one relationship, (B) A many-to-many relationship with nonkey attributes, (C) Reference data.

Normalized relations:

STUDENT(<u>Student_ID</u>, Campus_Address, <u>Application ID</u>)

APPLICATION(<u>Application ID</u>, Application_Date, Qualifications, <u>Student ID</u>)

Denormalized relation:

STUDENT(<u>Student ID</u>, Campus_Address, Application_Date, Qualifications) and Application_Date and Qualifications may be null

(*Note:* We assume Application_ID is not necessary when all fields are stored in one record, but this field can be included if it is required application data.)

A

Normalized relations:

VENDOR(<u>Vendor ID</u>, Address, Contact_Name)

ITEM(<u>Item ID</u>, Description)

PRICE QUOTE(<u>Vendor ID</u>, <u>Item ID</u>, Price)

Denormalized relations:

VENDOR(<u>Vendor ID</u>, Address, Contact_Name)

ITEM-QUOTE(<u>Vendor ID</u>, <u>Item ID</u>, Description, Price)

B

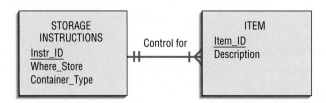

Normalized relations:

STORAGE(<u>Instr ID</u>, Where_Store, Container_Type)

ITEM(<u>Item ID</u>, Description, <u>Instr ID</u>)

Denormalized relation:

ITEM(<u>Item ID</u>, Description, Where_Store, Container_Type)

C

Literally hundreds of different file organizations and variations have been created, but we outline the basics of three families of file organizations used in most file management environments: sequential, indexed, and hashed, as illustrated in Figure 9-20. You need to understand the particular variations of each method available in the environment for which you are designing files.

Sequential File Organizations   In a **sequential file organization,** the rows in the file are stored in sequence according to a primary key value (see Figure 9-20A). To locate a particular row, a program must normally scan the file from the beginning until the desired row is located. A common example of a sequential file is the alphabetical list of persons in the white pages of a phone directory (ignoring any index that may be included with the directory). Sequential files are fast if you want to process rows sequentially, but they are essentially impractical for random row retrievals. Deleting rows can cause wasted space or the need to compress the file. Adding rows requires rewriting the file, at least from the point of insertion. Updating a row may also require rewriting the file, unless the file organization supports rewriting over the updated row only. Moreover, only one sequence can be maintained without duplicating the rows.

Sequential file organization
The rows in the file are stored in sequence according to a primary key value.

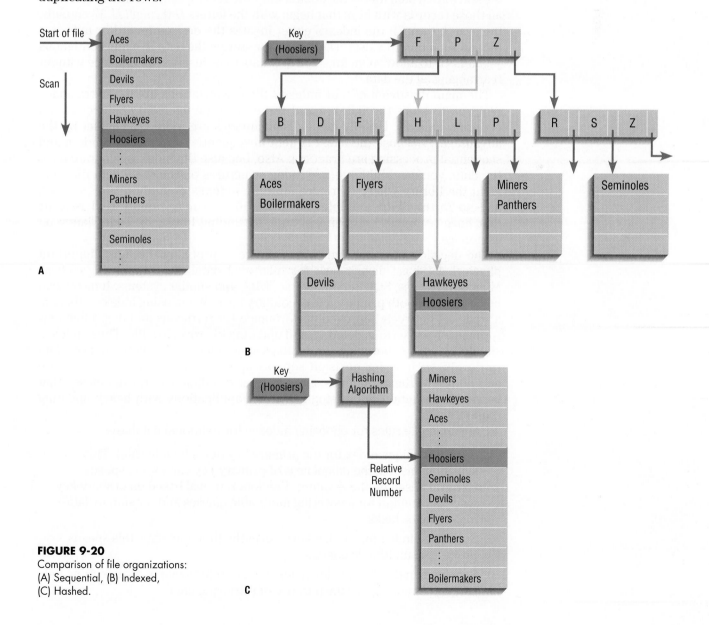

FIGURE 9-20
Comparison of file organizations:
(A) Sequential, (B) Indexed,
(C) Hashed.

Indexed file organization
The rows are stored either sequentially or nonsequentially, and an index is created that allows software to locate individual rows.

Index
A table used to determine the location of rows in a file that satisfy some condition.

Secondary key
One or a combination of fields for which more than one row may have the same combination of values.

Indexed File Organizations   In an **indexed file organization,** the rows are stored either sequentially or nonsequentially, and an index is created that allows the application software to locate individual rows (see Figure 9-20B). Like a card catalog in a library, an **index** is a structure that is used to determine the rows in a file that satisfy some condition. Each entry matches a key value with one or more rows. An index can point to unique rows (a primary key index, such as on the Product_ID field of a product table) or to potentially more than one row. An index that allows each entry to point to more than one record is called a **secondary key** index. Secondary key indexes are important for supporting many reporting requirements and for providing rapid ad hoc data retrieval. An example would be an index on the Finish field of a product table.

The example in Figure 9-20B, typical of many index structures, illustrates that indexes can be built on top of indexes, creating a hierarchical set of indexes, and the data are stored sequentially in many contiguous segments. For example, to find the record with key "Hoosiers," the file organization would start at the top index and take the pointer after the entry P, which points to another index for all keys that begin with the letters *G* through *P* in the alphabet. Then the software would follow the pointer after the H in this index, which represents all those records with keys that begin with the letters *G* through *H*. Eventually, the search through the indexes either locates the desired record or indicates that no such record exists. The reason for storing the data in many contiguous segments is to allow room for some new data to be inserted in sequence without rearranging all the data.

The main disadvantages of indexed file organizations are the extra space required to store the indexes and the extra time necessary to access and maintain indexes. Usually these disadvantages are more than offset by the advantages. Because the index is kept in sequential order, both random and sequential processing are practical. Also, because the index is separate from the data, you can build multiple index structures on the same data file (just as in the library where there are multiple indexes on author, title, subject, and so forth). With multiple indexes, software may rapidly find records that have compound conditions, such as finding books by Tom Clancy on espionage.

The decision of which indexes to create is probably the most important physical database design task for relational database technology, such as Microsoft Access, SQL Server, Oracle, DB2, and similar systems. Indexes can be created for both primary and secondary keys. When using indexes, there is a trade-off between improved performance for retrievals and degrading performance for inserting, deleting, and updating the rows in a file. Thus, indexes should be used generously for databases intended primarily to support data retrievals, such as for decision support applications. Because they impose additional overhead, indexes should be used judiciously for databases that support transaction processing and other applications with heavy updating requirements.

Here are some rules for choosing indexes for relational databases:

1. Specify a unique index for the primary key of each table (file). This selection ensures the uniqueness of primary key values and speeds retrieval based on those values. Random retrieval based on primary key value is common for answering multitable queries and for simple data-maintenance tasks.

2. Specify an index for foreign keys. As in the first guideline, this speeds processing multitable queries.

3. Specify an index for nonkey fields that are referenced in qualification and sorting commands for the purpose of retrieving data.

To illustrate the use of these rules, consider the following relations for Pine Valley Furniture:

PRODUCT(Product_Number, Description, Finish, Room, Price)
ORDER(Order_Number, Product_Number, Quantity)

You would normally specify a unique index for each primary key: Product_Number in PRODUCT and Order_Number in ORDER. Other indexes would be assigned based on how the data are used. For example, suppose that a system module requires PRODUCT and PRODUCT_ORDER data for products with a price below $500, ordered by Product_Number. To speed up this retrieval, you could consider specifying indexes on the following nonkey attributes:

1. Price in PRODUCT because it satisfies rule 3

2. Product_Number in ORDER because it satisfies rule 2

Because users may direct a potentially large number of different queries against the database, especially for a system with a lot of ad hoc queries, you will probably have to be selective in specifying indexes to support the most common or frequently used queries.

Hashed File Organizations   In **hashed file organization,** the address of each row is determined using an algorithm (see Figure 9-20C) that converts a primary key value into a row address. Although there are several variations of hashed files, in most cases the rows are located nonsequentially as dictated by the hashing algorithm. Thus, sequential data processing is impractical. On the other hand, retrieval of random rows is fast. Some of the issues in the design of hashing file organizations, such as how to handle two primary keys that translate into the same address, are beyond our scope (see Hoffer, Ramesh, and Topi [2011] for a thorough discussion).

Hashed file organization
The address for each row is determined using an algorithm.

Summary of File Organizations   The three families of file organizations—sequential, indexed, and hashed—cover most of the file organizations you will have at your disposal as you design physical files and databases. Table 9-3 summarizes the comparative features of these file organizations. You can use this table to help choose a file organization by matching the file characteristics and file processing requirements with the features of the file organization.

Designing Controls for Files

Two of the goals of physical table design mentioned earlier are protection from failures or data loss and security from unauthorized use. These goals are achieved primarily by implementing controls on each file. Data integrity controls, a primary type of control, was mentioned earlier in the chapter. Two other important types of controls address file backup and security.

It is almost inevitable that a file will be damaged or lost, because of either software or human errors. When a file is damaged, it must be restored to an accurate and reasonably current condition. A file and database designer has several techniques for file restoration, including:

- Periodically making a backup copy of a file
- Storing a copy of each change to a file in a transaction log or audit trail
- Storing a copy of each row before or after it is changed

For example, a backup copy of a file and a log of rows after they were changed can be used to reconstruct a file from a previous state (the backup copy) to its current values. This process would be necessary if the current file were so damaged that it could not be used. If the current file is operational but inaccurate,

TABLE 9-3:   Comparative Features of Sequential, Indexed, and Hashed File Organizations

Factor	File Organization		
	Sequential	**Indexed**	**Hashed**
Storage space	No wasted space	No wasted space for data, but extra space for index	Extra space may be needed to allow for addition and deletion of records
Sequential retrieval on primary key	Very fast	Moderately fast	Impractical
Random retrieval on primary key	Impractical	Moderately fast	Very fast
Multiple key retrieval	Possible, but requires scanning whole file	Very fast with multiple indexes	Not possible
Deleting rows	Can create wasted space or require reorganizing	If space can be dynamically allocated, this is easy, but requires maintenance of indexes	Very easy
Adding rows	Requires rewriting file	If space can be dynamically allocated, this is easy, but requires maintenance of indexes	Very easy, except multiple keys with same address require extra work
Updating rows	Usually requires rewriting file	Easy, but requires maintenance of indexes	Very easy

then a log of earlier images of rows can be used in reverse order to restore a file to an accurate but previous condition. Then a log of the transactions can be re-applied to the restored file to bring it up to current values. It is important that the information system designer make provisions for backup, audit trail, and row image files so that data files can be rebuilt when errors and damage occur.

An information system designer can build data security into a file by several means, including:

- Coding, or encrypting, the data in the file so that they cannot be read unless the reader knows how to decrypt the stored values

- Requiring data file users to identify themselves by entering user names and passwords, and then possibly allowing only certain file activities (read, add, delete, change) for selected users for selected data in the file

- Prohibiting users from directly manipulating any data in the file, and rather requiring programs and users to work with a copy (real or virtual) of the data they need; the copy contains only the data that users or programs are allowed to manipulate, and the original version of the data will change only after changes to the copy are thoroughly checked for validity

Security procedures such as these all add overhead to an information system, so only necessary controls should be included.

Physical Database Design for Hoosier Burger

A set of normalized relations and an associated E-R diagram for Hoosier Burger (Figure 9-16) were presented in the section "Logical Database Design for Hoosier Burger" earlier in this chapter. The display of a complete design of this database would require more documentation than space permits in this text, so we illustrate in this section only a few key decisions from the complete physical database.

As outlined in this chapter, to translate a logical database design into a physical database design, you need to make the following decisions:

- Create one or more fields for each attribute and determine a data type for each field.
- For each field, decide whether it is calculated, needs to be coded or compressed, must have a default value or input mask, or must have range, referential integrity, or null value controls.
- For each relation, decide whether it should be denormalized to achieve desired processing efficiencies.
- Choose a file organization for each physical file.
- Select suitable controls for each file and the database.

Remember, the specifications for these decisions are made in physical database design, and then the specifications are coded in the implementation phase using the capabilities of the chosen database technology. These database technology capabilities determine what physical database design decisions you need to make. For example, for Microsoft Access, which we assume is the implementation environment for this illustration, the only choice for file organization is indexed, so the file organization decision becomes on which primary and secondary key attributes to build indexes.

We illustrate these physical database design decisions only for the INVOICE table. The first decision most likely would be whether to denormalize this table. Based on the suggestions for possible denormalization presented in the chapter, the only possible denormalization of this table would be to combine it with the VENDOR table. Because each invoice must have a vendor, and the only additional data about vendors not in the INVOICE table is the Vendor_Name attribute, it is a good candidate for denormalization. Because Vendor_Name is not especially volatile, repeating Vendor_Name in each invoice for the same vendor will not cause excessive update maintenance. If Vendor_Name is often used with other invoice data when invoice data are displayed, then, indeed, it would be a good candidate for denormalization. So, the denormalized relation to be transformed into a physical table is:

INVOICE(Vendor_ID, Invoice_Number, Invoice_Date, Paid?, Vendor_Name)

The next decision can be what indexes to create. The guidelines presented in this chapter suggest creating an index for the primary key, all foreign keys, and secondary keys used for sorting and qualifications in queries. So, we create a primary key index on the combined fields Vendor_ID and Invoice_Number. INVOICE has no foreign keys. To determine what fields are used as secondary keys in query sorting and qualification clauses, we would need to know the content of queries. Also, it would be helpful to know query frequency, because indexes do not provide much performance efficiency for infrequently run queries. For simplicity, suppose only two frequently run queries reference the INVOICE table, as follows:

1. Display all the data about all unpaid invoices due this week.
2. Display all invoices sorted by vendor: show all unpaid invoices first, then all paid invoices, and order the invoices of each category in reverse sequence by invoice date.

In the first query, both the Paid? and Invoice_Date fields are used for qualification. Paid?, however, may not be a good candidate for an index because this field contains only two values. The systems analyst would need to discover what percentage of invoices on file are unpaid. If this value is more than 10 percent,

TABLE 9-4:   INVOICE Table Field Design Parameters for Hoosier Burger

	Physical Design Parameter				
Field	Data Type and Size	Format and Input Mask	Default Value	Validation Rule	Required, Zero Length
Vendor_ID	Number	Fixed with 0 decimals, 9999	N/A	< 0	Required, not 0 length
Invoice_Number	Text, 10	LL99–99999	N/A	N/A	Required, not 0 length
Invoice_Date	Date/Time	Medium date	= Date( )	> #1/1/2000	Not required
Paid?	Yes/No	N/A	False	N/A	Required
Vendor_Name	Text, 30	N/A	N/A	N/A	Required, may be 0 length

then an index on Paid? would not likely be helpful. Invoice_Date is a more discriminating field, so an index on this field would be helpful.

In the second query, Vendor_ID, Paid?, and Invoice_Date are used for sorting. Vendor_ID and Invoice_Date are discriminating fields (most values occur in less than 10 percent of the rows), so indexes on these fields will be helpful. Assuming less than 10 percent of the invoices on file are unpaid, then it would make sense to create the following indexes to make these two queries run as efficiently as possible:

> *Primary key index:* Vendor_ID and Invoice_Number
> *Secondary key indices:* Vendor_ID, Invoice_Date, and Paid?

Table 9-4 shows the decisions made for the properties of each field, based on reasonable assumptions about invoice data. Figure 9-4 illustrates a Microsoft Access table definition screen for the SHIPMENT table that includes the Invoice_Number field. It is the parameters on such a screen that must be specified for each field. Table 9-4 summarizes the field design parameters for the Invoice_Number field: size (width), format and input mask (picture), default value, validation rule (integrity control), and whether the field is required or is allowed zero length (null value controls); we have already indicated the indexing decision. Recall from Table 9-2 that the data type of Lookup Wizard implements referential integrity, but no foreign keys are in the INVOICE table because we combined the VENDOR table into the INVOICE table. We do not specify properties under the Lookup tab, which relates to additional data entry and display properties peculiar to Microsoft Access. Remember, we specify these parameters in physical database design, and it is in implementation that the Access tables would be defined using forms such as in Figure 9-4.

We do not illustrate security and other types of controls because these decisions are dependent on unique capabilities of the technology and a complex analysis of what data which users have the right to read, modify, add, or delete. This section illustrates the process of making many key physical database design decisions within the Microsoft Access environment.

Pine Valley Furniture WebStore: Designing Databases

Like many other analysis and design activities, designing the database for an Internet-based electronic commerce application is no different from the process followed when designing the database for other types of applications. In the last chapter, you read how Jim Woo and the Pine Valley Furniture development team designed the human interface for the WebStore. In this section, we examine the processes Jim followed when transforming the conceptual data model for the WebStore into a set of normalized relations.

Designing Databases for Pine Valley Furniture's WebStore

The first step Jim took when designing the database for the WebStore was to review the conceptual data model—the entity-relationship diagram—developed during the analysis phase of the SDLC (see Figure 7-13 for a review). Given that the diagram contained no associative entities or many-to-many relationships, he began by identifying four distinct entity types that he named:

CUSTOMER
ORDER
INVENTORY
SHOPPING_CART

Once reacquainted with the conceptual data model, he examined the lists of attributes for each entity. He noted that three types of customers were identified during conceptual data modeling, namely: corporate customers, home-office customers, and student customers. Yet, all were simply referred to as a "customer." Nonetheless, because each type of customer had some unique information (attributes) that other types of customers did not, Jim created three additional entity types, or subtypes, of customers:

CORPORATE
HOME_OFFICE
STUDENT

Table 9-5 lists the common and unique information about each customer type. As Table 9-5 implies, four separate relations are needed to keep track of customer information without having anomalies. The CUSTOMER relation is used to capture common attributes, whereas the additional relations are used to capture

TABLE 9-5: Common and Unique Information about Each Customer Type*

Common Information about ALL Customer Types		
Corporate Customer	**Home-Office Customer**	**Student Customer**
Customer ID	Customer ID	Customer ID
Address	Address	Address
Phone	Phone	Phone
E-mail	E-mail	E-mail
Unique Information about EACH Customer Type		
Corporate Customer	**Home-Office Customer**	**Student Customer**
Corporate name	Customer name	Customer name
Shipping method	Corporate name	School
Buyer name	Fax	
Fax		

*Having multiple "types" of an entity, with some sharing common attributes and each having unique attributes, is modeled in E-R diagrams as a subclass entity and is commonly referred to as an "is a" relationship (e.g., a customer is a corporate customer, a customer is a home-office customer, or a customer is a student customer). Please see a comprehensive database management text such as Hoffer, Ramesh, and Topi (2011) for more information on subclass entities and "is a" relationships.

information unique to each distinct customer type. In order to identify the type of customer within the CUSTOMER relation easily, a Customer_Type attribute is added to the CUSTOMER relation. Thus, the CUSTOMER relation consists of:

CUSTOMER(Customer_ID, Address, Phone, E-mail, Customer_Type)

In order to link the CUSTOMER relation to each of the separate customer types—CORPORATE, HOME_OFFICE, and STUDENT—they all share the same primary key, Customer_ID, in addition to the attributes unique to each, which results in the following relations:

CORPORATE(Customer_ID, Corporate_Name, Shipping_Method, Buyer_Name, Fax)
HOME_OFFICE(Customer_ID, Customer_Name, Corporate_Name, Fax)
STUDENT(Customer_ID, Customer_Name, School)

In addition to identifying all the attributes for customers, Jim also identified the attributes for the other entity types. The results of this investigation are summarized in Table 9-6. As described in Chapter 7, much of the order-related information is captured and tracked within PVF's Purchasing Fulfillment System. Therefore, the ORDER relation does not need to track all the details of the order because the Purchasing Fulfillment System produces a detailed invoice that contains all order details, such as the list of ordered products, materials used, colors, quantities, and other such information. In order to access this invoice information, a foreign key, Invoice_ID, is included in the ORDER relation. Additionally, to easily identify which orders belong to a specific customer, the Customer_ID attribute is also included in ORDER. Two additional attributes, Return_Code and Order_Status, are also included in ORDER. The Return_Code is used to track the return of an order more easily—or a product within an order—whereas Order_Status is a code used to represent the state of an order as it moves through the purchasing fulfillment process. These attributes result in the following ORDER relation:

ORDER(Order_ID, Invoice_ID, Customer_ID, Return_Code, Order_Status)

In the INVENTORY entity, two attributes—Materials and Colors—could take on multiple values but were represented as single attributes. For example, Materials represents the range of materials from which a particular inventory item could be constructed. Likewise, Colors is used to represent the range of possible

TABLE 9-6: Attributes for Order, Inventory, and Shopping Cart Entities

Order	Inventory	Shopping_Cart
Order_ID (primary key)	Inventory_ID (primary key)	Cart_ID (primary key)
Invoice_ID (foreign key)	Name	Customer_ID (foreign key)
Customer_ID (foreign key)	Description	Inventory_ID (foreign key)
Return_Code	Size	Material
Order_Status	Weight	Color
	Materials	Quantity
	Colors	
	Price	
	Lead_Time	

product colors. PVF has a long-established set of codes for representing materials and colors; each of these *complex* attributes is represented as a single attribute. For example, the value "A" in the Colors field represents walnut, dark oak, light oak, and natural pine, whereas the value "B" represents cherry and walnut. Using this coding scheme, PVF can use a single character code to represent numerous combinations of colors and results in the following INVENTORY relation:

INVENTORY(<u>Inventory_ID</u>, Name, Description, Size, Weight, Materials, Colors, Price, Lead_Time)

Finally, in addition to Cart_ID, each shopping cart contains the Customer_ID and Inventory_ID attributes so that each item in a cart can be linked to a particular inventory item and to a specific customer. In other words, both the Customer_ID and Inventory_ID attributes are foreign keys in the SHOPPING_CART relation. Recall that the SHOPPING_CART is temporary and is kept only while a customer is shopping. When a customer actually places the order, the ORDER relation is created and the line items for the order—the items in the shopping cart—are moved to the Purchase Fulfillment System and stored as part of an invoice. Because we also need to know the selected material, color, and quantity of each item in the SHOPPING_CART, these attributes are included in this relation, which results in the following:

SHOPPING_CART(<u>Cart_ID</u>, <u>Customer_ID</u>, <u>Inventory_ID</u>, Material, Color, Quantity)

Now that Jim had completed the database design for the WebStore, he shared all the design information with his project team so that the design could be turned into a working database during implementation. We read more about the WebStore's implementation in the next chapter.

Key Points Review

1. **Concisely define each of the following key database design terms: *relation, primary key, functional dependency, foreign key, referential integrity, field, data type, null value, denormalization, file organization, index*, and *secondary key*.**

   A relation is a named, two-dimensional table of data. Each relation consists of a set of named columns and an arbitrary number of unnamed rows. In logical database design, a relation corresponds to an entity or a many-to-many relationship from an E-R data model. One or more columns of each relation compose the primary key of the relation, values for which distinguish each row of data in the relation. A functional dependency is a particular relationship between two attributes. For a given relation, attribute B is functionally dependent on attribute A if, for every valid value of A, that value of A uniquely determines the value of B. The functional dependence of B on A is represented by A→B. The primary goal of logical database design is to develop relations in which all the nonprimary key attributes of a relation functionally depend on the whole primary key and nothing but the primary key. Relationships between relations are represented by placing the primary key of the table on the one side of the relationship as an attribute (also known as a foreign key) in the relation on the many side of the relationship. Foreign keys must satisfy referential integrity, which means that the value (or existence) of an attribute depends on the value (or existence) of the same attribute in another relation. The specifications for a database in terms of relations must be transformed into technology-related terms before the database can be implemented. A field is the smallest unit of stored data in a database and typically corresponds to an attribute in a relation. Each field has a data type, which is a coding scheme recognized by system software for representing organizational data. A null value for a field is a special field value, distinct from 0, blank, or any other value, that indicates that the value for the field is missing or otherwise unknown. Denormalization is an important process in designing a physical database, by which normalized relations are split or combined into physical tables based on affinity of use of rows and fields. A file organization is a technique for physically arranging the records of a physical file. Many types of file organizations utilize an index, which is a table (not related to the E-R diagram for the application) used to determine the location of rows in a file that satisfy some condition. An index can be created on a primary or a secondary key, which is one or a combination of fields for which more than one row may have the same combination of values.

2. **Explain the role of designing databases in the analysis and design of an information system.**

    Databases are defined during the systems design phase of the systems development life cycle. They are designed usually in parallel with the design of system interfaces. To design a database, a systems analyst must understand the conceptual database design for the application, usually specified by an E-R diagram, and the data requirements of each system interface (report, form, screen, etc.). Thus, database design is a combination of top-down (driven by an E-R diagram) and bottom-up (driven by specific information requirements in system interfaces) processes. Besides data requirements, systems analysts must also know physical data characteristics (e.g., length and format), frequency of use of the system interfaces, and the capabilities of database technologies.

3. **Transform an entity-relationship (E-R) diagram into an equivalent set of well-structured (normalized) relations.**

    An E-R diagram is transformed into normalized relations by following well-defined principles summarized in Table 9-1. For example, each entity becomes a relation and each many-to-many relationship or associative entity also becomes a relation. The principles also specify how to add foreign keys to relations to represent one-to-many relationships. You may want to review Table 9-1 at this point.

4. **Merge normalized relations from separate user views into a consolidated set of well-structured relations.**

    Separate sets of normalized relations are merged (this process is also called *view integration*) to create a consolidated logical database design. The different sets of relations come from the conceptual E-R diagram for the application, known human system interfaces (reports, screens, forms, etc.), and known or anticipated queries for data that meet certain qualifications. The result of merging is a comprehensive, normalized set of relations for the application.

Merging is not simply a mechanical process. A systems analyst must address issues of synonyms, homonyms, and dependencies between nonkeys during view integration.

5. **Choose storage formats for fields in database tables.**

    Fields in the physical database design represent the attributes (columns) of relations in the logical database design. Each field must have a data type and potentially other characteristics, such as a coding scheme to simplify the storage of business data, default value, input mask, range control, referential integrity control, or null value control. A storage format is chosen to balance four objectives: (1) minimize storage space, (2) represent all possible values of the field, (3) improve data integrity for the field, and (4) support all data manipulations desired on the field.

6. **Translate well-structured relations into efficient database tables.**

    Whereas normalized relations possess properties of well-structured relations, the design of a physical table attempts to achieve two goals different from those of normalization: efficient use of secondary storage and data-processing speed. Efficient use of storage means that the amount of extra (or overhead) information is minimized. So, file organizations, such as sequential, are efficient in the use of storage because little or no extra information, besides the meaningful business data, are kept. Data-processing speed is achieved by keeping storage data close together that are used together and by building extra information in the database that allows data to be quickly found based on primary or secondary key values or by sequence.

7. **Explain when to use different types of file organizations to store computer files.**

    Table 9-3 summarizes the performance characteristics of different types of file organizations. The systems analyst must decide which performance factors are most important for each application and the associated database. These factors are storage space, sequential retrieval speed, random-row retrieval speed, speed of retrieving data based on multiple key qualifications, and the speed to perform data maintenance activities of row deletion, addition, and updating.

8. **Describe the purpose of indexes and the important considerations in selecting attributes to be indexed.**

    An index is information about the primary or secondary keys of a file. Each index entry contains the key value and a pointer to the row that contains that key value. Using indexes involves a trade-off between improved performance for retrievals and degrading performance for inserting, deleting, and updating the rows in a file. Thus, indexes should be used generously for databases intended primarily to support data retrievals, such as for decision support applications. Because they impose additional overhead, indexes should be used judiciously for databases that support transaction processing and other applications with heavy updating requirements. Typically, you create indexes on a file for its primary key, foreign keys, and other attributes used in qualification and sorting clauses in queries, forms, reports, and other system interfaces.

Key Terms Checkpoint

Here are the key terms from the chapter. The page where each term is first explained is in parentheses after the term.

1. Calculated (or computed or derived) field (p. 295)
2. Data type (p. 294)
3. Default value (p. 296)
4. Denormalization (p. 298)
5. Field (p. 294)
6. File organization (p. 299)
7. Foreign key (p. 283)
8. Functional dependency (p. 282)
9. Hashed file organization (p. 303)
10. Homonym (p. 290)
11. Index (p. 302)
12. Indexed file organization (p. 302)
13. Input mask (p. 296)
14. Normalization (p. 281)
15. Null value (p. 297)
16. Physical file (p. 299)
17. Physical table (p. 297)
18. Pointer (p. 299)
19. Primary key (p. 276)
20. Recursive foreign key (p. 288)
21. Referential integrity (p. 284)
22. Relation (p. 280)
23. Relational database model (p. 280)
24. Second normal form (2NF) (p. 282)
25. Secondary key (p. 302)
26. Sequential file organization (p. 301)
27. Synonyms (p. 290)
28. Third normal form (3NF) (p. 283)
29. Well-structured relation (or table) (p. 280)

Match each of the key terms above with the definition that best fits it.

_____ 1. A named, two-dimensional table of data. Each relation consists of a set of named columns and an arbitrary number of unnamed rows.

_____ 2. A relation that contains a minimum amount of redundancy and allows users to insert, modify, and delete the rows without errors or inconsistencies.

_____ 3. The process of converting complex data structures into simple, stable data structures.

_____ 4. A particular relationship between two attributes.

_____ 5. A relation for which every nonprimary key attribute is functionally dependent on the whole primary key.

_____ 6. A relation that is in second normal form and has no functional (transitive) dependencies between two (or more) nonprimary key attributes.

_____ 7. An attribute that appears as a nonprimary key attribute in one relation and as a primary key attribute (or part of a primary key) in another relation.

_____ 8. An integrity constraint specifying that the value (or existence) of an attribute in one relation depends on the value (or existence) of the same attribute in another relation.

_____ 9. A foreign key in a relation that references the primary key values of that same relation.

_____ 10. Two different names that are used for the same attribute.

_____ 11. A single attribute name that is used for two or more different attributes.

_____ 12. The smallest unit of named application data recognized by system software.

_____ 13. A coding scheme recognized by system software for representing organizational data.

_____ 14. A field that can be derived from other database fields.

_____ 15. The value a field will assume unless an explicit value is entered for that field.

_____ 16. A pattern of codes that restricts the width and possible values for each position of a field.

_____ 17. A special field value, distinct from 0, blank, or any other value, that indicates that the value for the field is missing or otherwise unknown.

_____ 18. A named set of rows and columns that specifies the fields in each row of the table.

_____ 19. The process of splitting or combining normalized relations into physical

_____ tables based on affinity of use of rows and fields.

_____ 20. A named set of table rows stored in a contiguous section of secondary memory.

_____ 21. A technique for physically arranging the records of a file.

_____ 22. A field of data that can be used to locate a related field or row of data.

_____ 23. The rows in the file are stored in sequence according to a primary key value.

_____ 24. The rows are stored either sequentially or nonsequentially, and an index is created that allows software to locate individual rows.

_____ 25. A table used to determine the location of rows in a file that satisfy some condition.

_____ 26. One or a combination of fields for which more than one row may have the same combination of values.

_____ 27. The address for each row is determined using an algorithm.

_____ 28. An attribute whose value is unique across all occurrences of a relation.

_____ 29. Data represented as a set of related tables or relations.

Review Questions

1. What is the purpose of normalization?
2. List five properties of relations.
3. What problems can arise during view integration or merging relations?
4. How are relationships between entities represented in the relational data model?
5. What is the relationship between the primary key of a relation and the functional dependencies among all attributes within that relation?
6. How is a foreign key represented in relational notation?
7. Can instances of a relation (sample data) prove the existence of a functional dependency? Why or why not?
8. In what way does the choice of a data type for a field help to control the integrity of that field?
9. Contrast the differences between range control and referential integrity when controlling data integrity.

10. What is the purpose of denormalization? Why might you not want to create one physical table or file for each relation in a logical data model?
11. What factors influence the decision to create an index on a field?
12. Explain the purpose of data compression techniques.
13. What are the goals of designing physical tables?
14. What are the seven factors that should be considered in selecting a file organization?
15. What are the four key steps in logical database modeling and design?
16. What are the four steps in transforming an E-R diagram into normalized relations?

Problems and Exercises

1. Assume that at Pine Valley Furniture products consist of components, products are assigned to salespersons, and components are produced by vendors. Also assume that in the relation PRODUCT(Prodname, Salesperson, Compname, Vendor) Vendor is functionally dependent on Compname, and Compname is functionally dependent on Prodname. Eliminate the transitive dependency in this relation and form 3NF relations.
2. Transform the E-R diagram of Figure 7-20 into a set of 3NF relations. Make up a primary key and one or more nonkeys for each entity that does not already have them listed.
3. Transform the E-R diagram of Figure 9-21 into a set of 3NF relations.

4. Consider the list of individual 3NF relations that follow. These relations were developed from several separate normalization activities.

PATIENT(Patient_ID, Room_Number, Admit_Date,_Address)
ROOM(Room_Number, Phone, Daily_Rate)
PATIENT(Patient_Number, Treatment_Description, Address)
TREATMENT(Treatment_ID, Description, Cost)
PHYSICIAN(Physician_ID, Name, Department)
PHYSICIAN(Physician_ID, Name, Supervisor_ID)

a. Merge these relations into a consolidated set of 3NF relations. Make and state whatever

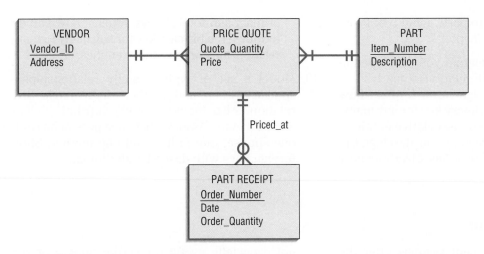

FIGURE 9-21
E-R diagram for Problem
and Exercise 3.

assumptions you consider necessary to resolve any potential problems you identify in
the merging process.
  b. Draw an E-R diagram for your answer to part a.

5. Consider the following 3NF relations about a
sorority or fraternity:

  MEMBER(<u>Member_ID</u>, Name, Address,
    Dues_Owed)
  OFFICE(<u>Office_Name</u>, Officer_ID,
    Term_Start_Date, Budget)
  EXPENSE(<u>Ledger_Number</u>,
    Office_Name, _Expense_Date, Amt_Owed)
  PAYMENT(<u>Check_Number</u>, Expense_Ledger_
    Number, Amt_Paid)
  RECEIPT(<u>Member_ID</u>, Receipt_Date,
    Dues_Received)
  COMMITTEE(<u>Committee_ID</u>, Officer_
    in_Charge)
  WORKERS(<u>Committee_ID</u>, <u>Member_ID</u>)

  a. Foreign keys are not indicated in these relations. Decide which attributes are foreign keys
  and justify your decisions.
  b. Draw an E-R diagram for these relations, using
  your answer to part a.
  c. Explain the assumptions you made about cardinalities in your answer to part b. Explain
  why it is said that the E-R data model is more
  expressive or more semantically rich than the
  relational data model.

6. Consider the following functional dependencies:

  Applicant_ID→Applicant_Name
  Applicant_ID→Applicant_Address
  Position_ID→Position_Title
  Position_ID→Date_Position_Opens
  Position_ID→Department
  Applicant_ID + Position_ID→Date_Applied
  Applicant_ID + Position_ID +
    Date_Interviewed?→

  a. Represent these attributes with 3NF relations.
  Provide meaningful relation names.
  b. Represent these attributes using an E-R diagram. Provide meaningful entity and relationship names.

7. Suppose you were designing a file of student
records for your university's placement office.
One of the fields that would likely be in this file is
the student's major. Develop a coding scheme for
this field that achieves the objectives outlined in
this chapter for field coding.

8. In Problem and Exercise 3, you developed integrated normalized relations. Choose primary
keys for the files that would hold the data for
these relations. Did you use attributes from the
relations for primary keys or did you design new
fields? Why or why not?

9. Suppose you created a file for each relation in your
answer to Problem and Exercise 3. If the following
queries represented the complete set of accesses
to this database, suggest and justify what primary
and secondary key indexes you would build.

  a. For each PART, list all vendors and their associated prices for that part.
  b. List all PART RECEIPTs, including related
  PART fields for all the parts received on a particular day.
  c. For a particular VENDOR, list all the PARTs and
  their associated prices that VENDOR can supply.

10. Suppose you were designing a default value for the
marriage status field in a student record at your
university. What possible values would you consider and why? How would the default value
change depending on other factors, such as type of
student (undergraduate, graduate, professional)?

11. Consider Figure 9-19B. Explain a query that
would likely be processed more quickly using the
denormalized relations rather than the normalized relations.

12. Consider your answers to parts a and b of Problem and Exercise 11 in Chapter 7.

   a. Transform the E-R diagram you developed in part a into a set of 3NF relations. Clearly identify primary and foreign keys. Explain how you determined the primary key for any many-to-many relationships or associative entities.
   b. Transform the E-R diagram you developed in part b into a set of 3NF relations. Clearly identify primary and foreign keys. Explain how you determined the primary key for any many-to-many relationships or associative entities.

13. Model a set of typical family relationships—spouse, father, and mother—in a single 3NF relation. Also include nonkey attributes name and birth date. Assume that each person has only one spouse, one father, and one mother. Show foreign keys with dashed underlining.

Discussion Questions

1. Many database management systems offer the ability to enforce referential integrity. Why would using such a feature be a good idea? Are there any situations in which referential integrity might not be important?

2. Assume you are part of the systems development team at a medium-sized organization. You have just completed the database design portion of the systems design phase, and the project sponsor would like a status update. Assuming the project sponsor is a VP in the marketing department, with only a high-level understanding of technical subjects, how would you go about presenting the database design you have just completed? How would your presentation approach change if the project sponsor were the manager of the database team?

3. Discuss what additional information should be collected during requirements analysis that is needed for file and database design and that is not especially useful for earlier phases of systems development.

4. Find out what database management systems are available at your university for student use. Investigate which data types these DBMSs support. Compare these DBMSs based upon data types supported and suggest which types of applications each DBMS is best suited for based on this comparison.

5. Find out what database management systems are available at your university for student use. Investigate what physical file and database design decisions need to be made. Compare this list of decisions to those discussed in this chapter. For physical database and design decisions (or options) not discussed in the chapter, investigate what choices you have and how you should choose among these choices. Submit a report to your instructor with your findings.

Case Problems

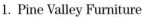

1. Pine Valley Furniture

   Development work on Pine Valley Furniture's new Customer Tracking System is proceeding according to plan and is on schedule. The project team has been busy designing the human interfaces, and you have just completed the new tracking system's Customer Profile Form, Products by Demographics Summary Report, and Customer Purchasing Frequency Report.

   Because you are now ready for a new task, Jim Woo asks you to prepare logical data models for the form and two reports that you have just designed and drop them by his office this afternoon. At that time, the two of you will prepare a consolidated database model, translate the Customer Tracking System's E-R data model into normalized relations, and then integrate the logical data models into a final logical data model for the Customer Tracking System.

   a. Develop logical data models for the form and two reports mentioned in the case scenario.
   b. Perform view integration on the logical models developed for part a.
   c. What view integration problems, if any, exist? How should you correct these problems?
   d. Have a fellow classmate critique your logical data model. Make any necessary corrections.

2. Hoosier Burger

   As the lead analyst on the Hoosier Burger project, you have had the opportunity to learn more about the systems development process, work with project team members, and interact with the system's end users, especially with Bob and

Thelma. You have just completed the design work for the various forms and reports that will be used by Bob, Thelma, and their employees. Now it is time to prepare logical and physical database designs for the new Hoosier Burger system.

During a meeting with Hoosier Burger project team members, you review the four steps in logical database modeling and design. It will be your task to prepare the logical models for the Customer Order Form, Customer Account Balance Form, Daily Delivery Sales Report, and Inventory Low-in-Stock Report. At the next meeting, the E-R model will be translated and a final logical model produced.

a. Develop logical models for each of the interfaces mentioned in the case scenario.
b. Integrate the logical models prepared for part a into a consolidated logical model.
c. What types of problems can arise from view integration? Did you encounter any of these problems when preparing the consolidated logical model?
d. Using your newly constructed logical model, determine which fields should be indexed. Which fields should be designated as calculated fields?

3. PlowMasters

PlowMasters is a locally owned and operated snow removal business. PlowMasters provides residential and commercial snow removal for clients throughout a large metropolitan area. Typical services include driveway and walkway snow removal, as well as parking lot snow maintenance for larger commercial clients.

PlowMasters' clientele has grown over the past several snow seasons. Recent heavy snowfall, coupled with a successful advertising campaign, has increased current demand even more, and this increase in demand is expected to continue. In order to provide faster, more efficient service, PlowMasters has hired your consulting company to design, develop, and implement a computer-based system. Your development team is currently preparing the logical and physical database designs for PlowMasters.

a. What are the four steps in logical database modeling and design?
b. Several relations have been identified for this project, including removal technician, customer, service provided, equipment inventory, and services offered. What relationships exist among these relations? How should these relationships be represented?
c. Think of the attributes that would most likely be associated with the relations identified in the part b. For each data integrity control method discussed in the chapter, provide a specific example.
d. What are the guidelines for choosing indexes? Identify several fields that should be indexed.

CASE: PETRIE'S ELECTRONICS

Designing Databases

Jim Watanabe, assistant director of IT for Petrie's Electronics and the manager of the "No Customer Escapes" customer loyalty system project, was walking down the hall from his office to the cafeteria. It was 4 P.M., but Jim was nowhere close to going home yet. The deadlines he had imposed for the project were fast approaching. His team was running behind, and he had a lot of work to do over the next week to try to get things back on track. He needed to get some coffee for the start of what was going to be a late night.

As Jim approached the cafeteria, he saw Sanjay Agarwal and Sam Waterston walking toward him. Sanjay was in charge of systems integration for Petrie's, and Sam was one of the company's top interface designers. They were both on the customer loyalty program team. They were having an intense conversation as Jim approached.

"Hi guys," Jim said.

"Oh, hi, Jim," Sanjay replied. "Glad I ran into you—we are moving ahead on the preliminary database designs. We're translating the earlier conceptual designs into physical designs."

"Who's working on that? Stephanie?" Jim asked. Stephanie Welch worked for Petrie's database administrator.

"Yes," Sanjay replied. "But she is supervising a couple of interns who have been assigned to her for this task."

"So how is that going? Has she approved their work?"

"Yeah, I guess so. It all seems to be under control."

"I don't want to second-guess Stephanie, but I'm curious about what they've done."

MEMO

To: Stephanie Welch

From: Xin Zhu & Anton Washington

Re: Preliminary physical database design for "No Customer Escapes"

Date: June 1, 2012

We were charged with converting the conceptual database designs for the customer loyalty system to physical database designs. We started with one of the initial ERDs (see Figure 7-1), designed at a very high level. The ERD identified six entities: Customer, Product, Service, Promotion, Transaction, and Coupon. We discovered that all of these entities are already defined in Petrie's existing systems. The only entity not already defined is Coupon. Product and Service are defined as part of the product database. Promotion is defined as part of the marketing database. Customer and Transaction are defined as part of the core database.

However, after considerable consideration, we are not sure if some of these already identified and defined entities are the same as those identified in the preliminary ERD we were given. Specifically, we have questions about Customer, Transaction and Promotion.

Customer: The Customer entity is more complex than it appears. There are several ways to think about the instances of this entity. For example, we can divide Customers into those who shop online and those who shop in the Brick-and-Mortar stores. And there is of course some overlap. The biggest distinction between these two groups is that we know the names of (and other information about) the Customers who shop online, but we may have very little identifying information about those who shop only in the stores. For example, if an individual shops only at a store and pays only with cash, that individual meets the definition of Customer (see Table 7-1), but we collect no data on that individual at all. We raise these issues to call attention to the relationship between Customers and members of the customer loyalty program: All members are Customers, but not all Customers are members. We suggest that the entity called Customer in the preliminary ERD be renamed 'Member,' as we think that is a better name for this entity. We are prepared to map out the table design when this change is approved.

Transaction: Petrie's already has a relational table called Transaction, but that applies to all transactions in all stores and online. The customer loyalty program focuses on the transactions of its Members, so the program involves only a subset of Transactions. We suggest that the ERD be redesigned to take this fact into account, and that what is now called Transaction be renamed 'Member Transaction.' The relational tables should then be designed accordingly.

Promotion: Petrie's already has a relational table called Promotion. Again, the customer loyalty program, while having some interest in general promotions, focuses primarily on promotions created specifically for Members of the program. What is called Promotion in the ERD is really a subset of all of Petrie's promotions. We recommend a name change to 'Member Promotion' with the associated relational table design.

Finally, for the Coupon entity, which is new, we note from the ERD that Coupon only has one relationship, and that is with the Customer. As it is a one-to-many relationship, the PK from Customer will be an FK in Coupon. We recommend the following table design:

COUPON (Coupon ID, Customer ID, Creation Date, Expiration Date, Value)

"Do you really have time to review interns' work?" Sanjay asked. "OK, let me send you the memo Stephanie sent me [PE Figure 9-1]."

"You're right, I don't have time," Jim said, "but I'm curious. It won't take long to read the memo, right?"

"OK, I'll send it as soon as I get back to my desk."

"OK, thanks." Jim walked on to the cafeteria, and he poured himself a big cup of coffee.

Case Questions

1. In the questions associated with the Petrie's Electronics case at the end of Chapter 7, you were asked to modify the E-R diagram given in PE Figure 7-1 to include any other entities and the attributes you identified from the Petrie's case. Review your answers to these questions, and add any additional needed relations to the document in PE Figure 9-1.

2. Study your answer to Question 1. Verify that the relations you say represent the Petrie's Electronics database are in third normal form. If they are, explain why. If they are not, change them so that they are.

3. The E-R diagram you developed in questions in the Petrie's Electronics case at the end of Chapter 7 should have shown minimum cardinalities on both ends of each relationship. Are minimum cardinalities represented in some way in the relations in your answer to Question 2? If not, how are minimum cardinalities enforced in the database?

4. Using your answer to Question 2, select data types, formats, and lengths for each attribute of each relation. Use the data types and formats supported by Microsoft Access. What data type should be used for nonintelligent primary keys?

5. Complete all table and field definitions for the Petrie's Electronics case database using Microsoft Access. Besides the decisions you have made in answers to the preceding questions, fill in all other field definition parameters for each field of each table.

6. The one decision for a relational database that usually influences efficiency the most is index definition. What indexes do you recommend for this database? Justify your selection of each index.

7. Using Microsoft Visio, develop an E-R diagram with all the supporting database properties for decisions you made in Questions 1–6. Can all the database design decisions you made be documented in Visio? Finally, use Visio to generate Microsoft Access table definitions. Did the table generation create the table definitions you would create manually?

ten

Systems Implementation and Operation

age fotostock/SuperStock

After studying this chapter, you should be able to:

- Describe the process of coding, testing, and installing an organizational information system and outline the deliverables and outcomes of the process.

- Apply four installation strategies: direct, parallel, single location, and phased installation.

- List the deliverables for documenting the system and for training and supporting users.

- Compare the many modes available for organizational information system training.

- Discuss the issues of providing support for end users.

- Explain why systems implementation sometimes fails.

- Explain and contrast four types of maintenance.

- Describe several factors that influence the cost of maintaining an information system.

318

Chapter Preview . . .

The implementation and operation phase of the systems development life cycle is the most expensive and time-consuming phase of the entire life cycle. This phase is expensive because so many people are involved in the process. It is time consuming because of all the work that has to be completed through the entire life of the system. During implementation and operation, physical design specifications must be turned into working computer code. Then the code is tested until most of the errors have been detected and corrected, the system is installed, user sites are prepared for the new system, and users must come to rely on the new system rather than the existing one to get their work done. Even once the system is installed, new features are added to the system, new business requirements and regulations demand system improvements, and corrections are made as flaws are identified from use of the system in new circumstances. These changes will have ripple effects, causing rework in many systems development phases. The seven major activities we are concerned with in this chapter are coding, testing, installation, documentation, training, support, and maintenance. These and other activities are highlighted in Figure 10-1. Our intent is not to explain how to program and test systems—most of you have already learned about writing and testing programs in other courses. Rather, this chapter shows you where coding and testing fit in the overall scheme of

FIGURE 10-1
The activities of the systems implementation and operation phase of the SDLC.

implementation and stresses the view of implementation as an organizational change process that is not always successful.

In addition, you will learn about providing documentation about the new system for the information systems personnel who will maintain the system; likewise, you will learn about providing documentation and conducting training for the system's users. Once training has ended and the system is accepted and used, you must provide a means for users to get answers to their additional questions and to identify needs for further training.

Your first job after graduation may well be as a maintenance programmer/analyst. Maintenance can begin soon after the system is installed.

A question many people have about maintenance relates to how long organizations should maintain a system. Five years? Ten years? Longer? This question has no simple answer, but it is most often an issue of economics. In other words, at what point does it make financial sense to discontinue updating an older system and build or purchase a new one? Upper IS management gives significant attention to assessing the trade-offs between maintenance and new development. In this chapter, we describe the maintenance process and the issues that must be considered when maintaining systems. At the end of the chapter, we describe the process of resolving a maintenance request at Pine Valley Furniture.

Systems Implementation and Operation

Systems implementation and operation is made up of seven major activities:

- Coding
- Testing
- Installation
- Documentation
- Training
- Support
- Maintenance

The purpose of these steps is to convert the final physical system specifications into working and reliable software and hardware, document the work that has been done, and provide help for current and future users and caretakers of the system. Usage of the system leads to changes, so during maintenance, users and others submit maintenance requests; requests are transformed into specific changes to the system; the system is redesigned to accept the changes; and the changes are implemented.

These steps are often done by other project team members besides analysts, although analysts may do some programming and other steps. Often a separate analyst and developer team from those who developed the original system is responsible for testing, documenting, training, and maintenance activities. In any case, analysts are responsible for ensuring that all of these various activities are properly planned and executed. We briefly discuss these activities in three groups:

1. Activities that lead to the system going into operation—coding, testing, and installation
2. Activities that are necessary for successful system operation—documenting the system and training and supporting users
3. Activities that are ongoing and needed to keep the system working and up to date—maintenance

The Processes of Coding, Testing, and Installation

Coding, as we mentioned before, is the process through which the physical design specifications created by the design team are turned into working computer code by the programming team. Depending on the size and complexity of the system, coding can be an involved, intensive activity. Once coding has begun, the testing process can begin and proceed in parallel. As each program module is produced, it can be tested individually, then as part of a larger program, and then as part of a larger system. You learn about the different strategies for testing later in the chapter. We should emphasize that although testing is done during implementation, you must begin planning for testing earlier in the project. Planning involves determining what needs to be tested and collecting test data. These activities are often done during the analysis phase, because testing requirements are related to system requirements.

Installation is the process during which the current system is replaced by the new system. It includes conversion of existing data, software, documentation, and work procedures to those consistent with the new system. Users must give up the old ways of doing their jobs, whether manual or automated, and adjust to accomplishing the same tasks with the new system. Users will sometimes resist these changes, and you must help them adjust. However, you cannot control all the dynamics of user-system interaction involved in the installation process.

Deliverables and Outcomes from Coding, Testing, and Installation

Table 10-1 shows the deliverables from the coding, testing, and installation processes. The most obvious outcome is the code itself, but just as important as the code is documentation of the code. Modern programming languages, such as Visual Basic, are said to be largely self-documenting. When standard naming and program design conventions are used, the code itself spells out much about the program's logic, the meaning of data and variables, and the locations where data are accessed and output. But even well-documented codes can be mysterious to maintenance programmers who must maintain the system for years after the original system was written and the original programmers have moved on to other jobs. Therefore, clear, complete documentation for all individual modules and programs is crucial to the system's continued smooth operation.

TABLE 10-1:   Deliverables from Coding, Testing, and Installation

Action	Deliverable
Coding	Code
	Program documentation
Testing	Test scenarios (test plan) and test data
	Results of program and system testing
Installation	User guides
	User training plan
	Installation and conversion plan
	Hardware and software installation schedule
	Data conversion plan
	Site and facility remodeling plan

Increasingly, automated tools are used to maintain the documentation needed by systems professionals.

The results of program and system testing are important deliverables from the testing process because they document the tests, as well as the test results. For example, what type of test was conducted? What test data were used? How did the system handle the test? The answers to these questions can provide important information for system maintenance as changes require retesting, and similar testing procedures will be used during the maintenance process.

The next two deliverables, user guides and the user training plan, result from the installation process. User guides provide information on how to use the new system, and the training plan is a strategy for training users so they can quickly learn the new system. The development of the training plan probably began earlier in the project, and some training on the concepts behind the new system may have already taken place. During the early stages of implementation, the training plans are finalized and training on the use of the system begins. Similarly, the installation plan lays out a strategy for moving from the old system to the new. Installation includes installing the system (hardware and software) at central and user sites. The installation plan answers such questions as when and where the new system will be installed, what people and resources are required, which data will be converted and cleansed, and how long the installation process will take. It is not enough that the system is installed; users must actually use it.

As an analyst, your job is to ensure that all of these deliverables are produced and done well, whether by you or by others. Coding, testing, and installation work may be done by IS professionals in your organization, by contractors, hardware designers, and, increasingly, by users. The extent of your responsibilities will vary according to the size and standards of the organization you work for, but your ultimate role includes ensuring that all the coding, testing, and installation work leads to a system that meets the specifications developed in earlier project phases.

The Processes of Documenting the System, Training Users, and Supporting Users

Although the process of documentation proceeds throughout the life cycle, it receives formal attention now, because once the system is installed, the analysis team's involvement in system development usually ceases. As the team is getting ready to move on to new projects, you and the other analysts need to prepare documents that reveal all of the important information you have learned about this system during its development and implementation. The two audiences for this final documentation are (1) the information systems personnel who will maintain the system throughout its productive life, and (2) the people who will use the system as part of their daily lives.

Larger organizations also tend to provide training and support to computer users throughout the organization, sometimes as part of a corporate university. Some of the training and support is directed to off-the-shelf software packages. For example, it is common to find courses on Microsoft Windows and Office in organization-wide training facilities. Analysts typically work with corporate trainers to provide training and support tailored to particular computer applications they have helped develop. Centralized information system training facilities tend to have specialized staff who can help with training and support issues. In smaller organizations that cannot afford to have well-staffed centralized training and support facilities, fellow users are the best source of training and support that users have, whether the software is customized or off the shelf.

TABLE 10-2: Deliverables from Documenting the System, Training Users, and Supporting Users

Documentation	User Training Modules
System documentation	Training materials
User documentation	Computer-based training aids
User Training Plan	**User Support Plan**
Classes	Help desk
Tutorials	Online help
	Bulletin boards and other support mechanisms

Deliverables and Outcomes from Documenting the System, Training Users, and Supporting Users

Table 10-2 shows the deliverables from documenting the system, training users, and supporting users. User documentation can be paper based, but it should also include computer-based modules. For modern information systems, this documentation includes any online help designed as part of the system interface. The development team should think through the user training process: Who should be trained? How much training is adequate for each training audience? What do different types of users need to learn during training? The training plan should be supplemented by actual training modules, or at least outlines of such modules, that at a minimum address the three questions stated previously. Finally, the development team should also deliver a user support plan that addresses such issues as how users will be able to find help once the information system has become integrated into the organization. The development team should consider a multitude of support mechanisms and modes of delivery. Each deliverable is addressed in more detail later in the chapter.

The Process of Maintaining Information Systems

Throughout this book, we have drawn the systems development life cycle as a circle where one phase leads to the next, with overlap and feedback loops. This means that the process of maintaining an information system is the process of returning to the beginning of the SDLC and repeating development steps, focusing on the needs for system change, until the change is implemented.

Four major activities occur within maintenance:

1. Obtaining maintenance requests
2. Transforming requests into changes
3. Designing changes
4. Implementing changes

Obtaining maintenance requests requires that a formal process be established whereby users can submit system change requests. Earlier in the book, we presented a user request document called a system service request (SSR). Most companies have some sort of document like an SSR to request new development, to report problems, or to request new system features for an existing system. When developing the procedures for obtaining maintenance requests, organizations must also specify an individual within the organization to collect these requests and manage their dispersal to maintenance personnel. The process of collecting and dispersing maintenance requests is described in much greater detail later in the chapter.

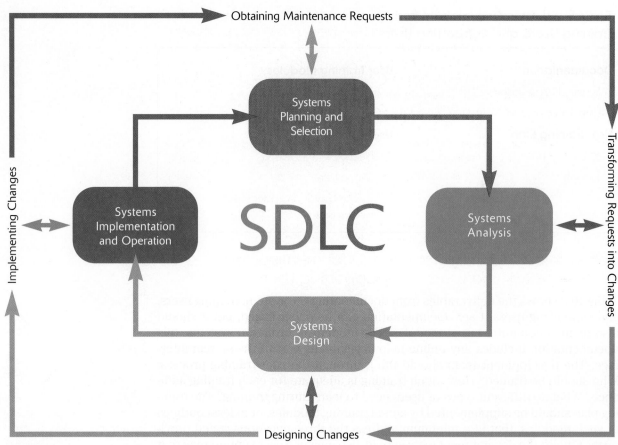

FIGURE 10-2
Maintenance activities in relation to the SDLC.

Once a request is received, analysis must be conducted to gain an understanding of the scope of the request. It must be determined how the request will affect the current system and the duration of such a project. As with the initial development of a system, the size of a maintenance request can be analyzed for risk and feasibility (see Chapter 4). Next, a change request can be transformed into a formal design change, which can then be fed into the maintenance implementation phase. Thus, many similarities exist between the SDLC and the activities within the maintenance process. Figure 10-2 equates SDLC phases to the maintenance activities described previously. The figure shows that the first phase of the SDLC—systems planning and selection—is analogous to the maintenance process of obtaining a maintenance request (step 1). The SDLC phase systems analysis is analogous to the maintenance process of transforming requests into a specific system change (step 2). The systems design phase of the SDLC, of course, equates to the designing changes process (step 3). Finally, the SDLC phase implementation and operation equates to implementing changes (step 4). This similarity between the maintenance process and the SDLC is no accident. The concepts and techniques used to develop a system initially are also used to maintain it.

Deliverables and Outcomes from Maintaining Information Systems

Because maintenance is basically a subset of the activities of the entire development process, the deliverables and outcomes from the process are the development of a new version of the software and new versions of all design documents and training materials developed or modified during the maintenance process.

All documents created or modified during the maintenance effort, including the system itself, represent the deliverables and outcomes of the process. Those programs and documents that did not change may also be part of the new system. Because most organizations archive prior versions of systems, all prior programs and documents must be kept to ensure the proper versioning of the system. This enables prior versions of the system to be recreated if needed. A more detailed discussion of configuration management and change control is presented later in the chapter.

Because of the similarities between the steps, deliverables, and outcomes of new development and maintenance, you may be wondering how to distinguish between these two processes. One difference is that maintenance reuses most existing system modules in producing the new system version. Other distinctions are that we develop a new system when there is a change in the hardware or software platform or when fundamental assumptions and properties of the data, logic, or process models change.

Software Application Testing

As we mentioned previously, analysts prepare system specifications that are passed on to programmers for coding. Testing software begins earlier in the systems development life cycle, even though many of the actual testing activities are carried out during implementation. During analysis, you develop an overall test plan. During design, you develop a unit test plan, an integration test plan, and a system test plan. During implementation, these various plans are put into effect, and the actual testing is performed.

The purpose of these written test plans is to improve communication among all the people involved in testing the application software. The plan specifies what each person's role will be during testing. The test plans also serve as checklists you can use to determine whether all testing steps have been completed. The overall test plan is not just a single document but is a collection of documents. Each of the component documents represents a complete test plan for one part of the system or for a particular type of test.

Some organizations have specially trained personnel who supervise and support testing. Testing managers are responsible for developing test plans, establishing testing standards, integrating testing and development activities in the life cycle, and ensuring that test plans are completed. Testing specialists help develop test plans, create test cases and scenarios, execute the actual tests, and analyze and report test results.

Seven Different Types of Tests

Software application testing is an umbrella term that covers several types of tests. Tests can be done with or without executing the code, and they may be manual or automated. Using this framework, we can categorize types of tests as shown in Table 10-3.

TABLE 10-3:   A Categorization of Test Types

	Manual	**Automated**
Without code execution	Inspections	Syntax checking
With code execution	Walkthroughs	Unit testing
	Desk checking	Integration testing
		System testing
		Stub testing

Inspection
A testing technique in which participants examine program code for predictable language-specific errors.

Let's examine each type of test in turn. **Inspections** are formal group activities in which participants manually examine code for occurrences of well-known errors. Syntax, grammar, and some other routine errors can be checked in early stages of coding by automated inspection software, so manual inspection checks are used for more subtle errors. Code inspection participants compare the code they are examining to a checklist of well-known errors for that particular language. Exactly what the code does is not investigated in an inspection. Code inspections have been used by organizations to detect from 60 to 90 percent of all software defects, as well as to provide programmers with feedback that enables them to avoid making the same types of errors in future work. The inspection process can also be used to ensure that design specifications are accomplished.

Unlike inspections, what the code does is an important question in a *walkthrough*. Using structured walkthroughs is an effective method of detecting errors in code. As you saw in Chapter 4, structured walkthroughs can be used to review many systems development deliverables, including design specifications and code. Whereas specification walkthroughs tend to be formal reviews, code walkthroughs tend to be informal. Informality makes programmers less apprehensive of criticism and, thus, helps increase the frequency of walkthroughs. Code walkthroughs should be done frequently when the pieces of work reviewed are relatively small and before the work is formally tested. If walkthroughs are not held until the entire program is tested, the programmer will have already spent too much time looking for errors that the programming team could have found much more quickly. Further, the longer a program goes without being subjected to a walkthrough, the more defensive the programmer becomes when the code is reviewed. Although each organization that uses walkthroughs conducts them differently, you can follow a basic structure that works well (see Figure 10-3).

It should be stressed that the purpose of a walkthrough is to detect errors, not to correct them. It is the programmer's job to correct the errors uncovered in a walkthrough. Sometimes it can be difficult for the reviewers to refrain from suggesting ways to fix the problems they find in the code, but increased experience with the process can help change reviewers' behavior.

Desk checking
A testing technique in which the program code is sequentially executed manually by the reviewer.

What the code does is also important in **desk checking,** an informal process where the programmer or someone else who understands the logic of the program works through the code with a paper and pencil. The programmer executes each instruction, using test cases that may or may not be written down. In one sense, the reviewer acts as the computer, mentally checking each step and its results for the entire set of computer instructions.

Syntax checking is typically done by a compiler. Errors in syntax are uncovered, but the code is not executed. For the other three automated techniques, the code is executed.

FIGURE 10-3
Guidelines for conducting a code walkthrough.

Source: Walkthrough based on Yourdon, 1989.

GUIDELINES FOR CONDUCTING A CODE WALKTHROUGH

1. Have the review meeting chaired by the project manager or chief programmer, who is also responsible for scheduling the meeting, reserving a room, setting the agenda, inviting participants, and so on.
2. The programmer presents his or her work to the reviewers. Discussion should be general during the presentation.
3. Following the general discussion, the programmer walks through the code in detail, focusing on the logic of the code rather than on specific test cases.
4. Reviewers ask to walk through specific test cases.
5. The chair resolves disagreements if the review team cannot reach agreement among themselves and assigns duties, usually to the programmer, for making specific changes.
6. A second walkthrough is then scheduled if needed.

The first such technique is **unit testing,** sometimes called *module* or *functional testing.* In unit testing, each module (roughly a section of code that performs a single function) is tested alone in an attempt to discover any errors that may exist in the module's code. Yet, because modules coexist and work with other modules in programs and systems, they must be tested together in larger groups. Combining modules and testing them is called **integration testing.** Integration testing is gradual. First you test the highest level, or coordinating module, and only one of its subordinate modules. The process assumes a typical structure for a program, with one highest-level, or main, module and various subordinate modules referenced from the main module. Each subordinate module may have a set of modules subordinate to it, and so on, similar to an organization chart. Next, you continue testing subsequent modules at the same level until all subordinate to the highest-level module have been successfully tested together. Once the program has been tested successfully with the high-level module and all of its immediate subordinate modules, you add modules from the next level one at a time. Again, you move forward only when tests are successfully completed. If an error occurs, the process stops, the error is identified and corrected, and the test is redone. The process repeats until the entire program—all modules at all levels—is successfully integrated and tested with no errors.

System testing is a similar process, but instead of integrating modules into programs for testing, you integrate programs into systems. System testing follows the same incremental logic that integration testing does. Under both integration and system testing, not only do individual modules and programs get tested many times, so do the interfaces between modules and programs.

Current practice (as previously outlined) calls for a top-down approach to writing and testing modules. Under a top-down approach, the coordinating module is written first. Then the modules at the next level are written, followed by the modules at the next level, and so on, until all of the modules in the system are done. Each module is tested as it is written. Because top-level modules contain many calls to subordinate modules, you may wonder how they can be tested if the lower-level modules haven't been written yet. The answer is **stub testing.** Stubs are two or three lines of code written by a programmer to stand in for the missing modules. During testing, the coordinating module calls the stub instead of the subordinate module. The stub accepts control and then returns it to the coordinating module.

System testing is more than simply expanded integration testing, where you are testing the interfaces between programs in a system rather than testing the interfaces between modules in a program. System testing is also intended to demonstrate whether a system meets its objectives. The system test is typically conducted by information systems personnel led by the project team leader, although it can also be conducted by users under the guidance of information systems personnel.

The Testing Process

Up to this point, we have talked about an overall test plan and seven different types of tests for software applications. We haven't said much about the process of testing itself. Two important things to remember about testing information systems are:

1. The purpose of testing is confirming that the system satisfies requirements.
2. Testing must be planned.

Testing is not haphazard. You must pay attention to many different aspects of a system, such as response time, response to extreme data values, response to no input, response to heavy volumes of input, and so on. You must test anything (within resource constraints) that could go wrong or be wrong with a system.

Unit testing
Each module is tested alone in an attempt to discover any errors in its code.

Integration testing
The process of bringing together for testing purposes all of the modules that a program comprises. Modules are typically integrated in a top-down, incremental fashion.

System testing
The bringing together for testing purposes of all the programs that a system comprises. Programs are typically integrated in a top-down, incremental fashion.

Stub testing
A technique used in testing modules, especially where modules are written and tested in a top-down fashion, where a few lines of code are used to substitute for subordinate modules.

FIGURE 10-4
Test case description
and summary form.

Pine Valley Furniture Company
Test Case Description and Summary

Test Case Number: Date:
Test Case Description:

Program/Module Name:
Testing State:
Test Case Prepared By:
Test Administrator:
Description of Test Data:

Expected Results:

Actual Results:

Explanation of Differences between Actual and Expected Results:

Suggestions for Next Steps:

At a minimum, you should test the most frequently used parts of the system and as many other paths through the system as time permits. Planning gives analysts and programmers an opportunity to think through all the potential problem areas, list these areas, and develop ways to test for problems. As indicated previously, one part of a test plan is creating a set of test cases, each of which must be carefully documented. See Figure 10-4 for an outline of a test case description and summary.

A test case is a specific scenario of transactions, queries, or navigation paths that represent a typical, critical, or abnormal use of the system. A test case should be repeatable so that it can be rerun as new versions of the software are tested. This is important for all codes, whether written in-house, developed by a contractor, or purchased. Test cases need to determine that new software works with other existing software with which it must share data. Even though analysts often do not do the testing, systems analysts, because of their intimate knowledge of applications, often make up or find test data. The people who create the test cases should not be the same people who coded and tested the system. In addition to a description of each test case, there must also be a summary of the test results, with an emphasis on how the actual results differed from the expected results. The testing summary will indicate why the results were different and what, if anything, should be done to change the software. Further, this summary will then suggest the need for retesting, possibly introducing new tests necessary to discover the source of the differences.

One important reason to keep such a thorough description of test cases and results is so that testing can be repeated for each revision of an application. Although new versions of a system may necessitate new test data to validate new features of the application, previous test data usually can and should be

FIGURE 10-5
NUnit, a unit testing framework for .NET.

reused. Results from use of the test data with prior versions are compared to new versions to show that changes have not introduced new errors and that the behavior of the system, including response time, is no worse.

Testing often requires a great deal of labor. Manual code reviews can be time-consuming and tedious work; and, most importantly, are not always the best solution. As such, special-purpose testing software, called a **testing harness,** has been developed for a variety of environments to help designers automatically review the quality of their code. In many situations, a testing harness greatly enhances, the testing process because they can automatically expand the scope of the tests beyond the current development platform, as well as be run every time with each new version of the software. For instance, with the testing harness called NUnit (see Figure 10-5), an open-source unit testing framework for .NET, a developer can answer questions such as: How stable is the code? Does the code follow standard rules? Will the code work across multiple platforms? When deploying large scale, multiplatform projects, automatic code review systems have become a necessity.

Testing harness
An automated testing environment used to review code for errors, standards violations, and other design flaws.

Acceptance Testing by Users

Once the system tests have been satisfactorily completed, the system is ready for **acceptance testing,** which is testing the system in the environment where it will eventually be used. Acceptance refers to the fact that users typically sign off on the system and "accept" it once they are satisfied with it. The purpose of acceptance testing is for users to determine whether the system meets their requirements. The extent of acceptance testing will vary with the organization and with the system in question. The most complete acceptance testing will include **alpha testing,** (also called *mock client testing*), where simulated but typical data are used for system testing; **beta testing,** in which live data are used in the users' real working environment; and a system audit conducted by the organization's internal auditors or by members of the quality assurance group.

Acceptance testing
The process whereby actual users test a completed information system, the end result of which is the users' acceptance of it once they are satisfied with it.

Alpha testing
User testing of a completed information system using simulated data.

Beta testing
User testing of a completed information system using real data in the real user environment.

During alpha testing, the entire system is implemented in a test environment to discover whether the system is overtly destructive to itself or to the rest of the environment. The types of tests performed during alpha testing include the following:

- *Recovery testing.* Forces the software (or environment) to fail in order to verify that recovery is properly performed.
- *Security testing.* Verifies that protection mechanisms built into the system will protect it from improper penetration.
- *Stress testing.* Tries to break the system (e.g., what happens when a record is written to the database with incomplete information or what happens under extreme online transaction loads or with a large number of concurrent users).
- *Performance testing.* Determines how the system performs on the range of possible environments in which it may be used (e.g., different hardware configurations, networks, operating systems); often the goal is to have the system perform with similar response time and other performance measures in each environment.

In beta testing, a subset of the intended users run the system in their own environments using their own data. The intent of the beta test is to determine whether the software, documentation, technical support, and training activities work as intended. In essence, beta testing can be viewed as a rehearsal of the installation phase. Problems uncovered in alpha and beta testing in any of these areas must be corrected before users can accept the system.

Installation

Installation
The organizational process of changing over from the current information system to a new one.

Direct installation
Changing over from the old information system to a new one by turning off the old system when the new one is turned on.

Parallel installation
Running the old information system and the new one at the same time until management decides the old system can be turned off.

Single location installation
Trying out a new information system at one site and using the experience to decide if and how the new system should be deployed throughout the organization.

Phased installation
Changing from the old information system to the new one incrementally, starting with one or a few functional components and then gradually extending the installation to cover the whole new system.

The process of moving from the current information system to the new one is called **installation**. All employees who use a system, regardless of whether they were consulted during the development process or not, must give up their reliance on the current system and begin to rely on the new system. Four different approaches to installation have emerged over the years:

- **Direct**
- **Parallel**
- **Single location**
- **Phased**

These four approaches are highlighted in Figure 10-6 and Table 10-4. The approach (or combination) an organization decides to use will depend on the scope and complexity of the change associated with the new system and the organization's risk aversion. In practice, you will rarely choose a single strategy to the exclusion of all others; most installations will rely on a combination of two or more approaches. For example, if you choose a single location strategy, you have to decide how installation will proceed there and at subsequent sites. Will it be direct, parallel, or phased?

Planning Installation

Each installation strategy involves converting not only software but also data and (potentially) hardware, documentation, work methods, job descriptions, offices and other facilities, training materials, business forms, and other aspects of the system. For example, it is necessary to recall or replace all the current system documentation and business forms, which suggests that the IS

FIGURE 10-6
Comparison of installation strategies: (A) Direct installation, (B) Parallel installation, (C) Single location installation (with direct installation at each location), (D) Phased installation.

department must keep track of who has these items so that they can be notified and receive replacement items.

Of special interest in the installation process is the conversion of data. Because existing systems usually contain data required by the new system, current data must be made error-free, unloaded from current files, combined with new data, and loaded into new files. Data may need to be reformatted to be consistent with more advanced data types supported by newer technology used to build the new system. New data fields may have to be entered in large quantities so that every record copied from the current system has all the new fields populated. Manual tasks, such as taking a physical inventory, may need to be done in order to validate data before they are transferred to the new files. The total data conversion

TABLE 10-4: Approaches to Information Systems Installation

Characteristics	Positive Aspects	Hazards/Risks
Direct Installation		
• Abrupt • "Cold turkey"	• Low cost • High interest in making installation a success • May be the only possible approach if new and existing systems cannot coexist in some form	• Operational errors have direct impact on users and organization • It may take too long to restore old system, if necessary • Time-consuming, and benefits may be delayed until whole system is installed
Parallel Installation		
• Old and new systems coexist • Safe	• New systems can be checked against old systems • Impact of operational errors are minimized because old system is also processing all data	• Not all aspects of new systems can be compared to old system • Very expensive because of duplication of effort to run and maintain two systems • Can be confusing to users • May be a delay until benefits result • May not be feasible because of costs or system size
Single Location Installation		
• Pilot approach • Middle-of-the-road approach • May involve a series of single location installations • Each location may be branch office, factory, or department	• Learning can occur and problems fixed by concentrating on one site • Limits potential harm and costs from system errors or failure to selected pilot sites • Can use early success to convince others to convert to new system	• Burden on IS staff to maintain old and new systems • If different sites require data sharing, extra programs need to be written to "bridge" the two systems • Some parts of organization get benefits earlier than other parts
Phased Installation		
• Staged, incremental, gradual, based on system functional components • Similar to bringing system out via multiple releases	• Allows for system development also to be phased • Limits potential harm and costs from system error or failure to certain business activities/functions • Risk spread over time • Some benefits can be achieved early • Each phase is small and more manageable	• Old and new systems must be able to work together and share data, which likely will require extra programming to "bridge" the two systems • Conversion is constant and may extend over a long period, causing frustration and confusion for users

process can be tedious. Furthermore, this process may require that current systems be shut off while the data are extracted so that updates to old data, which would contaminate the extract process, cannot occur.

Any decision that requires the current system to be shut down, in whole or in part, before the replacement system is in place must be done with care. Typically, off-hours are used for installations that require a lapse in system support. Whether a lapse in service is required or not, the installation schedule should be announced to users well in advance to let them plan their work schedules around outages in service and periods when their system support might be erratic. Successful installation steps should also be announced, and special procedures put in place so that users can easily inform you of problems they encounter during installation periods. You should also plan for emergency staff to be available in case of system failure so that business operations can be recovered and made operational as quickly as possible. Another consideration is the business cycle of the organization. Most organizations face heavy workloads at particular times of the year and relatively light loads at other times. A well-known example is the retail industry, where the busiest time of the year is the fall, right before the year's major gift-giving holidays. You wouldn't want to schedule installation of a new point-of-sale system to begin December 1, for a department store.

Planning for installation may begin as early as the analysis of the organization supported by the system. Some installation activities, such as buying new hardware, remodeling facilities, validating data to be transferred to the new system, and collecting new data to be loaded into the new system, must be done before the software installation can occur. Often the project team leader is responsible for anticipating all installation tasks and assigns responsibility for each to different analysts.

Each installation process involves getting workers to change the way they work. As such, installation should be looked at not as simply installing a new computer system, but as an organizational change process. More than just a computer system is involved—you are also changing how people do their jobs and how the organization operates.

Documenting the System

In one sense, every information systems development project is unique and will generate its own unique documentation. In another sense, though, system development projects are probably more alike than they are different. Each project shares a similar systems development life cycle, which dictates that certain activities be undertaken and that each of those activities be documented. Specific documentation will vary depending on the life cycle you are following, and the format and content of the documentation may be mandated by the organization you work for. Start developing documentation elements early, as the information needed is captured.

We can simplify the situation by dividing documentation into two basic types, system documentation and user documentation. **System documentation** records detailed information about a system's design specifications, its internal workings, and its functionality. System documentation can be further divided into internal and external documentation. **Internal documentation** is part of the program source code or is generated at compile time. **External documentation** includes the outcome of all of the structured diagramming techniques you have studied in this book, such as data-flow and entity-relationship diagrams. **User documentation** is written or other visual information about how an application system works and how to use it. Although not part of the code itself, external documentation can provide useful information to the primary users of system documentation—maintenance programmers. For example, data-flow diagrams provide a good overview of a system's structure. In the past, external documentation was typically discarded after implementation, primarily because it was considered too costly to keep up to date but today's integrated development environment makes it possible to maintain and update external documentation as long as desired.

System documentation
Detailed information about a system's design specifications, its internal workings, and its functionality.

Internal documentation
System documentation that is part of the program source code or is generated at compile time.

External documentation
System documentation that includes the outcome of structured diagramming techniques such as data-flow and entity-relationship diagrams.

User documentation
Written or other visual information about how an application system works, and how to use it.

Whereas system documentation is intended primarily for maintenance programmers, user documentation is intended mainly for users. An organization should have definitive standards on system documentation. These standards may include the outline for the project dictionary and specific pieces of documentation within it. Standards for user documentation are not as explicit.

User Documentation

User documentation consists of written or other visual information about an application system, how it works, and how to use it. An excerpt of online user documentation for Microsoft Visio appears in Figure 10-7. The documentation lists the item necessary to perform the task the user inquired about. The user controls how much of the help is shown.

Figure 10-7 represents the content of a reference guide, just one type of user documentation. Other types of user documentation include a quick reference guide, user's guide, release description, system administrator's guide, and acceptance sign-off. Most online reference guides allow you to search by topic area or by typing in the first few letters of your keyword. Reference guides are great for specific information (as in Figure 10-7) but are not as good for the broader picture of how to perform all the steps required for a given task. The quick reference guide provides essential information about operating a system in a short, concise format. Where computer resources are shared and many users perform similar tasks on the same machines (as with airline reservation or mail-order-catalog clerks), quick reference guides are often printed on index cards or as small books and mounted on or near the computer terminal. The purpose of a reference guide is to provide information on how users can use computer systems to perform specific tasks. The information in a user's guide is typically ordered by how often tasks are performed and how complex they are. Increasingly, software vendors are using Web sites to provide additional user-guide content. Figure 10-8 shows the Microsoft Visio help page. Web-based documentation allows the vendor to provide more up-to-date reference material without issuing new software CDs.

Because most software is reissued as new features are added, a release description contains information about a new system release, including a list of

FIGURE 10-7

Online user documentation for Microsoft Visio.

Source: Microsoft product screen shot(s). Reprinted with permission from Microsoft Corporation.

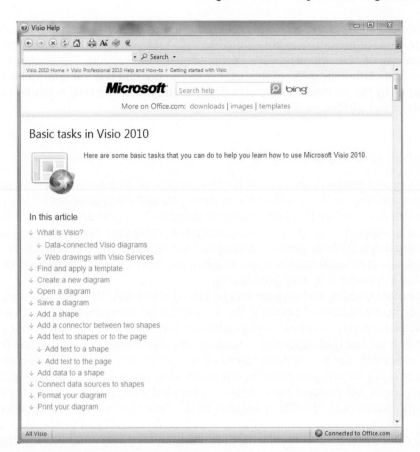

FIGURE 10-8
Structure of an online reference user's guide.

Source: Microsoft product screen shot(s). Reprinted with permission from Microsoft Corporation.

complete documentation for the new release, features and enhancements, known problems and how they have been dealt with in the new release, and information about installation. A system administrator's guide is intended primarily for a particular type of user—those who will install and administer a new system—and contains information about the network on which the system will run, software interfaces for peripherals such as printers, troubleshooting, and setting up user accounts. Finally, the acceptance sign-off allows users to test for proper system installation and then signify their acceptance of the new system and its documentation with their signatures.

Preparing User Documentation

User documentation, regardless of its content or intended audience, is now most often delivered online in hypertext format. In all its forms, user documentation is an investment that reduces training and consultation costs. As a future analyst, you need to consider the source of documentation, its quality, and whether its focus is on the information system's functionality or on the tasks the system can be used to perform.

The traditional source of user and system documentation has been the organization's information systems department. Until recently, the bulk of this documentation was system documentation, intended for analysts, programmers, and those who must maintain the system.

In today's end-user information systems environment, users interact directly with many computing resources; users have many options or querying capabilities from which to choose when using a system; and users are able to develop many local applications themselves. Analysts often serve as consultants for these local end-user applications. For end-user applications, the nature and purpose of documentation has changed from documentation intended for the maintenance programmer to documentation for the end user. Application-oriented documentation, whose purpose is to increase user understanding and utilization of the organization's computing resources, has also come to be important. Although some of this user-oriented documentation continues to be supplied by the information systems department, much of it now originates with vendors and with users themselves.

Training and Supporting Users

Support

Providing ongoing educational and problem-solving assistance to information system users. Support material and jobs must be designed along with the associated information system.

Training and **support** are critical for the success of an information system. As the person responsible for the new system, you and other analysts on the project team must ensure that high-quality training and support are available. Training and support help people adequately use computer systems to do their primary work. Without proper training and the opportunity to ask questions and gain assistance/consultation when needed, users will misuse, underuse, or not use the information system you develop.

Although training and support can be talked about as if they are two separate things, in organizational practice, the distinction between the two is not all that clear, as the two sometimes overlap. After all, both deal with learning about computing. It is clear that support mechanisms are also a good way to provide training, especially for intermittent users of a system. Intermittent or occasional system users are not interested in, nor would they profit from, typical user training methods. Intermittent users must be provided with "point-of-need support," specific answers to specific questions at the time the answers are needed. A variety of mechanisms, such as the system interface itself and online help facilities, can be designed to provide both training and support at the same time.

Training Information System Users

Many organizations tend to underinvest in computer skills training. It is true that some organizations institutionalize high levels of information system training, but many others offer no systematic training at all. Many studies show that training users to be effective with the systems they have now can be a cost-effective way to increase productivity, even more so than installing hardware and software upgrades.

The type of necessary training will vary by type of system and expertise of users. The list of potential topics from which you must determine whether training will be useful include the following:

- Use of the system (e.g., how to enter a class registration request)
- General computer concepts (e.g., computer files and how to copy them)
- Information system concepts (e.g., batch processing)
- Organizational concepts (e.g., FIFO inventory accounting)
- System management (e.g., how to request changes to a system)
- System installation (e.g., how to reconcile current and new systems during phased installation)

As you can see from this partial list, many topics go beyond simply how to use the new system. It may be necessary for you to develop training for users in other areas so that they will be ready, conceptually and psychologically, to use the new system. Some training, such as concept training, should begin early in the project because this training can assist in convincing users of the need for system and organizational change.

Each element of training can be delivered in a variety of ways. Table 10-5 lists the most common training methods used by information system departments.

TABLE 10-5:   Types of Training Methods

Method of Training

Formal courses—several people taught at the same time

Resident expert

E-learning/distance learning

Blended learning (combination of instructor-led training and e-learning)

Software help components

External sources, such as vendors

The most common delivery method for corporate training remains traditional instructor-led classroom training. Many times users turn to the resident expert and to fellow users for training. Users are more likely to turn to local experts for help than to the organization's technical support staff, because the local expert understands both the users' primary work and the computer systems they use. Given their dependence on fellow users for training, it should not be surprising that end users describe their most common mode of computer training as "self-training."

One conclusion from the experience with user training methods is that an effective strategy for training on a new system is first to train a few key users and then to organize training programs and support mechanisms that involve these users to provide further training, both formal and on-demand. Often, training is most effective if you customize it to particular user groups, and the lead trainers from these groups are in the best position for this task.

Increasingly, corporations are turning to e-learning as a key delivery mode for training. Although the term *e-learning* is not precisely defined, it generally means the same thing as distance learning, i.e., a formalized learning system designed to be carried out remotely, using computer-based electronic communication. You may have taken a distance learning course at your school, or you may have experience in on-campus classes with some of the dominant software packages used in e-learning, such as WebCT, Blackboard, or Desire2Learn. E-learning courses can be delivered over the Internet or over company intranets. Such courses can be purchased from vendors or prepared by the corporation's in-house training staff. E-learning is relatively inexpensive, compared to traditional classroom training, and it has the additional advantage of being available anytime from just about anywhere. Students can also learn at their own pace. E-learning systems can make available several different elements that enhance the learning experience, including simulations, online access to mentors and experts, e-books, net meetings, and video on-demand. Another trend in corporate training is blended learning, the combining of e-learning with instructor-led classroom training. A recent survey reported that over 80 percent of respondents were using e-learning or blended learning to train their employees. Half of the respondents in the study believed that e-learning would become the dominant training delivery method in their organizations by 2010.

Another training method listed in Table 10-5 is software help components. One common type is called an **electronic performance support system (EPSS).** Electronic performance support systems are online help systems that go beyond simply providing help—they embed training directly into a software package. An EPSS may take on one or more forms: It can be an online tutorial, provide hypertext-based access to context-sensitive reference material, or consist of an expert system shell that acts as a coach. The main idea behind the development of an EPSS is that the user never has to leave the application to get the benefits of training. Users learn a new system or unfamiliar features at their

Electronic performance support system (EPSS)
Component of a software package or application in which training and educational information is embedded. An EPSS may include a tutorial, expert system, and hypertext jumps to reference material.

own pace and on their own machines, without having to lose work time to attend remote group-training sessions. Furthermore, this learning is on-demand when the user is most motivated to learn, because the user has a task to do. EPSS is sometimes referred to as "just-in-time knowledge."

Supporting Information System Users

Historically, computing support for users has been provided in one of a few forms: paper, online versions of paper-based support, as well as help desks provided by vendors or resident experts within the same organization. As we stated earlier, support, whatever its form, has often been inadequate for users' needs. Yet users consider support to be extremely important.

As computing spreads throughout organizations, especially with the advent of personal computers, the need for support increased as more and more employees came to rely on computing to do their jobs. As organizations moved to client/server architectures, their need for support increased even more, and organizations relied more and more on vendor support. This increased need for support comes in part from the lack of standards governing client/server products and the resulting need to make equipment and software from different vendors compatible.

Issue tracking system
Typically a Web-based tool for logging, tracking, and assigning system bugs and change requests to developers.

Automated Issue Tracking   Bugs and change requests in any software release are inevitable. Previously, we talked about using a system service request (see also Chapter 3), a standard form for requesting systems development work. To automate this process, many organizations are deploying a Web-based **issue tracking system** to provide a systematic way to log, track, and assign system bugs and change requests to developers (see Figure 10-9); the types of information typically captured within an issue tracking system are summarized in Table 10-6.

Automating Support   As vendors have primarily shifted their offerings from expensive mainframe packages to inexpensive off-the-shelf software, they have found that they can no longer bear the cost of providing support for free. Most vendors now charge for support, and many have instituted toll-free numbers and other automated support mechanisms or sell customers unlimited support for a given monthly or annual charge. Common methods for automating support include online support forums (on private Web sites) and voice-response systems. Online support forums provide users access to information on new releases, bugs, and tips for more effective usage. Voice-response systems allow users to navigate option menus that lead to prerecorded messages about usage, problems, and workarounds. Organizations have established similar support mechanisms for systems developed or purchased by the organization. Internal e-mail and instant messaging can be used to support such capabilities within an organization.

Help desk
A single point of contact for all user inquiries and problems about a particular information system or for all users in a particular department.

Providing Support through a Help Desk   Whether assisted by vendors or going it alone, the center of support activities for a specific information system in many organizations is the help desk. A **help desk** is an information systems department function, staffed by IS personnel. The help desk is the first place users should call when they need assistance with an information system. The help desk staff either deals with the users' questions or refers the users to the most appropriate person.

Today, help desks are increasingly common as management comes to appreciate the special combination of technical skills and people skills needed to make good help desk staffers. Many software packages exist to automate the record keeping for a help desk. Records must be kept on each user contact, the content of the question or problem, and the status and resolution of the problem. Help desk managers use the software to track problems with different

FIGURE 10-9
Bugzilla is a popular Web-
based issue tracking system.

Bugzilla@Mozilla – Bug 65845 | incorporate code coverage info into link process | Last modified: 2010-04-10 13:21:31 PDT

Home | New | Browse | Search | [ ]   Search [?] | Reports | Requests | Help | New Account | Log In | Forgot Password

First Last Prev Next   No search results available

Bug 65845 - incorporate code coverage info into link process   Last Comment

Status:	UNCONFIRMED	**Reported:**	2001-01-18 09:41 PST by Chris Waterson
Whiteboard:		**Modified:**	2010-04-10 13:21 PDT (History)
Keywords:	embed, footprint	**CC List:**	34 users (show)

Product:	Core
Component:	Build Config
Version:	Trunk
Platform:	All All

See Also:

blocking-fennec:	---
blocking2.0:	---
status2.0:	---
blocking1.9.2:	---
status1.9.2:	---
blocking1.9.1:	---
status1.9.1:	---

Importance:	-- normal with 3 votes (vote)
Target Milestone:	---
Assigned To:	Nobody; OK to take it and work on it
QA Contact:	build-config
URL:	

Depends on:
Blocks: 7251 71874
Show dependency tree / graph

Attachments		
MOZ_COVERAGE work-in-progress (5.21 KB, patch) 2001-01-18 10:03 PST, Chris Waterson	no flags	Details | Diff
ZIP file containing a makefile, a C file, and an ordering file. (625 bytes, application/octet-stream) 2001-01-19 12:06 PST, Chris Waterson	no flags	Details
cleaner diffs, with MOZ_NO_COVERAGE (6.64 KB, patch) 2001-01-19 12:13 PST, Chris Waterson	no flags	Details | Diff
diffs used to collect coverage data (4.80 KB, patch) 2001-01-19 16:28 PST, Chris Waterson	no flags	Details | Diff
skanky perl script used to process `order.raw' file (677 bytes, text/plain) 2001-01-19 16:29 PST, Chris Waterson	no flags	Details
input to perl script that tells script where to smack `win32.order' files (2.78 KB, text/plain) 2001-01-19 16:29 PST, Chris Waterson	no flags	Details
config\trace.cpp, new file (2.83 KB, text/plain) 2001-01-19 16:32 PST, Chris Waterson	no flags	Details
new trace.cpp that makes sorted order files (6.03 KB, text/plain) 2001-02-01 18:50 PST, dprice (gone)	no flags	Details
final diffs (5.06 KB, patch) 2001-02-02 16:52 PST, dprice (gone)	no flags	Details | Diff
final version of trace.cpp (60.04 KB, text/plain) 2001-02-02 16:53 PST, dprice (gone)	no flags	Details
define /Gh independently of MOZ_DEBUG (543 bytes, patch) 2001-02-07 13:20 PST, Chris Waterson	no flags	Details | Diff
search for pdb files, only build trace.dll if moz_coverage (1.85 KB, patch) 2001-02-12 19:24 PST, dprice (gone)	no flags	Details | Diff
loging, guaranteed .pdb files and better demangling (2.72 KB, patch) 2001-04-06 21:48 PDT, dprice (gone)	no flags	Details | Diff
order.tgz: gzipped tar file containing source to tools (14.89 KB, application/octet-stream) 2001-06-12 17:42 PDT, Roger Chickering	no flags	Details
Add an attachment (proposed patch, testcase, etc.)		View All

Chris Waterson   2001-01-18 09:41:19 PST   Description

```
Per jband's suggestion, we should collect function usage information and use
the
windows linker's `/ORDER:@filename' flag to layout the function to minimize (or
at least reduce) the working set. Ideally, we could simply:

1. Do a `special' MOZ_COVERAGE build

2. Run the build and exercise a well-defined test suite that would get us
decent
coverage information.

3. Shut down the browser, at which point the coverage information (suitable
as input to the linker) would be dumped into each DLL's `build' directory.
```

information systems, assess help desk personnel efficiency and effectiveness, and identify users who require training.

Help desk personnel need to be good at communicating with users, by listening to their problems and intelligently communicating potential solutions.

TABLE 10-6:   Information Captured in an Issue Tracking System

Information in an Issue Tracking System	Rationale for Capturing This Information
Version of product	• Is used in the planning of the next version of the product • Specifically identifies problems that might carry over from different versions
Which customer has encountered the issue	• Tracks not only the issue but the origination of the issue • Allows for deeper analysis when designing a solution
Severity of the issue	• Allows developers to prioritize bugs and changes so that the most critical issues are addressed first
Who fixed the issue	• Creates accountability for the developers • Allows managers to track developer productivity
Who verified the fix	• Ensures that all software fixes are tested and retested for reliability • Provides a critical aspect of the system maintenance process

These personnel also need to understand the technology they are helping users with. It is crucial, however, that help desk personnel know when new systems and releases are being implemented and when users are being trained for new systems. Help desk personnel themselves should be well trained on new systems. One sure recipe for disaster is to train users on new systems but not train the help desk personnel these same users will turn to for their support needs.

Support Issues for the Analyst to Consider

Support is more than just answering user questions about how to use a system to perform a particular task or about the system's functionality. Support also consists of such tasks as providing for recovery and backup, disaster recovery, and PC maintenance; writing newsletters and offering other types of proactive information sharing; and setting up user groups. It is the responsibility of analysts for a new system to be sure that all forms of support are in place before the system is installed.

For medium-to-large organizations with active information system units, many of these issues are dealt with centrally. For example, users may be provided with backup software by the central information systems unit and a schedule for routine backup. Policies may also be in place for initiating recovery procedures in case of system failure. Similarly, disaster recovery plans are almost always established by the central IS unit. Also, IS unit specialists may be in charge of composing and transmitting newsletters or overseeing automated bulletin boards and organizing user groups.

When all of these (and more) services are provided by central IS, you must follow the proper procedures to include any new system and its users in the lists of those to whom support is provided. You must design training for the support staff on the new system, and you must make sure that system documentation will be available to it. You must make the support staff aware of the installation schedule. You must also keep these people informed as the system evolves. Similarly, any new hardware and off-the-shelf software have to be registered with the central IS authorities.

When no official IS support function is available to provide support services, you must come up with a creative plan to provide as many services as possible. You may have to write backup and recovery procedures and schedules, and the users' departments may have to purchase and be responsible for the maintenance of their hardware. In some cases, software and hardware maintenance may have to be outsourced to vendors or other capable professionals. In such situations, user interaction and information dissemination may have to be more informal than formal: informal user groups may meet over lunch or over a coffeepot rather than in officially formed and sanctioned forums.

Why Implementation Sometimes Fails

Despite the best efforts of the systems development team to design and build a quality system and to manage the change process in the organization, the implementation effort sometimes fails. Sometimes employees will not use the new system that has been developed for them, or if they do use the system, their level of satisfaction with it is low.

The conventional wisdom that has emerged over the years is that at least two conditions are necessary for a successful implementation effort: management support of the system under development and the involvement of users in the development process. Yet, despite the support and active participation of management and users, information systems implementation still sometimes fails.

Let's review some insights about the implementation process:

- *Risk.* User involvement in the development process can help reduce the risk of failure when the system is complex, but it can also make failure more likely when financial and time constraints affect the development process.
- *Commitment to the project.* The system development project should be managed so that the problem being solved is well understood and that the system being developed to deal with the problem actually solves it.
- *Commitment to change.* Users and managers must be willing to change behaviors, procedures, and other aspects of the organization.
- *Extent of project definition and planning.* The more extensive the planning effort, the less likely is implementation failure.
- *Realistic user expectations.* The more realistic a user's early expectations about a new system and its capabilities, the more likely it is that the user will be satisfied with the new system and actually use it.

Whether a system implementation fails or succeeds also depends on your definition of success. Although determining whether an implementation has been successful can be done in a number of ways, the two most common and trusted are the extent to which the system is used and the user's satisfaction with the system. Whether a user will actually use a new system depends on several additional factors:

1. How relevant the system is to the work the user performs.
2. System ease of use and reliability.
3. User demographics, such as age and degree of computer experience.
4. The more users can do with a system and the more creative ways they can develop to benefit from the system, the more they will use it. Then the more people use the system, the more likely they are to find even more ways to benefit from the system.
5. The more satisfied the users are with the system, the more they will use it. The more they use it, the more satisfied they will be.

It should be clear that, as an analyst and as someone responsible for the successful implementation of an information system, you have more control over some factors than others. For example, you have considerable influence over the system's ease of use and reliability, and you may have some influence over the levels of support that will be provided for users of the system. You have no direct control over a user's demographics, relevance of the system, management support, or the urgency of the problem to the user. However, you can't ignore these factors. You need to understand these factors well, because you will have to balance them with the factors you can change in your system design and implementation strategy. You may not be able to change a user's demographics or personal stake in a system, but you can help design the system and your implementation strategy with these factors in mind.

The factors mentioned so far are straightforward. For example, a lack of computer experience can make a user hesitant, inefficient, and ineffective with a system, leading to a system's not achieving its full potential benefit. If top management does not seem to care about the system, why should subordinates care? However, additional factors can be categorized as political, and may be more hidden, difficult to effect, and even unrelated to the system you are implementing, yet instrumental to the system's success.

The basis for political factors is that individuals who work in an organization have their own self-interested goals, which they pursue in addition to the goals of their departments and of their organizations. For example, people may act to increase their own power relative to that of their coworkers, and at other times, people will act to prevent coworkers with more power (such as bosses) from using that power or from gaining more. Because information is power, information systems are often seen as instruments of one's ability to influence and exert power. For example, an information system that provides information about the inventory and production capabilities of plant A to other plants, may be seen as undesirable to managers in plant A, even if this information makes the company operate more efficiently overall. Users in plant A may resist participation in systems development activities, may continue (if possible) to use old systems and ignore the new one, or may initiate delaying tactics to stall the installation of the new system (such as asking for more studies and analysis work to "perfect" the system). Thus, you must attempt to understand the history and politics around an information system and deal with negative political factors, as well as the more objective and operational ones.

Project Closedown

In Chapter 3, you learned about the various phases of project management, from project initiation to closing down the project. If you are the project manager and have successfully guided your project through all of the phases of the systems development life cycle presented so far in this book, you are now ready to close down your project. Although systems operation is just about to begin, the development project itself is over. As you will see in the following sections, maintenance can be thought of as a series of smaller development projects, each with its own series of project management phases.

As you recall from Chapter 3, your first task in closing down the project involves many different activities, from dealing with project personnel to planning a celebration of the project's ending. You will likely have to evaluate your team members, reassign most to other projects, and perhaps terminate others. As project manager, you will also have to notify all of the affected parties that the development project is ending and that you are now switching to operation and maintenance mode.

Your second task is to conduct post-project reviews with both your management and your customers. In some organizations, these postproject reviews follow formal procedures and may involve internal or electronic data processing (EDP) auditors. The point of a project review is to critique the project, its methods, its deliverables, and its management. You can learn many lessons to improve future projects from a thorough postproject review.

The third major task in project closedown is closing out the customer contract. Any contract that has been in effect between you and your customers during the project (or as the basis for the project) must be completed. This may involve a formal "signing-off" by the clients that your work is complete and acceptable. Maintenance activities will typically be covered under new contractual agreements. If your customer is outside of your organization, you will also likely negotiate a separate support agreement.

Some organizations conduct a post-implementation audit of a system shortly after it goes into operation, during, or shortly after project closedown. A system audit may be conducted by a member of an internal audit staff, responsible for checking any data-handling procedure change in the organization. Sometimes a system audit is conducted by an outside organization, such as a management consulting firm or a public accounting firm. The purpose of a system audit is to verify that a system works properly by itself and in combination with other systems. A system audit is similar to a system test but is done on a system in operation. A system audit not only checks that the operational system works accurately, but the audit is also likely to review the development process for the system. Such a process audit checks that sound practices were used to design, develop, and test the system. For example, a process audit will review the testing plan and summary of results. Errors found during an audit will generate requests for system maintenance, and in an extreme case, could force a system to cease operation.

As an analyst member of the development team, your job on this particular project ends during project closedown. You will likely be reassigned to another project dealing with some other organizational problem. During your career as a systems analyst, many of your job assignments will be to perform maintenance on existing systems. We cover this important part of the systems implementation and operation phase next.

Conducting Systems Maintenance

A significant portion of an organization's budget for information systems does not go to the development of new systems but to the maintenance of existing systems. We describe various types of maintenance, factors influencing the complexity and cost of maintenance, alternatives for managing maintenance, and the role of automated development tools during maintenance. Given that maintenance activities consume the majority of information systems–related expenditures, gaining an understanding of these topics will yield numerous benefits to your career as an information systems professional.

Types of Maintenance

You can perform several types of maintenance on an information system, as described in Table 10-7. By **maintenance,** we mean the fixing or enhancing of an information system. **Corrective maintenance** refers to changes made to repair defects in the design, coding, or implementation of the system. For example, if you purchase a new home, corrective maintenance would involve repairs made to things that had never worked as designed, such as a faulty electrical outlet or misaligned door. Most corrective maintenance problems surface soon after installation. When corrective maintenance problems arise, they are typically urgent and need to be resolved to curtail possible interruptions in normal business activities. Some corrective maintenance is due to incompatibilities between the new system and other information systems with which it must exchange data. Corrective maintenance adds little or no value to the organization; it simply focuses on removing defects from an existing system without adding new functionality.

Adaptive maintenance involves making changes to an information system to evolve its functionality to changing business needs or to migrate it to a

Maintenance
Changes made to a system to fix or enhance its functionality.

Corrective maintenance
Changes made to a system to repair flaws in its design, coding, or implementation.

Adaptive maintenance
Changes made to a system to evolve its functionality to changing business needs or technologies.

TABLE 10-7: Types of Maintenance

Type	Description	Approximate Percentage of Maintenance Effort
Corrective	Repair design and programming errors	70
Adaptive	Modify system to environmental changes	10
Perfective	Add new features or improve system performance	15
Preventive	Safeguard system from future problems	5

different operating environment. Within a home, adaptive maintenance might be adding storm windows to improve its energy efficiency. Adaptive maintenance is usually less urgent than corrective maintenance because business and technical changes typically occur over some period of time. Contrary to corrective maintenance, adaptive maintenance is generally a small part of an organization's maintenance effort but does add value to the organization.

Perfective maintenance involves making enhancements to improve processing performance, interface usability, or to add desired, but not necessarily required, system features ("bells and whistles"). In our home example, perfective maintenance would be adding a new room. Many system professionals feel that perfective maintenance is not really maintenance but new development.

Preventive maintenance involves changes made to a system to reduce the chance of future system failure. An example of preventive maintenance might be to increase the number of records that a system can process far beyond what is currently needed. In our home example, preventive maintenance could be painting the exterior to better protect the home from severe weather conditions. As with adaptive maintenance, both perfective and preventive maintenance are typically a much lower priority than corrective maintenance. Adaptive, perfective, and preventive maintenance activities can lead to corrective maintenance activities if not carefully designed and implemented.

Perfective maintenance
Changes made to a system to add new features or to improve performance.

Preventive maintenance
Changes made to a system to avoid possible future problems.

The Cost of Maintenance

Information systems maintenance costs are a significant expenditure. For some organizations, as much 60–80 percent of their information systems budget is allocated to maintenance activities. This proportion has risen from roughly 50 percent twenty years ago because many organizations have accumulated more and more older systems that require more and more maintenance. It means that you must understand the factors influencing the maintainability of systems. Maintainability is the ease with which software can be understood, corrected, adapted, and enhanced. Systems with low maintainability result in uncontrollable maintenance expenses.

Numerous factors influence the maintainability of a system. These factors, or cost elements, determine the extent to which a system has high or low maintainability. Of these factors, three are most significant: number of latent defects, number of customers, and documentation quality. The others—personnel, tools, and software structure—have noticeable, but less, influence.

- *Latent defects:* This is the number of unknown errors existing in the system after it is installed. Because corrective maintenance accounts for most maintenance activity, the number of latent defects in a system influences most of the costs associated with maintaining a system.

- *Number of customers for a given system:* In general, the greater the number of customers, the greater the maintenance costs. For example, if a system has only one customer, problem and change requests will come from only one source. Also, training, reporting errors, and support will be simpler. Maintenance requests are less likely to be contradictory or incompatible.

- *Quality of system documentation:* Without quality documentation, maintenance effort can increase exponentially. Quality documentation makes it easier to find code that needs to be changed and to understand how the code needs to be changed. Good documentation also explains why a system does what it does and why alternatives were not feasible, which saves wasted maintenance efforts.

- *Maintenance personnel:* In some organizations, the best programmers are assigned to maintenance. Highly-skilled programmers are needed because the maintenance programmer is typically not the original programmer and must quickly understand and carefully change the software.

- *Tools:* Tools that can automatically produce system documentation where none exists can also lower maintenance costs. Also, tools that can automatically generate new code based on system specification changes can dramatically reduce maintenance time and costs.

- *Well-structured programs:* Well-designed programs are easier to understand and fix.

Since the mid-1990s, many organizations have taken a new approach to managing maintenance costs. Rather than develop custom systems internally or through contractors, they have chosen to buy packaged application software. Although vendors of packaged software charge an annual maintenance fee for updates, these charges are more predictable and lower than those for custom-developed systems. Internal maintenance work is often still necessary when using packages. One major maintenance task is to make the packaged software compatible with other packages and internally developed systems with which it must cooperate. When new releases of the purchased package appear, maintenance may be needed to make all the packages continue to share and exchange data. Some companies are minimizing this effort by buying comprehensive packages, called *enterprise resource planning (ERP) packages*, which provide information services for a wide range of organizational functions (from human resources to accounting, manufacturing, and sales and marketing). Although the initial costs to install such ERP packages can be significant, they promise great potential for drastically reducing system maintenance costs.

Measuring Maintenance Effectiveness

Because maintenance can be so costly, it is important to measure its effectiveness. To measure effectiveness, you must measure these factors:

- Number of failures
- Time between each failure
- Type of failure

Measuring the number of and time between failures will provide you with the basis to calculate a widely-used measure of system quality. This measure is referred to as the **mean time between failures (MTBF)**. As its name implies, the MTBF measure shows the average length of time between the identification of one system failure until the next. Over time, you should expect the MTBF value to increase rapidly after a few months of use (and corrective maintenance) of the system. If the MTBF does not rapidly increase over time, it will be a signal to management that major problems exist within the system that are not being adequately resolved through the maintenance process.

Mean time between failures (MTBF)

A measurement of error occurrences that can be tracked over time to indicate the quality of a system.

A more revealing method of measurement is to examine the failures that are occurring. Over time, logging the types of failures provides a clear picture of where, when, and how failures occur. For example, knowing that a system repeatedly fails logging new account information to the database when a particular customer is using the system can provide invaluable information to the maintenance personnel. Were the users adequately trained? Is there something unique about this user? Is there something unique about an installation that is causing the failure? What activities were being performed when the system failed?

Tracking the types of failures also provides important management information for future projects. For example, if a higher frequency of errors occurs when a particular development environment is used, such information can help guide personnel assignments, training courses, or the avoidance of a particular package, language, or environment during future development. The primary lesson here is that without measuring and tracking maintenance activities, you cannot gain the knowledge to improve or know how well you are doing relative to the past. To manage effectively and to improve continuously, you must measure and assess performance over time.

Controlling Maintenance Requests

Another maintenance activity is managing maintenance requests. From a management perspective, a key issue is deciding which requests to perform and which to ignore. Because some requests will be more critical than others, some method of prioritizing requests must be determined.

Figure 10-10 shows a flowchart that suggests one possible method for dealing with maintenance change requests. First, you must determine the type of request. If, for example, the request is an error—that is, a corrective maintenance request— then a question related to the error's severity must be asked. If the error is "very severe," then the request has top priority and is placed at the top of a queue of tasks waiting to be performed on the system. If, however, the error is considered "not very severe," then the change request can be categorized and prioritized based upon its type and relative importance. Categorization and prioritization may be done by the same review panel or board that evaluates new system requests.

If the change request is not an error, then you must determine whether the request is to adapt the system to technology changes and/or business requirements or to enhance the system with new business functionality. Adaptation requests will also need to be evaluated, categorized, prioritized, and placed in the queue. Enhancement-type requests must first be evaluated for alignment with future business and information systems plans. If not aligned, the request will be rejected, and the requester will be informed. If the enhancement is aligned with business and information systems' plans, it can then be prioritized and placed into the queue of future tasks. Part of the prioritization process includes estimating the scope and feasibility of the change. Techniques used for assessing the scope and feasibility of entire projects should be used when assessing maintenance requests (see Chapter 4).

Managing the queue of pending tasks is an important activity. The queue of maintenance tasks is dynamic—growing and shrinking based upon business changes and errors. In fact, some lower-priority change requests may never be accomplished, because only a limited number of changes can be accomplished at a given time. In other words, changes in business needs between the time the request was made and when the task finally rises to the top of the queue may result in the request being deemed unnecessary or no longer important given current business directions.

Although each change request goes through an approval process as depicted in Figure 10-10, changes are usually implemented in batches, forming a new release of the software. It is too difficult to manage a lot of small changes. Further,

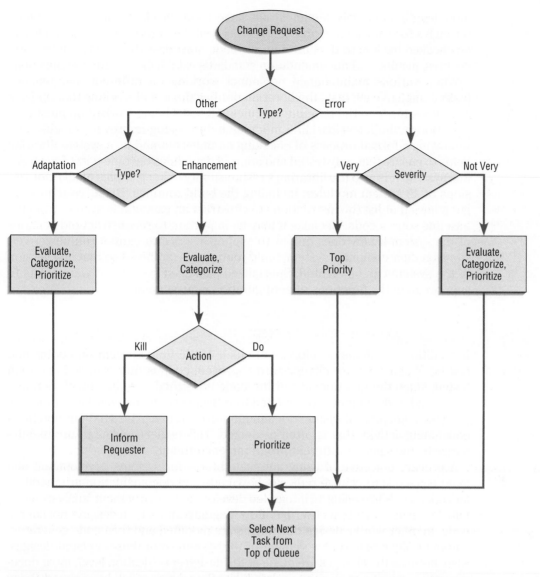

FIGURE 10-10
Flowchart showing how to control maintenance requests.

Source: Pressman, R.S. (2010). Software Engineering: A Practitioner's Approach. 7th ed. New York: McGraw Hill.

batching changes can reduce maintenance work when several change requests affect the same or highly related modules. Frequent releases of new system versions may also confuse users if the appearance of displays, reports, or data-entry screens changes.

Configuration Management

A final aspect of managing maintenance is **configuration management,** which is the process of ensuring that only authorized changes are made to a system. Once a system has been implemented and installed, the programming code used to construct the system represents the **baseline modules** of the system. In these software modules for the most recent version of a system, each module has passed the organization's quality assurance process and documentation standards. A **system librarian** controls the baseline source code modules. If maintenance personnel are assigned to make changes to a system, they must first check out a copy of the baseline system modules because no one is allowed to modify the baseline

Configuration management
The process of ensuring that only authorized changes are made to a system.

Baseline modules
Software modules that have been tested, documented, and approved to be included in the most recently created version of a system.

System librarian
A person responsible for controlling the checking out and checking in of baseline modules when a system is being developed or maintained.

modules directly. Only modules that have been checked out and have gone through a formal check-in process can reside in the library. Before any code can be checked back in to the librarian, the code must pass the quality-control procedures, testing, and documentation standards established by the organization.

When various maintenance personnel working on different maintenance tasks complete each task, the librarian notifies those still working that updates have been made to the baseline modules. All tasks being worked on must now incorporate the latest baseline modules before being approved for check-in. Following a formal process of checking modules out and in, a system librarian helps to ensure that only tested and approved modules become part of the baseline system. It is also the librarian's responsibility to keep copies of all prior versions of all system modules, including the build routines. **Build routines** are guidelines that list the instructions to construct an executable system from the baseline source code. Because it may be important to reconstruct old versions of the system if new ones fail, or to support users that cannot run newer versions on their computer system, build routines are archived so that any version of the system can be created. Specialized packaged system software exists to support all of the functions of configuration management.

Build routines
Guidelines that list the instructions to construct an executable system from the baseline source code.

Role of Automated Development Tools in Maintenance

In traditional systems development, much of the time is spent on coding and testing. When software changes are approved, code is first changed and then tested. Once the functionality of the code is verified, the documentation and specification documents are updated to reflect system changes. Over time, the process of keeping all system documentation current can be a tedious and time-consuming activity that is often neglected. This neglect makes future maintenance by the same or different programmers difficult.

A primary objective of using automated tools for systems development and maintenance is to change radically how code and documentation are modified and updated. When using an integrated development environment, analysts maintain design documents such as data-flow diagrams and screen designs, not source code. In other words, design documents are modified and then code generators automatically create a new version of the system from these updated designs. Also, because the changes are made at the design-specification level, most documentation changes such as an updated data-flow diagram will have already been completed during the maintenance process itself. One of the biggest advantages to using these tools, for example, is the benefits during system maintenance.

In addition to using general automated tools for maintenance, two special-purpose tools, reverse engineering and reengineering tools, are primarily used to maintain older systems. These tools are often referred to as *design recovery tools* because their primary benefit is to create high-level design documents of a program by reading and analyzing its source code. When original documentation is not available, these tools can save considerable maintenance time by helping maintenance personnel to understand program and data structures.

Web Site Maintenance

All of the discussion on maintenance in this chapter applies to any type of information system, no matter on what platform it runs. Some special issues and procedures are needed for Web sites, however, because of their nature and operational status. These issues and procedures include:

- *24 × 7 × 365:* Most Web sites are never purposely down. In fact an e-commerce Web site has the advantage of continuous operation. Thus, maintenance of pages and the overall site usually must be done without taking the site off-line. However, it may be necessary to lock out use of pages in a portion of a Web site while changes are made to those pages. Inserting a "Temporarily Out of Service" notice on the main page of the section being maintained and disabling all links within that segment is a common approach. Alternatively, references to the main page of the section can be temporarily rerouted to an alternative location where the current pages are kept while maintenance is performed to create new versions of those pages. The really tricky nuance is keeping the site consistent for a user during a session: that is, it can be confusing to a user to see two different versions of a page within the same online session. Browser caching functions may bring up an old version of a page even when that page changes during the session. One precaution against confusion is locking, as previously explained. Another approach is to not lock a page being changed but to include a date and time stamp of the most recent change. Giving the page visitor an indication of the change may reduce confusion.

- *Check for broken links:* Arguably the most common maintenance issue for any Web site (besides changing the content of the site) is validating that links from site pages (especially for links that go outside the source site) are still accurate. Periodic checks need to be performed to make sure active pages are found from all links. Various software such as CyberSpyder (www.cyberspyder.com) or Google Webmaster (www.google.com/webmasters) provide such checking features. In addition, periodic human checks need to be performed to make sure that the content found at a still-existing referenced page is still the intended content.

- *Reregistration:* It may be necessary to reregister a Web site with search engines when the content of your site significantly changes. Reregistration may be necessary for visitors to find your site based on the new or changed content.

- *Future editions:* One of the most important issues to address to ensure effective Web site use is to avoid confusing visitors. Especially frequent visitors can be confused if the site is constantly changing. To avoid confusion, you can post indications of future enhancements to the site and, as with all information systems, you can batch changes to reduce the frequency of site changes.

Maintaining an Information System at Pine Valley Furniture

Early one Saturday evening, Juanita Lopez, head of the manufacturing support unit of the purchasing department at Pine Valley Furniture (PVF), was developing a new four-week production schedule to prepare purchase orders for numerous material suppliers. She was working on Saturday evening because she was leaving the next day for a long-overdue two-week vacation to the Black Hills of South Dakota. Before she could leave, however, she needed to prepare purchase orders for all material requirements for the next four weeks so that orders could be placed during her absence. She was using the Purchasing Fulfillment System to assist her with this activity.

Midway through the process of developing a new production schedule, the system failed and could not be restarted. When she tried to restart the program, an error message was displayed on the terminal:

Data Integrity Error: Corrupt or missing supplier file.

Given that her plane for Rapid City left in less than 12 hours, Juanita had to figure out some way to overcome this catastrophic system error. Her first thought was to walk over to the offices of the information systems development group within the same building. When she did, she found no one there. Her next idea was to contact Chris Ryan, the project manager for the development and maintenance of the system. She placed a call to Chris's home and found that he was at the grocery store but would be home soon. Juanita left a message for Chris to call her ASAP at the office.

Within 30 minutes, Chris returned the call and was on his way into the office to help Juanita. Although not a common occurrence, it is not the first time that Chris has gone into the office to assist users when systems have failed during off-hours. Chris was looking forward to the day when he could handle all problems from home using a home PC and secure, high-speed Internet connection as he had been able to do when he needed to scan data files for errors or issue a command to restore a database. Based on Juanita's explanation of the problem and a few quick inquiries from his home PC, Chris decided he had better make the trip to the office where he had a variety of tools at his disposal.

PVF's systems development methodology for performing system maintenance is a formal process in which a user must first write a system service request (SSR) before maintenance is performed. After it is reviewed by the project manager, it is then forwarded to the Systems Priority Board. For catastrophic problems requiring instant correction so as not to delay normal business operations, the project manager has the discretion to circumvent the normal request process. After arriving on the scene, reviewing the error messages, and learning of Juanita's pending vacation, Chris believed that the failure with the Purchasing Fulfillment System was an instance where he could circumvent the normal maintenance process. His quick investigation suggested a failure in a new version of a system module that had been installed late on Friday afternoon. Chris noticed that the automated development tool records showed that this replacement module had not been tested against a standard test data set related to the type of work Juanita was doing, which made him suspect that it was the source of the problem. After patching the system to make it run, he would have to go back and document and test his changes so that they conformed to the development standards of PVF.

Over the next two hours, Chris used system backups to rebuild the supplier database. He reinstalled a previous version of the system's potentially faulty module (stored in the system library) that seemed more reliable, and then he quickly ran a test data set to check that the patches would hold the system together for now. He had to refresh himself on how to mount a tape cartridge on which the backup supplier data had been archived. Juanita was able to complete her task on time to easily make her flight the next morning. She thanked Chris for "going beyond the call of duty." Her appreciation made Chris feel good, but he was still uneasy. When making the "quick fix" on the system, he did not perform carefully planned testing, nor did he confirm what had caused the error. He knew that the system could fail at any time. He did, however, have a copy of all of Juanita's actions just prior to the system failure. He hoped that through a careful review of those actions he would be able to learn why the system failed. But that would be a job for Monday morning.

PINE
VALLEY
FURNITURE

Pine Valley Furniture WebStore: Systems Implementation and Operation

In the last chapter, you read how Jim Woo and the Pine Valley Furniture development team transformed the conceptual data model for the WebStore into a set of normalized relations. Here we examine how the WebStore system was tested before it was installed and brought online.

Systems Implementation and Operation for Pine Valley Furniture's WebStore

The programming of all WebStore software modules is now complete. The programmers extensively tested each unique module, and it was now time to perform a system-wide test of the WebStore. In this section, we examine how test cases were developed, how bugs were recorded and fixed, and how alpha and beta testing was conducted.

Developing Test Cases for the WebStore   To begin the systemwide testing process, Jim and the PVF development team developed test cases to examine every aspect of the system. Jim knew that system testing, like all other aspects of the SDLC, needed to be a tightly structured and planned process. Before opening the WebStore to the general public, every module and component of the system needed to be tested within a controlled environment. Based upon his experience in implementing other systems, Jim felt that they would need to develop approximately 150–200 separate test cases to fully examine the WebStore. To help focus the development of test cases and to assign primary responsibility to members of his team to specific areas of the system, Jim developed the following list of testing categories:

- *Simple functionality:* Add to cart, list section, calculate tax, change personal data
- *Multiple functionality:* Add item to cart and change quantity, create user account, and change address
- *Function chains:* Add item to cart, check out, create user account, purchase
- *Elective functions:* Returned items, lost shipments, item out-of-stock
- *Emergency/crisis:* Missing orders, hardware failure, security attacks

The development group broke into five separate teams, each working to develop an extensive set of cases for each of the testing categories. Each team had one day to develop its test cases. Once developed, each team would lead a walkthrough so that everyone would know the totality of the testing process and to facilitate extensive feedback to each team so that the testing process would be as comprehensive as possible. To make this point, Jim stated, "What happens when a customer repeatedly enters the same product into the shopping cart? Can we handle that? What happens when the customer repeatedly enters and then removes a single product? Can we handle that? Although some of these things are unlikely to ever occur, we need to be confident that the system is robust enough to handle any type of customer interaction. We must develop every test case necessary to give us confidence that the system will operate as intended, 24/7!"

A big part of successful system testing is to make sure that no information is lost and that all tests are described in a consistent way. Jim provided all teams with a standard form for documenting each case and for recording the results of each test. This form had the following sections:

Test Case ID
Category/Objective of Test
Description
System Version
Completion Date
Participant(s)
Machine Characteristics (processor, operating system, memory, browser, etc.)
Test Result
Comments

The teams also developed standard codes for each general type of test that was used to create the Test Case ID. For example, all tests related to "simple functionality" were given an ID with SF as a prefix and a number as the suffix—for example, SF001. The teams also developed standards for categorizing, listing objectives, and writing other test-form contents. Establishing these standards assured that the testing process would be documented consistently.

Bug Tracking and System Evolution   An outcome of the testing process is the identification of system bugs. Consequently, in addition to setting a standard method for writing and documenting test cases, Jim and the teams established several other rules to ensure a smooth testing process. Experienced developers have long known that an accurate bug tracking process is essential for rapid troubleshooting and repair during the testing process. You can think of bug tracking as creating a "paper trail" that makes it much easier for programmers to find and repair the bug. To make sure that all bugs were documented in a similar way, the team developed a bug tracking form that had the following categories:

> Bug Number (simple incremental number)
> Test Case ID That Generated the Bug
> Is the Bug Replicable?
> Effects
> Description
> Resolution
> Resolution Date
> Comments

The PVF development team agreed that bug fixes would be made in batches, because all test cases would have to be redone every time the software was changed. Redoing all the test cases each time the software is changed is done to ensure that in the process of fixing the bug, no other bugs were introduced into the system. As the system moves along in the testing process—as batches of bugs are fixed—the version number of the software is incremented. During the development and testing phases, the version is typically below the "1.0" first release version.

Alpha and Beta Testing the WebStore   After completing all system test cases and resolving all known bugs, Jim moved the WebStore into the alpha testing phase where the entire PVF development team and personnel around the company would put the WebStore through its paces. To motivate employees throughout the company to participate actively in testing the WebStore, several creative promotions and giveaways were held. All employees were given a T-shirt with the motto "I shop at the WebStore, do you?" Additionally, all employees were given $100 to shop at the WebStore and were offered a free lunch for their entire department if they found a system bug while shopping on the system. Also during alpha testing, the development team conducted extensive recovery, security, stress, and performance testing. Table 10-8 provides a sample of the types of tests performed.

After completing alpha testing, PVF recruited several of their established customers to help in beta testing the WebStore. As real-world customers used the system, Jim was able to monitor the system and fine-tune the servers for optimal system performance. As the system moved through the testing process, fewer and fewer bugs were found. After several days of "clean" usage, Jim felt confident that it was now time to open the WebStore for business.

WebStore Installation   Throughout the testing process, Jim kept PVF management aware of each success and failure. Fortunately, because Jim and the development team followed a structured and disciplined development process, they experienced far more successes than failures. In fact, he was now confident that the WebStore was ready to go online and would recommend to PVF's top management that it was now time to "flip the switch" and let the world enter the WebStore.

TABLE 10-8:   Sample of Tests Conducted on the WebStore during Alpha Testing

Test Type	Sample of Tests Performed
Recovery	Unplug main server to test power backup system.
Security	Switch off main server to test the automatic switching to backup server.
Stress	Try to purchase without being a customer.
Performance	Try to examine server directory files both within the PVF domain and when connecting from an outside Internet service provider.
	Have multiple users simultaneously establish accounts, process purchases, add to shopping cart, remove from shopping cart, etc.
	Examine response time using different connection speeds, processors, memory, browsers, and other system configurations.
	Examine response time when backing up server data.

Key Points Review

1. **Describe the process of coding, testing, and converting an organizational information system and outline the deliverables and outcomes of the process.**

   Coding is the process whereby the physical design specifications created by the design team are turned into working computer code by the programming team. Once coding has begun, the testing process can begin and proceed in parallel. As each program module is produced, it can be tested individually, then as part of a larger program, and then as part of a larger system. Installation is the process during which the current system is replaced by the new system. This includes conversion of existing data, software, documentation, and work procedures to those consistent with the new system. The deliverables and outcomes from coding, testing, and conversion are program and system code with associated documentation; testing plans, data, and results; and installation user guides, training plan, and conversion plan for hardware, software, data, and facilities.

2. **Apply four installation strategies: direct, parallel, single location, and phased installation.**

   Direct installation is the changing over from the old information system to a new one by turning off the old system when the new one is turned on. *Parallel installation* means running the old information system and the new one at the same time until management decides the old system can be turned off. *Single location installation* is trying out

a new information system at one site and using the experience to decide if and how the new system should be deployed throughout the organization. *Phased installation* is changing from the old information system to the new one incrementally, starting with one or a few functional components and then gradually extending the installation to cover the whole new system. Often, a combination or hybrid of these four strategies is employed for a particular information system installation. The approach (or combination) an organization decides to use depends on the scope and complexity of the change associated with the new system and the organization's risk aversion.

3. **List the deliverables for documenting the system and for training and supporting users.**

   The deliverables are system and user documentation; user training plan for classes and tutorials; user training materials, including computer-based training aids; and a user support plan, including such elements as a help desk, online help materials, bulletin boards, and other support mechanisms.

4. **Compare the many modes available for organizational information system training.**

   While formal instructor led courses is the most common method of training, other approaches include: resident experts, software help components, e-learning/distance learning, and external sources such as vendors. Increasingly, organizations are using e-learning/distance learning to meet their employee training needs.

5. **Discuss the issues of providing support for end users.**

Support is more than just answering user questions about how to use a system to perform a particular task or about the system's functionality. Support also consists of such tasks as providing for recovery and backup, disaster recovery, and PC maintenance; writing newsletters and offering other types of proactive information sharing; and setting up user groups. It is the responsibility of analysts for a new system to be sure that all forms of support are in place before the system is installed. For medium-to-large organizations with active information system units, many of these issues are dealt with centrally. When no official IS support function is available to provide support services, you must come up with a creative plan to provide as many services as possible. You may have to write backup and recovery procedures and schedules, and the users' departments may have to purchase and be responsible for the maintenance of their hardware. In some cases, software and hardware maintenance may have to be outsourced to vendors or other capable professionals.

6. **Explain why systems implementation sometimes fails.**

Even well-executed systems development projects, which have identified the right requirements and designed and installed a sound system, can fail. Research and experience have shown that management support of the system under development and the involvement of users in the development process can be important but are not sufficient to achieve success. In addition, users must have a commitment to the project and a commitment to change. Poorly done project definition and planning can set up a project for failure. Users also must have realistic and consistent expectations of the system's capabilities. Of course, the system must be relevant to the work the user performs. Also important are the ease of use and reliability of the system and user demographics,

such as age and degree of computer experience. The more users can do with a system and the more creative ways they can develop to benefit from the system, the more they will use it. Then more use leads users to find even more ways to benefit from the system. The more satisfied the users are with the system, the more they will use it. The more they use it, the more satisfied they will be.

7. **Explain and contrast four types of maintenance.**

Corrective maintenance repairs flaws in a system's design, coding, or implementation. *Adaptive maintenance* implements changes to a system to evolve its functionality to changing business needs or technologies. *Perfective maintenance* adds new features or improves system performance. *Preventive maintenance* avoids possible future problems. Corrective maintenance is the most frequent, by far, and should occur primarily shortly after a system release is installed. Corrective maintenance must be made, and usually quickly. Adaptive maintenance also usually must be done. Some adaptive maintenance and all perfective and preventive maintenance are discretionary and must be categorized and prioritized.

8. **Describe several factors that influence the cost of maintaining an information system.**

The factors that influence the cost of maintaining an information system are: (1) latent defects, which are unknown errors existing in the system after it is installed; (2) number of customers for a given system; (3) quality of system documentation; (4) maintenance personnel; (5) tools that can automatically produce system documentation where none exists; and (6) well-structured programs. The most influential of these are latent defects, number of customers, and quality of documentation. Also, some companies have adopted a strategy of using packaged application software, especially enterprise resource planning systems, to reduce maintenance costs.

Key Terms Checkpoint

Here are the key terms from the chapter. The page where each term is first explained is in parentheses after the term.

1. Acceptance testing (p. 329)
2. Adaptive maintenance (p. 343)
3. Alpha testing (p. 329)
4. Baseline modules (p. 347)
5. Beta testing (p. 329)
6. Build routines (p. 348)
7. Configuration management (p. 347)
8. Corrective maintenance (p. 343)
9. Desk checking (p. 326)
10. Direct installation (p. 330)
11. Electronic performance support system (EPSS) (p. 337)
12. External documentation (p. 333)
13. Help desk (p. 338)
14. Inspection (p. 326)
15. Installation (p. 330)

16. Integration testing (p. 327)
17. Internal documentation (p. 333)
18. Issue tracking system (p. 338)
19. Maintenance (p. 343)
20. Mean time between failures (MTBF) (p. 345)

21. Parallel installation (p. 330)
22. Perfective maintenance (p. 344)
23. Phased installation (p. 330)
24. Preventive maintenance (p. 344)
25. Single location installation (p. 330)
26. Stub testing (p. 327)
27. Support (p. 336)

28. System documentation (p. 333)
29. System librarian (p. 347)
30. System testing (p. 327)
31. Testing harness (p. 329)
32. Unit testing (p. 327)
33. User documentation (p. 333)

Match each of the key terms with the definition that best fits it.

_____ 1. A testing technique in which participants examine program code for predictable language-specific errors.

_____ 2. A testing technique in which the program code is sequentially executed manually by the reviewer.

_____ 3. Component of a software package or application in which training and educational information is embedded. An EPSS may include a tutorial, expert system, and hypertext jumps to reference material.

_____ 4. Written or other visual information about how an application system works, and how to use it.

_____ 5. Changing over from the old information system to a new one by turning off the old system when the new one is turned on.

_____ 6. Changes made to a system to evolve its functionality to changing business needs or technologies.

_____ 7. Each module is tested alone in an attempt to discover any errors in its code.

_____ 8. The organizational process of changing over from the current information system to a new one.

_____ 9. A measurement of error occurrences that can be tracked over time to indicate the quality of a system.

_____ 10. System documentation that includes the outcome of structured diagramming techniques such as data-flow and entity-relationship diagrams.

_____ 11. The process whereby actual users test a completed information system, the end result of which is the users' acceptance of it once they are satisfied with it.

_____ 12. Guidelines that list the instructions to construct an executable system from the baseline source code.

_____ 13. Changes made to a system to avoid possible future problems.

_____ 14. Detailed information about a system's design specifications, its internal workings, and its functionality.

_____ 15. Running the old information system and the new one at the same time until management decides the old system can be turned off.

_____ 16. The process of bringing together for testing purposes all of the modules that a program comprises. Modules are typically integrated in a top-down, incremental fashion.

_____ 17. Changes made to a system to add new features or to improve performance.

_____ 18. A technique used in testing modules, especially modules that are written and tested in a top-down fashion, where a few lines of code are used to substitute for subordinate modules.

_____ 19. Software modules that have been tested, documented, and approved to be included in the most recently created version of a system.

_____ 20. A person responsible for controlling the checking out and checking in of baseline modules when a system is being developed or maintained.

_____ 21. Changing from the old information system to the new one incrementally, starting with one or a few functional components and then gradually extending the installation to cover the whole new system.

_____ 22. The process of ensuring that only authorized changes are made to a system.

_____ 23. The bringing together for testing purposes of all the programs that a system comprises. Programs are typically integrated in a top-down, incremental fashion.

_____ 24. Changes made to a system to fix or enhance its functionality.

_____ 25. System documentation that is part of the program source code or is generated at compile time.

_____ 26. Providing ongoing educational and problem-solving assistance to information system users. Support material and jobs must be designed along with the associated information system.

_____ 27. User testing of a completed information system using real data in the real user environment.

_____ 28. Changes made to a system to repair flaws in its design, coding, or implementation.

_____ 29. Trying out a new information system at one site and using the experience to decide if and how the new system should be deployed throughout the organization.

_____ 30. User testing of a completed information system using simulated data.

_____ 31. A single point of contact for all user inquiries and problems about a particular information system or for all users in a particular department.

_____ 32. An automated testing environment used to review code for errors, standards violations, and other design flaws.

_____ 33. Typically a Web-based tool for logging, tracking, and assigning system bugs and change requests to developers.

Review Questions

1. What are the deliverables from coding, testing, and installation?
2. Explain the testing process for code.
3. What are the four approaches to installation? Which is the most expensive? Which is the most risky? How does an organization decide which approach to use?
4. List and define the factors that are important to successful implementation efforts.
5. What is the difference between system documentation and user documentation?
6. List and define the various methods of user training.
7. Describe the delivery methods many vendors employ for providing support.
8. List the steps in the maintenance process and contrast them with the phases of the systems development life cycle.
9. What are the different types of maintenance and how do they differ?
10. Describe the factors that influence the cost of maintenance. Are any factors more important? Why?
11. What types of measurements must be taken to gain an understanding of the effectiveness of maintenance? Why is tracking mean time between failures an important measurement?
12. Describe the process for controlling maintenance requests. Should all requests be handled in the same way or are there situations when you should be able to circumvent the process? If so, when and why?
13. What is meant by *configuration management*? Why do you think organizations have adopted the approach of using a systems, librarian?

Problems and Exercises

1. Consider the reasons implementations fail. For at least three of these reasons, explain why this happens, if there is one (or more) type of implementation likely to minimize the occurrence, and if there is one (or more) type of installation more likely to induce failure for this reason.
2. Two members of your project development team are disagreeing about the relative importance of training and documentation. Sam strongly believes that training is far more important because it will ensure the successful implementation of the information system and that the early usage is a positive experience. Pat encounters that the user documentation is far more important because its impact can help not only the current users, but also future users. Which do you think is right, and why?
3. Why is it important to keep a history of test cases and the results of those test cases even after a system has been revised several times?
4. What is the purpose of electronic performance support systems? How would you design one to support a word processing package? A database package?
5. Due to advances in technology and widespread computer literacy, many organizations use e-learning extensively to train employees. If you were managing a system implementation and had to train on a limited budget, you may find yourself choosing between e-learning or conducting face-to-face training with a subset of users who would then train their departments (called train-the-trainers). Which would you choose and why?
6. Is it good or bad for corporations to rely on vendors for computing support? List arguments both for and against reliance on vendors as part of your answer.
7. Suppose you were responsible for establishing a training program for users of Hoosier Burger's inventory control system (described in previous

chapters). Which forms of training would you use? Why?

8. Suppose you work in a senior management position for a large corporation. A member of your team has suggested that your company outsource the help desk functions. Would you support a plan to outsource your help desk? Support your answer.

9. If you were an analyst on a project team developing a new information system and you were given the task of organizing the user documentation, you would probably not be able to create all of the content by yourself from memory. List three sources you would tap for the documentation and explain how you would have to modify it for end-users.

10. In what ways is a request to change an information system handled differently from a request for a new information system?

11. What can a systems analyst do to reduce the frequency of corrective maintenance, the most common form of maintenance?

12. What other information should be collected on a system service request for maintenance as opposed to a system service request for a new system?

13. What can a systems analyst do to facilitate future maintenance?

14. Suppose an information system was developed following a rapid application development approach like prototyping. How might maintenance be different than if the system had been developed following the traditional life cycle? Why?

15. This chapter contains a warning that maintenance activities could lead to further corrective maintenance work if not carefully designed and implemented. What processes or procedures can organizations use to reduce the likelihood of this occurring?

Discussion Questions

1. If possible, ask a systems analyst you know or have access to about implementation. Ask what the analyst believes is necessary for a successful implementation. Compare what the analyst believes are the factors that influence successful implementation to the factors discussed in this chapter.

2. Talk with people you know who use computers in their work. Ask them to get copies of the user documentation they rely on for the systems they use. Analyze the documentation. Would you consider it good or bad? Support your answer. Whether good or bad, how might you improve it?

3. Volunteer to work for a shift at a help desk at your school's computer center. Keep a journal of your experiences. What kind of users did you have to deal with? What kinds of questions did you get? Do you think help desk work is easy or hard? What skills are needed by someone in this position?

4. Let's say your professor has asked you to help him or her train a new secretary on how to prepare class notes for electronic distribution to class members. Your professor uses word processing software and an e-mail package to prepare and distribute the notes. Assume the secretary knows nothing about either package. Prepare a user task guide that shows the secretary how to complete this task.

5. Study an information systems department with which you are familiar or to which you have access. How does this department measure the effectiveness of systems maintenance? What specific metrics are used, and how are these metrics used to effect changes in maintenance practices? If a history of measurements has been collected over several years, how can changes in the measurements be explained?

Case Problems

1. Pine Valley Furniture

Pine Valley Furniture's Customer Tracking System is now entering the final phases of the systems development life cycle. It is a busy time for the project team; project team members are busy coding, testing, training end users, and finalizing the system's documentation.

To enhance your learning experience, Jim Woo has asked you to participate in the implementation process. As a result of this assignment, you have been attending all meetings concerning coding, testing, installation, end-user training, and documentation. During several of these meetings, the installation strategies, necessary end-user training, and required documentation have been discussed. You recall from your recent systems analysis and design course that several options for each of these areas are available.

a. Locate a technical-writing article on the Web. Briefly summarize this article.
b. Which installation options are available for the Customer Tracking System? Which would you recommend?
c. How can you determine if implementation has been successful?
d. What conditions are necessary for a successful implementation effort?

2. Hoosier Burger

The development of Hoosier Burger's information system is nearing completion. At recent project meetings, the types of testing, training, documentation, and installation strategies appropriate for Hoosier Burger have been discussed. The end users have little computer experience and thus, require several types of training and supporting documentation.

Fred Jones, one of the project's team members, has recommended using a direct installation approach. Because Hoosier Burger's information system is relatively small, he feels that the direct approach is the best installation strategy to pursue. The new system could be installed at the beginning of the week and be up and running for the weekend traffic. However, Paula Freeman does not like this idea. She feels that a parallel approach is more appropriate. She worries that if the system crashes, it may be difficult to return to the old system.

a. What types of training will Hoosier Burger's end users need?
b. What types of documentation would you recommend for Hoosier Burger's end users?

c. Which installation strategy would you recommend pursuing?
d. What support issues should be considered?

3. Kitchen Plus

Kitchen Plus is one of the nation's top kitchenware producers. The company has several product lines, including cookware, small appliances, cutlery, and tableware. Over the past several years, the company has watched its market share begin to slip. Several information system projects were rushed into development, including an MRP project. Kitchen Plus executives felt that the new MRP system would enable the company to reduce escalating costs, especially in the areas of inventory, labor, and shipping.

The new MRP system has just been installed, and it is now time to close down the project. As project manager, one of your tasks is to evaluate project team members. Most of the team members performed well, and their work is exemplary. However, Joe McIntire's performance is a different story. Joe was asked to complete several tasks for this project, assisting with interviewing, diagramming, testing, and documentation preparation. Several end users called and complained about Joe's interrogation methods. Additionally, his diagrams were incomplete, sloppily done, and not completed by the due date. During the testing phase, Joe took a week off from work; Pauline Applegate was assigned to take over Joe's duties.

a. Identify the tasks involved in project closedown.
b. How would you evaluate Joe's performance?
c. What types of maintenance problems can you expect from this information system?
d. What factors will influence the maintainability of this system?

CASE: PETRIE'S ELECTRONICS

Systems Implementation and Operation

Jim Watanabe was in his new car, driving down I-5, on his way to work. He dreaded the phone call he knew he was going to have to make.

The original go-live date for a pilot implementation of Petrie's Electronics' new customer relationship management (CRM) system was July 31. That was only six weeks away, and Jim knew there was no way they were going to be ready. The XRA CRM they were

licensing turned out to be a lot more complex than they had thought. They were behind schedule in implementing it. Sanjay Agarwal, who was a member of Jim's team and who was in charge of systems integration for Petrie's, wanted Jim to hire some consultants with XRA experience to help with implementation. So far, Jim had been able to stay under budget, but missing his deadlines and hiring some consultants would push him over his budget limit.

It didn't help that John Smith, the head of marketing, kept submitting requests for changes to the original specifications for the customer loyalty program. As specified in the project charter, the new system was supposed to track customer purchases, assign points for cumulative purchases, and allow points to be redeemed for "rewards" at local stores. The team had determined that those rewards would take the form of dollars-off coupons. Customers who enrolled in the program would be given accounts that they could access from Petrie's Web site. When they signed on, they could check their account activity to see how many points they had accumulated. If they had earned enough points, they were rewarded with a coupon. If they wanted to use the coupon, they would have to print it out on their home printers and bring it in to a store to use on a purchase. The team had decided long ago that keeping everything electronic saved Petrie's the considerable costs of printing and mailing coupons to customers.

But now marketing had put in a change request that would give customers a choice of having coupons mailed to them automatically or printing them from the Web site at home. This option, while nice for customers, added complexity to the XRA system implementation, and it added to the costs of operation. Jim had also learned yesterday from the marketing representative on his team, Sally Fukuyama, that now Smith wanted another change. Now he wanted customers to be able to use the coupons for online purchases from Petrie's Web site. This change added a whole new layer of complexity, affecting Petrie's existing systems for ordering online, in addition to altering yet again the implementation of the XRA CRM.

As if that wasn't enough, Carmen Sanchez was now telling Jim that she would not be ready to let the team pilot the system in her Irvine store. Carmen was saying her store would not be ready by the end of July. Maybe that wouldn't matter, since they were going to miss the go-live date for the pilot. But Carmen was hinting she would not be ready for months after that. It seemed as if she didn't want her store to be used for the pilot at all. Jim didn't understand it. But maybe he should try to find another store to use as the pilot site.

Jim was almost at his exit. Soon he would be at the office, and he would have to call Ella Whinston and tell her the status of the project. He would have to tell her that they would miss the go-live date, but in a way it didn't matter since he didn't have a pilot location to go live at. In addition to going over schedule, he was going to have to go over budget, too. He didn't see any way they would be ready for the pilot anytime close to when they had scheduled, unless he hired the consultants Sanjay wanted. And he would have to stop the latest change request filed by marketing. Even more important, he would have to keep the rumored change request, about using coupons for online purchases, from being submitted in the first place.

Maybe, just maybe, if he could hire the consultants, fight off the change requests, and get Carmen to cooperate, they might be ready to go live with a pilot in Irvine on October 15. That gave him four months to complete the project. He and the team were going to have to work hard to make that happen.

Jim realized he had missed his exit. Great, he thought, I hope it gets better from here.

Case Questions

1. Why don't information systems projects work out as planned? What causes the differences between the plan and reality?

2. Why is it important to document change requests? What happens if a development team doesn't?

3. When a project is late, do you think that adding more people to do the work helps or not? Justify your answer.

4. What is the role of a pilot project in information systems analysis? Why do you think the Petrie's team decided to do a pilot project before rolling out the customer loyalty system for everyone?

5. Information systems development projects are said to fail if they are late, go over budget, or do not contain all of the functionality they were designed to have. Is the customer loyalty program a failure? Justify your answer. If not, how can failure be prevented? Is it important to avert failure? Why or why not?

Appendix A

Object-Oriented Analysis and Design*

After studying this appendix, you should be able to:

- Define the following key terms: *association, class diagram, event, object, object class, operation, sequence diagram, state, state transition, Unified Modeling Language,* and *use case.*
- Describe the concepts and principles underlying the object-oriented approach.
- Develop a simple requirements model using use-case diagrams.
- Develop a simple object model using class diagrams.
- Develop simple requirements models using state and sequence diagrams.

The Object-Oriented Modeling Approach

In Chapters 1 through 10, you learned about traditional methods of systems analysis and design. You also learned how to use data-flow diagrams and entity-relationship diagrams to model your system. In some environments, an object-oriented rather than a traditional approach is needed. This appendix covers the techniques and graphical diagrams that systems analysts use for object-oriented analysis and design. As with the traditional modeling techniques, the deliverables from project activities using object-oriented modeling are data-flow and entity-relationship diagrams and repository descriptions. A major characteristic of these diagrams in object-oriented modeling is how tightly they are linked with each other. The object-oriented modeling approach provides several benefits, including:

1. The ability to tackle more challenging problem domains
2. Improved communication among users, analysts, designers, and programmers
3. Reusability of analysis, design, and programming results
4. Increased consistency among the models developed during object-oriented analysis, design, and programming

An object-oriented systems development life cycle consists of a progressively developing representation of a system component (what we will call an *object*) through the phases of analysis, design, and implementation. In the early stages of development, the model built is abstract, focusing on external qualities of the application system such as data structures, timing and sequence of processing operations, and how users interact with the system. As the model evolves, it becomes more and more detailed, shifting the focus to how the system will be built and how it should function.

In the analysis phase, a model of the real-world application is developed showing its important properties. It abstracts concepts from the application

---

*The original version of this appendix was written by Professor Atish P. Sinha.

domain and describes what the intended system must do, rather than how it will be done. The model specifies the functional behavior of the system, independent of concerns relating to the environment in which it is to be finally implemented. In the design phase, the application-oriented analysis model is adapted and refined to suit the target implementation environment. That is followed by the implementation phase, where the design is implemented using a programming language and/or a database management system. The techniques and notations that are incorporated into a standard object-oriented language are called the **Unified Modeling Language (UML).**

The techniques and notations within UML include:

- Use cases, which represent the functional requirements or the "what" of the system
- Class diagrams, which show the static structure of data and the operations that act on the data
- State diagrams, which represent dynamic models of how objects change their states in response to events
- Sequence diagrams, which represent dynamic models of interactions between objects

The Unified Modeling Language (UML) allows the modeler to specify, visualize, and construct the artifacts of software systems, as well as business models. It builds upon and unifies the semantics and notations of leading object-oriented methods and has been adopted as an industry standard.

The UML notation is useful for graphically depicting object-oriented analysis and design models. It not only allows you to specify the requirements of a system and capture the design decisions, but it also promotes communication among key persons involved in the development effort. A developer can use an analysis or design model expressed in the UML notation to communicate with domain experts, users, and other stakeholders. To represent a complex system effectively, the model developed needs to have a small set of independent views of the system. UML allows you to represent multiple views of a system using a variety of graphical diagrams, such as the use-case diagram, class diagram, state diagram, sequence diagram, and collaboration diagram. The underlying model integrates those views so that the system can be analyzed, designed, and implemented in a complete and consistent fashion.

We first show how to develop a use-case model during the requirements analysis phase. Next, we show how to model the static structure of the system using class and object diagrams. You then learn how to capture the dynamic aspects using state and sequence diagrams. Finally, we provide a brief description of component diagrams, which are generated during the design and implementation phases.

Use-Case Modeling

Use-case modeling is applied to analyze the functional requirements of a system. Use-case modeling is done in the early stages of system development (during the analysis phase) to help developers understand the functional requirements of the system without worrying about how those requirements will be implemented. The process is inherently iterative; developers need to involve the users in discussions throughout the model development process and finally come to an agreement on the requirements specification.

A use-case model consists of actors and use cases. An **actor** is an external entity that interacts with the system (similar to an external entity in data-flow diagramming). It is someone or something that exchanges information with the system. A **use case** represents a sequence of related actions initiated by an

Unified Modeling Language (UML)
A notation that allows the modeler to specify, visualize, and construct the artifacts of software systems, as well as business models.

Actor
An external entity that interacts with the system (similar to an external entity in data-flow diagramming).

Use case
A sequence of related actions initiated by an actor; it represents a specific way to use the system.

Appendix A   Object-Oriented Analysis and Design   **363**

actor; it is a specific way of using the system. An actor represents a role that a user can play. The actor's name should indicate that role. Actors help you to identify the use cases they carry out.

During the requirements analysis stage, the analyst sits down with the intended users of the system and makes a thorough analysis of what functions they desire from the system. These functions are represented as use cases. For example, a university registration system has a use case for class registration and another for student billing. These use cases, then, represent the typical interactions the system has with its users.

In UML, a use-case model is depicted diagrammatically, as in Figure A-1. This **use-case diagram** is for a university registration system, which is shown as a box. Outside the box are four actors—Student, Registration clerk, Instructor, and Bursar's office—that interact with the system (shown by the lines touching the actors). An actor is shown using a stick figure with its name below. Inside the box are four use cases—*Class registration*, *Registration for special class*, *Prereq courses not completed*, and *Student billing*—which are shown as ellipses with their names inside. These use cases are performed by the actors outside the system.

A use case is always initiated by an actor. For example, *Student billing* is initiated by the Bursar's office. A use case can interact with actors other than the one that initiated it. The *Student billing* use case, although initiated by the Bursar's office, interacts with the Students by mailing them tuition invoices. Another use case, *Class registration*, is carried out by two actors, Student and Registration clerk. This use case performs a series of related actions aimed at registering a student for a class.

The numbers on each end of the interaction lines indicate the number of instances of the use case with which the actor is associated. For example, the Bursar's office causes many (*) *Student billing* use-case instances to occur, each one for exactly one student.

A use case represents a complete functionality. You should not represent an individual action that is part of an overall function as a use case. For example, although submitting a registration form and paying tuition are two actions performed by users (students) in the university registration system, we do not show them as use cases, because they do not specify a complete course of events; each of these actions is executed only as part of an overall function or

Use-case diagram
A diagram that depicts the use cases and actors for a system.

FIGURE A-1
Use-case diagram for a university registration system drawn using Microsoft Visio.

use case. You can think of "Submit registration form" as one of the actions of the *Class registration* use case, and "Pay tuition" as one of the actions of the *Student billing* use case.

A use case may participate in relationships with other use cases. An *extends relationship*, shown in Microsoft Visio as a line with a hollow triangle pointing toward the extended use case and labeled with the "<<extends>>" symbol, extends a use case by adding new behaviors or actions. In Figure A-1, for example, the *Registration for special class* use case extends the *Class registration* use case by capturing the additional actions that need to be performed in registering a student for a special class. Registering for a special class requires prior permission of the instructor, in addition to the other steps carried out for a regular registration. You may think of *Class registration* as the basic course, which is always performed—independent of whether the extension is performed or not—and *Registration for special class* as an alternative course, which is performed only under special circumstances.

Another example of an extends relationship is that between the *Prereq courses not completed* and *Class registration* use cases. The former extends the latter in situations where a student registering for a class has not taken the prerequisite courses.

Figure A-2 shows a use-case diagram for Hoosier Burger. The Customer actor initiates the *Order food* use case; the other actor involved is the Service Person. A specific scenario would represent a customer placing an order with a service person.

So far you have seen one kind of relationship, extends, between use cases. Another kind of relationship is *included*, which arises when one use case references another use case. An include relationship is also shown diagrammatically as a dashed line with a hollow arrowhead pointing toward the use case that is being used; the line is labeled with the "<<include>>" symbol. In Figure A-2, for example, the include relationship between the *Reorder supplies* and *Track sales and inventory data* use cases implies that the former uses the latter while

FIGURE A-2
Use-case diagram for a Hoosier Burger system.

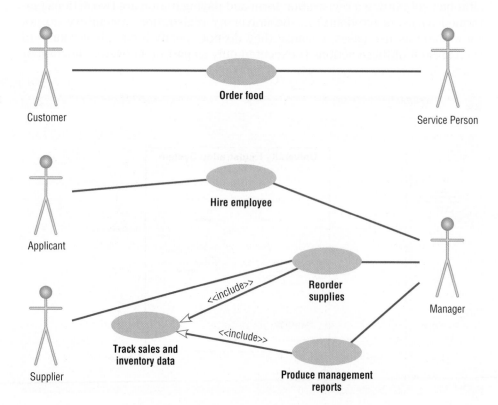

executing. Simply put, when a manager reorders supplies, the sales and inventory data are tracked. The same data are also tracked when management reports are produced, so there is another include relationship between the *Produce management reports* and *Track sales and inventory data* use cases.

The *Track sales and inventory data* is a generalized use case, representing the common behavior among the specialized use cases, *Reorder supplies* and *Produce management reports*. When *Reorder supplies* or *Produce management reports* is performed, the entire *Track sales and inventory data* is used.

Object Modeling: Class Diagrams

In the object-oriented approach, we model the world in objects. An **object** is an entity that has a well-defined role in the application domain and has state, behavior, and identity. An object is a concept, abstraction, or thing that makes sense in an application context. An object could be a tangible or visible entity (e.g., a person, place, or thing); it could be a concept or event (e.g., Department, Performance, Marriage, Registration, etc.); or it could be an artifact of the design process (e.g., User Interface, Controller, Scheduler, etc.).

An object has a state and exhibits behavior through operations that can examine or affect its state. The **state** of an object encompasses its properties (attributes and relationships) and the values those properties have, its **behavior** represents how an object acts and reacts. An object's state is determined by its attribute values and links to other objects. An object's behavior depends on its state and the operation being performed. An operation is simply an action that one object performs upon another in order to get a response.

Consider the example of a student, Mary Jones, represented as an object. The state of this object is characterized by its attributes, say, name, date of birth, year, address, and phone, and the values these attributes currently have. For example, name is "Mary Jones," year is "junior," and so on. Its behavior is expressed through operations such as calc-gpa, which is used to calculate a student's current grade point average. The Mary Jones object, therefore, packages both its state and its behavior together.

All objects have an identity, that is, no two objects are the same. For example, if two Student instances have the same name and date of birth, they are essentially two different objects. Even if those two instances have identical values for all the attributes, the objects maintain their separate identities. At the same time, an object maintains its own identity over its life. For example, if Mary Jones gets married and changes her name, address, and phone, she will still be represented by the same object.

You can depict an **object class** (a set of objects that shares a common structure and a common behavior) graphically in a class diagram as in Figure A-3A. A **class diagram** shows the static structure of an object-oriented model: the object classes, their internal structure, and the relationships in which they participate. In UML, a class is represented by a rectangle with three compartments separated by horizontal lines. The class name appears in the top compartment, the list of attributes in the middle compartment, and the list of operations in the bottom compartment of a box. The figure shows two classes, Student and Course, along with their attributes and operations.

Objects belonging to the same class may also participate in similar relationships with other objects, for example, all students register for courses and, therefore, the Student class can participate in a relationship called *registers-for* with another class called *Course*.

An **object diagram,** also known as an *instance diagram*, is a graph of instances that are compatible with a given class diagram. In Figure A-3B, we have shown an object diagram with two instances, one for each of the two

Object
An entity that has a well-defined role in the application domain and has state, behavior, and identity.

State
A condition that encompasses an object's properties (attributes and relationships) and the values those properties have.

Behavior
Represents how an object acts and reacts.

Object class
A set of objects that shares a common structure and a common behavior.

Class diagram
A diagram that shows the static structure of an object-oriented model: the object classes, their internal structure, and the relationships in which they participate.

Object diagram
A graph of instances that are compatible with a given class diagram.

FIGURE A-3
UML class and object diagrams:
(A) Class diagram showing two
classes, (B) Object diagram with
two instances.

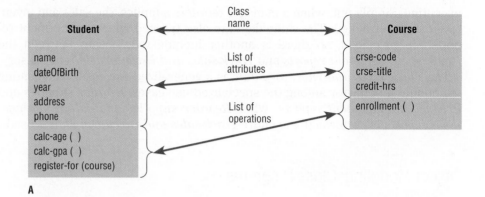

A

Student

name
dateOfBirth
year
address
phone

calc-age ( )
calc-gpa ( )
register-for (course)

Class
name

List of
attributes

List of
operations

Course

crse-code
crse-title
credit-hrs

enrollment ( )

B

Mary Jones:Student

name=Mary Jones
dateOfBirth=4/15/1978
year=junior
. . .

MIS385:Course

crse-code=MIS385
crse-title=Database Mgmt
credit-hrs=3

classes that appear in Figure A-3A. A static object diagram is an instance of a class diagram, providing a snapshot of the detailed state of a system at a point in time.

In an object diagram, an object is represented as a rectangle with two compartments. The names of the object and its class are underlined and shown in the top compartment using the following syntax: objectname:classname. The object's attributes and their values are shown in the second compartment. For example, we have an object called Mary Jones, who belongs to the Student class. The values of the name, dateOfBirth, and year attributes are also shown.

An **operation,** such as calc-gpa in Student (see Figure A-3A), is a function or a service that is provided by all the instances of a class. It is only through such operations that other objects can access or manipulate the information stored in an object. The operations, therefore, provide an external interface to a class; the interface presents the outside view of the class without showing its internal structure or how its operations are implemented. This technique of hiding the internal implementation details of an object from its external view is known as **encapsulation** or *information hiding.*

Representing Associations

An **association** is a relationship among object classes. As in the E-R model, the degree of an association relationship may be one (unary), two (binary), three (ternary), or higher (*n*-ary), as shown in Figure A-4. An association is depicted as a solid line between the participating classes. The end of an association where it connects to a class is called an **association role.** A role may be explicitly named with a label near the end of an association (see the "manager" role in Figure A-4A). The role name indicates the role played by the class attached to the end near which the name appears. For example, the manager role at one end of the Manages relationship implies that an employee can play the role of a manager.

Each role has a **multiplicity,** which indicates how many objects participate in a given association relationship. In a class diagram, a multiplicity specification is

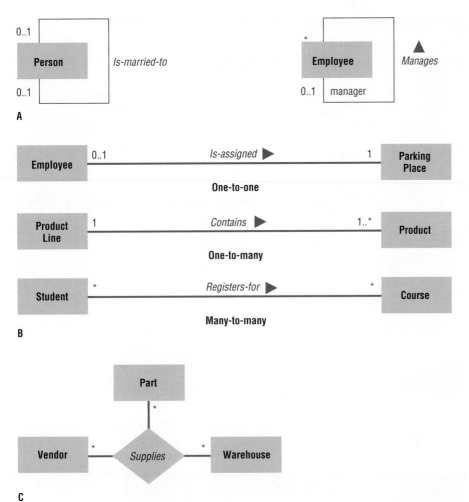

FIGURE A-4
Examples of association relationships of different degrees: (A) Unary, (B) Binary, (C) Ternary.

shown as a text string representing an interval (or intervals) of integers in the following format: lower bound..upper bound. The interval is considered to be closed, which means that the range includes both the lower and upper bounds. In addition to integer values, the upper bound of a multiplicity can be a star character (*), which denotes an infinite upper bound. If a single integer value is specified, it means that the range includes only that value.

The most common multiplicities in practice are 0..1, *, and 1. The 0..1 multiplicity indicates a minimum of 0 and a maximum of 1 (optional one), whereas * (or equivalently, 0..*) represents the range from 0 to infinity (optional many). A single 1 stands for 1..1, implying that exactly one object participates in the relationship (mandatory one).

Figure A-4B shows three binary relationships: *Is-assigned* (one-to-one), *Contains* (one-to-many), and *Registers-for* (many-to-many). A solid triangle next to an association name shows the direction in which the association is read. For example, the *Contains* association is read from Product Line to Product.

Figure A-4C shows a ternary relationship called *Supplies* among Vendor, Part, and Warehouse. As in an E-R diagram, we represent a ternary relationship using a diamond symbol and place the name of the relationship there.

The class diagram in Figure A-5A (known as a *static structure chart* in Microsoft Visio) shows binary associations between Student and Faculty,

FIGURE A-5
Examples of binary association
relationships: (A) University
example (a static structure chart
in Microsoft Visio), (B) Customer
order example.

A

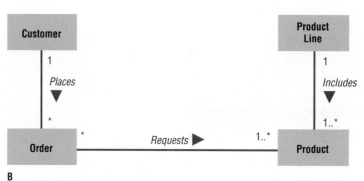

B

between Course and Course Offering, between Student and Course Offering, and between Faculty and Course Offering. The diagram shows that a student may have an adviser, whereas a faculty member may advise up to a maximum of ten students. Also, although a course may have multiple offerings, a given course offering is scheduled for exactly one course. Notice that a faculty member can play two roles: instructor and adviser. Figure A-5B shows another example of a class diagram, that for a customer order, using standard UML notation.

Representing Generalization

In the object-oriented approach, you can abstract the common features (attributes and operations) among multiple classes, as well as the relationships they participate in, into a more general class. This process is known as *generalization*. The classes that are generalized are called *subclasses*, and the class they are generalized into is called a *superclass*.

Consider the example shown in Figure A-6A. Here, the three types of employees are hourly employees, salaried employees, and consultants. The features that are shared by all employees—empName, empNumber, address, dateHired, and printLabel—are stored in the Employee superclass, whereas the

A

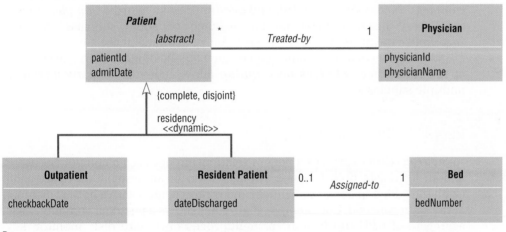

B

FIGURE A-6
Examples of
generalization,
inheritance, and
constraints: (A) Employee
superclass with three
subclasses, (B) Abstract
patient class with two
concrete subclasses.

features peculiar to a particular employee type are stored in the corresponding subclass (e.g., hourlyRate and computeWages of Hourly Employee). A generalization path is shown as a solid line from the subclass to the superclass, with a hollow arrowhead at the end of, and pointing toward, the superclass. You can show a group of generalization paths for a given superclass as a tree with multiple branches connecting the individual subclasses, and a shared segment with a hollow arrowhead pointing toward the superclass. In Figure A-6B, for instance, we have combined the generalization paths from Outpatient to Patient, and from Resident Patient to Patient, into a shared segment with an arrowhead pointing toward Patient.

You can indicate the basis of a generalization by specifying a discriminator next to the path. A discriminator shows which property of an object class is being abstracted by a particular generalization relationship. For example, in Figure A-6A, we discriminate the Employee class on the basis of employment type (hourly, salaried, consultant).

A subclass inherits all the features from its superclass. For example, in addition to its own special features—hourlyRate and computeWages—the Hourly Employee subclass inherits empName, empNumber, address, dateHired, and printLabel from Employee. An instance of Hourly Employee will store values for the attributes of Employee and Hourly Employee and, when requested, will apply the printLabel and computeWages operations.

Inheritance is one of the major advantages of using the object-oriented model. It allows code reuse: There is no need for a programmer to write code that has already been written for a superclass. The programmer writes only code that is unique to the new, refined subclass of an existing class. Proponents of the object-oriented model claim that code reuse results in productivity gains of several orders of magnitude.

Notice that in Figure A-6B the Patient class is in italics, implying that it is an abstract class. An **abstract class** is a class that has no direct instances but whose descendants may have direct instances. A class that can have direct instances (e.g., Outpatient or Resident Patient) is called a **concrete class.**

The Patient abstract class participates in a relationship called *Treated-by* with Physician, implying that all patients, outpatients and resident patients alike, are treated by physicians. In addition to this inherited relationship, the Resident Patient class has its own special relationship called *Assigned-to* with Bed, implying that only resident patients may be assigned to beds. Semantic constraints among the subclasses can be expressed using the *complete*, *incomplete*, *disjoint*, and *overlapping* keywords. *Complete* means that every instance must be an instance of some subclass, whereas *incomplete* means that an instance may be an instance of the superclass only. *Disjoint* means that no instance can be an instance of more than one subclass at the same time, whereas *overlapping* allows concurrent participation in multiple subclasses.

Representing Aggregation

An **aggregation** expresses a *part-of* relationship between a component object and an aggregate object. It is a stronger form of an association relationship (with the added "part-of" semantics) and is represented with a hollow diamond at the aggregate end. For example, Figure A-7 shows a personal computer as an aggregate of CPU (up to four for multiprocessors), hard disk, monitor, keyboard, and other objects. Note that aggregation involves a set of distinct object instances, one of which contains or is composed of the others. For example, a Personal Computer object is related to (consists of) CPU objects, one of its parts. In contrast, generalization relates to object classes: An object (e.g., Mary Jones) is simultaneously an instance of its class (e.g., Graduate Student) and its superclass (e.g., Student).

Abstract class
A class that has no direct instances but whose descendants may have direct instances.

Concrete class
A class that can have direct instances.

Aggregation
A *part-of* relationship between a component object and an aggregate object.

FIGURE A-7
Example of aggregation.

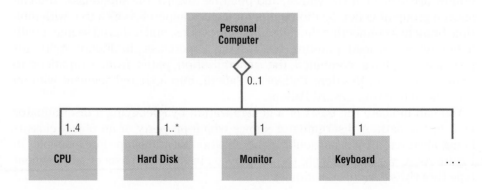

Dynamic Modeling: State Diagrams

In this section, we show you how to model the dynamic aspects of a system from the perspective of state transitions. In UML, state transitions are shown using state diagrams. A state diagram depicts the various state transitions or changes an object can experience during its lifetime, along with the events that cause those transitions.

A *state* is a condition during the life of an object during which it satisfies some condition(s), performs some action(s), or waits for some event(s). The state changes when the object receives some event; the object is said to undergo a **state transition.** The state of an object depends on its attribute values and links to other objects.

An **event** is something that takes place at a certain point in time. It is a noteworthy occurrence that triggers a state transition. Some examples of events are: a customer places an order, a student registers for a class, a person applies for a loan, and a company hires a new employee. For the purpose of modeling, an event is considered to be instantaneous, though, in reality, it might take some time. A state, on the other hand, spans a period of time. An object remains in a particular state for some time before transitioning to another state. For example, an Employee object might be in the Part-time state (as specified in its employment-status attribute) for a few months, before transitioning to a Full-time state, based on a recommendation from the manager (an event).

In UML, a state is shown as a rectangle with rounded corners. In Figure A-8, for example, we have shown different states of a Student object, such as Inquiry, Applied, Approved, Rejected, and so on. This state diagram shows how the object transitions from an initial state (shown as a small, solid, filled circle) to other states when certain events occur or when certain conditions are satisfied. When a new Student object is created, it is in its initial state. The event that created the object, inquires, and transitions it from the initial state to the Inquiry state. When a student in the Inquiry state submits an application for admission,

State transition
The changes in the attributes of an object or in the links an object has with other objects.

Event
Something that takes place at a certain point in time; it is a noteworthy occurrence that triggers a state transition.

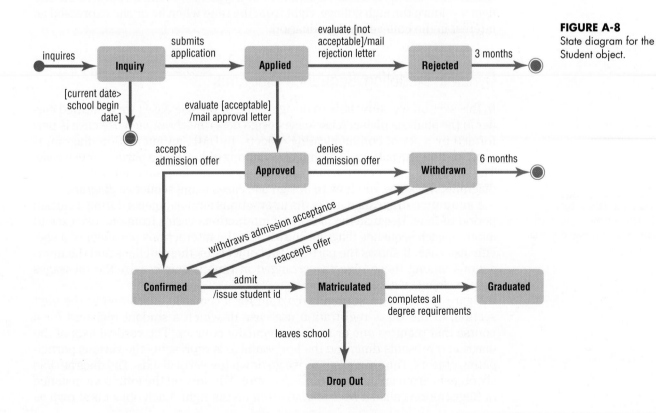

FIGURE A-8
State diagram for the Student object.

the object transitions to the Applied state. The transition is shown as a solid arrow from Inquiry (the source state) to Applied (the target state), labeled with the name of the event, Submits application.

A transition may be labeled with a string consisting of the event name, parameters of the event, guard condition, and action expression. A transition, however, does not have to show all the elements; it shows only those relevant to the transition. For example, we label the transition from Inquiry to Applied with simply the event name. But, for the transition from Applied to Approved, we show the event name (evaluate), the guard condition (acceptable), and the action taken by the transition (mail approval letter). It simply means that an applicant is approved for admission if the admissions office evaluates the application and finds it acceptable. If acceptable, a letter of approval is mailed to the student. The guard condition is shown within square brackets, and the action is specified after the "/" symbol.

If the evaluate event results in a not-acceptable decision (another guard condition), a rejection letter is mailed (an action), and the Student object undergoes a state transition from the Applied to the Rejected state. It remains in that state for three months before reaching the final state. In the diagram, we have shown an elapsed-time event, three months, indicating the amount of time the object waits in the current state before transitioning. The final state is shown as a bull's eye: a small, solid, filled circle surrounded by another circle. After transitioning to the final state, the Student object ceases to exist.

Notice that the Student object may transition to the final state from two other states: Inquiry and Withdrawn. For the transition from Inquiry, we have not specified any event name or action, but we have shown a guard condition, current date > school begin date. This condition implies that the Student object ceases to exist beyond the first day of school unless, of course, the object has moved in the meantime from the Inquiry state to some other state.

The state diagram shown in Figure A-8 captures all the possible states of a Student object, the state transitions, the events or conditions that trigger those transitions, and the associated actions. For a typical student, it captures the student's sojourn through college, right from the time when he or she expressed an interest in the college until graduation.

Dynamic Modeling: Sequence Diagrams

In this section we show how to design some of the use cases we identified earlier in the analysis phase. A use-case design describes how each use case is performed by a set of communicating objects. In UML, an interaction diagram is used to show the pattern of interactions among objects for a particular use case. The two types of interaction diagrams are sequence diagrams and collaboration diagrams. We show you how to design use cases using sequence diagrams.

Sequence diagram
A depiction of the interactions among objects during a certain period of time.

A **sequence diagram** depicts the interactions among objects during a certain period of time. Because the pattern of interactions varies from one use case to another, each sequence diagram shows only the interactions pertinent to a specific use case. It shows the participating objects by their lifelines and the interactions among those objects—arranged in time sequence—by the messages they exchange with one another.

Figure A-9 shows a sequence diagram for a scenario, discussed in the next section, of the Class registration use case in which a student registers for a course that requires one or more prerequisite courses. The vertical axis of the diagram represents time, and the horizontal axis represents the various participating objects. Time increases as we go down the vertical axis. The diagram has six objects, from an instance of Registration Window on the left, to an instance of Registration called *a New Registration* on the right. Each object is shown as

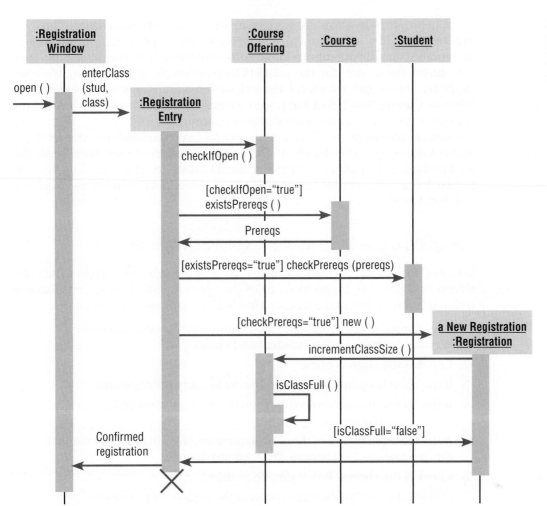

FIGURE A-9
Sequence diagram
for a class registration
scenario with
prerequisites.

a vertical line called the *lifeline;* the lifeline represents the object's existence over a certain period of time. An object symbol—a box with the object's name underlined—is placed at the head of each lifeline.

A thin rectangle, superimposed on the lifeline of an object, represents an activation of the object. An **activation** shows the time period during which the object performs an operation, either directly or through a call to some subordinate operation. The top of the rectangle, which is at the tip of an incoming message, indicates the initiation of the activation, and the bottom, its completion.

Objects communicate with one another by sending messages. A message is shown as a solid arrow from the sending object to the receiving object. For example, the checkIfOpen message is represented by an arrow from the Registration Entry object to the Course Offering object.

There are different types of messages. Each type is indicated in a diagram by a particular type of arrowhead. A **synchronous message,** shown as a solid arrowhead, is one for which the caller has to wait for the receiving object to complete executing the called operation before it itself can resume execution. An example of a synchronous message is checkIfOpen. When a Registration Entry object sends this message to a Course Offering object, the latter responds by executing an operation called checkIfOpen (same name as the message). After the execution of this operation is completed, control is transferred back to the calling operation within Registration Entry with a return value of "true" or "false."

Activation
The time period during which an object performs an operation.

Synchronous message
A type of message in which the caller has to wait for the receiving object to finish executing the called operation before it can resume execution itself.

A synchronous message always has an associated return message. The message may provide the caller with some return value(s) or simply acknowledge to the caller that the operation called has been successfully completed. We have not shown the return for the checkIfOpen message; it is implicit. We have explicitly shown the return for the existsPrereqs message from Registration Entry to Course. The tail of the return message is aligned with the base of the activation rectangle for the existsPrereqs operation.

A **simple message** simply transfers control from the sender to the recipient without describing the details of the communication. As we have seen, the return of a synchronous message is a simple message. The "open" message in Figure A-9 is also a simple message; it simply transfers control to the Registration Window object.

Simple message
A message that transfers control
from the sender to the recipient
without describing the details
of the communication.

Designing a Use Case with a Sequence Diagram

Let's see how we can design use cases. We will discuss the sequence diagram, shown in Figure A-9, for an instance of the *Class registration* use case, one in which the course has prerequisites. Here's a description of this scenario:

1. Registration Clerk opens the registration window and enters the registration information (student and class).
2. Check if the class is open.
3. If the class is open, check if the course has any prerequisites.
4. If the course has prerequisites, then check if the student has taken all of those prerequisites.
5. If the student has taken those prerequisites, then register the student for the class, and increment the class size by one.
6. Check if the class is full; if not, do nothing.
7. Display the confirmed registration in the registration window.

In response to the "open" message from Registration Clerk (external actor), the Registration Window pops up on the screen, and the registration information is entered. A new Registration Entry object is created, which then sends a checkIfOpen message to the Course Offering object (representing the class the student wants to register for). The two possible return values are true or false. In this scenario, the assumption is that the class is open. We have, therefore placed a guard condition, checkIfOpen = "true," on the message existsPrereqs. The guard condition ensures that the message will be sent only if the class is open. The return value is a list of prerequisites; the return is shown explicitly in the diagram.

For this scenario, the fact that the course has prerequisites is captured by the guard condition, existsPrereqs = "true." If this condition is satisfied, the Registration Entry object sends a checkPrereqs message, with "prereqs" as an argument, to the Student object to determine if the student has taken those prerequisites. If the student has taken all the prerequisites, the Registration Entry object creates an object called a *New Registration*, which denotes a new registration.

Next, a New Registration sends a message called incrementClassSize to Course Offering in order to increase the class size by one. The incrementClassSize operation within Course Offering then calls upon isClassFull, another operation within the same object. Assuming that the class is not full, the isClassFull operation returns control to the calling operation with a value of "false." Next, the incrementClassSize operation completes and relinquishes control to the calling operation within a New Registration.

Finally, on receipt of the return message from a New Registration, the Registration Entry object destroys itself (the destruction is shown with a large X) and sends a confirmation of the registration to the Registration Window. Note that Registration Entry is not a persistent object; it is created on the fly to control the sequence of interactions and is deleted as soon as the registration is completed. In between, it calls several other operations within other objects by sequencing the following messages: checkIfOpen, existsPrereqs, checkPrereqs, and new.

Apart from the Registration Entry object, *a New Registration* is also created during the time period captured in the diagram. The messages that created these objects are represented by arrows pointing directly toward the object symbols. For example, the arrow representing the message called *new* is connected to the object symbol for a New Registration. The lifeline of such an object begins when the message that creates it is received (the vertical line is hidden behind the activation rectangle).

Moving to Design

When you move to design, you start with the existing set of analysis models and keep adding technical details. For example, you might add several interface classes to your class diagrams to model the windows that you will later implement using a GUI graphical user interface development tool such as Visual C# or Java. You would define all the operations in detail, specifying the procedures, signatures, and return values completely. If you decide to use a relational DBMS, you need to map the object classes and relationships to tables, primary keys, and foreign keys. The models generated during the design phase will therefore be much more detailed than the analysis models.

Figure A-10 shows a three-layered architecture, consisting of a User Interface package, a Business Objects package, and a Database package. The packages represent different generic subsystems of an information system. The dashed arrows represent the dependencies among the packages. For example, the User Interface package depends on the Business Objects package; the packages participate in a client-supplier relationship. If you make changes to some of the business objects, the interface (e.g., screens) might change.

A package consists of a group of classes. Classes within a package are cohesive. That is, they are tightly coupled. The packages themselves should be loosely coupled so that changes in one package do not affect the other packages a great deal. In the architecture of Figure A-10, the User Interface package contains all the windows, the Business Objects package contains the problem-domain objects that you identified during analysis, and the Database package contains a Persistence class for data storage and retrieval. In the university registration system that we considered earlier, the User Interface package could include Microsoft Windows class libraries for developing different types of windows. The Business Objects package would include all the domain classes, such as Student, Course, Course Offering, Registration, and so on. If you are using an SQL server, the classes in the Database package would contain operations for data storage, retrieval, and update (all using SQL commands).

During design, you would also refine the other analysis models. For example, you may need to show the interaction between a new window object you introduced during design and the other existing objects in a sequence diagram. Also, once you have selected a programming language for each of the operations shown in the sequence diagram, you should provide the exact names that you will be using in the program, along with the names of all the arguments.

In addition to the types of diagrams you have seen so far, two other types of diagrams—component diagrams and deployment diagrams—are pertinent during the design phase. A **component diagram** shows the software components or modules and their dependencies. For example, you can draw a component diagram showing the modules for source code, binary code, and executable

Component diagram
A diagram that shows the software components or modules and their dependencies.

FIGURE A-10
An example of UML packages and dependencies.

FIGURE A-11

A component diagram for class registration.

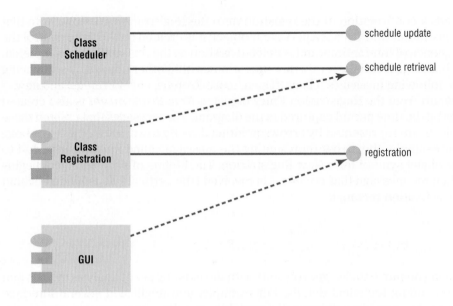

code and their dependency relationships. Figure A-11 shows a component diagram for the university registration system. In this figure, three software components have been identified: Class Scheduler, Class Registration, and GUI. The small circles in the diagram represent interfaces. The registration interface, for example, is used to register a student for a class, and the schedule update interface is used for updating a class schedule.

Another type of diagram, a deployment diagram (not illustrated), shows how the software components, processes, and objects are deployed into the physical architecture of the system. It shows the configuration of the hardware units (e.g., computers, communication devices) and how the software (components, objects, etc.) is distributed across the units. For example, a deployment diagram for the university registration system might show the topology of nodes in a client/server architecture and the deployment of the Class Registration component to a Windows NT Server and of the GUI component to client workstations.

When the design phase is complete, you move on to the implementation phase where you code the system. If you are using an object-oriented programming language, translating the design models to code should be relatively straightforward. Programming of the system is followed by testing. The system is developed after going through multiple iterations, with each new iteration providing a better version of the system. The models that you developed during analysis, design, and implementation are navigable in both directions.

Key Points Review

1. **Define the following key terms: *association, class diagram, event, object, object class, operation, sequence diagram, state, state transition, Unified Modeling Language, and use case.***

   An association is a relationship among object classes. A class diagram shows the static structure of an object-oriented model: the object classes, their internal structure, and the relationships in which they participate. An event is something that takes place at a certain point in time; it is a noteworthy occurrence that triggers a state transition. An object is an entity that has a well-defined role in the application domain and has state, behavior, and identity; an object class is a set of objects that share a common structure and a common behavior. An operation is a function or a service that is provided by all the instances of a class. A sequence diagram depicts the interactions among objects during a certain period of time. A state encompasses an object's properties (attributes and relationships) and the values those properties have; a state transition is the changes the attributes of an object or the links an object has with other objects. The Unified Modeling Language (UML) is a notation that allows the modeler to specify, visualize, and construct the artifacts of software systems, as well as business models. A use case is a complete sequence of related actions initiated by an actor; it represents a specific way to use the system.

2. **Describe the concepts and principles underlying the object-oriented approach.**

    The fundamental concept of the object-oriented approach is that we can model the world as a set of related objects with their associated states—attributes and behaviors. Through different uses of an object, the object's state changes. The internal implementation details of an object can be hidden from external view by the technique of encapsulation. A class of objects may be a superset or subset of other classes of objects, forming a generalization hierarchy or network of object classes. In this way an object may inherit the properties of the superclasses to which it is related. An object may also be a part of another more aggregate object.

3. **Develop a simple requirements model using use-case diagrams.**

    A use-case diagram consists of a set of related actions initiated by actors. A use case represents a complete functionality, not an individual action. A use case may extend another use case by adding new behaviors or actions. A use case may use another use case when one use case calls on another use case.

4. **Develop a simple object model using class diagrams.**

    A class diagram shows the static structure of object classes, their internal structure, and the relationships in which they participate. The structure of a class includes its name, attributes, and operations. Each object has an object identifier separate from its attributes. An object class can be either abstract (having no direct instances) or concrete (having direct instances). Object classes may have associations similar to relationships in the entity-relationship notation with multiplicity and degree. The end of an association where it connects to a class is labeled with an association role. A class diagram can also show the generalization relationships between object classes, and subclasses can be complete or incomplete and disjoint or overlapping. In addition, a class diagram may show the aggregation association among object classes.

5. **Develop simple requirements models using state and sequence diagrams.**

    State and sequence diagrams show the dynamic behavior of a system. A state diagram shows all the possible states of an object and the events that trigger an object to transition from one state to another. A state transition occurs by changes in the attributes of an object or in the links an object has with other objects. An object begins in an initial state and ends in a final state. A state may have a guard condition, which checks that certain object properties exist before the transition may occur. When a state transition occurs, specified actions may take place. A sequence diagram depicts the interactions among objects during a certain period of time. The vertical axis of the diagram represents time (going down the axis), and the horizontal axis represents the various participating objects. Each object has a lifeline, which represents the object's existence over a certain period. Objects communicate with one another by sending messages. Among the different types of messages are synchronous (for which the caller has to wait for the receiving object to complete the called operation before the caller can resume execution) and simple (for which control is transferred from the sender to the recipient).

Key Terms Checkpoint

Here are the key terms from the appendix. The page where each term is first explained is in parentheses after the term.

1. Abstract class (p. 370)
2. Activation (p. 373)
3. Actor (p. 362)
4. Aggregation (p. 370)
5. Association (p. 366)
6. Association role (p. 366)
7. Behavior (p. 365)
8. Class diagram (p. 365)
9. Component diagram (p. 375)
10. Concrete class (p. 370)
11. Encapsulation (p. 366)
12. Event (p. 371)
13. Multiplicity (p. 366)
14. Object (p. 365)
15. Object class (p. 365)
16. Object diagram (p. 365)
17. Operation (p. 366)
18. Sequence diagram (p. 372)
19. Simple message (p. 374)
20. State (p. 365)
21. State transition (p. 371)
22. Synchronous message (p. 373)
23. Unified Modeling Language (UML) (p. 362)
24. Use case (p. 362)
25. Use-case diagram (p. 363)

Match each of the key terms above with the definition that best fits it.

_____ 1. A diagram that depicts the use cases and actors for a system.

_____ 2. Something that takes place at a certain point in time; it is a noteworthy occurrence that triggers a state transition.

_____ 3. The time period during which an object performs an operation.

_____ 4. A set of objects that share a common structure and a common behavior.

_____ 5. A notation that allows the modeler to specify, visualize, and construct the artifacts of software systems, as well as business models.

_____ 6. A type of message in which the caller has to wait for the receiving object to finish executing the called operation before it can resume execution itself.

_____ 7. The end of an association where it connects to a class.

_____ 8. A graph of instances that are compatible with a given class diagram.

_____ 9. The changes in the attributes of an object or in the links an object has with other objects.

_____ 10. An entity that has a well-defined role in the application domain and has state, behavior, and identity.

_____ 11. A diagram that shows the software components or modules and their dependencies.

_____ 12. An external entity that interacts with the system (similar to an external entity in data-flow diagramming).

_____ 13. A complete sequence of related actions initiated by an actor; it represents a specific way to use the system.

_____ 14. A *part-of* relationship between a component object and an aggregate object.

_____ 15. An indication of how many objects participate in a given relationship.

_____ 16. The technique of hiding the internal implementation details of an object from its external view.

_____ 17. A function or a service that is provided by all the instances of a class.

_____ 18. A condition that encompasses an object's properties (attributes and relationships) and the values those properties have.

_____ 19. Represents how an object acts and reacts.

_____ 20. A diagram that shows the static structure of an object-oriented model: the object classes, their internal structure, and the relationships in which they participate.

_____ 21. A relationship among object classes.

_____ 22. A class that has no direct instances but whose descendants may have direct instances.

_____ 23. A class that can have direct instances.

_____ 24. A depiction of the interactions among objects during a certain period of time.

_____ 25. A message that transfers control from the sender to the recipient without describing the details of the communication.

Review Questions

1. Compare and contrast the object-oriented analysis and design models with structured analysis and design models.
2. Give an example of an abstract use case. Your example should involve at least two other use cases and show how they are related to the abstract use case.
3. Explain the use of association role for an association on a class diagram.
4. Give an example of generalization. Your example should include at least one superclass and three subclasses, and a minimum of one attribute and one operation for each of the classes. Indicate the discriminator and specify the semantic constraints among the subclasses.
5. Give an example of aggregation. Your example should include at least one aggregate object and three component objects. Specify the multiplicities at each end of all the aggregation relationships.
6. Give an example of state transition. Your example should show how the state of the object undergoes a transition based on some event.

Problems and Exercises

1. The use-case diagram shown in Figure A-1 captures the Student billing function but does not contain any function for accepting tuition payment from students. Revise the diagram to capture this functionality. Also, express some common behavior among two use cases in the revised diagram by using include relationships.
2. Suppose that the employees of the university are not billed for tuition. Their spouses do not get a full-tuition waiver but pay for only 25 percent of

the total tuition. Extend the use-case diagram of Figure A-1 to capture these situations.

3. Draw a class diagram, showing the relevant classes, attributes, operations, and relationships for the following situation (if you believe that you need to make additional assumptions, clearly state them for each situation).

A laboratory has several chemists who work on one or more projects. Chemists may also use certain kinds of equipment on each project. Attributes of Chemist include name and phoneNo. Attributes of Project include projectName and startDate. Attributes of Equipment include serialNo and cost. The organization wishes to record assignDate (the date when a given equipment item was assigned to a particular chemist working on a specified project) and totalHours (the total number of hours the chemist has used the equipment for the project). The organization also wants to track the usage of each type of equipment by a chemist. It does so by computing the average number of hours the chemist has used that equipment on all assigned projects. A chemist must be assigned to at least one project and to one equipment item. A given equipment item need not be assigned, and a given project need not be assigned either a chemist or an equipment item.

4. An organization has been entrusted with developing a Registration and Title system that maintains information about all vehicles registered in a particular state. For each vehicle that is registered with the office, the system has to store the name, address, telephone number of the owner, the start date and end date of the registration, plate information (issuer, year, type, and number), sticker (year, type, and number), and registration fee. In addition, the following information

is maintained about the vehicles themselves: the number, year, make, model, body style, gross weight, number of passengers, diesel powered (yes/no), color, cost, and mileage. If the vehicle is a trailer, diesel powered and number of passengers are not relevant. For travel trailers, the body number and length must be known. The system needs to maintain information on the luggage capacity for a car, maximum cargo capacity and maximum towing capacity for a truck, and horsepower for a motorcycle. The system issues registration notices to owners of vehicles whose registrations are due to expire after two months. When the owner reviews the registration, the system updates the registration information on the vehicle.

a. Develop a static object model by drawing a class diagram that shows all the object classes, attributes, operations, relationships, and multiplicities. For each operation, show its argument list.

b. Draw a state diagram that captures all the possible states of a Vehicle object, right from the time the vehicle was manufactured until it goes to the junkyard. In drawing the diagram, you may make any necessary assumptions, as long as they are realistic.

c. Select any state or event from the high-level state diagram that you have drawn and show its fine structure (substates and their transitions) in a lower-level diagram.

d. One of the use cases for this application is *Issue registration renewal notice*, which is performed once every day. Draw a sequence diagram, in generic form, showing all possible object interactions for this use case.

Appendix B

Agile Methodologies

After studying this appendix, you should be able to:

- Define Agile Methodologies.
- Explain when to use Agile Methodologies and when to use engineering-based approaches to systems development.
- Define eXtreme Programming.
- Discuss the Agile Methodologies approach to systems requirements determination, design specifications, and the combination of coding and testing.

The Trend to Agile Methodologies

Systems analysis and design, or systems development, has gone through three major phases since its inception. The first phase was undisciplined, where developers were seen as geniuses and artists. This phase was marked by a lack of documentation and development tools and by a high degree of dependence on the developer for the continued ongoing operation of the system he or she had created. As computing became more sophisticated, so, too, did the requirements for business applications. More and more, businesses began to see their systems as investments. The era of the developer-as-artist was replaced with the era of developer-as-engineer. Seeing information systems development as engineering brought a great deal of discipline to the theory and practice of developing systems. Principles from engineering, such as factoring and decomposition, as well as prototyping were applied to the systems development process. Documentation, rigorous testing, structured tools and techniques, and computer-based tools all became standard parts of analysis and design. This engineering-based view spawned the structured analysis and structured design approaches to development from which many of the tools and techniques used in this book are derived.

Although the engineering approach is still in use today, to many critics it has become bloated and slow, no longer as useful in a global economy that runs on Internet time. The convergence of the object-oriented approach and the Internet economy set the stage for the current major phase in systems development. Relying on object-orientation and the need for speed, the new approach sacrifices the milestones and multiple phases of the engineering approach, favoring instead close cooperation between developers and clients, combining many life cycle phases into few phases, and having multiple rapid releases of software. Although many individual methods reflect the new approach, collectively they are called the **Agile Methodologies.**

In this appendix, you will be introduced broadly to the Agile Methodologies, and we will focus on the most well-known Agile Methodology, eXtreme Programming, as an example of the approach. First, we describe Agile Methodologies and how they differ from the traditional engineering-based systems development approaches presented in the rest of this book. We describe when Agile methods are appropriate and when traditional approaches fit best. We then discuss eXtreme Programming and its key principles. The remainder of the

Agile Methodologies
A family of development methodologies characterized by short iterative cycles and extensive testing; active involvement of users for establishing, prioritizing, and verifying requirements; and a focus on small teams of talented, experienced programmers.

appendix illustrates how requirements determination, design specifications, and combining coding and testing are handled in the Agile Methodologies, and what has been learned about Agile Methodologies in practice.

Agile Methodologies

Many different individual methodologies come under the umbrella of Agile Methodologies, including the Crystal family of methodologies, Adaptive Software Development, Scrum, Feature Driven Development, and eXtreme Programming.

In February 2001, many of the proponents of these alternative approaches to systems analysis and design met in Utah in the United States to reach a consensus on many of the underlying principles their various approaches contained. This consensus turned into a document they called "The Agile Manifesto" (Figure B-1). The Agile Methodologies share three key principles: (1) a focus on adaptive rather

FIGURE B-1
The Agile Manifesto.

(From Fowler & Highsmith, 2001. Used by permission.) © 2001, the above authors. This declaration may be freely copied in any form, but only in its entirety through this notice.

The Manifesto for Agile Software Development

Seventeen anarchists* agree:

We are uncovering better ways of developing software by doing it and helping others do it. Through this work we have come to value:

- Individuals and interactions over processes and tools
- Working software over comprehensive documentation
- Customer collaboration over contract negotiation
- Responding to change over following a plan

That is, while we value the items on the right in the list above, we value the items on the left more.

We follow the following principles:

- Our highest priority is to satisfy the customer through early and continuous delivery of valuable software.
- Welcome changing requirements, even late in development. Agile processes harness change for the customer's competitive advantage.
- Deliver working software frequently, from a couple of weeks to a couple of months, with a preference to the shorter timescale.
- Business people and developers work together daily throughout the project.
- Build projects around motivated individuals. Give them the environment and support they need, and trust them to get the job done.
- The most efficient and effective method of conveying information to and within a development team is face-to-face conversation.
- Working software is the primary measure of progress.
- Agile processes promote sustainable development. The sponsors, developers, and users should be able to maintain a constant pace indefinitely.
- Continuous attention to technical excellence and good design enhances agility.
- Simplicity—the art of maximizing the amount of work not done—is essential.
- The best architectures, requirements, and designs emerge from self-organizing teams.
- At regular intervals, the team reflects on how to become more effective, then tunes and adjusts its behavior accordingly.

*Kent Beck, Mike Beedle, Arie van Bennekum, Alistair Cockburn, Ward Cunningham, Martin Fowler, James Grenning, Jim Highsmith, Andrew Hunt, Ron Jeffries, Jon Kern, Brian Marick, Robert C. Martin, Steve Mellor, Ken Schwaber, Jeff Sutherland, Dave Thomas (www.agileAlliance.org)

than predictive methodologies, (2) a focus on people rather than roles, and (3) a self-adaptive process.

The Agile Methodologies group argues that software development methodologies adapted from engineering generally do not fit well with the reality of developing software. In the engineering disciplines, such as civil engineering, requirements tend to be well understood. Once the creative and difficult work of design is completed, construction becomes more predictable. In addition, construction may account for as much as 90 percent of the total project effort. For software, on the other hand, requirements are rarely understood well, and they change continually during the lifetime of the project. Construction may account for as little as 15 percent of the total project effort, leaving design to constitute as much as 50 percent of the project effort. Applying techniques that work well for predictable, stable projects, such as building a bridge, tend not to work well for fluid design-heavy projects, such as writing software, say the Agile Methodology proponents. What are needed are methodologies that embrace change and that are able to deal with a lack of predictability. One mechanism for dealing with a lack of predictability, which all Agile Methodologies share, is iterative development. Iterative development focuses on the frequent production of working versions of a system that have a subset of the total number of required features. Iterative development provides feedback to customers and developers alike.

Second, the focus on people in Agile Methodologies is a focus on individuals rather than on the roles that people perform. The roles that people fill, of systems analyst or tester or manager, are not as important as the individuals who fill those roles. Fowler argues that the focus on engineering principles applied to systems development has resulted in a view of people as interchangeable units instead of a view of people as talented individuals, each of whom has something unique to bring to the development team.

Third, the Agile Methodologies also promote a self-adaptive software development process. As software is developed, the process used to develop it should be refined and improved. Development teams can discover these improvements through a review process, often associated with the completion of iterations. The implication is that, as processes are adapted, you would not expect to find a single monolithic methodology within a given corporation or enterprise. Instead, you would find many variations of the methodology, each of which reflects the particular talents and experience of the team using it.

Agile Methodologies are not for every project. An Agile or adaptive process is recommended if your project involves:

- Unpredictable or dynamic requirements
- Responsible and motivated developers
- Customers who understand and will get involved

On the other hand, a more engineering-oriented predictable process may be necessary if the development team exceeds 100 people and the project is operating under a fixed-price or fixed-scope contract. Thus, organizations need various approaches for developing information systems, depending upon the characteristics of the system and the development team.

Although not universally agreed on, the key differences in development approaches are listed in Table B-1, based on work by Boehm and Turner (2004). These five key factors can be used to help determine which development approach would work best for a particular project.

As you can see from Table B-1, the size of the systems development project is a key indicator of whether Agile Methodologies are appropriate. Agile methods fit much better with smaller projects than with larger ones. Traditional methods are preferred for large projects and for those dealing with safety-critical systems, such as the control systems for nuclear power plants and missile

TABLE B-1: Five Critical Factors That Distinguish Agile and Traditional Approaches to Systems Development

Factor	Agile Methods	Engineering-Based Methods
Size	Well-matched to small products and teams. Reliance on tacit knowledge limits scalability.	Methods evolved to handle large products and teams. Hard to tailor down to small projects.
Criticality	Untested on safety-critical products. Potential difficulties with simple design and lack of documentation.	Methods evolved to handle highly critical products. Hard to tailor down to low-criticality products.
Dynamism	Simple design and continuous refactoring are excellent for highly dynamic environments but are a source of potentially expensive rework for highly stable environments.	Detailed plans and Big Design Up Front are excellent for highly stable environments but are a source of expensive rework for highly dynamic environments.
Personnel	Requires continuous presence of a critical mass of scarce experts. Risky to use non-Agile people.	Needs a critical mass of scarce experts during project definition but can work with fewer later in the project, unless the environment is highly dynamic.
Culture	Thrives in a culture where people feel comfortable and empowered by having many degrees of freedom (thriving on chaos).	Thrives in a culture where people feel comfortable and empowered by having their roles defined by clear practices and procedures (thriving on order).

Source: Boehm & Turner, 2004. Used by permission.

launch pads. The reason for using engineering-based methods for safety-critical systems is that they have been proven to work well with such systems. Another variable that differentiates between Agile and traditional approaches is dynamism. Agile methods work well when the target system is to operate in a volatile and fluid environment, where business conditions are turbulent and frequently changing. Because of the large amount of planning that is part of them, traditional approaches work best where the system being developed operates in a stable environment. You read about how Agile Methodologies stress the importance of individuals rather than roles. The implication is that an Agile approach may not work so well unless there is a critical mass of agility experts. Finally, Agile methods will work best in an organization culture that thrives on uncertainty, rapid change, and chaos. Traditional methods work where organizational roles are clearly defined and change little.

One of the best-known and most written-about Agile Methodologies is called *eXtreme Programming*. Developed by Kent Beck in the late 1990s, eXtreme Programming illustrates many of the central philosophies of this new approach to systems development. We use eXtreme Programming as an example of the central ideas common to many Agile methods and present it next in more detail.

eXtreme Programming

eXtreme Programming is distinguished by its short development cycles, its incremental planning approach, its focus on automated tests written by programmers and customers to monitor the process of development, and its reliance on an evolutionary approach to development that lasts throughout the lifetime of the system. One of the key emphases of eXtreme Programming is its use of two-person programming teams, described here, and having a customer on-site during the development process. The relevant parts of eXtreme Programming that relate to design specifications are: (1) how planning, analysis, design, and construction are all fused together into a single phase of activity, and (2) its unique way of capturing and presenting system requirements and design specifications. All phases of the life cycle converge together into a series of activities based on the basic processes of coding, testing, listening, and designing.

Under this approach, coding and testing are intimately related parts of the same process. The programmers who write the code also write the tests. The emphasis is on testing those things that can break or go wrong, not on testing everything. Code is tested soon after it is written. The overall philosophy behind eXtreme Programming is that code will be integrated into the system it is being developed for and tested within a few hours after it has been written. Code is written, integrated into the system, and then tested. If all the tests run successfully, then development proceeds. If not, the code is reworked until the tests are successful.

Another part of eXtreme Programming that makes the code-and-test process work more smoothly is the practice of pair programming. All coding and testing is done by two people working together, writing code and writing tests. Pair programming is not one person typing while the other one watches. Rather, the two programmers work together on the problem they are trying to solve, exchanging information and insight and sharing skills. Compared to traditional coding practices, the advantages of pair programming include: (1) more (and better) communication among developers, (2) higher levels of productivity, (3) higher-quality code, and (4) reinforcement of the other practices in eXtreme Programming, such as the code-and-test discipline. Although the eXtreme Programming process has its advantages, just as with any other approach to systems development, it is not for everyone and is not applicable to every project.

The Heart of the Systems Development Process

The systems development life cycle used in this book provides a convenient way to see the systems development process and helps to organize this book. The different phases are clearly defined, their relationships to each other are well specified, and the sequencing of phases from one to the next, from beginning to end, has a compelling logic. In the Agile Methodologies, current practice combines the activities traditionally thought of as belonging to analysis, design, and implementation into a single process. Instead of systems requirements being produced in analysis, system specifications being created in design, and coding and testing being done at the beginning of implementation, current practice combines all of these activities into a single analysis-design-code-test process (Figure B-2). These activities are the heart of systems development, as we suggest in Figure B-3. This combination of activities started with rapid application development (RAD), which you read about in Chapter 1, and is seen in many of the Agile Methodologies.

In the rest of this appendix, we will focus on the heart of systems development—analysis, design, and implementation—from the perspective of the Agile Methodologies. Note that Figure B-3 shows two arrows between analysis and design.

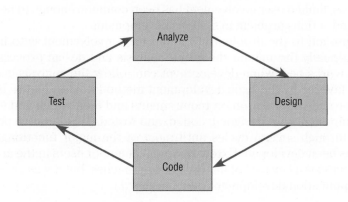

FIGURE B-2
The analysis-design-code-test loop.

FIGURE B-3
The heart of systems development.

These arrows denote the iteration between these two activities, which is at the core of developmental agility. In the next sections you will read about the iteration between analysis and design and where certain aspects of implementation fit it. The first section is about requirements determination. The second section is about design specifications, and the last section is about the combination of coding and testing in implementation. As you read before, many flavors of the Agile Methodologies are available. We will illustrate how these methodologies work primarily with the eXtreme Programming approach, but we will also reference Agile Usage-Centered Design, originally developed by Larry Constantine and adapted for Agile Methodologies by Jeff Patton.

Requirements Determination

Three requirements determination techniques are presented in this section. The first is continual user involvement in the development process, a technique that works especially well with small and dedicated development teams. The second approach is a JAD-like process called Agile Usage-Centered Design. The third approach is the Planning Game, which was developed as part of eXtreme Programming.

Continual User Involvement One of the criticisms of the traditional engineering-based approach to systems development is that users were involved only in the early stages of analysis. Once requirements had been gathered from them, the users were not involved again in the process until the system was being installed and they were asked to sign off on it. Typically, by the time users saw the system again, it was nothing like what they had imagined. Also, given how their business processes had changed since analysis had ended, the system most likely did not adequately address user needs. To some extent, this view of limited user participation is a stereotype of the traditional approach to development. Nonetheless, limited user involvement has been common enough to be perceived as a real and serious problem in systems development.

One approach to the problem of limited user involvement is to involve the users continually throughout the entire analysis and design process. Such an approach works best when development can follow the analysis-design-code-test cycle favored by the Agile development methodologies (Figure B-1), as the user can provide information on requirements and then watch and evaluate as those requirements are designed, coded, and tested. This iterative process can continue through several cycles until most of the major functionality of the system has been developed. Extensive involvement of users in the analysis and design process is a key part of many Agile approaches, but it was also a key part of rapid application development (see Chapter 1).

Continual user involvement was a key aspect of the success of Boeing's Wire Design and Wire Install system for the 757 aircraft (Bedoll, 2003). The system was intended to support engineers who customize plane configurations for customers, allowing them to analyze whether all 50,000 wires can possibly be installed on a 757. A previous attempt at building a similar system took more than three years, and the resulting system was never used. The second attempt, relying on Agile methods, resulted in a system that was in production after only six weeks. One of the keys to success was a user liaison who spent half of his time with the small development team and half with the other end users. In addition to following the analysis-design-code-test cycle, the team also had weekly production releases. The user liaison was involved every step of the way. Obviously, for such a requirements determination to succeed, the user who works with the development team must be especially knowledgeable, but he or she must also be in a position to give up his or her normal business responsibilities in order to become so heavily involved in a system's development.

Agile Usage-Centered Design   Continual user involvement in systems development is an excellent way to ensure that requirements are captured accurately and are immediately implemented in system design. However, such constant interaction works best when the development team is small, as was the case in the previous Boeing example. Also, it is not always possible to have continual access to users for the duration of a development project. So Agile developers have come up with other means for effectively involving users in the requirements determination process. One such method is called Agile Usage-Centered Design, a process with nine steps, which we have adapted and presented as eight steps in Table B-2.

Notice how similar the overall process is to a JAD meeting (see Chapter 5). All of the experts are gathered together and work with the help of the facilitator. What's unique about the Agile Usage-Centered Design is the process that

TABLE B-2:   Steps in the Agile Usage-Centered Design Method for Requirements Determination

1. Gather a group of people, including analysts, users, programmers, and testing staff, and sequester them in a room to collaborate on this design. Include a facilitator who knows this process.

2. Give everyone a chance to vent about the current system and to talk about the features everyone wants in the new system. Record all of the complaints and suggestions for change on whiteboards or flip charts for everyone to see.

3. Determine what the most important user roles would be. Determine who will be using the system and what their goals are for using the system. Write the roles on 3 × 5 cards. Sort the cards so that similar roles are close to each other. Patton (2002) calls this a *role model*.

4. Determine what tasks user roles will have to complete in order to achieve their goals. Write these down on 3 × 5 cards. Order tasks by importance and then by frequency. Place the cards together based on how similar the tasks are to each other. Patton calls this a *task model*.

5. Task cards will be clumped together on the table based on their similarity. Each clump of cards is called an *interaction context*.

6. For each task card in the interaction context, write a description of the task directly on the task card. List the steps that are necessary to complete the task. Keep the descriptions conversational to make them easy to read. Simplify.

7. Treat each clump as a tentative set of tasks to be supported by a single aspect of the user interface, such as a screen, page, or dialog, and create a paper-and-pencil prototype for that part of the interface. Show the basic size and placement of the screen components.

8. Take on a user role and step through each task in the interaction context as modeled in the paper-and-pencil prototype. Make sure the user role can achieve its goals by using the prototype. Refine the prototype accordingly.

supports it, with a focus on user roles, user goals, and the tasks necessary to achieve those goals. Then tasks are grouped and turned into paper-and-pencil prototypes before the meeting is over. Requirements captured from users and developers are captured as prototyped system screens. The two most effective aspects of this approach are the venting session, which lets everyone get their complaints out in the open, and the use of 3×5 cards, which serve as very effective communication tools. As with any analysis and design process or technique, however, Agile Usage-Centered Design will not work for every project or for every company.

The Planning Game   The techniques used for requirements determination in eXtreme Programming are captured in the Planning Game. The Planning Game is really just a stylized approach to development that seeks to maximize fruitful interaction between those who need a new system and those who build it. The players in the Planning Game, then, are Business and Development. Business is the customer and is ideally represented by someone who knows the processes to be supported by the system being developed. Development is represented by those actually designing and constructing the system. The game pieces are what Beck calls "Story Cards." These cards are created by Business and contain a description of a procedure or feature to be included in the system. Each card is dated and numbered and has space on it for tracking its status throughout the development effort.

    The Planning Game has three phases: exploration, commitment, and steering (Figure B-4). In exploration, Business creates a Story Card for something it wants the new system to do. Development responds with an estimation of how long it would take to implement the procedure. At this point, it may make sense to split a Story Card into multiple Story Cards, as the scope of features and procedures becomes clearer during discussion. In the commitment phase, Business sorts Story Cards into three stacks, one for essential features, one for features that are not essential but would still add value, and one for features that would be nice to have. Development then sorts Story Cards according to risk, based on how well they can estimate the time needed to develop each feature.

FIGURE B-4
eXtreme Programming's
Planning Game.

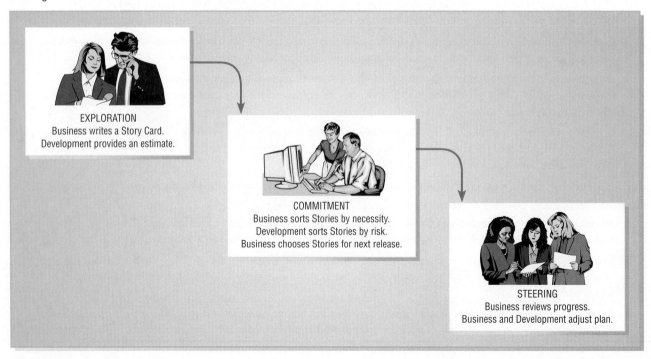

EXPLORATION
Business writes a Story Card.
Development provides an estimate.

COMMITMENT
Business sorts Stories by necessity.
Development sorts Stories by risk.
Business chooses Stories for next release.

STEERING
Business reviews progress.
Business and Development adjust plan.

Business then selects the cards that will be included in the next release of the product. In the final phase, steering, Business has a chance to see how the development process is progressing and to work with Development to adjust the plan accordingly. Steering can take place as often as once every three weeks.

The Planning Game between Business and Development is followed by the Iteration Planning Game, played only by programmers. Instead of Story Cards, programmers write Task Cards, which are based on Story Cards. Typically, several Task Cards are generated for each Story Card. The Iteration Planning Game has the same three phases as the Planning Game: exploration, commitment, and steering. During exploration, programmers convert Story Cards into Task Cards. During commitment, they accept responsibility for tasks and balance their workloads. During steering, the programmers write the code for the feature, test it, and if it works, they integrate the feature into the product being developed. The Iteration Planning Game takes place during the time intervals between steering phase meetings in the Planning Game.

You can see how the Planning Game is similar in some ways to Agile Usage-Centered Design. Both rely on participation by users, rely on cards as communication devices, and focus on tasks the system being designed is supposed to perform. Although these approaches differ from some of the more traditional ways of determining requirements, such as interviews and prototyping, many of the core principles are the same. Customers, or users, remain the source for what the system is supposed to do. Requirements are still captured and negotiated. The overall process is still documented, although the extent and formality of the documentation may differ. Given the way requirements are identified and recorded and broken down from stories to tasks, design specifications can easily incorporate the characteristics of quality requirements: completeness, consistency, modifiability, and traceability.

Design Specifications

With their focus on working software over documentation, the Agile Methodologies promote rapid iterative movement between design and coding. Design specifications are captured as part of the design process itself, evolving with each iteration through the cycle of analysis-design-code-test (see Figure B-2), leaving little room in the process for documenting the design with paper or diagrams or in any other way than the code itself.

At one extreme, then, a project using only Agile Methodologies would not produce design specifications of any kind other than the code. At the other extreme, where more traditional or engineering-based methodologies are used, detailed and complete design specifications would be generated. These specifications would then be handed over to programming and testing teams once they were complete. Many choices are also available between these extremes. Whether a systems development project is organized in terms of Agile or more traditional methodologies depends on many different considerations. If a project is considered to be high risk, highly complex, and has a development team made up of hundreds of people, then more traditional methods will apply. Less risky, smaller, and simpler development efforts lend themselves more to Agile methods. Other determining factors include organizational practice and standards and the extent to which different parts of the system will be contracted out to others to develop. Obviously, the larger the proportion of the system that will be farmed out, the more detailed the design specifications will need to be so subcontractors can understand what is needed.

Agile Methodologies go from requirements to functional design directly to code, where the design specifications are immediately captured and then tested. Lengthy text specifications, computer-based specification tools, and intermediate diagrams, such as structure charts, tend to be ignored in favor of capturing design specifications directly in the code itself. You just read that in eXtreme Programming, users generate stories that serve as the basis for system functions and features. These user requirements are not consolidated into a single, detailed, and complete design specification, as would be expected in an engineering-based development effort. Instead, requirements serve as the basis for a design that is captured in code and then tested (Figure B-2). As the founder of eXtreme Programming says, "Code is the one artifact that development absolutely cannot live without. . . . It turns out that code can be used to communicate—expressing tactical intent, describing algorithms, pointing to spots for possible future expansion and contraction" (Beck, 2000, pp. 44–45). After testing, all of the code that works may be integrated at the end of each working day, and working versions of the system will be released frequently, as often as once per week in some cases. eXtreme Programming developers design and build working systems in short amounts of time (relative to traditionally organized methods), and they do it without written or diagrammatic design specifications. eXtreme Programming employs two particular techniques that are used to continually improve the quality of the design as developers continue to iterate through the analysis-design-code-test cycle. These techniques are **simple design** and **refactoring.**

Simple design is exactly what it sounds like: keeping the design simple. For many developers and programmers, it is too easy to look ahead and try to anticipate changes in how the system will work and to design accordingly for these changes. Many times, those anticipated future conditions never materialize, and the time and effort that went into designing for the uncertain future is wasted. According to Beck (2000), design should focus on solving the immediate problem, not on solving future problems that may or may not occur. eXtreme Programming has four constraints that pertain to what Beck means by the simplest design:

> **Simple design**
> Creating uncomplicated software and software components that work to solve the current problem rather than creating complicated software designed for a future that may not come.

> **Refactoring**
> Making a program simpler after adding a new feature.

- The system must communicate everything you want it to communicate.
- The system must contain no duplicate code.
- The system should have the fewest possible classes.
- The system should have the fewest possible methods.

Classes and methods refer to object-oriented programming and design (see Appendix A), and in the nonobject world, these last two constraints could correspond to tables in a relational database and in lines of code that model processes in a system, respectively.

Refactoring is related to the overall goal of simple design in eXtreme Programming. Refactoring is nothing more than simplifying a system, typically after a new feature or set of features have been added. As more features are added to a system, it becomes more complex, and this complexity will be reflected in the code. After a time of increasing complexity, eXtreme Programming developers stop and redesign the system. The system must still pass the test cases written for it after it has been simplified, so rework continues until the tests can be passed. Different forms of refactoring include simplifying complex statements, abstracting solutions from reusable code, and removing duplicate code. Refactoring and the continuing simplification it implies reflects the iterative nature of eXtreme Programming and the other Agile Methodologies. As development progresses and the system gets closer to being ready for production, the iterations and the evolution of the system slow, a process Beck calls *productionizing.* A system ready to go into production is ready to be released to users, either customers ready to buy the software or internal users.

Implementation

Although coding and testing are in many ways part of the same process, it is not uncommon in large and complicated systems development environments to find the two practices separated from each other. You have seen examples of this case in Chapter 10. Big companies and big projects often have dedicated testing staff who develop test plans and then use the plans to test software after it has been written. You have already seen how many different types of testing there are, and you can deduce from that how elaborate and extensive testing can be. With eXtreme Programming and other Agile Methodologies, coding and testing are intimately related parts of the same process, and the programmers who write the code also write the tests. The general idea is that code is tested soon after it is written. If the code passes the tests, then it is integrated into the system. If it does not pass, the code is reworked until it does pass.

What We've Learned about Agile Methodologies

Agile methods have been in use since "The Agile Manifesto" was issued in 2001, and some were in use even before that. We saw one example, at Boeing, where Agile methods were successful. In the years that Agile methods have been used, what have we learned about their use in organizations? What can managers do to try to ensure that Agile methods really do work? Several studies have investigated Agile methods in practice.

One study, a survey of over 100 Agile projects, found three primary critical success factors for Agile development. The first is delivery strategy, which refers to the continuous delivery of working software in short time scales. The second is following Agile software engineering practices. That means managers and programmers must continually focus on technical excellence and simple design. The third critical success factor is team capability, which refers to the Agile principle of building projects around motivated individuals.

Another study found that, once implemented, Agile methods can lead to improved job satisfaction and productivity on the part of programmers. They can also lead to increased customer satisfaction, even though the role of on-site customer representative can be tiring and so not sustainable for very long. Agile methods tend to work best in small projects. In some instances, it may make sense to combine them with traditional development methods.

The best programmers for Agile methods have faith in their own abilities and good interpersonal skills and trust. To succeed, Agile teams need to balance a high level of individual autonomy with a high level of team responsibility and corporate responsibility. However, high levels of team autonomy are a two-edged sword. On the one hand, highly autonomous teams tend to be more efficient. They are able to take actions that reduce the time, cost, and resources needed to develop a system. In fact, Agile projects undertaken by efficient teams tended to come in on time, on budget, and with the needed software functionality. On the other hand, highly autonomous teams also have more ability to say no to new user demands. Users may not be entirely happy with the resulting system if too many of their demands are declined.

A detailed study of one Agile development effort showed that some of the key principles of Agile development had to be modified to help ensure success. For example, in the Agile project studied, pair programming was not always used, especially when resources were needed elsewhere. Second, the process of writing the test case first and then the code was followed until the system became too complex. Third, the customer was not located in the same place as the programmers. Instead, the customer stayed in contact through regular meetings and continual e-mail and phone communication. Even with these modifications, the resulting system was considered a success—fewer than ten updates were issued because of errors and none were issued because of implementing the wrong functionalities. Working together, the users and developers were able to clarify system requirements and create a user interface that was easy to learn and use.

In conclusion, Agile development offers managers and programmers more choice in their efforts to produce good systems that come in on time and at or under budget. Agile methods are here to stay, and over time, we will come to understand them better, as well as how best to use them for the benefit of developers and users.

Key Points Review

1. **Define Agile Methodologies.**

   The Agile Methodologies, a collection of related methodologies for systems development, rely on object-orientation and the need for speed. This approach sacrifices the milestones and multiple phases of the engineering approach currently common in systems development, favoring instead close cooperation between developers and clients, combining many life cycle phases into few phases, and having multiple rapid releases of software. Although many individual methods reflect the new approach, collectively they are called the *Agile Methodologies*. These individual methods have in common a focus on adaptive methodologies, people instead of roles, and an overall self-adaptive development process.

2. **Explain when to use Agile Methodologies and when to use engineering-based approaches to systems development.**

   First, Agile methods fit much better with smaller projects than with larger ones. Traditional methods are preferred for large projects and for those dealing with safety-critical systems. Second, Agile methods work well when the target system is to operate in a volatile and fluid environment, where business conditions are turbulent and frequently changing. Because of the large amount of planning that is part of them, traditional approaches work best where the system being developed operates in a stable environment. Third, because Agile Methodologies stress the importance of individuals rather than roles, an Agile approach may not work as well unless a critical mass of people is trained to use Agile methods. Finally, Agile methods will work best in an organization culture that thrives on uncertainty, rapid change, and chaos. Traditional methods work where organizational roles are clearly defined and change little.

3. **Define eXtreme Programming.**

   eXtreme Programming was developed by Kent Beck in the late 1990s. eXtreme Programming is distinguished by its short development cycles, its incremental planning approach, its focus on automated tests written by programmers and customers to monitor the process of development, and its reliance on an evolutionary approach to development that lasts throughout the lifetime of the system. One of the key emphases of eXtreme Programming is its use of two-person programming teams. A second emphasis is having a customer on-site during the development process. The techniques used for requirements determination in eXtreme Programming are captured in the Planning Game, a stylized approach to development that seeks to maximize fruitful interaction between those who need a new system and those who build it. Other important aspects of eXtreme Programming are simple design and refactoring.

4. **Discuss the Agile Methodologies approach to systems requirements determination, design specifications, and the combination of coding and testing.**

   Three methods for requirements determination from an Agile Methodologies perspective were presented in this appendix: (1) continual user involvement in the development process, a technique that works especially well with small and dedicated development teams; (2) Agile Usage-Centered Design, a JAD-like approach; and (3) the Planning Game, developed as part of eXtreme Programming. Agile Methodologies promote rapid iterative movement between design and coding, so design specifications are captured as part of the design process itself. Specifications evolve with each iteration, through the cycle of analysis-design-code-test, leaving little room in the process for documenting the design with paper or diagrams or in any way other than the code itself. For Agile Methodologies, coding and testing are intimately related parts of the same process, and the programmers who write the code also write the tests. The general idea is that code is tested soon after it is written.

Key Terms Checkpoint

Here are the key terms from the appendix. The page where each term is first explained is in parentheses after the term.

1. **Agile Methodologies (p. 381)**   2. **Refactoring (p. 390)**   3. **Simple design (p. 390)**

Match each of the key terms above with the definition that best fits it.

_____ 1. Making a program simpler after adding a new feature.

_____ 2. Creating uncomplicated software and software components that work to solve the current problem rather than creating complicated software designed for a future that may not come.

_____ 3. A family of development methodologies characterized by short iterative cycles and extensive testing; active involvement of users for establishing, prioritizing, and verifying requirements; and a focus on small teams of talented, experienced programmers.

Review Questions

1. What are Agile Methodologies?
2. Describe the three stages that information systems development has passed through.
3. What is the heart of the systems development process? How does it fit within the larger SDLC framework?
4. Explain eXtreme Programming.
5. What is continual user involvement?
6. What is Agile Usage-Centered Design? How is it used for requirements determination?
7. What is the Planning Game, and what is it used for?
8. How are design specifications handled in the Agile Methodologies?
9. What is simple design? What is refactoring?
10. Explain how testing differs in the Agile Methodologies and in traditional approaches.
11. What have we learned about Agile development methods in practice?

Problems and Exercises

1. When should you use an Agile method, and when should you use an engineering-based method for developing a system? Support your answer.
2. Find books and articles on some of the other Agile Methodologies, such as Scrum and Feature Driven Development. Compare what you find to what you have read in this appendix about eXtreme Programming. Write a report that illustrates the similarities and differences in these approaches.
3. How widespread are the Agile Methodologies in the information technology industry? Research this question and write a report that explains what you find.
4. Using the World Wide Web, find a company or firm near you where the Agile Methodologies are in use. Interview developers to find out what their approach to development looks like. Prepare a report based on your findings.
5. Assume you have been given the task of leading a team developing an online order-entry system. What would your project look like using the structured techniques featured in this book? What would your project look like using an Agile method? Compare and contrast these two different approaches to developing this system. Be sure to include important considerations, such as project duration, personnel issues, and the quantity and quality of involvement of the client.

References

Chapter 1: The Systems Development Environment

Aktas, A. Z. *Structured Analysis and Design of Information Systems.* Upper Saddle River, NJ: Prentice Hall, 1987.

Bohm, C., and I. Jacopini. "Flow Diagrams, Turing Machines, and Languages with only Two Formation Rules." *Communications of the ACM* 9 (May 1966): 366–71.

Bourne, K. C. "Putting Rigor Back in RAD." *Database Programming & Design* 7 (8) (August 1994): 25–30.

Coy, P. "The Future of Work." *BusinessWeek* (March 22, 2004): 50–52.

DeMarco, T. *Structured Analysis and System Specification.* Upper Saddle River, NJ: Prentice Hall, 1979.

Fowler, M. "The New Methodology." April 2003. Accessed April 23, 2011, www.martinfowler.com/articles/newMethodology.html.

Gallivan, M. J., D. P. Truex, and L. Kvasny. "Changing Perspectives in IT Skill Sets 1988–2003: A Content Analysis of Classified Advertising." *Data Base for Advances in Information Systems* 35 (3) (2004): 64–87.

Mumford, E. "Participative Systems Design: A Structure and Method." *Systems, Objectives, Solutions* 1 (1) (1981): 5–19.

Naumann, J. D., and A. M. Jenkins. "Prototyping: The New Paradigm for Systems Development." *MIS Quarterly* 6 (3) (1982): 29–44.

Vegso, J. "BLS Projects IT Work Force to Add a Million New Jobs Between 2004 and 2014." *CRA Bulletin.* Accessed January 1, 2008, www.cra.org/wp/index.php?p=70.2006.

Yourdon, E., and L. L. Constantine. *Structured Design.* Upper Saddle River, NJ: Prentice Hall, 1979.

Chapter 2: The Sources of Software

Applegate, L. M., and R. Montealegre. "Eastman Kodak Company: Managing Information Systems Through Strategic Alliances." Harvard Business School, Case 9-192-030. Cambridge, MA: President and Fellows of Harvard College, 1991.

Basili, V. R., L. C. Briand, and W. L. Melo. "How Reuse Influences Productivity in Object-Oriented Systems." *Communications of the ACM* 39 (10) (1996): 104–116.

Computer History Museum. "Timeline of Computer History." Accessed December 24, 2003, www.computerhistory.org.

Cowley, S. "JP Morgan Cancels $5bn IBM Outsourcing Deal." *ComputerWeekly.com* (September 16, 2004). Accessed October 27, 2004, www.computerweekly.com.

DeSouza, K. C., Y. Awazu, and A. Tiwana. "Four Dynamics for Bringing Use Back into Software Reuse." *Communications of the ACM*, 49 (1) (2006): 96–100.

"ERP Market Share and Evaluation." 2010. Accessed April 23, 2011, whatiserp.net/erp-comparison/erp-vendor-evaluation-2010.

Ewing. "Strong Numbers and New Products for SAP." *Spiegel Online International.* Accessed April 23, 2011, http://www.spiegel.de/international/business/0,1518,495579,00.html.

Flinders, K. 2010. "IT Will Become More Strategic as Outsourcers Industrialise IT Foundations." *ComputerWeekly.com* (September 20, 2010). Accessed April 23, 2011, www.computerweekly.com/blogs/inside-outsourcing/2010/09/it-will-become-more-strategic-as-outsourcers-industrialise-it-foundations.html.

Grinter, R. E. "From Local to Global Coordination: Lessons from Software Reuse." In *Proceedings of Group '01*, 144–153. Boulder, CO: Association for Computing Machinery, SIGGROUP, 2001.

Griss, M. "Reuse Comes in Several Flavors." Flashline white paper. Accessed February 10, 2004, www.flashline.com.

Kim, Y., and E. A. Stohr. "Software Reuse: Survey and Research Directions." *Journal of MIS* 14 (4) (1998): 113–147.

King, J., and B. Cole-Gomolski. 1999. "IT Doing Less Development, More Installation, Outsourcing." *Computerworld* (January 25, 1999). Accessed December 28, 2003, www.computerworld.com.

King, R. "The Outstanding Upstarts." *BusinessWeek Online* (July 31, 2007). Accessed April 23, 2011, www.businessweek.com/print/technology/content/jul2007/tc20070730_998591.htm.

King, R. 2008. "How Cloud Computing is Changing the World." *BusinessWeek Online* (August 4, 2008). Accessed April 23, 2011, http://www.businessweek.com/print/technology/content/aug2008/tc2008082_445669.htm.

Mackie, K. 2009. "Report: Microsoft Key to IT Jobs Growth." *Redmondmag.com* (October 5, 2009). Accessed April 23, 2011, http:// redmondmag.com/articles/2009/10/05/report-microsoft-key-to-it-jobs-growth.aspx.

"Microcomputer Procurement Guidelines." *Public Works* 125 (April 15, 1994): G23 1.

Royce, W. *Software Project Management: A Unified Framework.* Boston: Addison-Wesley, 1998.

Vaughn-Nichols, S. J. "Linux Server Market Share Keeps Growing." Linux-Watch.com (May 29, 2007). Accessed January 24, 2008, www.linux-watch.com/news/NS5369154346.html.

Wilcox, J., and M. A. Farmer. "Microsoft to Unveil Software-for-Rent Strategy." *CNETNews.com* (July 14, 2000). Accessed April 23, 2011, news.cnet.com.

Chapter 3: Managing the Information Systems Project

Abdel-Hamid, T. K., K. Sengupta, and C. Swett. "The Impact of Goals on Software Project Management: An Experimental Investigation." *MIS Quarterly* (23) (1999): 4.

Boehm, B. W. *Software Engineering Economics.* Upper Saddle River, NJ: Prentice Hall, 1981.

Boehm, B., et al. Software Cost Estimation with COCOMO II. Upper Saddle River, NJ: Prentice Hall, 2000.

Butler, J. "Automating Process Trims Software Development Fat." *Software Magazine* 14 (8) (August 1994): 37–46.

Fuller, M. A, J. S. Valacich, and J. F. George. *Information Systems Project Management.* Upper Saddle River, NJ: Prentice Hall, 2008.

George, J. F., D. Batra, J. S. Valacich, and J. A. Hoffer. *Object-Oriented Analysis and Design.* 2d ed. Upper Saddle River, NJ: Prentice Hall, 2004.

Grupe, F. H., and D. F. Clevenger. "Using Function Point Analysis as a Software Development Tool." *Journal of Systems Management* 42 (December 1991): 23–26.

Guinan, P. J., J. G. Cooprider, and S. Faraj. "Enabling Software Development Team Performance During Requirements Definition: A Behavioral versus Technical Approach." *Information Systems Research* 9 (2) (1998): 101–25.

Hoffer, J. A., V. Ramesh, and H. Topi. *Modern Database Management.* 10th ed. Upper Saddle River, NJ: Prentice Hall, 2011.

Keil, M., B. C. Y. Tan, K. K. Wei, T. Saarinen, V. Tuunainen, and A. Wassenaar. "A Cross-Cultural Study on Escalation of Commitment Behavior in Software Projects." *MIS Quarterly* (24) (2000): 2.

Kettelhut, M. C. "Avoiding Group-Induced Errors in Systems Development." *Journal of Systems Management* 42 (December 1991): 13–17.

King, J. "IT's Global Itinerary: Offshore Outsourcing Is Inevitable." Accessed September 15, 2003, www.cio.com. Information verified September 17, 2003.

Kirsch, L. J. "Software Project Management: An Integrated Perspective for an Emerging Paradigm." In *Framing the Domains of IT Management: Projecting the Future from the Past.* Edited by R. W. Zmud, Chapter 15, 285–304. Cincinnati, OH: Pinnaflex Educational Resources.

Murch, R. *Project Management: Best Practices for IT Professionals.* Upper Saddle River, NJ: Prentice Hall, 2001.

Project Management Institute. *Work Breakdown Structures.* Newton Square, PA: Project Management Institute, 2001.

Rettig, M. "Software Teams." *Communications of the ACM* 33 (10) (1990): 23–27.

Verma, V. K. *Human Resource Skills for the Project Manager.* Newtown Square, PA: Project Management Institute, 1996.

Verma, V. K. *Managing the Project Team.* Newton Square, PA: Project Management Institute, 1997.

Wideman, R. M. *Project and Program Risk Management.* Newton Square, PA: Project Management Institute, 1992.

Chapter 4: Systems Planning and Selection

Applegate, L. M., R. D. Austin, and F. W. McFarlan. *Corporate Information Strategy and Management.* 7th ed. Boston: Irwin/McGraw-Hill, 2007.

Atkinson, R. A. "The Motivations for Strategic Planning." *Journal of Information Systems Management* 7 (4) (1990): 53–56.

Carlson, C. K., E. P. Gardner, and S. R. Ruth. "Technology-Driven Long-Range Planning." *Journal of Information Systems Management* 6 (3) (1989): 24–29.

DeGiglio, M. "Measure for Measure: The Value of IT." Accessed June 17, 2003, www.cio.com. Information verified April 23, 2011.

Dewan, S., S. C. Michael, and C-K. Min. "Firm Characteristics and Investments in Information Technology: Scale and Scope Effects." *Information Systems Research* 9 (3) (1998): 219–232.

Hasselbring, W. "Information System Integration." *Communications of the ACM* 43 (6) (2000): 33–38.

IBM. "Business Systems Planning." In *Advanced System Development/Feasibility Techniques.* Edited by J. D. Couger, M. A. Colter, and R. W. Knapp, 236–314. New York: Wiley, 1982.

Kerr, J. "The Power of Information Systems Planning." *Database Programming & Design* 3 (December 1990): 60–66.

King, J. "IT's Global Itinerary: Offshore Outsourcing Is Inevitable." Accessed September 15, 2003, www.cio.com. Information verified September 17, 2003.

King, J. L., and E. Schrems. "Cost Benefit Analysis in Information Systems Development and Operation." *ACM Computing Surveys* 10 (1) (1978): 19–34.

Kirsch, L. J. "Software Project Management: An Integrated Perspective for an Emerging Paradigm." In *Framing the Domains of IT Management: Projecting the Future from the Past.* Edited by R. W. Zmud, Chapter 15, 285–304. Cincinnati, OH: Pinnaflex Educational Resources, 2000.

Lederer, A. L., and J. Prasad. "Nine Management Guidelines for Better Cost Estimating." *Communications of the ACM* 35 (2) (1992): 51–59.

Luftman, J. N. *Managing the Information Technology Resource.* With C.V. Bullen, D. Liao, E. Nash, and C. Neumann. Upper Saddle River, NJ: Prentice Hall, 2004.

McKeen, J. D., T. Guimaraes, and J. C. Wetherbe. "A Comparative Analysis of MIS Project Selection Mechanisms." *Data Base* 25 (February 1994): 43–59.

Parker, M. M., and R. J. Benson. *Information Economics.* Upper Saddle River, NJ: Prentice Hall, 1988.

Parker, M. M., and R. J. Benson. "Enterprisewide Information Management: State-of-the-Art Strategic Planning." *Journal of Information Systems Management* 6 (Summer 1989): 14–23.

Porter, M. *Competitive Strategy: Techniques for Analyzing Industries and Competitors.* New York: Free Press, 1980.

Porter, M. *Competitive Advantage.* New York: Free Press, 1985.

Pressman, R. S. *Software Engineering.* 5th ed. New York: McGraw-Hill, 2001.

Radosevich, L. "Can You Measure Web ROI?" *Datamation* (July 1996): 92–96.

Ross, J., and D. Feeny. "The Evolving Role of the CIO." In *Framing the Domains of IT Management: Projecting the Future from the Past.* Edited by R. W. Zmud, Chapter 19, 385–402. Cincinnati, OH: Pinnaflex Educational Resources.

Segars, A. H., and V. Grover. "Profiles of Strategic Information Systems Planning." *Information Systems Planning* 10 (3) (1999): 199–232.

Shank, J. K., and V. Govindarajan. *Strategic Cost Management.* New York: Free Press, 1993.

Sowa, J. F., and J. A. Zachman. "Extending and Formalizing the Framework for Information Systems Architecture." *IBM Systems Journal* 31 (3) (1992): 590–616.

Yourdon, E. *Structured Walkthroughs.* 4th ed. Upper Saddle River, NJ: Prentice Hall, 1989.

Zachman, J. A. "A Framework for Information Systems Architecture." *IBM Systems Journal* 26 (March 1987): 276–92.

Chapter 5: Determining System Requirements

Carmel, E. "Supporting Joint Application Development with Electronic Meeting Systems: A Field Study." Unpublished doctoral dissertation, University of Arizona, 1991.

Carmel, E., J. F. George, and J. F. Nunamaker, Jr. "Supporting Joint Application Development (JAD) with Electronic Meeting Systems: A Field Study." In *Proceedings of the Thirteenth International Conference on Information Systems,* 223–32. Dallas, TX, December 1992.

Carmel, E., R. Whitaker, and J. F. George. "Participatory Design and Joint Application Design: A Transatlantic Comparison." *Communications of the ACM* 36 (June 1993): 40–48.

Davenport, T. H. *Process Innovation: Reengineering Work through Information Technology.* Boston: Harvard Business School Press, 1993.

Dennis, A. R., J. F. George, L. Jessup, J. F. Nunamaker, Jr., and D. R. Vogel. "Information Technology to Support Electronic Meetings." *MIS Quarterly* 12 (December 1988): 591–624.

Dobyns, L., and C. Crawford-Mason. *Quality or Else.* Boston: Houghton Mifflin, 1991.

Hammer, M., and J. Champy. *Reengineering the Corporation.* New York: Harper Business, 1993.

Lucas, M. A. "The Way of JAD." *Database Programming & Design* 6 (July 1993): 42–49.

Mintzberg, H. *The Nature of Managerial Work.* New York: Harper & Row, 1973.

Moad, J. "After Reengineering: Taking Care of Business." *Datamation* 40 (20) (1994): 40–44.

Wood, J., and D. Silver. *Joint Application Design.* New York: Wiley, 1989.

Chapter 6: Structuring System Requirements: Process Modeling

Celko, J. "I. Data Flow Diagrams." *Computer Language* 4 (January 1987): 41–43.

DeMarco, T. *Structured Analysis and System Specification.* Upper Saddle River, NJ: Prentice Hall, 1979.

Gane, C., and T. Sarson. *Structured Systems Analysis.* Upper Saddle River, NJ: Prentice Hall, 1979.

Gibbs, W. W. "Software's Chronic Crisis." *Scientific American* 271 (September 1994): 86–95.

Hammer, M., and J. Champy. *Reengineering the Corporation.* New York: Harper Business, 1993.

Yourdon, E. *Managing the Structured Techniques.* 4th ed. Upper Saddle River, NJ: Prentice Hall, 1989.

Yourdon, E., and L. L. Constantine. *Structured Design.* Upper Saddle River, NJ: Prentice Hall, 1979.

Chapter 7: Structuring System Requirements: Conceptual Data Modeling

Aranow, E. B. "Developing Good Data Definitions." *Database Programming & Design* 2 (8) (1989): 36–39.

Booch, G. *Object-Oriented Analysis and Design with Applications.* 2d ed. Redwood City, CA: Benjamin Cummings, 1994.

Bruce, T. A. *Designing Quality Databases with IDEF1X Information Models.* New York: Dorset House, 1992.

Chen, P. P-S. "The Entity-Relationship Model—Toward a Unified View of Data." *ACM Transactions on Database Systems* 1 (March 1976): 9–36.

Codd, E. F. "A Relational Model of Data for Large Relational Databases." *Communications of the ACM* 13 (6) (1970): 77–87.

Dutka, A. F., and H. H. Hanson. *Fundamentals of Data Normalization.* Reading, MA: Addison-Wesley, 1989.

Finkelstein, R. "Breaking the Rules Has a Price." *Database Programming & Design* 1 (June 1988): 11–14.

Fleming, C. C., and B. von Halle. "An Overview of Logical Data Modeling." *Data Resource Management* 1 (1) (1990): 5–15.

Fowler, M. *UML Distilled: A Brief Guide to the Object Modeling Language.* 2d ed. Reading, MA: Addison-Wesley, 2000.

Gibson, M., C. Hughes, and W. Remington. "Tracking the Trade-Offs with Inverted Lists." *Database Programming & Design* 2 (January 1989): 28–34.

Gottesdiener, E. "Turning Rules into Requirements." *Application Development Trends* 6 (7) (1999): 37–50.

Hay, D. *Data Model Patterns: Conventions of Thought.* New York: Dorset House, 1996.

Hoffer, J. A., V. Ramesh, and H. Topi. *Modern Database Management.* 10th ed. Upper Saddle River, NJ: Prentice Hall, 2011.

Inmon, W. H. "Using the Generic Data Model." Accessed January 12, 2004, www.dmreview.com/master.cfm?NavID=55&EdID=4820.

Kimball, R., and M. Ross. *The Data Warehouse Toolkit: The Complete Guide to Dimensional Data Modeling.* 2d ed. New York: Wiley, 2002.

Moody, D. "The Seven Habits of Highly Effective Data Modelers." *Database Programming & Design* 9 (October 1996): 57, 58, 60–62, 64.

Rodgers, U. "Denormalization: Why, What, and How?" *Database Programming & Design* 2 (12) (1989): 46–53.

Rumbaugh, J., M. Blaha, W. Premerlani, F. Eddy, and W. Lorensen. *Object-Oriented Modeling and Design.* Upper Saddle River, NJ: Prentice Hall, 1991.

Sandifer, A., and B. von Halle. "A Rule by Any Other Name." *Database Programming & Design* 4 (2) (1991a): 11–13.

Sandifer, A., and B. von Halle. "Linking Rules to Models." *Database Programming & Design* 4 (3) (1991b): 13–16.

Silverston, L. *The Data Model Resource Book. Vol. 1. A Library of Universal Data Models for All Enterprises.* New York: Wiley, 2001a.

Silverston, L. *The Data Model Resource Book. Vol 2. A Library of Data Models for Specific Industries.* New York: Wiley, 2001b.

Silverston, L. "A Universal Data Model for Relationship Development," Accessed April 23, 2011, http://www.information-management.com/issues/20020301/4820-1.html

Storey, V. C. "Relational Database Design Based on the Entity-Relationship Model." *Data and Knowledge Engineering* 7 (1) (1991): 47–83.

Teorey, T. J., D. Yang, and J. P. Fry. "A Logical Design Methodology for Relational Databases Using the Extended Entity-Relationship Model." *Computing Surveys* 18 (2) (1986): 197–221.

UML Notation Guide. Document accessed at http://www.scribd.com/doc/8365836/UML-Notation-Guide. Copyright held by Rational Software Corporation, Microsoft Corporation, Hewlett-Packard Company, Oracle Corporation, Sterling Software, MCI Systemhouse Corporation, Unisys Corporation, ICON Computing, IntelliCorp, i-Logix, IBM Corporation, ObjecTime Limited, Platinum Technology Incorporated, Ptech Incorporated, Taskon A/S, Reich Technologies, Softeam. Accessed April 23, 2011.

Chapter 8: Designing the Human Interface

Apple Computer. *Macintosh Human Interface Guidelines.* Reading, MA: Addison-Wesley, 1993.

Ash, T. *Landing Page Optimization: The Definitive Guide to Testing and Tuning for Conversion.* New York: Sybex, 2008.

Benbasat, I., A. S. Dexter, and P. Todd. "The Influence of Color and Graphical Information Presentation in a Managerial Decision Simulation." *Human-Computer Interaction* 2 (1986): 65–92.

Blattner, M., and E. Schultz. "User Interface Tutorial." Presented at the 1988 Hawaii International Conference on System Sciences, Kona, Hawaii, January 1988.

Carroll, J. M. *Designing Interaction.* Cambridge: Cambridge University Press, 1991.

Castro, E. *XML for the World Wide Web.* Berkeley, CA: Peachpit Press, 2001.

Cooper, A., and R. M. Reimann. *About Face 2.0: The Essentials of Interaction Design.* New York: Wiley, 2003.

Dumas, J. S. *Designing User Interfaces for Software.* Upper Saddle River, NJ: Prentice Hall, 1988.

Hoffer, J. A., V. Ramesh, and H. Topi. *Modern Database Management.* 10th ed. Upper Saddle River, NJ: Prentice Hall, 2011.

Jarvenpaa, S. L., and G. W. Dickson. "Graphics and Managerial Decision Making: Research Based Guidelines." *Communications of the ACM* 31 (6) (1988): 764–74.

Johnson, J. 2007. GUI Bloopers 2.0: Common User Interface Design Don'ts and Dos. 2nd ed. New York: Morgan Kaufmann.

Lazar, J. *User-Centered Web Development: Theory into Practice.* Sudbury, MA: Jones & Bartlett, 2004.

Lindholm, C., and T. Keinonen. *Mobile Usability: How Nokia Changed the Face of the Mobile Phone.* Chicago: McGraw-Hill Professional, 2003.

Loveday, L. and S. Niehaus. *Web Design for ROI: Turning Browsers into Buyers and Prospects into Leads.* Indianapolis, IN: New Riders, 2007.

McCracken, D. D., R. J. Wolfe, and J. M. Spoll. *User-Centered Web Site Development: A Human-Computer Interaction Approach.* Upper Saddle River, NJ: Prentice Hall, 2003.

McKay, E. N. *Developing User Interfaces for Microsoft Windows.* Redmond, WA: Microsoft Press, 1999.

Nielsen, J. "Marginalia of Web Design." April 23, 2011; www.useit.com/alertbox/9611.html.

Nielsen, J. "Loyalty on the Web." April 23, 2011; www.useit.com/alertbox/9708a.html.

Nielsen, J. "Using Link Titles to Help Users Predict Where They Are Going." April 23, 2011a; www.useit.com/alertbox/980111.html.

Nielsen, J. "Personalization Is Over-Rated." April 23, 2011b; www.useit.com/alertbox/981004.html.

Nielsen, J. "Web Pages Must Live Forever." April 23, 2011c; www.useit.com/alertbox/981129.html.

Nielsen, J. "User Interface Directions for the Web." *Communications of the ACM*, 42 (1) (1999a), 65–71.

Nielsen, J. "Trust or Bust: Communicating Trustworthiness in Web Design." April 23, 2011b; www.useit.com/alertbox/990307.html.

Nielsen, J., and H. Loranger. *Prioritizing Web Usability.* Indianapolis, IN: New Riders, 2006.

Norman, K. L. *The Psychology of Menu Selection.* Norwood, NJ: Ablex, 1991.

Seffah, A., and H. Javahery. *Multiple User Interfaces: Cross Platform Applications and Context-Aware Interfaces.* New York: Wiley, 2003.

Shneiderman, B., C. Plaisant, M. Cohen, and S. Jacobs. *Designing the User Interface.* 5th ed. Reading, MA: Addison-Wesley, 2009.

Snyder, C. *Paper Prototyping: The Fast and Easy Way to Design and Refine User Interfaces.* San Francisco: Morgan Kaufmann Publishers, 2003.

Sun Microsystems. *Java Look and Feel Design Guidelines.* Reading, MA: Addison-Wesley, 1999.

Veeny, D. *Get to the Top on Google.* London: Nicholas Brealey Publishing, 2008.

Chapter 9: Designing Databases

Babad, Y. M., and J. A. Hoffer. "Even No Data Has a Value." *Communications of the ACM* 27 (August 1984): 748–56.

Codd, E. F. "A Relational Model of Data for Large Relational Databases." *Communications of the ACM* 13 (June 1970): 77–87.

Gibson, M., C. Hughes, and W. Remington. "Tracking the Trade-Offs with Inverted Lists." *Database Programming & Design* 2 (January 1989): 28–34.

Hoffer, J. A., V. Ramesh, and H. Topi. *Modern Database Management.* 10th ed. Upper Saddle River, NJ: Prentice Hall, 2011.

Navathe, S., R. Elmasri, and J. Larson. "Integrating User Views in Database Design." *Computer* (January 1986): 50–62.

Rodgers, U. "Denormalization: Why, What, and How?" *Database Programming & Design* 2 (12) (December 1989): 46–53.

Viehman, P. "24 Ways to Improve Database Performance." *Database Programming & Design* 7 (2) (February 1994): 32–41.

Chapter 10: Systems Implementation and Operation

Bell, P., and C. Evans. *Mastering Documentation.* New York: Wiley, 1989.

Bloor, R. "The Disappearing Programmer." *DBMS* 7 (9) (August 1994): 14–16.

Brooks, F. P., Jr. *The Mythical Man-Month.* Anniversary edition. Reading, MA: Addison-Wesley, 1995.

Cole, K., O. Fischer, and P. Saltzman. "Just-in-Time Knowledge Delivery." *Communications of the ACM* 40 (7) (1997): 49–53.

Crowley, A. "The Help Desk Gains Respect." *PC Week* 10 (November 15, 1993): 138.

Dillon, N. "Internet-Based Training Passes Audit." *Computerworld* (November 3, 1997): 47–48.

Eason, K. *Information Technology and Organisational Change.* London: Taylor & Francis, 1988.

Galvin, T. "Industry Report." *Training* (October 2002): 24–33.

Ginzberg, M. J. "Early Diagnosis of MIS Implementation Failure: Promising Results and Unanswered Questions." *Management Science* 27 (4) (1981): 459–78.

Ginzberg, M. J. "Key Recurrent Issues in the MIS Implementation Process." *MIS Quarterly* 5 (2) (June 1981): 47–59.

Hanna, M. "Using Documentation as a Life-Cycle Tool." *Software Magazine* (December 1992): 41–46.

Henderson, J. C., and M. E. Treacy. "Managing End-User Computing for Competitive Advantage." *Sloan Management Review* (Winter 1986): 3–14.

Ives, B., and M. H. Olson. "User Involvement and MIS Success: A Review of Research." *Management Science* 30 (5) (1984): 586–603.

Jones, C. "How to Measure Software Costs." *Application Development Trends* (May 1997): 32–36.

Kaplan, S. "Now Is the Time to Pull the Plug on Your Legacy Apps." *CIO Magazine.* (March 15, 2002). Accessed April 23, 2011, www.cio.com.

Kim, K-J., C. J. Bonk, and T. T. Zeng. "Surveying the Future of Workplace E-Learning: The Rise of Blending, Interactivity, and Authentic Learning." *eLearn Magazine* (2005). Available at http://www.elearnmag.org/subpage.cfm?article=5-1&section=research. Accessed April 23, 2011.

Kling, R., and S. Iacono. "Desktop Computerization and the Organization of Work." *Computers in the Human Context.* Edited by T. Forester, 335–56. Cambridge, MA: MIT Press, 1989.

Lee, D. M. S. "Usage Pattern and Sources of Assistance for Personal Computer Users." *MIS Quarterly,* 10 (December 1986): 313–25.

Markus, M. L. "Implementation Politics: Top Management Support and User Involvement." *Systems, Objectives, Solutions* 1 (4) (1981): 203–15.

Martin, E. W., C. V. Brown, D. W. DeHayes, J. A. Hoffer, and W. C. Perkins. *Managing Information Technology: What Managers Need to Know.* 4th ed. Upper Saddle River, NJ: Prentice Hall, 2002.

Mosley, D. J. *The Handbook of MIS Application Software Testing.* Englewood Cliffs, NJ: Yourdon Press, 1993.

Nelson, R. R., and P. H. Cheney. "Training End Users: An Exploratory Study." *MIS Quarterly* 11 (December 1987): 547–59.

Pressman, R. S. *Software Engineering: A Practitioner's Approach.* 5th ed. New York, NY: McGraw-Hill, 2001.

Schrage, M. "Unsupported Technology: A Prescription for Failure." *Computerworld* 27 (May 10, 1993): 31.

Schurr, A. "Support Is No. 1." *PC Week* 10 (November 15, 1993): 126.

Tait, P., and I. Vessey. "The Effect of User Involvement on System Success: A Contingency Approach." *MIS Quarterly* 12 (1) (March 1988): 91–108.

Torkzadeh, G., and W. J. Doll. "The Place and Value of Documentation in End-User Computing." *Information & Management* 24 (3) (1993): 147–58.

Yourdon, E. *Managing the Structured Techniques.* 4th ed. Upper Saddle River, NJ: Prentice Hall, 1989.

Appendix A: Object-Oriented Analysis and Design

Booch, G. *Object-Oriented Analysis and Design with Applications.* 2d ed. Redwood City, CA: Benjamin Cummings, 1994.

Coad, P., and E. Yourdon. *Object-Oriented Analysis.* 2d ed. Upper Saddle River, NJ: Prentice Hall, 1991.

Coad, P., and E. Yourdon. *Object-Oriented Design.* Upper Saddle River, NJ: Prentice Hall, 1991.

Eriksson, H., and M. Penker. *UML Toolkit.* New York: Wiley, 1998.

Fowler, M. *UML Distilled: A Brief Guide to the Object Modeling Language.* Reading, MA: Addison-Wesley, 2000.

Jacobson, I., M. Christerson, P. Jonsson, and G. Overgaard. *Object-Oriented Software Engineering: A Use-Case Driven Approach.* Reading, MA: Addison-Wesley, 1992.

Rumbaugh, J., M. Blaha, W. Premerlani, F. Eddy, and W. Lorensen. *Object-Oriented Modeling and Design.* Upper Saddle River, NJ: Prentice Hall, 1991.

UML Document Set. Version 1.0. Santa Clara, CA: Rational Software Corp., January 1997.

UML Notation Guide. Version 1.0. Santa Clara, CA: Rational Software Corp., January 1997.

Appendix B: Agile Methodologies

Beck, K. *eXtreme Programming eXplained.* Upper Saddle River, NJ: Addison-Wesley, 2000.

Bedoll, R. "A Tale of Two Projects: How 'Agile' Methods Succeeded After 'Traditional' Methods Had Failed in a Critical System-Development Project." In *Proceedings of 2003 XP/Agile Universe Conference* (2003). Accessed September 19, 2003, www.agileuniverse.com/home.

Boehm, B., and R. Turner. *Balancing Agility and Discipline.* Boston: Addision-Wesley, 2004.

Chow, T., and D-B. Cao. "A Survey Study of Critical Success Factors in Agile Software Projects." *Journal of Systems and Software* 81 (2008): 961–971.

Constantine, L. "Process Agility and Software Usability: Toward Lightweight Usage-Centered Design." *Information Age* (August/September 2002).

Dyba, T., and T. Dingsoyr. "Empirical Studies of Agile Software Development: A Systematic Review." *Information and Software Technology* 50 (2008): 833–859.

Fowler, M. "The New Methodology." April 2003. Accessed April 23, 2011, www .martinfowler.com/articles/ newMethodology.html.

Fruhling, A., and G. J. De Vreede. "Field Experiences with eXtreme Programming: Developing an Emergency Response System." *Journal of MIS* 22 (4) (2006): 39–68.

Lee, G., and W. Xia. "Toward Agile: An Integrated Analysis of Quantitative and Qualitative Field Data on Software Development Agility." *MIS Quarterly* 34 (1) (2010): 87–114.

Martin, R. C. "Iterative and Incremental Development (IID)." Accessed April 23, 2011, www.objectmentor.com/resources/ articleIndex.

Patton, J. "Designing Requirements: Incorporating Usage-Centered Design into an Agile SW Development Process." In *XP/Agile Universe 2002.* Edited by D. Wells and L. Williams, 1–12. LNCS 2418. Berlin: Springer-Verlag, 2002.

Glossary of Acronyms

Note: Some acronyms are abbreviations for entries in the Glossary of Terms. For these and some other acronym entries, we list in parentheses the chapter or appendix in which the associated term is defined or introduced. Other acronyms are generally used in the information systems field and are included here for your convenience.

1:1   One-to-one (7)

1:*N*   One-to-many (7)

1NF   First normal form (9)

2NF   Second normal form (9)

3NF   Third normal form (9)

ACM   Association for Computing Machinery

ATM   Automated teller machine

AT&T   American Telephone & Telegraph

BEA   Break-even analysis (4)

BPP   Baseline project plan (3)

BPR   Business process reengineering (5)

CASE   Computer-aided software engineering (1)

CD   Compact disc

CD-ROM   Compact disc read-only memory

CIO   Chief information officer

COBOL   COmmon Business Oriented Language

COCOMO   COnstruction COst Model (3)

CPU   Central processing unit

CRMS   Customer relationship management system

CTS   Customer Tracking System

DB2   Data Base 2

DBMS   Database management system (8)

DFD   Data-flow diagram (6)

EC or E-commerce   Electronic commerce (4)

EDI   Electronic data interchange (4)

EDS   Electronic Data Systems (1)

E-mail   Electronic mail

EPSS   Electronic performance support system (10)

E-R   Entity-relationship (7)

ERD   Entity-relationship diagram (7)

ERP   Enterprise resource planning (2)

ET   Estimated time (3)

FIFO   First in, first out

GE   General Electric

GUI   Graphical user interface

HTML   Hypertext markup language

IBM   International Business Machines (1)

IDC   International Data Corporation

I/O   Input/output

IS   Information systems (1)

IT   Information technology

JAD   Joint application design (1)

LAN   Local area network

MIS   Management information system

M:*N*   Many-to-many

MRP   Material requirements planning

MTBF   Mean time between failures (10)

NBDS   Natural Best Delivery Service

NPV   Net present value (4)

OO   Object-oriented

OOAD   Object-oriented analysis and design (A)

PC   Personal computer

PCB   Printed circuit board (1)

PD   Participatory design (1)

PDA   Personal digital assistant

PERT   Program evaluation review technique (3)

PSS   Project scope statement

PV   Present value (4)

PVF   Pine Valley Furniture (1)

RAD   Rapid application development (1)

RFP   Request for proposal (2)

RFQ   Request for quote (2)

ROI   Return on investment (4)

SaaS   Software as a service

SAP   Systems, Applications, and Products (1)

SDK   System development kit

SDLC   Systems development life cycle (1)

SPTS   Sales Promotion Tracking System (3)

SQL   Structured Query Language

SSR   System service request (3)

TCP/IP   Transmission control protocol/Internet protocol

TQM   Total quality management

TVM   Time value of money (4)

UML   Unified Modeling Language (A)

URL   Uniform resource locator

USD   U.S. dollars

WBS   Work breakdown structure (3)

XML   Extensible Markup Language

YTD   Year-to-date

Glossary of Terms

Abstract class A class that has no direct instances but whose descendants may have direct instances.

Acceptance testing The process whereby actual users test a completed information system, the end result of which is the users' acceptance of it once they are satisfied with it.

Action stubs That part of a decision table that lists the actions that result for a given set of conditions.

Activation The time period during which an object performs an operation.

Actor An external entity that interacts with the system (similar to an external entity in data-flow diagramming).

Adaptive maintenance Changes made to a system to evolve its functionality to changing business needs or technologies.

Aggregation A *part-of* relationship between a component object and an aggregate object.

Agile Methodologies A family of development methodologies characterized by short iterative cycles and extensive testing; active involvement of users for establishing, prioritizing, and verifying requirements; and a focus on small teams of talented, experienced programmers.

Alpha testing User testing of a completed information system using simulated data.

Application software Software designed to process data and support users in an organization. Examples of application software include spreadsheets, word processors, and database management systems.

Association A relationship among object classes.

Association role The end of an association where it connects to a class.

Associative entity An entity type that associates the instances of one or more entity types and contains attributes that are peculiar to the relationship between those entity instances.

Attribute A named property or characteristic of an entity that is of interest to the organization.

Audit trail A record of the sequence of data entries and the date of those entries.

Balancing The conservation of inputs and outputs to a data-flow diagram process when that process is decomposed to a lower level.

Baseline modules Software modules that have been tested, documented, and approved to be included in the most recently created version of a system.

Baseline project plan (BPP) A major outcome and deliverable from the project initiation and planning phase. It contains the best estimate of the project's scope, benefits, costs, risks, and resource requirements.

Behavior Represents how an object acts and reacts.

Beta testing User testing of a completed information system using real data in the real user environment.

Binary relationship A relationship between instances of two entity types.

Boundary The line that marks the inside and outside of a system and that sets off the system from its environment.

Break-even analysis A type of cost-benefit analysis to identify at what point (if ever) benefits equal costs.

Build routines Guidelines that list the instructions to construct an executable system from the baseline source code.

Business case A written report that outlines the justification for an information system. The report highlights economic benefits and costs and the technical and organizational feasibility of the proposed system.

Business process reengineering (BPR) The search for, and implementation of, radical change in business processes to achieve breakthrough improvements in products and services.

Calculated (or computed or derived) field A field that can be derived from other database fields.

Candidate key An attribute (or combination of attributes) that uniquely identifies each instance of an entity type.

Cardinality The number of instances of entity B that can (or must) be associated with each instance of entity A.

Class diagram A diagram that shows the static structure of an object-oriented model: the object classes, their internal structures, and the relationships in which they participate.

Closed-ended questions Questions in interviews and on questionnaires that ask those responding to choose from among a set of specified responses.

Cloud computing The provision of computing resources, including applications, over the Internet, so customers do not have to invest in the computing infrastructure needed to run and maintain the resources.

COCOMO A method for estimating a software project's size and cost.

Cohesion The extent to which a system or subsystem performs a single function.

Component An irreducible part or aggregation of parts that makes up a system; also called a *subsystem*.

Component diagram A diagram that shows the software components or modules and their dependencies.

Computer-aided software engineering (CASE) Software tools that provide automated support for some portion of the systems development process.

Conceptual data model A detailed model that shows the overall structure of organizational data but is independent of any database management system or other implementation considerations.

Concrete class A class that can have direct instances.

Condition stubs That part of a decision table that lists the conditions relevant to the decision.

Configuration management The process of ensuring that only authorized changes are made to a system.

Constraint A limit to what a system can accomplish.

Context diagram A data-flow diagram of the scope of an organizational system that shows the system boundaries, external entities that interact with the system, and the major information flows between the entities and the system.

Cookie crumbs A technique for showing a user where they are in a Web site by placing a series of "tabs" on a Web page that show a user where they are and where they have been.

Corrective maintenance Changes made to a system to repair flaws in its design, coding, or implementation.

Coupling The extent to which subsystems depend on each other.

Critical path The shortest time in which a project can be completed.

Critical path scheduling A scheduling technique in which the order and duration of a sequence of task activities directly affect the completion date of a project.

Data-flow diagram (DFD) A graphic that illustrates the movement of data between external entities and the processes and data stores within a system.

Data store Data at rest, which may take the form of many different physical representations.

Data type A coding scheme recognized by system software for representing organizational data.

Decision table A matrix representation of the logic of a decision, which specifies the possible conditions for the decision and the resulting actions.

Decomposition The process of breaking the description of a system down into small components; also known as *functional decomposition*.

Default value The value a field will assume unless an explicit value is entered for that field.

Degree The number of entity types that participate in a relationship.

Deliverable An end product in a phase of the systems development life cycle (SDLC).

Denormalization The process of splitting or combining normalized relations into physical tables based on affinity of use of rows and fields.

Design strategy A particular approach to developing an information system. It includes statements on the system's functionality, hardware and system software platform, and method for acquisition.

Desk checking A testing technique in which the program code is sequentially executed manually by the reviewer.

DFD completeness The extent to which all necessary components of a data-flow diagram have been included and fully described.

DFD consistency The extent to which information contained on one level of a set of nested data-flow diagrams is also included on other levels.

Dialogue The sequence of interaction between a user and a system.

Dialogue diagramming A formal method for designing and representing human-computer dialogues using box and line diagrams.

Direct installation Changing over from the old information system to a new one by turning off the old system when the new one is turned on.

Discount rate The interest rate used to compute the present value of future cash flows.

Disruptive technologies Technologies that enable the breaking of long-held business rules that inhibit organizations from making radical business changes.

Economic feasibility A process of identifying the financial benefits and costs associated with a development project.

Electronic commerce (EC or E-commerce) Internet-based communication and other technologies that support day-to-day business activities.

Electronic data interchange (EDI) The use of telecommunications technologies to transfer business documents directly between organizations.

Electronic performance support system (EPSS) Component of a software package or application in which training and educational information is embedded. An EPSS may include a tutorial, an expert system, and hypertext jumps to reference material.

Encapsulation The technique of hiding the internal implementation details of an object from its external view.

Enterprise resource planning (ERP) system A system that integrates individual traditional business functions into a series of modules so that a single transaction occurs seamlessly within a single information system rather than in several separate systems.

Entity A person, place, object, event, or concept in the user environment about which the organization wishes to maintain data.

Entity instance (instance) A single occurrence of an entity type.

Entity-relationship diagram (E-R diagram) A graphical representation of the entities, associations, and data for an organization or business area; it is a model of entities, the associations among those entities, and the attributes of both the entities and their associations.

Entity type A collection of entities that share common properties or characteristics.

Environment Everything external to a system that interacts with the system.

Event Something that takes place at a certain point in time; it is a noteworthy occurrence that triggers a state transition.

External documentation System documentation that includes the outcome of structured diagramming techniques, such as data-flow and entity-relationship diagrams.

Extranet Internet-based communication to support business-to-business activities.

Feasibility study Determines whether the information system makes sense for the organization from an economic and operational standpoint.

Field The smallest unit of named application data recognized by system software.

File organization A technique for physically arranging the records of a file.

Foreign key An attribute that appears as a nonprimary key attribute in one relation and as a primary key attribute (or part of a primary key) in another relation.

Form A business document that contains some predefined data and may include some areas where additional data are to be filled in; typically based on one database record.

Formal system The official way a system works, as described in organizational documentation.

Functional dependency A particular relationship between two attributes. For a given relation, attribute B is functionally dependent on attribute A if, for every valid value of A, that value of A uniquely determines the value of B. The functional dependence of B on A is represented by $A \rightarrow B$.

Gantt chart A graphical representation of a project that shows each task as a horizontal bar whose length is proportional to its time for completion.

Gap analysis The process of discovering discrepancies between two or more sets of data-flow diagrams or discrepancies within a single DFD.

Hashed file organization The address for each row is determined using an algorithm.

Help desk A single point of contact for all user inquiries and problems about a particular information system or for all users in a particular department.

Homonym A single attribute name that is used for two or more different attributes.

Identifier A candidate key that has been selected as the unique, identifying characteristic for an entity type.

Incremental commitment A strategy in systems analysis and design in which the project is reviewed after each phase, and continuation of the project is rejustified in each of these reviews.

Index A table used to determine the location of rows in a file that satisfy some condition.

Indexed file organization The rows are stored either sequentially or nonsequentially, and an index is created that allows software to locate individual rows.

Indifferent condition In a decision table, a condition whose value does not affect which actions are taken for two or more rules.

Informal system The way an organization actually works.

Information systems analysis and design The process of developing and maintaining an information system.

Input mask A pattern of codes that restricts the width and possible values for each position of a field.

Inspections A testing technique in which participants examine program code for predictable language-specific errors.

Installation The organizational process of changing over from the current information system to a new one.

Intangible benefit A benefit derived from the creation of an information system, that cannot be easily measured in dollars or with certainty.

Intangible cost A cost associated with an information system, that cannot be easily measured in terms of dollars or with certainty.

Integration testing The process of bringing together for testing purposes all of the modules that a program comprises. Modules are typically integrated in a top-down, incremental fashion.

Interface Point of contact where a system meets its environment or where subsystems meet each other.

Internal documentation System documentation that is part of the program source code or is generated at compile time.

Internet A network of interconnected individual networks that use a common protocol to communicate with one another; a global computing network to support business-to-consumer electronic commerce.

Interrelated Dependence of one part of the system on one or more other system parts.

Intranet Internet-based communication to support business activities within a single organization.

Issue tracking system Typically a Web-based tool for logging, tracking, and assigning system bugs and change requests to developers.

JAD session leader The trained individual who plans and leads joint application design sessions.

Joint application design (JAD) A structured process in which users, managers, and analysts work together for several days in a series of intensive meetings to specify or review system requirements.

Key business processes The structured, measured set of activities designed to produce a specific output for a particular customer or market.

Legal and contractual feasibility The process of assessing potential legal and contractual ramifications due to the construction of a system.

Level-0 diagram A data-flow diagram that represents a system's major processes, data flows, and data stores at a high level of detail.

Level-n diagram A DFD that is the result of n-nested decompositions of a series of subprocesses from a process on a level-0 diagram.

Lightweight graphics The use of small simple images to allow a Web page to be displayed more quickly.

Maintenance Changes made to a system to fix or enhance its functionality.

Mean time between failures (MTBF) A measurement of error occurrences that can be tracked over time to indicate the quality of a system.

Modularity Dividing a system up into chunks or modules of a relatively uniform size.

Multiplicity An indication of how many objects participate in a given relationship.

Multivalued attribute An attribute that may take on more than one value for each entity instance.

Network diagram A diagram that depicts project tasks and their interrelationships.

Normalization The process of converting complex data structures into simple, stable data structures.

Null value A special field value, distinct from 0, blank, or any other value, that indicates that the value for the field is missing or otherwise unknown.

Object An entity that has a well-defined role in the application domain and has state, behavior, and identity.

Object class A set of objects that share a common structure and a common behavior.

Object diagram A graph of instances that are compatible with a given class diagram.

One-time cost A cost associated with project initiation and development, or system start-up.

Open-ended questions Questions in interviews and on questionnaires that have no prespecified answers.

Operation A function or a service that is provided by all the instances of a class.

Operational feasibility The process of assessing the degree to which a proposed system solves business problems or takes advantage of business opportunities.

Outsourcing The practice of turning over responsibility for some or all of an organization's information systems applications and operations to an outside firm.

Parallel installation Running the old information system and the new one at the same time until management decides the old system can be turned off.

Participatory design (PD) A systems development approach that originated in northern Europe, in which users and the improvement of their work lives are the central focus.

Perfective maintenance Changes made to a system to add new features or to improve performance.

PERT A technique that uses optimistic, pessimistic, and realistic time estimates to calculate the expected time for a particular task.

Phased installation Changing from the old information system to the new one incrementally, starting with one or a few functional components and then gradually extending the installation to cover the whole new system.

Physical file A named set of table rows stored in a contiguous section of secondary memory.

Physical table A named set of rows and columns that specifies the fields in each row of the table.

Pointer A field of data that can be used to locate a related field or row of data.

Political feasibility The process of evaluating how key stakeholders within the organization view the proposed system.

Present value The current value of a future cash flow.

Preventive maintenance Changes made to a system to avoid possible future problems.

Primary key An attribute whose value is unique across all occurrences of a relation.

Primitive DFD The lowest level of decomposition for a data-flow diagram.

Process The work or actions performed on data so that they are transformed, stored, or distributed.

Process modeling Graphically representing the processes that capture, manipulate, store, and distribute data between a system and its environment and among components within a system.

Project A planned undertaking of related activities, having a beginning and an end, to reach an objective.

Project charter A short, high-level document prepared for both internal and external stakeholders to formally announce the establishment of the project and to briefly describe its objectives, key assumptions, and stakeholders.

Project closedown The final phase of the project management process, which focuses on bringing a project to an end.

Project execution The third phase of the project management process, in which the plans created in the prior phases (project initiation and planning) are put into action.

Project initiation The first phase of the project management process, in which activities are performed to assess the size, scope, and complexity of the project and to establish procedures to support later project activities.

Project management A controlled process of initiating, planning, executing, and closing down a project.

Project manager A systems analyst with a diverse set of skills—management, leadership, technical, conflict management, and customer relationship—who is responsible for initiating, planning, executing, and closing down a project.

Project planning The second phase of the project management process, which focuses on defining clear, discrete activities and the work needed to complete each activity within a single project.

Project scope statement A document prepared for the customer that describes what the project will deliver and that outlines generally at a high level all work required to complete the project.

Project workbook An online or hard-copy repository, for all project correspondence, inputs, outputs, deliverables, procedures, and standards, that is used for performing project audits, orienting new team members, communicating with management and customers, identifying future projects, and performing postproject reviews.

Prototyping Building a scaled-down version of the desired information system.

Purpose The overall goal or function of a system.

Rapid application development (RAD) Systems development methodology created to radically decrease the time needed to design and implement information systems.

Recurring cost A cost resulting from the ongoing evolution and use of a system.

Recursive foreign key A foreign key in a relation that references the primary key values of that same relation.

Refactoring Making a program simpler after adding a new feature.

Referential integrity An integrity constraint specifying that the value (or existence) of an attribute in one relation depends on the value (or existence) of the same attribute in another relation.

Relation A named, two-dimensional table of data. Each relation consists of a set of named columns and an arbitrary number of unnamed rows.

Relational database model Data represented as a set of related tables or relations.

Relationship An association between the instances of one or more entity types that is of interest to the organization.

Repeating group A set of two or more multivalued attributes that are logically related.

Report A business document that contains only predefined data; it is a passive document used only for reading or viewing; typically contains data from many unrelated records or transactions.

Repository A centralized database that contains all diagrams, forms and report definitions, data structures, data definitions, process flows and logic, and definitions of other organizational and system components; it provides a set of mechanisms and structures to achieve seamless data-to-tool and data-to-data integration.

Request for proposal (RFP) A document provided to vendors to ask them to propose hardware and system software that will meet the requirements of a new system.

Resources Any person, group of people, piece of equipment, or material used in accomplishing an activity.

Reuse The use of previously written software resources, especially objects and components, in new applications.

Rules That part of a decision table that specifies which actions are to be followed for a given set of conditions.

Schedule feasibility The process of assessing the degree to which the potential time frame and completion dates for all major activities within a project meet organizational deadlines and constraints for effecting change.

Scribe The person who makes detailed notes of the happenings at a joint application design session.

Second normal form (2NF) A relation for which every nonprimary key attribute is functionally dependent on the whole primary key.

Secondary key One or a combination of fields for which more than one row may have the same combination of values.

Sequence diagram A depiction of the interactions among objects during a certain period of time.

Sequential file organization The rows in the file are stored in sequence according to a primary key value.

Simple design Creating uncomplicated software and software components that work to solve the current problem rather than creating complicated software designed for a future that may not come.

Simple message A message that transfers control from the sender to the recipient without describing the details of the communication.

Single location installation Trying out a new information system at one site and using the experience to decide if and how the new system should be deployed throughout the organization.

Slack time The amount of time that an activity can be delayed without delaying the project.

Source/Sink The origin and/or destination of data; sometimes referred to as external entities.

State A condition that encompasses an object's properties (attributes and relationships) and the values those properties have.

State transition The changes in the attributes of an object or in the links an object has with other objects.

Stub testing A technique used in testing modules, especially modules that are written and tested in a top-down fashion, where a few lines of code are used to substitute for subordinate modules.

Support Providing ongoing educational and problem-solving assistance to information system users. Support material and jobs must be designed along with the associated information system.

Synchronous message A type of message in which the caller has to wait for the receiving object to finish executing the called operation before it can resume execution itself.

Synonyms Two different names that are used for the same attribute.

System A group of interrelated procedures used for a business function, with an identifiable boundary, working together for some purpose.

System documentation Detailed information about a system's design specifications, its internal workings, and its functionality.

System librarian A person responsible for controlling the checking out and checking in of baseline modules when a system is being developed or maintained.

Systems analysis Phase of the SDLC in which the current system is studied and alternative replacement systems are proposed.

Systems analyst The organizational role most responsible for the analysis and design of information systems.

Systems design Phase of the SDLC in which the system chosen for development in systems analysis is first described independently of any computer platform (logical design) and is then transformed into technology-specific details (physical design) from which all programming and system construction can be accomplished.

Systems development life cycle (SDLC) The series of steps used to mark the phases of development for an information system.

Systems development methodology A standard process followed in an organization to conduct all the steps necessary to analyze, design, implement, and maintain information systems.

Systems implementation and operation Final phase of the SDLC, in which the information system is coded, tested, and installed in the organization, and in which the information system is systematically repaired and improved.

Systems planning and selection The first phase of the SDLC, in which an organization's total information system needs are analyzed and arranged, and in which a potential information systems project is identified and an argument for continuing or not continuing with the project is presented.

System testing The bringing together for testing purposes of all the programs that a system comprises. Programs are typically integrated in a top-down incremental fashion.

Tangible benefit A benefit derived from the creation of an information system, that can be measured in dollars and with certainty.

Tangible cost A cost associated with an information system, that can be easily measured in dollars and with certainty.

Technical feasibility A process of assessing the organization's ability to construct a proposed system.

Template-based HTML Templates to display and process common attributes of higher-level, more abstract items.

Ternary relationship A simultaneous relationship among instances of three entity types.

Testing harness An automated testing environment used to review code for errors, standards violations, and other design flaws.

Third normal form (3NF) A relation that is in second normal form and has no functional (transitive) dependencies between two (or more) nonprimary key attributes.

Time value of money (TVM) The process of comparing present cash outlays to future expected returns.

Unary relationship (recursive relationship) A relationship between the instances of one entity type.

Unified Modeling Language (UML) A notation that allows the modeler to specify, visualize, and construct the artifacts of software systems, as well as business models.

Unit testing Each module is tested alone in an attempt to discover any errors in its code.

Use case A complete sequence of related actions initiated by an actor; it represents a specific way to use the system.

Use-case diagram A diagram that depicts the use cases and actors for a system.

User documentation Written or other visual information about how an application system works, and how to use it.

Walkthrough A peer group review of any product created during the systems development process; also called a *structured walkthrough*.

Well-structured relation (table) A relation that contains a minimum amount of redundancy and allows users to insert, modify, and delete the rows without errors or inconsistencies.

Work breakdown structure The process of dividing the project into manageable tasks and logically ordering them to ensure a smooth evolution between tasks.

Index

Page references with f indicate figures; those with t represent tables.